Bernstein-Ratner, N. (1987). The phonology of parent child speech. In K. Nelson & A. van Kleeck (Eds.), *Children's Language: Vol. 6.* Hillsdale, NJ: Erlbaum.

Bernstein-Ratner, N., & Pye, C. (1984). Higher pitch in baby talk is not universal: Acoustic evidence from Quiche Mayan. *Journal of Child Language, 11*, 515-522.

Bishop, D. V. M. (1982). *The test of reception of grammar* . University of Manchester: Medical Research Council.

Bliss, L. (1988). The development of modals. *The Journal of Applied Developmental Psychology, 9*, 253-261.

Bloom, L. (1970). *Language development: Form and function in emerging grammars* . Cambridge, MA: MIT Press.

Bloom, L. (1973). *One word at a time: The use of single word utterances* . The Hague: Mouton.

Bloom, L. (1975). Language development. In F. Horowitz (Ed.), *Review of child development research.* (Vol. 4) Chicago: University of Chicago Press.

Blum-Kulka, S., & Snow, C. (1992). Developing autonomy for tellers, tales, and the telling in family narrative events. *Journal of Narrative and Life History, 2*, 187-217.

Bohannon, J. N., & Marquis, A. L. (1977). Children's control of adult speech. *Child Development, 48*, 1002-1008.

Bohannon, N., & Stanowicz, L. (1988). The issue of negative evidence: Adult responses to children's language errors. *Developmental Psychology, 24*, 684-689.

Bolinger, D. (1986). *Intonation and its parts: Melody in spoken English* . Stanford, CA: Stanford University Press.

Braine, M. D. S. (1976). Children's first word combinations. *Monographs of the Society for Research in Child Development, 41*, (Whole No. 1).

Branigan, G. (1979). Some reasons why successive single word utterances are not. *Journal of Child Language, 6*, 411-421.

Brown, R. (1973). *A first language: The early stages* . Cambridge, MA: Harvard.

Bush, C. M., Edwards, M. L., Luckan, J. M., Stoel, C. M., Macken, M. A., & Peterson, J. D. (1973). *On specifying a system for transcribing consonants in child language* . Unpublished mss. Stanford: Stanford University.

Carlson-Luden, V. (1979). *Causal understanding in the 10-month-old.* Unpublished doctoral dissertation, University of Colorado at Boulder.

Carterette, E. C., & Jones, M. H. (1974). *Informal Speech: Alphabetic and Phonemic texts with statistical analyses and tables* . Berkeley, Ca: University of California Press.

Chafe, W. (Ed.). (1980). *The Pear stories: Cognitive, cultural, and linguistic aspects of narrative production* . Norwood, NJ: Ablex.

Chafe, W. (1987). Cognitive constraints on information flow. In R. Tomlin (Ed.), *Coherence and grounding in discourse.* Philadelphia: Benjamins.

Chomsky, C. (1969). *The acquisition of syntax in children from 5 to 10* . Cambridge, MA: MIT Press.

Cipriani, P., Pfanner, P., Chilosi, A., Cittadoni, L., Ciuti, A., Maccari, A., Pantano, N., Pfanner, L., Poli, P., Sarno, S., Bottari, P., Cappelli, G., Colombo, C., & Veneziano, E. (1989). *Protocolli diagnostici e terapeutici nello sviluppo e nella patologia del linguaggio.* (1/84 Italian Ministry of Health): Stella Maris Foundation.

Clahsen, H. (1982). *Spracherwerb in der Kindheit: Eine Untersuchung zur Entwicklung der Syntax bei Kleinkindern* . Tübingen: Gunter Narr.

Clark, E. (1979). Building a vocabulary: Words for objects, actions and relations. In P. Fletcher & M. Garman (Eds.), *Language acquisition: Studies in first language development.* New York: Cambridge University Press.

Clark, E. (1987). The Principle of Contrast: A constraint on language acquisition. In B. MacWhinney (Ed.), *Mechanisms of Language Acquisition.* Hillsdale, N.J.: Erlbaum.

Clark, E. V. (1978a). Awareness of language: Some evidence from what children say and do. In R. J. A. Sinclair & W. Levelt (Eds.), *The child's conception of language*. Berlin: Springer Verlag.

Clark, E. V. (1978b). Discovering what words can do. In W. J. D. Farkas & K. Todrys (Eds.), *Papers from the parasession on the lexicon*. Chicago: Chicago Linguistic Society.

Clark, E. V. (1982a). Language change during language acquisition. In M. E. Lamb & A. L. Brown (Eds.), *Advances in child development: Vol. 2*. Hillsdale: N. J.: Lawrence Erlbaum.

Clark, E. V. (1982b). The young word maker: A case study of innovation in the child's lexicon. In E. Wanner & L. R. Gleitman (Eds.), *Language acquisition: The state of the art*. Cambridge: Cambridge University Press.

Clark, R. (1976). A report on methods of longitudinal data collection. *Journal of Child Language*, *3*, 457-461.

Comrie, B., & Corbett, G. (Eds.). (1992). *The Slavonic Languages* . London: Routledge.

Conti-Ramsden, G., & Dykins, J. (1989). *Mother-child interaction with language-impaired children and their siblings* . Manchester: University of Manchester.

Crystal, D. (1969). *Prosodic systems and intonation in English* . Cambridge: Cambridge University Press.

Crystal, D. (1975). *The English tone of voice: Essays in intonation, prosody and paralanguage* . London: Edward Arnold.

Crystal, D., Fletcher, P., & Garman, M. (1989). *The grammatical analysis of language disability. Second Edition.*. London: Cole and Whurr.

Dale, P., Bates, E., Reznick, S., & Morisset, C. (1989). The validity of a parent report instrument. *Journal of Child Language*, *16*, 239-249.

Davidson, R., Kline, S., & Snow, C. E. (1986). Definitions and definite noun phrases: Indicators of children's decontextualized language skills. *Journal of Research in Childhood Education*, *1*, 37-48.

De Houwer, A. (1990). *The acquisition of two languages: A case study* . New York: Cambridge University Press.

Demetras, M. (1989a). *Changes in parents' converational responses: A function of grammatical development.* Paper presented at the ASHA, St. Louis, MO.

Demetras, M. (1989b). *Working parents conversational responses to their two-year-old sons.* Unpublished doctoral dissertation, University of Arizona.

Demetras, M., Post, K., & Snow, C. (1986). Feedback to first-language learners. *Journal of Child Language*, *13*, 275-292.

Deuchar, M., & Clark, A. (1992). *Bilingual acquisition of the voicing contrast in word-initial stop consonants in English and Spanish.* Cognitive Science Research Report 213: University of Sussex.

Dore, J. (1977). "Oh Them Sheriff": a pragmatic analysis of children's response to questions. In S. Ervin-Tripp, & C. Mitchell-Kernan (Eds.), *Child Discourse*. New York: Academic Press.

Dore, J., Franklin, M. B., Miller, R. T., & Ramer, A. L. H. (1976). Transitional phenomena in early language acquisition. *Journal of Child Language*, *3*, 13-28.

Dunn, L. M., Dunn, L. M., Whetton, C., & Pintillie, D. (1982). *The British Picture Vocabulary Scale* . Windsor: NFER.

Edwards, J. (1992). Computer methods in child language research: four principles for the use of archived data. *Journal of Child Language*, *19*, 435-458.

Edwards, M. L., & Bernhardt, B. H. (1973). *Phonological analyses of the speech of four children with language disorders*. Unpublished mss. Stanford: Stanford University.

Ehlich, K., & Rehbein, J. (1976). Halbinterpretative Arbeitstranskription (HIAT). *Linguistische Berichte*, *45*, 24-41.

Ekman, P., & Friesen, W. (1969). The repertoire of nonverbal behavior: Categories, origins, usage, and coding. *Semiotica*, *1*, 47-98.

Ekman, P., & Friesen, W. (1978). *Facial action coding system: Investigator's guide* . Palo Alto, CA: Consulting Psychologists Press.

Elbers, L. (1985). A tip-of-the-tongue experience at age two? *Journal of Child Language*, *12*, 353-365.

Elbers, L., & Wijnen, F. (1992). Effort, production skill, and language learning. In C. Ferguson, L. Menn, & C. Stoel-Gammon (Eds.), *Phonological development: Models, research, implications.* Parkton, MD: York.

Ervin-Tripp, S. (1979). Children's verbal turn-taking. In E. Ochs & B. Schieffelin (Eds.), *Developmental pragmatics.* New York: Academic Press.

Feldman, H., Keefe, K., & Holland, A. (1989). Language abilities after left hemisphere brain injury: A case study of twins. *Topics in Special Education*, *9*, 32-47.

Fletcher, P. (1985). *A child's learning of English* . Oxford: Blackwell.

Fletcher, P., & Garman, M. (1988). Normal language development and language impairment: Syntax and beyond. *Clinical Linguistics and Phonetics*, *2*, 97-114.

Fosnot, S. M., & Spajik, S. (1994). Vocal development in 6- to 36-month-old children at risk and not at risk to stutter. *UCLA Working Papers in Phonetics*, *89*.

Francis, W., & Kucera, H. (1982). *Frequency analysis of English usage: Lexicon and grammar* . Boston: Houghton Mifflin.

Garvey, C. (1979). An approach to the study of children's role play. *The Quarterly Newsletter of the Laboratory of Comparative Human Cognition*, *12*.

Garvey, C., & Hogan, R. (1973). Social speech and social interaction: Egocentrism revisited. *Child Development*, *44*, 562-568.

Gathercole, V. (1980). *Birdies like birdseed the bester than buns: A study of relational comparatives and their acquisition.* Unpublished doctoral dissertation, University of Kansas.

Gathercole, V. (1986). The acquisition of the present perfect: explaining differences in the speech of Scottish and American children. *Journal of Child Language*, *13*, 537-560.

Gerken, L. (1991). The metrical basis for children's subjectless sentences. *Journal of Memory and Language*, *30*, 431-451.

Gerken, L., Landau, B., & Remez, R. E. (1990). Function morphemes in young children's speech perception and production. *Developmental Psychology*, *26*(2), 204-216.

Geverink, N. A., Noldus, L. P., Pluim, M. D., & Ødberg, F. O. (1993). A new technique for the integrated analysis of behavioral data and physiological measurements: Matching time series of discrete events and continuous signals. In M. Nichelmann, H. K. Wierenga, & S. Braun (Eds.), *Proceedings of the International Congress of Applied Ethology.* Berlin.

Gillis, S., & Verhoeven, J. (1992). Developmental aspects of syntactic complexity in two triplets. *Antwerp Papers in Linguistics*, *69*.

Gleason, J. B. (1980). The acquisition of social speech and politeness formulae. In H. Giles, W. P. Robinson, & S. M. P. (Eds.), *Language: Social psychological perspectives.* Oxford: Pergamon.

Gleason, J. B., & Greif, E. (1983). Men's speech to young children. In B. Thorne, C. Kramerae, & N. Henley (Eds.), *Language, Gender and Society.* Rowley, MA: Newbury.

Gleason, J. B., Perlmann, R. Y., & Greif, E. B. (1984). What's the magic word? Learning language through routines. *Discourse Processes*, *6*, 493-502.

Goldman-Eisler, F. (1968). *Psycholinguistics: Experiments in spontaneous speech* . New York: Academic Press.

Gopnik, M. (1989). Reflections on challenges raised and questions asked. In P. R. Zelazo & R. G. Barr (Eds.), *Challenges to developmental paradigms.* Hillsdale, NJ: Erlbaum.

Greif, E. B., & Gleason, J. B. (1980). Hi, thanks and goodbye: More routine information. *Language in Society*, *9*, 159-166.

Guthrie, L. F. (1983). *Learning to use a new language: Language functions and use by first grade Chinese-Americans* . Oakland: ARC Associates.

Guthrie, L. F. (1984). Contrasts in teachers' language use in a Chinese-English bilingual classroom. In J. Hanscombe, R. Orem, & B. Taylor (Eds.), *On TESOL '83: The question of control.* Washington, DC: TESOL.

Guthrie, L. F., & Guthrie, G. P. (1988). Teacher language use in a Chinese bilingual classroom. In S. Goldman & H. Trueba (Eds.), *Becoming literate in English as a second language.* Norwood, NJ: Ablex.

Haggerty, L. (1929). What a two-and-one-half-year-old child said in one day. *Journal of Genetic Psychology*, *38*, 75-100.

Hall, W. S., Nagy, W. E., & Linn, R. (1984). *Spoken words: Effects of situation and social group on oral word usage and frequency* . Hillsdale, NJ: Erlbaum.

Hall, W. S., Nagy, W. E., & Nottenburg, G. (1981). *Situational variation in the use of internal state words* . Champaign, IL: University of Illinois.

Hall, W. S., & Tirre, W. C. (1979). *The communicative environment of young children: Social class, ethnic and situational differences* . Champaign, IL: University of Illinois.

Halliday, M. (1966). Notes on transitivity and theme in English: Part 1. *Journal of Linguistics*, *2*, 37-71.

Halliday, M. (1967). Notes on transitivity and theme in English: Part 2. *Journal of Linguistics*, *3*, 177-274.

Halliday, M. (1968). Notes on transitivity and theme in English: Part 3. *Journal of Linguistics*, *4*, 153-308.

Halliday, M., & Hasan, R. (1976). *Cohesion in English* . London: Longman.

Hargrove, P. M., Holmberg, C., & Zeigler, M. (1986). Changes in spontaneous speech associated with therapy hiatus: A retrospective study. *Children Language Teaching and Therapy*, *2*, 266-280.

Hausser, R. (1990). Principles of computational morphology. *Computational Linguistics*, 47.

Hayashi, M. (1993). *A longitudinal study of the language development in bilingual children.* Unpublished doctoral dissertation, University of Århus.

Hayes, D. P. (1988). Speaking and writing: Distinct patterns of word choice. *Journal of Memory and Language*, *27*, 572-585.

Heath, S. (1983). *Ways with words: Language, life and work in communities and classrooms* . Cambridge: Cambridge University Press.

Hicks, D. (1990). Kinds of texts: Narrative genre skills among children from two communities. In A. McCabe (Ed.), *Developing narrative structure.* Hillsdale, NJ: Lawrence Erlbaum.

Higginson, R., & MacWhinney, B. (1990). *CHILDES/BIB: An annotated bibliography of child language and language disorders* . Hillsdale, NJ: Erlbaum.

Higginson, R. P. (1985). *Fixing-assimilation in language acquisition.* Unpublished doctoral dissertation, Washington State University.

Hirsh-Pasek, K., Trieman, R., & Schneiderman, M. (1984). Brown and Hanlon revisited: mother sensitivity to grammatical form. *Journal of Child Language*, *11*, 81-88.

Hoff-Ginsberg, E. (1985). Some contributions of mothers' speech to their children's syntactic growth. *Journal of Child Language* , *12*, 367-385.

Holland, A., Miller, J., Reinmuth, O., Bartlett, C., Fromm, D., Pashek, G., Stein, D., & Swindell, C. (1985). Rapid recovery from aphasia: A detailed language analysis. *Brain and Language*, *24*, 156-173.

Hooshyar, N. (1985). Language interaction between mothers and their nonhandicapped children, mothers and their Down Syndrome children, and mothers and their language-impaired children. *International Journal of Rehabilitation Research*, *4*, 475-477.

Hooshyar, N. (1987). The relationship between maternal language parameters and the child's language constancy and developmental condition. *International Journal of Rehabilitation Research, 10*, 321-324.

Ingram, D. (1989). *First language acquisition* . New York: Cambridge.

Isaacs, S. (1930). *Intellectual growth in young children* . London: Routledge and Kegan Paul.

Isaacs, S. (1933). *Social development in young children* . London: Routledge and Kegan Paul.

Jefferson, G. (1984). Transcript notation. In J. Atkinson & J. Heritage (Eds.), *Structures of social interaction: Studies in conversation analysis.* Cambridge: Cambridge University Press.

Johannsen, H. S., Schulze, H., Rommel, D., & Häge, A. (1992). Ätiologie und Verlaufsbedingungen des kindlichen Stotterns. Darstellung einer laufenden Längsschnittstudie. *Folia Phoniatrica, 44*, 34-35.

Johnson, M. (1986). *A computer-based approach to the analysis of child language data.* Unpublished doctoral dissertation, University of Reading.

Jones, M. H., & Carterette, E. C. (1963). Redundancy in children's free-reading choices. *Journal of Verbal Learning and Verbal Behavior, 2*, 489-493.

Karmiloff-Smith, A. (1986). From meta-processes to conscious access: Evidence from children's metalinguistic and repair data. *Cognition, 23*, 95-147.

Kearney, G., & McKenzie, S. (1993). Machine interpretation of emotion: Design of memory-based expert system for interpreting facial expressions in terms of signaled emotions. *Cognitive Science, 17*, 589-622.

Keefe, K., Feldman, H., & Holland, A. (1989). Lexical learning and language abilities in preschoolers with perinatal brain damage. *Journal of Speech and Hearing Disorders, 54*, 395-402.

Kent, R. D., & Shriberg, L. D. (1982). *Clinical Phonetics* . New York: Macmillan.

Klausen, T., Subritzky, M. S., & Hayashi, M. (1992). Initial production of inflections in bilingual children. In G. Turner & D. Messer (Eds.), *Critical influences on language acquisition and development.* London: Macmillan.

Korman, M. (1984). Adaptive aspects of maternal vocalizations in differing contexts at ten weeks. *First Language, 5*, 44-45.

Kuczaj, S. (1976). *-ing, -s and -ed: A study of the acquisition of certain verb inflections.* Unpublished doctoral dissertation, University of Minnesota.

Lee, L. (1974). *Developmental Sentence Analysis* . Evanston, IL: Northwestern University Press.

Lehmann, C. (1982). Directions for interlinear morphemic translations. *Folia Linguistica, 16*, 119-224.

Leiter, R. G. (1969). *The Leiter International Performance Scale* . Chicago: Stoelting.

Leopold, W. (1949). *Speech development of a bilingual child: a linguist's record: Vol. 3. Grammar and general problems in the first two years* . Evanston, IL: Northwestern University Press.

MacWhinney, B. (1974). *How Hungarian children learn to speak.* Unpublished doctoral dissertation, University of California, Berkeley.

MacWhinney, B. (1975). Pragmatic patterns in child syntax. *Stanford Papers And Reports on Child Language Development, 10*, 153-165.

MacWhinney, B. (1985). Grammatical devices for sharing points. In R. Schiefelbusch (Ed.), *Communicative competence: Acquisition and intervention.* Baltimore, MD: University Park Press.

MacWhinney, B. (1989). Competition and lexical categorization. In R. Corrigan, F. Eckman, & M. Noonan (Eds.), *Linguistic categorization.* New York: Benjamins.

MacWhinney, B., & Bates, E. (1978). Sentential devices for conveying givenness and newness: A cross-cultural developmental study. *Journal of Verbal Learning and Verbal Behavior, 17*, 539-558.

MacWhinney, B., & Osser, H. (1977). Verbal planning functions in children's speech. *Child Development*, *48*, 978-985.

MacWhinney, B., & Snow, C. (1990). The Child Language Data Exchange System: An update. *Journal of Child Language*, *17*, 457-472.

Masur, E., & Gleason, J. B. (1980). Parent-child interaction and the acquisition of lexical information during play. *Developmental Psychology*, *16*, 404-409.

Menn, L., & Gleason, J. B. (1986). Babytalk as a stereotype and register: Adult reports of children's speech patterns. In J. A. Fishman (Ed.), *The Fergusonian Impact, Volume I*. Berlin: Mouton de Gruyter.

Miller, J., & Chapman, R. (1983). *SALT: Systematic Analysis of Language Transcripts, User's Manual*. Madison, WI: University of Wisconsin Press.

Miranda, E., Camp, L., Hemphill, L., & Wolf, D. (1992). *Developmental changes in children's us of tense in narrative*. Paper presented at the Boston University Conference on Language Development, Boston.

Moerk, E. (1972). Factors of style and personality. *Journal of Psycholinguistic Research*, *1*, 257-268.

Moerk, E. (1983). *The mother of Eve - As a first language teacher*. Norwood, N.J.: ABLEX.

Montes, R. (1987). *Secuencias de clarificación en conversaciones con niños*. (Morphe 3-4): Universidad Autónoma de Puebla.

Montes, R. G. (1992). *Achieving understanding: Repair mechanisms in mother-child conversations*. Unpublished doctoral dissertation, Georgetown University.

Narasimhan, R. (1981). *Modeling language behavior*. Berlin: Springer.

Nelson, K. E., Denninger, M. S., Bonvilian, J. D., Kaplan, B. J., & Baker, N. D. (1984). Maternal input adjustments and non-adjustments as related to children's linguistic advances and to language acquisition theories. In A. D. Pellegrini & T. D. Yawkey (Eds.), *The development of oral and written language in social contexts*. Norwood, N.J.: Ablex Publishing Corporation.

Nelson, L., & Bauer, H. (1991). Speech and language production at age 2: Evidence for tradeoffs between linguistic and phonetic processing. *Journal of Speech and Hearing Research*, *34*, 879-892.

Ninio, A., Snow, C., Pan, B., & Rollins, P. (1994). Classifying communicative acts in children's interactions. *Journal of Communicative Disorders*, *27*, 157-188.

Ninio, A., & Wheeler, P. (1986). A manual for classifying verbal communicative acts in mother-infant interaction. *Transcript Analysis*, *3*, 1-83.

Noldus, L. (1991). The Observer: A software system for collection and analysis of observational data. *Behavior Research Methods, Instrument, and Computers*, *23*, 415-429.

Noldus, L. P., van de Loo, E. H., & Timmers, P. H. (1989). Computers in behavioural research. *Nature*, *341*, 767-768.

Ochs, E. (1979). Transcription as theory. In E. Ochs & B. Schieffelin (Eds.), *Developmental pragmatics*. New York: Academic.

Oshima-Takane, Y., & MacWhinney, B. (1994). *Japanese CHAT Manual*. Montreal: McGill University.

Peters, A. (1983). *The units of language acquisition*. New York: Cambridge University Press.

Peters, A. (1987). The role of imitation in the developing syntax of a blind child. *Text*, *7*, 289-311.

Piaget, J. (1952). *The origins of intelligence in children*. New York: International Universities Press.

Pittenger, R., Hockett, C., & Danehy, J. (1960). *The first five minutes*. Ithaca, NY: Martineau.

Plunkett, K. (1985). *Preliminary approaches to language development*. Århus, Denmark: Århus University Press.

Plunkett, K. (1986). Learning strategies in two Danish children's language development. *Scandinavian Journal of Psychology, 27*, 64-73.

Plunkett, K., & Strömqvist, S. (1992). The acquisition of Scandinavian languages. In D. I. Slobin (Ed.), *The crosslinguistic study of language acquisition: Volume 3.* Hillsdale, NJ: Lawrence Erlbaum Associates.

Post, K. (1992). *The Language Learning Environment of Laterborns in a Rural Florida Community.* Unpublished doctoral dissertation, Harvard University.

Post, K. (1994). Negative evidence. In J. Sokolov & C. Snow (Eds.), *Handbook of Research in Language Development Using CHILDES.* Hillsdale, NJ: Lawrence Erlbaum Associates.

Pullum, G., & Ladusaw, W. (1986). *Phonetic symbol guide.* Chicago: University of Chicago Press.

Quirk, R., Greenbaum, S., Leech, G., & Svartvik, J. (1985). *A comprehensive grammar of the English language* . London: Longman.

Rinsland, H. (1945). *A basic vocabulary of elementary school children* . New York: Macmillan.

Romero, S., Santos, A., & Pellicer, D. (1992). *The construction of communicative competence in Mexican Spanish speaking children (6 months to 7 years)* . Mexico City: University of the Americas.

Rondal, J. (1978). Maternal speech to normal and Down's Syndrome children matched for mean length of utterance. In C. E. Meyers (Ed.), *Quality of life in severely and profoundly mentally retarded people: Research foundations for improvement.* Washington, DC: American Association on Mental Deficiency.

Rondal, J. A. (1985). *Adult-child interaction and the process of language understanding* . New York: Praeger.

Rondal, J. A., Bachelet, J. F., & Peree, F. (1985). Analyse du langage et des interactions verbales adulte-enfant. *Bulletin d'Audiophonologie, 5-6*, 507-536.

Ryder, N. B., & Westhoff, C. F. (1971). *Reproduction in the United States in 1965* . Princeton, NJ: Princeton University Press.

Sachs, J. (1983). Talking about the there and then: The emergence of displaced reference in parent-child discourse. In K. E. Nelson (Ed.), *Children's language, Vol. 4.* Hillsdale, N.J.: Lawrence Erlbaum.

Scarborough, H. S. (1990). Index of productive syntax. *Applied Psycholinguistics, 11*, 1-22.

Schaerlaekens, A., & Gillis, S. (1987). *De taalverwerving van het kind: een hernieuwde orientatie in het Nederlandstalig onderzoeks* . Groningen: Wolters-Noordhoff.

Schaerlaekens, A. M. (1972). A generative transformational model of language acquisition. *Cognition, 2*, 371-376.

Schaerlaekens, A. M. (1973). *The two-word sentence in child language* . The Hague: Mouton.

Sinclair, H. (1982). *Los bebés y las cosas* . Buenos Aires: Gedisa.

Slobin, D. (1977). Language change in childhood and in history. In J. Macnamara (Ed.), *Language learning and thought.* New York: Academic Press.

Slobin, D. (1982). Universal and particular in the acquisition of language. In E. Wanner & L. Gleitman (Eds.), *Language acquisition: The state of the art.* New York: Cambridge University Press.

Slobin, D. I. (1972). *Leopold's bibliography of child language: Revised and augmented edition* . Bloomington, IN: Indiana University Press.

Snow, C. E. (1972). Mothers' speech to children learning language. *Child Development, 43*, 549-565.

Snow, C. E. (1989). Imitativeness: a trait or a skill? In G. Speidel & K. Nelson (Eds.), *The many faces of imitation.* New York: Reidel.

Sokolov, J., & MacWhinney, B. (1990). The CHIP framework: Automatic coding and analysis of parent-child conversational interaction. *Behavioral Research Methods, Instruments, and Computers, 22,* 151-161.

Sokolov, J., & Snow, C. (Eds.). (1994). *Handbook of research in language development using CHILDES* . Hillsdale, NJ: Erlbaum.

Sparrow, S., Balla, D., & Cichetti, D. (1984). *Vineland Adaptive Behavior Scales: Interview Edition* . Circle Pines, MN: American Guidance Service.

Stemberger, J. (1985). *The lexicon in a model of language production* . New York: Garland.

Stemberger, J. P. (1989). Speech errors in early child language production. *Journal of Memory and Language, 28,* 164-188.

Stephany, U. (1986). Modality. In P. Fletcher & M. Garman (Eds.), *Language Acquisition. Vol. 2.* Cambridge: Cambridge University Press.

Stephany, U. (1992). Grammaticalization in first language acquisition. *Zeitschrift für Phonetik, Sprachwißenschaft, und Kommunikationsforschung, 45,* 289-303.

Stephany, U. (1995). The acquisition of Greek. In D. I. Slobin (Ed.), *The crosslinguistic study of language acquisition. Vol. 4.* Hillsdale, NJ: Lawrence Erlbaum.

Stern, C., & Stern, W. (1907). *Die Kindersprache* . Leipzig: Barth.

Stiles, W. B. (1992). *Describing talk: A taxonomy of verbal response modes* . Newbury Park: Sage.

Stine, E. L., & Bohannon III, J. N. (1983). Imitations, interactions, and language acquisition. *Journal of Child Language, 10,* 589-603.

Strömqvist, S., Richtoff, U., & Anderson, A.-B. (1993). Strömqvist's and Richtoff's corpora: A guide to longitudinal data from four Swedish children. *Gothenburg Papers in Theoretical Linguistics, 66.*

Suppes, P. (1973). The semantics of children's language. *American Psychologist, 88,* 103-114.

Suppes, P., Smith, R., & Leveillé, M. (1973). The French syntax of a child's noun phrases. *Archives de Psychologie, 42,* 207-269.

Svartvik, J., Eeg-Olofsson, M., Forsheden, O., Oreström, B., & Thavenius, C. (1982). *Survey of spoken English: Report on research 1975-1981* . Lund: Gleerup/Liber.

Tager-Flusberg, H., Calkins, S., Nolin, T., Bamberger, T., Anderson, M., & Chandwick-Dias, A. (1990). A longitudinal study of language acquisition in autistic and Down Syndrome children. *Journal of Autism and Developmental Disorders, 20,* 1-21.

Templin, M. (1957). *Certain language skills in children* . Minneapolis, MN: University of Minnesota Press.

Trager, G. (1958). Paralanguage: A first approximation. *Studies in Linguistics, 13,* 1-12.

Uzgiris, I., & Hunt, J. (1975). *Toward ordinal scales of psychological development in infancy* . Champaign, IL: University of Illinois Press.

Van Houten, L. (1986). *Role of maternal input in the acquisition process: The communicative strategies of adolescent and older mothers with their language learning children.* Boston: Eleventh Annual Boston University Conference on Language Development.

Van Kampen, N. J. (1994). The learnability of the left branch condition, *Linguistics in the Netherlands.*

Velasco, P. (1989). *The relationship between decontextualized oral language skills and reading comprehension in bilingual children.* Unpublished doctoral dissertation, Harvard Graduate School of Education.

Velasco, P., & Snow, C. (1990). *Bilingual children's performance in Spanish and English on decontextualized language tasks.* . Unpublished mss. Cambridge, MA: Harvard Graduate School of Education.

Volterra, V. (1972). Prime fasi di sviluppo della negazione nel linguaggio infantile. *Archivio di Psicologia, Neurologia e Psichiatria, 33,* 16-53.

Volterra, V. (1976). A few remarks on the use of the past participle in child language. *Journal of Italian Linguistics*, 2, 149-157.

Volterra, V. (1984). Waiting for the birth of a sibling: The verbal fantasies of a two year old boy. In I. Bretherton (Ed.), *Symbolic Play*. New York: Academic Press.

Wagner, K. R. (1974). *Die Sprechsprache des Kindes. Teil 1: Theorie und Analyse* . Düsseldorf: Pädagogische Verlag Schwan.

Wagner, K. R. (1985). How much do children say in a day? *Journal of Child Language*, 12, 475-487.

Warren-Leubecker, A. (1982). *Sex differences in speech to children*. Unpublished doctoral dissertation, Georgia Institute of Technology.

Warren-Leubecker, A., & Bohannon, J. N. (1984). Intonation patterns in child-directed speech: Mother-father speech. *Child Development*, 55, 1379-1385.

Weissenborn, J. (1985). Ich weiss ja nicht von hier aus, wie weit es von da hinten ist: Makroräume in der kognitiven und sprachlichen Entwicklung des Kindes. In H. Schweizer (Ed.), *Sprache und Raum*. Stuttgart: Metzlersche.

Weissenborn, J. (1986). Learning how to become an interlocutor: The verbal negotiation of common frames of reference and actions in dyads of 7- to 14-year-old children. In J. Cook-Gumperz (Ed.), *Children's worlds and children's language*. The Hague: Mouton.

Weist, R., & Witkowska-Stadnik, K. (1986). Basic relations in child language and the word order myth. *International Journal of Psychology*, 21, 363-381.

Weist, R., Wysocka, H., Witkowska-Stadnik, K., Buczowska, E., & Konieczna, E. (1984). The defective tense hypothesis: On the emergence of tense and aspect in child Polish. *Journal of Child Language*, 11, 347-374.

Wells, C. G. (1981). *Learning through interaction: The study of language development* . Cambridge: Cambridge University Press.

Wijnen, F. (1988). Spontaneous word fragmentations in children: Evidence for the syllable as a unit in speech production. *Journal of Phonetics*, 16, 187-202.

Wijnen, F. (1990a). The development of sentence planning. *Journal of Child Language*, 17, 550-562.

Wijnen, F. (1990b). *On the development of language production mechanisms*. Unpublished doctoral dissertation, University of Nijmegen.

Wijnen, F. (1992). Incidental word and sound errors in young speakers. *Journal of Memory and Language*, 31, 734-755.

Wilson, A. J., & Zeitlyn, D. (in press). The distribution of person-referring terms in natural conversation. *Research on Language and Social Interaction*.

Wilson, B., & Peters, A. M. (1988). What are you cookin' on a hot?: Movement Constraints in the Speech of a Three-Year-Old Blind Child. *Language*, 64, No.2, 249-273.

Wode, H. (1974). Natürliche Zweitsprachigkeit: Probleme, Aufgaben, Perspektiven. *Linguistische Berichte*, 32, 15-36.

Wode, H. (1977). Four early stages in the development of LI negation. *Journal of Child Language*, 4, 87-102.

Wode, H. (1978). The L1 vs L2 acquisition of English interrogation. *Indian Journal of Applied Linguistics*, 4, 31-46.

Wode, H. (1979). Operating principles and "universals" in L1, L2, and FLT. *International Review of Applied Linguistics*, 17, 217-231.

Wode, H. (1980). Grammatical intonation in child language. In L. R. Waugh & C. Schooneveld (Eds.), *The melody of language*. Baltimore, MD: University Park Press.

Wode, H. (1981). Language-acquisitional universals: A unified view of language acquisition. In H. Winitz (Ed.), *Native language and foreign language acquisition*. (Proceedings of the New York Academy of Sciences Vol. 379) New York: New York Academy of Sciences.

Wode, H. (1987). The rise of phonological coding abilities for the mental representation of lexical items. In H. Bluhme & G. Hammarström (Eds.), *Descriptio linguistica.* Tübingen: Narr.

Wode, H., & Allendorff, S. (1981). Some overgeneralizations in the L1 acquisition of interrogative pronouns. *International Review of Applied Linguistics, 19*, 31-44.

Wulfeck, B., Bates, E., Juarez, L., Opie, M., Friederici, A., MacWhinney, B., & Zurif, E. (1989). Pragmatics in aphasia: Crosslinguistic evidence. *Language and Speech, 32*, 315-336.

Zimmerman, I. L., Steiner, V. G., & Pond, R. E. (1979). *The pre-school language scale .* London: Merrill.

Index

The CHILDES Project:

Tools for Analyzing Talk

Second Edition

Brian MacWhinney
Carnegie Mellon University

LEA **LAWRENCE ERLBAUM ASSOCIATES, PUBLISHERS**
1995 Hillsdale, New Jersey   Hove, UK

Lawrence Erlbaum Associates, Inc., Publishers
365 Broadway
Hillsdale, New Jersey 07642

CHILDES postal address:

Child Language Data Exchange System
Department of Psychology
Carnegie Mellon University
Pittsburgh, PA 15213 USA
Phone: (412) 268-3793
Fax: (412) 268-7251
e-mail: brian@andrew.cmu.edu

Library of Congress Cataloging-in-Publication Data

MacWhinney, Brian.
   The CHILDES project : tools for analyzing talk / Brian MacWhinney.
--2nd ed.
    p. cm.
   Includes bibliographical references (p.   ) and index.
   ISBN 0-8058-2027-2 (alk. paper)
   1. Children--Language--Data processing. 2. Language acquisition--
Research--Data processing. I. Title.
LB1139.L3M24 1995
155.4'136'0285--dc20   95-2714
                                      CIP

Printed in the United States of America

10 9 8 7 6 5 4 3 2 1

Contents

Contents

Preface

Language acquisition research thrives on data collected from spontaneous interactions in naturally occurring situations. It is easy to turn on a taperecorder or videotape, and, before you know it, you will have accumulated a library of dozens or even hundreds of hours of naturalistic interactions. But simply collecting data is only the beginning of a much larger task, because the process of transcribing and analyzing naturalistic samples is extremely time-consuming and often unreliable. In this book, we will examine a set of computational tools designed to facilitate the sharing of transcript data, increase the reliability of transcriptions, and automate the process of data analysis. These new computational tools have brought about revolutionary changes in the way that research is conducted in the child language field. Moreover, they have equally revolutionary potential for the study of second language learning, adult conversational interactions, sociological content analyses, and language recovery in aphasia. Although the tools are of wide applicability, this book concentrates on their use in the child language field, hoping that researchers from other areas can make the necessary analogies to their own topics.

The Beginnings of Transcript Analysis

The first attempts to track the spontaneous interactions of children with their parents were stimulated by Darwin's detailed studies of gestural communication in his son. Researchers like Preyer, Ament, and the Sterns used Darwin's baby biography method to track the emergence of the first words and utterances. By writing their observations on note cards or by taking down notes at the end of the day, these researchers compiled daily accounts of the development of language in their own children. The most comprehensive of these biographies is the detailed and fully organized four-volume account by Leopold of the language development of his two English-German bilingual children. Other important works in this tradition include Gvozdev, Kenyeres, Szuman, Guillaume, and Ronjat.

Anyone who has attempted to follow a child about with a pen and a notebook soon realizes how much detail is missed and how the notetaking process interferes with the ongoing interactions. In the late 1950's, researchers began to abandon the pencil and the notebook for the audio taperecorder. In fact, much of the excitement in the 1960's regarding new directions in child language research was fueled directly by the great increase in raw data that was possible through use of taperecordings and typed transcripts. This increase in data had an additional, seldom discussed consequence. In the period of the baby biography, the final published account closely resembled the original data base of note cards. In this sense, there was no major gap between the observational database and the published database. In the period of typed transcripts, a wider gap emerged. The size of the transcripts produced in the 60's and 70's made it impossible to publish the full unanalyzed corpora. Instead, researchers were forced to publish only high-level analyses based on data that was not available to others. This led to a lamentable situation in which the raw empirical database for the field was kept only in private stocks, unavailable for general public examination. Clearly, what was needed was some better way of sharing data between research projects.

The Concept of Data Sharing

The dream of establishing a system for sharing child language transcript data has a long history, and there were several individual efforts to share data early on. For example, Roger Brown's original Adam, Eve, and Sarah transcripts (Brown, 1973) were typed onto stencils and mimeographed in multiple copies. The extra copies were lent to and analyzed by a wide variety of researchers – some of them (Moerk, 1983) attempting to disprove the conclusions drawn from those data by Brown himself! In addition, of course, to the copies lent out or given away for use by other researchers, a master copy – never lent and in principle never marked on – has been retained in Roger Brown's files as the ultimate historical archive.

Such storing and lending of hard copies of transcripts formed an historical precedent for the establishment of a true, comprehensive, international, crosslinguistic child language data exchange system, but a revolution in the basic conception of such a system was made possible by the emergence of computers as tools for storage, analysis, and communication. In the traditional model, everyone took his copy of the transcript home, developed his or her own coding scheme, applied it (usually by making pencil markings directly on the transcript), wrote a paper about the results and, if very polite, sent a copy to Roger. The original database remained untouched. The nature of each individual's coding scheme and the relationship among any set of different coding schemes could never be fully plumbed.

The dissemination of transcript data allowed us to see more clearly the limitations involved in our analytic techniques. As we began to compare handwritten and typewritten transcripts, problems in transcription methodology, coding schemes, and cross-investigator reliability became more apparent. But, just as these new problems arose, a major technological opportunity appeared. Using microcomputer word-processing systems, researchers started to enter transcript data into computer files that could then be easily duplicated, edited, and analyzed by standard data-processing techniques. Rather than serving primarily as an "archive" or historical record, a computer database can become a constantly growing data set, enriched by every user. Moreover, a focus on a shared database can lead to additional advances in methodology. At first, the possibility of utilizing shared transcription formats, shared codes, and shared analysis programs shone only as a faint glimmer on the horizon, against the fog and gloom of handwritten tallies, fuzzy dittoes, and idiosyncratic coding schemes. Slowly, against this backdrop, the idea of a computerized data exchange system began to emerge.

It was within this conceptual background that the Child Language Data Exchange System (CHILDES) system was conceived. The origin of the system can be traced back to the summer of 1981 when Dan Slobin, Willem Levelt, Susan Ervin-Tripp, and Brian MacWhinney discussed the possibility of creating an archive for typed, handwritten, and computerized transcripts to be located at the Max-Planck Institut für Psycholinguistik in Nijmegen. In 1983, the MacArthur Foundation funded meetings of developmental researchers in which Elizabeth Bates, Brian MacWhinney, Catherine Snow, and other child language researchers discussed the possibility of soliciting MacArthur funds to support a data exchange system. In January of 1984, the MacArthur Foundation awarded a two-year grant to Carnegie Mellon University for the establishment of the Child Language Data Exchange System with Brian MacWhinney and Catherine Snow as Principal Investigators. These funds provided for the entry of data into the system and for the convening of a meeting of an Advisory Board for the System.

The Three Tools

The reasons for developing a computerized exchange system for language data are immediately obvious to anyone who has produced or analyzed transcripts. With such a system, we can address these three basic goals:

1. to provide more data for more children from more ages, speaking more languages;
2. to obtain better data in a consistent and fully-documented transcription system; and
3. to automate the process of data analysis.

The CHILDES system has addressed each of these goals by developing three separate, but integrated, tools. The first tool is the **CHAT** transcription and coding format. The second tool is the **CLAN** package of analysis programs, and the third tool is the CHILDES database itself.[1] These three tools are like the legs of a three-legged stool. The transcripts in the database have all been put into the **CHAT** transcription system. The **CLAN** programs are designed to make full use of the **CHAT** format to facilitate a wide variety of searches and analyses. Many research groups are now using both **CHAT** and **CLAN** to enter new data sets. Eventually, these new data sets will be available to other researchers as a part of the growing CHILDES database. In this way, **CHAT**, **CLAN**, and the database function as a coarticulated set of complementary tools.

Some Words of Appreciation

The construction of the database has depended upon the generosity of the dozens of scholars listed in chapter 27. The **CLAN** programs are the brain child of Leonid Spektor. Spektor began his work by relying on extensions to the public domain **HUM** concordance package generously provided to us by Bill Tuthill at the University of California at Berkeley. The **HUM** package served as a solid base during the initial period of development, although no **HUM** code is contained in the current version. In addition, the **SALT** transcription system of Miller and Chapman (1983) provided solid initial guidelines regarding basic practices in transcription and analysis. We also derived ideas for the **MODREP** and **PHONFREQ** programs from aspects of the **PAL** analysis system developed by Cliff Pye.

Darius Clynes ported **CLAN** to the Macintosh and added a variety of features specific to the Macintosh, including a facility for building **CLAN** commands through dialog boxes. Jeffrey Sokolov wrote the **CHIP** program and the **CLAN** tutorial given in chapter 24 was constructed by Pam Rollins, Barbara Pan, and Catherine Snow. Mitzi Morris designed the **MOR** analyzer and the morphological rules upon which it depends.

Jane Desimone, Mary MacWhinney, Jane Morrison, Kim Roth, and Gergely Sikuta worked many long hours bringing the CHILDES database into conformity with the **CHAT** coding system. Helmut Feldweg provided an enormous service by supervising a parallel effort with the German and Dutch data sets. Mike Blackwell, Julia Evans, Kris Loh, Mary MacWhinney, Lucy Hewson, and Gergely Sikuta helped with the seemingly never-ending task of checking and formatting this book. Barbara Pan, Jeff Sokolov, and Pam Rollins also provided a reading of the final draft. Steven Gillis, Kim Plunkett, and Sven Strömqvist have helped propagate the CHILDES system at universities in Northern and Central Europe. Gillis has also built a **MOR** system for Dutch and established a CHILDES

---

[1] Acronyms and other names for computer programs and computer systems, such as **CHAT**, **CLAN**, or **FREQ** are given in bold face in small caps. The acronym CHILDES is given in standard capital letters, since it does not indicate just a computer program of format, but a complete system for data exchange and analysis.

file server at the University of Antwerp. Yuriko Oshima-Takane has established a vital group of child language researchers using CHILDES to study the acquisition of Japanese.

Catherine Snow played a pivotal role throughout the formation of the CHILDES system in shaping policy and direction, helping in the building of the database, organizing workshops, and determining the shape of CHAT and CLAN. We also received a great deal of extremely helpful input from a variety of other sources regarding the CHAT codes described in Part I. Some of the most detailed comments have come from George Allen, Elizabeth Bates, Nan Bernstein-Ratner, Giuseppe Cappelli, Paola Cipriani, Annick De Houwer, Jane Desimone, Jane Edwards, Julia Evans, Judi Fenson, Paul Fletcher, Steven Gillis, Kristen Keefe, Mary MacWhinney, Jon Miller, Barbara Pan, Lucia Pfanner, Kim Plunkett, Catherine Snow, Jeff Sokolov, Leonid Spektor, Joseph Stemberger, Frank Wijnen, and Antonio Zampolli. Comments developed in Edwards (1992) were useful in shaping parts of chapters 1, 4, 5, and 6. George Allen was the principal author of the PHONASCII system (Allen, 1988).

The CHILDES system has an ongoing commitment to the further refinement of the codes, programs, and database. Detailed comments and critiques are solicited from all interested parties. This work is currently supported by grants from the National Institute of Child Health and Human Development (NICHHD).

How to Use this Book

This book is intended primarily as a manual for users of the three CHILDES tools. Chapters 1 through 17 provide a manual for CHAT; Chapters 18 through 24 provide a manual for CLAN; and chapters 25 through 32 are a guide to the database. Different users will wish to approach these tools in different orders. Users interested primarily in producing new child language transcript data will want to focus on learning to use the CHAT and CLAN tools. Working alongside a computer, they will first learn to enter transcripts in CHAT using the CED editor and then how to run CLAN programs on the data they have entered. These users will need to have copies of the CLAN programs. They will also want to make extensive use of the guide to the use of the CHILDES tools by Sokolov and Snow (1994)..

A second group of users will be most interested in analyzing data already available in the CHILDES database. These users will want to focus first on the guide to the database in Chapters 25-32. Using this guide and following the instructions in Chapter 25, they can get copies of the data either on CD-ROM or using anonymous FTP. They will then want to scan the description of CHAT in chapter 2 in order to understand the basic coding conventions used in the database. Then, they will want to look over the description of the CLAN programs with an eye toward determining how the programs can help them analyze and quantify patterns in the database.

A third group of users may be most interested in the CHILDES tools as ways of teaching language analysis to students. These users will want to construct additional materials that will guide students through the learning of CHAT and CLAN and will encourage them to explore the current database to test out particular hypotheses. Several of the chapters in the guide to the use of the CHILDES tools (Sokolov & Snow, 1994) will help students in specific applications of CHAT and CLAN.

The CHILDES system was not intended to address all issues in the study of language learning or even to be used by all students of spontaneous interactions. The CHAT system is comprehensive, but it is not ideal for all purposes. The CLAN programs are powerful, but they cannot solve all analytic problems. It is not the goal of CHILDES to be everything to everybody or to force all research into some uniform mold. Forced uniformity, even on the level of transcription standards, would be a great disservice to scientific progress. It is important for researchers to pursue a variety of approaches to the study of language learning. Indeed, we estimate that the three CHILDES tools will never be used by at least half of the researchers in the field of child language. There are three common reasons why individual researchers may not find CHILDES useful:

1. some researchers may have already committed themselves to use of another transcription system;
2. some researchers may have collected so much data that they can work for many years without needing to collect more data and without comparing their own data to other researchers' data; and
3. some researchers may not be interested in studying spontaneous speech.

Of these three reasons for not needing to use the three CHILDES tools, the third is the most frequent. For example, researchers studying comprehension would only be interested in CHILDES data when they wish to compare findings arising from studies of comprehension with patterns occurring in spontaneous production.

Changes and the Future

The CHILDES tools have been extensively tested for ease of application, accuracy, and reliability. However, change is fundamental to the research enterprise. Researchers are constantly pursuing better ways of coding and analyzing data. It is important that the CHILDES tools keep progress with these changing requirements. For this reason, there will be revisions to **CHAT, CLAN,** and the database as long as the CHILDES project is active. Some of the important directions for the future are discussed in Chapter 35.

1. Principles of Transcription

The **CHAT** system is a standardized format for computerized transcripts of face-to-face conversational interactions. Face-to-face interactions may be between children and their parents, between a doctor and a patient, or between a teacher and second language learners. Despite the differences between interactions of these different types, there are enough features common to the various forms of face-to-face interaction to make the idea of a general transcription system reasonable. The system being proposed here is designed for use with both normal and disordered populations. It can be used with learners of all types, including children, second language learners, and adults recovering from aphasic disorders. The system provides options for basic discourse transcription, as well as detailed phonological and morphological analysis. The system bears the acronym "CHAT" which stands for Codes for the Human Analysis of Transcripts. **CHAT** is the standard transcription system for the CHILDES (Child Language Data Exchange System) Project. With the exception of a few corpora of historical interest, all of the transcripts in the CHILDES database are in **CHAT** format. In addition, approximately 60 groups of researchers around the world are currently actively involved in new data collection and transcription using the **CHAT** system. Eventually the data collected in these projects will be contributed to the database. The **CHAT** system is specifically designed to facilitate the subsequent automatic analysis of transcripts by the **CLAN** programs that will be discussed in chapters 18 to 24.

1.1. The Promise of Computerized Transcription

Public inspection of experimental data is a crucial prerequisite for serious scientific progress. Imagine how genetics would function if every experimenter had their own individual strain of peas or drosophila and refused to allow them to be tested by other experimenters. What would happen in geology, if every scientist kept their own set of rock specimens and refused to compare them with those of other researchers? In some fields the basic phenomena in question are so clearly open to public inspection that this is not a problem. The basic facts of planetary motion are open for all to see, as are the basic facts underlying Newtonian mechanics.

Unfortunately, in language studies, a free and open sharing and exchange of data has not always been the norm. In earlier decades, researchers often jealously guarded their field notes from a particular language community of subject type, refusing to share them openly with the broader community. Various justifications were given for this practice. It was sometimes claimed that other researchers would not fully appreciate the nature of the data or that they might misrepresent crucial patterns. Sometimes, it was claimed that only someone who had actually participated in the community or the interaction could understand the nature of the language and the interactions. In some cases, these limitations were real and important. However, such restrictions on the sharing of data inevitably impede the progress of the scientific study of language learning.

Within the field of language acquisition studies it is now understood that the advantages of sharing data outweigh the potential dangers. The question is no longer whether data should be shared, but rather how they can be shared in a reliable and responsible fashion. The computerization of transcripts opens up the possibility for many types of data sharing and analysis that otherwise would have been impossible. However, the full exploitation of this opportunity requires the development of a standardized system for data transcription and analysis.

1.2. Some Words of Caution

Before we examine the **CHAT** system, we need to consider certain dangers involved in computerized transcriptions. These dangers arise from the need to compress a complex set of spoken and nonspoken messages into the extremely narrow channel required for the computer. In most cases, these dangers also exist when one creates a typewritten or handwritten transcript. Let us look at some of the dangers surrounding this enterprise.

1.2.1. The Dominance of the Written Word

Perhaps the greatest danger facing the transcriber is the tendency to treat spoken language as if it were written language. The decision to write out stretches of vocal material using the forms of written language involves a major theoretical commitment. As Ochs (1979) showed so clearly, these decisions inevitably turn transcription into a theoretical enterprise. The most difficult bias to overcome is the tendency to map every form spoken by a learner – be it a child, an aphasic, or a second language learner – onto a set of standard lexical items in the adult language. Transcribers tend to assimilate nonstandard learner strings to standard forms of the adult language. For example, when a child says "put on my jamas," the transcriber may instead enter "put on my pajamas," reasoning unconsciously that "jamas" is simply a childish form of "pajamas." This type of regularization of the child form to the adult lexical norm can lead to misunderstanding of the shape of the child's lexicon. For example, it could be the case that the child uses "jamas" and "pajamas" to refer to two very different things (Clark, 1987; MacWhinney, 1989).

There are two types of errors possible here. One involves mapping a learner's spoken form onto an adult form when, in fact, there was no real correspondence. This is the problem of *overregularization*. The second type of error involves failing to map a learner's spoken form onto an adult form when, in fact, there is a correspondence. This is the problem of *underregularization*. The goal of transcribers should be to avoid both the Scylla of overregularization and the Charybdis of underregularization. Steering a course between these two dangers is no easy matter. A transcription system can provide devices to aid in this process, but it cannot guarantee safe passage.
Transcribers also often tend to assimilate the shape of sounds spoken by the learner to the shapes that are dictated by morphosyntactic patterns. For example, Fletcher (1985) noted that both children and adults generally produce "have" as "uv" before main verbs. As a result, forms like "might have gone" assimilate to "mightuv gone." Fletcher believed that younger children have not yet learned to associate the full auxiliary "have" with the contracted form. If we write the children's forms as "might have," we then end up mischaracterizing the structure of their lexicon. To take another example, we can note that, in French, the various endings of the verb in the present tense are distinguished in spelling, whereas they are homophonous in speech. If a child says /mAnZ/ "eat," are we to transcribe it as first person singular *mange*, as second person singular *manges*, or as the imperative *mange?* If the child says /mAnZe/, should we transcribe it as the infinitive *manger*, the participle *mangé*, or the second person formal *mangez* ?

CHAT deals with these problems by providing a uniform way of transcribing discourse phonemically called UNIBET. Using UNIBET, we can code "mightuv" as /maItUv/ and *mangez/manger/mangé* as /mAnZe/. It is a pity that phonological transcriptions are not more widely used, because they offer a level of accuracy that is difficult to obtain in other ways. However, for those who wish to avoid the work involved in phonemic transcription, **CHAT** also allows for the specification of nonstandard lexical forms, so that the form "mightav" would be universally recognized as the spelling of the contracted form of "might have." For the French example, **CHAT** allows for a general neutral suffix written as *-e*. Using this, we would write *mang-e*, rather than *mang-ez*, *mang-é*, or *mang-er*.

As a supplement to the use of UNIBET codes, the **CED** editor supports transcription in standard IPA characters. **CED** also allows the user to link a full digitized audio record of the interaction directly to the transcript. This is the system called "sonic **CHAT**". With these sonic **CHAT** links, it is possible to double click on a sentence and hear its sound immediately. Having the actual sound produced by the child directly available in the transcript takes some of the burden off of the transcription system. However, whenever computerized analyses are based not on the original audio signal, but on transcribed orthographic forms, one must continue to understand the limits of transcriptions conventions.

1.2.2. The Misuse of Standard Punctuation

Transcribers have a tendency to write out spoken language with the punctuation conventions of written language. Written language is organized into clauses and sentences delimited by commas, periods, and other marks of punctuation. Spoken language, on the other hand, is organized into tone units clustered about a tonal nucleus and delineated by pauses and tonal contours (Crystal, 1969; Crystal, 1975; Halliday, 1966; Halliday, 1967; Halliday, 1968). Work on the discourse basis of sentence production (Chafe, 1980; Chafe, 1987; Jefferson, 1984; MacWhinney, 1985) has demonstrated a close link between tone units and ideational units. Retracings, pauses, stress, and all forms of intonational contours are crucial markers of aspects of the utterance planning process. Moreover, these features also convey important sociolinguistic information. Within special markings or conventions, there is no way to directly indicate these important aspects of interactions.

One way of dealing with punctuation bias is to supplement UNIBET phonological coding with prosodic markings that indicate tonal stress and rises and falls in intonation. For those who do not wish to construct a complete phonological transcription, **CHAT** makes available a set of prosodic markers that can be combined either with standard words or with a phonological transcription to code the details of tone units and contours. In addition, **CHAT** provides a set of conventions for marking retracings, pauses, and errors. Again, having the actual audio record available through the sonic **CHAT** feature in the **CED** editor helps keep a link between the transcript and the original data.

1.2.3.   The Advantages of Working with a Videotape

Whatever form a transcript may take, it will never contain a fully accurate record of what went on in an interaction. A transcript of an interaction can never fully replace an audiotape, because an audiotape of the interaction will always be more accurate in terms of preserving the actual details of what transpired. By the same token, an audio recording can never preserve as much detail as a video recording with a high-quality audio track. Audio recordings record none of the nonverbal interactions that often form the backbone of a conversational interaction. Hence, they systematically exclude a source of information that is crucial for a full interpretation of the interaction. Although there are biases involved even in a videotape, it is still the most accurate record of an interaction that we have available. For those who are trying to use transcription to capture the full detailed character of an interaction, it is imperative that transcription be done from a videotape and the videotape be repeatedly consulted during all phases of analysis.

The **CED** editor is currently being extended to facilitate its use with videotapes. Our plan is to make available a floating window in the shape of a VCR controller that can be used to rewind the videotape and to enter time stamps from the videotape into the **CHAT** file.

1.3.   Transcription and Coding

It is important to recognize the difference between *transcription* and *coding*. Transcription focuses on the production of a written record that can lead us to understand, albeit only vaguely, the flow of the original interaction. Transcription must be done directly off an audiotape or, preferably, a videotape. Coding, on the other hand, is the process of recognizing, analyzing and taking note of phenomena in transcribed speech. Coding can often be done by referring only to a written transcript. For example, the coding of parts of speech can be done directly from a transcript without listening to the audiotape. For other types of coding, such as speech act coding, it is imperative that coding be done while watching the original videotape.

The **CHAT** system includes conventions for both transcription and coding. When first learning the system, it is best to focus on learning how to transcribe. The **CHAT** system offers the transcriber a large array of coding options. Although few transcribers will need to use all of the options, everyone needs to understand how basic transcription is done on the "main line." Additional coding is done principally on the secondary or "dependent" tiers. As transcribers work more with their data, they will include further options from the secondary or "dependent" tiers. However, the beginning user should focus first on learning to correctly use the conventions for the main line. The manual includes several sample transcripts to help the beginner in learning the transcription system.

2. The CHAT Transcription System

2.1. The Goals of a Transcription System

Like other forms of communication, transcription systems are subjected to a variety of communicative pressures. The view of language structure developed by Slobin (1977) sees structure as emerging from the pressure of three conflicting charges or goals. On the one hand, language is designed to be **clear**. On the other hand, it is designed to be **processible** by the listener and quick and **easy** for the speaker. Unfortunately, ease of production often comes in conflict with clarity of marking. The competition between these three motives leads to a variety of imperfect solutions that satisfy each goal only partially. Such imperfect and unstable solutions characterize the grammar and phonology of human language (Bates & MacWhinney, 1982). Only rarely does a solution succeed in fully achieving all three goals.

Slobin's view of the pressures shaping human language can be extended to analyze the pressures shaping a transcription system. In many regards, a transcription system is much like any human language. It needs to be clear in its markings of categories, while still preserving readability and ease of transcription. However, unlike a human language, a transcription system needs to address two types audiences. One audience is the human audience of transcribers, analysts, and readers. The other audience is the digital computer and its programs. In order to successfully deal with these two audiences, a system for computerized transcription needs to achieve the following goals:

1. **Clarity**: Every symbol used in the coding system should have some clear and definable real-world referent. The relation between the referent and the symbol should be consistent and reliable. Symbols that mark particular words should always be spelled in a consistent manner. Symbols that mark particular conversational patterns should refer to actual patterns consistently observable in the data. In practice, codes will always have to steer between the Scylla of overregularization and the Charybdis of underregularization discussed earlier. Distinctions must avoid being either too fine or too coarse. Another way of looking at clarity is through the notion of **systematicity**. Systematicity is a simple extension of clarity across transcripts or corpora. Codes, words, and symbols must be used in a consistent manner across transcripts. Ideally, each code should always have a unique meaning independent of the presence of other codes or the particular transcript in which it is located. If interactions are necessary, as in hierarchical coding systems, these interactions need to be systematically described.
2. **Readability**: Just as human language needs to be easy to process, so transcripts need to be easy to read. This goal often runs directly counter to the first goal. In the CHILDES system, we have attempted to provide a variety of CHAT options that will allow a user to maximize the readability of a transcript. We have also provided CLAN tools that will allow a reader to suppress the less readable aspects in transcript when the goal of readability is more important than the goal of clarity of marking.
3. **Ease of data entry**: As distinctions proliferate within a transcription system, data entry becomes increasingly difficult and error-prone. The CLAN programs provide three tools for dealing with this problem. One is a program called **CHECK** that verifies the syntactic accuracy of a transcript. The second is a mode of the

CED editor that provides computer assistance for applying a coding scheme to a transcript. The third is a program called **MOR** which provides automatic morphological analysis of the words in a transcript.

2.2. Learning to Use CHAT

CHAT is designed to provide options for users on two levels – basic and advanced. The basic level of **CHAT** is called min**CHAT**. Everyone should start out first learning min**CHAT**.

2.2.1. minCHAT and minDOS

At the basic level, **CHAT** requires a minimum of coding decisions. This minimalist version of **CHAT**, called min**CHAT**, is discussed in section 2.3. Min**CHAT** looks much like other intuitive transcription systems that are in general use in the fields of child language and discourse analysis. It makes sense for the new user to focus on the use of min**CHAT** and to ignore the rest of this manual at first. However, eventually, many users will find that there is something that they want to be able to code that goes beyond min**CHAT**. At that point, the next chapters to read are chapters 4, 7, and 8, which explain the remaining details of the basic coding of words on the main line.

The beginning user also has to become familiar with the basic use of a microcomputer. For users working with a Macintosh computer, this means learning how to navigate around on the desktop and how to use the mouse to open up menus and select items. For users working with machines running MS-DOS, this means learning how to use these DOS commands: **type, dir, cd, path, mkdir, rmdir, delete, copy,** and **rename.** We refer to this restricted set of DOS commands as minDOS. Acquainting yourself with minDOS requires patience and a careful reading of your MS-DOS manuals. While learning minDOS, you also need to learn the **CED** text editor.

2.2.2. Analyzing One Small File

For researchers who are just now beginning to use **CHAT** and **CLAN**, there is perhaps one single suggestion that can save literally hundreds of hours of possibly wasted time. The suggestion is to transcribe and analyze one single small file completely and perfectly before launching a major program of transcription and analysis. The idea is that you should learn just enough about min**CHAT**, minDOS, and min**CLAN** to see your path through these four crucial steps:
1. entry of a small set of your data into a **CHAT** file using **CED**,
2. successful running of the **CHECK** program inside **CED** to guarantee accuracy in your **CHAT** file,
3. development of a series of codes that will interface with the particular **CLAN** programs most appropriate for your analysis, and
4. running of the relevant **CLAN** programs, so that you can be sure that the results you will get will properly test the hypotheses you wish to develop.

If you go through these steps first, you can guarantee in advance the successful outcome of your project. You can avoid ending up in a situation in which you have transcribed hundreds of hours of data in a way that simply does not match correctly with the input requirements for the **CLAN** programs.

2.2.3. midCHAT

After having learned min**CHAT**, the learner is ready to move on to mid**CHAT**. Before doing that, it is probably a good idea to learn the basics of **CLAN**. To do this, first consult chapter 18 which introduces the CLAN system. To begin, you will want to learn CLAN only up to the level of minCLAN, which corresponds to the minCHAT level. However, once you have learned midCHAT, it also makes sense to learn the rest of the CLAN system. Learning midCHAT involves mastering additional material in chapters 4, 5, 7, and 8. This material includes the following aspects of transcription:

1. the use of canonical spellings (chapter 4),
2. using explanations on the main line (chapter 8),
3. marking omitted words and morphemes (chapters 4 and 5),
4. indicating suffixes and prefixes on the main line (chapter 5),
5. marking utterance incompletion (chapter 7) and overlap (chapter 8), and
6. marking retracings and errors (chapter 8).

Having mastered the CHAT manual through chapter 8, the learner has picked up all of the basic CHAT conventions. In many cases, the transcriber may not need to learn any more about CHAT. However, there are five topic areas for which researchers will have to look at other chapters.

1. **Phonological Transcription.** If your research deals with speech that diverges strongly from the standard in phonological terms, you will want to make use of some form of phonological transcription. This is often important when you are dealing with very young children, language-impaired subjects, dialect speakers, and second language learners. If you need to do phonological transcription, first read chapter 10, which describes a system for phonemic transcription, including codes for stress and tone contours. If this level of detail is insufficient, the full extended IPA phonetic system given in chapter 11 may be needed.

2. **Speech Acts**. If your research focuses on speech acts, you will wish to work out a system of the sort outlined in chapter 13. That chapter provides only a sketch of a fuller set of codes that will be provided in future versions of CHAT.

3. **Error Analysis**. If your research deals with the analysis of phonological, morphological, syntactic, or semantic errors, you will want to read chapter 12, which presents a system for the detailed coding of errors. That chapter has a number of examples given at the end and there are further examples of error coding that can be found in chapter 15. Even if you do not use this full system, you may wish to mark errors using the asterisk symbol on the main line.

4. **Timing Analyses**. If you wish to construct detailed analyses of pause times and the times for spoken material, you will want to look at the use of the %tim coding line discussed in chapter 9.

5. **Morphological Analysis**. If you wish to analyze the child's learning of morphological markings, you will first want to look at the main line coding of morphemes discussed in chapter 5. However, for those who want to go beyond the simple tabulation of types of markings, it is better to use the complete system for morphological and syntactic coding presented in chapter 14.

Finally, there will be researchers who find that none of the CHAT conventions properly express the categories that they wish to code. In such cases, researchers can create their own CHAT codes, following the basic principles discussed in chapter 9.

2.2.4.   Problems with Forced Decisions

Transcription and coding systems often force the user to make difficult distinctions. For example, a system might make a distinction between grammatical ellipsis and ungrammatical omission. However, it may often be the case that the user cannot decide in a given case whether an omission is grammatical or not. In that case, it may be helpful to have some way of blurring the distinction in the particular case. **CHAT** has certain symbols that can be used when a categorization cannot be made. It is important to remember that many of the **CHAT** symbols are entirely optional. Whenever you feel that you are being forced to make a distinction, check with the manual to see whether the particular coding choice is actually required. If it is not required, then simply omit the code altogether.

2.3.   minCHAT

This section describes the minimum set of standards for a **CHAT** file. Files that follow these standards can use most aspects of the **CLAN** programs effectively. The basic requirements for min**CHAT** involve the form of the file, the form of utterances, the writing of documentation, and the use of ASCII symbols.

2.3.1.   The Form of Files

There are several minimum standards for the form of a min**CHAT** file. These standards must be followed for the **CLAN** programs to run successfully on **CHAT** files:

1.   When doing normal coding in English, every character in the file must be in the basic ASCII character set (see the following section).

2.   Every line must end with a carriage return.

3.   The first line in the file must be an @Begin header line.

4.   The last line in the file must be an @End header line.

5.   There must be an @Participants header line listing three-letter codes for each participant, the participant's name, and the participant's role.

6.   Lines beginning with * indicate what was actually said. These are called "main lines." Each main line should code one and only one utterance. When a speaker produces several utterances in a row, code each with a new main line.

7.   After the asterisk on the main line comes a three-letter code in upper case letters for the participant who was the speaker of the utterance being coded. After the three-letter code comes a colon and then a tab.

8.   What was actually said is entered starting in the ninth column.

9.   Lines beginning with the % symbol can contain anything. Typically, these lines include codes and commentary on what was said. They are called "dependent tier" lines.

10. Dependent tier lines begin with the % symbol. Then comes a three-letter code in lower case letters for the dependent tier type, such as "pho" for phonology, a colon, and then a tab. The text of the dependent tier begins in the ninth column.

11. Continuations of main lines and dependent tier lines begin with a tab.

2.3.2. The Form of Utterances

In addition to these minimum requirements for the form of the file, there are certain minimum ways in which utterances and words should be written on the main line:

1. Utterances should end with an utterance terminator. The basic utterance terminators are the period, the exclamation mark, and the question mark.

2. Commas should be used sparingly.

3. Use upper case letters only for proper nouns and the word "I." Do not use upper case letters for the first words of sentences. This will facilitate the identification of proper nouns. However, for languages like German that use capitalization to mark part of speech, this restriction can be modified so that only nouns are capitalized.

4. Unintelligible words with an unclear phonetic shape should be transcribed as **xxx.**

5. If you wish to note the phonological form of an incomplete or unintelligible phonological string, write it out with an ampersand, as in **&guga.**

6. Incomplete words can be written with the omitted material in parentheses, as in **(be)cause** and **(a)bout.**

Here is a sample that illustrates these principles. This file is syntactically correct and uses the minimum number of **CHAT** conventions while still maintaining compatibility with the **CLAN** analysis programs.

```
@Begin
@Participants:    ROS Ross Child, BRI Brian Father
*ROS: why isn't Mommy coming?
%com: Mother usually picks Ross up around 4 PM.
*BRI: don't worry.
*BRI: she'll be here soon.
*ROS: good.
@End
```

For further examples of minCHAT coding see chapter 15.

2.3.3. The Documentation File

CHAT files typically record a conversational sample collected from a particular set of speakers on a particular day. Sometimes researchers study a small set of children repeatedly over a long period of time. This is a *longitudinal* study. For such studies, it is best to break up **CHAT** files into one collection for each child. Such a collection of files constitutes a *corpus*. A corpus can also be composed of a group of files from different groups of speakers when the focus is on a *cross-sectional* sampling of larger numbers of language learners from various age groups. In either case, each corpus should be accompanied by a documentation file. By convention, the name for this file should be

"00readme.doc". The name of this file begins with two zeroes in order to assure that it appears first in directory listings. This "readme" file should contain a basic set of facts that are indispensable for the proper interpretation of the data by other researchers. The minimum set of facts that should be in each "00readme.doc" file are:

1. **Acknowledgments.** There should be a statement that asks the user to cite some particular reference when using the corpus. For example, researchers using the Adam, Eve, and Sarah corpora from Roger Brown and his colleagues are asked to cite Brown (1973). In addition, all users can cite this manual as the source for the CHILDES system in general.

2. **Restrictions.** If the data is being contributed to the CHILDES system, contributors can set particular restrictions on the use of their data. For example, researchers may ask that they be sent copies of articles that make use of their data. Many researchers have chosen to set no limitations at all on the use of their data.

3. **Warnings.** This documentation file should also warn other researchers about limitations on the use of the data. For example, if an investigator paid no attention to correct transcription of speech errors, this should be noted.

4. **Pseudonyms.** The 00readme.doc file should also include information on whether informants gave informed consent for the use of their data and whether pseudonyms have been used to preserve informant anonymity. In general, real names should be replaced by pseudonyms. This replacement may not be desirable when the subject of the transcriptions is the researcher's own child.

5. **History.** There should be detailed information on the history of the project. How was funding obtained? What were the goals of the project? How was data collected? What was the sampling procedure? How was transcription done? What was ignored in transcription? Were transcribers trained? Was reliability checked? Was coding done? What codes were used? Was the material computerized? How?

6. **Codes.** If project-specific codes are being used, these should be described.

7. **Biographical data.** Where possible, extensive demographic, dialectological, and psychometric data should be provided for each informant. There should be information on topics such as age, gender, siblings, schooling, social class, occupation, previous residences, religion, interests, friends, and so forth. Information on where the parents grew up and the various residences of the family is particularly important in attempting to understand sociolinguistic issues regarding language change, regionalism, and dialect. Without detailed information about specific dialect features, it is difficult to know whether these particular markers are being used throughout the language or just in certain regions.

8. **Table of contents.** There should be a brief index to the contents of the corpora. This could be in the form of a list of files with their dates and the age of the target children involved. If MLU data are available for the children, these should be included. Such data are often extremely helpful to other researchers in making an initial judgment regarding the utility of a data set for their particular research objectives.

9. **Situational descriptions.** General situational descriptions such as the shape of the child's home and bedroom can be included in the readme file. More specific

situational information should be included in each separate file, as discussed in chapter 3.

2.3.4. Checking Syntactic Accuracy

Each **CLAN** program runs a very superficial check to see if a file conforms to minCHAT. This check looks only to see that each line begins with either @, *, %, a tab or a space. This is the minimum that the **CLAN** programs must have to function. However, the correct functioning of many of the functions of **CLAN** depends on adherence to further standards for minCHAT. In order to make sure that a file matches these minimum requirements for correct analysis through the **CLAN** programs, researchers should run each file through the **CLAN** program called **CHECK**. The program can be run directly inside the **CED** editor, so that you can verify the accuracy of your transcription as you are producing it. The **CHECK** program will detect errors such as failure to start lines with the correct symbols, use of incorrect speaker codes, or missing @Begin and @End symbols. **CHECK** can also be used to find errors in **CHAT** coding beyond those discussed in this chapter. Using the **CHECK** program is like brushing your teeth. It may be hard to remember to use the program, but the more you use it the easier it becomes and the better the final results.

2.3.5. ASCII, extended ASCII, and Special Characters

By default, **CHAT** files are in ASCII code. Basic ASCII is composed of these 96 printing symbols:

```
a b c d e f g h i j k l m n o p q r s t u v w x y z
A B C D E F G H I J K L M N O P Q R S T U V W X Y Z
1 2 3 4 5 6 7 8 9 0 - = [ ] ' ` ; / \ . ,
! @ # $ % ^ & * ( ) _ + { } " ~ : ? | > <
```

This core set of characters is constant across computers, but the next 128 characters used on many computers are not standardized. These additional 128 characters are called "extended ASCII".

The **CED** editor allows users to create standard ASCII files for language like English and Dutch that can be represented with only ASCII characters. For many other languages, additional fonts and characters are needed and **CED** provides support for these additional characters on both Macintosh and MS-DOS computers.

3. File Headers

The three major components of a CHAT transcript are the file headers, the main tier, and the dependent tiers. In this chapter we discuss creating the first major component – the file headers. A computerized transcript in CHAT format begins with a series of "header" lines, which tells us about things such as the date of the recording, the names of the participants, the ages of the participants, the setting of the interaction, and so forth. Most of these header lines occur only at the very beginning of the file. These are what we call "constant headers," because they refer to information that is constant throughout the file. Other headers can occur along within the main body of the file. These "changeable headers" refer to information that varies during the course of the interaction.

A header is a line of text that gives information about the participants and the setting. All headers begin with the "@" sign. Some headers require nothing more than the @ sign and the header name. These are "bare" headers such as @Begin or @New Episode. However, most headers require that there be some additional material. This additional material is called an "entry." Headers that take entries must have a colon, which is then followed by one or two tabs and the required entry. By default, tabs are usually understood to be placed at eight-character intervals. The only purpose for the tabs is to improve the readability of the file header information. The material up to the colon is called the "header name." In the example following, "@Age of CHI:" and "@Date:" are both header names.

```
@Age of CHI:    2;6.14
@Date:      25-JAN-1983
```

The text that follows the header name is called the "header entry." In the example cited earlier, "2;6.14" and "25-JAN-1983" are the header entries. The header name and the header entry together are called the "header line." The header line should never have a punctuation mark at the end. In CHAT, only utterances actually spoken by the subjects receive final punctuation.

This chapter presents a set of headers that researchers have considered important. You may find this list incomplete. It that case, CHAT allows you to add to it. You may also find many of the headers unnecessary. Except for the @Begin, @Participants, and @End headers, none of the headers are required and you should feel free to use only those headers that you feel are needed for the accurate documentation of your corpus.

3.1. Obligatory Headers

CHAT uses three types of headers – obligatory, constant, and changeable. There are only three obligatory headers – @Begin, @Participants, and @End. Without these obligatory headers, the CLAN programs will not run correctly.

@Begin

This header is placed at the beginning of the file. It is needed to guarantee that no material has been lost at the beginning of the file. This is a "bare" header that takes no entry and uses no colon.

@Participants:
This header must be included as the second line in the file. It lists all of the actors within the file. The entry for this header is XXX Name Role, XXX Name Role, ..., XXX Name Role. XXX stands for the three-letter speaker ID. Here is an example of a completed @Participants header line:

```
@Participants:  SAR  Sue_Day  Target_Child,  CAR  Carol  Mother
```

Participants are identified by three elements: their speaker ID, their name and their role:

1. **Speaker ID.** The speaker ID is usually composed of three letters. The code may be based either on the participant's name, as in *ROS or *BIL, or on her role, as in *CHI or *MOT. In this type of identifying system, several different children could be indicated as *CH1, *CH2, *CH3, and so on. Speaker IDs must be unique because they will be used to identify speakers both in the main body of the transcript and in other headers. In many transcripts, three letters are enough to distinguish all speakers. However, even with three letters, some ambiguities can arise. For example, suppose that the child being studied is named Mark (MAR) and his mother is named Mary (MAR). They would both have the same speaker ID and you would not be able to tell who was talking. So you must change one speaker ID. You would probably want to change it to something that would be easy to read and understand as you go through the file. A good choice is that speaker's role. In this example, Mary's speaker ID would be changed to MOT (Mother). You could change Mark's speaker ID to CHI, but that would be misleading if there are other children in the transcript. So a better solution would be to use MAR and MOT as shown in the following example:

```
@Participants:  MAR  Mark  Target_Child,  MOT  Mary  Mother
```

Combinations of speaker and addressee can be indicated by combining three-letter codes, as in *CHI-MOT or *CHI-FAT for the child talking to the Mother or the child talking to the Father.

2. **Name.** The speaker's name can be omitted. If the **CLAN** programs find only a three-letter ID and a role, they will assume that the name has been omitted. In order to preserve anonymity, it is often useful to include a pseudonym for the name, since the pseudonym will also be used in the body of the transcript. For the **CLAN** programs to correctly parse the participants line, multiple-word name definitions such as "Sue Day" need to be joined in the form "Sue_Day".

3. **Role.** After the ID and name, you type in the role of the speaker. There are a fixed set of roles specified in the file used by the **CHECK** program and we recommend trying to use these fixed roles whenever possible. The roles given in that file are: Target_child, Child, Mother, Father, Brother, Sister, Sibling, Grandmother, Grandfather, Aunt, Uncle, Cousin, Family_Friend, Playmate, Visitor, Student, Teacher, Investigator, Examiner, Observer, Camera_Operator Doctor, Nurse, Patient, Client, Subject, Unidentified, Adult, Teenager, Non_Human, OffScript, and Narrator. All of these roles are hard-wired into the **depfile** used by the **CHECK** program. It is impossible to list all of the roles that one might wish to use. Therefore, if one of these standard roles does not work, it would be best to use one of the generic age roles, like Adult, Child, or Teenager. Then, the exact nature of the role can be put in the place of the name, as in these examples:

```
@Participants:    TBO  Toll_Booth_Operator  Adult,
```

```
AIR  Airport_Attendant  Adult,  SI1 First_Sibling  Sibling,
SI2  Second_Sibling  Sibling,  OFF MOT_to_INV OffScript,
NON  Computer_Talk  Non_Human
```

@End
Like the @Begin header, this header uses no colon and takes no entry. It is the only
constant header that is not placed at the beginning of the file. Instead, it is placed at the end
of the file. It is needed to guarantee that no material has been lost at the end of the file.
Experience has shown that adding this header provides an important safeguard against the
very real danger of undetected file truncation during copying.

3.2. Constant Headers

The second set of **CHAT** headers are the nonobligatory constant headers that contain useful
information that is constant throughout the file. These headers are placed at the beginning
of the file before any of the actual spoken utterances. Constant headers indicate such basic
information as the speaker's age, socioeconomic status, or date of birth – information that
is unlikely to change during the course of the recording session. A given researcher may
be interested in the use of personal pronouns by middle class, male 2-year-olds. Having
this information readily accessible allows us to search the database more efficiently. The
following list of constant headers is arranged alphabetically.

@Age of XXX:
This header specifies a speaker's age in years, months and days. Age is typically entered
for the Target Child and his or her siblings, but could be entered for any speaker. The
XXX symbol stands for the three-letter speaker ID. The entry for the @Age header is
given in the form years;months.days as in 2;11.17 for 2 years, 11 months, and 17 days.
This syntax is different from that used to represent dates.

You can figure out a child's age if you know the date of the transcript and the child's date
of birth. Suppose that John (JOH) was born on May 12, 1978 and the date of the
transcript is September 20, 1984. First, you calculate the number of full years since he
was born. From May of 1978 to May of 1984 (Johnny's last birthday) is 6 years. Then
you calculate the number of full months since his last birthday. From May 12, 1984 to
September 12, 1984 is 4 months. Then you calculate the number of days from that day.
From September 12 to September 20, 1984 is 8 days. So John's age would be 6 years, 4
months and 8 days. This same computation can also be done by the **DATES** program
discussed in Chapter 21. Here is an example of the completed header line:

```
@Age of JOH:  6;4.8
```
If you do not know the child's age in days, you can simply use years and months, as in
this example:

```
@Age of JOH:     6;4.
```
If you do not know the months, you can use this form:

```
@Age of JOH:     6;
```

@Birth of XXX:

This header gives the date of birth of the speaker. The speaker is indicated by the three-letter speaker ID in place of the XXX. The entry for this header is day-month-year. Notice that the day comes first and the month second. In this notation, January 23, 1973 is reformatted as 23-JAN-1973. In all dates, months should be upper case and abbreviated as follows: JAN, FEB, MAR, APR, MAY, JUN, JUL, AUG, SEP, OCT, NOV, DEC. Here is an example of an @Birth header line:

```
@Birth of SAR: 23-JUL-1961
```

@Coder:

This line identifies the people who transcribed and coded the file. Having this indicated is often helpful later when questions arise. It also provides us with a way of expressing appreciation to the people who have taken the time to make the data available for further study.

@Education of XXX:

The entry for this header is the speaker's highest grade in school. Education is indicated by the integers from 0 to 20, where the numbers after 12 indicate years of college. The speaker is indicated by the speaker ID in place of the XXX. For example, if the speaker was in her second year of graduate school, this would be represented as "18." Here is an example of an @Education line:

```
@Education of MOT: 18
```

@Filename:

This header gives the name of the computer file, as a safeguard against accidental file renaming.

@ID:

The **STATFREQ** program uses this header to assign a unique code to each individual child or file across a larger set of files. If you plan to use the **STATFREQ** program, you can develop a general coding scheme and enter values for @ID headers. Here is an example of this type of header:

```
@ID:   1.25.8.2=NIC
```

This sets the ID for the speaker Nicolette to 1.25.8.2 for this file. In this scheme the first 1 might indicate that the speaker is a child. The 25 might indicate that this is file number 25 for this corpus. The 8 might indicate that this is age level 8, and so on.

@Language:

This head is used to indicate the main language of the transcript.

@Language of XXX:
This header can be used to indicate the primary language of the various participants. In order to describe the basic language of a particular interaction, it is best to use the @bg and @eg markers that work with the **GEM** program. When language switching is even more intense, it may be necessary to include a %lan: dependent tier for each utterance indicating the language of the utterance. Ideas for constructing such a tier are given in chapter 9.

@SES of XXX:
This header describes the socioeconomic status of the child's family. The child is indicated by the speaker ID in place of the XXX. To enter the family's socioeconomic status, use standard adjectives such as: welfare, lower, working, lower-middle, middle, upper-middle, upper. Here is an example of a completed @SES header:

```
@SES  of  SAR:  working
```

@Sex of XXX:
This header indicates the gender of the speaker, Male or Female. The speaker is indicated by the three-letter speaker ID in place of the XXX. Here is an example of a completed @Sex header line:

```
@Sex  of  SAR:  female
```

@Warning:
This header is used to warn the user about certain defects or peculiarities in the collection and transcription of the data in the file. Some typical warnings are as follows:
1. These data are not useful for the analysis of overlaps, because overlapping was not accurately transcribed.
2. These data contain no information regarding the context. Therefore they will be inappropriate for many types of analysis.
3. Retracings and hesitation phenomena have not been accurately transcribed in these data.
4. These data have been transcribed, but the transcription has not yet been double-checked.
5. This file has not yet passed successfully through the **CHECK** program.

3.3. Changeable Headers

Changeable Headers can occur either at the beginning of the file along with the constant headers or else in the body of the file. Changeable Headers contain information that can change within the file. For example, if the file contains material that was recorded on only one day, the @Date header would occur only once at the beginning of the file. However, if the material contains some material from a later day, the @Date header would be used again later in the file to indicate the next date. These headers appear, then, at the point within the file where the information changes. The list that follows is alphabetical.

@Activities:
This header describes the activities involved in the situation. The entry is a list of component activities in the situation. Suppose the @Situation header reads, "Getting ready to go out," the @Activities header would list what was involved in this, such as putting on coats, gathering school books and saying good-bye.

@Bg and **@Bg:**
These headers are used to mark the beginning of a "gem" for analysis by the **CLAN GEM** program. If there is a colon, you must follow the colon with a tab and then one or more code words.

@Bck:
Diary material that was not originally transcribed in the **CHAT** format often has explanatory or backgrounding material placed before a child's utterance. When converting this material to the **CHAT** format, it is sometimes impossible to decide whether this backgrounding material occurs before, during, or after the utterance. In order to avoid having to make these decisions after the fact, one can simply enter it in a background header. Here is an example:
```
@Bck:  Rachel  was  fussing  and  pointing  toward  the  cabinet
       where  the  cookies  are  stored.
*RAC:  cookie  [/]    cookie.
```

@Comment:
This header can be used as an all-purpose comment line. Any type of comment can be entered on an @Comment line. When the comment refers to a particular utterance, use the %com line discussed in chapter 9. When the comment refers to more general material, use the @Comment header. If the comment is intended to apply to the file as a whole, place the @Comment header along with the constant headers before the first utterance.

Instead of trying to make up a new coding tier name for a special purpose type of information, it is best to use the @Comment field, as in this example:
```
@Comment: Gestational  age  of  MAR  is  7  months
@Comment: Birthweight  of  MAR  is  6  lbs.  4  oz.
```

@Date:
This header indicates the date of the interaction. The entry for this header is given in the form day-month-year. The date is abbreviated in the same way as in the @Birth header entry. Here is an example of a completed @Date header line.
```
@Date:   1-JUL-1965
```
This form includes information on the century. This is needed to distinguish reliably data collected at the beginning of this century, such as the data of Stern and Stern, from data that will be collected in the early part of the next century.

@Eg and **@Eg:**
These headers are used to mark the end of a "gem" for analysis by the **CLAN GEM** program. If there is a colon, you must follow the colon with a tab and then one or more code words.

@G:
This header is used to mark "gems" with their tags when no nesting or overlapping of gems occurs and when the +n switch is used in **GEM**.

@Location:
This header should include the city, state or province, and country in which the interaction took place. Here is an example of a completed header line.
```
@Location:  Boston,  MA,  USA
```

@New Episode
This header simply marks the fact that there has been a break in the recording and that a new episode has started. It is a "bare" header that is used without a colon, because it takes no entry. There is no need to mark the end of the episode, because the @New Episode header indicates both the end of one episode and the beginning of another.

@Room Layout:
This header outlines room configuration and positioning of furniture. This is especially useful for experimental settings. The entry should be a description of the room and its contents. Here is an example of the completed header line.
```
@Room  Layout:  Kitchen;  Table  in  center  of  room  with
                window  on  west  wall,  door  to  outside  on
                north  wall
```

@Situation:
This changeable header describes the general setting of the interaction. It applies to all the material that follows it until a new @Situation header appears. The entry for this header is a standard description of the situation. Try to use standard situations such as: "breakfast," "outing," "bath," "working," "visiting playmates," "school," or "getting ready to go out." Here is an example of the completed header line:
```
@Situation:  Tim  and  Bill  are  playing  with  toys  in  the
             hallway.
```

There should be enough situational information given to allow the user to reconstruct the situation as much as possible. Who is present? What is the layout of the room or other space? What is the social role of those present? Who is usually the caregiver? What activity is in progress? Is the activity routinized and, if so, what is the nature of the routine? Is the routine occurring in its standard time, place, and personnel configuration? What objects are present that affect or assist the interaction? It will also be important to include relevant ethnographic information that would make the interaction interpretable to the user of the database. For example, if the text is parent-child interaction before an observer, what is the culture's evaluation of behaviors such as silence, talking a lot, displaying formulaic skills, defending against challenges, and so forth?

@Tape Location:

This header indicates the specific tape ID, side and footage. This is very important for identifying the tape from which the transcription was made. The entry for this header should include the tape ID, side and footage. Here is an example of this header:

```
@Tape Location: tape74, side a, 104
```

@Time Duration:

It is often necessary to indicate the time at which the audiotaping began and the amount of time that passed during the course of the taping. The following header indicates these facts:

```
@Time Duration: 12:30-13:30
```

This header provides the absolute time during which the taping occurred. For most projects what is important is not the absolute time, but the time of individual events relative to each other. This sort of relative timing is provided by coding on the %tim dependent tier in conjunction with the @Time Start header described next.

@Time Start:

If a transcript is keeping track of elapsed time in detail on the %tim tier, the @Time Start header can be used to indicate the absolute time when the timing marks begin. If a new @Time Start header is placed into the middle of the transcript, this "restarts" the clock. Here is an example of the use of this header:

```
@Time Start: 12:30
```

4. Transcribing Words

Words are the basic building blocks of all sentential and discourse structures. By studying the development of word use, we can learn an enormous amount about the growth of syntax, discourse, morphology, and conceptual structure. However, in order to realize the full potential of computational analysis of word usage, we need to follow certain basic rules. In particular, we need to make sure that we spell words in a consistent manner. If we sometimes use the form "doughnut" and sometimes use the form "donut," we are being inconsistent in our representation of this particular word. If such inconsistencies are repeated throughout the lexicon, we can make computerized analysis inaccurate and misleading. One of the major goals of **CHAT** analysis is to maximize systematicity and minimize inconsistency. This chapter spells out some rules and heuristics designed to achieve this goal for word-level transcription.

In the introduction, we discussed some of the problems involved in mapping the speech of language learners onto standard adult forms. One solution to this problem would be to avoid the use of words altogether by transcribing everything in phonetic or phonemic notation. But this solution would make the transcript difficult to read and analyze. A great deal of work in language learning is based on searches for words and combinations of words. If we want to conduct these lexical analyses, we have to try to match up the child's production to actual words. Work in the analysis of syntactic development also requires that the text be analyzed in terms of lexical items. Without a clear representation of lexical items and the ways that they diverge from the adult standard, it may be impossible to conduct lexical and syntactic analyses computationally. Even for those researchers who do not plan to conduct lexical analyses, it is extremely difficult to understand the flow of a transcript if no attempt is made to relate the learner's sounds to items in the adult language.

At the same time, attempts to force adult lexical forms onto learner forms can seriously misrepresent the data. The solution to this problem is to devise ways to indicate the various types of divergences between learner forms and adult standard forms. Note that we use the term "divergences" rather than "error." Although both learners (MacWhinney & Osser, 1977; Stemberger, 1989) and adults clearly do make errors (Stemberger, 1985), most of the divergences between learner forms and adult forms are due to structural aspects of the learner's system.

This chapter discusses the various tools that **CHAT** provides to mark some of these divergences of child forms from adult standards. The basic types of codes for divergences that we discuss are:
1. special learner form markers,
2. codes for unidentifiable material,
3. codes for incomplete words,
4. ways of treating formulaic use of words, and
5. conventions for standardized spellings.

Before we begin our discussion of these conventions, we will quickly review the basic form of the main line.

4.1. The Form of the Main Line

In **CHAT**, words are transcribed on the main speaker tier. This is the line that tells us what the participants said. Each main tier line begins with an asterisk. Then follows a three letter speaker ID, a colon and a tab. The transcription of what was said begins in the ninth column, after the tab. The remainder of the main tier line is composed primarily of a series of words. Words are defined as a series of ASCII characters separated by spaces. In this chapter we discuss the principles governing the transcription of words. In **CLAN**, all characters that are not punctuation markers are potentially parts of words. The default punctuation set includes the space and these characters:

$$, \cdot ; ? ! [ ] < >$$

None of these characters or the space can be used within words. Other nonletter characters such as the plus sign (+) or the at sign (@) can be used within words to express special meanings. This punctuation set applies to the main lines and all coding lines with the exception of the %pho and %mod lines which use the UNIBET and PHONASCII systems described in chapters 10 and 11. Because those systems make use of punctuation markers for special characters, only the space can be used as a delimiter on the %pho and %mod lines. As the **CLAN** manual explains, this default punctuation set can be changed for particular analyses.

4.2. Special Learner Form Markers

When attached at the end of a word, the symbol "@" is used in conjunction with one or two additional letters to further distinguish and categorize the word. Here is an example of the use of the @ symbol:

```
*SAR:  I got a bingbing@c.
```

Here the child has invented the form "bingbing" to refer to a toy. The word "bingbing" is not in the dictionary and must be treated as a special form. It is the responsibility of the transcriber to create a file called 0lexicon.doc for each child that provides glosses for such forms.

The @c form illustrated in this example is only one of many possible special learner form markers that can be devised. The following table lists some of these markers that we have found useful. However, this categorization system is only meant to be suggestive, not exhaustive. Researchers may wish to add further distinctions or ignore some of the categories listed. The particular choice of markers and the decision to code a word with a marker form is one that is made by the transcriber, not by **CHAT**. The basic idea is that words marked with the special learner form markers will be treated as words by the **CLAN** programs and not as fragments.

Letters	Categories	Example	Meaning	You Code As
@b	babbling	abame	-	abame@b
@c	child-invented form	gumma	sticky	gumma@c
@d	dialect form	younz	you	younz@d
@f	family-specific form	bunko	broken	bunko@f
@fp	filled pause	huh	-	huh@fp
@i	interjection, interactional	uhhuh	-	uhhuh@i
@l	letter	b	letter b	b@l
@n	neologism	breaked	broke	breaked@n
@o	onomatopoeia	woof woof	dog barking	woof@o
@p	phonol. consistent form	aga	-	aga@p
@pr	phrasal repetition	its a, its a	-	its+a@pr
@s	second-language form	istenem	my God	istenem@s
@sl	sign language	apple sign	apple	apple@sl
@sas	sign & speech	word & sign	apple	apple@sas
@t	test word	wug	small creature	wug@t
@u	UNIBET transcription	binga	-	bIN6@u
@	general special form	gongga	-	gongga@

We can define these special markers in the following ways:

1. **Babbling** can be used to mark both low-level early babbling and high-level sound play in older children. These forms have no obvious meaning and are used just to have fun with sound.

2. **Child-invented forms** are words created by the child sometimes from other words without obvious derivational morphology. Sometimes they appear to be sound variants of other words. Sometimes their origin is simply obscure. However, the child appears to be convinced that they have meaning and adults sometimes come to use these forms themselves.

3. **Dialect form.** In general, the coding of phonological dialect variations should be minimized, since it often makes transcripts more difficult to read and analyze. However, general phonological variation can be noted in the 00readme.doc file.

4. **Family-specific forms** are much like child-invented forms that have been taken over by the whole family. Sometimes the source of these forms are children, but they can also be older members of the family. Sometimes the forms come from variations of words in another language. An example might be the use of "undertoad" to refer to some mysterious being in the surf, although the word was simply "undertow" initally.

5. **Filled pauses.** For most purposes, there is no need to add the @fp marker at the end of filled pauses represented by forms like "uh" or "mmm". However, for detailed studies of children with fluency deficits it may be useful to add this additional marking.

6. **Interjections** can be indicated in standard ways, making the use of the @i notation usually not necessary. Instead of transcribing "ahem@i," one can simply transcribe "ahem" following the conventions listed later.

7. **Letters** can either be transcribed with the @l marker or simply as single-character words.

8. **Neologisms** are meant to refer to morphological coinages, whereas monomorphemic nonce forms are either child-invented forms, family-specific forms, or test words.

9. **Onomatapoeic forms** include animal sounds and attempts to imitate natural sounds.

10. **Phonological consistent forms** are early forms that are phonologically consistent, but whose meaning is unclear to the transcriber. Usually these forms have some relation to small function words.
11. **Phrasal repetition**. Like the @fp form, this marker is mainly only useful for studies that focus particularly on children with fluency problems. By using this marker, it is often easier to include and exclude phrasal repetitions in particular analyses.
12. **Second-language forms** derive from some language not usually used in the home.
13. **Sign language** use can be indicated by the @s.
14. **Sign and speech** use can be indicate by @sas.
15. **Test words** are nonce forms generated by the investigators to test the productivity of the child's grammar.
16. **UNIBET transcription** can be given on the main line by using the @u marker. However, if many such forms are being noted, it may be better to construct a @pho line.
17. **General special forms.** This category can be used when all of the above fail. However, its use should generally be avoided.

Later in this chapter we present a set of standard spellings of such words for English that make use of @d and @i largely unnecessary. However, in languages where such a list is not available, it may be necessary to use forms with @d or @i.

The @b, @u, and @w markers allow the transcriber to represent words and babbling words phonologically on the main line and have them treated as full lexical items by CLAN programs such as **FREQ** and **MLU** . This should only be done when the analysis requires that the phonological string be treated as a word and it is unclear which standard morpheme corresponds to the word. If a phonological string should not be treated as a full word, it should be marked by a beginning & and the @b, @u, or @w endings should not be used. Also, if the transcript includes a complete %pho line for each word (see chapter 10) and the data are intended for phonological analysis, it is better to use yy (see the next section) on the main line and then give the phonological form on the %pho line.

Family-specific forms are special words used only by the family. These are often derived from child forms that are adopted by all family members. They also include certain "caregiverese" forms that are not easily recognized by the majority of adult speakers, but which may be common to some areas or some families. Family-specific forms can be used by either adults or children.

The @n marker is intended for morphological neologisms and overregularizations, whereas the @c marker is intended to mark nonce creation of stems. Of course, this distinction is somewhat arbitrary and incomplete. Whenever a child-invented form is clearly onomatopoeic, use the @o coding instead of the @c coding. A fuller characterization of neologisms can be provided by the error coding system given in chapter 12.

If transcribers find it difficult to distinguish between child-invented forms, onomatopoeia, and familial forms, they can use the @ symbol without any following letter. In this way, they can at least indicate the fact that the preceding word is not a standard item in the adult lexicon.

4.3. Codes for Unidentifiable Material

During the process of transcribing from audiotape, often we cannot map a sound or group of sounds onto either a conventional word or a non-conventional word. This can occur when the audio signal is so weak or garbled that you cannot even identify the sounds being used. Other times you can recognize the sounds that the speaker is using, but cannot map the sounds onto words. Sometimes you choose not to transcribe a passage because it is irrelevant to the interaction. Sometimes the person makes a noise or performs an action instead of speaking, and sometimes a person breaks off before completing a recognizable word. All of these problems can be dealt with by using certain special symbols for those items that cannot be easily related to words. These symbols are typed in lower case and are preceded and followed by spaces. When standing alone on a text tier, they should be followed by a period, unless it is clear that the utterance was a question or a command.

Unintelligible Speech   xxx / xx

Use the symbol xxx when you cannot hear or understand what the speaker is saying. If you believe you can distinguish the number of unintelligible words, you may use several xxx strings in a row. Here is an example of the use of the xxx symbol:

```
*SAR:   xxx.
*MOT:   what?
*SAR:   I want xx.
```

Sarah's first utterance is fully unintelligible. Her second utterance includes some unintelligible material along with some intelligible material.

The **CLAN** programs will ignore the xxx symbol when computing mean length of utterance and other statistics. If you want unintelligible material included in such counts, use the symbol xx instead of xxx. If you want to have several words included, use as many occurrences of xx as you wish.

Unintelligible Speech with %pho   yyy / yy

Use the symbol yy or yyy when you cannot hear or understand what the speaker is saying and you wish to represent its phonological form on a %pho line which is being consistently used throughout the transcript. If you are not consistently creating a %pho line, you should use the @u or & notations instead. If you believe you can distinguish the number of unintelligible words, and you wish to treat each word-like string as a word, use yy rather than yyy. Each yy form will be counted as a word by the **CLAN** programs. Here is an example of the use of yy:

```
*SAR:   yy yy a ball.
%pho:   ta g6 6 bal
```

The first two words cannot be matched to particular words, but their phonological form is given on the %pho line.

Untranscribed Material   w w w

This symbol must be used in conjunction with an %exp tier which is discussed in chapter 9. This symbol is used on the main line to indicate material that a transcriber does not know how to transcribe or does not want to transcribe. For example, it could be that the material is in a language that the transcriber does not know. This symbol can also be used when a speaker says something that has no relevance to the interactions taking place and the experimenter would rather ignore them. For example, www could indicate a long conversation between adults that would be superfluous to transcribe. Here is an example of the use of this symbol:

```
*MOT:   www.
%exp:   talks  to  neighbor  on  the  telephone
```

Actions without Speech   0

This symbol is used when the speaker performs some action that is not accompanied by speech. Notice that the symbol is the numeral zero "0," NOT the capital letter "O." Here is an example of the correct usage of this symbol:

```
*FAT:   where's  your  doll?
*DAV:   0  [=!  cries].
```

If the transcriber wishes to code the phonetics of the crying, it would be better to insert yyy on the main tier. Do not use the zero, if there is any speech on the tier. The zero can also be used to provide a place to attach a dependent tier.

Phonological Fragment   &

The & can be used at the beginning of a string to indicate that the following material is being transcribed in correct phonological form in UNIBET and is not to be treated as a word by the **CLAN** programs. It is important not to include any of the three utterance terminators -- the exclamation mark, the question mark, or the period -- since **CLAN** will treat these as utterance terminators. This form of notation is useful when the speaker stutters or breaks off before completing a recognizable word (false starts). The utterance "t- t- c- can't you go" is transcribed as follows:

```
*MAR:   &t  &t  &k  can't  you  go?
```

Note that the form &k is being used instead of &c, because the notation is in UNIBET. The ampersand can also be used for nonce and nonsense forms:

```
*DAN:   &glNk  &glNk.
%com:   weird  noises
```

Material following the ampersand symbol will be ignored by certain **CLAN** programs, such as the MLU program, which computes Mean Length of Utterance. If you want to have the material treated as a word, use the @u form of notation instead (see the previous section).

Unless you specifically attempt to search for strings with the ampersand, the **CLAN** programs will not see them at all. If you want a program such as **FREQ** to count all of the instances of phonological fragments, you would have to add a switch such as +s"&*".

Best Guess at a Word   [?]

This symbol is a scoped symbol discussed in fuller detail in chapter 8. It can be used to indicate that the previous word or group of words are simply the transcriber's best guess at what was being said and there is some doubt in the transcriber's mind whether this guess is correct.

4.4. Codes for Incomplete and Omitted Words

Words may also be incomplete or even fully omitted. We can judge a word to be incomplete when enough of it is produced for us to be sure what was intended. Judging a word to be omitted is often much more difficult.

Noncompletion of a Word   ()

When a word is incomplete, but the intended meaning seems clear, insert the missing material within parentheses. This notation can also be used to derive a consistent spelling for commonly shortened words, such as "(un)til" and "(be)cause. " Items that are coded in this way will be treated as full words by the CLAN programs.   For programs such as FREQ, the parentheses will essentially be ignored and "(be)cause" will be treated as if it were "because."   The CLAN programs also provide ways of either including or excluding the material in the parentheses, depending on the goals of the analysis.

```
     *RAL:   I   been   sit(ting)   all   day.
```
Note that coding omissions in this way involves important theoretical decisions, some of which are discussed in the next section.

The inclusion or exclusion of material enclosed in parentheses is well-supported by the CLAN programs and this same notation can also be used for other purposes when necessary. For example, studies of fluency may find it convenient to code the number of times that a word is repeated directly on that word, as in this example with three repetitions of the word "dog".

```
     *JEF:        that's   a   dog(/3).
```

Omitted Word   0word

The coding of word omissions is an extremely difficult and unreliable process. Many researchers will prefer not to even open up this particular can of worms. On the other hand, researchers in language disorders and aphasia often find that the coding of word omissions is crucial to particular theoretical issues. In such cases, it is important that the coding of omitted words be done in as clear a manner as possible.

To code an omission, the zero symbol "0" is placed before a word on the text tier. If what is important is not the actual word omitted, but its part of speech, then a code for the part of speech can follow the zero. (These codes are listed in chapter 14). The decision to code a word as missing is, of course, one that must be based on the transcriber's judgment. Similarly, the identity of the omitted word is always a guess. The best guess is placed on the main line. This item would be counted for scoping conventions, but it would not be included in the MLU (mean length of utterance) count. Here is an example of its use.

```
     *EVE:   I   want   0to   go.
```

It is, of course, very difficult to know when a word has been omitted. However, the following criteria can be used to help make this decision for English data:

1. 0art: Unless there is a missing plural, a common noun without an article is coded as 0art.
2. 0v: Sentences with no verbs can be coded as having missing verbs. Of course, often the omission of a verb can be viewed as a grammatical use of ellipsis.

3. Oaux: In standard English, sentences like "he running" clearly have a missing auxiliary.
4. Osubj: In English, every finite verb requires a subject.
5. Opobj: Every preposition requires an object. However, often a preposition may be functioning as an adverb. The coder must look at the verb to decide whether a word is functioning as a preposition as in "John put on Opobj" or an adverb as in "Mary jumped up."

In English, there are seldom solid grounds for assigning codes like Oadj, Oadv, Oobj, Oprep, or Odat.

Incorrect Omission   0*word

The basic zero symbol implies nothing about the correctness or incorrectness of the omission. In order to make this further distinction, the symbols 0*word and 00word are used. The 0*word symbol is used when the omission is clearly ungrammatical and the transcriber wishes to code that fact.

Ellipsis   00word

Often the omission of a word is licensed by the standard grammatical and discourse patterns of the language. For example, answers to questions usually involve ellipsis of the presupposed part of the question. In order to indicate ellipsis, two zeroes are placed before the word that is ellipsed, as in 00verb.

```
*FAT:  where  did  you  go?
*ABE:  00sub  00verb  0*prep  the  store.
```

Of course, the marking of ellipsis raises many theoretical and interpretive questions whose resolution is beyond the scope of the present system.

4.5. Conventions for Standardized Spellings

There are a number of common words in the English language that cannot be found in the dictionary or whose lexical status is vague. For example, how should letters be spelled? What about numbers and titles? What is the best spelling "doggy" or "doggie," "yeah" or "yah," and "pst" or "pss?" If we can increase the consistency with which such forms are transcribed, we can improve the quality of automatic lexical analyses. Within the **CLAN** system, programs like **FREQ** and **COMBO** provide output based on searches for particular word strings. If a word is spelled in an indeterminate number of variant ways, researchers who attempt to analyze the occurrence of that word will inevitably end up with inaccurate results. For example, if a researcher wants to trace the use of the pronoun "you," it might be necessary to search not only for "you," "ya," and "yah," but also for all the assimilations of the pronouns with verbs such as "didya/dicha/didcha" or "couldya/couldcha/coucha." Without a standard set of rules for the transcription of such forms, accurate lexical searches could become impossible. On the other hand, there is no reason to avoid using these forms if a set of standards can be established for their use. Other programs rely on the use of dictionaries of words. If the spellings of words are indeterminate, the analyses produced will be equally indeterminate. For that reason, it is helpful to specify a set of standard spellings for marginal words. This section lists some of these words with their standard orthographic form.

The forms in these lists all have some conventional lexical status in standard American English. In this regard, they differ from the various nonstandard forms indicated by the special form markers @b, @c, @f, @l, @n, @o, @p, and @s. Because there is no clear limit to the number of possible babbling forms, onomatopoeic forms, or neologistic forms, there is no way to provide a list of such forms. In contrast, the words given in this section are fairly well known to most speakers of the language, and many can be found in unabridged dictionaries. The list given here is only a beginning; over time, we intend to continue to add new forms.

Some of the forms use parentheses to indicate optional material. For example, the exclamation "yeek" can also be said as "eek." When a speaker uses the full form, the transcriber types in "yeek," and when the speaker uses the reduced form the transcriber types "(y)eek." When the **CLAN** programs come to analyzing the transcripts, the parentheses can be ignored and both "yeek" and "eek" will be retrieved as instances of the same word. Parentheses can also be used to indicate missing fragments of suffixes. Thus, both the morphemicized (see chapter 5 form "do-in(g)") and the nonmorphemicized form "doing" are legal ways of transcribing the form "doin." The majority of the words listed can be found in the form given in *Webster's Third New International Dictionary*. Those forms that cannot be found in Webster's Third are indicated with an asterisk. The asterisk should not be used in actual transcription.

4.5.1. Letters

CLAN offers two ways of transcribing letters. The recommended form uses the @l symbol after the letter. For example, the letter "b" would be b@l. Some transcribers find this notational form cumbersome. They may wish to use the somewhat more ambiguous, but still useful short form for letters. In the short form, the names of the letters in English can be written out as single characters with the exception of the letter "a," which is needed for the article and the letter "i," which is needed for the pronoun. By writing out the letter "a" as "ay" and the letter "i" as "iy," the names of the letters in the English alphabet become: ay b c d e f g h iy j k l m n o p q r s t u v w x y z. Here is an example of the use of these conventions:

```
*MOT:   could you please spell your name?
*MAR:   it's m@l a@l r@l k@l.
```

The simpler, more ambiguous form would be:

```
*MOT:   could you please spell your name?
*MAR:   it's m ay r k.
```

If you are using the ambiguous form, you should also use the spelling "aye" for the affirmative exclamation, rather than the rarer form "ay." As noted in the dictionary, the plural for the word for the letters of the alphabet "abc" is "abcs."

4.5.2. Acronyms

Acronyms should be transcribed by using the component letters as a part of a compound form. Thus, USA can be written as "U+s+a." In this case, the first letter is capitalized in order to mark it as a proper noun. However, the acronym "p+js" for "pajamas" is not capitalized. If no confusion can occur, the compound markers can be omitted. The recommended way of transcribing the common name for television is just "tv". On the other hand, it is better to include the plus sign for acronyms of children's names, as in "C+J" for the nickname for "Charles James". The plus sign is also needed for combinations such as "m+and+ms" for the M&M candy. These forms are similar to non-acronyms such as "bye+and+bye".

Acronyms that are not actually spelled out when produced in conversation should be written as words. Thus "UNESCO" would be written as "Unesco." The capitalization of the first letter is used to indicate the fact that it is a proper noun. There must be no periods inside acronyms and titles, since these can be confused with utterance delimiters. Thus, the acronym USA can be transcribed as "u s ay," if the transcriber wants to emphasize the fact that it is being produced as a series of letters.

4.5.3. Numbers and Titles

Numbers should be written out in words. For example, the number 256 could be written as "two hundred and fifty six," "two hundred fifty six," "two five six," or "two fifty six," depending on how it was pronounced. It is best to use the form "fifty six" rather than "fifty-six," because the hyphen is used in **CHAT** to indicate morphemicization. If you want to emphasize the fact that a number is a single lexical item, you can treat it as a compound using the form two+hundred+and+fifty+six. Other strings with numbers are monetary amounts, percentages, times, fraction, logarithms, and so on. All should be written out in words, as in "eight thousand two hundred and twenty dollars" for $8220, "twenty nine point five percent" for 29.5%, "seven fifteen" for 7:15, "ten o'clock ay m" for 10:00 AM, and "four and three fifths" for 4 3/5.

Titles such as "Dr." or "Mr." should be written out in their full capitalized form as "Doctor" or "Mister," as in "Doctor Spock" and "Mister Rogers." For "Mrs." use the form "Missus."

4.5.4.   Kinship Forms

The following table lists some of the most important kinship address forms in standard American English. The forms with asterisks cannot be found in *Webster's Third New International Dictionary*.

Child	Formal		Child	Formal
Da(da)	Father		Mommy	Mother
Daddy	Father		Nan	Grandmother
Gram(s)	Grandmother		Nana	Grandmother
Grammy	Grandmother		*Nonny	Grandmother
Gramp(s)	Grandfather		Pa	Father
*Grampy	Grandfather		Pap	Father
Grandma	Grandmother		Papa	Father
Grandpa	Grandfather		Pappy	Father
Ma	Mother		Pop	Father
Mama	Mother		Poppa	Father
Momma	Mother		*Poppy	Father
Mom	Mother			

4.5.5.   Shortenings

One of the biggest problems that the transcriber faces is the tendency of speakers to drop sounds out of words. For example, a speaker may leave the initial "a" off of "about," saying instead "'bout". In **CHAT**, this shortened form is represented as (a)bout. The **CLAN** computer analysis programs can easily ignore the parentheses and treat the word as "about." Alternatively, they can treat the word as a spelling variant, depending on how they are instructed. Many common words have standard shortened forms. Some of the most frequent are given below. The basic notational principle illustrated in that table can be extended to other words as needed. All of these words can be found in *Webster's Third New International Dictionary*.

(a)bout	don('t)	(h)is	(re)frigerator
an(d)	(e)nough	(h)isself	(re)member
(a)n(d)	(e)spress(o)	-in(g)	sec(ond)
(a)fraid	(e)spresso	nothin(g)	s(up)pose
(a)gain	(es)presso	(i)n	(th)e
(a)nother	(ex)cept	(in)stead	(th)em
(a)round	(ex)cuse	Jag(uar)	(th)emselves
ave(nue)	(ex)cused	lib(r)ary	(th)ere
(a)way	(e)xcuse	Mass(achusetts)	(th)ese
(be)cause	(e)xcused	micro(phone)	(th)ey
(be)fore	(h)e	(pa)jamas	(to)gether
(be)hind	(h)er	(o)k	(to)mato
b(e)long	(h)ere	o(v)er	(to)morrow
b(e)longs	(h)erself	(po)tato	(to)night
Cad(illac)	(h)im	prob(ab)ly	(un)til
doc(tor)	(h)imself	(re)corder	wan(t)

More extreme types of shortenings include: "(what)s (th)at" which becomes "sat" "y(ou) are" which becomes "yar" and "d(o) you" which becomes "dyou." Representing these forms as shortenings rather than as nonstandard words facilitates standardization and the automatic analysis of transcripts.

4.5.6. Assimilations

Words such as "gonna" for "going to" and "whynt cha" for "why don't you" involve complex sound changes, often with assimilations between auxiliaries and the infinitive or a pronoun. For forms of this type, **CHAT** allows the transcriber to place the assimilated form on the main line followed by a fuller form in square brackets, as in the form:

```
gonna [: going to]
```

The **CLAN** programs then allow the user to either analyze the material preceding the brackets or the material following the brackets, as described in Chapters 8 and 21. An extremely incomplete list of assimilated forms is given below. All of the forms are marked with asterisks, because none are found in *Webster's Third New International Dictionary*.

NonStandard	Standard	NonStandard	Standard
*coulda(ve)	could have	*mighta	might have
*dunno	don't know	*need(t)a	need to
*dyou	do you	*nere	in here
*gimme	give me	*oughta	ought to
*gonna	going to	*posta	supposed to
*gotta	got to	*shoulda(ve)	should have
*hadta	had to	*sorta	sort of
*hasta	has to	*sorta	sort of
*hafta	have to	*wanna	want to
*kinda	kind of	*wassup	what's up
*lemme	let me	*whaddya	what did you
*lotsa	lots of		

Forms involving alterations of "you" to "cha", "chu" or "ya" can be represented by having "ya", "chu", and "cha" as alternative spellings for "you". Thus, transcribers can choose to either enter "could cha" or "couldcha [: could you]". If you have chosen to represent "yu" as "ya", you must remember to include "cha", "chu", and "ya" in your search lists. A more convenient and systematic way of representing some of these forms is by noting omitted letters with parenteses as in: "gi(ve) me" for "gimme", "le(t) me" for "lemme", or "d(o) you" for "dyou".

4.5.7. Exclamations

Exclamations and interjections, such as "aah" and "gosh" are very frequent. However, because their phonological shape varies so much, they often have an unclear lexical status. The following table provides standard shapes for these words. For consistency, these forms should be used even when the actual phonological form diverges from the standardizing convention, as long as the variant is perceived as related to the standard. Words that are marked with an asterisk cannot be found in *Webster's Third New International Dictionary*.

Exclamation	Meaning	Exclamation	Meaning
*aah	relief, joy	*pst	listen here
*ahhah	discovery	sh	silence
aw	sympathy	*tsk	shame
golly	gee whiz	tut	pity
gosh	gee whiz	ugh	disgust, effort
ha(h)	triumph	*uhoh	trouble
*haha	amusement, derision	vroom	car noise
*heehee	amusement, derision	whee	exuberance
*mmm	tasty, good	wow	amazement
*num	tasty	yea	a cheer
*nummy	tasty	(y)eek	fear
*numnum	tasty	y(o)ikes	mild fear
ouch	sudden pain	yum	tasty
ow	hurt	yummy	tasty
oy	dismay	yumyum	tasty

4.5.8. Interactional Markers

Another set of interjections, such as *uhhuh* and *yep*, signal agreement, disagreement, and pauses. A sampling of these forms is given below. Words that are marked with an asterisk cannot be found in *Webster's Third New International Dictionary*.

Marker	Function	Marker	Function
ahem	ready to speak	nah	no
*emem	I don't know	uhhuh	yes
*er	pause	*uhhum	yes indeed
*hunmmm	no	*uhuh	no
*hunhunh	no	*uh	pause (any vowel)
huh	questioning	um	pause
hmm	thinking, waiting	ye(a)h	yes
hmm?	questioning	*yeahhuh	yes (contradicting)
*mmhm	yes	yep	yes
nope	no	yup	yes
*nuhuh	strong no	whoops	blunder

4.5.9. Spelling Variants

There are a number of words that are misspelled so frequently that the misspellings seem as acceptable as the standard spellings. These include "altho" for standard "although," "donut" for "doughnut," "tho" for "though," "thru" for "through," and "abc's" for "abcs." Transcribers should use the standard spellings for these words.

In general, it is best to avoid the use of monomorphemic words with apostrophes. For example, it is better to use the form "mam" than the form "ma'am". However, apostrophes must be used in English for multimorphemic contractions such as "I'm" or "don't".

4.5.10. Colloquial Forms

Colloquial and slang forms are often listed in the dictionary. Examples include "telly" for television and "rad" for "radical." The following table lists some such colloquial forms with their corresponding standard forms. Words that are marked with an asterisk cannot be found in *Webster's Third New International Dictionary*.

Form	Meaning
doggone	problematic
*fuddy+duddy	old-fashioned person
*grabby	grasping (adj)
*hon	honey(name)
*humongous	huge
looka	look
lookit	look!

Form	Meaning
okeydokey	allright
*telly	television
thingumabob	thing
thingumajig	thing
tinker+toy	toy
who(se)jigger	thing
whatchamacallit	thing

4.5.11. Baby Talk

Baby talk or "caregiverese" forms include onomatopoeic words, such as "choochoo," and diminutives, such as "froggie" or "thingie." In the following table, diminutives are given in final "-ie" except for the common forms "doggy," "kitty," "potty," "tummy," and "dolly." Wherever possible, use the suffix "-ie" for the diminutive and the suffix "-y" for the adjectivalizer. Table 4-7 does not include the hundreds of possible diminutives with the "-ie" suffix simply attached to the stem, as in "eggie," "footie," "horsie," and so on. Nor does it attempt to list forms such as "poopy," which use the adjectivalizer "-y" attached directly to the stem. Words that are marked with an asterisk cannot be found in *Webster's Third New International Dictionary*.

Baby Talk	Standard	Baby Talk	Standard
*beddie(bye)	go to sleep	*nunu	hurt
*blankie	blanket	*night(ie)+night	good night
booboo	injury, hurt	*owie	hurt
boom	fall	pantie	underpants
byebye	good-bye	pee	urine, urinate
choochoo	train	peekaboo	looking game
*cootchykoo	tickle	*peepee	urine, urinate
*dark+time	night, evening	*peeyou	smelly
doggy	dog	poo(p)	defecation, defecate
dolly	doll	*poopoo	defecation, defecate
*doodoo	feces	potty	toilet
*dumdum	stupid	rockabye	sleep
*ew	unpleasant	scrunch	crunch
*footie+ballie	football	*smoosh	smash
gidd(y)up	get moving	(t)eensy(w)eensy	little
goody	delight	(t)eeny(w)eeny	little
guck	unpleasant	*teetee	urine, urinate
*jammie	pajamas	titty	breast
*kiki	cat	tippytoe	on tips of toes
kitty	cat	tummy	stomach, belly
lookee	look yee!	ugh	unpleasant
*moo+cow	cow	*(wh)oopsadaisy	surprise or mistake

4.5.12. Dialectal Variants

Other variant pronunciations, such as "dat" for "that," involve standard dialectal sound substitutions without deletions. Unfortunately, using these forms can make lexical retrieval very difficult. For example, a researcher interested in the word "together" will seldom remember to include "tagether" in the search string. There are four ways to deal with this problem. The first is to carefully add each variant word in the transcript to the 0lexicon.doc file, which also contains other nonstandard forms. Because these variant forms are, in nearly all cases, nonhomographic with other words, researchers analyzing the transcript will simply need to include the variant in their search lists. An exception to this is "den" for "then," which is already the standard word for an animal's burrow. A second solution to this problem is to follow each variant form with the standard form, as given below using the [: replacement] notation discussed in chapter 8. A third solution is to create a UNIBET transcription of the whole interaction, preferably linked to a full sonic **CHAT** digitized audio record. In transcripts where the speakers have strong dialectal influences, this is probably the best solution. The fourth solution is to ignore the dialectal variation and simply transcribe the standard form. If this is being done, the practice must be clearly noted in the "00readme.doc" file.

Variant	Standard	Variant	Standard
caint	can't	hows about	how about
da	the	nutin	nothing
dan	than	sumpin	something
dat	that	ta	to
de	the	tagether	together
dese	these	tamorrow	tomorrow
deir	their	weunz	we
deirselves	themselves	whad	what
dem	them	wif	with
demselves	themselves	ya	you
den	then	yall	you all
dere	there	yer	your
dey	they	youse	you all
dis	this	yinz	you all
dose	those	younz	you all
fer	for	ze	the
git	get	zis	this
gon	going	zat	that
hisself	himself		

4.5.13. Disambiguating Homophones in Japanese

Because Japanese Kanji script provides a direct disambiguation of homophones, Japanese readers are accustomed to having the different meanings kept clearly separate. To preserve this in **CHAT**, one can place the English meaning after the Japanese form as in these examples of common Japanese homophones from the Japanese **CHAT** manual (Oshima-Takane & MacWhinney, 1994).

Word	Meaning 1	Meaning 2
e	e(picture)	e(handle)
ga	ga(moth)	-
ka	ka(mosquito)	-
kara	kara(empty)	kara(shell)
ne	ne(price)	ne(root)
ni	ni(two)	-
no	no(field)	-
o	o(tail)	-
to	to(door)	-
wa	wa(circle)	-
yo	yo(night)	yo(world)

In these examples, forms such as "ga" or "yo" in the second column are not translated, since they are grammatical particles.

4.5.14. Punctuation in French and Italian

The standard use of the apostrophe to mark truncation is preserved in French and Italian. In French, when a word begins with a vowel, this leads in some cases to the disappearance of the final vowel of the preceding word, as in "l' ami" and not "le ami". The vowel -e is elided, and in standard spelling, the two words are linked together by an apostrophe without a space. When transcribing these forms into **CHAT**, it is important to add a space after the apostrophe, in order to allow for direct searching for the elided pronouns and articles and in order to make more accurate morpheme counts and analyses. In particular, the following strings must be followed by a space: c' , d' , j' , l' , m' , n' , qu' , s' , t' , and y' .

For similar reasons, the dashes that are used in words such as "est-ce" or "qu'est-ce" should be replaced with spaces. Thus, these forms should be transcribed as "est ce" and "qu' est ce". In other cases, such as "abat-jour", the French hyphen indicates a true compound and should be replaced by the plus symbol, as in "abat+jour".

5. Transcribing Morphemes on the Main Line

Some students of language learning are interested in studying the development of morphological markings and the concepts underlying those markings. **CHAT** provides two ways to conduct morphological analysis. Superficial morphological analysis can be conducted by breaking words up into morphemes on the main line. For deeper morphological analysis, the %mor line should be used instead. In this chapter, we discuss morphological analysis on the main line. Chapter 14 discusses morphological analysis on the %mor line.

Individual words in the main line may be subjected to morphological analysis or "morphemicization." In order to indicate the ways that words on the main line are composed from morphemes, **CHAT** uses the symbols -, +, #, ~, &, and 0. These same six symbols are also used for parallel purposes on the %mor line. However, on the %mor line these symbols are a part of a more extensive system. For more accurate morphemic analysis, particularly in languages other than English, we recommend creating a complete morphemic analysis on the %mor tier. If this is done, no morphemicization need be done on the main line. Morphemicization on the main line is intended mostly for initial morphemic analysis or general quantitative characterization of morphological development.

5.1. Codes for Morphemicization

Suffix marker   -

A single dash is used to indicate the attachment of a suffix to a stem.

```
*ALL:   I  like-ed  dog-s.
```

Prefix Marker   #

Prefixes are followed by a number sign, as in this example:
```
*AUS:  un#tie  my  shoe  please.
```

Some common prefixes include: un#, re#, dis#, over#, under#, pre#, post#, inter#, quasi#, non#, and pseudo#. Some of these will, of course, occur only rarely in the speech of young children.

Compound Marker   +

Use this symbol to indicate segmentation of compounds or to mark rote forms.
```
*MAR:   I  like  Star+wars.
*EVE:  put+this  ball.
```

Compounds that are usually written as one word, such as "birthday" or "rainbow," should not be segmented. Those compounds that are generally separated by a hyphen in English orthography should be separated by a + symbol in **CHAT** transcription (e.g., "jack-in-the-box" should be transcribed as "jack+in+the+box"). Rote forms to be counted as a single morpheme may also be joined with a + symbol (e.g., all+right). Of course, the decision to count multiword strings as rote forms or unanalyzed chunks presupposes an extensive analysis of the individual child's productive uses. This decision is not easily made at the transcription level, and may be better addressed by subsequent lexical analyses. By default, the MLU program does not treat the plus symbol as a morpheme delimiter.

Because the dash is used in **CHAT** to indicate suffixation, it is important to avoid confusion between the standard use of the dash in compounds such as "blue-green" and the use of the dash in **CHAT**. To do this, use the compound marker to replace the dash or hyphen, as in "blue+green" instead of "blue-green." In other languages, this becomes even more important. For example, French "la-bas" should be written as "la+bas."

Clitic Marker   ~

The tilde can be used on the main line to indicate clitics. This can be done with suffixed clitics as in Italian *da~me~lo* "give me it" or with preposed clitics as in Italian *me~lo~dai* "he gives me it."

Fusion Marker   &

If the transcriber wants to morphemicize not only regular verbs such as "jumped" (into *jump-ed*) but also "sang," it is necessary to use the ampersand & to mark the fact that the past tense marking "-ed" has fused with the stem. Using this marker, "sang" is coded as *sing&ed* and "doesn't" as *do&es-'nt*. Note that this use of the ampersand within words is quite different from its use at the beginning of words to mark phonological fragments.

Omitted Affix   -0affix

The decision to code a word as missing is, as we noted earlier, very difficult. However, the decision to code an affix as missing can be based on somewhat more solid grounds:

1. -0ing: If a progressive auxiliary occurs with the verb and there is no "ing" as in "John is run," one can judge that there is a missing "-ing."
2. -0ed: If a verb stem occurs by itself and the referent appears to be past tense, then there is sufficient reason to judge that there is a missing "-0ed."
3. -0s: Omission of the plural on nouns is indicated when:
    (a) a singular noun is preceded by any plural quantifier (two, some, many) or demonstrative (these, those),
    (b) when the verbal auxiliary marks plurality of the subject (dog are running, dog were running),
    (c) when the referent is plural in the context and there is no reason to believe that the child has selected out a single referent. It is admittedly difficult to find solid grounds for applying the last of these three criteria.
4. -0's: Omission of the possessive is most easily detected when two nouns that are not a standard compound occur together with no possessive and are serving as a constituent of the verb, as in "I found Mommy sock." However, when the two nouns occur without a verb, as in "Mommy sock," it is not possible to know whether or not there is a missing possessive.

5.2. Standard Forms for Affixes and Clitics

In order to facilitate easy coding on the main line for English, we have devised a full set of **CHAT** affix markers. Most of these forms are written much as they are in standard English. However, to avoid ambiguity, we write out some forms as full words. Below we list the inflectional suffixes for English, some common derivational suffixes and prefixes, and the contracted auxiliaries and negatives. Additional forms can be found in Chapter 24.

Inflectional Suffixes for English

Suffix	Function	Suffix	Function
-ed	past	-'s	possessive
-en	participle	-s'	plural possessive
-es	third person singular	-s	plural
-ing	progressive	-'	zero possessive

Derivational Suffixes for English

Suffix	Function	Suffix	Function
-able	adjectivalizer	-(i)fy	verbalizer
-al	adjectivalizer	-(i)ty	nominalizer
-ary	adjectivalizer	-ize	verbalizer
-er	comparative	-less	without
-est	superlative	-ly	adverbializer
-ful	adjectivalizer	-ment	nominalizer
-ic	adjectivalizer	-ness	nominalizer
-ie	diminutive	-(t)ion	nominalizer
		-y	adjectivalizer

Derivational Prefixes for English

Prefix	Meaning	Prefix	Meaning
anti#	against	pre#	before
dis#	reversal	pro#	in favor of
ex#	previous	re#	repetitive
mis#	erroneously	un#	reversal

Contractions for English

Contraction	Long Form	Contraction	Long Form
-'d	would, had	-'ll	will
-'does	does	-'m	am
-'has	has	-'nt	not
-'is	is	-'re	are
-'iscop	is (cop)	-'us	us (let's)
-'isaux	is (aux)	-'ve	have

Here is an example of the use of these symbols:

```
*MOT:   Bob-'s   truck.
*MOT:   the   boy-s'   truck.
*MOT:   Bob-'ll   have   to   get   some   milk.
*MOT:   I   do-'nt   want   any   bananas.
*MOT:   You   can-'nt   get   the   ball   now.
*MOT:   He   does-'nt   want   a   dog.
```

Suffixes can be combined in words such as "learn-er-s" or "un#think-able-ity." Words with special learner form markers of the type given in chapter 4 can also be morphemicized. Thus, the plural of the word "bingbing@c" could be given as either "bingbings@c" or "bingbing@c-s." The letter "m" can be pluralized in the long form "m@l-s" or the short form "m-s."

5.3. Placing Morphemicizations in Brackets

The suffixes -en, -s, -est, -er, -es, and -ed also have the irregular forms &en, &s, &est, &er, &es, and &ed. Applying these irregular markings directly can decrease readability. Therefore, for these irregular forms, transcribers should use the [: text] replacement notation to indicate the morphemicization, as in this example:

```
*CHI:   Mommy's   [:   Mommy-'isaux]   gone   [:   go&en]   to   the
        store.
```

Seven of the suffixes can take the phonological shape of final "s." These include -s (plural), -'s (possessive), -s' (plural possessive), -'is, -'us, -'does, and -'has. If the transcriber wants to distinguish the auxiliary and copula forms of "-'is", the forms "-isaux" and "-iscop" can be used. If a transcriber wants to avoid making a distinction between the four contracted verbal forms, the general verbal contraction form -is can be used. Here are some alternative transcriptions:

```
*MOT:   Bob-'is   go-ing   to   the   park.
*MOT:   Bob's   [:   Bob-'isaux]   go-ing   to   the   park.
*FRA:   Bob-'is   a   nice   boy.
*FRA:   Bob's   [:   Bob-'iscop]   a   nice   boy.
*BEE:   Bob-'is   gone   home.
*BEE:   Bob's   [:   Bob-'has]   gone   home.
*TOM:   what-'is   that   mean?
*TOM:   what's   [:   What-'does]   that   mean?
```

By default, the **CLAN** programs replace the material before the square brackets with the material in the square brackets. If you do not want this replacement to be done, you can use the +r5 switch described in chapter 23.

6. Utterances and Tone Units

The basic units of **CHAT** transcription are the morpheme, the word, and the utterance. In addition, some transcribers may be interested in marking tone units. In the previous two chapters we examined principles for transcribing words and morphemes. In this chapter we examine ways of delimiting utterances and tone units.

6.1. One Utterance or Many?

Early child language is rich with repetitions. For example, a child may often say the same word or group of words eight times in a row without changes. The **CHAT** system provides mechanisms for coding these repetitions into single utterances. However, at the earliest stages, it may be misleading to try to compact these multiple attempts into a single line. Consider five alternative ways of transcribing a series of repeated words.

1. Simple transcription of the words as several items in a single utterance:

   ```
   *CHI:  milk  milk  milk  milk.
   ```

2. Transcription of the words as items in a single utterance, separated by commas:

   ```
   *CHI:  milk,  milk,  milk,  milk.
   ```

3. Transcription of the words as items in a single utterance, but separated by prosodic delimiters (see later in this Chapter):

   ```
   *CHI:  milk -,  milk -,  milk -,  milk.
   ```

4. Treatment of the words as a series of attempts to repeat the single word:

   ```
   *CHI:  milk [/]  milk [/]  milk [/]  milk [/].
   ```

5. Treatment of the words as separate utterances.

   ```
   *CHI:  milk.
   *CHI:  milk.
   *CHI:  milk.
   *CHI:  milk.
   ```

These five forms of transcription will lead to markedly different analytic outcomes. Consider the ways in which the five forms will lead to different results in the **MLU** program. The first three forms will all be counted as having one utterance with four morphemes for an MLU of 4.0. The fourth form will be counted as having one utterance with one morpheme for an MLU of 1.0. The fifth form will be counted as having four utterances each with one morpheme for an MLU of 1.0.

Admittedly, not all analyses depend crucially on the computation of MLU, but problems with deciding how to compute MLU point to deeper issues in transcription and analysis. In order to compute MLU, one has to decide what is a word and what is an utterance and these are two of the biggest decisions that one has to make when transcribing and analyzing child language. In this sense, the computation of MLU serves as a methodological tripwire for the consideration of these two deeper issues. Other analyses, including lexical, syntactic, and discourse analyses also require that these decisions be made clearly and consistently. However, because of its conceptual simplicity, the MLU index places these problems into the sharpest focus.

The first three forms of transcription all make the basic assumption that there is a single utterance with four morphemes. Given the absence of any clear syntactic relation between the four words, it seems difficult to defend use of this form of transcription, unless the transcriber explicitly declares that the data should not be used to compute syntactic and sentential measures.

The fourth form of transcription treats the successive productions of the word "milk" as repeated attempts to produce a single word. This form of transcription makes sense if there is clear evidence that the child was having trouble saying the word. If there is no evidence that the word is really a repetition, it would seem best to use the fifth form of transcription. Studies of early child syntax have emphasized the extent to which the child is subject to constraints on utterance length (Bloom, 1973; Bloom, 1975; Gerken, 1991; Gerken, Landau & Remez, 1990). If one decides to count all repetitions of single words as full productions, it would seem that one is overestimating the degree of syntactic integration being achieved by the child. On the other hand, some researchers have argued that treatment of words as separate utterances in the earliest stages of language acquisition tends to underestimate the level of syntactic control being achieved by the child (Branigan, 1979; Elbers & Wijnen, 1992; Wijnen, 1990a).

The **CLAN** programs provide a partial solution to this dilemma. In cases where the researcher wants to use separate utterances for each word, the programs will treat each utterance as having a single morpheme. If the fourth form of transcription with repetition marks is used, the programs will, by default, treat the utterance as having only one morpheme. However, there is an option that allows the user to override this default and treat each word as a separate morpheme. This then allows the researcher to compute two different MLU values. The analysis with repetitions excluded could be viewed as the one which emphasizes syntactic structure and the one with repetitions included could be viewed as the one which emphasizes productivity measures.

The example we have been discussing involves a simple case of word repetition. In other cases, researchers may want to group together non-repeated words for which there is only partial evidence of syntactic or semantic combination. Consider the contrast between these next two examples. In the first example, the presence of the conjunction "and" motivates treatment of the words as a syntactic combination:

```
*CHI:  red,  yellow,  blue,  and  white.
```

However, without the conjunction, the words are best treated as separate utterances:

```
*CHI:  red.
*CHI:  yellow.
*CHI:  blue.
*CHI:  white.
```

As the child gets older, the solidification of intonational patterns and syntactic structures will give the transcriber more reason to group words together into utterances and to code retracings and repetitions as parts of larger utterances.

A somewhat separate, but related, issue is the treatment of interactional markers and other "communicators" such as "yes", "sure", "well", and "now."   In general, it seems best to group these markers together with the utterances to which they are most closely bound intonationally.   However, it only makes sense to do this if the utterances are contiguous in discourse.   Here are some examples:

```
*CHI:   no,  Mommy  no  go.
*CHI:   no  Mommy  go.
*CHI:   no  #  Mommy  go.
```

However, in other cases, it makes sense to transcribe "no" by itself.

```
*CHI:   no
*MOT:   why  not?
*CHI:   Mommy  go.
```

6.2.   Discourse Repetition

In the previous section, we discussed problems involved in deciding whether a group of words should be viewed as one utterance or as several.   This issue moves into the background when the word repetitions are broken up by the conversational interactions or by the child's own actions.   Consider these two examples:

```
*MOT:   what  do  you  drink  for  breakfast"
*CHI:   milk.
*MOT:   and  what  do  you  drink  for  lunch?
*CHI:   milk.
*MOT:   how  about  for  dinner?
*CHI:   milk.
*MOT:   and  what  is  your  favorite  thing  to  drink  at
        bedtime?
*CHI:   milk.
```

Or the child may use a single utterance repeatedly, but each time with a slightly different purpose.   For example, when putting together a puzzle, the child may pick up a piece and ask:

```
*CHI:   where  does  this  piece  go?
```

This may happen ten times in succession.   In both of these examples, it seems unfair from a discourse point of view to treat each utterance as a mere repetition.   Instead, each is functioning independently as a full communication.   One may want to mark the fact that the lexical material is repeated, but this should not affect other quantitative measures.

6.3.   Basic Utterance Terminators

The basic **CHAT** utterance terminators are the period, the question mark, and the exclamation mark.   **CHAT** requires that there be only one utterance on each main line.   In order to mark this, each utterance must end with one of these three utterance terminators. However, a single main line utterance may extend for several computer lines, as in this example:

```
*CHI:   this.
*MOT:   if  this  is  the  one  you  want,  you  will  have  to  take
        your  spoon  out  of  the  other  one.
```

The utterance in this main tier extends for two lines in the computer file. When it is necessary to continue an utterance on the main tier onto a second line, the second line *must begin with a tab*. The **CLAN** programs are set to expect no more than 2000 characters per main line, dependent tier, or header line.

Period   .

A period marks the end of an unmarked (declarative) utterance. Here are some examples of unmarked utterances:

```
*SAR:   I got cold.
*SAR:   pickle.
*SAR:   no.
```

For correct functioning of the **CLAN** programs, periods should be eliminated from abbreviations. Thus "Mrs." should be written as "Mrs" and "E.T." should become "E+t". Only proper nouns and the word "I" and its contractions are capitalized. Words that begin sentences are not capitalized.

Question   ?

The question mark indicates the end of a question. A question is an utterance that uses a wh-question word, subject–verb inversion, or a tag question ending. Here is an example of a question:

```
*FAT:   is that a carrot?
```

The question mark can also be used after a declarative sentence when it is spoken with the rising intonation of a question.

Exclamation   !

An exclamation point marks the end of an imperative or emphatic utterance. Here is an example of an exclamation:

```
*MOT:   sit down!
```

If this utterance were to be conveyed with final rising contour, it would instead be:

```
*MOT:   sit down?
```

6.4. Tone Unit Marking

The terminators discussed in this section and the next are chiefly relevant to those researchers who wish to mark prosodic groupings in discourse.

In spoken language, words cluster into tone units (Crystal, 1969; Crystal, 1975). Each tone group has a stressed syllable as its nucleus. Additional syllables may cluster around this nucleus with a variety of intonational contours. In order to indicate the grouping of words into tone units and the shape of intonational contours, transcribers need to mark: (a) the identity of the accented syllable, (b) the identity of stressed syllables, and (c) the direction of the tone on the accented or nuclear syllable. If one is writing out sentences by hand, the nicest way of transcribing tone movements is to use arrow symbols as in Crystal (1975), Fletcher (Fletcher, 1985), or Svartvik, Eeg-Olofsson, Forsheden, Oreström, and Thavenius (1982). These symbols could be supplemented by a musical notation scheme of the type used by Bolinger (1986) or Crystal (1969). However, none of these systems of notation can be inserted directly in computer files based on ASCII code. Although the system of Svartvik et al. is designed for computer use, it goes outside the boundaries of ASCII code and requires special purpose printing routines. In ASCII, one cannot place an arrow over a letter or raise a word higher on the page by turning the platen of a typewriter. Instead, we need to devise a set of codes that can represent the distinctions used by workers such as Bolinger, Crystal, Fletcher, and Svartvik et al. while still obeying the constraints of the ASCII system. In CHAT, these codes are available in two forms. In this chapter, we discuss a set of codes for main line coding of tone units and pitch movement. A parallel set of symbols exist for coding with UNIBET on the %pho line. The marking of stressed syllables is handled in the next chapter.

6.4.1. Terminated Tone Units

The three basic terminators can be further qualified to mark particular intonational contours. Those tone unit terminators which end with one of these three symbols are treated as utterance terminators when they occur at the end of the main line in CHAT. This means that the first four contours cited later are also treated by the CLAN programs as utterance terminators.

Rising Contour   -?

This symbol is used to indicate final rising contour. It is placed at the end of the tone unit, but is understood as applying to the tone group clustered about the preceding accented syllable or nucleus. This is the intonation pattern typically found in questions. It is treated by the CLAN programs as an utterance terminator.

Falling Contour   -.

This symbol is used to indicate final falling contour. This is the standard intonation pattern of declarative sentences. It is treated by the CLAN programs as an utterance terminator.

Rise–Fall Contour   -'.

This symbol is used to indicate final rise–fall contour. It is treated by the CLAN programs as an utterance terminator.

Fall–Rise Contour   -,.

This symbol is used to indicate final fall–rise contour. It is treated by the CLAN programs as an utterance terminator.

6.4.2. Nonterminated Tone Units

If the final punctuation on a tone unit does not include an utterance terminator, the CLAN programs do not treat it as a terminated utterance. Thus, the following two symbols can be used to indicate tone units that do not terminate utterances.

Level Contour   -,

This symbol is used to indicate final level contour. This contour often indicates nonfinality and is sometimes represented by a comma. It is not treated by the **CLAN** programs as an utterance terminator. If a series of phrases are joined together into a single utterance, this symbol or the previous one should be used to indicate nonfinal contour. Following Fletcher (1985), these terminal contours and stress symbols can be combined as in this example. (The use of slashes is discussed in the next chapter.)

```
*SON:  /you play -, /snakes and ladders -, //me -.
*FAT:  yes -, /I'll play -, /snakes and //ladders  -.
*FAT:  /where -, //is it -?
*SON:  /over //there -.
*FAT:  /will you //get it -?
*SON:  and //that -. # and //that -.
*FAT:  //yes -.
```

There are no examples in this passage of words with stress or accent on the second syllable. For such words, the slashes would be placed right in the middle of the word. The **CLAN** programs can be instructed to ignore the slashes and the contour markers when performing morphemic searches.

Low Level Contour   -_

This symbol is used to indicate low level final contour. Like the previous symbol, it is not treated by the **CLAN** programs as an utterance terminator.

6.5. The Comma

Transcriptions of spontaneous interactions have often tended to overuse the comma. It has often been used to mark five major utterance features at once: syntactic juncture, conceptual juncture, pausing, intonational drop, and even clause boundary. **CHAT** attempts to mark each of these functions differently. For example, pausing is marked by #; utterance and clause boundaries are marked by periods and question marks; and a level intonational contour is marked by the -, symbol. Once all of these functions have been broken out, there is then a clear and legitimate role for the comma as a marker of the standard forms of syntactic juncture, such as appositives and nonrestrictive relatives.

Syntactic Juncture   ,

The comma can be used to mark syntactic juncture.

Tag Question   ,,

A double comma can also be used to mark tag questions for easy retrieval.

```
*MOT:  you're coming home soon,, aren't you?
```

6.6. Pauses

Transcribers frequently want to be able to mark the pauses that occur both within and between tone units. Pauses that are marked only by silence are coded on the main line with the symbol #.

Unfilled Pause

Longer pauses can be represented as ## and a very long pause can be ###. Alternatively, you can add an estimate of pause length by adding a word after the # symbol as in #long. This example illustrates these forms:
```
*SAR:  I  don't  #  know  -.
*SAR:  #long  what  do  you  ###  think  -?
```

If you want to be exact, you can code the exact length of the pauses, following the # in minutes, seconds, and parts of seconds. The minutes are placed before a colon with the seconds following the colon. Parts of seconds are given after an underscore symbol. If there is no colon, it is assumed that the pause lasts under a minute. If there is no underscore, it is assumed that milliseconds are not being measured. However, a number for the seconds is obligatory. The following example codes pauses lasting .5 seconds, one minute and 13.41 seconds, and two seconds, respectively:
```
*SAR:  I  don't  #0_5  know  -.
*SAR:  #1:13_41  what  do  you  #2  think  -?
```

Researchers may wish to distinguish fluent pauses from disfluent pauses. Fluent pauses occur at grammatical junctures where commas are general used. They also occur at other sites that are determined by discourse rules. Pauses that occur elsewhere are typically considered to be disfluent. Disfluent pauses can be marked with the symbol #d. Making the distinction between fluent and disfluent pauses overt helps to guarantee the correct use of a marker for fluent pauses. Here are some examples:
```
*CHI:  well  -.
*CHI:  #  how  I  felt  about  that  -?
*CHI:  I  had  to  //put  #d  in  my  arms  -.
*CHI:  because  I  had  to  //put  on  a  special  coat  -.
*MOT:  we'll  see  -.
*MOT:  #long  maybe  to//morrow  -.
*CHI:  my  brother  does-'nt  //sleep  #dlong  so  much  now  -.
```

Lengthening   -:

This symbol is used to indicate lengthening or drawling of the previous word.

6.7. Special Utterance Terminators

In addition to the three basic utterance terminators, **CHAT** provides a series of more complex utterance terminators to mark various special functions. These special terminators all begin with the + symbol and end with one of the three basic utterance terminators.

Trailing Off   +...

The trailing off or incompletion marker is the terminator for an incomplete but not interrupted utterance. Trailing off occurs when speakers shift attention away from what they are saying, sometimes even forgetting what they were going to say. Usually the trailing off is followed by a pause in the conversation. After this lull, the speaker may continue with another utterance or a new speaker may produce the next utterance. Here is an example of an incompleted utterance:

```
*SAR:  smells good enough for +...
*SAR:  what is that?
```

If the speaker does not really get a chance to trail off before being interrupted by another speaker, then use the interruption marker +/. rather than the incompletion symbol. Do not use the incompletion marker to indicate either simple pausing #, repetition [/] , or retracing [//]. Note that utterance fragments coded in this way will be counted as complete utterances for analyses such as **MLU**, **MLT**, and **CHAINS**. If your intention is to avoid treating these fragments as complete utterances, then you should use the symbol [/-] discussion in chapter 8.

Interruption   +/.

This symbol is used for an utterance which is incomplete because one speaker is interrupted by another speaker. Here is an example of an interruption:

```
*MOT:  what did you +/.
*SAR:  Mommy.
```

The notion of interruption is to be taken very broadly. However, some researchers may wish to distinguish between an invited interruption and an uninvited interruption. An invited interruption may occur when one speaker is prompting his addressee to complete the utterance. This should be marked by the ++ symbol for other-completion, which is given later. Uninvited interruptions should be coded with the symbol +/.

Self-Interruption   +//.

Some researchers wish to be able to distinguish between incompletions involving a trailing off and incompletions involving an actual self-interruption. When an incompletion is not followed by further material from the same speaker, the +... symbol should always be selected. However, when the speaker breaks off an utterance and starts up another, the +//. symbol can be used, as in this example:

```
*SAR:  smells good enough for +//.
*SAR:  what is that?
```

There is no hard and fast way of distinguishing cases of trailing off from self-interruption. For this reason, some researchers prefer to avoid making the distinction. Researchers who wish to avoid making the distinction, should use only the +... symbol.

Interruption of Question   +/?

If the utterance being interrupted is a question, you can use the +/? symbol.

Quotation on Next Line   +"/.

During story reading and similar activities, a great deal of talk may involve direct quotation. In order to mark off this material as quoted, a special symbol can be used, as in the following example:

```
*CHI:   and  then  the  little  bear  said  +"/.
*CHI:   +"  please  give  me  all  of  your  honey.
*CHI:   +"  if  you  do,  I'll  carry  you  on  my  back.
```

The use of the +"/. symbol is linked to the use of the +" symbol. Breaking up quoted material in this way allows us to maintain the rule that each separate utterance should be on a separate line. This form of notation is only used when the material being quoted is a complete clause or sentence. It is not needed when single words are being quoted in noncomplement position. In those cases the ["] symbol can be used. Note that, from the viewpoint of syntactic analysis, the first line in the previous example is not a complete utterance, because the complement is contained in the material quoted on the following lines.

Quotation Precedes   +".

This symbol is used when the material being directly quoted precedes the main clause, as in the following example:

```
*CHI:   +"  please  give  me  all  of  your  honey.
*CHI:   the  little  bear  said  +".
```

6.8. Utterance Linkers

There is another set of symbols that can be used to mark other aspects of the ways in which utterances link together into turns and discourse. These symbols are not utterance terminators, but utterance initiators, or rather "linkers." They indicate various ways in which an utterance fits in with an earlier utterance. Each of these symbols begins with the plus sign.

Quoted Utterance   +"

This symbol is used in conjunction with the +"/. and +". symbols discussed earlier. It is placed at the beginning of an utterance that is being directly quoted.

Quick Uptake   +^

Sometimes an utterance of one speaker follows quickly on the heels of the last utterance of the preceding speaker without the customary short pause between utterances. An example of this is:

```
*MOT:   why  did  you  go?
*SAR:   +^  I  really  didn't.
```

Self-completion   +,

The symbol +, can be used at the beginning of a main tier line to mark the completion of an utterance after an interruption. In the following example, it marks the completion of an utterance by CHI after interruption by EXP. Note that the incompleted utterance must be terminated with the incompletion marker.

```
*CHI:  so after the tower +...
*EXP:  yeah.
*CHI:  +, I go straight ahead.
```

Other-completion   ++

A variant form of the +, symbol is the ++ symbol which marks "latching" or the completion of another speaker's utterance, as in the following example:

```
*HEL:  if Bill had known +...
*WIN:  ++ he would have come.
```

7. Prosody Within Words

CHAT also provides codes for marking stressing, lengthening, and pausing within words. The stressing of a particular word can be indicated in two ways. One way is to mark the stress levels of particular stressed syllables. Three levels of stress marking are available for this purpose.

Stressed Syllable   /

A single forward slash is used to indicate the placement of stress on the following syllable. It is placed right inside the word, as in **rhi/noceros.**

Primary Stressed Syllable   //

A double slash indicates the placement of strong nuclear accent on the following syllable. This is the nuclear accent that forms the center of a tone group. If the word "rhinoceros" is the center of a tone group, it would be marked as **rhi//noceros.**

Contrastively Stressed Syllable   ///

A triple apostrophe is used to indicate very strong contrastive stress, as in **rhi///noceros.**

A second way of marking stress refers not to a particular syllable, but to a word or a group of words. This way of indicating stress uses the symbols [!] and [!!]. This method is discussed in chapter 8.

Lengthened Syllable   :

A colon within a word indicates the lengthening or drawling of a syllable, as in this example:
```
MOT:    baby  want  bana:nas?
```

Pause between Syllables   ::

A pause between syllables may be indicated by two colons, as in this example:
```
MOT:   is that  a  rhin::oceros?
```

Be careful not to confuse a pause in the middle of a word with lengthening or drawling. There is no special **CHAT** symbol for a filled pause. Instead words like "uh" and "um" are used to mark filled pauses. The exact written form of these fillers is given in chapter 4.

8. Scoped Symbols

Up to this point, the symbols we have discussed are inserted at single points in the transcript. They refer to events occurring at particular points during the dialogue. There is another major class of symbols that refers not to particular points in the transcript, but to stretches of speech. These symbols are enclosed in square brackets and the material to which they relate can be enclosed in angle brackets. The material in the square brackets functions as a descriptor of the material in angle brackets. If a scoped symbol applies only to the single word preceding it, the angle brackets need not be marked, because the CLAN programs consider that the material in square brackets refers to a single preceding word when there are no angle brackets. Depending on the nature of the material in the square brackets, the material in the angle brackets may be automatically excluded from certain types of analysis, such as MLU counts, and so forth. Scoped symbols are useful for marking wide variety of relations, including paralinguistics, explanations, and retracings.

Paralinguistic Material   [=! text]

Paralinguistic events, such as "coughing," "laughing," or "yelling" can be marked by using square brackets, the =! symbol, a space, and then text describing the event.
```
*CHI:  that's  mine  [=!  cries].
```

This means that the child cries while saying the word "mine." If he cries throughout, the transcription would be:
```
*CHI:  <that's  mine>  [=!  cries].
```

In order to indicate crying with no particular vocalization, you can use the 0 symbol, as in this example:
```
*CHI:  0  [=!  crying].
```
However, use of the 0 symbol is not necessary and many transcribers find it distracting. The above example could just as well be coded as simply:
```
*CHI:  [=!  crying].
```

Alternatively, laughing and other similar vocalizations can be marked using the %par line which is discussed later. This same format of [=! text] can also be used to describe prosodic characteristics such as "glissando" or "shouting" that are best characterized with full English words. Paralinguistic effects such as soft speech, yelling, singing, laughing, crying, whispering, whimpering, and whining can also be noted in this way. For a full set of these terms and details on their usage, see Crystal (1969) or Trager (1958). Here is another example:
```
*NAO:  watch  out  [=!  laughs].
```

Stressing   [!]

This symbol can be used without accompanying angle brackets to indicate that the preceding word is stressed. If a whole string of words is stressed, they should be enclosed in angle brackets.

Contrastive Stressing [!!]

This symbol can be used without accompanying angle brackets to indicate that the preceding word is contrastively stressed. If a whole string of words is contrastively stressed, they should be enclosed in angle brackets.

Quotation Mark ["]

This symbol marks a metalinguistic reference to a word or phrase. The metalinguistic reference must be surrounded by angle brackets, if it is more than a single word long. Here is an example of its use:

```
*MAR:  what  does  <unca  banana>  ["]  mean?
```

This symbol is not intended for use in marking complete direct quotations. When a speaker cites a whole utterance from some other speaker as quoted, use the +"/. and +" symbols discussed in chapter 6.

Explanation [= text]

This symbol is used for brief explanations on the text tier. This symbol is helpful for specifying the deictic identity of objects and people.

```
*MOT:  don't  look  in  there  [= closet]!
```

Explanations can be more elaborate as in this example:

```
*ROS:  you  don't  scare  me  anymore
       [= don't  scare  me  anymore!].
```

An alternative form for transcribing this, which is discussed in chapter 9, is:

```
*ROS:  you  don't  scare  me  any  more.
%exp:  means  to  say  "Don't  scare  me  anymore!"
```

Replacement [: text]

In chapter 4 we discussed the use of a variety of nonstandard forms such as "gonna" and "hafta." In chapter 5 we examined ways of morphemicizing words directly on the main line. However, words such as "gonna" and irregular forms such as "went" cannot easily be morphemicized as they stand. In order to morphemicize such words, the transcriber can use replacement symbol that allows the CLAN programs to substitute a morphemicized form for the form actually produced. Here is an example:

```
*BEA:  when  ya  gonna  [: go-ing to]  stop  doin(g)  that?
*CHA:  whyncha  [: why do-'nt you]  just  be  quiet!
```

In this example, "gonna" is followed by its morphemicized replacement in brackets. The colon that follows the first bracket provides instructions to the CLAN programs that perform morphological analysis that the material in brackets should replace the preceding word. There must be a space following the colon, in order to keep this symbol separate from other symbols that use letters after the colon. This example also illustrates two other ways in which CHAT and CLAN deal with nonstandard forms. The lexical item "ya" is treated as a lexical item distinct from "you." However, the semantic equivalence between "ya" and "you" is maintained by the formalization of a list of dialectal spelling variations.

The string "doin(g)" is treated by the analysis programs as if it were "doing." This is done by simply having the programs ignore the parentheses, unless they are given instructions to pay attention to them, as discussed in chapter 23. From the viewpoint of **CLAN**, a form like "doin(g)" is much like an incomplete form such as "broth(er)."

In order for replacement to function properly, nothing should be placed between the replacing string and the string to be replaced. For example, one should use the form:

```
    go-ed  [:  went]  [*]
```
rather than:
```
    go-ed  [*]  [:  went]
```

Omissions   [0 text]

In chapter 4, we used the symbols 0word, 0*word, and 00word to code for omitted words, incorrectly omitted words, and ellipsed words. However, some users may find this form of coding difficult to read. To solve this problem, it is possible to use the forms [0 text], [0* text], and [00 text] instead. The two forms are equivalent.

Translation   [:=x text]

This symbol is used to translate words spoken in a secondary language. Here is an example from Leopold (1949):

```
    *HIL:  spiel@s  [:=g  game]  house,  knock  down.
```
There is no space here between the colon and the equals sign. In this example, the German word *Spiel* "game" is first given a special form marker @s which indicates that it is a second language form. Then the English translation is given in brackets. The :=g symbol indicates that the word comes from German. If there are several languages being mixed in a transcript, each can be given its own letter, but this must be marked in the 00readme.doc file.

Alternative Transcription   [=? text]

Sometimes it is difficult to choose between two possible transcriptions for a word or group of words. In that case an alternative transcription can be indicated in this way:

```
    *CHI:  we  want  <one  or  two>  [=?  one  too].
```

Dependent Tier on Main Line   [%xxx: text]

The various dependent tiers discussed in chapter 9 can be placed directly on the main line. This is useful when it is important to refer to a particular set of words, rather than the utterance as a whole, as in this example:

```
    *RES:  would  all  of  you  <who  have  not  had  seconds>
           [%gpx:  looks  at  Timmy]  come  up  to  the  front  of  the
           line?
```

Comment on Main Line   [% text]

Instead of placing comment material on a separate %com line, it is possible to place comments directly on the main line using the % symbol in brackets. Here is an example of this usage:

```
*CHI:   I  really  wish  you  wouldn't  [%  said  with  strong
        raising  of  eyebrows]  do  that.
```

A word of warning regarding comments on the main line. Overuse of this particular notational form can make a transcript difficult to read and analyze. Because placing a comment directly onto the main line tends to highlight it, this form should only be used for material that is crucial to the understanding of the main line.

Code on Main Line   [$text]

We do not recommend that you include codes on the main line. However, if you find it necessary to place codes directly onto the main line, you should enclose them in square brackets. By default, they will apply to the immediately preceding word. If you want them to refer to a longer stretch of material, you should enclose that material in angle brackets. This form of notation is used by the **SALTIN** program to translate in-line SALT codes. Here is an example:

```
*ADA:      All  of  them  [$TRO]  go  in  here.
```

Best Guess   [?]

Often audio tapes are hard to hear because of interference from room noise, recorder malfunction, vocal qualities, and so forth. Nonetheless, the transcriber often thinks that, through the noise, they can recognize what is being said. The fact that there is some residual uncertainty about this "best guess" is indicated by using this symbol to mark either the single preceding word or the previous group of words enclosed in angle brackets.

```
*SAR:  I  want  a  frog  [?].
```

In this example, the word that is unclear is "frog." In general, when there is a symbol in square brackets that takes scoping and there are no preceding angle brackets, then the single preceding word is the scope. When more than one word is unclear, you can surround the unclear portion in angle brackets as in the following example:

```
*SAR:  <going  away  with  my  mommy>  [?]  ?
```

Overlap Follows   [>]

During the course of a conversation, speakers often talk at the same time. Transcribing these interactions can be trying. This and the following two symbols are designed to help sort out this difficult transcription task. The "overlap follows" symbol indicates that the text enclosed in angle brackets is being said at the same time as the following speaker's bracketed speech. They are talking at the same time. This code must be used in combination with the "overlap precedes" symbol, as in this example:

```
*MOT:  no  #  Sarah  #  you  have  to  <stop  doing  that>  [>]  !
*SAR:  <Mommy  I  don't  like  this>  [<].
*SAR:  it  is  nasty.
```

Using these overlap indicators does not preclude making a visual indication of overlap in the following way:

```
*MOT:   no # Sarah # you have to <stop doing that> [>]  !
*SAR:                             <Mommy I don't like this> [<].
*SAR:   it is nasty.
```

The visual indication of the overlap will be ignored by the **CLAN** programs, which treat any sequence of more than one spaces as if they were a single space.

Overlap precedes   [<]

The "overlap precedes" symbol indicates that the text enclosed in angle brackets is being said at the same time as the preceding speaker's bracketed speech. This code must be used in combination with the "overlap follows" symbol. Sometimes several overlaps occur in a single sentence. It is then necessary to use numbers to identify these overlaps, as in this example:

```
*SAR:   and the <doggy was> [>1] really cute and it <had to
        go> [>2] into bed.
*MOT:   <why don't you> [<1]  ?
*MOT:   <maybe we could> [<2].
```

If this sort of intense overlapping continues, it may be necessary to continue to increment the numbers as long as needed to keep everything straight. However, once one whole turn passes with no overlaps, the number counters can be reinitialized to "1."

Overlap Follows and Precedes <text> [<>]

This symbol indicates that the text enclosed in angle brackets is being overlapped by the bracketed speech of the following speaker and by the bracketed utterance of the preceding speaker. It must be used in conjunction with the previous two symbols to indicate the overlapped utterances of more than two speakers. The three symbols, used together, would look like this:

```
*ROS:   well then # four +/.
*MAR:   hey wait.
*MAR:   you were <scared> [>].
*ROS:   +, [//] <five> [<>]
*MAR:   <I> [<] wasn't really scared.
```

Using spacing to provide additional clarity, these overlaps could be represented in this way:

```
*ROS:   well then # four +/.
*MAR:   hey wait.
*MAR:   you were <scared> [>]
*ROS:   +,          [//] <five> [<>]
*MAR:                    <I> [<] wasn't really scared.
```

Constructing transcripts with this careful spatial representation of overlap is a time-consuming business. However, if you want to include a visual representation of this type, it is best to do so using the space bar, rather than tabs, because using tabs in the middle of the line can cause problems for **CLAN**.

Retracing Without Correction   [/]

Often speakers repeat words or even whole phrases (Goldman-Eisler, 1968; MacWhinney & Osser, 1977). The [/] symbol is used in those cases when a speaker begins to say something, stops and then repeats the earlier material without change. The material being retraced is enclosed in angle brackets. If there are no angle brackets, the **CLAN** programs assume that only the preceding word is being repeated. In a retracing without correction, it is necessarily the case that the material in angle brackets is the same as the material immediately following the [/] symbol. Here is an example of this.

```
*BET:  <I wanted>  [/]  I wanted  to  invite  Margie.
```

If there are pauses and fillers between the initial material and the retracing, they should be placed after the retracing symbol, as in:

```
*HAR:  it's  [/]  #  um  #  it's  [/]  it's  like  #  a  um  #  dog.
```

When a word or group of words is repeated several times with no fillers, all of the repetitions except for the last are placed into a single retracing, as in this example:

```
*HAR:  <it's  it's  it's>  [/]  it's  like  #  a  um  #  dog.
```

By default, all of the **CLAN** programs except **MLU**, **MLT**, and **MODREP** include repeated material. This default can be changed by using the +r6 switch. An alternative way of indicating several repetitions of a single word uses this form:

```
*HAR:  it's(/4)  like  #  a  um  #  dog.
```

This forms indicates directly on the word the fact that it has been repeated four times. If this form is used, it is not possible to get a count of the repetitions to be added to MLU. However, since this is not usually desirable anyway, there are good reasons to use this more compact form when single words are repeated.

Retracing With Correction   [//]

This symbol is used when a speaker starts to say something, stops, repeats the basic phrase, changes the syntax but maintains the same idea. Usually, the correction moves closer to the standard form, but sometimes it moves away from it. The material being retraced is enclosed in angle brackets. If there are no angle brackets, the **CLAN** programs assume that only the preceding word is being retraced. In retracing with correction, it is necessarily true that the material in the angle brackets is different from what follows the [//] symbol. Here is an example of this:

```
*BET:  <I  wanted>   [//]   uh  I  thought  I  wanted  to  invite
       Margie.
```

Retracing with correction can combine with retracing without correction, as in this example:

```
*CHI:  <the  fish  are>  [//]  the  [/]  the  fish  are  swimming.
```

Sometimes retracings can become quite complex and lengthy. This is particularly true in speakers with language disorders. It is important not to underestimate the extent to which retracing goes on in such transcripts. The example from a Wernicke's aphasic given in chapter 15 illustrates the extent to which retracing can occur. By default, all of the **CLAN** programs except **MLU**, **MLT**, and **MODREP** include retraced material. This default can be changed by using the +r6 switch.

False Start without retracing   [/-]

The symbols [/] and [//] are used when a false start is followed by a complete repetition or by a partial repetition with correction. If the speaker terminates an incomplete utterance and starts off on a totally new tangent, this can be coded with the [/-] symbol:
```
*BET:  <I wanted>  [/-]  uh when is Margie coming?
```

If the material is coded in this way only one utterance will be counted by the CLAN programs. If the coder wishes to treat the fragment as a separate utterance, the symbols +... and +//. that were discussed in Chapter 6 should be used instead.

By default, all of the CLAN programs except MLU, MLT, and MODREP include repeated material. This default can be changed by using the +r6 switch.

Unclear Retracing Type   [/?]

This symbol is used primarily when using the CLAN program called SALTIN to reformat from SALT files to CHAT files. SALT does not distinguish between filled pausing (#) repetitions ([/]), and retracings ([//]); all three phenomena and possible others are treated as "mazes." Because of this, SALTIN uses the [/?] symbol to translate SALT mazes into CHAT hesitation markings.

Error Marking   [*]

Most of the work of coding for errors is done on the %err line. However, all errors that are to be coded on the %err line must be marked with the [*] symbol on the main line. This symbol can be given multiword scope. However, most often the scope of the error is a single word and the scope can be omitted. Usually, this symbol occurs right after the error. In repetitions and retracing with errors in the initial part of the retracing, the [*] symbol is placed before the [/] mark. If the error is in the second part of the retracing, the [*] symbol goes after the [/]. In error coding, the form actually produced is placed on the main line and the target form is given on the %err line.

The corrections made by retracings are sometimes errors themselves. Here are two examples from aphasic patients:
```
*PAT:  the boy was on the <tree stamp>  [*]  [//]  tree
       stump.
*PAT:  <he's vacuu(m)ing the>  [//]  #  he's vadgering  [*]
       the grass.
```

8.1. Postcodes

The symbols we have discussed so far in this chapter usually refer to words or groups of words. CHAT also allows for codes that refer to entire utterances. These codes are placed into square brackets following the final utterance delimiter. They always begin with a plus sign.

Postcodes   [+ text]

Postcodes have the same form as generic comments within utterances. The transcriber can make up any postcode symbol desired; there is no predefined set of postcodes. Postcodes differ from scoped codes in that they are assumed, by default, to apply to the utterance as a whole, as in this example:

```
*CHI:      not this one. [+ neg] [+ req] [+ inc]
```

In many cases it is better to put codes of this type on separate coding lines, as discussed in chapter 9. However, there are times when it is best to use postcodes. They are important in translating from SALT format to CHAT format. Because the scope and type of codes is often unclear in SALT, it usually makes most sense to place them as postcodes. Postcodes are also helpful in including or excluding utterances from analyses of turn length or utterance length by MLT and MLU. The postcodes, [+ bch] and [+ trn], when combined with the -s and +s+ switch, can be used for this purpose.

Excluded Utterance   [+ bch]

Sometimes we want to have a way of marking utterances that are not really a part of the main interaction, but are in some "back channel." For example, during an interaction that focuses on a child, the mother may make a remark to the investigator. We might want to exclude remarks of this type from analysis by MLT and MLU, as in this interaction:

```
*CHI:      here one.
*MOT:      no   -, here.
%sit:       the  doorbell  rings.
*MOT:      just  a  moment.   [+ bch]
*MOT:      I'll get it.    [+ bch]
```

In order to exclude the utterances marked with [+ bch], the -s"[+ bch]" switch must be used with MLT and MLU.

Included Utterance   [+ trn]

The [+ trn] postcode can force the CLAN MLT program to treat an utterance as a turn when it would normally not be treated as a turn. For example, utterances containing only "0" are usually not treated as turns. However, if one believes that the accompanying nonverbal gesture constitutes a turn, one can note this using [+ trn], as in this example:

```
*MOT:      where  is  it?
*CHI:      0. [+ trn]
%act:      points  at  wall.
```

Later, when counting utterances with the MLT program, one can use the +s+"[+ trn]" switch to force counting of actions as turns, as in this command:

```
mlt +s+"[+  trn]"  sample.cha
```

9. Dependent Tiers

In the previous chapters, we have examined how **CHAT** can be used to create file headers and to code the actual words of the interaction on the main line. The third major component of a **CHAT** transcript is the ancillary information given on the dependent tiers. Dependent tiers are lines typed below the main line that contain codes, comments, events and descriptions of interest to the researcher. It is important to have this material on separate lines, because the extensive use of complex codes in the main line would make it unreadable. There are many codes that refer to the utterance as a whole. Using a separate line to mark these avoids having to indicate their scope or cluttering up the end of an utterance with codes.

It is important to emphasize that no one expects any researcher to code all tiers for all files. **CHAT** is designed to provide options for coding, not requirements for coding. These options constitute a common set of coding conventions that will allow the investigator to represent those aspects of the data that are most important. It is often possible to transcribe the main line without making much use at all of dependent tiers. However, for some projects, dependent tiers are crucial.

All dependent tiers should begin with the percent symbol (%) and should be in lower case letters. As in the main line, dependent tiers consist of a tier code and a tier line. The dependent tier code is the percent symbol, followed by a three letter code ID and a colon. The dependent tier line is the text entered after the colon which describes fully the elements of interest in the main tier. Except for the %mor and %syn tiers, these lines do not require ending punctuation. Here is an example of a main line with two dependent tiers:

```
*MOT:   well  go get  it!
%spa:   $IMP  $REF  $INS
%mor:   ADV|well . V|go&PRES   V|get&PRES   PRO|it!
```

The first dependent tier indicates certain speech act codes and the second indicates a morphemic analysis with certain part of speech coding. Coding systems have been developed for some dependent tiers. Often, these codes begin with the symbol $. If there is more than one code, they can be put in strings with only spaces separating them as in:

```
%spa:  $IMP  $REF  $INS
```

Multiple dependent tiers may be added in reference to a single main line, giving you as much richness in descriptive capability as is needed.

9.1. Standard Dependent Tiers

Users can make up any new dependent tier that they need for their analyses. Each dependent tier should be used to code consistently for a particular type of data. The shape of any new tiers should be discussed in detail in the 00readme.doc file. New tiers also have to be added to the "depfile" used by the **CHECK** program, as discussed in chapter 21.

Most users will find that they can simply use the dependent tiers that are pre-defined in this chapter. Here we list all of the dependent tier types that have been proposed for child language data. It is unlikely that a given corpus would ever be transcribed in all of these ways. The listing that follows is alphabetical.

%act: This tier describes the actions of the speaker or the listener. Here is an example of text accompanied by the speaker's actions.

```
*ROS:    I  do  it!
%act:    runs  to  toy  box
```

The %act tier can also be used in conjunction with the 0 symbol when actions are performed in place of speaking:

```
*ADA:    0.
%act:    kicks  the  ball
```

In chapter 4 we saw how this could also be coded as:

```
*ADA:    0  [%act:  kicks  the  ball].
```

And if one does not care about preserving the identification of the information as an action, the following form can be used:

```
*ADA:    0  [%  kicks  the  ball].
```

The choice among these three forms depends on the extent to which the coder wants to keep track of a particular type of dependent tier information. The first form preserves this best and the last form fails to preserve it at all. Actions also include gestures, such as nodding, pointing, waving, and shrugging.

%add: This tier describes who talks to whom. Use the three-letter identifier given in the participants header to identify the addressees.

```
*MOT:    be  quiet.
%add:    ALI,  BEA
```

In this example, Mother is telling Alice and Beatrice to "be quiet." A simpler way of coding addressee is to use combined speaker ID's such as *MOT-ALI or *MOT-BEA or even *MOT-BEI for various combinations of speakers and addressees. The decision to use either a full %add line or these combined codes is up to the transcriber.

%alt: This tier is used to provide an alternative possible transcription. If the transcription is intended to provide an alternative for only one word, it may be better to use the main line form of this coding tier in the form [=? text].

%cod: This is the general purpose coding tier. It can be used for mixing codes into a single tier for economy or ease of entry. Here is an example.

```
*MOT:    you  want  Mommy  to  do  it?
%cod:    $MLU=6  $NMV=2  $RDE  $EXP
```

%**com**: This is the general purpose comment tier. One of its many uses is to note occurrence of a particular construction type, as in this example:

```
*EVE:    that's nasty # is it?
%com:    note tag question
```

Notations on this line should usually be in common English words, rather than codes. If special symbols and codes are included, they should be placed in quotation marks, so that the **CHECK** program does not flag them as errors.

%**def**: This tier is needed only for files that are reformatted from the SALT system by the **SALTIN** program.

%**eng**: This line provides a fluent, nonmorphemicized, English translation for non-English data.

```
*MAR:    yo no tengo nada.
%eng:    I don't have anything.
```

%**err**: This tier codes errors using the system discussed in depth in chapter 12.

%**exp**: This explanation tier is useful for specifying the deictic identity of objects or individuals. Brief explanations can also appear on the main line, enclosed in square brackets and preceded by a "=" followed by a space, as discussed in chapter 8.

%**fac**: This tier codes facial actions. Ekman and Friesen (1969; 1978) have developed a complete and explicit system for the coding of facial actions. This system takes about 100 hours to learn to use and provides extremely detailed coding of the motions of particular muscles in terms of facial action units. Recently, Kearney and McKenzie (1993) have developed tools for machine interpretation of emotions using the system of Ekman and Friesen.

%**flo**: This tier codes a "flowing" version of the transcript that is as free as possible of transcription conventions and which reflects a minimal number of transcription decisions. Here is an example of a %flo line:

```
*CHI:    <I do-'nt> [//] I do-'nt wanna [: want to]
         look in a [*] badroom [*] or Bill-'s room.
%flo:    I don't I don't wanna look in a badroom or
         Bill's room.
%err:    a /A/ -> the /DA/ ; badroom /baedrUm/ ->
         bathroom /baeTrUm/
```

Most researchers would agree that the %flo line is easier to read than the *CHI line. However, it gains readability by sacrificing precision and utility for computational analyses. The %flo line has no records of retracings; words are simply repeated. There is no regularization to standard morphemes. Standard English orthography is used to give a general impression of the nature of phonological errors. There is no need to enter this line by hand, because there is a **CLAN** program that can enter it automatically by comparing the main line to the other coding lines. However, when dealing with very difficult speech such as that of Wernicke's aphasics (particularly in other languages), the transcriber may find it useful to first type in this line as a kind of notepad from which it is then possible to create the main line and the %err line.

%gls: This tier can be used to provide a "translation" of the child's utterance into the adult language. Unlike the %eng tier, this tier does not have to be in English. It should use an explanation in the target language. This tier differs from the %flo tier in that it is being used not to simplify the form of the utterance, but to explain what might otherwise be unclear. Finally, this tier differs from the %exp tier in that it is not used to clarify deictic reference or the general situation, but to provide a target language gloss of immature learner forms.

%gpx: This tier codes gestural and proxemic material. Some transcribers find it helpful to distinguish between general activity that can be coded on the %act line and more specifically gestural and proxemic activity, such as nodding or reaching, which can be coded on the %gpx line.

%int: This tier codes intonations, using standard language descriptions.

%lan: This tier can be used to code the nature of the language of the utterance, the language of the preceding speaker and the dominant language of the speaker and addressee. For example, a code such as $DGDG or $D:G:D:G might indicate an utterance by a Dutch speaker in response to another Dutch speaker who had used German. See the discussion of the %add tier for other approaches to this coding. The exact shape of the codes on this tier will probably be project-specific. For a good example of a system of this type see De Houwer (1990).

%mod: This tier is used in conjunction with the %pho tier to code the phonological form of the adult target or model for each of the learner's phonological forms.

%mor: This tier codes morphemic semantics in accord with the system outlined in chapter 14. Here is an example of the %mor tier:

```
*MAR:    I wanted a toy.
%mor:    PRO|I&1S V|want-PAST DET|a&INDEF N|toy.
```

%par: This tier codes paralinguistic behaviors such as coughing, crying.

%pho: This dependent tier is used to describe phonological phenomena. When the researcher is only attempting to describe particular phonological errors, the %err line should be used instead. The %pho line is to be used when the entire utterance is being coded or when there is no reason to interpret some nonstandard speech string as an error. In order to code data phonemically or phonetically, the symbols of IPA must be translated to ASCII. Chapter 10 describe a system for translating a subset of IPA into ASCII for the phonemes of English. This system is called the UNIBET. Systems like UNIBET can also be devised for other languages. Here is an example of the %pho tier in use. The symbols in the tier line are in UNIBET.

```
*SAR:    I got a boo+boo.
%pho:    /ai gat V bubu/
```

There are two main uses for the %pho line. One use is the transcription of occasional difficult stretches that the transcriber can render phonemically, but which have no obvious morphemic analysis. The other use is for a more extended transcription of a complete text on the phonemic level as in the work of Carterette and Jones (1974).

For more serious phonological analysis, the PHONASCII system described in chapter 11 should be used instead of UNIBET. When doing more extended coding, the transcriber may wish to do most of the transcription in UNIBET and particular segments in greater detail in PHONASCII. The %pho line should not be used as the only transcription of phonological errors, because this is done on the %err line.

%**sit**:   This tier describes situational information relevant only to the utterance. There is also an @Situation header. Situational comments that relate more broadly to the file as a whole or to a major section of the file should be placed in a @Situation header.

```
*EVE:    what that?
*EVE:    woof@o woof@o.
%sit:    dog is barking
```

%**spa**:   This tier is for speech act coding. Many researchers wish to transcribe their data with reference to speech acts. Speech act codes describe the function of sentences in discourse. Often researchers express a preference for the method of coding for speech acts. Many systems for coding speech acts have been developed. A set of speech act codes adapted from the system of Ninio and Wheeler (1986) is provided in chapter 13.

%**syn**:   This tier is used to code syntactic structure, as discussed in chapter 14.

%**tim**:   This tier is for time stamp coding. Often it is necessary to give time readings during the course of taping. These readings are given relative to the time of the first utterance in the file. The time of that utterance is taken to be time 00:00:00. Its absolute time value can be given by the @Time Start header. Elapsed time from the beginning of the file is given in hours:minutes:seconds. Thus, a %tim entry of 01:20:55 indicates the passage of one hour, twenty minutes, and 55 seconds from time zero. If you only want to track time in minutes and seconds, you can use the form minutes:seconds, as in 09:22 for nine minutes and 22 seconds.

```
*MOT:    where are you?
%tim:    00:00:00

...        (40 pages of transcript follow and then)

*EVE:    that one.
%tim:    01:20:55
```

If there is a break in the interaction, it may be necessary to establish a new time zero. This is done by inserting a new @Time Start header.

9.2. Creating Additional Dependent Tiers

There are no restrictions on the creation of additional dependent tiers. Researchers have found tiers, such as %par for paralinguistics or %gpx for gestural-proxemic, to be extremely useful. For a transcript of language on a farm, one might want to make up a tier for animal noises and call it %ani. When devising additional tiers, the codes and markings should always be based on printing ASCII symbols. In addition, use the $ symbol to indicate unitary codes. The names for new tiers and the codes for those tiers must also be entered into the "depfile" used by the **CHECK** program.

9.3. Synchrony Relations

For dependent tiers whose codes refer to the entire utterance, it is often important to distinguish whether events occur before, during, or after the utterance.

< bef >   Occurrence before

If the comment refers to something that occurred immediately before the utterance in the main line, you may use the symbol <bef>, as in this example:
```
*MOT:  it is her turn.
%act:  <bef> moves to the door
```

< aft >   Occurrence after

If a comment refers to something that occurred immediately after the utterance, you may use the form <aft>. In this example, Mother opened the door after she spoke:
```
*MOT:  it is her turn.
*MOT:  go ahead.
%act:  <aft> opens the door
```

If neither < bef > or < aft > are coded, it is assumed that the material in the coding tier occurs during the whole utterance or that the exact point of its occurrence during the utterance is not important.

Although **CHAT** provides transcribers with the option of indicating the point of events using the %com tier and <bef> and <aft> scoping, it may often be best to use the @Comment header tier instead. The advantage of using the @Comment header is that it indicates in a clearer manner the point at which an activity actually occurs. For example, instead of the form:
```
*MOT:  it is her turn.
%act:  <bef> moves to the door
```
one could use the form:
```
@Comment:  Mot moves to the door.
*MOT:  it is her turn.
```

The third option provided by **CHAT** is to code comments in square brackets right on the main line, as in this form:
```
*MOT:  [% Mot moves to the door] it is her turn.
```

Of these alternative forms, the second seems to be the best in this case.

< $=n >   Following sentences

When material on a dependent tier refers to a whole string of utterances, the scope of its application may be indicated by using the symbol < $=n >, where **n** is the number of following utterances to which the tier refers. For example, in the following excerpt, the mother has her arms extended to the child throughout three utterances.
```
*MOT:  want to come sit in my lap?
%act:  <$=2> MOT extends arms in direction of CHI
*MOT:  come on.
*MOT:  hop up.
```

9.4. Code-switching and Voice-switching

Transcription is easiest when speakers avoid overlaps, speak in full utterances, and use a single standard language throughout. However, the real world of conversational interactions is seldom so simple and uniform. One particularly challenging type of interaction involves code-switching between two or even three different languages. In some cases, it may be possible to identify a default language and to mark a few words as intrusions into the default language. In other cases, mixing and switching are more intense.

CHAT provides several ways of dealing with code switching. The selection of some or all of these methods of notation depends primarily on the user's needs for retrieval of codes during analysis.

1. The languages spoken by the various participants can be noted with the @Language of XXX header tier.
2. As noted in chapter 4, individual words may be identified with the @s terminator to indicate their second language status. The exact identity of the second language can be coded as needed. For example, words in French could be noted as @f and words in German as @g. In the limiting case, it would be possible to mark every single word in a French-German bilingual transcript as either @f or @g. Of course, doing this would be tedious, but it would provide a complete key for eventual retrieval and study.
3. If needed, the @f and @g markers can be further expanded with replacement symbols as discussed in Chapter 8. For example, one can have:
   ```
   spiel@g  [:=g  game]
   ```
4. It is possible to use the six-letter code for the main tier as an easy way of indicating the matrix language being used for each utterance. For example, *CHIGG could indicate the child speaking German to a German speaker and *CHIGF could indicate the child speaking German to a French speaker. Retrieval during analysis would then rely on the use of the +t switch, as in +t*CHIG*, +t*CHUGG, and +t*CHI*.
5. The %lan dependent tier can be used to code the status of the main language of each utterance and the presence of additional material. If desired, aspects of the %add tier can be coded together with the %lan tier to indicate the primary language of the addressees.
6. The system of "gem" markers can also be used to indicate the beginnings and ends of segments of discourse in particular languages.
7. A large database may consist of files in certain well-specified interaction types. For example, conversations with the mother may be in German and those with the father in French. If this is the case, the careful selection of file names such as "ger01.cha" and "fre01.cha" can be used to facilitate analysis.

These techniques are all designed to facilitate the retrieval of material in one language separately from the other. The choice of one method over another will depend on the nature of the material being transcribed and the eventual goals of the analysis.

Problems similar to those involved in code-switching occur in studies of narratives where a speaker may assume a variety of roles or voices. For example, a child may be speaking either as the dragon in a story or as the narrator of the story or as herself. These different roles are most easily coded by marking the six-character main line code with forms such as *CHIDRG, *CHINAR, and *CHISEL for child-as-dragon, child-as-narrator, and child-as-self. However, the other forms discussed above for noting code-switching can also be used for these purposes.

10. UNIBETs

Young children's phonological productions often differ from the adult standard in interesting and important ways. Sometimes a researcher may not want to assume that the sounds made by a child correspond to any adult forms at all. In such cases, researchers may wish to code the phonological shapes of words or word-like strings.

Earlier versions of the **CLAN** programs relied heavily on systems for coding phonological data in ASCII characters. However, two major changes in the programs have decreased the extent to which transcribers need to rely on ASCII characters for transcription. The first change is the modification of the **CED** text editor to permit inclusion of characters in fonts based on the International Phonetic Alphabet or IPA (Pullum & Ladusaw, 1986). Rather than coding these characters in ASCII, it is now possible to code them directly in IPA. Second, the ability of the **CED** text editor to make reference to full digitized sound makes it less important in some cases to have a full phonological transcription.

Despite these changes, it is still often useful to have a simple way of representing phonemes in ASCII which does not require installation of the complete IPA font. We call this system a UNIBET. In this chapter we present UNIBET systems for several languages.

10.1. A UNIBET for English

For single character phonemic (not phonetic) coding on the %err and %pho tiers, researchers may want to use the following ASCII translations of IPA symbols. Most of the symbols were taken from a draft report of the ALVEY Speech Group sent to us by Dr. Bladon of the Oxford Phonetics Laboratory and then modified by George Allen. There have been two earlier versions of this proposal. The current proposal supersedes the earlier ones.

UNIBET strings on the main line are marked by @u, as noted in chapter 4. Main line use of UNIBET is intended to be fairly limited. Any extensive transcription with UNIBET should be done on the %pho line. When making use of UNIBET on the main line, none of the utterance delimiter symbols such as ! or ? should be included in UNIBET strings. In order to permit coding of the glottal stop within main line UNIBET strings, we represent it with the character "7".

Most phonemes are single characters; exceptions are the "standard" digraphic diphthongs (/ai,au,oi/), r-colored vowels, affricates, and British schwa on- and off-glides. A consonant or vowel may be coded as "long" rather than doubled, by use of colon. Spaces should be inserted between words, and various internal boundaries (syllable /$/, morpheme /#/, and word /##/) may be marked as desired. Syllabic stress is coded in three levels, /"/ for primary pitch accent, /'/ for secondary (heavy unaccented), and no code for weak syllables. This code is placed at the beginning of the syllable to which it applies. There are three phonemic terminal contours, falling declarative contour, which is coded by a period, rising interrogative contour which is coded by a question mark, and continuative contour which is coded by a dash. These codes are placed at the end of the fluent phrase, and the contour is presumed to begin at the last pitch-accented (/"/) syllable in the phrase. Phrase-internal intonation contours are not coded. A rhythmic boundary marked by the turnstile symbol (I) is presumed to follow any of the three terminal intonation contours and thus need not be coded; a hesitation (|H) should always be coded, however, because there is no terminal contour code to signal its presence.

Because UNIBET only codes phonemic types, there are no symbols for sub-phonemic segments such as flaps. An exception to this principle is made for the glottal stop, because of its phonologically unique nature. Two sorts of phonemes are coded with more than one character, these are affricates and diphthongs. The reason for this is both practical and theoretical. Adding additional single unit codes for the affricates and diphthongs is difficult within the ASCII set and use of the digraphs seldom causes major problems with these characters in practice. Affricates are coded by the digraphs /tS/ for the coda of "catch" and /dZ/ for the coda of "judge." All UNIBET sequences are enclosed in slashes. GA stands for General American and RP stands for Standard Southern British. The symbols for diphthongs are not intended to always stand in a one-to-one relation with the monophthongs to which they most closely correspond. Thus the vowel of "boy" is given as /oi/ rather than /OI/, because the former corresponds more closely to standard orthography as requires fewer keystrokes. The names for the IPA correlates of these symbols are taken from Pullum and Ladusaw (1986), although the term "lower-case" is omitted from the names.

IPA –> UNIBET translations for English

Consonants			
UNIBET	*IPA Symbol*	*IPA Name*	*Example Word(s)*
p	p	p	**p**it
b	b	b	**b**it
m	m	m	**m**itt
t	t	t	**t**ip
d	d	d	**d**ip
n	n	n	**n**ip
k	k	k	pi**ck**
g	g	g	pi**g**
N	ŋ	eng	pi**ng**
f	f	f	**f**ew
v	v	v	**v**iew
T	θ	theta	e**th**er
D	ð	eth	ei**th**er
s	s	s	**s**ue
z	z	z	**z**oo
S	ʃ	esh	**sh**oe
Z	ʒ	yogh	plea**s**ure
tS	tʃ	t-esh	ca**tch**
dZ	dʒ	d-yogh	**j**u**dg**e
h	h	h	**h**op
w	w	w	**w**itch
W	ʍ	inverted w	**wh**ich
r	r	r	**r**ip
l	l	l	**l**ip
j	j	j	**y**ip

Monophthongs			
UNIBET	*IPA Symbol*	*IPA Name*	*Example Word(s)*
i	i	i	h**ee**d, b**ea**t
I	ɩ	iota	h**i**d, b**i**t
e	e	e	h**ay**ed, b**ai**t
E	ɛ	epsilon	h**ea**d, b**e**t
&	æ	ash	h**a**d, b**a**t
u	u	u	wh**o'd**, b**oo**t
U	ɷ	closed omega	h**oo**d, f**oo**t
o	o	o	h**oe**d, b**oa**t (GA)
O	ɔ	open o	h**aw**ed, b**ought** (GA) h**oar**d (RP)
A	ʌ	inverted v	b**u**d, b**u**t
a	a	a	m**a**, h**o**d, h**o**t(GA) h**ar**d (RP)
3	ɜ	reversed epsilon	h**er**d (RP)
6	ə	schwa	**a**bove
Q	ɒ	-	h**o**d (RP)

IPA –> UNIBET translations for English (cont.)

Diphthongs		
UNIBET	*IPA Symbols*	*Example Word(s)*
ai	ai	hide, bite
au	au	howdy, bout
oi	oi	ahoy, boy
6U	əo	hoed (RP)

R Sounds		
UNIBET	*IPA Symbols*	*Example Word(s)*
ir	ir	here (GA)
er	ɛr	hare (GA)
ar	ar	hard (GA)
or	or	hoard (GA)
ur	ur	moor (GA)
3r	ɜr	herd, hurt (GA)
i6	iə	here (RP)
e6	eə	hare (RP)
u6	uə	moor (RP)

Suprasegmentals, etc.		
UNIBET	*IPA Symbols*	*Meaning*
$		syllable boundary
#		morpheme boundary
##		word boundary
|		rhythmic juncture
|H		hesitation
7	?	glottal stop
"		pitch accent (primary)
'		heavy (secondary)
!		emphatic
.		falling terminal
?		rising terminal
-		continuation terminal
:	:	long, geminate

10.2. Sample Transcriptions using UNIBET.

These examples use spaces to separate words. Contour markers are also preceded by spaces and follow the words to which they apply. This allows for easier morphemic sorting of phonological shapes by the **CLAN** programs.

```
*CHI:   I  don't  wanna  go.
%pho:   'ai  dont  "wan6  'go  .

*CHI:   you  better  believe  it!
%pho:   'yu  "bEt3r  b6!liv  It  .

*CHI:   I  said  "why  choose"   not  "white  shoes".
%pho:   'ai  'sEd  "Wai  "tSuz  .|  'nat  'Wait  "Suz  -

*CHI:   &wa  was  it  Mrs  Robin's  son  or  Mrs  Robinson?
%pho:   w6  |H  w6z  It  'mIs6z  "rab6nz  "sAn  -|  'or'mIs6z
        "rab6ns6n  .

*CHI:   it's  a  very  hardened  murderer  we've  got  here.
%pho:   Its  6  "veri  "hard6nd  "m3rd3r$3r  'wiv  'gat  'hir  -
```

10.3. UNIBET and CLAN

When using **CLAN** programs such as **FREQ** or **COMBO** with UNIBET strings it is important to remember that UNIBET is case-sensitive. The UNIBET "N" and "n" symbols refer to two different phonemes. The **CLAN** programs are set up so that, for the %pho and %mod tiers, the default analyses are case-sensitive.

10.4. UNIBETs for Other Languages

UNIBETs for the various major languages can be devised along similar lines. They all use suprasegmentals as in English. As in English, diphthongs and affricates can be coded as digraphs.

10.4.1. Dutch

The system for Dutch was proposed by Steven Gillis of the University of Antwerp. The Dutch UNIBET closely matches the DISC system used by the CELEX project in Nijmegen. Segments used only in borrowings are not listed. The orthographic types given are not meant to be exhaustive.

UNIBET	IPA	Orthography	Example	Full UNIBET
a	aː	aa, a	laat	lat
A	ɑ	a	lat	lAt
e	eː	ee, e	leeg	lek
E	ɛ	e	leg	lEk
6	ə	e (i, ij)	de	d6
i	iː	ie	liep	lip
I	ɩ	i	lip	lIp
o	oː	oo	boom	bom
O	ɔ	o	bom	bOm
y	y	u, uu	vuur	vyr
Y	œ	u	bus	bYs
u	uː	oe	boek	buk
3	øː	eu	neus	n3s
Ei	ɛi	ei, ij	wijs	wEIs
8y	œy	ui	huis	hUIs
Au	ɑu	ou	koud	kAut

p	p	p	pak	pAk
b	b	b	bak	bAk
t	t	t	tak	tAk
d	d	d	dak	dAk
k	k	k (c)	kat	kAt
g	g	k	zakdoek	zAgduk
f	f	f	fee	fe
v	v	v (w)	vee	ve
s	s	s	sok	sOk
z	z	z	zak	zAk
x	x	ch (g)	licht	lIxt
G	ɣ	g	geen	Gen
m	m	m	meer	mer
n	n	n	neer	ner
N	ŋ	ng	lang	lAN
l	l	l	lat	lAt
r	R, r	r	rat	rAt
S	ʃ	sj	sjaal	Sal
Z	ʒ	ge, dj, gie	garage	GAraZ6
h	h	h	had	hAt
j	j	j	jas	jAs
w	ʋ	w	wat	wAt

10.4.2. French

The system for French was proposed by Christian Champaud of the CNRS, Paris.

UNIBET	IPA	Orthography	Example	Full UNIBET
a	a	a	table	/tabl/
A	ɑ	a	pas	/pA/
6	ə	e	me	/m6/
e	e	e (ê, é)	parler	/parle/
E	ɛ	è (ê, ei)	père	/pEr/
i	i	i (y)	rire	/rir/
Y	y	û	mûr	/mYr/
o	o	o (au, eau)	mot	/mo/
O	ɔ	o (u)	robe	/rOb/
8	œ	eu	fleur	/fl8r/
3	ø	eu	feu	/f3/
u	u	ou	courir	/kurir/
a~	ã	an (am, en, em)	maman	/mAma~/
e~	ẽ	in	matin	/mAte~/
o~	õ	on,om	selon	/selo~/
8~	œ̃	un, um	parfum	/parf8~/

p	p	p (pp)	patin	/pate~/
b	b	b (bb)	balle	/bal/
m	m	m (mm)	maison	/mezo~/
t	t	t (tt,th)	tour	/tur/
d	d	d (dd)	dame	/dam/
n	n	n (nn)	nager	/naZe/
k	k	c (cc)	carte	/kart/
g	g	g (gg, gu, c)	goût	/gu/
f	f	f (ff, ph)	carafe	/karaf/
v	v	v (w)	veux	/v3/
s	s	s (ss, sc, ce, ti, ç)	si	/si/
l	l	l (ll)	livre	/livr/
N	ɲ	gn	gagner	/gaNe/
r	ʁ	r (rr)	rue	/ru/
z	z	z (s)	gazon	/gazo~/
Z	ʒ	g (ge, j)	plongeon	/plo~Zo~/
S	ʃ	ch	chemin	/Seme~/
w	w	oi (ou, w, oy)	oiseau	/wazo/
W	ɥ	ui	huile	/Wil/
j	j	i (ll, y, il)	miel	/mjel/

10.4.3. German

The German UNIBET was proposed by Helmut Feldweg of the University of
Braunschweig. It omits some phonemes found in borrowings from French and English, as
well as the first letters in "Oase", "Etage", and "Ökonomisch".

UNIBET	IPA	Orthography	Example	Full UNIBET
a	aː	a	klar	/klar/
A	a	a	hat	/hAt/
e	eː	e	Mehl	/mel/
E	ɛ	e	Bett	/bEt/
6	ə	e	Beginn	/b6gIn/
i	iː	ie	Lied	/lid/
I	ɪ	i	Mitte	/mIt6/
o	oː	oo	Boot	/bot/
O	ɔ	o	Glocke	/glOk6/
c	øː	ö	Möbel	/mcb6l/
C	œ	ö	Götter	/gCt6r/
u	uː	u	Hut	/hut/
U	ʊ	u	Pult	/pUlt/
y	yː	ü	für	/fyr/
Y	ʏ	ü	Pfütze	/PYZ6/
1	ai	ei	weit	/v1t/
2	au	au	Haut	/h2t/
3	ɔy	eu	freut	/fr3t/

p	p	p	Pakt	/pAkt/
b	b	b	Bad	/bad/
t	t	t	Tag	/tak/
d	d	d	dann	/dan/
k	k	k	kalt	/kalt/
g	g	g	Gast	/gast/
f	f	f	falsch	/falS/
v	v	w	Welt	/vElt/
s	s	s	Gas	/gas/
z	z	s	Suppe	/zup6/
x	x ç	ch	ich ach	/ix/ /ax/
m	m	m	Maß	/mas/
n	n	n	Naht	/nat/
N	ŋ	ng	Klang	/klaN/
l	l	l	Last	/last/
r	ʀ, r	r	Ratte	/rat6/
S	ʃ	sch	Schiff	/SIf/
Z	ʒ	ge	Genie	/ZEni/
h	h	h	Hand	/hAnd/
j	j	j	Jacke	/jak6/
P	pf	pf	Pferd	/PErd/
T	ts	Z	Zahl	/Tal/
J	tʃ	tsch	Matsch	/mAJ/
G	dʒ	G,j	Gin	/GIn/

10.4.4. Italian

The system for Italian was proposed by Umberta Bortolini of the CNR, Padova.

UNIBET	IPA	Orthography	Example	full UNIBET
a	a	a	altro	/ˈaltro/
e	e	e	pesca	/ˈpeska/
E	ɛ	e	pesca	/ˈpEska/
i	i	i	spianti	/ˈspianti/
j	j	i	spianti	/ˈspjanti/
o	o	o	botte	/ˈbot:e/
O	ɔ	o	botte	/ˈbOt:e/
u	u	u	acuita'	/akuit"a/
w	w	u	equita'	/ekwit"a/
p	p	p	pane	/ˈpane/
b	b	b	bravo	/ˈbravo/
m	m	m	mio	/ˈmio/
t	t	t	tutti	/ˈtut:i/
d	d	d	dopo	/ˈdopo/
n	n	n	notte	/ˈnot:e/
k	k	c, ch, q	casa	/ˈkasa/
g	g	g, gh	gara	/ˈgara/
f	f	f	fare	/ˈfare/
v	v	v	valore	/va"lore/
s	s	s	sano	/ˈsano/
z	z	s	rosa	/ˈrOza/
S	ʃ	sc	scena	/ˈSena/
l	l	l	luna	/ˈluna/
L	ʎ	gl	egli	/ˈeL:i/
N	ŋ	gn	ogni	/ˈoN:i/
r	r	r	rosa	/ˈrOza/
ts	ts	z	stanza	/ˈstantsa/
dz	dz	z	pranzo	/ˈprandzo/
tS	tʃ	c, ci	cena	/ˈtSena/
dZ	dʑ	g, gi	giro	/ˈdZiro/

10.4.5. Japanese

Yasushi Terao of Tokoha Gakuen Tanki Daigaku has proposed the following UNIBET for Japanese. Double or long letters are indicated with colons (i:, e:, u:, o:, a:, p:, k:, s:, S:, t:, tS:, and m:).

ASCII	Orthog.	Example	Engl.Transl	Full UNIBET
i	i	ike	pond	ike
e	e	eki	station	eki
u	u	uma	horse	uma
o	o	obake	ghost	obake
a	a	atama	head	atama
6	6	6kooki@b	airplane	6ko:ki
p	p	papa	daddy	papa
b	b	banana	banana	banana
m	m	mame	beans	mame
t	t	taki	waterfall	taki
d	d	daiku	carpenter	daiku
n	n	nami	wave	nami
k	k	kagami	mirror	kagami
g	g	gakkoo	school	gak:o:
N	n(moraic)	san	three	saN
F	f	fune	ship	Fune
s	s	sakana	fish	sakana
z	z	zasshi	magazine	zaS:i
S	sh	shinsetsu	kindness	SiNsetsu
Z	j	junjo	order	juNjo
ts	ts	kutsu	shoe	kutsu
tS	ch	kuchi	mouth	kutSi
h	h	hana	flower	hana
x	h	hiza	knee	xiza
w	w	watashi	I	wataSi
dt	r	remon	lemon	dtemoN
j	y	yama	mountain	jama
T	T	so:deTu@u	yes (polite)	so:deTu
D	D	Dodtayaki	jam pancake	Dodtajaki
pj	py	happyaku	eight hundred	hap:jaku
bj	by	byooki	sickness	bjo:ki
mj	my	myaku	pulse	mjaku
nj	ny	nyuushi	exam	nju:Si
kj	ky	kyaku	guest	kjaku
gj	gy	gyakuten	reversal	gjakuteN
dtj	ry	ryakugo	abbreviation	dtjakugo

10.4.6. Portuguese (Brazilian)

The system for Brazilian Portuguese was proposed by Leonor Scliar-Cabral and Giovanni Secco of the Federal University of Santa Catarina, Florianópolis. The symbol "R" is used to cover a wide range of sociolinguistic variants: velar and glottal fricatives, trilled sounds, alveolar retroflex and so on.

UNIBET	IPA	Orthography	Example	full UNIBET
A	ɐ	a	bo**la**	'bOlA
a	a	a, á	**ga**to	'gatu
E	ɛ	e, é	**te**to	'tEtu
e	e	e, ê	**de**do	'dedu
i	i	i, í, e	le**ve**	'lEvi
O	ɔ	o, ó	**bo**la	'bOla
o	o	o, ô	**bo**lo	'bolu
u	u	u, o	**nu**	nu
6~	ɐ̃	ã, am, an	l**ã**	l6~
e~	ẽ	em, en	**tem**po	'te~pu
i~	ĩ	im, in	**lim**po	'li~pu
o~	õ	õ, om, on	**ton**to	'to~tu
u~	ũ	um, un	**um**	u~
p	p	p	**pa**to	'patu
b	b	b	**bo**ca	'bokA
tS	ʧ	t	**ti**a	'tSiA
t	t	t	**te**to	'tEtu
dZ	ʤ	d	**di**a	dZiA
d	d	d	**de**do	'dedu
k	k	c, qu	**ca**sa	'kazA
g	g	g, gu	**ga**to	'gatu
f	f	f	**fa**ca	'fakA
v	v	v	**vi**da	'vidA
s	s	s ss c ç sc sç x xc z	**se**lo	'selu
z	z	z, s, x	**ze**ro	'zEdtu
S	ʃ	ch, x, z , s	**cha**ve	'Savi
Z	ʒ	g, j, z, s	**ge**lo	'Zelu
m	m	m	**ma**la	'malA
n	n	n	**no**ve	'nOvi
N	ɲ	nh	u**nh**a	'uNA
l	l	l	**la**do	'ladu
L	ʎ	lh	mi**lh**o	'miLu
r	ɾ	r	ca**r**o	'karu
R	x, ʀ, χ, ɣ	r, rr	**ro**sa	'ROzA
j	j̃	i, ~e	pa**i**	paj
w	w̃	u, l, ~o	se**u**	sew

10.4.7. Spanish

The system for Castillian Spanish was proposed by Brian MacWhinney. Capital letters are used for vowels in closed syllables. The open-closed distinction for /e/ and /o/ is not phonemic and is highly variable, but some researchers may wish to mark it nonetheless. If the distinction is not important, use the lower case vowels only. The letter "x" can be represented as "ks". No separate symbol is provided for the "n" of "banco."

UNIBET	IPA	Orthography	Example	full UNIBET
a	a	a	gato	'gato
E	ɛ	e	papel	pa'pEl
e	e	e	se	'se
i	i	i, y	comí	ko'mi
O	ɔ	o	menor	mE'nOr
o	o	o	boca	'boka
u	u	u	pura	'pura
p	p	p	pato	'pato
b	b	b, v	embargo	em'bargo
v	v	b, v	hablar	ha'vlar
t	t	t	todo	'toDo
d	d	d	dedo	'dEDo
D	ð	d	dedo	'dEDo
T	θ	c, z	cena	'Tena
C	tʃ	ch	chicle	'Cikle
k	k	c, k	casa	'kasa
g	g	g	gato	'gato
G	ɣ	g, j, x	gente	'Gente
f	f	f	fino	'fino
s	s	s, z	solo	'solo
m	m	m, n	mala	'mala
n	n	n	novio	'novio
N	ɲ	ñ	cañon	ka'Non
l	l	l	lado	'lado
y	y	y, ll	ya	'ya
L	ʎ	ll	villa	'viLa
w	w	u	cuando	'kwando
r	r	r	rosa	'rosa
R	ʀ	r, rr	perro	'peRo

10.5. Romanization of Cyrillic

Comrie and Corbett (1992) have summarized the Cyrillic characters of Ukrainian, Serbian, Russian, Belorussian, and Bulgarian. To their list, we have added a set of ASCII forms. The meanings of the column headers are as follows:

Cyril: This is the Cyrillic character in upper and lower case.

Lang: This is the language that uses this characters. The dash symbol means all Slavonic Cyrillic orthographies use this character.

CHAT: This is the character string that will be stored in a **CHAT** file by **CED**. **CED** requires the Cyrillic II font from Linguist's Software. In addition, the @Language symbol must be entered in the transcript to distinguish automatically the alternatives used by various Cyrillic languages.

ASC: This is the form that some users may decide to use if they are restricted to using ASCII characters and are not hoping to see Cyrillic characters in **CED**. However, use of the **CHAT** form is recommended over this form.

Tra: These are the transliteration symbols used by Comrie and Corbett. Some of these are ASCII characters, but some are non-ASCII Roman-based characters.

Cyril	Lang	CHAT	ASC	Tra	Cyril	Lang	CHAT	ASC	T
Аа	-	a	a	a	Њњ	Mac.,Serbian	^nj	nj	
Бб	-	b	b	b	Оо	-	o	o	
Вв	-	v	v	v	Пп	-	p	p	
Гг	-	g	g	g	Рр	-	r	r	
Гг	Bel., Ukr.	h	h	h	Сс	-	s	s	
Гг	Ukrainian	g	g	g	Тт	-	t	t	
Дд	-	d	d	d	Ћћ	Serbian	^c'	c'	
Ђђ	Serbian	^dh	dh	∂	Ќќ	Macedonian	^k'	k'	
Ѓѓ	Macedonian	^g'	g'	g;	Уу	-	u	u	
Ее	-	e	e	e	Ўў	Belorussian	^uc	u'	
Ёё	Bel., Ru.	^jo	jo	ё	Фф	-	f	f	
Єє	Ukrainian	^je	je	je	Хх	-	x	x	
Жж	-	^zh	zh	z=	Хх	Mac.,Serbian	h	h	
Ѕѕ	Macedonian	^dz	dz	dz	Цц	-	c	c	
Зз	-	z	z	z	Чч	-	^ch	ch	
Ии	-	i	i	i	Џџ	Mac.,Serbian	^dz	dzh	d
Йй	Ukrainian	y	y	y	Шш	-	^sh	sh	
Іі	Bel., Ukr.	i	i	i	Щщ	Ru., Ukr.	^sc	sch	s=
Її	Ukrainian	^i"	i"	ï	Щщ	Bulgarian	^st	sht	
Јј	Mac.,Serbian	j	j	j	Ъъ	Russian	"	"	
Йй	-	j	j	j	Ъъ	Bulgarian	^ac	ac	
Кк	-	k	k	k	Ыы	Bel., Ru.	y	y	
Лл	-	l	l	l	Ьь	-	'	'	
Љљ	Mac.,Serbian	^lj	lj	lj	Ээ	Bel., Ru.	^e'	e'	
Мм	-	m	m	m	Юю	-	^ju	ju	
Нн	-	n	n	n	Яя	-	^ja	ja	

11. PHONASCII – by George Allen

UNIBETs are not adequate for more detailed analysis of early child speech, because they fail to provide sufficient phonetic detail. To address this need, George Allen has devised the PHONASCII system, which provides an ASCII translation of symbols with at least the power of the International Phonetic Alphabet (IPA). This system is to be used for coding on the %pho (phonetic) tier within a **CHAT** file.

11.1. Coding PHONASCII Segment Strings

The basic form of a PHONASCII segment is:

```
BS,d1,d2,...,dnSP
```

where "BS" is the base symbol, "d1" through "dn" are (optional) diacritics, and "SP" is one or more spaces (a caret ^ is also an accepted terminator). Base symbols are the consonant and vowel codes shown in section 11.2 and 11.3, and the diacritics are shown in section 11.4. Thus, IPA [p] would be coded as "p " or "p^" (no brackets, and a terminating space or caret), a palatalized [p] would be coded p,j or p,j^, and a long, breathy, nasalized [i] would be coded i,:,hv,n or i,:,hv,n^/. The order of the diacritics is usually unimportant, but the separating commas and the terminating space or caret are crucial. Any number of spaces or carets may be used to terminate the segment string, so long as no spaces or carets occur within such a string (e.g. between the base symbol and its diacritics). Henceforth, in this document only spaces will be used as terminators. Unlike UNIBET, the space delimiter in PHONASCII is used to separate segments, not words.

PHONASCII codes consist in all cases of one or two characters. Two or more base symbols can be tied together into a complex symbol by the ligature /_/. Thus, a double stop [p]+[t] is coded as /p_t/ (or /t_p/), and vowels can be strung together into di- and triphthongs, such as /I_6/ for the vowel in r-less pronunciations of "here". To code such a diphthong as an onglide or an offglide, use the diacritic "gl" with the glide element. Thus, to code the schwa as an offglide from the preceding [I], /I_6,gl/ would be used. If a schwa onglide is intended, then /6,gl_I/ would be used. In many cases, PHONASCII leaves ambiguous (as does IPA) whether the multiple articulation is simultaneous or sequential. In the case of vowels, however, the order is clearly implied.

Cover symbols are used for segments whose presence is clear but whose identity is not. Thus a fricative-like consonant is coded as /FR/, an unidentified stop would be /ST/, and so on. Additional identifiable features may be added as diacritics, so that a voiced nasal stop of unidentifiable place would be coded /ST,n/, voicing being redundant.

Parentheses are also used to code segments and diacritics whose presence or identity is questionable. Thus, if a final [z] is devoiced, it is coded as /z,-v/; whereas if it is only partially devoiced, its coding would be /z,(-v)/. Likewise, the base symbol itself can be questioned, as with a nearly inaudible initial [h], which could be coded as /(h)/. As with the UNIBET, comments may be inserted into the PHONASCII string between square brackets [].

11.1.1. Coding PHONASCII Suprasegmentals

Virtually any phonetic feature may be used as a prosody or suprasegmental. A prosody begins with a left curly bracket ("{"), followed by the code for the feature involved, and terminates with at least one space or caret. This feature is then understood to continue until the matching right curly bracket ("}") appears. The feature code may be omitted from the closing right curly bracket if the context makes clear which left curly bracket is its match. Thus, a nasal prosody may be coded as /{n ... }(n)/, but if another prosody intervenes, such as breathy voice /{hv ... }(hv)/, then the closing labels must be included (e.g. /{n ... {hv ... }n ... }hv/. As with the segmentals each bracket, whether labeled or not, ends with a terminating space or caret.

Four suprasegmental features, viz. weight, tone, intonation, and rhythm, have their own special codes. Each of these may be introduced by a left curly bracket, as described earlier. In addition, however, because weight and tone are features of the syllable, these two may be introduced by the syllable boundary mark "$". Thus both "{S3" and "$S3" stand for "heavy syllable". Intonation and rhythm are properties of the phrase, however, and thus demand the use of curly brackets. Weight and tone may be combined, separated by commas, with a single "$".

The feature "weight" is used here instead of "stress", because of the ambiguity associated with the latter term in phonetics literature. The letter "S" is used in the code, however, because "stress" is easier to remember. This feature is most appropriately associated with tonic languages, such as English or German, in which the intensity and/or duration of some syllables is greater than others, along with associated pitch and articulatory (allophonic) variations. PHONASCII uses a five-level code, plus an extra code for emphasis, though more levels can be created by using intermediate numbers, such as /S2.5/, for a syllable that is probably heavy but has some feature(s) associated with lightness.

Tone is the syllabic feature associated with distinctive pitch levels and/or contours. Thus, a high falling contour would be coded as /$T5V, whereas a low–mid falling–rising contour would be coded /$T2v/. Either the level or the contour may be coded without the other, because they use different symbols. The five levels and five contours shown in section 11.6. are probably enough for coding children's utterances, no matter what the target language. If needed, however, intermediate pitch levels can be created using fractional numbers, and complex pitch contours can be coded as sequences of numbers and the five contours shown, optionally tied with ligatures.

Intonation contours, because they are associated with phrases, can be more complex than the five possibilities offered. Here again, however, these more complex contours can be coded as sequences of the simple ones, joined by optional ligatures. Because these contours are phonetic, there is no need to associate them with rhythmic boundaries. Instead, a contour can be terminated and a new one begun at any point in the transcription, thereby permitting enough variety to capture virtually any pitch contour. As with tones, moreover, either the level or the contour may be coded without the other, with no ambiguity resulting.

Whenever weight or tone is coded, the associated syllable boundary should be marked with "$" to avoid any ambiguity in the meaning of the "T" or "S". Without the "$", these codes might be confused with segmental codes, even though the syntax of their use differs. If the precise location of the syllable boundary is ambiguous, any ambisyllabic segments (usually intervocalic consonants or glides) can be marked with the "AS" diacritic.

11.2. Consonants

This is the IPA Symbol set followed by the PHONASCII equivalents.

	Manner											
	Stops									Glot		
Place	-asp	+asp	nas	fric	affric	appx	lat	flap	tr	ej	im	vel
labial	p b		m	Φ β	pφ bβ	wɾɥ				p'	ɓ	⊙
lingualabial												
labiodental			ɱ	f v	pf bv	ʋ						
interdental				θ ð								
dental	t d							ɾ	r			ɻ
apicoalveolar	t d		n	s z	ts dz			ɾ	r	t'	ɗ	ʄ ɺ
laminoalveolar												
lateral alv.				ɬ ɮ		1		ɺ				
retroflex	ʈ ɖ		ɳ	ʂ ʐ̥		ɻ	ɭ					ɕ
palatoalveolar				ʃ ʒ	tʃ dʒ							
laminopal'alv.												
palatal	c ɟ		ɲ	ç j	çx jx	j	ʎ					ɕ
prevelar												
velar	k g		ŋ	x ɣ	kx ɣx	ɰ				k'	ɠ	
labial velar	k͡p g͡b			ʍ		w						
uvular	q ɢ		ɴ	χ ʁ	qχ ʁχ	ʁ			ʀ			
pharyngeal				ħ ʕ								
glottal	ʔ			h ɦ								

	Manner											
	Stops									Glottal		
Place	-asp	+asp	nas	fric	affric	appx	lat	flap	tr	ej	im	vel
labial	p b	ph bh	m	F V	pF bV	V\			bb	p?	b?	
lingualabial	pt bd		mn	FT VD								
labiodental			mv	f v	pf bv							
interdental				T D								
dental	td dd		nd	sd zd			ld					
apicoalveolar	t d	th dh	n	s z	ts dz		l	dt	rr	t?	d?	t!
laminoalveolar				ss zz			ll					
lateral alv.	tl dl		nl	ls lz					lt			l!
retroflex	tr dr		nr	sr zr		r	lr	rt				
palatoalveolar				S Z	tS dZ							
laminopal'alv.				SS ZZ								
palatal	c J	ch Jh	nj	c\ J\	cx Jx	j , y/	lj			c?	J?	c!
prevelar	kk gg											
velar	k g	kh gh	ng	x g\	kx gx	Rg				k?	g?	k!
labial velar	kp gb		nm			w						
uvular	q G	qh Gh	N	X G\	qX GX	R			RR	q?	G?	
pharyngeal				H Hv								
glottal	?			h hv								

11.2.1. Stops

p, ph, b, bh: Here and elsewhere, single letter bases add "h" to signify aspiration (if voiceless) or breathiness (if voiced). This convention is justified on the ground that [p,t,k] occur so often in both aspirated and unaspirated form that adding "h" as a diacritic would be unnecessarily cumbersome. For two-letter bases there is no choice, i.e., the "h" must be added as a diacritic, because PHONASCII codes are at most two characters long.

t, td, d, dd: Alveolar is the single letter form, with "d" added to the dentals, because a majority of our data will be from English, in which the alveolars are more common.

J: This looks much like its IPA equivalent and is a single letter. It also maintains the connection between letters based on "j" and the palatal region.

kk, gg: This category is felt by some paedophoneticians to be necessary.

mv: Because there is no generic "hook" symbol, the [m] is "coarticulated" with a [v].

ng: IPA uses "N" for the uvular; "ng" is appropriate on orthographic grounds for the velar nasal.

mg: Lacking a one-letter velar nasal, the velar "g" is added to the bilabial nasal to make a labial velar nasal.

11.2.2. Fricatives

F, V: Although "B" looks like the IPA voiced bilabial, "P" doesn't look at all like its voiceless cognate. A different relationship is therefore used here, namely that [F] and [V] are "close relatives" of their lower case counterparts.

T, D: These single letter codes do not look very much like fricatives, but explicit reference to theta and edh would require an "h" (or "H"), whose meaning is very different elsewhere throughout the code. One alternative would be to attach the "D" interdental diacritic, thus creating "tD, dD, nD, sD, zD, and lD".

ss, zz, SS, ZZ: Doubling of the base consonant is used for the lower frequency codes.

ls, lz: The "natural" order (manner first, place second, as in [sd,sr,sj]) is reversed because [lz] looks a lot like its IPA equivalent.

c\, J\, g\, G\: The "\" here represents "lowered", or "more open articulation," for which IPA uses a down-caret right superscript. This use of "\" occurs elsewhere among the consonants and as a diacritic.

H, Hv, h, hv: Here the "v" represents "voiced", as in its use as a diacritic.

11.2.3. Other Consonant Types

pF, bV: "PF,BV" might work as well, because both sets require two characters plus a SHIFT. Lower case "p" and "b" are preferable, however, because these letters correspond to the correct place of articulation.

cx, Jx, kx, gx, qX, GX: Of these only "kx" and "qX" are "correct," i.e., they correspond to their IPA equivalents. Because the voiced fricatives are already two-character symbols ("J\, g\, G\"), there is little choice but to "borrow" the (voiceless) friction "x,X". Of these "Jx" is the worst, because its friction is incorrect in both place and voicing. Nevertheless, they ought to be usable in this form, because friction is all that's really needed here.

V\: This labial approximant is a "more open" articulation of the voiced fricative, again using "\".

y/: This rounded palatal approximant goes the other way, a "close articulation" of the high front rounded vowel "y". Hence, "/" is used to signify "raised" or "closer" articulation. As with "\", this symbol can also be used as a diacritic.

R, Rg: The correct IPA symbol is upside down "R". Right side up is close and the "g" is then attached to signify velarity.

dt, lt, rt: Adding "t" makes it a tap. Other systems have used /td/ or /TD/ for the alveolar tap, but there is no real conflict. "t" is also the diacritic for tapping or flapping.

bb, rr, RR: One letter for the approximant, two for the trill. This goes somewhat against IPA, but not against logic, because a trill is a repeated sound.

p?, b?, etc: "?" signifies "glottalic," i.e., the voiceless ones are the ejectives and the voiced ones the implosives. As a diacritic, "?" is used for "laryngealization," thus maintaining the correspondence.

t!, l!, c!, k!: Some orthographic systems, such as Bushman, use "!" to signal a click, an appropriately startling code. "k!" is added to the standard trio to signify velar release of the velic closure.

11.3. Vowels

This is the IPA vowel set:

	Front		Central		Back	
	-round	+round	-round	+round	-round	+round
High	i	y	ɨ	ʉ	ɯ	u
	ɪ	ʏ	ɘ		ɤ	ʊ
Mid	e	ø	ə	ɵ	ʌ	o
	ɛ	œ	ɜ		ɐ	ɔ
Low	æ	ɶ	a	ɐ	ɑ	ɒ

And these are the PHONASCII equivalents:

	Front		Central		Back	
	-round	+round	-round	+round	-round	+round
High	i	y	i-	u-	uu	u
	I	Y	e-		UU	U
Mid	e	oe	6	o-	oo	o
	E	oE	3		A	O
Low	ae	OE	a	a-	aa	ao

Additional symbols include:
    Diphthongs: aI, aU, OI, 6U
    Glides: eI, oU, ar, Ir, Er, Or, Ur, I6, E6, U6
    Rhotic vowel: 3r

a-, e-, i-, o-, u- : The intended reading of the minus sign here is "bar", as in "barred i", "barred o", and "barred u". However, the minus is also used for two other central vowels in the form a- and e-. In these two cases there is no bar in the IPA notation, but they are still variants of more common forms.

6: The "6" is close to a left-to-right reversed schwa.

a, aa: The "a" retains its correct IPA value, and it is also more common than [aa] in early child speech.

uu, UU, oo: Although the doubled vowels seem more rounded than their single letter counterparts, the model here is the IPA high back unrounded vowel.

A: Some systems use "V" for this vowel. The virtues of "A" are its overall shape (it is a lambda with a bar) and its orthographic relationship to other neighboring symbols, all based in some way on the letter "a".

Other vowels: Special letter codes are available for commonly occurring diphthongs and glides in the "standard" dialects of English. As noted in the section on coding conventions, ligatures and diacritics must be used for any other vowel sequences.

11.4. Diacritics

Symbol	Meaning
V\	labialized
(+)w	rounded
<>	spread
pr	protruded
d	dentalized
D	interdentalized
ap	apical
lm	laminal
dr	dorsal
j	palatalized
g	velarized
G	uvularized
H	pharyngealized
?	glottalized
(+)n	nasalized
-n	denasalized
n+	prenasalized
n-	nasal release
ne	nasal emission
(+)l	lateralized
l-	lateral release
r	retroflexed, rhoticized
-r	derhoticized
f	fricated
s	stopped
t	tapped,flapped
rr	trilled
qr	quick release
lk	leaky (stop)
wh	whistled
wt	wet

Symbol	Meaning
/,up	raised
\,dn	lowered
<,fr	fronted
>,bk	backed
.	half long
:	long
::	overlong
-	short/checked
--	very short
=	unreleased
(+)v	voiced
-v	devoiced
hv	breathy (murmured)
?v	creaky (laryngealized)
h(-)	(post-) aspirated
h+	preaspirated
-h	de-/unaspirated
v>	ingressive
v<	egressive
?>	implosive
?<	ejective
!(>)	velaric (ingressive)
AS	ambisyllabic
$	syllabic
gl	glide (vocalic)
os	on-/offset (consonantal)
L	lenis (weak)
LL	very weak
F	fortis (strong)
FF	very strong

11.5. Cover Symbols

CN	consonant
VL	vowel
AP	approximant
RS	resonant
FR	fricative
ST	stop
NS	nasal snort
SC	staccato
UN	undefinable noise

+v,-v,-n: A "+" or "-" **before** a symbol indicates presence versus absence of the feature in question. The "+" may be omitted from a diacritic when it is redundant (i.e. its intent is clear), as in "(+)w", "(+)n", and so forth.

n+,n-,h+,h-:   A "+" or "-" **after** a symbol indicates presence of the feature in question at the onset versus offset of the base segment.

V\, w, d, D, j, g, G, H,?   These diacritics derive from their meanings as base symbols.

/, \, <, >, up, dn, ft, bk
Because the meanings of "/" and "\" are not self-evident, abbreviations of "up, down, front, back" are also available. "ft" is used rather than "fr", which might be confused with "fricative".

11.6. Prosodies and Suprasegmentals

[ ] - The paired delimiters are either square brackets or curly braces.
Syllable boundary is marked by $.
Syllable weight is coded as the letter "S" followed by n,where n =
If additional delicacy is needed, fractional numbers, such as 2.5, may be used.

```
1  -  light
2  -  possibly  light,  possibly  heavy
3  -  heavy
4  -  possibly  heavy,  possibly  accented
5  -  (pitch)  accented
!  -  emphasized
```

Tone

It is necessary to be able to code either levels or contours (or both) in a given transcription. To do this, tone is coded as the letter "T" followed by l and c, where l =

```
1  -  low
2  -  low-mid
3  -  mid
4  -  high-mid
5  -  high
```

and where c=

```
r    rise
f    fall
l    level
b    rise-fall
v    fall-rise
```

Ligature may be used to code sequences of tones.

Intonation

Because intonation is a phrasal phenomenon, it should be coded above the syllable, even if the utterance is only one syllable long. Hence the requirement for the use of brackets. Intonation is coded with the letter "I" followed by l and c, as cited earlier.

Rhythm is coded as:

```
Q   - quick (fast)          |  - pause
QQ  - very fast             |H - hesitation pause
S   - slow                  |B - breath pause
SS  - very slow             |F - filled pause
AC  - accelerando           IR - irregular rhythm
DC  - decelerando
```

"Quick" (Q) is used instead of "fast" (F) to avoid confusion with "fortis". Note that if "strong/weak" (S/W) were used as diacritics instead of "fortis/lenis", then something besides "slow" (S) would have to be used.

11.7. Sample Transcriptions

IPA transcriptions, on which these PHONASCII codings are based, are shown in full in Allen (1988).

Sample transcripts using PHONASCII segments:

```
*TXT:  systems  apart  from  these
%pho:  s I s t 6 m z 6 ph ar t f r 6 m D i z

*TXT:  nonstandard  usage
%pho:  n aa n s t ae n d 3r d j u s i- dZ

*TXT:  there  would  be  no  objection
%pho:  D Er w U d b i n oU 6 b dZ E k S 6 n
```

Sample transcripts using PHONASCII diacritics:

```
*TXT:  don't  believe  him
%pho:  d o,n,- ? b l,$ i,: v i-,n m

*TXT:  playing  in  the  garden
%pho:  p l,(-v) e_I,n ng I,n nd D 6 g ar d n,$

*TXT:  up  to  last  season
%pho:  A p,= t 6 l ae s,:,AS i z n,$
```

Sample transcripts using PHONASCII suprasegmentals:

```
*TXT: don't believe him!
%pho: {T4- $S3 d o,n ? $ b l,$ } {I5\ $S! i,: v i-,n m }

*TXT: I don't wanna go
%pho: {T3/ $S3 ? aI $S2 d }n o,- } {I5\ $S5 w a n   6 $S3
g oU }

*TXT: humpty dumpty?
%pho: {?v $S5,T1- h A,n m $S3} {T4- p i,- ? |H $S5,T1- d
 A,n m $S3} {T3/ p i,: }
```

Additional examples from Kent and Shriberg (1982):

```
*TXT:  hammer
%pho: h ae,n,> m_b,os 3r

*TXT:  pencils
%pho: p E,n n s,d o,< z,d,-v

*TXT:  roller skates
%pho: r,-r o_U l 3r,-r s k e-I t s,wh
```

The next three examples are from Bush, Edwards, Luckan, Stoel, Macken, and Peterson (1973). Items are elicited VCV's.

```
*TXT:  /anja/
%pho: aa,?v nj,-,//,AS a

*TXT:  /atSa/
%pho: aa,- tS,j,lm_j,os aa

*TXT:  /uko/
%pho: u_k,os,> k,> FR,wt o,-,\
```

The following examples are from Edwards and Bernhardt (1973):

```
*TXT:  frog
%pho: $S5  p,os_f,w,\_w,os O_6,gl kh

*TXT:  grasshopper
%pho: $S5 g A s,g,\,> $S3 h A $S3 ? I,w ?

*TXT:  elephant
%pho: $S5 E $S3 ? U_u,gl ? $S3 w,f,\ A,? n th_U,-v,os

*TXT:  fish
%pho: $S5  f,s,//,D ae_E,gl_t,d,=,os

*TXT:  lamp
%pho: $S5  l,gl_j,gl_E,\ p_x,os_6,-v,os
```

The next examples are from a Swedish 2-year-old's naming of a series of pictures (George Allen, personal communication). The English gloss is given in comment brackets on the *TXT line:

```
*TXT:   katt [% cat].
%pho:   {T5_3\ kh a t,. } [far from mike]

*TXT:   en docka [% a doll].
%pho:   $T4- n,$ $T4_3\ O,. k,.,AS $T4_2\ a

*TXT:   känguru [% kangaroo].
%pho:   {I4_5/ th E,n,/,. ng,. g I,- } $T5_3\ th,(r) U

*TXT:   ett # badkar [% a bathtub]
%pho:   $T5- ? E,.,/,(hv) (|) $T3- b O,. $T5_3\ k @1 ao
        r_I, gl,-v @2 [infant crying between @1 and @2]

*TXT:   en- en- en mot- en mo- en- en motorcykel
        [% a motorcycle]
%pho:   $T4- ae n |H $T3_4/ E,- n |H $T4- lj E n,. $T4_3\
m o,/ (h) t |H $T4_3\ a,<,n m o |H $T4- a,<,. n |H [I4- a
n m o,. t,. 6 s,d i ] $T4_2\ k E l E,-v
```

12. Error Coding

The **CHAT** error coding system was designed with the assistance of Joseph Stemberger. All of the examples of speech errors used in this chapter come from Stemberger's collection of natural speech errors (Stemberger, 1985).

The [*] symbol is used the mark the presence of an error on the main line and this error is then analyzed and categorized in detail on the %err line. The **CHAT** system for error coding is designed with several goals in mind:

1.   the system must indicate what the speaker actually said,

2.   the system must indicate in some way that what the speaker said was an error,

3.   the system must allow the transcriber to indicate what the correct or target forms should have been,

4.   the coding should facilitate retrieval oriented both toward target forms and actually produced forms, and

5.   the system must allow the analyst to indicate theoretically interesting aspects of the error by delineating the source of the error, the processes involved, and the type of the error in theoretical terms.

Researchers who are not trained in speech error theory will want to focus primarily on the first four goals. If the initial transcription meets these first four goals, then it will always be possible to produce new theoretical analyses at some later date.

12.1. Coding Format

On the main line, the transcriber places the [*] symbol after the error to indicate that the form preceding it was an error. Let us consider some examples from an aphasic patient. If the patient describes a picture of a dog with the word "cat," we code this on the main line as follows:

```
*PAT:     a  cat  [*].
```

The shape of the target is coded on the %err line in the following way.

```
*PAT:     a  cat  [*].
%err:     cat  =  dog  ;
```

Here, the sequence of elements on the %err line is:

```
erroneous  form  =  target  form
```

Often errors are corrected by the speaker. In such cases we need to code both the presence of an error and the nature of the retracing. For example, in the following example, the error is marked with the asterisk and the retracing is marked by angle brackets.

```
*PAT:  a  <cat  [*]  uh>  [//]  dog
```

If the error involves more than just the word before the [*], it is necessary to use angle brackets to indicate the complete error.

The transcriber must make sure that each error is followed immediately by the [*] symbol, and that each error is coded separately on the %err line. It is not absolutely necessary to code errors on the %err line. However, if the %err line is used, it is crucial to mark each error with the [*] symbol on the main line. Every error marked on the main line by an asterisk must be coded separately on the %err line. If this is not done, the **CLAN** programs will not be able to construct the proper correspondence between the two lines. The following elements must always be present in the error analysis on the %err line:

1.   the error in the form actually said,

2.   the symbol =,

3.   the target,

4.   a series of statements regarding possible sources that may have induced the error, using the $= symbol and parentheses to indicate the focus of the source,

5.   various codes for the error, and

6.   the semicolon symbol to mark the end of the codes for an error.

If the error involves nonstandard phonological forms, the transcriber should put the UNIBET representation of the actual form and the target in slashes directly after them. There is no need to provide UNIBET representations for standard lexical items unless the error involves a phonological change between standard lexical items. Let us take as an example of a phonological error a case where a subject is describing a picture of a boy hitting a dog and says "higging" for "hitting." This is coded as:

```
*PAT:  a  boy  higging  [*]  a  dog.
%err:  higging  /hIgIN/  =  hitting  /hItIN/  $=hItI(N)
       $PHO  $ANT  ;
```

When the target is not clear it can be followed by a question mark in brackets [?]. If the coder has no idea at all what the target might be, the [?] alone is sufficient. For example, the patient may respond to a question from the doctor saying in Italian "doctore fare" where the verb "fare" (= to do) could have as its target "ha fatto," "fa," or any of a number of the other forms in the conjugational paradigm for the verb. Here, we cannot really know what the target is. We may put down "ha fatto" as our best guess, but we realize that other forms are possible.

```
*PAT:  dottore  fare  [*]
%err:  fare  =  ha  fatto  [?]  ;
```

Finally, consider the case where the patient is describing in English a picture of a mouse crying and says "eagles, eagles going." There is no clear relation between "eagles" and any aspect of the picture. In this case, we code the target as simply [?]:

```
*PAT:  eagles  [*]  [/]  eagles  [*]  going
%err:  eagles  =  [?]  ;  eagles  =  [?]  ;
```

Note that each separate occurrence of the same error is coded in full. The semicolon separates the two codings. If you want to avoid having to enter and analyze repeated error entries for repeated errors, you can use this form of notation instead:

```
*PAT:  eagles(/2)  [*]  going
%err:  eagles  =  [?]  ;
```

In general, any number of errors may be coded on a single %err line, as long as there is one [*] symbol for each error and each coding on the %err line is separated by a semicolon.

So far, the types of errors we have been discussing are all **substitutions** which involve the use of one form for another. The other major types of morphemic error are **loss** and **addition** . "Loss" is just another name for "omission" or "deletion." Here is an example of loss:

```
*CHI:  I  want  two  candy  [*].
%err:  candy  =  candies  $MOR  $LOS  ;
```

And here is an example of addition:

```
*CHI:  I  want  a  candies  [*].
%err:  candies  =  candy  $MOR  $ADD  ;
```

Occasionally, a single form involves two major types of errors. For example, the following error from an Italian child involves both a phonological and an inflectional error. In this case, the second level of the error is coded after an additional = after which appears the second level of the target at the same locus. The second = symbol is not preceded by a second transcription of the error.

```
*CHI:  tei  [*]  aduto  [*].
%err:  tei  /tei/  =  sei  /sei/   $PHO  $SUB  $CON  =  sono  $NFL  ;
       aduto  =  caduto  $PHO  $LOS  ;
```

Here the singular form "sei" was used instead of the correct verb "sono" . In addition, "sei" was misarticulated as "tei" and "caduto" was misarticulated as "aduto".

If there is a clearly identifiable lexical or phonological source for the error, the identity of this source can be coded by using the $= symbol. If the source is a whole word, insert the whole word after the $=. If the source is one or more parts of a word, surround those parts with parentheses as in $=(l)asts. An example of this is the following exchange error:

```
*SHE:  in  the  lakes  [*]  cities  [*].
%err:  lakes  /leiks/  =  late  /leit/  $=/si(ks)tiz/=cities
  $PHO  $EX1  $CC  ;  cities  /sItiz/  =  sixties  /sIkstiz/
  $PHO  $EX2  $CC
```

In this example, the source is itself a target that never appears. The notation $=/si(ks)tiz/=cities is to be read as follows: the source of the error is the target of the form "cities" which has the phonological shape /sikstiz/ for which the particular source is the sequence /ks/ which is noted by the parentheses. In most cases there is no reason to include the form after the second equals sign. However, in some complicated errors it is nice to have this option so that the nature of the source is made maximally clear. When there are two or more sources for an error, as typically happens in blends, the various sources are listed separated only by commas (see the following examples). Admittedly, coding of the sources of errors is not an easy matter. If the transcriber prefers, the task of identifying sources can be left to others. However, if this is done, a note to this effect should be put in the 00readme.doc file or in an @Warning header.

12.2. Specific Error Codes

Having completed the coding of the error up to this point, the transcriber can choose whether or not to further analyze the error in terms of particular error codes. For those who wish to do further analysis, this section provides an initial set of codes. Researchers will surely wish to add to this set. If they do add new codes, they will also need to enter these codes in the "depfile" used by the CHECK program. The codes are given in capital letters, but they can be entered in lower case, if this is easier. Except for the symbols in the UNIBET systems, CHAT coding is not case-sensitive.

General Codes: The highest level codes distinguish between a phonological error, a lexical error, a morphological error, a syntactic error, and various complex types. If both phonological and lexical influences are suspected, both codes can be used. Some general codes are as follows:

$PHO	error involving specific phonological units
	example: gutter = butter
$LEX	choice of the wrong word on a semantic basis
	example: coat = sweater
$SYN	syntactic error, accomodation, stranding, etc.
$MOR	omissions, additions, and substitutions of closed-class items
	example: jump = jumped
$ALL	morphophonological errors in allosegments or allomorphs
	example: guve = gave
$CWFA	complex word finding attempts as in Wernicke's aphasia
	example: a binny, a figgy, a fig, no an eagey
$MAL	malapropism (mix of phonological and lexical sources)
	example: croutons = coupons
$INT	intonational error usually detected during a retraced false start
$NW	nonword with an unknown or unclear basis
	example: griff
$CIR	circumlocution, as in Wernicke's aphasia
	example: do with car = drive

Type Codes: After the general level codes, the analyst should classify the error into at least one of the following error types:

$ADD	addition (lexical addition should be coded with just the ! symbol)
	example: blunch = bunch
$LOS	loss (lexical loss should be coded with just the 0 symbol)
	example: garet = garnet
$SUB	substitution
	example: batter = tatter
$HAP	haplology
	example: Sancisco -> San Francisco
$BLE	a blend
	example: flaste = flavor + taste
$EX1	first part of an exchange error
$EX2	second part of an exchange error
	example: broudy klight = cloudy bright
$SH1	first part of a shift error
$SH2	second part of a shift error
	example: people different = different people
$ANT	anticipation – an item is produced early and also where it belongs
	example: bould be = would be
$PER	perseveration – a item is produced late and also where it belongs
	example: would we = would be
$A/P	both anticipation and perseveration are possible
	example: thingle = single thing
$ACH	an chain in which A anticipates B which anticipates C
$PCH	a chain in which C perseverates B which perseverates A
$INC	the production is incomplete
$UNC	the analyst finds it unclear how to classify the error type

Phonological Codes: The following codes are used to further characterize $PHO errors:

$VOW	error involving a vowel or diphthong
	example: bonny = bunny
$CON	error involving consonants
	example: munny = bunny
$CC	error involving consonant clusters
	example: tickle = trickle
$SYL	error where the target or source are syllables
	example: perfacial performance = spatial performance
$FEA	error involving particular features
	example: munny = bunny
$STS	error involving stress
	example: capiTULate = caPITulate
$MRA	moraic error in Japanese and other mora languages
$TON	error involving tone

Morphological Codes: The following codes are used to further characterize $MOR errors:

$PRE	error involving prefix
	example: misforgiving = unforgiving
$SUF	error involving suffix
	example: taked = taken
$NFX	error involving infix
$NFL	error involving inflection
	example: taked = taken
$DER	error involving derivational processes
	example: misforgiving = unforgiving
$RED	error involving morphological reduplication
	example: sevenses = sevens
$AGA	error of agreement where agreer is wrong
	example: el palma
$AGC	error of agreement where controller is wrong
	example: la palmo
$AGB	error with both agreer and controller wrong
	example: el palmo
$REG	regularization
	example: eated = ate
$FUL	full regularization
	example: throwed = threw
$PAR	partial regularization
	example: threwed = threw
$HAR	vowel harmony error
	example: ablakek = ablakok

Syntactic Codes: The following codes are used to further characterize $SYN errors:

$ACC	error where accommodation was present
	example: a apper = an 'A'
$STR	error where affixes are stranded
	example: the flood was roaded = the road was flooded
$SBL	syntactic blend
	example: thingle = single thing
$POS	position error
	example: gave it him = gave him it

12.3. Hesitation Codes

CHAT allows you to code hesitation phenomena directly on the main line, using symbols such as # for pause or [//] for retracing. Some researchers may also want to indicate these various hesitation phenomena by separate codes on the %err line. To do this, the following codes can be used:

$ISR	initial segment repetition
$WR	word repetition
$MWR	multiple word repetition
$RFS	retraced false start
$UNP	unfilled pause
$FIP	filled pause
$FRG	word fragment

12.4. Examples

This section provides a series of examples that show how the codes given in this chapter are intended to be used.

```
*JOE:  is it broudy [*] klight [*] ?
%err:  broudy /braUdi/ = cloudy /klaUdi/ $=/(br)aIt/ = klight
       $PHO  $EX1  $CC  ;  klight  /klaIt/  =  bright  /braIt/
       $=/(kl)aUdi/=   broudy $PHO $EX2 $CC  ;

*SHE:  I got <a paper> [*] on my test [*].
%err:  a  paper  =  an  A  $=paper=test  $LEX  $EX1  $ACC  ;
       test = paper $LEX $EX2 $SUB  ;

*SHE:  the flood [*] was roaded [*].
%err:  flood  =  road  $=flooded=roaded  $STE  $EX1  $STR  ;
       roaded = flooded $=road=flood $STE $EX2 $STR ;

*SHE:  he bould [*] re [*] real +...
%err:  bould /bUd/ = would /wUd/ $=/(b)i/=re $PHO $ANT $CHN ;
       re /ri/ = be /bi/ $=/(r)il/ $PHO $SUB $DANT $CON $CHN;

*SHE:  you think Pulina [*]  Lat [*]  Chow lasts +...
%err:  Pulina  /pulin6/  =  Purina  /purin6/  $=(1)&sts
       $PHO  $ANT  $SUB  $CON  ; Lat /l&t/ = Rat /r&t/ $=(1)&sts
       $PHO  $ANT  $SUB  $CON  ;

*JIM:  +... in the blite [*]  block experiment.
%err:  blite  /blaIt/  =  bite  /baIt/  $=/b(1)Qk/  $PHO  $ANT
       $ADD $CON ;

*BEA:  oh # we pant [*]  peas every spring.
%err:  pant  /pAnt/  =  plant  /plAnt/  $=/p()iz/  $PHO  $ANT
       $LOS $CON ;
```

```
*KAT:   perfacial [*]    performance.
%err:   perfacial /p3feISVl/    =    spatial    /speIsVl/
        $=/(p3f)ormVns/ $PHO $ANT $SUB $CON $SYL $MIX ;

*SHE:   you don't atk [*]   mad.
%err:   atk /&tk/ = act /&kt/ $PHO $SH1 $SH2 $CON ;

*SHE:   I knit my sweater [*]   Michelle a scarf.
%err:   sweater = sister $=scarf $ANT $SUB $LEX<7> $SND<4>;

*SHE:   it has a very nice flaste [*].
%err:   flaste /fleIst/    =    taste    /teIst/    $=flavor,taste
        $LEX $BLN ;

*SHE:   I haven't found a thingle [*] yet.
%err:   thingle    /TiNgl/    =    single    thing    /siNglTiN/
        $=single thing $LEX $SBL $A/P ;

*SHE:   he relax [*] when you go away.
%err:   relax = relaxes $LOS $SUF $NFL ;

*SHE:   I  carefully  looked  at  them  and  <choosed  [*]>
        [//] chose that one.
%err:   choosed = chose   $MOR $SUF $NFL $REG $FUL ;

*SPE:   it tooked [*] a while.
%err:   tooked = took   $MOR $SUF $NFL $SUB $REG $PAR ;

*JEA:   the infant <tucks [*]>   [//] touches the nipple.
%err:   tucks = touches   $PHO $SUB $ACC ;

*JOE:   did a lot of people [*]   different [*] see it?
%err:   people  =  different  $=people=different  $LEX  $SH1  ;
        different = people $=different=people $LEX $SH2 ;

*SHE:   uhoh # where it [*] is [*]?
%err:   it = is $LEX $SH1 ;   is = it $LEX $SH2 ;
```

13. Speech Act Codes

One way of coding speech acts is to separate out the component of illocutionary force from those aspects that deal with interchange types. One can also distinguish a set of codes that relate to the modality or means of expression. Codes of these three types can be placed together on the %spa tier. One form of coding precedes each code type with an identifier, such as "x" for interchange type and "i" for illocutionary type. Here is an example of the combined use of these various codes:

```
*MOT:  are you okay?
%spa:  $x:dhs  $i:yq
```

Alternatively, one can combine the codes in a hierarchical system, so that the previous example would have only the code $dhs:yq. Choice of different forms for codes depends on the goals of the analysis, the structure of the coding system, and the way the codes interface with the **CLAN** programs.

Users will often need to construct their own coding schemes. However, one scheme that has received extensive attention is one proposed by Ninio and Wheeler (1986). Ninio, Snow, Pan, and Rollins (1994) have provided a simplified version of the Ninio and Wheeler system called INCA-A, or Inventory of Communicative Acts – Abridged. The next two sections give the categories of interchange types and illocutionary forces in the proposed INCA-A system.

13.1. Interchange Type Categories

Code	Category	Function
CMO	comforting	to comfort and express sympathy for misfortune.
DCA	discussing clarification of action	to discuss clarification of hearer's nonverbal communicative acts.
DCC	discussing clarification of comm.	to discuss clarification of hearer's ambiguous verbal communication or a confirmation of the speaker's understanding of it.
DFW	discussing the fantasy world	to hold a conversation within fantasy play.
DHA	directing hearer's attention	to achieve joint focus of attention by directing hearer's attention to objects, persons and events in the environment.
DHS	discussing hearer's sentiments	to hold a conversation about hearer's non-observable thoughts and feelings.

DJF	discussing a joint focus of attention	to hold a conversation about something in the environment that both participants are attending to, e.g., objects; persons; ongoing actions of hearer and speaker; ongoing events.
DNP	discussing the non-present	to hold a conversation about topics which are not observable in the environment, e.g., past and future events and actions, distant objects and persons, abstract matters. (Excluding conversations about inner states.)
DRE	discussing a recent event	to hold a conversation about immediately past actions and events.
DRP	discussing the related-to-present	to discuss non-observable attributes of objects or persons present in the environment or to discuss past or future events related to those referents.
DSS	discussing speaker's sentiments	to hold a conversation about speaker's non-observable thoughts and feelings.
MRK	marking	to express socially expected sentiments on specific occasions such as thanking, apologizing, or to mark some event.
NCS	negotiate copresence and separation	to manage the transition.
NFA	negotiating an activity in the future	to negotiate actions and activities in the far future.
NIA	negotiating the immediate activity	to negotiate the initiation, continuation, ending and stopping of activities and acts; to direct hearer's and speaker's acts; to allocate roles, moves, and turns in joint activities.
NIN	non-interactive speech	speaker engages in private speech or produces utterances which are clearly not addressed to present hearer.
NMA	negotiate mutual attention	to establish mutual attentiveness and proximity or withdrawal.
PRO	performing verbal moves	to perform moves in a game or other activity by uttering the appropriate verbal forms.

PSS	negotiating possession of objects	to determine or discuss who is the possessor of an object.
SAT	showing attentiveness	to demonstrate that speaker is paying attention to hearer.
TXT	read written text	to read or recite written text aloud.
OOO	unintelligible utterances	unknown function.
YYY	uninterpretable utterances	unknown function.

13.2. Categories of Illocutionary Force

1.   Directives and responses

AC   Answer calls; show attentiveness to communications.
AD   Agree to carry out act requested or proposed by other.
AL   Agree to do for the last time.
CL   Call attention to hearer by name or by substitute exclamations.
CS   Counter-suggestion; an indirect refusal.
DR   Dare or challenge hearer to perform action.
GI   Give in; accept other's insistence or refusal.
GR   Give reason; justify a request for action, refusal or prohibition.
RD   Refuse to carry out act requested or proposed by other.
RP   Request, propose, or suggest an action for hearer, or for hearer and speaker.
RQ   Yes/no question about hearer's wishes and intentions which functions as a suggestion.
SS   Signal to start performing an act, such as running or rolling a ball. Pace performance of acts by hearer.
WD   Warn of danger.

2.   Speech elicitations and responses

CX   Complete text, if so demanded.
EA   Elicit onomatopoeic or animal sounds.
EI   Elicit imitation of word or sentence by modelling or by explicit command.
EC   Elicit completion of word or sentence.
EX   Elicit completion of rote-learned text.
RT   Repeat or imitate other's utterance.
SC   Complete statement or other utterance in compliance with request eliciting completion.

3.   Commitments and responses

FP   Ask for permission to carry out act.
PA   Permit hearer to perform act.
PD   Promise.
PF   Prohibit/forbid/protest hearer's performance of an act.
SI   State intent to carry out act by speaker; description of one's own on-going activity.
TD   Threaten to do.

4. Declarations and responses

DC   Create a new state of affairs by declaration.
DP   Declare make-believe reality.
ND   Disagree with a declaration.
YD   Agree to a declaration.

5. Markings and responses

CM   Commiserate, express sympathy for hearer's distress.
EM   Exclaim in distress, pain.
EN   Express positive emotion.
ES   Express surprise.
MK   Mark occurrence of event (thank, greet, apologize, congratulate, mark ending of an
       action, and so forth).
TO   Mark transfer of object to hearer.
XA   Exhibit attentiveness to hearer.

6. Statements and responses

AP   Agree with proposition or proposal expressed by previous speaker.
CN   Count.
DW   Disagree with proposition expressed by previous speaker.
ST   State or make a declarative statement.
WS   Express a wish.

7. Questions and responses

AQ   Aggravated question, expression of disapproval by restating a question.
AA   Answer in the affirmative to yes/no question.
AN   Answer in the negative to yes/no question.
EQ   Eliciting question (e.g., hmm?).
NA   Intentionally non-satisfying answer to question.
QA   Answer a question with a wh-question.
QN   Ask a product-question (wh-question).
RA   Refuse to answer.
SA   Answer a wh-question by a statement.
TA   Answer a limited-alternative question.
TQ   Ask a limited-alternative yes/no question.
YQ   Ask a yes/no question.
YA   Answer a question with a yes/no question.

8. Performances

PR   Perform verbal move in game.
TX   Read or recite written text aloud.

9. Evaluations

AB   Approve of appropriate behavior. Express positive evaluation of hearer's or
       speaker's acts.
CR   Criticize or point out error in nonverbal act.

DS   Disapprove, scold, protest disruptive behavior. Express negative evaluation of hearer's or speaker's behavior as inappropriate.
ED   Exclaim in disapproval.
ET   Exclaim in surprise or enthusiasm, express enthusiasm for hearer's performance.
PM   Praise for motor acts, i.e. for nonverbal behavior.

10.   Demands for clarification

RR   Request to repeat utterance.

11.   Text editing

CT   Correct, provide correct verbal form in place of erroneous one.

12.   Vocalizations

YY   Utter a word-like utterance without clear function.
00   Unintelligible vocalization.

There are some other, more general, speech act codes that have been widely used in child language research and which can be encountered in some of the corpora in the CHILDES database. These general codes should not be combined with the more detailed INCA-A codes.

ELAB	Elaboration
EVAL	Evaluative
IMIT	Imitation
N	Negation
NR	No response
Q	Question
REP	Repetition (=RT)
YN	Yes-No Question

14. Morphosyntactic Coding

Many students of child language are interested in examining the role of universals in language acquisition. To test for the impact of universals, researchers need to examine the development of grammatical marking and syntax in corpora from different languages. If such research is to be conducted efficiently, it must be made available to computational analysis. This requires that there be a level of representation that uses a standard set of morphosyntactic codings. This chapter presents a system for constructing such a representation, using the %mor and the %syn tier.

14.1. Morphological Coding

It is now possible to automatically generate a %mor tier from a main tier by using the **MOR** program. At present the files for **MOR** distributed with the **CLAN** programs can only handle English transcriptions. However, additional materials for other languages are also available. **MOR** creates a %mor tier with a one-to-one correspondence between words on the main line and words on the %mor tier. In order to achieve this one-to-one correspondence, the following rules are observed:

1. Each word on the %mor line is separated by spaces to correspond to a space-delimited word on the main line.
2. Utterance delimiters are preserved on the %mor line to facilitate readability and analysis.
3. Retracings and repetitions are excluded from this one-to-one mapping, as are nonwords such as xxx or strings beginning with &. When word repetitions are marked in the form word(/3), the material in parens is stripped off and the word is considered as a single form.
4. When a replacing form is indicated on the main line with the form [: text], the material on the %mor line corresponds to the replacing material in the square brackets, not the material that is being replaced. For example, if the main line has **gonna [: going to]**, the %mor line will code **going to.**
5. The [*] symbol that is used on the main line to indicate errors is not duplicated on the %mor line. However, morphological errors of omission and commission can be coded on the %mor line using the symbols *0 and * respectively. If a morphological error can be coded on the %mor line without using the %err line, there is no need to insert the [*] on the main line.

The basic scheme for coding of words on the %mor line is:

```
part-of-speech|
stem
=english   (optional)
&fusionalsuffix
#prefix
-suffix
```

Items of this shape can be further combined using the delimiter + is for words in a compound and the delimiter ~ for clitics.

When a word has several prefixes and/or several suffixes, these should be listed in the order of their occurrence within the word. The English translation of the stem is not a part of the morphology, but is included for convenience in retrieval and data entry.

Now let us look in greater detail at the nature of each of these types of coding. Throughout this discussion, bear in mind that all coding is done on a word-by-word basis.

14.2. Part of Speech Codes

The morphological codes on the %mor line begin with a part-of-speech code. The basic scheme for the part-of-speech code is:

```
syntactic   category:sub-category
```

Additional fields can be added, using the colon character as the field separator. The sub-category fields contain information about syntactic features of the word which are not marked overtly. For example, you may wish to code the fact that Italian "andare" is an intransitive verb even though there is no single morpheme which signals intransitivity. You can do this by using the part-of-speech code **v:intrans**, rather than by inserting a separate morpheme.

In order to avoid redundancy, information which is marked by a prefix or suffix isn't incorporated into the part-of-speech code, since this information will be found to the right of the I delimiter.

The following set of top-level part-of-speech codes has been developed for English and is currently being used by the **MOR** program.

Adjective	ADJ
Adverb	ADV
Communicator	CO
Conjunction	CONJ
Determiner	DET
Infinitive marker *to*	INF
Noun	N
Proper Noun	N:PROP
Number	NUM
Particle	PTL
Preposition	PREP
Pronoun	PRO
Quantifier	QN
Verb	V
Auxiliary verb, including modals	V:AUX
WH words	WH

These codes can be given in either upper case, as in **ADJ**, or lower case, as in **adj**. In general, **CHAT** codes are not case-sensitive.

The particular codes presented above are the ones that are used by the **MOR** program for automatic morphological tagging of English. Individual researchers will need to define a system of part-of-speech codes that correctly reflects their own research interests and theoretical commitments. Languages that are typologically quite different from English may have to use very different part of speech categories. Quirk et al. (1985) explain some of the intricacies of part-of-speech coding.

14.3. Stems

Every word on the %mor tier must include a "lemma" or stem as part of the morpheme analysis. The stem is found on the right hand side of the | delimiter, following any pre-clitics or prefixes. If the transcript is in English, this can be simply the canonical form of the word. For nouns, this is the singular. For verbs, it is the infinitive. If the transcript is in another language, it can be the English translation. A single form should be selected for each stem. Thus, the English indefinite article is coded as **det|a** with the lemma "a" whether or not the actual form of the article is "a" or "an." When the stem is a special word, such as a nonce form marked with the @n symbol, then the full nonce form together with its @n should be put after the | symbol, as in **N|bahbi@n**.

When English is not the main language of the transcript, the transcriber must decide whether or not to use English stems. Using English stems has the advantage that it makes the corpus more available to English-reading researchers. To show how this is done, take the German phrase "wir essen":

```
*FRI:   wir  essen.
%mor:   pro|wir=we   v|ess=eat-INF.
```

Some projects may have reasons to avoid using English stems, even as translations. In this example, "essen" would be simply **v|ess-INF**. Other projects may wish to use only English stems and no target language stems. Sometimes there are multiple possible translations into English. For example, German "Sie"/sie" could be either "you", "she", or "they". Choosing a single English meaning helps fix the German form. However, when it is not clear which form to choose, the alternatives can be indicated by a second equals sign, as in "=she=they."

14.4. Affixes and Clitics

Affixes and clitics are coded in the position in which they occur with relation to the stem. The morphological status of the affix should be identified by the following delimiters: - for a suffix, # for a prefix, ~ for a clitic and **&** for fusional or infixed morphology. These four markers have the same meaning on the %mor tier as in the main line morphemicization system presented in Chapter 5.

The **&** is used to mark affixes that are not realized in a clearly isolable phonological shape. For example, the form "men" cannot be broken down into a part corresponding to the stem "man" and a part corresponding to the plural marker, since one cannot say that the vowel "e" marks the plural. For this reason, the word is coded as **n|man&PL**. The past forms of irregular verbs may undergo similar ablaut processes, as in "came", which is coded **v|come&PAST**, or they may undergo no phonological change at all, e.g. "hit", which is coded **v|hit&PAST** Sometimes there may be several codes indicated with the **&** after the stem. For example, the form "was" is coded **v|be&PAST&13s**.

Clitics are marked by a tilde, as in **v|parl=speak&IMP:2S~pro|DAT:MASC:SG** for Italian "parlagli" and **pro|it~v|be&3s** for English "it's." Note that part of speech coding is repeated for clitics. Both clitics and contracted elements are coded with the tilde. The use of the tilde for contracted elements extends to forms like "sul" in Italian, "ins" in German, or "rajta" in Hungarian in which prepositions are merged with articles or pronouns.

Affix and clitic codes are based either on Latin forms for grammatical function or English words corresponding to particular closed-class items. The following set of affix and clitic codes is used by the **MOR** program for automatic morphological tagging of English.

Inflectional morphemes	
adjective suffix *er, r*	CP
adjective suffix *est, st*	SP
noun suffix *ie*	DIM
noun suffix *s, es*	PL
noun suffix *'s, '*	POSS
verb suffix *s, es*	3S
verb suffix *ed, d*	PAST
verb suffix *ing*	PROG
verb suffix *en*	PERF
Derivational morphemes	
adjective and verb prefix *un*	UN
adverbializer *ly*	LY
nominalizer *er*	ER
noun prefix *ex*	EX
verb prefix *dis*	DIS
verb prefix *mis*	MIS
verb prefix *out*	OUT
verb prefix *over*	OVER
verb prefix *pre*	PRE
verb prefix *pro*	PRO
verb prefix *re*	RE
Clitic codes	
noun phrase post-clitic *'d*	v:aux|would, v|have&PAST
noun phrase post-clitic *'ll*	v:aux|will
noun phrase post-clitic *'m*	v|be&1S, v:aux|be&1S
noun phrase post-clitic *'re*	v|be&PRES, v:aux|be&PRES
noun phrase post-clitic *'s*	v|be&3S, v:aux|be&3S
verbal post-clitic *n't*	neg|not

14.5. Compounds

In chapter 5 we discussed the marking of compounds on the main line. For coding on the %mor line, matters get even more complex. Here are some words that we might want to treat as compounds: *San+Diego+Zoo, Mister+Frog, sweat+shirt, tennis+court, bathing+suit, high+school, play+ground, choo+choo+train, rock+'n+roll,* and *High+street.* There are also many idiomatic phrases that could be best analyzed as compounds. Here are some examples: *a+lot+of, all+of+a+sudden, at+last, for+sure, kind+of, of+course, once+and+for+all, once+upon+a+time, so+far,* and *lots+of.*

On the %mor tier is it necessary to assign a part-of-speech label to the entire compound, and to identify the constituent stems, plus any inflectional affixes or clitics. For example, the word *choo+choo+trains* is coded on the %mor tier as **n\|choo+choo+train-PL**.

In order to preserve the one-to-one correspondance between words on the main line and words on the %mor tier, words which are not marked as compounds on the main line should not be coded as compounds on the %mor tier. For example, if the words "come here" are used as a rote form, then they should be written as "come+here" on the main tier. On the %mor tier this will be coded as **v|come+here**. It makes no sense to code this as **v|come+adv|here**, since that analysis would contradict the claim that this pair functions as a single unit. It is sometimes difficult to assign a part-of-speech code to a morpheme. In the usual case, the part-of-speech code should be chosen from the same set of codes used to label single words of the language. For example, the idiomatic phrases listed above can be coded: **qn|a+lot+of**, **adv|all+of+a+sudden**, **adv|at+last**, **co|for+sure**, **adv:int|kind+of**, **adv|once+and+for+all**, **adv|once+upon+a+time**, **adv|so+far**, and **qn|lots+of**.

14.6. Sample Morphological Tagging for English

The following table describes and illustrates the set of word classes for English which are of general interest to the researcher. The %mor tier examples correspond to the labellings which are produced by the **MOR** program for the words in question. It is possible to augment or simplify this set, either by creating additional word categories, or by adding to additional fields to the part-of-speech label, as discussed above.

Description	Example	%mor tier
ADJECTIVES		
adjective	big	adj|big
adjective, comparative	bigger, better	adj|big-CP, adj|good&CP
adjective, superlative	biggest, best	adj|big-SP, adj|good&SP
ADVERBS		
adverb	well	adv|well
adverb, ending in ly	quickly	adv|quick-ADVR
intensifying adverb	very, rather	adv:int|very, adv:int|rather
post-qualifying adverb	enough, indeed	adv|enough, adv|indeed
locative adverb	here, then	adv|here, adv|then
COMMUNICATORS		
communicator	aha	co|aha
CONJUNCTIONS		
coordinating conjunction	and, or	conj:coord|and, conj:coord|or
subordinating conjunction	if, although	conj:subord|if, conj:coord|although
pragmatic conjuction	but	conj:prag|but
DETERMINERS		
determiner (number unspecified)	some, any, no	det|some, det|no
determiner, singular	a, the, this	det|a, det|this
determiner, plural	these, those	det|these, det|those
determiner, conjunctive	either, neither	det|either, det|neither
determiner, possessive	my, your, her, our, their	det:poss|my

INFINITIVE		
infinitive marker *to*	to	inflto

NOUNS		
noun, mass or singular common	cat, coffee	nlcat, nlcoffee
noun, plural	cats	nlcat-PL
noun, possessive	cat's	nlcat-POSS
noun, plural possessive	cats'	nlcat-PL-POSS
proper noun	Mary	n:proplMary
proper noun, plural	Marys	n:proplMary-PL
proper noun, possessive	Mary's	n:proplMary-POSS
proper noun, plural possessive	Marys'	n:proplMary-PL-POSS
locative noun, (adverbial noun)	home, west, tomorrow	nlhome, nlwest, nltomorrow

NUMERALS		
cardinal number	two	numltwo
ordinal number	second	adjlsecond

PARTICLES		
particle	up	ptllup

PREPOSITIONS		
preposition	in	preplin

PRONOUNS		
personal pronouns	I, me, we, us, he, him, it	prolI, prolme, prolwe, prolus
reflexive pronouns	myself, ourselves, themselves	pro:refllmyself
possessive pronouns	mine, yours, his, ours	pro:posslmine, pro:posslhis
demonstrative pronouns	that, this, these, those	pro:demlthat
indefinite pronoun	everybody, nothing,	pro:indefleverybody
indefinite pronoun, possessive	everybody's	pro:indefleverybody-POSS
existential pronoun	there	pro:existlthere

QUANTIFIERS		
quantifier	half, all	qnlhalf, qnlall

VERBS		
verb, base form	walk, run	vlwalk, vlrun
verb, 3rd singular present tense	walks, runs	vlwalk-3S, vlrun-3S
verb, past tense	walked, ran	vlwalk-PAST, vlrun&PAST
verb, present participle	walking, running	vlwalk-PROG, vlrun-PROG
verb, past participle	walked, run, fallen	vlwalk-PAST, vlrun&PERF, vlfall-PERF
modal auxiliary verbs	can, could, must	v:auxlcan, v:auxlcould, v:auxlmust

BE		
be, base form	be	v|be, v:aux|be
be, 1st singular present tense	am, 'm	v|be&1S, v:aux|be&1S
be, 3rd singular present tense	is, 's	v|be&3S, v:aux|be&3S
be, present tense	are	v|be&PRES, v:aux|be&PRES
be, 1st or 3rd singular past tense	was	v|be&PAST&13S, v:aux|be&PAST&13S
be, past tense	were	v|be&PAST, v:aux|be&PAST
be, present participle	being	v|be-PROG, v:aux|be-PROG
be, past participle	been	v|be&PERF, v:aux|be&PERF
special tagset for *do*		
do, base form	do	v|do, v:aux|do
do, 3rd singular present tense	does	v|do&3S, v:aux|do&3S
do, past tense	did	v|do&PAST, v:aux|do&PAST
do, present participle	doing	v|do-PROG, v:aux|do-PROG
do, past participle	done	v|do&PERF, v:aux|do&PERF
special tagset for *have*		
have, base form	have	v|have, v:aux|have
have, 3rd singular present tense	has	v|have&3S, v:aux|have&3S
have, past tense	had	v|have&PAST, v:aux|have&PAST
have, present participle	having	v|have-PROG, v:aux|have-PROG
have, past participle	had	v|have&PAST, v:aux|have&PAST
WH words		
wh question pronoun	who, whom, what	wh:pro|who
wh determiner	what, which, whose	wh:det|what
wh adverb	how, when	wh:adv|how
wh relative pronoun	who, whom, which, that, whose	wh:rel|who

Inasmuch as it is sometimes difficult to decide what part of speech a word belongs to, we offer the following overview of the different part of speech labels used in the standard English grammar.

Adjectives. Adjectives modify nouns, either pre-nominally, or predicatively. Unitary compound modifiers such as "good-looking" should be labeled as adjectives.

Adverbs. The term adverb is used to cover a heterogenous class of words including: manner adverbs, which generally end in -*ly* ; locative adverbs which include expressions of time and place; intensifiers which modify adjectives; and post-head modifiers such as **indeed** and **enough**.

Communicators. The term comminucator is used for interactive and communicative forms which fulfill a variety of functions in speech and conversation. Many of these are formulaic expressions such as **hello, good-morning, good-bye, please, thank-you**. Also included in this category are words used to express emotion, as well as imitative and onomatopeic forms, such as **ah, aw, boom, boom-boom, icky, wow, yuck,** and **yummy**.

Conjunctions. Conjunctions conjoin two or more words, phrases, or sentences. Coordinating conjunctions include: **and, but, or**, and **yet**. Subordinating conjunctions include: **although, because, if, unless,** and **until**.

Determiners. Determiners include articles, and definite and indefinite determiners. Possessive determiners such as **my** and **your** are tagged **det:poss**.

Infinitive marker. When **to** is used with an infinitive verb it is tagged **inflto**.

Nouns. Common nouns are tagged with **n**, proper nouns (names of people, places, fictional characters, brand-name products) are tagged with **n:prop**.

Negative marker *not* . The negation marker **not** is tagged **neglnot**.

Numbers. Cardinal numbers are labelled **num**. Ordinal numbers are adjectives.

Particles.

Prepositions. Prepositions are labelled **prep**. When classifying a word as a preposition, make sure that it is part of a prepositional phrase. When a preposition is not a part of a phrase, it should be coded as a particle or an adverb.

Quantifiers. The quantifiers of English include **each, every, all**, **some**, and similar items.

14.7. Error Coding on the %mor Tier

When an item on the main line is incorrect in either phonological or semantic terms, the coding of that item on the %mor line should be based on its target, as given in the %err line. If there is no clear target, the form should be represented with xxx, as in the following example:

```
*PAT:   the catty [*] was on a eaber [*].
%mor:   det|the *n|kitty v|be&PAST prep|on
        det|a *n|xxx.
%err:   catty = kitty $BLE $=cat,kitty ; eaber = [?]
```

In this example the symbol * on the %mor line indicates the presence of an error, in this case a stem error. The detailed analysis of this error should be conducted on the %err line. In order to facilitate the analysis of overuse and underuse of grammatical markers, the symbol *0 can be used to indicate omission and the symbol * can be used to indicate incorrect usage, as in the following examples:

```
*CHI:   dog is eat.
%mor:   *0det|the n|dog v:aux|be&PRES v|eat-*0PROG.

*PAT:   the dog was eaten [*] the bone.
%mor:   det|the n|dog v:aux|be&PAST&3S v|eat-*PERF det|the
n|bone.
%err:   eaten = eating $MOR $SUB
```

Here is an example of coding on the %mor line that indicates how the omission of an auxiliary is coded:

```
*BIL:  he  going.
%mor:  pro|he  *0v|be&3S  v|go-prog.
```

Note that the missing auxiliary is not coded on the main line, because this information is available on the %mor line. If a noun is omitted, there is no need to also code a missing article. Similarly, if a verb is omitted, there is no need to also code a missing auxiliary.

14.8. Coding Syntactic Structure

The syntactic role of each word can be notated before its part-of-speech on the %mor line. However, in order to capture syntactic groupings, it is better to code syntactic structure on the %syn line. Clauses are enclosed in angle brackets and their type is indicated in square brackets, as in the following example:

```
*CHI:  if  I  don't  get  all  the  cookies  you  promised  to  give
       me,  I'll  cry.
%syn:  <C  S  X  V  M  M  D  <  S  V  <  R  V  I  >  [CP]  >  [RC]  >  [CC]  <
       S  V  >  [MC].
```

In this notation, each word plays some syntactic role. The rules for achieving one-to-one correspondence to words on the main line apply to the %syn line also. Higher order syntactic groupings are indicated by the bracket notation. The particular syntactic codes used in this example come from the following list. This list is not complete and researchers may need to devise additional codes, particularly for languages other than English.

A	Adverbial Adjunct	V	Verb
C	Conjunction	X	Auxiliary
D	Direct Object	AP	Appositive Phrase
I	Indirect Object	CC	Coordinate Clause
M	Modifier	CP	Complement
P	Preposition	MC	Main Clause
R	Relativizer/Inf	PP	Prepositional Phrase
S	Subject	RC	Relative Clause

The proposals for syntactic coding given in this section are extremely preliminary and will need significant further development.

14.9. Codes For Grammatical Morphemes

It is not possible to provide an exhaustive list of all of the concepts expressed in all of the morphological systems of the world's languages. However, abbreviations for the names of some of the most frequent concepts can be found in a list first constructed by Lehmann (1982). The codes are given in capital letters, but they can also be used in lower case, because **CHAT** coding is not case-sensitive. Codes that refer to parts of speech, rather than grammatical markings, are noted with asterisks.

Code	Meaning
1	First Person
2	Second Person
3	Third Person
1S	First Person Singular
2S	Second Person Singular
3S	Third Person Singular
1P	First Person Plural
1PI	First Plural Inclusive
1PE	First Plural Exclusive
2P	Second Person Plural
3P	Third Person Plural
ABESS	abessive ('without X')
ABL	ablative('from X')
ABS	absolutive
ABST	abstract
ACC	accusative
ACH	achieve "manage-to"
ACT	active
ADESS	adessive('toward X')
ADJ	adjective, adjectival*
ADJR	adjectivalizer
ADP	adposition*
ADV	adverb(ial)*
ADVR	adverbializer
ADVN	adverbial noun*
ADVERS	adversative
ADVR	adverbializer
AFFECT	affective
AFF	affirmative
AGTV	agentive
AG	agent
AGR	agreement
AL	alienable
ALL	allative
ALLOC	allocutive
ANA	anaphoric
ANI	animate
ANT	antipassive

AORIST	aorist
APPL	applicative
ART	article*
ASP	aspect
ASS	assertive
AT	attributor
ATTEN	attenuative
AUG	augmentative
AUX	auxiliary*
BEN	benefactive
CARD	cardinal number
CAT	catenative
CAUS	causative
CESS	cessive "stop"
CGN	conjugational marker
CIRC	circumstantial
CLFR	classifier
CLIT	clitic*
CMPLR	complementizer
CMN	common
CMPLX	complex (morphologically)
COLL	collective
COM	comitative "together"
COMPL	completive
CONC	concessive
COND	conditional
CONJ	conjunction*
CONN	connective
CONSEC	consecutive
CONT	continuous, continuative
COO	coordinating
COP	copula*
CORR	correlative
COU	count
CP	comparative
DAT	dative
DCLN	declensional marker
DECL	declarative
DEF	definite
DEICT	deictic

DEM	demonstrative
DESID	desiderative
DET	determiner*
DIM	diminutive
DIREC	directional
DIST	distal
DISTR	distributive
DO	direct object
DU	dual
DUB	dubitative
DUR	durative
DYN	dynamic (nonstative)
ELAT	elative ('out of X')
EMPH	emphatic
EMPTY	empty
EPIT	epithet
ERG	ergative
ESS	essive ('as X')
EVE	event
EV	evidential
EXCL	exclusive
EXIST	existential
FACT	factive, factitive
FEM	feminine
FIN	finite
FNL	final (goal)
FOC	focus
FREQ	frequentative
FUT	future
GEN	genitive ('of X')
GENER	generic
GER	gerund
HAB	habitual
HE	head
HON	honorific
HORT	hortative
HUM	human
ILL	illative ('into X')
IMM	imminent
IMP	imperative
IMPF	imperfective
IMPRS	impersonal
INAL	inalienable
INANI	inanimate
INCPT	inceptive
INCH	inchoative
INCL	inclusive
INDEF	indefinite
INESS	inessive ('in X')

INF	infinitive*
INFER	inferential
INJ	injunctive
INSTR	instrumental
INTNS	intensifier
INT	interrogative
INTENT	intentive
INTERJ	interjection*
INTRANS	intransitive
INVIS	invisible
IO	indirect object
IPFV	imperfective
IRR	irrealis
ITER	iterative
JUSS	jussive
LAT	lative ('moving to')
LOC	locative
MAIN	main
MAN	manner
MASC	masculine
MASS	mass
MEAS	measure
MP	mediopassive
MDL	modal
MOD	modifier
N	noun*
NARR	narrative
NEG	negative
NEUT	neuter
NEUTRAL	neutral
NR	nominalizer
NOM	nominative
NOML	nominal
NH	nonhuman
NONPAST	nonpast
NONVIR	nonvirile
NUM	numeral, numeric
OBJ	object
OBL	oblique
OBLIG	obligatory
OPT	optative
ORD	ordinal numeral ('first')
OTHER	other
PART	participle*
PARTIT	partitive
PASS	passive
PAST	past
PASTPT	past participle
PAT	patient

PEJ	pejorative
PERF	perfect
PFV	perfective ('already')
PERM	permissive ('may')
PL	plural
PLACE	place
POL	polite
POSS	possessive (X's)
POST	postposition*
POT	potential
PP	past participle
PRE	prefix
PREP	preposition*
PRES	present
PRESPT	present participle
PRESUM	presumptive
PRH	prohibitive
PRO	pronoun*
PROG	progressive
PROL	prolative ('along X')
PROP	proper
PROS	prospective ('by tomorrow')
PROT	protracted ('keep on ')
PRET	preterite
PROX	proximal
PSBL	possible
PTL	particle*
PURP	purposive
QUE	question
QUANT	quantifier*
QUOT	quotative
REAL	realized, nonfuture
RECENT	recent
RECIP	reciprocal
REFL	reflexive
REL	relative*
REM	remote

REPET	repetition
REPORT	reportative
RES	resultative
RETRO	retrospective
SEQ	sequential
SG	singular
SIMUL	simultaneous
SS	same subject
SPEC	specific
STAT	stative
SUBJ	subject
SUBJV	subjunctive
SUBL	sublative ('onto X')
SUBOR	subordinating
SUFF	suffix
SUG	suggestive
SUPER	superessive ('on X')
SP	superlative
TANG	tangible
TEMP	temporal, time
TERM	terminative
TNS	tense
TOP	topic
TRANS	transitive
TRANSL	translative ('becomingX')
TRY	try or strive to achieve
USIT	usitative
VAL	validator
VR	verbalizer
VIS	visible
V	verb*
VIR	virile
VOC	vocative
VOL	volitional
WH	wh-question word
YN	yes-no question word

14.10.   Parts of Speech and Markedness Conventions

The codes for the grammatical morphemes should be taken from the basic set given in the last section wherever possible. New elements for grammatical concepts not in Lehmann's list can be made up by using capitalized abbreviations as in POSSR for the Hungarian possessor genitive. For each language, markedness conventions can be set up so that zero morphs need not be rendered in the %mor line. These conventions should be included in the file entitled 0morcodes.doc attached to the corpus. For example, the unmarked form of the noun in English is the singular and we would want to avoid entering -SG for every singular noun in English. Another type of markedness statement refers to the neutralization of a distinction. For example, the gender distinction is neutralized in the plural in German. Thus one can code German plural possessive "der" as DET|der&DEF:GEN:PL|. These marking conventions should be stated in the file 0morcodes.doc attached to the corpus. This file should also have a complete listing of the grammatical morphemes of the language and their proper transcription in the *%mor* line. Examples of transcribed forms should also be discussed in this 0morcodes.doc file. Examples of markedness conventions are given later.

In addition to these quasi-universal codes, we have also developed some special codes for German and Hungarian. These codes are given in the next two subsections.

14.10.1.   Specialized Codes for Hungarian

Markedness conventions	
N, ADJ, ART	SG, NOM, INDEF
POSS	thing possessed is singular
V	INDEF, PRES, INDIC, 3S
Person on V	agrees with person of subject
Conjugation	agrees with definiteness of object

Nominal Derivations		
-s	DAA	futós
-s	DNA	erös
-és	DVN	fözés
-ság	DAN	szabadság
-ó	DVN	fogó
-atlan	ABSE	erötlen (absentative)
-andó	PROG	teendö
-va	COMPL	futva
-ék	FAMIL	Paliék
-né	WIFE	Nagyné
-cska, -ka	DIM	fiucska
-ú	DNA	kezü

Case markings	
-m	POSSR:1S
-d	POSSR:2S
-ja	POSSR:3S
-nk	POSSR:1P
-tok	POSSR:2P
-juk	POSSR:3P
-é	POSS:NM
-i	POSS:PL
-ban	INESS
-nál	ADESS
-on	SUPER
-tól	ABL
-ról	DEL
-hoz	ALL
-ba	ILL
-ból	ELAT
-ra	SUB
-nak	DAT or DAT:POSR
-val	INSTR
-t	ACC
-ig	TERM
-kor	TEMP
-szor	MULT

Verb	Inflections
-ok	1S
-sz	2S
-ik	3S (only for -ik)
-unk	1P
-tok	2P
-nak	3P
-om	1S:DEF
-od	2S:DEF
-ja	3S:DEF
-juk	1P:DEF
-játok	2P:DEF
-ják	3P:DEF
-tam	1S:PAST
-tál	2S:PAST
-t	3S:PAST
-tunk	1P:PAST
-tatok	2P:PAST
-tak	3P:PAST

Verbal	Inflections
-tam	1S:PAST:DEF
-tad	2S:PAST:DEF
-ta	3S:PAST:DEF
-tuk	1P:PAST:DEF
-tátok	2P:PAST:DEF
-ták	3P:PAST:DEF
-jak	1S:IMP
-jál	2S:IMP
-jon -j	3S:IMP (ikes)
-junk	1P:IMP
-jatok	2P:IMP
-janak	3P:IMP
-jam	1S:DEF:IMP
-jad	2S:DEF:IMP
-d	3S:DEF:IMP
-juk	1P:DEF:IMP
-játok	2P:DEF:IMP
-ják	3P:DEF:IMP

Verbal	Inflections
-nék	1S:COND
-nál	2S:COND
-na	3S:COND
-nánk	1P:COND
-nátok	2P:COND
-nának	3P:COND
-nám	1S:DEF:COND
-nád	2S:DEF:COND
-ná	3S:DEF:COND
-nánk	1P:DEF:COND
-nátok	2P:DEF:COND
-nák	3P:DEF:COND
Stems	
van	COP
volna	COND
-ja	POSSD:3S
-om	POSSD:1S

Examples:

csinál-tam volna	V	do-1S:PAST PART	COND
láss-átok	V	see&IMP-2P
kér-ni fog-ok	V	ask-INF V	FUT-1S
áll-t-am	V	stand-PAST-DEF:1S
igyál	V	drink&IMP:2S
lett	V	COP&PAST
meg#esz-em	V	#COMP+eat&DEF-1S
dolgoz-ni fog-ok	V	work-INF V	FUT-1S
el fogok menni	PART	away V	FUT-1S V	go-INF
edd	V	eat&2S:IMP:DEF
ettem	V	eat&1S:PAST

14.10.2.   Specialized Codes for German

Markedness conventions	
Nouns	singular
Pronouns	nominative
Verbs	present indicative
Strong past	person is unknown
Plural	person is unknown

Article markings	
der	DEF:MASC:NOM:SG
	DEF:FEM:GEN:SG
	DEF:NEU:GEN:PL
	DEF:GEN:PL
die	DEF:FEM:NOM:SG
	DEF:NOM:PL
	DEF:ACC:PL
das	DEF:NEU:NOM:SG
	DEF:NEU:ACC:SG
dem	DEF:MASC:DAT:SG
	DEF:NEU:DAT:SG
den	DEF:MASC:ACC:SG
	DEF:DAT:PL
des	DEF:MASC:GEN:SG
	DEF:NEU:GEN:SG

Nominal markings	
-s	PL
-en	PL
-e	PL
"-e	PL

Adjective markings	
-er	MASC:NOM:SG
	FEM:GEN:SG
	GEN:PL
-e	FEM:NOM:SG
	NOM:PL
	ACC:PL
	WEAK ??
-es	NEU:NOM:SG
	NEU:ACC:SG
-em	MASC:DAT:SG
	NEU:DAT:SG
-en	MASC:ACC:SG
	DAT:PL
	WEAK ??
-es	MASC:GEN:SG
	NEU:GEN:SG

Verbal markings	
-en	INF
-t	PAST
-e	1S
-(e)st	2S
-(e)t	3S
-en	1P
-(e)t	2P
-en	3P
ge-	PAST:PART
-t	PAST:PART

15. Examples of Transcribed Data

```
@Begin
@Warning:        UNFINISHED TRANSCRIPT
@Filename:       boys85.cha
@Participants:   MAR Mark Child, ROS Ross Child, MOT Mary Mother,
        FAT Brian Father
@Date:  12-FEB-1985
@Sex of MAR:     male
@Sex of ROS:     male
@Tape Location:  Side A
@Warning:    This transcript is quite incomplete.
                 Side B has not yet been touched.
@Situation:       Breakfast table
*MAR:    what does alert mean?
%snd:    "Boys85" 8719 9938
*FAT:    <what do you mean> [//] what is it are you asking for?
%snd:    "Boys85" 10917 12665
*ROS:    alert [!] alert!
%snd:    "Boys85" 12429 14206
*FAT:    alert means like it's time for a fire alert.
%snd:    "Boys85" 14535 17347
*MOT:    well let [/] let but wait let uh.
%snd:    "Boys85" 16767 18446
*ROS:    yeah [= yes].
%snd:    "Boys85" 17934 18498
*MOT:    Ross was speaking.
%snd:    "Boys85" 18821 20438
*MAR:    no xxx a little song.
%snd:    "Boys85" 19201 22335
%par:    <1w> whine
*MOT:    Ross said it's when something's going on and something is wrong.
%snd:    "Boys85" 23032 26501
*ROS:    its my song.
%snd:    "Boys85" 24540 26029
*FAT:    <what song> [//] Ross's little song.
%snd:    "Boys85" 26291 28511
*ROS:    yeah.
%snd:    "Boys85" 27522 27901
*ROS:    ok sing us a song.
%snd:    "Boys85" 28851 30422
*FAT:    sing us a song.
%snd:    "Boys85" 31216 31918
*ROS:    I will.
%snd:    "Boys85" 31250 31860
*MAR:    no.
%snd:    "Boys85" 32953 33620
*MAR:    this is for xxx.
%snd:    "Boys85" 35382 37441
*MOT:    well maybe you're not saying it right.
%snd:    "Boys85" 39133 40686
*MOT:    maybe we don't have the right word.
```

```
%snd:    "Boys85" 40663 42170
*ROS:    yeah [= yes].
%snd:    "Boys85" 42329 42824
*MOT:    give us the song and &m [//] then maybe we can figure out what
         word it is.
%snd:    "Boys85" 42785 45964
*FAT:    yeah.
%snd:    "Boys85" 42939 43341
*FAT:    uhhum.
%snd:    "Boys85" 45653 46067
*FAT:    uhhum.
%snd:    "Boys85" 46393 46772
*MAR:    well and it has the elephant and the snake and the monkey on it.
%snd:    "Boys85" 47086 52048
*MAR:    it go?
%snd:    "Boys85" 52307 53410
*MOT:    how's it go?
%snd:    "Boys85" 53802 54722
*MAR:    uh # did you &kn [//] you'll hear it wh(en) [/] if I turn on the
         alarm after school.
%snd:    "Boys85" 55867 65555
*MOT:    just sing it.
%snd:    "Boys85" 65820 66579
*MAR:    uhhum.
%snd:    "Boys85" 67064 67501
*FAT:    0.
%snd:    "Boys85" 67220 70579
%com:    singing song about "I want to be like you oo oo (monkey)".
*MOT:    0.
%snd:    "Boys85" 69324 70245
%com:    singing the song
*MAR:    yeah like that.
%snd:    "Boys85" 70383 71821
*FAT:    and then what does it say in it?
%snd:    "Boys85" 73029 74733
*MAR:    uh.
%snd:    "Boys85" 76377 76700
*FAT:    where does it say alert?
%snd:    "Boys85" 76964 77942
*FAT:    I learn to be someone like you [% singing].
%snd:    "Boys85" 78688 82518
%com:    thinks that "alert" is really "I learn" in song
*MAR:    yeah.
%snd:    "Boys85" 81563 81943
*FAT:    I learn [!].
%snd:    "Boys85" 82543 83532
*MAR:    I learn [!] like you.
%snd:    "Boys85" 83936 86754
*FAT:    if I learn.
%snd:    "Boys85" 85546 86651
@End
```

Example 2 is an English Broca's aphasic

```
@Begin
@Participants:   PAT Patient, INV Investigator
@Age of PAT:     47;0.
@Sex of PAT:     male
@SES of PAT:     middle
@Date:  22-MAY-1978
@Comment:        Group is Broca
@Filename:       B72
@Coder: JMF
@Situation:      Given/New task
@G:              3c = bunny is eating banana, 3b = squirrel eating banana,
                 3a = monkey eating banana
*PAT:    0a rabbits [*] # 0a squirrel # 0a monkeys [*].
%flo:    rabbits, squirrel, monkeys.
%mor:    DET|0 N|*rabbit DET|0 N|squirrel DET|0 N|*monkey.
%err:    rabbits = rabbit $SUB ; monkeys = monkey $SUB ;
*INV:    is anything happening?
*PAT:    0a <bananas [*] bananas [*]> [/] bananas [*].
%flo:    bananas, bananas, bananas.
%mor:    DET|0 N|*banana.
%err:    bananas = banana $SUB ; bananas = banana $SUB ;
         bananas = banana $SUB ;
@G:      2a = boy is running, 2b = boy is swimming, 2c = boy is skiing
*PAT:    0boy jogging # 0boy swimming # 0boy <swimming [*] no # no>[//]
         skiing.
%flo:    jogging, swimming, swimming...no, no...skiing.
%mor:    N|0 V|jog-PROG N|0 V|swim-PROG N|0 V|ski-PROG.
%err:    swimming = skiing $SUB ;
@G:      9a = cat is giving flower to boy
*PAT:    0a boy # uh 0a cat # uh flowers [*] +...
%flo:    boy, uh, cat, uh, flowers...
%mor:    DET|0 N|boy INTERJ|uh DET|0 N|cat INTERJ|uh N|*flower.
%err:    flowers = flower $SUB ;
@G:      9b = cat is giving flower to bunny
*PAT:    0a rabbits [*] # 0a flowers [*] # 0a cat +...
%flo:    rabbits, flowers, cat...
%mor:    DET|0 N|*rabbit DET|0 N|*flower DET|0 N|cat.
%err:    rabbits = rabbit $SUB ; flowers = flower $SUB ;
@G:      9c = cat is giving flower to dog
*PAT:    0a dog # 0a flowers [*] # 0a cat.
%flo:    dog, flowers, cat.
%mor:    DET|0 N|dog DET|0 N|*flower DET|0 N|cat.
%err:    flowers = flower $SUB ;
@G:      8a = lady giving present to girl, 8c = lady giving mouse to
         girl, 8b = lady giving truck to girl
*PAT:    0a boy [*] [//] girl # school [*] # 0a rat # 0a <boy [*] no>[//]
         girl [/] girl truck # girl +...
%flo:    boy, girl, school...rat, boy, no...girl...girl, truck...girl...
%mor:    DET|0 N|girl N|*xxx DET|0 N|rat DET|0 N|girl N|truck N|girl.
%err:    boy = girl $SUB ; school = [?] $SUB ; boy = girl $SUB ;
@G:      7a = cat is on table
*PAT:    0a cat girl [*]   0on 0the table.
%flo:    cat girl table.
%mor:    DET|0 N|cat N|*xxx PREP|0 DET|0 N|table.
%err:    girl = [?] $SUB $PER ;
```

```
@G:      7c = cat is on chair
*PAT:    0a cat 0on 0a chair.
%flo:    cat chair.
%mor:    DET|0 N|cat PREP|0 DET|0 N|chair.
@G:      7b = cat is on bed
*PAT:    0a chair [*] 0on 0a bed.
%flo:    chair bed.
%mor:    DET|0 N|*cat PREP|0 DET|0 N|bed.
%err:    chair = cat $SUB $PER ;
@G:      6c = dog is under car
*PAT:    0a car 0on 0a dog.
%flo:    car dog.
%mor:    DET|0 N|car PREP|0 DET|0 N|dog.
@G:      6a = dog is in car
*PAT:    0a car window.
%flo:    car window.
%mor:    DET|0 ADJ|car N|window.
@G:      6b = dog is on car
*PAT:    0 car # [=! writes hood] hood [*].
%flo:    car...hood.
%mor:    DET|0 ADJ|car N|*roof.
%err:    hood = roof $SUB ;
@G:      5b = girl is eating donut, 5a = girl is eating apple,
         5c = girl is eating ice cream
*PAT:    0girl eating pizza # apple # ice+cream.
%flo:    eating pizza, apple, ice cream.
%mor:    N|0 V|eat-PROG N|pizza N|apple N|ice+cream.
@G:      5b& = girl is eating donut
*PAT:    cookies [*].
%flo:    cookies.
%mor:    N|*cookie.
%err:    cookies = cookie $SUB ;
@G:      4b = boy is hugging dog
*PAT:    0a boy # 0a dog.
%flo:    boy...dog.
%mor:    DET|0 N|boy DET|0 N|dog.
@G:      4a = boy is kissing dog
*PAT:    0a boy # 0a dog # [=! writes kiss] kiss.
%flo:    boy...dog...kiss.
%mor:    DET|0 N|boy DET|0 N|dog V|kiss.
@G:      boy is kicking dog
*PAT:    0a dog <kiss [*] no> [//] 0gets kick.
%flo:    dog kiss...no kick.
%mor:    DET|0 N|dog AUX|0 V|kick.
%err:    kiss = kick $SUB ;
@G:      1c = bunny is crying, 1a = bear is crying, 1b = mouse is crying
*PAT:    0a rabbits [*] # [=! writes bear] 0a N|bear # 0a mouse.
%flo:    rabbits...bear, mouse.
%mor:    DET|0 N|*rabbit DET|0 N|bear DET|0 N|mouse.
%err:    rabbits = rabbit $SUB ;
*INV:    anything happening?
*PAT:    tears.
%flo:    tears.
%mor:    N|tear-PL.
@End
```

16. Recording and Transcription Techniques

This chapter offers some suggestions on techniques and equipment for recording and transcribing. Four words of advice stand out as most important. First, it is important to structure the recording session in a way that maximizes the naturalness of the interaction. Second, it is crucial to avoid excessive background noise. Third, the production of a high-quality transcript requires the use of high-quality recording and playback equipment. Fourth, it is important to learn to use the **CED** editor for transcription and coding. In this chapter, we also recommend specific types of equipment for recording and transcription.

16.1. Techniques for Recording

By using a small portable casette taperecorder with a small external microphone, one can minimize the extent to which one intrudes on natural interactions. If you are running the taperecorder on internal batteries, make sure to check their level before the recording session. Try to avoid adjusting the taperecorder during the session. If you know your equipment well, you will not have to worry about its functioning. Simply set it in place and then try to forget about it. Try to avoid recording near traffic or other external noises.

When recording, try to minimize spurious background noises or noises caused from bumping the microphone onto hard surfaces or jostling the microphone cord. Try to keep the microphone out of clear view so that the child will not try to talk directly into it. Use a volume level that is about well below the distortion level. The needle should never cross over into the red area.

You can also use the taperecorder as a notebook. You can record commentary directly onto the tape when the child is not talking and you are in a different room. You can begin each casette with a statement of the date, the year, the name of the child, the nature of the setting, and so on. This practice is very helpful in identifying tapes that have been otherwise mislabeled.

16.2. Recording Equipment

In the earlier days of audio recording, high-quality portable equipment was expensive and difficult to locate. Now, fortunately, good quality equipment is cheap and widely available. For ease of use and quality of recording, the SONY Professional Walkman stereo cassette recorder is an excellent choice. Some features to look for in a audiocassette recorder are: a tape footage counter, a high signal/noise ratio and a wide frequency response range. In some cases you may want to have a VU meter to monitor volume, but doing this will interfere with the naturalness of the recording situation.

It is important to never use the built-in microphone in a taperecorder. These microphones inevitably pick up the motor noise of the recorder itself. A good choice for an external microphone is the SONY ECM-929LT low-impedance electret condensor microphone. The batteries for the ECM-929LT are standard hearing aid batteries, which can be purchased in packs of six. There are many electret condensor microphones on the market that will perform as well as the SONY. With small portable sets of this type, it is easy to turn recordings on and off without interfering with the natural flow of the interaction. Decisions about when to sample speech and whether to attempt to keep the recording equipment out of the child's view depend highly on the goals of the project. For some discussions of these issues see Clark (1976).

Be careful to avoid the lower quality tapes, even those from well-known manufacturers. Instead, try to select the high-quality nonmetallic tapes. Metal tape can be used on the Walkman, but it requires setting a special switch. Metal cassette tapes are fairly expensive and add little quality beyond that available from very high-quality nonmetallic tape. The best length for most purposes is the 90-minute length that is also the most readily available in stores.

16.3. Transcribing Equipment

Audiotapes can be played back either through headphones or through sound systems. The cheapest way to get high-quality playback is to use headphones. Moreover, playing back the cries and yells common in interactions with children over a sound system can lead to complaints from office mates and neighbors. People differ in their preferences for transcribing headphones. Some prefer the lightweight walkman-type headphones. These are comfortable, but they allow in ambient noise, which can interfere with listening. Most people doing transcribing for long periods prefer the padded headphones. Here, you can often get units that are well-padded, but still lightweight and comfortable. A crucial factor in deciding which type of headphones to use is the environment in which the transcription will take place. If the room will be fairly quiet, then the lightweight ones are probably better. If there will be other noise or talking in the room while you are transcribing, the heavier headphones may be necessary.

It is important to use a high-quality transcribing machine. A good machine allows you to repeat sections of the tape easily. A feature that aids in this repeated playback is a foot pedal with a backwards winding action. The pedal is operated with your foot so that you do not have to remove your hands from the keyboard to operate the transcriber. When you remove your foot from the pedal, the tape automatically moves back a small specified amount. Using a foot pedal and the automatic replay facility, one can repeatedly play back short stretches of speech to identify difficult words. The Sony BH-75, a highly reliable machine, allows you to control the amount of tape that will rewind each time you stop. It also allows you to slow down the replay for accuracy in transcription. We are not aware of any videorecorder that permits rapid repeated replay of segments for transcription. However, when transcribing from video, a video cassette recorder with four heads can produce good quality in still frames. This can facilitate attention to nonverbal configurations.

An even better system for transcribing involves the use of computer digitized sounds and the "sonic CHAT" mode of CED. A drawback to the use of digitized audio is the significantly higher expense involved. However, with computers that already have multimedia capacities, the incremental cost involved in transcribing with sonic CHAT is not that large.

16.4. Creating ASCII Files with WordPerfect

We recommend use of the **CED** editor and discourage use of editors like Word Perfect. However, if Word Perfect must be used, the following procedure will create reasonable results.

1. Start WordPerfect.

2. Use Text In/Out (CTRL-F5) instead of normal retrieve. Choose the option that allows you to "retrieve in DOS text file" format. Tell it which file to retrieve. (See following note for files not in DOS text file format to start with.)

3. With the cursor at the top of the file, press SHIFT-F8 (Format or Format Line, depending on which version you're in). Choose Margins. Set the left margin to 0. (Not all versions of WordPerfect permit margin setting and this setting is not always required.)

4. Save the file by using Text In/Out (CTRL-F5), Option 1 (to save in DOS text file format).

5. Exit WordPerfect.

Even if you've saved a WordPerfect file in DOS text file format before (with the left margin changed to 0), you still have to change the margins each time you retrieve it (that is, WordPerfect doesn't save the zero left margin setting). Also, the first time you retrieve a nonDOS text file (such as a transcript you created or modified in WordPerfect), you have to retrieve it in the normal way (i.e., Text In/Out doesn't work for nonDOS text files). Then save it using Text In/Out to create the DOS text file version. An additional problem caused by using WordPerfect is that it is difficult to maintain tabs at the beginning of lines. When the **CHECK** program fails to find these tabs, it will complain. This problem can be solved by using the **+g2** switch in the **CHECK** program. Version 5.0 of WordPerfect also allows you to get around this problem by selecting option 3 in the Generic Save option.

17. CHAT Symbol Summary

| Obligatory Headers – Chapter 3 |

| Symbol | Description |

@**Begin** — marks the beginning of a file
@**End** — marks the end of the file
@**Participants:** — lists actors in a file

| Constant Headers – Chapter 3 |

@**Age of XXX:** — marks a speaker's age
@**Birth of XXX:** — shows date of birth of speaker
@**Coder:** — people doing transcription and coding
@**Educ of XXX:** — indicates educational level of speaker
@**Filename:** — shows name of file
@**ID:** — code for **STATFREQ** analyses
@**Language:** — the principal language of the transcript
@**Language of XXX:** — language(s) spoken by a given participant
@**SES of XXX:** — indicates socioeconomic status of speaker
@**Sex of XXX:** — indicates gender of speaker
@**Warning:** — marks defects in file

| Changeable Headers – Chapter 3 |

@**Activities:** — component activities in the situation
@**Bg** and @**Bg:** — begin gem
@**Bck:** — backgrounding information
@**Comment:** — comments
@**Date:** — date of the interaction
@**Eg** and @**Eg:** — end gem
@**G:** — simple gems
@**Location:** — geographical location of the interaction
@**New Episode:** — point at which a new episode begins and old one ends
@**Room Layout:** — configuration of furniture in room
@**Situation:** — general atmosphere of the interaction
@**Tape Location:** — footage markers from tape
@**Time Duration:** — beginning and end times
@**Time Start:** — beginning time

Word Symbols – Chapter 4

Symbol	Description
@	special form markers
x x x	unintelligible speech, not treated as a word
x x	unintelligible speech, treated as a word
y y y	unintelligible speech transcribed on %pho line, not treated as a word
y y	unintelligible speech transcribed on %pho line, treated as a word
www	untranscribed material
0	actions without speech
&	phonological fragment
[?]	best guess (see also chapter 8)
()	noncompletion of a word
0word	omitted word
0*word	ungrammatical omission
00word	(grammatical) ellipsis

Morpheme Symbols – Chapter 5

-	suffix marker
#	prefix marker
+	compound or rote form marker
~	clitic marker
&	fusion marker
-0	omitted affix
-0*	incorrectly omitted affix

Utterance and Tone Unit Terminators – Chapter 6

.	period
?	question
!	exclamation
-?	rising final contour
-.	falling final contour
-!.	rise-fall final contour
-,.	fall-rise final contour
-,	level final contour
-_	low level final contour
,	syntactic juncture
,,	tag question
#	pause between words
-:	previous word lengthened

Special Terminators and Linkers – Chapter 6	

Symbol	Description
+...	trailing off
+/.	interruption
+//.	self-interruption
+/?	interruption of a question
+"/.	quotation follows on next line
+".	quotation precedes
+"	quoted utterance follows
+^	quick uptake
+,	self-completion
++	other-completion

Prosody within Words – Chapter 7	

/	stress
//	accented nucleus
///	contrastive stress
:	lengthened syllable
::	pause between syllables

Scoped Symbols – Chapter 8	

[=! text]	paralinguistics, prosodics
[!]	stressing
[!!]	contrastive stressing
["]	quotation marks
[= text]	explanation
[: text]	replacement
[0 text]	omission
[:=x text]	translation
[=? text]	alternative transcription
[%xxx: text]	dependent tier on main line
[% text]	comment on main line
[$text]	code on main tier
[?]	best guess (also see chapter 4)
[>]	overlap follows
[<]	overlap precedes
[<>]	overlap follows and precedes
[>number]	overlap follows and overlaps are enumerated
[<number]	overlap precedes and overlaps are enumerated
[/]	retracing without correction
[//]	retracing with correction
[/-]	false start without retracing
[/?]	unclear retrace type
[*]	error marking
[+ text]	postcode

Dependent Tiers – Chapter 9

Symbol	Description
%act:	actions
%add:	addressee
%alt:	alternative transcription
%cod:	general purpose coding
%com:	comments by investigator
%def:	codes from SALT
%eng:	English translation
%err:	error coding
%exp:	explanation
%fac:	facial actions
%flo:	flowing version
%gls:	target language gloss for unclear utterance
%gpx:	gestural and proxemic activity
%int:	intonation
%mod:	model or target phonology
%mor:	morphemic semantics
%par:	paralinguistics
%pho:	phonetic transcription
%sit:	situation
%spa:	speech act coding
%syn:	syntactic structure notation
%tim:	time stamp coding

Symbols for Coding on Dependent Tiers – Chapter 9

/.../	delimiters for phonetic notation
$	indicates codes
<$=N >	occurs for N following utterances
<bef>	occurrence before an utterance
<aft>	occurrence after an utterance

Error Coding – Chapter 12

$ =	source of an error in the %err line
=	placed between error and target
;	separates errors on %err line

Coding on the %mor tier – Chapter 14

I	follows part-of-speech on %mor line
&	nonconcatenated morpheme in %mor line
+ (Plus)	compound delimiter on %mor line
- (Dash)	suffix delimiter on %mor line
:	feature fusion on %mor line
~ (Tilde)	clitic delimiter on %mor line
0	precedes omitted element
0 *	precedes incorrectly omitted element
0 0	precedes (grammatically) ellipsed element

18. Introduction to CLAN

This chapter and the four following chapters are designed to help you use a set of computer programs called **CLAN**. The **CLAN** programs were written at Carnegie Mellon University by Leonid Spektor. The acronym **CLAN** stands for Computerized Language ANalysis. These programs are designed to allow you to perform a large number of automatic analyses on transcript data. The analyses include frequency counts, word searches, co-occurrence analyses, MLU counts, interactional analyses, text changes, and so on. The programs have been designed specifically to analyze transcript data that have been formatted according to the **CHAT** system of the Child Language Data Exchange System. Although many of the programs can be run on ASCII files of any type, they function most smoothly and provide the most accurate output when used with **CHAT** files.

The programs have been written in the C programming language and are available for MS-DOS and Macintosh. The basic commands of the **CLAN** programs are the same for both MS-DOS and Macintosh. However, the shape of the environment or "shell" within which you issue these commands is different for the two different operating systems.

18.1. Learning minCLAN

The core set of **CLAN** commands and options constitute the *minCLAN* system. In order to learn minCLAN, you need to follow these steps:

1. **Learn minCHAT.** You will need to understand the basic parts of a **CHAT** file and the basic principles of **CHAT**, as discussed in the first few chapters of this manual.

2. **Learn minDOS or minMAC.** In order to use **CLAN** effectively with MS-DOS, you will need to review certain basic MS-DOS commands. We can refer to the basic MS-DOS commands that you need to know as "minDOS." The commands of minDOS are: **type, dir,cd, path, mkdir, rmdir, delete, copy,** and **rename**. Acquainting yourself with minDOS requires patience. Please read your MS-DOS manuals carefully. Gaining a good understanding of minDOS is important for successful use of **CLAN**.

   On the Macintosh, learning minMAC involves learning the basic operations of clicking on options and icons, dragging, cutting, pasting, and highlighting fields.

3. **Install CLAN on your machine**. Chapter 19 will explain how to install **CLAN** on your MS-DOS machine. Chapter 20 explains how to install **CLAN** on a Macintosh machine.

4. **Learn CED**. You should learn to use the **CED** editor for all work that you do with **CLAN**. Initially, you only need to learn how to use **CED** in the basic "CHAT mode". The use of the **CED** editor is discussed in section 21.1.

5. **Learn to use FREQ**. Once you have installed **CLAN** and have learned to use minCHAT, minDOS, and the **CED** editor, you are ready to learn to use the **CLAN** programs themselves. It is best to begin by focussing on a single program. For this purpose, we recommend beginning with the versatile **FREQ** program. Read the description of **FREQ** in section 22.9. Then sit down at the computer and try

the program out on the "sample.cha" file provided on the distribution diskettes. At this point, you will also need to read the section in the next chapter on the general rules for composing **CLAN** commands.

6. **Learn how to use all the options for** FREQ. Learning to use FREQ involves trying it out with all the various options or switches that can modify its usage. You can find these options by simply typing:

    ```
    freq
    ```

    Try working through the use of each option.

7. **Learn how to use redirecting and limiting with** FREQ. Redirecting involves the use of the redirect arrow **>** **and >>** to send the output to a single file. The single arrow overwrites material already in the file, whereas the double arrow appends new material at the end of material already in the file. If you want to send the output to several files, use the **+f** switch instead. Limiting involves the use of the **+t/-t** and **+s/-s** switches to focus in on a particular set of utterances. However, when a **FREQ** analysis is not actually involved, limiting should be done using **COMBO** and **KWAL**.

8. **Learn to use four additional commands**. After learning to use **FREQ**, you may wish to continue by learning **CHECK, GEM, KWAL**, and **MLU**. You can learn these four programs by reading their descriptions in chapter 21.

This will give you a good control over the minCLAN system. Try working with just this much of the **CLAN** system until you feel that you have it thoroughly mastered. Once you have completed that, go ahead on your own and test out the remaining **CLAN** commands. At this point, you will want to get a copy of the Handbook of Research on Language Acquisition Using CHILDES by Sokolov and Snow (1994) that provides excellent tutorials on all aspects of the use of **CLAN** in real research projects.

19. CLAN with DOS

Many **CLAN** users work on machines that run the MS-DOS operating system. **CLAN** has been designed to run both under the basic MS-DOS system and under the extended DOS-based system called Windows.

19.1. Installing CLAN

Before installing **CLAN** on your hard disk, make sure that you have at least 2 megabytes of free disk space. You can do this by using the DOS **chkdsk** command. If space is tight, you will need to delete unused files. Once this is done, make sure that you are on the hard drive where you want to install the files. The DOS system sets this to c: for your boot drive. However, you can also install the files on some other hard drive.

If you have obtained your copy of **CLAN** on a diskette, you can insert the diskette marked "**CLAN**" or "**CLAN1**" into your floppy disk drive, which is often called **a:** and then enter the following commands:

```
copy  a:install.bat
install  a
```

If your floppy disk drive is b: or some other letter, substitute that letter for the letter "a" above. The first command copies the file "install.bat" from your a: floppy drive to your current working directory on your hard drive. That file contains a series of commands that will install **CLAN**. When it is run, old versions of **CLAN** files will be overwritten. So, if you have some old customized coding files, you may wish to rename them or move them to another directory first. The second command runs those commands and does the installation. The program may ask you several times to insert the next diskette. When there are no more diskettes, you will need to type control-C to stop the installation program. You will then be asked whether you want to quit the batch file, and you should respond with the letter "y" for "yes".

If you have retrieved **CLAN** by anonymous FTP, you should move the clan.tar file into a directory called c:\childes\clan. If you need to create this directory, do so by using the **mkdir** command. You also need to have a copy of the tar.exe program in c:\childes\clan. You can retrieve this program through anonymous FTP. Then, you will need to untar the clan.tar file using this command:

```
tar  xvf  clan.tar
```

If you are getting **CLAN** from the CHILDES CD-ROM, then you will need to copy the directory structure present on the CD-ROM to your hard drive. You do this by positioning yourself in the c:\childes\clan directory. If you need to create this directory, do so by using the mkdir command. Then you issue this DOS command:

```
xcopy  d:\msdos\clan\*.*/s
```

At the end of the installation, you should have all of the **CLAN** programs with .exe extensions in a directory called c:\childes\clan\bin and the remaining files in a directory called c:\childes\clan\lib.

Once **CLAN** has been installed, the DOS variable called "path" must be set. Setting the path variable tells DOS where to "look for" the programs. This allows you to specify directories for DOS to search through for a program if it was not found in the present directory. In order to run the **CLAN** programs you must add the specification \childes\CLAN\bin to your path. The best way to do this is to use some text editor with which you are familiar to modify the "autoexec.bat" file on your boot drive. If you do not have an autoexec.bat file or if you do not have the path variable defined in your autoexec.bat file, then this is what you have to add to your file:

```
PATH=C:\CHILDES\CLAN\BIN;
```

If you already have a path variable defined, then you need to add this to it:

```
C:\CHILDES\CLAN\BIN;
```

Remember to separate directory names with a semicolon and to end the line with a semicolon. While you are editing your autoexec.bat file, you should also add the following line, in order to get the **RECALL** program to work:

```
recall  -i
```

When you are finished modifying your "autoexec.bat" file, you should reboot your machine and the new path specifications will take effect. You may wish to read the section entitled "PATH" in the MS-DOS manual chapter entitled "DOS Commands" for a fuller explanation of setting the path. Pay particular regard to the discussions under the subheadings "BatchFile Commands" and "The AUTOEXEC.BAT File."

19.2. Working with Directories

As you work on the computer, you will find that it becomes necessary to organize your computer files into directories and subdirectories. The role played by directories and subdirectories can best be explained by an analogy. Suppose that all of your projects, proposals, and data are sitting on top of your desk. It is very difficult to find anything. Imagine taking all the projects, data and proposals and putting them into several filing cabinets. One filing cabinet has data, one has proposals, and so on. Then suppose you look into the filing cabinet with your data sheets and realize that all your data is still mixed up. In order to organize your data further, you decide to designate the top drawer of one of the cabinet for all the data that pertain to longitudinal studies and the bottom drawer for cross-sectional studies. Then, within a single drawer, you make further divisions by particular studies. The organizational system you have now devised has a four-level structure. Organizing physical files in this way is similar to organizing computer files into directories and subdirectories. Suppose you had some files on your computer. Some of them contain different kinds of data, some contain proposals, projects, and so forth. You can take all the data and put in its own directory. Then you can go into this directory and divide the data into separate subdirectories for cross-sectional and longitudinal data. So, using directories and subdirectories helps you to organize your work.

Directories and subdirectories are arranged hierarchically on the computer. The top directory, also called the root directory, contains the files described on the installation disk: "config.sys," "ansi.sys," "autoexec.bat," and perhaps a few other files. The names of the first level of directories should be there also. To obtain a list of what is in a directory, type the DOS command, **dir**. As you organize your directories, you can name them whatever you want, but it is helpful to name them something that is representative of their contents.

In the example cited earlier, you might name the directory with the data in it "data." You create a directory or subdirectory by using the DOS command, `mkdir`. So, to create the directory for CHILDES data, you would type:

```
mkdir   childes
```

You can access the directory you've created by using the DOS command, `chdir` or `cd` for short and the name of the directory. The command to access the directory named `childes` is:

```
cd   childes
```

You create a subdirectory in the same way as you create a directory, but you must be *in* the directory where you want the subdirectory to reside. So, to create subdirectories for French and English data in the new directory "childes," you must first be in "childes\data." Use the command `mkdir` and the name "french." Then use the command `mkdir` and the name "english." This results in the creation of two subdirectories "french" and "english," respectively. You can also construct a subdirectory called "clan" in the same way then put subdirectories within it for the library and the programs.

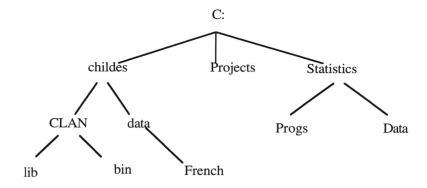

To get back up to a higher directory, you use the `cd` command followed by two periods:

```
cd   ..
```

You need to be able to move your files from place to place. Suppose you have some files called "sachs01.cha," "sachs02.cha," and so forth located in your root directory and you want to move those files to your "english" subdirectory. The easiest way to do that is to first go to your root directory. You can do this from any place in your tree structure by simply typing:

```
cd   \
```

Then copy the files to "english" with this command:

```
copy   *.cha   \childes\english
```

The asterisk is a "wild card" which is used to indicate anything that matches. Any file ending with .cha will match *.cha, including sample.cha, george8.cha, or chacha.cha.

MS-DOS will display messages telling you that the files are copying. After the copy is complete you can delete the files on the top level with this command:

```
delete  *.cha
```

You will need to understand all aspects of filenames and the use of tree-structured directories.

19.3. Default Directories

In MS-DOS, **CLAN** expects to find the programs in c:\childes\clan\bin. It also expects to find your library files in c:\childes\clan\lib. Make sure that you set up your directories in this way. If you use the install program, this will be done for you automatically. As long as you continue to work on the c: disk, **CLAN** will know how to find your programs and library files. If you move to working on another disk, the system will know how to find your **CLAN** files on c:.

CLAN uses a variety of library files for different programs. When searching for these files, it will look first for the default file name (such as "depfile") in your current directory and then in the library directory. After that, if you have given the file a particular non-default name, it will look for that name in your current directory and then in the library directory.

19.4. CLAN commands

CLAN programs take **CHAT** files as input and produce either new **CHAT** files or data summaries as output. In order to make a **CLAN** program run on a file, you must type in a command at the DOS prompt. Each command must contain a minimum of three elements. These elements are:

1. the *name* of the program,

2. any *options* you select for the program, and

3. the name of the *files(s)* on which the program will run.

These elements are typed on the command line and are separated by a single space. The only requirement on the order of these elements is that the program name should appear first. The switches may appear in any order and the name of the file on which the program will run can appear before or after any switch. It is possible to list any number of files, although typically users either examine one file at a time or a group of files such as *.cha. If the DOS command line gets too long for your screen, you can continue it on the next line using the dash symbol.

The top line of the following example contains a correctly entered **CLAN** command. The lines below label the individual parts of the command line.

```
> freq  +f +i   adam35.cha
  |     |        |
Prompt  Options
     Program    Filename
```

Chapter 21 describes the various programs and what they do. Chapter 22 describes the options or switches and how to use them. After you type the command and strike the return or enter key, the program begins to run.

In **CLAN**, files have three-letter extension names that are designed to correspond to the name of the particular program that was run on the file. For example, if you run the **MLU** program on a file called "adam15.cha," the program will create an output file called "adam15.mlu." Try running **MLU** on "sample.cha" using the command:

```
mlu  +f  sample.cha
```

The program sends the output of the program to a different file, called "sample.mlu", thus not altering or destroying the original data.

If you want the programs to run on more than one file at a time, you must use an asterisk (*) in the file name specification. The asterisk is used to call up filenames in sequence. Suppose that you want to run a program on Roger Brown's entire Sarah corpus. You could run the program on "sarah001.cha", and when it's finished run it on "sarah002.cha", and so forth. This task, however, requires constant monitoring and repeated typing of commands. You could, instead, type "sarah*.cha" or even "*.cha" and the program would run sequentially on all of the Sarah corpus in the current directory. This is a very powerful tool for working on large amounts of data.

19.5. Command Line Interpretation

The interpretation of **CLAN** commands is strictly controlled by certain basic aspects of MS-DOS that cannot be overridden. In particular, the interpretation of wild cards and capitalization is fixed by the MS-DOS Command Interpreter. In order to guarantee the correct interpretation of **CLAN** commands, we recommend these two basic principles:

1. Type all commands and switches in lower case. Sometimes upper case characters will also work, but this is unpredictable.

2. Use double quotes around all arguments for switches, as in +s"dog*" instead of +sdog*.

3. If you want to actually search for a quote sign, surround the material being searched for with single quotes, as in +s'[+ "]'.

19.6. Redirection

Redirecting involves the use of the redirect arrow >, >>, and >& to send the output of an analysis to a single file. An example of the use of this function would be this command:

```
freq   sample.cha   >    myanalyses
freq   sample.cha   >>   myanalyses
freq   sample.cha   >&   myanalyses
```

These threee forms have slightly different results.
1. The single arrow overwrites material already in the file.
2. The double arrow appends new material to the file, placing it at the end of material already in the file.
3. The single arrow with the ampersand writes both the analyses of the program and various system messages to the file.

If you want to send the output from analyses of a whole collection of files each to a separate file, use the **+f** switch instead.

19.7. Getting Help

If there is something that you do not understand about **CLAN**, one thing you can do is to try to find the answer to your problem in this manual. If your question is about a particular program, look in chapter 21. If your question is about the correct use of an option, look in chapter 22. If you are working at the computer and you do not have a manual nearby, you can access some limited forms of online help, however detailed help is only available through use of the manual.

In order to access online help, you simply type the name of the program without any further options and without a file name. The computer will then provide you with a brief description of the program and a list of the most common options. For example, just type **FREQ** and a carriage return and see what happens.

20. CLAN with Macintosh

CLAN will run on any Macintosh from the MacPlus onward. To install Macintosh CLAN, first create a new folder on your hard disk called CLAN. Then just copy everything on the CLAN distribution disk into that folder. In addition to the basic CLAN program and the CED editor, you should have a folder of files called "lib." It is best not to modify the files in the "lib" directory or to add new files to that directory. If you want to test out the programs on files like "sample.cha", you can copy them over to your working directory.

CLAN is designed to work in a similar fashion for MS-DOS and the Macintosh. However, Macintosh CLAN provides you with additional facilities not available in the MS-DOS version. You can launch CLAN by double-clicking on its icon. Once you are within CLAN, you get a right arrow (>) prompt. You can type in CLAN commands to this prompt.

20.1. Setting Directories

After you have launched CLAN and before you start constructing individual CLAN commands, it is a good idea to set the location of your working directory and your library directory. In order to set your working directory, you need to click on the Files menu in the top Menu bar. This will open up a pull-down menu and you should drag your cursor down to the Set Work Dir option and then release. The other options in the middle of the Files menu allow you to set the library directory. It is crucial to always set these two directories whenever you work with CLAN. If you do not set them, either you or CLAN will often become confused.

20.2. Specifying Files

There are three ways of specifying your input files.

1. The simplest way is to set your working directory and then refer to the files by name. You can set your working directory by clicking on an option in the Files menu. For example, once you have set your directory to **HardDisk:childes:clan:lib** where "sample.cha" is located, you can type:

    ```
    freq  sample.cha
    ```

    If you want to refer to a collection of files in that directory, you can use wild cards in file names, as in:

    ```
    freq  *.cha
    ```

2. You can also select files using the @Input Files menu command which is found under the File Option in the top menu bar. Selecting this option brings up a dialog box that allows you to navigate around to find files. Once you have selected a group of input files in this way, you can then later refer to these files as a group by simply using the symbol @ in your CLAN command, as in this example:

    ```
    freq  @
    ```

You can put many diverse files together using the @ symbol. For example, you could include all the *.cha files in one directory along with all the *.txt files in another.

3. You can specify a complete Macintosh path description, as in this example:

```
chstring  +s"this"  "that"  HD:Clan:lib:sample.cha
```

You may use spaces or special characters in folder names. Do not use any nonASCII character with filenames, and put single quotes around them if they contain a space.

20.3. Selecting an Editor

You can configure **CLAN** to call up an editor by typing the "set editor" command. We recommend that you use **CED** as your **CLAN** editor. A dialog will come up in which you will locate the editor you wish to use. Find the **CED** editor and double-click on it. Once **CED** is selected as your editor, you can use the "edit" command to open files. For example, you can use the command "edit *.cha."

20.4. Shell Commands

On the Macintosh, **CLAN** runs within a "shell" that duplicates some of the operating systems features found in UNIX or DOS. There are a variety of **CLAN** shell commands that you can give at the prompt in order to change your folder or directory, get information, or launch a new program. You can get the following online listing of these commands by typing **help**.

Command	Function
accept TEXT	allow TEXT type input files
accept ALL	allow any type of input file
batch filename	execute a set of batch commands in a file
cd ..	move up one directory
cd FolderName	change to a folder within current directory
cd HardDiskName:	move to top level
copy [-q] source destination	copy files, -q prompts you to verify, -r is recursive
del [-q] filename	delete file, -q prompts you to verify
dir	show contents of current directory
edit filename	open up files using the editor set by "set editor"
help	displays this "commands" file
launch programname	launches a Macintosh application
list	lists the files currently under the @ sign
log	display previous commands and messages
noisy	set prompt to display programs, directories, file names, and settings
quiet	set prompt to minimal
quit	quit **CLAN**
recall	call up a list of previous commands
ren [-qluct] oldfile newfile	rename file, -q prompts you to verify
	-l changes filenames to lowercase
	-u changes filenames to uppercase
	-cMSWD changes creator to, say, MSWD

	-tTEXT changes file type to, say, TEXT
set creator 'XXXX'	set output file type to XXXX
set editor	select an editor
set font fontname	change screen font type
set size fontsize	change screen font size
set recursion ON	enable recursive file searches through all directories under those specified
version	displays **CLAN** version number
!	launches a program if you provide the program's full path after the !
#	calls up a batch file if you provides the programs's full path after the #

Left and right arrows move the cursor left and right on the command line.
Up and down arrows rotate through the previous commands.

Let us look at each of these shell commands to see how they work.

1. **accept –** If you only want to have **CLAN** look at files that the Macintosh calls TEXT files, then type: accept text. If you want to set this back to all files, type: accept all.
2. **batch –** This command should be followed by the name of a file in your working directory. Each line of the file is then executed as a **CLAN** command.
3. **cd –** This command allows you to change directories. With two dots, you can move up one directory. If you type a folder's name and the folder is in the current folder, you can move right to that folder. If you type a folder's absolute address, you can move to that folder from any other folder. For example, the command **cd HardDisk:Applications:CLAN** will take you to the **CLAN** directory.
4. **copy –** If you want to copy files without going back to the Finder, you can simply use this command. The -q option asks to make sure you want to make the copy.
5. **del –** This command allows you to delete files. When you ask to do this and you have overtly turned recursion on, **CLAN** asks whether you are serious, because this can be quite destructive. **It can even remove all files on your hard disk. Please be careful!**
6. **dir –** This command lists all the files in your current directory.
7. **edit –** Once you have selected an editor using the "set editor" command, you can then specify the name of a file in your current working directory and type "edit filename."
8. **help –** This command displays the current list of commands.
9. **list –** This command lists the files that are currently in your input files list.
10. **log –** This command brings up a window in which you can view the output of earlier commands. This is particularly useful if you want to avoid writing lengthy output to files.
11. **noisy –** This command provides you with extra information regarding your settings each time you hit a carriage return. To turn this off, type "quiet" or "normal."
12. **normal –** Normal mode prints out available **CLAN** commands along with your working directory.
13. **quiet –** The **CLAN** program is distributed with the quiet mode turned on.
14. **quit –** This exits from **CLAN**.
15. **recall –** This command gives you a list of your previous commands. To repeat them use the up and down arrows.
16. **ren –** This is a fairly powerful command that allows you to change file names in a variety of ways. You can change case by using -u for upper and -l for lower. You can change extensions by using wildcards in file names. The -c and -t switches

allow you to change the creator signature and file types recognized by Macintosh. Usually, you will want to have TEXT file types. **CLAN** produces these by default and you should seldom need to use the -t option. You will find that the -c option is more useful. If you want a set of files to have the icon and ownership for Microsoft Word, you should use this command:

```
ren  -cMSWD  *.cha  *.cha
```

If you have to have spaces in these names, surround them with single quotes. For example, to change ownership to the MPW shell, you would need quotes in order to include the additional fourth space character:

```
ren  -c'MPS '  *.cha  *.cha
```

Or you could rename a series of files with names like "child.CHA (Word 5)", using this command:

```
ren  '*.CHA  (Word  5)'  '*.cha'
```

17. **set creator** – This specifies the default setting for the creator type of output files produced by **CLAN**. For example, if you type: set creator 'MCED', all output files will be owned by **CED** and will have the **CED** icon.
18. **set font** – This sets the font for screen display, i.e. set font geneva.
19. **set size** – This sets the point size of the font, i.e. set size 12.
20. **set recursion** – Setting this ON enables recursive file searches and recursive execution of **CLAN** programs. We do not recommend use of this option.
21. **version** – This tells you the date when the current version of **CLAN** was compiled.

Redirection and piping work in Macintosh **CLAN** just as they do in UNIX and MS-DOS (see the description for MS-DOS). The rename command can use the asterisk as a wildcard for files in which there is a period, as in *sample.cha*. It will not work properly if there is more than one period.

On the Macintosh, long lines can be continued simply by expanding the window to the right. If the window grows too big for your screen you can grab the top bar and move it to the left.

20.5. Using the Menus

CLAN provides several pull-down menus in the menu bar.

1. **File Menu**. The two options at the top of the Files menu – **Set Work Dir** and **Set Library Dir** – allow you to set the working directory and the library directory. It is crucial to always set these directories whenever you work with **CLAN**. If you do not set them, either you or **CLAN** may become confused. The **Fonts** option allows you to see the font you are currently working with and change it to another font, if you so desire. The **@Input Files** menu allows you to create a list of files regardless of their location, to be used as inputs for **CLAN** programs. Once you have added one or more file(s) to this list you may simply type @ instead of a filename on a command line. For example:

    ```
    chstring +s"this" "that" @
    ```

    Do not try to use @ if you have moved one of your input files. Make sure you always remove files using the **Clear** option. You may quit **CLAN** by choosing the **Quit** item or by typing Command-q. (The command key is the one with the apple on it -- ⌘-q.)

2. **Edit Menu**. This menu works exactly the same as Edit Menus in other Macintosh applications. You may cut and paste to and from the **CLAN** output or files to any other application. You may also paste onto the command line.

3. **Dialogs Menu**. Another way of composing **CLAN** commands is to use the Dialogs Menu. You click on the Dialogs word and pull down the menu. You then select the program for which you wish to build a command and release the mouse. Two windows then come up. One is titled "Command we are building" and the other is used to begin composing the command. At this point, you simply follow through selecting options in the standard Macintosh way. This way of composing commands is particularly useful for new users, although advanced users may also find this method useful, when they have forgotten some of the switches for a given program.

21. The Programs

This chapter provides detailed descriptions of the programs, listed in alphabetical order. As you read through the sections that follow, it will be helpful if you can test out on your own computer the specific command examples given in the descriptions. Most of these commands are designed to run correctly on the "sample.cha" file that is provided on the distribution diskettes.

The various options that work with each program are also listed and described in this chapter. However, more detailed description of the options that apply to several programs can be found in chapter 22.

21.1. CED – The CHILDES Editor

CED is a full-fledged ASCII-oriented editor that is specifically designed to work cooperatively with CHAT files. CED serves at least these seven functions:

1. In the **non-CHAT** mode [E-], CED functions as a basic ASCII editor for non-CHAT files.

2. In **CHAT editor** mode [E], CED facilitates the typing of new CHAT files and the editing of existing CHAT files. In both of the editor modes, CHAT produces only ASCII output, including extended ASCII.

   When specific language kits are installed on the Apple Macintosh, CED can also create files that mix character sets such as Japanese Kanji, Chinese Hanzi, IPA, or Cyrillic with standard ASCII characters.

3. **EDITOR** mode also allows you to check the file for accuracy by running the CHECK program inside the CED editor.

4. In **Coder** mode [C], CED provides coders with a systematic way of inserting codes from a predefined coding menu.

5. In **Disambiguator** mode, CED allows users to disambiguate the output of the MOR program on the %mor line.

6. In **Sonic Transcriber** mode (with waveform displayed), CED allows the transcriber to directly link the transcript to a digitized sound file. A wave form is displayed at the bottom of the screen and the beginnings and ends of sounds are indicated in the transcript with millisecond values. Sounds may be directly played from the transcript.

7. In **Sonic Playback** mode, the waveform display is turned off and the machine plays back the entire transcript, one utterance after another, while moving the cursor and adjusting the screen to continually display the current utterances. This has somewhat the effect of "following the bouncing ball" as in the old sing-along cartoons.

There are a series of commands for switching each of these modes on and off.

21.1.1. Editor Mode

To begin learning **CED**, it is best to begin in Editor mode. You can start working with **CED** by editing a copy of a simple **CHAT** file, such as sample.cha. You should stay in this mode until you learn the basic editing commands. Basic cursor movements can be controlled through the arrow keys on both MS-DOS and Macintosh. In addition, there is a set of commands modelled on those used in the EMACS editor. Word Perfect users will find that many of these commands also have been bound to the standard Word Perfect keystrokes.

Cursor movement commands:

Command	Movement
Control-f	forward a character
Control-b	backward a character
ESC-f	forward a word
ESC-b	backward a word
Control-l (then number)	go to particular line number
Control-n	forward a line
Control-p	backward a line
Control-e	end of line
Control-a	beginning of line
Control-v	forward a page
ESC-v	backward a page
ESC-<	beginning of file
ESC->	end of file
ESC-,	beginning of window
ESC-.	end of window
Control-z	move text one line up
ESC-z	move text one line down

Commands controlling insertion, deletion, and undoing:

Command	Functions
ESC-d	delete previous character
ESC-d	delete next word
ESC-backspace	delete previous word
Control-d	delete next character
<normal delete key>	delete previous character
Control-k	delete to the end of line
Control-y	reinsert previous deletion
Control-x Control-u	undo the previous command

Commands controlling window and file operations:

Command	Functions
Control-x Control-s	save the current file under its current name
Control-x Control-w	write out the current file with a new name
Control-x Control-c	exit **CED**
Control-x Control-v	read in a file to work with, leave current file
Control-x Control-f	read in a second read-only buffer
Control-x Control-r	redisplay the screen
Control-x Control-z	enlarge the editor window if you can
Control-x z	shrink the editor window if you can

Standard Macintosh equivalents for various commands include ⌘-s (save) for control-x control-s, ⌘-q (quit) for control-x control-c, ⌘-n (newfile) for control-x control-v, ⌘-x (cut) for control-k, ⌘-v (paste) for control-y, and ⌘-c (copy) for control-k, ⌘-p (print) to print, and ⌘-z (undo) for control-x control-u. All of these commands are also available through the menu bar.

In MS-DOS there is a system of command completion that helps in locating files. To use command completion, type a partial name and then press the space bar and a fuller name will be inserted if it is unambiguous.

Help Commands:

There are several commands in **CED** that help you in getting information on commands, keys, or your position in a file.

ESC-? or ESC-/	get help on some command
ESC-h	create a file listing command bindings
ESC-k	rebind a command to a new key
ESC-p	display cursor position in lines
ESC-w	write key bindings to a file
ESC-x version	get the **CED** number

Additional Commands:

Control-s	search forward for a string
Control-r	search in reverse for a string
ESC-r	query-replace
Control-x control-t	tier exclusion or inclusion
ESC-k	rebind a command to a new key
ESC-n	create an automatic insertion
Control-w	make an automatic string insertion

Several of these additional commands are in fact complex additional functions, involving additional options:

Query-replace. This function (ESC-r) provides an additional set of symbols to control the search process. They are:

!	replace all of them
n	do not replace current occurrence
CR (carriage return)	do not replace current occurrence
sp - (space bar)	replace current occurrence
^G	abort this command

Tier exclusion. This function (control-x control-t) allows you to focus your attention on only the tiers you are currently coding. Or you can exclude all dependent tiers. For example, if you want to exclude the %mor tier, you type control-x control-t. Then you type "e" to exclude a tier and %mor for the morphological tier. If you want to exclude all tiers, you type just %. To reset the tiers and to see them all, you type control-x control-t and then "r".

Automatic string insertion. This facility is used for automatic insertion of speaker codes or tier codes. ESC-n will ask for a string number (0-9) and a string to associate with this number. This command lets you specify some constant string like *CHI: that you would want to insert in a text without having to type it out every time. Once you have made these bindings, you can use control-w to retrieve them where needed. Command-w will ask for a string number (0-9) of the constant, pre-defined, string that you want to insert at a current cursor position.

Running CHECK inside CED. By typing ESC-L, you can fire up the **CHECK** program from inside **CED**. **CHECK** is used to verify the accurate use of the various conventions of the **CHAT** transcription system. The **CHECK** program will read in your depfile and start checking your file for errors. If you run **CHECK** frequently inside **CED** while transcribing a file, you can minimize any problems that might arise from incorrect use of **CHAT** coding.

21.1.2. Non-Roman and Non-ASCII Characters in CED

CED provides extensive support for the display of non-ASCII Roman-based characters such as á, ñ, or ç, as well as non-Roman characters from Cyrillic, Japanese, Chinese and other languages. This support is available for MS-DOS and Macintosh systems, using either system-provided fonts, or special fonts available from vendors. In all cases, **CED** displays these fonts correctly, but the underlying file is saved in ASCII characters according to the principles summarized in Chapter 9.

Here is an example of a file in Spanish:

```
@Begin
@Participants:  CHI Target_Child, MOT Mother
*CHI:    hasta mañana
*MOT:    ¿qué? creo que sí.
@End
```

When this file is saved to disk, it will actually look like this in another ASCII editor:

```
@Font:      Monaco:9
@Begin
@Participants:  CHI Target_Child, MOT Mother
*CHI:       hasta ma^n~ana
*MOT:       ¿qu^e'? creo que s^i'.
@End
```

This file will look the same on both MS-DOS and the Macintosh when it is read into **CED.**

In Cyrillic, one can create a file like this in **CED:**

```
@Begin
@Participants:          CHI Target_Child, MOT Mother
*CHI:       молоко?
*MOT:       нет.
@End
```

This file is produced using the Cyrillic II font from Linguist's Software at (206) 775-1130, fax (206) 771-5911 in Tacoma, WA. This font maintains full mapping of Roman ASCII characters along with additional characters for Cyrillic. When this file is viewed by another editor, it will look like this:

```
@Font:      CyrillicII:9
@Begin
@Participants:  CHI Target_Child, MOT Mother
*CHI:       ÏÓÎÓÍÓ?
*MOT:       ÍÂÚ.
@End
```

Unfortunately, many of the other fonts from Linguist's Software will not work properly with **CLAN,** since they do not retain a subset of the basic ASCII characters. For Japanese and Chinese, the font systems that will work are the Japanese Language Kit and the Chinese Language Kit available from Apple. We have not yet found font systems for Korean, Arabic, or Hebrew that have the correct mappings for ASCII.

In order to use the International characters available in MS-DOS, you must add this line to your "config.sys" file:

device=c:\dos\display.sys con=(ega,437)

This line enables you to change fonts. You must have the display.sys file located in your \dos directory or in some other path you wish to specify. **CED** will then be able to use the DOS "mod con" command to load the right font for you. If you have two keyboards and are planning to switch back and forth between them, you can use the "keyb" DOS command, as described in the DOS manual.

21.1.3. CED Preferences and Options

On the Macintosh, you can set preferences by pulling down the "Edit" menu and selecting "Options". The following dialog box then pops up:

```
┌─────────────────────────────────────────────────────┐
│                     CED options                      │
│  Checkpoint every: │50 │  0 – turns off checkpoint    │
│ ┌Codes file:┐      No file selected                  │
│ └───────────┘                                        │
│ ┌Key-bind file:┐   No file selected                  │
│ └──────────────┘                                     │
│                                                      │
│  ☒ Do not create backup file                         │
│  ☐ Do not start in Editor mode                       │
│  ☐ Show cursor position in percentages               │
│  ☒ always auto-wrap long lines                       │
│                                                      │
│  CHAT mode: ☐ always   ☐ never   ☒ auto              │
│ ┌─────────┐                      ┌────────┐          │
│ │   OK    │                      │ Cancel │          │
│ └─────────┘                      └────────┘          │
└─────────────────────────────────────────────────────┘
```

Under MS-DOS, you can set similar options, by using command line switches along with the basic "ced" command. The options for **CED** are:

1. **+a:** Always auto-wrap long lines.

2. **+bN:** Number of words before auto-saving. To turn off auto-saving enter +b0.

3. **-d:** Don't create a backup file.

4. **-e:** Don't start up in Editor mode.

5. **+h:** Display this help message.

6. **+k:** Specify a key bindings file. The default is "cedkeys.lst".

7. **+lN:** Determine how to rearrange codes on the basis of frequency of usage.
      +l1: move frequent code to top
      +l2: move frequent code up one step

8. **+p:** Display the current position of the cursor in terms of percentage of the file.

9. **+s:** When reading in a "codes.lst" file, make copies of codes across branches.

10. **+tS:** Set the name for the next speaker to be the value of "S".

10. **+w:** File is in **CHAT**.

11. **-w:** File is non-**CHAT**.

12. **-v:** Display the version number and compilation date.

These same options can be included in the top line of the "codes.lst" file that you use when working in "Coder mode", as we will see below.

21.1.4. Mode Toggling

Another set of commands allows you to switch between the various modes -- Coder, Editor, **CHAT**, non-**CHAT**, and Sonic **CHAT**. By default, **CED** starts up in **CHAT** Editor mode.

1. ESC-m toggles back and forth between **CHAT** and non-**CHAT** mode. **CHAT** mode facilitates indentation and other aspects of editing.
2. ESC-e toggles the switch between Editor and Coder mode. If **CED** cannot find your codes file, it will complain and ask you to locate your coding file. If you decide to change your coding file, you will need to type ESC-5 on MS-DOS to help it locate the new coding file. On the Macintosh, a dialog comes up to help you find the file.
3. ESC-0 toggles back and forth between Sonic **CHAT** and non-sonic **CHAT** modes.
4. ESC-2 toggles back and forth between Disambiguator mode and standard Editor mode.
5. ESC-8 turns on Sonic Playback mode. A single mouse-click pauses playback and a double mouse-click terminates Playback mode and throws you back to your previous mode.

21.1.5. Sonic Transcriber Mode

Currently, sonic **CHAT** mode works only on the Macintosh. You can use sonic **CHAT** immediately to listen to sounds from files with a %snd tier already coded. The example file for this is "boys85" and "boys85.cha". On the Macintosh, you can place your cursor on the sentence you want to hear. Then you hold down the key and click the mouse. The sound will play immediately. If the "boys85" file is not in the same folder as "boys85.cha", **CED** will ask you to locate the "boys85" sound file on your hard disk.

If your transcript does not yet have a %snd line, you will need to use Sonic Transcriber mode to construct it. In order to bring up the wave-form editor, you must be in Editor mode [E] and have already created your sound file. You then type ESC-0 and **CED** will ask you to locate the sound file. Once you have selected it, the wave-form comes up, starting at the beginning of the file. Several functions are available at this point:

1. **Sound playing from a line.** The facility of directly playing from a line is disabled when the waveform is available. Instead, you need to first activate the correct waveform segment (as in 2) and then play from the waveform (as in 3).
2. **Waveform activation.** In order to bring up the waveform associated with a particular utterance, you need to triple-click on the utterance and the waveform will redisplay. Then you can play it, as in (3) below.
3. **Sound playing from the waveform.** When a segment of the waveform is highlighted, you can play it by holding down the key and clicking the mouse. At this point, it does not matter where your cursor is positioned.
4. **Waveform demarcation.** You can move the borders of a highlighted region by holding down the shift key and moving the border with the mouse.
5. **Relinking.** When you are happy about the extent of the highlighted waveform, you can click on the "s" button to the left of the waveform display and a new millisecond value for the segment will appear in the %snd line in the editor window.

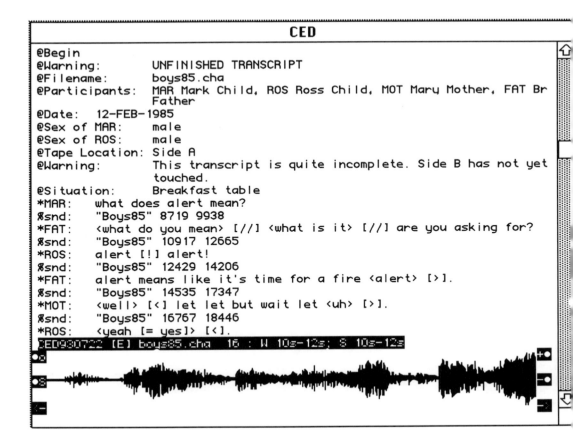

21.1.6. Sonic Playback Mode

For any file that has been coded in Sonic **CHAT**, Sonic Playback mode plays through each utterance in a file in sequence, highlighting each utterance as it goes. This allows you to hear the transcript as you read it. ESC-8 turns on Sonic Playback mode. Before turning on Sonic Playback mode, you have to turn off Sonic Transcriber mode. If you do not, **CED** will complain and ask you to turn it off. You turn off Sonic Transcriber mode with ESC-0. Then type ESC-8 again. Once Sonic Playback mode is on, playback will begin at the current cursor position. So, make sure that you click on the place where you want to start playback before you enter ESC-8. A single mouse-click pauses Sonic Playback and a double mouse-click terminates Playback mode and throws you back to your previous mode. You can start Sonic Playback again by positioning the cursor where you want it and entering ESC-8 again.

If you only want to listen to a single utterance or a few utterances, rather than lots of utterances in sequence, you can do this without using ESC-8. Simply position your cursor on the utterance you want to listen to and type ESC-1 or ⌘-mouseclick. As in the other form of Sonic Playback, you need to have Sonic Transcriber mode turned off to do this.

21.1.7. Disambiguator Mode

ESC-2 toggles back and forth between disambiguator mode and standard editor mode. In disambiguator mode, each ambiguous interpretation on a %mor line is broken into its alternative possibilities at the bottom of the CED screen. The user double-clicks on the correct option and it is inserted.

21.1.8. Coder Mode

Once you have learned to use CED in editor mode, you may wish to learn to use it in coder mode. To start out learning coder mode, place yourself into the /lib directory where you should find the "sample.cha" file and the "codes.exp" sample codes file. Before starting CED, make a copy of the "codes.exp" file and name the copy "codes.lst". We ask you to go through this renaming process in order to make sure that you understand the difference between a "codes.lst" file you create for your own coding systems and the "codes.exp" example file we distribute. Before renaming the codes.exp file, make sure that there is no "codes.lst" file in this directory that you want to preserve. Next, create a copy of "sid.cha" and call it "sidcode.cha". Then bring up CED by typing:

```
ced  sidcode.cha
```

On the Macintosh, you should be able to just double-click on the file and CED will be launched. What you will then see on the screen is a window of text from the test file. Near the bottom is a highlighted line that looks something like this:

```
CED  [E]  [CHAT]  sidcode.cha   1
```

Entering Codes

In order to begin coding, you first want to set your cursor on the first utterance you want to code. In the sidcode.cha file, this would be the first Mother utterance, beginning "I-'ll tell you what." Once you have placed the cursor anywhere on this line, you are ready to leave editor mode and start coding. Type ESC-e and you should be placed into coder mode.

Now the coding tier that you entered in your codes.lst file is shown at the bottom of the CED screen. If you click on the tier symbol with the mouse, CED will automatically insert the appropriate coding tier header (e.g. %spa), a colon and a tab on the line following the main line. It will also display all the codes at the top level of your coding scheme.

```
┌─────────────────────────────────────────────────────────────────────────┐
│                                  CED                                      │
├───────────────────────────────────────────────────────────────────────────
│ @Begin
│ @Participants:   MOT Kelly Mother, NIC Nicolette Child
│ @Age of NIC: 1;10.4
│ @Group of MOT:   Adolescent
│ @Sex of NIC:     Female
│ @ID:      1.25.8.2=NIC
│ @ID:      2.25.8.2=MOT
│ *MOT:     hey Nicky  wanna [: want to] see what other neat toy-s there are?
│ %spa:     $INI:sel:in $RFI:tes:ve
│ *NIC:     yeah. [+ Q]
│ %spa:     $RES:sel:ve $DES:tes:ve
│ @bg
│ *MOT:     you wanna [: want to]  see a [*] more toy-s?
│ %err:     a = some $LEX
│ %spa:     $RDE:sel:non $RFI:xxx:in $POS
│ *NIC:     yeah. [+ Q]
│ %spa:     $RES:sel:in $DES:tes:non
│ %add:     mot
│ *MOT:     oh # I see.
│ ▐CED930722 [C] sample.cha* 15▌
│  ▐:DUE▌ :OTH
│   :ANS
│   :COM
│   :ACK
└─────────────────────────────────────────────────────────────────────────┘
```

Now you have a set of coding choices available. At first, only the top level of the coding hierarchy is available. One particular code will be highlighted. To get a quick overview of your coding choices, type ESC-s several times in succession and you will see the various levels of your coding hierarchy. Then return back to the top level to make your first selection. When you are ready to select a top-level code, click on it with your mouse. Once you have selected a code on the top level of the hierarchy, **CED** moves down to the next level and you repeat the process until that complete code is constructed. To test this out, try to construct the code $POS:COM:VE.

You may also type the first letter or two of the code you desire (instead of using arrow keys or the mouse) in order to highlight the appropriate code. (For example, if NIA is the only code you have that begins with NI, typing NI would highlight the code NIA for you. You need not type the $ or : part of the code; it will be supplied automatically).

If the coding scheme you entered in codes.lst is hierarchical, but you do not wish to code lower levels, press ESC-c to signal that you have completed the current code. You may then enter any subsequent codes for the current tier.

Once you have entered all the codes for a particular tier, press ESC-c to signal that you are finished coding the current tier. You may then either highlight a different coding tier relevant to the same main line, or move on to code another main line. To move on to another main line, you may use the arrow keys to move the cursor or you may automatically proceed to next main speaker tier by pressing Control-t. Typing Control-t will move the cursor to the next main line, insert the highlighted dependent coding tier, and position you to select a code from the list of codes given. If you want to undo the results of typing Control-t, type Control-t again. Try out these various commands now to get a sense of how they work.

If you want to code data for only one speaker, you can restrict the way in which control-t works by using ESC-t to reset the set-next-tier-name function. For example, you confine the operation of the coder to only the *CHI lines, by typing ESC-t and then entering CHI. You can only do this when you are ready to move on to the next line.

If you receive the message "Finish coding current tier" in response to a command (as, for example, when trying to change to editor mode), use ESC-c (SHIFT-F4) to extricate yourself from the coding process. At that point, you can re-issue your original command. Here is a summary of the commands for controlling the coding window. There are single-key functions for each of these on MS-DOS.

All Systems	MS-DOS	Function
Control-c	Enter,Insert	insert highlighted code at cursor
ESC-c	F4	finish coding current code
ESC-c	SHIFT-F4	finish coding current tier
Control-t	F5	finish coding current tier and go to the next
ESC-t		restrict coding to a particular speaker
ESC-ESC		go to the next speaker
ESC-s		show subcodes under cursor
Control-g	F1	cancel illegal command
ESC-5	ESC-5	find codes.lst file

Setting up your codes.lst file

When you are ready to begin serious coding, you will want to create your own codes.lst file to replace our sample. The first line of your codes.lst file should be something like:

\ +b50 +d +l1 +s1

The options on the main line were described in the section above on **CED** options. In this example, the +b option sets the checkpoint buffer (that is, the interval at which the program will automatically back up the work you've done so far in that session). If you find the interval is too long or too short, you can adjust it by changing the value of b.

The +d option tells **CED** not to keep a ".bak" backup of your original **CHAT** file.

The +l option re-orders the presentation of the codes based upon their frequency of occurrence. There are three values of the +l option:

0	leave codes without frequency ordering
1	move most frequent code to the top
2	move codes up one level by frequency

If you use the +s option, the program assumes that all of the codes at a particular level have the same codes symmetrically nested within them. For example, a "codes.lst" list such as

```
\  +l1  +s1  +b50
$MOT
  :POS
    :Que
    :Res
  :NEG
$CHI
```

would be a shorter way of specifying that there are the following codes:

```
$MOT:POS:Que
$MOT:POS:Res
$MOT:NEG:Que
$MOT:NEG:Res
$CHI:POS:Que
$CHI:POS:Res
$CHI:NEG:Que
$CHI:NEG:Res
```

It is not necessary to explicitly type out each of the eight combinations of codes. With the +s1 switch turned on, each code at a particular level is copied across the branches so that all of the siblings on a given level have the same set of offspring.

If you want to include a real space character at the beginning of one of your codes, you should precede it with a quote. For example, to include spaces before the $MOT and $CHI codes, the previous short form of the codes.lst file should be changed to look like this:

```
\   +l1  +s1  +b50
'   $MOT
  :POS
    :Que
    :Res
  :NEG
'   $CHI
```

If not all codes at a given level occur within each of the codes at the next highest level, each individual combination must be spelled out explicitly in "codes.lst" and the +s option should not be used. When you are running **CED** in this non-symmetrical mode, the program creates two files to facilitate processing: *.cod and *.bin. You do not need to touch these files; in fact you should not modify them, since they are maintained by the program. They will be created in the same directory as "codes.lst".

Setting up the "codes.lst" properly is the trickiest part about Coder's Workbench. Once properly specified, however, it rarely requires modification (unless your coding scheme changes, or you want to change the checkpoint buffer increment). If you have problems getting **CED** to work, chances are the problem is with your "codes.lst" file.

21.1.9. Time Coding with The Observor

CED also includes a facility for including time codes from a videotape. Currently this facility is only supported in conjunction with use of The Observer (Geverink, Noldus, Pluim & Ødberg, 1993; Noldus, 1991; Noldus, van de Loo & Timmers, 1989).   The Observer is a separate software package developed by Noldus Information Technology. In order to make use of the Link program, one needs The Observer, version 3.0, Base Package for DOS, which costs $1,225. The package can be tried out on a 30-day loan basis at no charge. Noldus Information Technology can be reached at this address:

Noldus Information Technology
Costerweg 5
P. O. Box 268
6700 AG Wageningen
The Netherlands
email noldus@rcl.wau.nl
fax: 31-(0)8370-24496

21.1.10.   Command Reference

All **CED** commands can also be entered by their names. This is done by typing ESC-x followed by the name of the command. The program will help you by completing your typing once the string becomes unambiguous. You can create a list of available commands on your own computer by typing ESC-w and the program will then write out the available commands and store them in a file. The complete list of **CED** functions and their default key bindings is as follows:

```
CTRLX_Prefix: ^X
ESC_Prefix: ESC
abort: ^G
bind-key-to: ESC-K ESC-k
chat-mode: ESC-M ESC-m
check-with-default-depfile: ESC-L ESC-l
check-with-new-depfile: ^X-^L
commands-execute: ESC-X ESC-x
commands-save-keys-bindings: ESC-W ESC-w
commands-store-list-to-file: ESC-H ESC-h
cursor-backward-word: ESC-B ESC-b
cursor-beginning-of-file: ESC-<
cursor-beginning-of-line: ^A
cursor-beginning-of-window: ESC-,
cursor-down: ^N ^_
cursor-end-of-file: ESC->
cursor-end-of-line: ^E
cursor-end-of-window: ESC-.
cursor-forward-word: ESC-F ESC-f
cursor-left: ^B ^\
cursor-next-page: ^V
cursor-previous-page: ESC-V ESC-v
cursor-right: ^F ^]
cursor-up: ^P ^^
delete-line: ^K
delete-next-character: ^D
```

delete-next-word: ESC-D ESC-d
delete-previous-character: ^H F-133
delete-previous-word: ESC-^H
deleted-restore: ^Y
describe-key: ^X-^K
disambiguate-mor-tier: ESC-2
display-percent-of-file: ESC-P ESC-p
editor-mode-toggle: ESC-E ESC-e
editor-window-enlarge: ^X-^Z
editor-window-shrink: ^X-Z ^X-z
enter-ascii-code: ESC-G ESC-g
exit: ^X-^C
file-get-new-codes: ESC-5
file-get-second: ^X-^F
file-save-current: ^X-^S
file-switch-to-second: ESC-A ESC-a
file-visit: ^X-^V
file-write-new-name: ^X-^W
finish-coding-current-code-or-tier: ESC-C ESC-c
finish-current-tier-goto-next: <Coder mode only:> f F ^T
get-time-code:
goto-line: ^L
goto-next-speaker: ESC-ESC
help: ESC-/ ESC-?
insert-highlighted-code-at-cursor: <Coder mode only:> j J ^C
macro-insert-string: ^W
macro-set-string: ESC-N ESC-n
move-code-cursor-down: + =
move-code-cursor-up: -
redisplay-screen: ^X-^R
search-forward: ^S
search-reverse: ^R
select-tiers: ^X-^T ^X-T ^X-t
set-next-tier-name: ESC-T ESC-t
show-paragraph-marks:
show-subcodes-under-cursor: ESC-S ESC-s
sound-change-file-name: ESC-9
sound-mode-play-only: ESC-1
sound-mode-transcribe: ESC-0
sound-play-from-now-on: ESC-8
string-replace: ESC-Q ESC-R ESC-q ESC-r
undo-previous-command: ^X-^U
version:
window-move-one-line-down: ^Z
window-move-one-line-up: ^Q ESC-Z ESC-z

21.2. CHAINS – Sequences of Interactional Codes

The **CHAINS** program is used to track sequences of interactional codes. These codes must be entered by hand on a single specified coding tier. In order to test out **CHAINS**, you may wish to try the file called "chains.cha" which contains the following sample data.

```
@Begin
@Participants:   CHI  Sarah  Target_child,  MOT  Carol  Mother,
FAT  Bob  Father
*MOT:  sure  go  ahead  [c].
%wld:  $A
%spa:  $nia:gi
*CHI:  can  I?  [c]  can  I  really  [c].
%wld:  $A  $D.  $B.
%spa:  $nia:fp  $nia:yq.
%sec:  $ext  $why.  $mor.
*FAT:  you  do  [c]  or  you  don't  [c].
*MOT:  you  do  [c].
%wld:  $B  $C.
%spa:  $nia:pa
*MOT:  that's  it  [c].
%wld:  $C
%spa:  $nia:pa
@End
```

The symbol [c] in this file is used to delimit clauses. Currently, its only role is within the context of the **CHAINS** program. The %wld coding tier is a project-specific tier used to code possible worlds, as defined by narrative theory. The %spa, %sec, and %wld tiers have periods inserted to indicate the correspondence between [c] clausal units on the main line and sequences of codes on the dependent tier.

To change the order in which codes are displayed in the output, create a file called "codes.ord". This file could be located in either your working directory or in the "\childes\clan\lib" directory. **CHAINS** will automatically find this file, no option is required. If the file is not found then the codes are displayed in an alphabetical order, as before. In the codes.ord file, list all codes in any order you like, one code per line. You can list more codes than could be found in any one file. But if you do not list all the codes, the missing codes will be inserted in alphabetical order.

For our first **CHAINS** analysis of this file, let us look at the %spa tier. If you run the command:

```
chains  +t%spa  chains.cha
```

you will get a complete analysis of all chains of individual speech acts for all speakers, as in the following output:

```
Speaker markers:  1=*MOT, 2=*CHI, 3=*FAT
```

$nia:fp	$nia:gi	$nia:pa	$nia:yq	line #
0	1	0	0	3
2	0	0	2	6
0	0	1	0	11

0	0	1	0	14

ALL speakers:

	$nia:fp	$nia:gi	$nia:pa	$nia:yq
# chains	1	1	1	1
Avg leng	1.00	1.00	2.00	1.00
Std dev	0.00	0.00	0.00	0.00
Min leng	1	1	2	1
Max leng	1	1	2	1

Speakers *MOT:

	$nia:fp	$nia:gi	$nia:pa	$nia:yq
# chains	0	1	1	0
Avg leng	0.00	1.00	2.00	0.00
Std dev	0.00	0.00	0.00	0.00
Min leng	0	1	2	0
Max leng	0	1	2	0
SP Part.	0	1	1	0
SP/Total	0.00	1.00	1.00	0.00

Speakers *CHI:

	$nia:fp	$nia:gi	$nia:pa	$nia:yq
# chains	1	0	0	1
Avg leng	1.00	0.00	0.00	1.00
Std dev	0.00	0.00	0.00	0.00
Min leng	1	0	0	1
Max leng	1	0	0	1
SP Part.	1	0	0	1
SP/Total	1.00	0.00	0.00	1.00

Speakers *FAT:

	$nia:fp	$nia:gi	$nia:pa	$nia:yq
# chains	0	0	0	0
Avg leng	0.00	0.00	0.00	0.00
Std dev	0.00	0.00	0.00	0.00
Min leng	0	0	0	0
Max leng	0	0	0	0
SP Part.	0	0	0	0
SP/Total	0.00	0.00	0.00	0.00

It is also possible to use the +s switch to merge the analysis across the various speech act codes. If you do this, alternative instances will still be reported, separated by commas. Here is an example:

```
chains  +d  +t%spa  chains.cha  -t*FAT  +s$nia:%
```

This command should produce the following output. Note that the Father has been excluded from this analysis by use of the -t*FAT switch.

```
Speaker markers:  1=*MOT, 2=*CHI

$nia:                              line #
1 gi                                 3
2 fp, yq                             6
```

```
1 pa                                      11
1 pa                                      14

ALL speakers:
          $nia:

# chains  1
Avg leng  5.00
Std dev   0.00
Min leng  5
Max leng  5

Speakers  *MOT:
          $nia:

# chains  2
Avg leng  1.50
Std dev   0.50
Min leng  1
Max leng  2
SP Part.  1
SP/Total  0.60

Speakers  *CHI:
          $nia:

# chains  1
Avg leng  2.00
Std dev   0.00
Min leng  2
Max leng  2
SP Part.  1
SP/Total  0.40
```

It is possible to use **CHAINS** to track two coding tiers at a time. For example, one can look at chains across both the %cod and the %sec tiers by using the following command. This command also illustrates the use of the +c switch which allows the user to define units of analysis lower than the utterance. In the example file, the [c] symbol is used to delimit clauses. The following command makes use of this marking:

```
chains  +c"[c]"  +d  +t%cod  chains.cha  +t%sit  -t*fat
```

The output from this analysis should be as follows:

```
Speaker markers:  1=*MOT, 2=*CHI

$a                $b                $c              $d                  line #
1                                                                        3
2 $ext $why                                         2 $ext $why          6
                  2 $mor                                                 6
                  1                 1                                    11
                                    1                                    14

ALL speakers:
          $a                $b              $c              $d

# chains  1                 1               1               1
Avg leng  2.00              2.00            2.00            1.00
```

Std dev	0.00	0.00	0.00	0.00
Min leng	2	2	2	1
Max leng	2	2	2	1

Speakers *MOT:				
	$a	$b	$c	$d
# chains	1	1	1	0
Avg leng	1.00	1.00	2.00	0.00
Std dev	0.00	0.00	0.00	0.00
Min leng	1	1	2	0
Max leng	1	1	2	0
SP Part.	1	1	1	0
SP/Total	0.50	0.50	1.00	0.00

Speakers *CHI:				
	$a	$b	$c	$d
# chains	1	1	0	1
Avg leng	1.00	1.00	0.00	1.00
Std dev	0.00	0.00	0.00	0.00
Min leng	1	1	0	1
Max leng	1	1	0	1
SP Part.	1	1	0	1
SP/Total	0.50	0.50	0.00	1.00

1. **+c:** The default unit for **CHAINS** analysis is the utterance. You can use the +c switch to track some unit type other than utterances. The other unit type must be delimited in your files with some other punctuation symbol which you specify after the +c, as in +c"[c]" which uses the symbol [c] as a unit delimiter. If you have a large set of delimiters you can put them in a file and use the form +c@filename. To see how this switch operates try out the command given in the last illustration:

   ```
   chains +c"[c]" +d +t%wld chains.cha +t%sec -t*fat
   ```

2. **+d**: Use this switch to change zeroes to spaces in the output. The last command given above illustrates this switch.

   ```
   chains +d +t%spa chains.cha -t*FAT +s$nia:%
   ```

   The +d1 value of this switch works the same as +d, while also displaying every input line in output.

3. **+f/-f:** Send output to the screen or to a file. The default value of this switch is -f which sends output to the screen. If you want to send the output to a file, you must use the +f switch. The letters placed after the +f will be used as the file extension name.

4. **+k**: Make analyses case-sensitive.

5. **+m:** By default **CLAN** leaves the output files in your current working directory. The +m switch tells **CLAN** to store output files in the directory where the corresponding input files were found.

6. **+p**: Redefine the punctuation set.

7. **+s/-s**: This option is used to specify particular codes to track. For example, +s$b, will track only the $b code. A set of codes to be tracked can be placed in a file and tracked using the form +s@filename. In the examples given earlier, the following command was used to illustrate this feature:

```
chains  +d  +t%spa  chains.cha  -t*FAT  +s$nia:%
```

8. **+t/-t**: Particular dependent tiers can be included or excluded by using the +t or -t option immediately followed by the tier code. **CHAINS** requires that you specify at least one coding tier. If you do not, **CLAN** will give you an error message.

9. **+u**: By default, when the user has specified a series of files on the command line, the analyses are performed on each individual file. The program ends up reporting results for each data file separately. If the +u option is used, the program combines the input data found in all the specified files into one set and outputs results for that set as a whole.

10. **+wN**: Sets the width between columns to N characters.

11. **+y**: Work on non**CHAT** files.

12. **+z**: Work on a specified range of words or utterances. See the description of +z in chapter 22 for ways of specifying ranges.

21.3. CHECK – Verifying Data Accuracy

Checking the syntactic accuracy of a file can be done in two ways. One method is to work within the **CED** program. In **CED**, you can start up the **CHECK** program by just typing ESC-L. Alternatively, you can run **CHECK** outside **CED** as a separate program. The **CHECK** program checks the syntax of the specified **CHAT** files. If errors are found, the offending line is printed, followed by a description of the problem.

CHECK makes two passes through each **CHAT** file. On the first pass it checks the overall structure of the file. It makes sure that the file begins with @**Begin** and ends with @**End,** that each line starts with either *, @, %, or a tab, and that colons are used properly with main lines, dependent tiers, and headers that require entries. If errors are found at this level, **CHECK** reports the problem and stops, because further processing would be misleading. If there are problems on this level, you will need to fix them before continuing with **CHECK**. Errors on the first level can mask the detection of further errors on the second level. It is important not to think that a file has passed **CHECK** until all errors have been removed.

The second pass checks the detailed structure of the file. To do this, it relies heavily on the "depfile". That file, which was distributed with **CLAN**, lists the legitimate **CHAT** headers and dependent tier names as well as many of the strings allowed within the main line and the various dependent tiers. When running **CHECK**, you should have the "depfile" located either in the directory you are working in or in \childes\clan\lib (or /childes/clan/lib on UNIX). On the Macintosh, the depfile should be kept inside the \lib folder. If the programs cannot find the "depfile" on the Macintosh, they will query you for its location.

In order to maintain consistency in the use of **CHAT** across projects, we ask you to avoid modification of the "depfile". We occasionally make some additions to the "depfile" to reflect new uses of **CHAT**, but we try to be conservative in regards to these changes. If you need to extend **CHAT** in particular ways, you can create a file called "00depadd" which you should place into the same directory as the files being checked. **CHECK** will automatically pick up the additional codes in this file and use them to amplify the standard "depfile". If you use a "00depadd" file, it should remain with the data files as a form of documentation of the particular divergences from standard **CHAT**.

In order to work effectively with **CHECK**, and in order to create lines in a "00depadd" file, it is helpful to understand the format of the depfile. The "depfile" is, in effect, a short hand summary of the bulk of the **CHAT** system. The three components of the file are the definitions for headers, the main line, and the dependent tiers.

Currently, the header definitions in the "depfile" are as follows:

```
@Activities:          *
@Age of #:                    @d<yy;>  @d<yy;mm.>  @d<yy;mm.dd>  -
@Bck:       *
@Begin
@BG
@BG:        *  =  $*
@Birth of #:          @d<dd-lll-yyyy>
@Blank
@Coding:              *
@Coder:     *
@Comment:                     *  "*  -
@Date:      @d<dd-lll-yyyy>   -
```

```
@DSS
@DSS:      Start
@Education of #:             *
@EG
@EG:       *  =  $*
@End
@Filename:          *
@Font:     *
@G:        *  =
@Group of #:         *
@ID:       *
@Indent
@Language:          *
@Language of #:  *
@Location:          *
@New  Episode
@Participants:   Target_child  Child  Mother  Father  Brother
   Sister  Sibling  Grandmother  Grandfather  Aunt  Uncle  Cousin
   Family_Friend  Playmate  Visitor  Student  Teacher
   Babysitter  Housekeeper  Investigator  Examiner  Observer
   Clinician  Therapist  Camera_Operator  Doctor  Nurse  Patient
   Client  Subject  Unidentified  Adult  Teenager  Boy  Girl
   Non_Human  Toy  OffScript  Text  Narrator
@Room  Layout:       *
@SES of #:           *
@Sex of #:           *
@Situation:         *  "*  _
@Stim:     *  =
@Tape  Location:    *
@Time  Duration:    @t<hh:mm-hh:mm>   @t<hh:mm:ss-hh:mm:ss>
@Time  Start:       @t<hh:mm:ss>  @t<mm:ss>
@Transcriber:       *
@Warning:           *  [*]
```

Headers such as @BG or @End without following colons are assumed to have no additional following text. Headers such as @Location have a colon and a following asterisk. This asterisk allows for any text in which words begin with alphanumeric symbols. If the user needs to add additional symbols, they can be added after the asterisk. For example, the entry for @Comment also allows for words beginning with double quotation marks and for dashes. In order to allow for words beginning with double quotation marks, the symbol "* is used where the * stands for any material after the double quotation mark. If, for example, a user needs to also allow for an equals sign on the @Comment line, this line could be added to the "00depadd" file:

```
@Comment:    =
```

The shape of date and age entries in headers can be determined by using formats such as yy;mm.dd to indicate the age of a child. In this form, each letter indicates a possible field. The "y" indicates the year; the "m" indicates a month; and the "d" indicates a day. Lower case letters indicate numbers and upper case letters indicate letters. For dates, the standard form is @d<dd-MMM-yyyy>, as in 14-NOV-1956. For ages, the standard form is @d<yy;mm.dd>, as in 2;5.17. For timing, the standard form is @t<hh:mm-hh:mm>, as in 12:15-4:30. The name of a particular participant such as "MOT" or "CHI" is indicated in headers such as "Age of #" by the # sign.

Following the header definitions, there is a set of definitions for possible main line symbols. The standard "depfile" is oriented toward coding in English and includes many English prefixes and suffixes. Any string beginning with a letter is accepted by **CHECK** as a word. However, strings beginning with symbols like the dash and the square bracket must be exhaustively listed. Suffixes are coded by using the notation *-suffix and prefixes are coded by using the notation *prefix#.

```
*:      *  *-0*  *-able  *-al  *-ary  *-er  *-ed  *-en  *-er  *-es
        *-est
        *-ful  *-ic  *-ie  *-ify  *-ity  *-ize  *-ing  *-less  *-ly
        *-ment  *-ness  *-s  *-'s  *-s'  *-tion  *-y
        *-'d  *-'does  *-'has  *-'had  *-'ll  *-'m  *-'nt  *-'re
        *-'is  *-'iscop  *-'isaux  *-'us  *-'ve  *&*
        *un#  *re#  *dis#  *mis#  *pro#  *anti#  *ex#  *pre#
        *over#   *under#  *mono#  *quasi#
        -  -?  -.  -^  -'  -''  -''  -`  -,  -_  -:  #*
        +  ++  +"  +".  +...  +/.  +//.  +,  +^  +"/.  +/?
        [=!  *]  [=  *]  ["]  [:  *]  [:=*]  [=?  *]  [\%*]  [#*]
        [?]  [>*]  [<*]  [<>]  [+  *]  [$*]  [0  *]  [0  *  *]
        [/]  [//]  [///]  [/?]  [\*]  [!]  [!!]
        $*  ^*  &*  *&ed  0*  */*  *//*  *///*
        @*@u  6*@u  3*@u  *@b  *@c  *@d  *@f  *@i  *@l
        *@n  *@o  *@p  *@s  *@sl  *@sas  *@u  *@w  *@
```

Following the definition for the main line are a series of definitions for the dependent tiers. These have the same form as the definitions for the main line, although they differ in content.

```
%act:  *  $=*  "*  [?]
%add:  *  $=*
%alt:  *  [?]
%cod:  *  $=*  $*
%com:  *  $=*  "*  -  /*  =  '*  ^*  [=?  *]  [=  *]  [?]
%def:  *  $*  =
%eng:  *  [\%  *]  [=  *]  "*  +...
%err:  *  [?]  $PHO  $LEX  $SYN  $MOR  $ALL  $CWFA  $MAL  $CIR  $ADD
       $LOS  $SUB  $BLE  $HAP  $EX1  $EX2  $SH1  $SH2  $ANT    $PER    $A/P
       $ACH  $PCH   $INC  $UNC  $VOW  $CON   $CC   $SYL  $FEA  $STS
       $MR  $TON  $PRE  $SUF  $NFX   $NFL  $DER  $RED  $AGA  $AGC  $AGB
       $AGR  $REG  $FUL  $PAR  $HAR  $ACC  $STR  $SBL  $POS  $ISR  $RISR
       $WR  $MWR  $RFS  $UNP  $FIP  =  &*  @*  /*  $=/*
%exp:  *  "*  [=  *]  [?]  =
%fac:  *
%flo:  *  +...
%gls:  *  [/]  [//]  [%  *]  [?]
%gpx:  *  $*  "*
%int:  *  $=*
%lan:  *
%mod:  *  [IGN]
%mor:  *  $*  [UTD]  \**
%par:  *  $=*  "*
%pho:  *  `*  ~*  !*  @*  #*  $*  %*  ^*  &*    (*  )*  _*  +*  -*  =*  {*
       }*  [*  ]*  \*  |*  /*  ?*  >*  <*  ,*  .*  :*  ;*
%sit:  *  $=*  "*
%spa:  *  $=*  $*
%syn:  *  $*
%tim:  @t<hh:mm:ss>   @t<mm:ss>
```

If you have a very restricted set of words that you are allowing on a given dependent tier and you want **CHECK** to be even more cautious, you should remove the asterisk or the $* and list the acceptable words or codes exhaustively in a "00depadd" file.

The %mor line includes the special symbol [UTD] which is designed to allow for the inclusion of all utterance delimiters. The %mod line includes the special symbol [IGN] which is designed to turn off all checking of characters on a particular dependent tier.

Each main tier must start with a speaker ID in the **@Participants** list to be considered correct. Only the first three characters of the speaker ID field are checked, thereby allowing for extended combinations such as *CHI-MOT in the ID field. **CHECK** looks at things like the presence of delimiters, correct structure of scoping symbols, matching of paired delimiters, and the validity of the codes on the line.

The options for **CHECK** are:

1. **+c:** By default, **CHECK** will look in your directory for a "00depadd" file. However, if you wish to use some other name for your "depadd" file, you need to use this switch and follow it with the name of your file.

2. **+d:** This switch attempts to suppress repeated warnings of the same error type. It is convenient to use this in your initial runs when you file has consistent repeated divergences from standard **CHAT** form. However, you must be careful not to rely on this switch, because it will mask many types of errors you will eventually want to correct. The +d1 value of this switch represses errors even more severely to only one of each type.

3. **+e:** This switch allows the user to select a particular type of error for checking. To find the numbers for the different errors, type:

    ```
    check +e
    ```

    Then look for the error type you want to track, such as error #16, and type:

    ```
    check +e16 *.cha
    ```

4. **+f/-f:** Send output to the screen or to a file. The default value of this switch is -f which sends output to the screen. If you want to send the output to a file, you must use the +f switch. The letters placed after the +f will be used as the file extension name.

5. **+g1/-g1:** Setting +g1 turns on the treatment of prosodic contour markers such as -. or -? as utterance delimiters, as discussed in chapter 6. Setting -g1 sets the treatment back to the default which is to not treat these codes as delimiters.

    +g2/-g2: By default, **CHECK** requires tabs after the colon on the main line and at the beginning of each line. However, versions of Word Perfect before 5.0 cannot write out text files that include tabs. Other non-ASCII editors may may also have this problem. To get around the problem, you can set the -g2 switch in **CHECK** which stops checking for tabs. If you want to turn this type of checking back on, use the +g2 switch.

        +g3/-g3: Without the +g3 switch, **CHECK** does minimal checking for the correctness of the internal contents of words. With this switch turned on, the program makes sure that words do not contain numbers, capital letters, or spurious apostrophes.

6.   **+m**: By default **CLAN** leaves the output files in your current working directory. The +m switch tells **CLAN** to store output files in the directory where the corresponding input files were found.

7.   **+pF**: Use a punctuation file.

8.   **+t/-t**: Include or exclude a particular tier.

To get an idea of how **CHECK** operates, try this command:

```
check   sample.cha
```

Try adding a few errors to the file and rerunning **CHECK**. For a fuller experience in using **CHECK**, try running it on kid10.cha. That file has a large number of **CHAT** errors. If you can get it in correct **CHAT** format and run it cleanly through **CHECK**, you have certainly mastered the use of **CHECK** to verify **CHAT** format.

Once you are finished using **CHECK** to verify the accuracy of your files, you may wish to run through yet another type of accuracy checking. This involves using the **FREQ** program to create a listing of all the words in your transcript or set of transcripts. It is often easy to scan through such a listing and spot remaining errors in the spelling of codes or words. If this additional checking with **FREQ** picks up any consistent errors, you can change them using **CHSTRING**. For some further ideas on verifying the accuracy of your **CLAN** commands, see chapter 26.

Some Hints for Using CHECK:

1. Use **CHECK** early and often, particularly when you are learning to code in **CHAT**. When you begin transcribing, check your file inside the **CED** editor using ESC-l, even before it is complete. When **CHECK** complains about something, you can learn right away how to fix it before continuing with the same error.
2. Learn how to enter **CHAT** extensions in a "00depadd" file. Try to avoid adding symbols such as * or *$ too liberally, because you will then lose the ability to trap certain types of errors on coding lines.
3. If you are being "overwhelmed" by **CHECK** errors, you can use the +d1 switch to limit error reports to one of each type. Or you can focus your work first on eliminating main line errors by using the -t% switch.
4. Use a powerful text editor that allows you to examine two files at a time in two different windows. One file should be your **CHAT** file and the other should be the file that is output from **CHECK**. If you cannot open two windows, you will have to print out the **CHECK** file and this can be quite cumbersome.
5. Make sure that you know how to use your text editor to go to a particular line number. Most good text editors have this as a built-in function, although a few popular editors such as MS-Word do not have this function. Make sure that your editor has this function.
6. Learn how to use the query-replace function in your text editor to make general changes and **CHSTRING** to make changes across sets of files.

21.4. CHIP – Analysis of Interaction – Jeff Sokolov

CHIP is a program written by Jeffrey Sokolov. The program analyzes specified pairs of utterances. CHIP has been used to explore parental input, the relationship between speech acts and imitation, and individual differences in imitativeness in both normal and language-impaired children. Researchers who publish work based on the use of this program should cite Sokolov and MacWhinney (1990). There are four major aspects of CHIP to be described: (1) the tier creation system, (2) the coding system, (3) the technique for defining substitution classes, and (4) the nature of the summary statistics.

The Tier Creation System

CHIP compares two specified utterances and produces an analysis which it then inserts onto a new coding tier. The first utterance in the designated utterance pair is the "source" utterance and the second is the "response" utterance. The response is compared to the source. Speakers are designated by the +b and +c codes. An example of a minimal CHIP command is as follows:

```
chip +bMOT +cCHI chip.cha
```

Let us imagine that this command runs on the following seven-utterance file which is distributed with CLAN as "chip.cha".

```
@Begin
@Participants:    MOT Mother, CHI Child
*MOT: what-'is  that?
*CHI: hat.
*MOT: a hat!
*CHI: a hat.
*MOT: and what-'is this?
*CHI: a hat !
*MOT: yes that-'is the hat .
@End
```

The output from running this simple CHIP command on this short file is as follows:

```
*MOT:      what-'is that ?
*CHI:      hat .
%chi:      $NO_REP $REP = 0.00
*MOT:      a hat !
%asr:      $NO_REP $REP = 0.00
%adu:      $EXA:hat $ADD:a $EXPAN $DIST = 1 $REP = 0.50
*CHI:      a hat .
%csr:      $EXA:hat $ADD:a $EXPAN $DIST = 2 $REP = 0.50
%chi:      $EXA:a-hat $EXACT $DIST = 1 $REP = 1.00
*MOT:      and what-'is this ?
%asr:      $NO_REP $REP = 0.00
%adu:      $NO_REP $REP = 0.00
*CHI:      a hat !
%csr:      $EXA:a-hat $EXACT $DIST = 2 $REP = 1.00
%chi:      $NO_REP $REP = 0.00
*MOT:      yes that-'is the hat .
%asr:      $NO_REP $REP = 0.00
```

```
%adu:        $EXA:hat $ADD:yes-that-'is-the $DEL:a $DIST = 1
             $REP = 0.25
```

The output also includes a long set of summary statistics which are discussed later. In the first part of this output, **CHIP** has introduced four different dependent tiers:
1. **%chi**: This tier is an analysis of the child's response to an adult's utterance, so the adult's utterance is the source and the child's utterance is the response.
2. **%adu**: This tier is an analysis of the adult's response to a child's utterance, so the child is the source and the adult is the response.
3. **%csr**: This tier is an analysis of the child's self repetitions. Here the child is both the source and the response.
4. **%asr**: This tier is an analysis of the adult's self repetitions. Here the adult is both the source and the response.

By default, **CHIP** produces all four of these tiers. However, through the use of the **-n** option, the user can limit the tiers that are produced. Three combinations are possible:
1. You can use both **-ns** and **-nb**. The **-ns** switch excludes both the **%csr** tier and the **%asr** tier. The **-nb** switch excludes the **%adu** tier. Use of both switches results in an analysis which computes only the **%chi** tier.
2. You can use both **-ns** and **-nc**. The **-ns** switch excludes both the **%csr** tier and the **%asr** tier. The **-nc** switch excludes the **%chi** tier. Use of both of these switches results in an analysis which computes only the **%adu** tier.
3. You can use both **-nb** and **-nc**. This results in an analysis which produces only the **%csr** and the **%asr** tiers.

It is not possible to use all three of these switches at once.

The Coding System

The **CHIP** coding system includes aspects of several earlier systems (Bohannon & Stanowicz, 1988; Demetras, Post & Snow, 1986; Hirsh-Pasek, Trieman & Schneiderman, 1984; Hoff-Ginsberg, 1985; Moerk, 1983; Nelson, Denninger, Bonvilian, Kaplan & Baker, 1984). It differs from earlier systems in that it computes codes automatically. This leads to increases in speed and reliability, but certain decreases in flexibility and coverage.

The codes produced by **CHIP** indicate lexical and morphological additions, deletions, exact matches and substitutions. The codes are as follows:

$ADD	additions of N continuous words
$DEL	deletions of N continuous words
$EXA	exact-matches of N continuous words
$SUB	substitutions of N continuous words from within a specified word-list
$MADD	morphological addition based on matching word stem
$MDEL	morphological deletion based on matching word stem
$MEXA	morphological exact-match based on matching word stem
$MSUB	morphological substitution based on matching word stem
$DIST	the distance the response utterance is from the source
$NO_REP	the source and response do not overlap
$LO_REP	the overlap between source and response is below a user-specified minimum
$EXACT	source-response pairs with no additions, deletions, or substitutions
$EXPAN	source-response pairs with exact-matches and additions but no deletions or substitutions
$REDUC	source-response pairs with exact-matches and deletions but no additions or substitutions

$SUBST	source-response pairs with only exact-matches and substitutions
$FRO	an item from the word list has been fronted
$REP	The percentage of repetition between source and response. Computed by dividing the number of overlapping stems by the total number of stems in the response.

Let us take the last line of the chip.cha file as an example:

```
*MOT:  yes that-'is the hat  .
%asr:  $NO_REP $REP = 0.00
%adu:  $EXA:hat   $ADD:yes-that-'is-the  $DEL:a  $DIST  =  1
       $REP  =  0.25
```

The %adu dependent tier indicates that the adult's response contained an EXAct-match of the string "hat," the ADDition of the string "yes-that-'is-the" and the DELetion of "a." The DIST=1 indicates that the adult's response was "one" utterance from the child's, and the repetition index for this comparison was 0.25 (1 matching stem divided by 4 total stems in the adult's response).

CHIP also takes advantage of **CHAT**-style morphological coding. Upon encountering a word, the program determines the word's stem and then stores any associated prefixes or suffixes along with the stem. During the coding process, if lexical stems match exactly, the program then also looks for additions, deletions, repetitions, or substitutions of attached morphemes.

Word Class Analysis

In the standard analysis of the last line of the "chip.cha" file, the fact that the adult and the child both use a definite article before the noun "hat" is not registered by the default **CHIP** analysis. However, it is possible to set up a substitution class for small groups of words such as definite articles or modal auxiliaries that will allow **CHIP** to track such within-class substitutions, as well as to analyze within-class deletions, additions, or exact repetitions. To do this, the user must first create a file containing the list of words to be considered as substitutions. For example to code the substitution of articles, the file distributed with **CLAN** called "articles" containing "a" and "the" can be used. Both the +g option and the +h (word-list filename) options are used, as in the following example:

```
chip  +cCHI  +bMOT  +g  +harticles  chip.cha
```

The output of this command for the last two lines of "chip.cha" will add a $SUB field to the %adu tier:

```
*CHI:  a  hat!
*MOT:  yes  that-'is  the  hat.
%adu:  $EXA:hat $ADD:yes-that-'is $SUB:the $DIST = 1
       $REP  =  0.25
```

The +g option enables the substitutions, and the +harticle option directs **CHIP** to examine the word list previously created by the user. Note that the %adu now indicates that there was an EXAct repetition of "hat", an ADDition of the string "yes that-'is" and a within-class substitution of "the" for "a." If the substitution option is used, EXPANsions and REDuctions are tracked for the included word list only. In addition to modifying the dependent tier, using the substitution option also effects the summary statistics that are produced. With the substitution option, the summary statistics will be calculated relative only to the word list included with +h switch. In many cases, you will want to run **CHIP** analyses both with and without the substitution option and compare the contrasting analyses.

You can also use **CLAN** iterative limiting techniques to increase the power of your **CHIP** analyses. If you are interested in isolating and coding those parental responses that were expansions involving closed-class verbs, you would first perform a **CHIP** analysis and then use **KWAL** to obtain a smaller collection of examples. Once this smaller list is obtained, it may be handcoded and then once again resubmitted to another **KWAL** or **FREQ** analysis. This notion of iterative analysis is extremely powerful and takes full advantage of the benefits of both automatic and manual coding.

Summary Statistics

In addition to analyzing utterances and creating separate dependent tiers, **CHIP** also produces a set of summary statistics. These statistics include absolute and proportional values for each of the coding categories for each speaker type which are outlined below. This example is from a run on the "chip.cha" sample file.

chip.cha	Measure	ADU	CHI	ASR	CSR
chip.cha	Total number of utterances: 7				
chip.cha	Total Responses	3	3	3	2
chip.cha	Overlap	2	1	0	2
chip.cha	No Overlap	1	2	3	0
chip.cha	%_Overlap	0.67	0.33	0.00	1.00
chip.cha	Avg_Dist	1.00	1.00	0.00	2.00
chip.cha	Rep_Index	0.38	1.00	0.00	0.75
chip.cha	ADD_OPS	2	0	0	1
chip.cha	DEL_OPS	1	0	0	0
chip.cha	EXA_OPS	2	1	0	2
chip.cha	%_ADD_OPS	0.40	0.00	0.00	0.33
chip.cha	%_DEL_OPS	0.20	0.00	0.00	0.00
chip.cha	%_EXA_OPS	0.40	1.00	0.00	0.67
chip.cha	ADD_WORD	4	0	0	1
chip.cha	DEL_WORD	1	0	0	0
chip.cha	EXA_WORD	2	2	0	3
chip.cha	%_ADD_WORDS	0.57	0.00	0.00	0.25
chip.cha	%_DEL_WORDS	0.14	0.00	0.00	0.00
chip.cha	%_EXA_WORDS	0.29	1.00	0.00	0.75
chip.cha	MORPH_ADD	0	0	0	0
chip.cha	MORPH_DEL	0	0	0	0
chip.cha	MORPH_EXA	0	0	0	0
chip.cha	MORPH_SUB	0	0	0	0
chip.cha	%_MORPH_ADD	0.00	0.00	0.00	0.00
chip.cha	%_MORPH_DEL	0.00	0.00	0.00	0.00
chip.cha	%_MORPH_EXA	0.00	0.00	0.00	0.00
chip.cha	%_MORPH_SUB	0.00	0.00	0.00	0.00
chip.cha	AV_WORD_ADD	2.00	0.00	0.00	1.00
chip.cha	AV_WORD_DEL	1.00	0.00	0.00	0.00
chip.cha	AV_WORD_EXA	1.00	2.00	0.00	1.50
chip.cha	EXACT	0	1	0	1
chip.cha	EXPAN	1	0	0	1
chip.cha	REDUC	0	0	0	0

```
chip.cha    %_EXACT          0.00 1.00 0.00 0.50
chip.cha    %_EXPAN          0.50 0.00 0.00 0.50
chip.cha    %_REDUC          0.00 0.00 0.00 0.00
```

- **Columns**: The first column is the filename, the second is an abbreviated name for the statistic, the third is the child-adult data, the fourth is the adult-child data, the fifth is for adult-adult self-repetitions, and the sixth is for child-child self-repetitions.

- **Total Number of Utterances**: The number of utterances for all speakers regardless of the number of intervening utterances and speaker identification.

- **Total Responses**: The total number of responses for each speaker type regardless of amount of overlap.

- **Overlap**: The number of responses in which there is an overlap of each least one word-stem in the source and response utterances.

- **No Overlap**: The number of responses in which there is NO overlap between the source and response utterances.

- **Avg_Dist**: The sum of the DIST values divided by the total number of overlapping utterances.

- **%_Overlap**: The percentage of overlapping responses over the total number of responses.

- **Rep_Index**: Average proportion of repetition between the source and response utterance across all the overlapping responses in the data.

- **ADD_OPS, DEL_OPS, EXA_OPS, SUB_OPS:** The total (absolute) number of add, delete, exact, or substitution operations for all overlapping utterance pairs in the data.

- **%_ADD_OPS, %_DEL_OPS, %_EXA_OPS, %_SUB_OPS**: The numerator in these percentages is the operator being tracked and the denominator is the sum of all four operator types.

- **ADD_WORD, DEL_WORD, EXA_WORD, SUB_WORD**: The total (absolute) number of add, delete, exact, or substitution words for all overlapping utterance pairs in the data.

- **%_ADD_WORDS,%_DEL_WORDS, %_EXA_WORDS, %_SUB_WORDS**: The numerator in these percentages is the word operator being tracked and the denominator is the sum of all four word operator types.

- **MORPH_ADD, MORPH_DEL, MORPH_EXA, MORPH_SUB**: The total number of morphological changes on exactly-matching stems.

- **%_MORPH_ADD, %_MORPH_DEL, %_MORPH_EXA, %_MORPH_SUB**: The total number of morphological changes divided by the number of exactly-matching stems.

- **AV_WORD_ADD, AV_WORD_DEL, AV_WORD_EXA**: The average number of words per operation across all the overlapping utterance pairs in the data.

$$AV\_WORD\_ADD = \#\_added\_words/\#\_ADD\_OPS$$
$$AV\_WORD\_DEL = \#\_deleted\_words/\#\_DEL\_OPS$$
$$AV\_WORD\_EXA = \#\_exact\_words/\#\_EXA\_OPS$$
$$AV\_WORD\_SUB = \#\_substituted\_words/\#\_SUB\_OPS$$

- **FRONTED, %_FRONTED**: The number and percentage (based on class overlapping responses) of lexical items from the word-list that have been fronted.

- **EXACT, %_EXACT**: The number and percentage (based on overlapping responses) of exactly-matching responses.

- **EXPAN, %_EXPAN**: The number and percentage (based on overlapping responses) of responses containing only exact-matches and additions.

- **REDUC, %_REDUC**: The number and percentage (based on overlapping responses) of responses containing only exact-matches and deletions.

- **SUBST, %_SUBST**: The number and percentage (based on overlapping responses) of responses containing only exact-matches and substitutions.

The options for **CHIP** are:

1. **+b**: Specify that speaker ID S is an "adult." The speaker does not actually have to be an adult. The "b" simply indicates a way of keeping track of one of the speakers.

2. **+c**: Specify that speaker ID S is a "child." The speaker does not actually have to be a child. The "c" simply indicates a way of keeping track of one of the speakers.

3. **+d**: Using +d with no further number outputs only coding tiers, which are useful for iterative analyses. Using +d1 outputs only summary statistics, which can then be sent to a statistical program.

4. **+f/-f**: Send output to the screen or to a file. The default value of this switch is -f which sends output to the screen. If you want to send the output to a file, you must use the +f switch. The letters placed after the +f will be used as the file extension name. The default extension name .chp.

5. **+g**: Enable the substitution option. This option is meaningful in the presence of a word-list in a file specified by the +h/-h switch, because substitutions are coded with respect to this list.

6. **+h/-h**: The target file is specified after the letter "h." Words to be included (with +h) or excluded (with -h) are searched for in the target file. The use of an include file enables **CHIP** to compare ADD and DEL categories for any utterance pair analyses to determine if there are substitutions within word classes. For example the use of a file containing a list of pronouns would enable **CHIP** to determine that the instances of ADD of "I" and DEL of "you" across a source and response utterance are substitutions within a word class.

Standard **CLAN** wildcards may be used anywhere in the word list. When the transcript uses **CHAT**-style morphological coding (e.g., I-'ve), only words from the word list file will match to stems in the transcript. In other words, specific morphology may not be traced within a word list analysis. Note that all of the operation and word-based summary statistics are tabulated with respect to the word list only. The word list option may be used for any research purpose including grammatical word-classes, number terms, color terms, or mental verbs. Note also that the -h option is useful for excluding certain terms such as "okay" or "yeah" from the analysis. Doing this often improves the ability of the program to pick up matching utterances.

7. **+k**: Make analyses case-sensitive.

8. **+m**: By default **CLAN** leaves the output files in your current working directory. The +m switch tells **CLAN** to store output files in the directory where the corresponding input files were found.

9. **-n**: This switch has three values: **-nb**, **-nc,** and **-ns**. See above for a discussion of the use of these switches in combination.

10. **+p**: Redefine the punctuation set.

11. **+qN**: Set the utterance window to N utterances. The default window is seven utterances. **CHIP** identifies the source-response utterances pairs to code. When a response is encountered, the program works backwards (through a window determined by the +q option) until it identifies the most recent potential source utterance. Only one source utterance is coded for each response utterance. Once the source-response pair has been identified, a simple matching procedure is performed.

12. **+r**: This switch has several different levels which allow you to specify how to treat omissions of parts of words, text replacement, prosodic delimiters, and retracings. For details see chapter 22.

13. **+t/-t**: Particular dependent tiers can be included or excluded by using the +t option immediately followed by the tier code. By default, **CHIP** excludes the header and dependent code tiers from the search and output. This option should be used with caution as **CLAN** omits the specified tier prior to any subsequent **CHIP** analyses. For example using the -t*MOT would exclude all mother utterances and only child self repetitions would be computed. Adding +t% and +t* will duplicate the entire transcript in the output.

14. **+u**: Treat all specified files as one large file.

15. **+x**: Set the minimum repetition index for coding.

21.5. CHSTRING – Altering Strings in Files

This program changes one string to another string in an ASCII text file. **CHSTRING** is useful when you want to correct spelling, change subjects' names to preserve anonymity, update codes, or make other uniform changes to a transcript. This changing of strings can also be done on a single file using a text editor. However **CHSTRING** is much faster and allows you to make a whole series of uniform changes in a single pass over many files.

It is important to note that **CHSTRING** is string-oriented, as opposed to word-oriented. This means that the program treats "the" as the letters "t", "h", and "e" rather than a single unique word "the." Searching for "the" with this program will result in retrieving words such as "other", "bathe", "there", and so forth. Using spaces can help you to limit your search. Knowing this will help you to specify the changes that need to be made on words. By default, **CHSTRING** works only on the text and not on the dependent tiers or the headers.

The options for **CHSTRING** are:

1. **+c**: Often, many changes need to be made in data. You can do this by using a text editor to create an ASCII text file containing a list of words to be changed and what they should be changed to. This file should conform to this format:

```
"  old  string  "  "  new  string  "
"  old  word  "      "  new  word  "
```

The default name for the file listing the changes is "changes.txt." That is, if you don't specify a filename at the +c option, the program searches for a file named "changes.txt". If you want to name the file containing the changes something other than "changes.txt", that filename should follow the +c. For example, if your file is called "mywords.txt," then the option takes the form **+cmywords.txt**.

To test out the operation of CHSTRING, try creating the following file called "changes.txt":

```
"  the  "  "  wonderful  "
"  eat  "  "  quark  "
```

Then try running this file on the sample.cha file with the command:

```
chstring  +c  sample.cha
```

Check over the results to see if they are correctly done.

If you need to include the double quotation symbol in your search string, use a pair of single quote marks around the search and replacement strings in your include file. Also, note that you can include extended ASCII symbols in your search string. For example, the following "changes.txt" file would convert German text with extended ASCII characters to basic ASCII:

```
"ä"    '^a"'
"ö"    '^o"'
"ü"    '^u"'
"ß"    '^ss'
```

2. **+d:** This option turns off a number of **CHSTRING** clean-up actions. It turns off the deletion of blank lines, the removal of blank spaces, the removal of empty dependent tiers, the replacement of spaces after headers with a tab, and the wrapping of long lines. All it allows is the replacement of individual strings.

3. **+f/-f:** Write output to a file or send it to the screen. The letters that are placed after the +f will be used as the file extension name. **CHSTRING** is the only program for which the +f value is the default. For the other programs, the default value is -f. If you don't want the output to be sent to a file, you should use -f. If you want the output sent to a file with the extension .str, then you do not have to type anything and all this will happen automatically.

4. **+l:** Work only on material that is to the left of the colon which follows the tier ID.

5. **+m:** By default **CLAN** leaves the output files in your current working directory. The +m switch tells **CLAN** to store output files in the directory where the corresponding input files were found.

6. **+n:** Work only on material that is to the right of the colon which follows the tier ID.

7. **+p:** This option allows you to redefine the punctuation set. Because **CHSTRING** treats punctuation as a space, changes in the punctuation set can help in specifying strings to be changed.

8. **+q:** **CHAT** requires that a three letter speaker code, such as *MOT:, be followed by a tab. Often, this space is filled by three spaces instead. Although this is undetectable visually, the computer recognizes tabs and spaces as separate entities. The **+q** option brings the file into conformance with **CHAT** by replacing the spaces with a tab.

9. **+r:** Work only on material that is to the right of the colon which follows the tier ID.

10. **+s:** Sometimes you need to change just one word, or string, in a file(s). These strings can be put directly on the command line following the **+s** option. For example, if you wanted to mark all usages of the word "gumma" in a file as child-based forms, the option would look like this:

    ```
    +s"  gumma  "  "  gumma@c  "
    ```

    Please note the format of the previous example command line. The original string "gumma" has spaces around it and is delimited by double quotes. There is a space separating the quotes surrounding the replacement string "gumma@c" from the original. The replacement string is also delimited by double quotes and surrounded by spaces.

    If either the original or the replacement string contains a double quote ("), then the whole string must be put between single quotes (').

11. **+t/-t:** Particular dependent tiers can be included or excluded by using the +t and -t options immediately followed by the tier code. Suppose you only want to make changes on the %spa tier. Then you can use a command of this form:

```
chstring  -t*  +t%spa  +s"$INI"  "$INIT"  sample.cha
```

Note that you must specifically exclude the main tier with the -t* switch, since the main tier is usually included in **CLAN** programs by default. Unlike the other **CLAN** programs, **CHSTRING** is case-sensitive and the strings following the +s need to be given the correct capitalization. If you want to work on all the main speaker tiers and their dependent tiers, it is unnecessary to include the +t* option, because speaker tiers are included by default. If you want to make changes on coding tiers, you have to use the +t% option. If you are using UNIX, remember that % and * are treated as special characters and need to be "quoted." If you want to work only on the %spa tier of only MOT, then you can add +t*MOT as a further specification.

```
chstring  -t*  +t*MOT  +t%spa  +s"$INI"  "$INIT"  sample.cha
```

Note that the +t*MOT switch limits the search to only the lines spoken by the mother. Then the -t* switch further limits the search to exclude the main line of the mother. Thus, -t* functions in a different way from -t*CHI which will simply exclude all of the utterances of CHI and the associated dependent tiers.

12. **+x**: The default setting of **CHSTRING** does not treat the asterisk (*), the underline (_), and the backslash (\) as metacharacters, because treating them as metacharacters can often lead to bad results. Therefore, if the user really wants to use them as metacharacters, **CLAN** requires this switch to be overtly set. Using this option will make **CHSTRING** interpret these characters as metacharacters.

13. **+y**: Work on nonCHAT files. Unlike some of the other **CLAN** programs, **CHSTRING** works well on nonCHAT files. The +y value works on lines and the +y1 value works on utterances as delimited by periods, question marks, and exclamation marks.

CAUTION: **CHSTRING** is potentially the most dangerous of the **CLAN** programs. Used incorrectly, it can lead to serious losses of important data. You must be quite careful when defining changes. If you do not accurately show the strings to be changed, including spaces, the results can be disastrous. Consider what happens when changing all occurrences of "yes" to "yeah". If you use this command:

```
chstring  +s"yes"  "yeah"  myfile.cha
```

every single occurrence of the sequence of letters y-e-s will be changed. This includes words, such as "yesterday," "eyes," and "polyester" which would become "yeahterday," "eyeah," and "polyeahter" respectively. Spaces should be inserted around strings in order for the program to make the proper changes. A better version of this line would look like this:

```
chstring  +s" yes "  " yeah "  myfile.cha
```

Please note also that this option will cause all possible occurrences of the *word* "yes" to be changed. It will also change those occurrences when followed by punctuation, because the program recognizes final punctuation as a space. By default, **CHSTRING** works only on the text and not on the dependent tiers or the headers.

21.6. COLUMNS – Display of CHAT Files in Columns

When viewing printed versions of **CHAT** files, it is often helpful to have a visual display which can separate out the contributions of the child from those of the other speakers. A traditional way of doing this is to place the child's utterances in the left column, the other speakers' utterances in a middle column, and commentary in the right column. In order to reformat a **CHAT** file in this way, you can run the **COLUMNS** program. For example, if you want to get columned output for the first five utterances in the sample file, you can use this command:

```
columns  +h  +nNIC  +z5u  sample.cha
```

This should produce output much like this:

```
                                         hey Nicky wanna [: want to] see what
                                         other neat toy-s there are?
                                         %spa: $INI:sel:in $RFI:tes:ve
yeah. [+ Q]
%spa:  $RES:sel:ve $DES:tes:ve

                                         you wanna [: want to] see a [*] more toy-s?
                                         %err: a = some $LEX
                                         %spa: $RDE:sel:non $RFI:xxx:in
yeah. [+ Q]
%spa:  $RES:sel:in $DES:tes:non
%add:  mot

                                         oh # I see.
                                         %spa: $INI:xxx:non $CR:sel:in
```

In this output, the child's speech is in the left column, the mother's is in the right, with the dependent tiers placed under the main tiers.

If you want to have the dependent tiers placed into a separate column, you can add the +d switch, as in this command:

```
columns  +h  +d  +nNIC  +z5u  sample.cha
```

which will yield this output:

```
            hey Nicky wanna
            [: want to] see what
             other neat toy-s there
            are?
                                                     %spa: $INI:sel:in
                                                     $RFI:tes:ve
yeah. [+ Q]
                                                     %spa: $RES:sel:ve
                                                     $DES:tes:ve

            you wanna [: want to]
            see a [*] more toy-s?

                                                     %err: a = some $LEX
```

```
                                                    %spa: $RDE:sel:non
                                                    $RFI:xxx:in
yeah. [+ Q]
                                                    %spa: $RES:sel:in
                                                    $DES:tes:non
                                                    %add: mot
                 oh # I see.
                                                    %spa: $INI:xxx:non
                                                    $CR:sel:in
```

You can add speaker ID codes by omitting the +h switch. You can also suppress the comments column altogether by adding a -t switch. In order to use the space of the omitted comments column, you can change the columns for the second speaker to the second 36 columns by using +b40 and +c76. You can move the mother's utterances to the left column by using the +nMOT switch instead of +nNIC. The next example shows these changes:

```
    columns  +nMOT  -t%  +z5u  +b40  +c76  sample.cha
```

The output of this version of the command is simply:

```
*MOT: hey Nicky wanna [: want to] see
what other neat toy-s there are?
                                            *NIC: yeah. [+ Q]
*MOT: you wanna [: want to] see a [*]
more toy-s?
                                            *NIC: yeah. [+ Q]
```

Finally, for those who want to see as little **CHAT** coding and headers as possible, it is possible to pipe the file through **FLO** using a command such as the following:

```
    flo +d sample.cha | columns +nNIC +z5u +h +b40 +c76
```

This command will produce this type of very simple output:

```
                              hey Nicky wanna see what other
                              neat toys there are ?
yeah .
                              you wanna see a more toys ?
yeah .
                              oh I see .
```

The options for **COLUMNS** are:

1. **+b**: Set the column in which the second speaker's utterances should start to N, as in +b40 to start the second speaker in the fortieth column.

2. **+c**: Set the column in which the dependent tiers should start to N, as in +c60 to start the dependent tiers in the sixtieth column.

3. **+d**: Display the dependent tiers in a separate column.

4. **+f/-f**: Send output to the screen or to a file. The default value of this switch is -f which sends output to the screen. If you want to send the output to a file, you

must use the +f switch. The letters placed after the +f will be used as the file extension name. When you work on a collection of files, this switch sends each of the resultant analyses to a separate file. If you want a single merged analysis for a collection of files, use the redirecting symbol (>) instead.

5. **+h**: Do not include the tier name in the output

6. **+k**: Make analyses case-sensitive.

7. **+m:** By default **CLAN** leaves the output files in your current working directory. The +m switch tells **CLAN** to store output files in the directory where the corresponding input files were found.

8. **+n**: You must always use this switch in order to tell the program which speaker should be placed in the first column. For example, +nNIC will select the speaker Nicolette in the sample.cha file.

9. **+p**: Redefine the punctuation set.

10. **+r**: This switch has several different levels which allow you to specify how to treat omissions of parts of words, text replacement, prosodic delimiters, and retracings. For details see chapter 22.

11. **+t/-t**: Particular dependent tiers can be included or excluded by using the +t or -t options immediately followed by the tier code.

12. **+z**: Work on a specified range of words or utterances. See the description of +z in chapter 22 for ways of specifying ranges.

21.7. COMBO – Boolean Searching

COMBO provides the user with ways of composing Boolean search strings to match patterns of letters, words, or groups of words in the data files. This program is particularly important for researchers who are interested in syntactic analysis. The search strings are specified with either the +s/-s option or in a separate file. When learning to use **COMBO**, what is most tricky is learning how to specify the correct search strings.

21.7.1. Composing Search Strings

Boolean searching uses algebraic symbols to better define words or combinations of words to be searched for in data. **COMBO** uses regular expressions to define the search pattern. The Boolean operators are: *followed-by*, *or* and *not*. In combination with the three logical operators, **COMBO** also uses three metacharacters: *, _, and \ . These six special symbols are listed in the following table.

Meaning	Symbol
immediately FOLLOWED by	^
inclusive OR	+
logical NOT	!
repeated character	*
single character	_
quoting	\

Inserting the *followed-by* operator between two strings causes the program to search for the first string followed by the second string. The *or* operator inserted between two strings causes the program to search for either of the two strings. In this case, it is not necessary for both of them to match the text to have a successful match of the whole expression. Any one match is sufficient. The *not* symbol inserted before a string causes the program to match a string of text that does not contain that string.

The items of the regular expression will be matched to the items in the text *only* if they directly follow one another. For example, the expression `big^cat` will match only the word "big" directly followed by the word "cat" as in "big cat". To find the word "big" followed by the word "cat" immediately or otherwise, use the metacharacter "*" between the items "big" and "cat", as in `big^*^cat`. This expression will match, for example, "big black cat". Notice that, in this example, the asterisk ends up matching not just any string of characters, but any string of words or characters up to the point where "cat" is matched. The "*" alone **cannot** be used in conjunction with the +g or +x option.

In combination with the logical operators (^ + !), you can use the metacharacters *, _ , and \. The asterisk (*), when used by itself within a word, stands for any number of characters. When used in the form ^*^, it stands for any number of words. The underline (_) is used to "stand in for" for any *single* character. If you want to match any *single* word, you can use the underscore with the asterisk as in +s"_*." which will match any single word followed by a period. For example, in the string "cat.", the underscore would match "c", the asterisk would match "at" and the period would match the period.

The backslash (\) is used to quote either the asterisk or the underline. That is, when you want to search for the actual characters * and _, rather than using them in their "official capacity" as metacharacters, you insert the \ character before them. Using metacharacters can be quite helpful in defining search strings. Suppose you want to search for the words "weight", "weighs", "weighing" "weighed" and "weigh". You could use the "weigh*" string to find all of the previously mentioned forms. Metacharacters may be used anywhere in the search string.

When **COMBO** finds a match to a search string, it prints out the entire utterance in which the search string matched, along with any previous context or following context that had been included with the +w or -w switches. This whole area printed out is what we will call the "window."

21.7.2. Examples of Search Strings

The following command searches the sample.cha file and prints out the window which contains the word "want" when it is directly followed by the word "to."

```
combo  +swant^to  sample.cha
```

If you are interested not just in cases where "to" immediately follows "want," but also cases where it follows eventually, you can use the following command syntax:

```
combo  +s"want^*^to"  sample.cha
```

The next command searches the file and prints out any window that contains both "want" and "to" in any order:

```
combo  +s"want^to"  +x  sample.cha
```

The next command searches sample.cha and sample2.cha for the words "wonderful" or "chalk" and prints the window that contains either word:

```
combo  +s"wonderful+chalk"  sample*.cha
```

The next command searches sample.cha for the word "neat" when it is *not* directly followed by the words "toy" or "toy-s." Note that you need the *followed by* symbol (^) in addition to the *not* symbol (!) in order to clearly specify the exact nature of the search you wish to be performed.

```
combo  +s"neat^!toy*"  sample.cha
```

In this next example, the **COMBO** program will search the text for either the word "see" directly followed by the word "what" or all the words matching "toy*."

```
combo  +s"see^(what+toy*)"  sample.cha
```

You can use parentheses in order to group the search strings unambiguously as in the next example.

```
combo  +s"what*^(other+that*)"  sample.cha
```

This command causes the program to search for words matching "what" followed by either the word "that" or the word "other." An example of the types of strings that would be found are: "what that," "what's that," and "what other." It will not match "what is that" or "what do you want." Parentheses are necessary in the command line because the program reads the string from left to right. Parentheses are also important in the next example.

```
combo  +s"the^*^!grey^*^(dog+cat)"  sample2.cha
```

This command causes the program to search the file "sample2.cha" for the word "the" followed, immediately or eventually, by any word or words, except the word "grey." This combination is then to be followed by either the word "dog" or the word "cat." Thus, the intention of this search is to find strings like "the big dog" or "the boy with a cat," and not to match strings like "the big grey cat." Note the use of the parentheses in the example. Without parentheses around "dog+cat," the program would match simply "cat." In this example, the sequence ^*^ is used to indicate "immediately or later." If we had used only the symbol ^ instead of the ^*^, we would only have matched strings in which the word immediately following "the" was not "grey."

21.7.3. Referring to Files in Search Strings

Inside the +s switch, one can include reference to one, two, or even more groups of words that are listed in separate files. For example, you can look for combinations of prepositions with articles by using this switch:

```
+s@preps^@arts
```

To use this form, you first need to create a file of prepositions called "preps" with one preposition on each line and a file of articles called "arts" with one article on each line. By maintaining files of words for different parts of speech or different semantic fields, you can use **COMBO** to achieve a wide variety of syntactic and semantic analyses. Some suggestions for words to be grouped into files are given in Chapter 22 on Word Lists. Some particularly easy lists to create would be those including all the modal verbs, all the articles, or all the prepositions. When building these lists, remember the possible existence of dialect and spelling variations such as "dat" for "that".

21.7.4. Cluster pairs in COMBO

Most computer search programs work on a single line at a time. If these programs find a match on the line, they print it out and then move on. Because of the structure of **CHAT**, and the relation between the main line and the dependent tiers, it is more useful to have the **CLAN** programs work on "clusters" instead of lines. The notion of a cluster is particularly important for search programs, such as **COMBO** and **KWAL**. A cluster can be defined as a single utterance by a single speaker, along with all of its dependent tiers. By default, **CLAN** programs work on a single cluster at a time. For **COMBO**, one can extend this search scope to a pair of contiguous clusters by using the +b switch. However, this switch should only be used when cross-cluster matches are important, since addition of the switch tends to slow down the running of the program.

21.7.5. Searching for Clausemates

When conducting analyses on the %syn tier, researchers often want to make sure that the matches they locate are confined to "clausemate" constituents. Consider the following two %syn tiers:

```
%syn:  ( S V L ( O V ) )
%syn:  ( S V ( S V O ) )
```

If we want to search for all Subjects (S) followed by Objects (O), we want to make sure that we match only patterns of the type found in the embedded clause in the second example. If we use a simple search pattern such as +sS^*^O", we will match the first example as well as both clauses in the second example. In order to prevent this, we need to add parenthesis checking to our search string. The string then becomes:

```
+s"S^*^(!\(+!\))^*^O
```

This will only find Subjects that are followed by Objects without intervening parentheses. In order to guarantee the correct detection of parentheses, they must be surrounded by spaces on the %syn line.

21.7.6. Tracking Final Words

In order to find the final words of utterances, you need to use the complete delimiter set in your **COMBO** search string. You can do this with this syntax (\!+?+.) where the parentheses enclose a set of alternative delimiters. In order to specify the single word that appears before these delimiters, you can use the asterisk wild card preceded by an underline. Note that this use of the asterisk treats it as referring to any number of letters, rather than any number of words. By itself, the asterisk in **COMBO** search strings usually means any number of words, but when preceded by the underline, it means any number of characters. Here is the full command:

```
combo    +s"_*^(\!+?+.)"     sample.cha
```

This can then be piped to **FREQ** if the +d2 switch is used.

```
combo    +s"_*^(\!+?+.)"   +d2   sample.cha   |   freq
```

21.7.7. Limiting with COMBO

Often researchers want to limit their analysis to some particular group of utterances. **CLAN** provides the user with a series of switches within each program for doing the simplest types of limiting. For example, the +t/-t switch allows the user to include or exclude whole tiers. However, sometimes these simple mechanisms are not sufficient and the user will have to use **COMBO** or **KWAL** for more detailed control of limiting. **COMBO** is the most powerful program for limiting, because it has the most versatile methods for string search using the +s switch. Here is an illustration. Suppose that, in the file "sample.cha," you want to find the frequency count of all the speech act codes associated with the speaker *MOT when this speaker used the phrase "want to" in an utterance. To accomplish this analysis, use this command:

```
combo   +t*MOT   +t%spa   sample.cha   +s"want^to"   +d   |   freq
```

The +t*MOT switch (UNIX users should add double quotes) tells the program to select only the main lines associated with the speaker *MOT. The +t%spa tells the program to add the %spa tier to the *MOT main speaker tiers. By default, the dependent tiers are excluded from the analysis. Then follows the file name, which can appear anywhere after the program name. The +s"want^to" then tells the program to select only the *MOT clusters that contain the phrase "want to". The +d option tells the program to output the matching clusters from the file "sample.cha" without any non-**CHAT** identification information. Then the results are sent through a "pipe" indicated by the "|" symbol to the

FREQ program, which conducts an analysis on the main line.   The results could also be piped on to other programs such as **MLU** or **KEYMAP** or they can be stored in files.

Sometimes researchers want to maintain a copy of their data that is stripped of the various coding tiers. This can be done by this type of command in either **COMBO** or **KWAL**:

```
combo  +o@  -t%  +f  *.cha
```

The +o switch controls the addition of the header material that would otherwise be excluded from the output and the -t switch controls the deletion of the dependent tiers. It is also possible to include or exclude invidual speakers or dependent tiers by providing additional +t or -t switches. The best way to understand the use of limiting for controlling data display is to to try out the various options on a small sample file.

The options for **COMBO** are:

1.   **+b**: **COMBO** usually works on only one cluster at a time. However, when you want to look at a contiguous pair of clusters, you can use this switch.

2.   **+d**: Normally, **COMBO** outputs the location of the tier where the match occurs. When the +d switch is turned on you can output only each matched sentence in a simple legal **CHAT** format. The +d1 switch outputs legal **CHAT** format along with line numbers and file names. The +d2 switch outputs legal **CHAT** format, but with only the actual words matched by the search string, along with @Comment headers that are ignored by other programs. Try these commands:

```
combo   +s"want^to"   sample.cha
combo   +s"want^to"   +d  sample.cha
combo   +s"want^to"   +d1  sample.cha  |  freq
combo   +d2  +s"_*^."  sample.cha  |  freq
```

This final command provides a useful way of searching for utterance final words and tabulating their frequency.

2.   **+f/-f**: Send output to the screen or to a file. The default value of this switch is -f which sends output to the screen. If you want to send the output to a file, you must use the +f switch. The letters placed after the +f will be used as the file extension name.

3.   **+g**: Unlike **CHSTRING**, which only operates in string-oriented mode, **COMBO** can operate in either string-oriented or word-oriented mode. The default mode is word-oriented. **COMBO** can be converted to a string-oriented program by using the +g option. Word-oriented search assumes that the string of characters requested in the search string is surrounded by spaces or other word delimiting characters. The string-oriented search does not make this assumption: It sees a string of characters simply as a string of characters.   In most cases, there is no need to use this switch, because the default word-oriented mode is usually more useful.

The interpretation of metacharacters varies depending on the search mode. In word-oriented mode, an expression with the asterisk metacharacter, such as `air*^plane`, will match "air plane" as well as "airline plane" or "airy plane". It will not match "airplane" because, in word-oriented mode, the program expects to find to words. It will not match "air in the plane" because the text is broken into words by assuming that all adjacent nonspace characters are part of the same word, and a space marks the end of that word. You can think of the search string "air" as a signal for the computer to search for the expressions: `_air_`, `_air.`, `air?`, `air!`, and so forth, where the underline indicates a space.

The same expression `air*^plane` in the string-oriented search will match "airline plane," "airy plane," "air in the plane" or "airplane" in the examples. They will all be found because the search string, in this case, specifies the string consisting of the letters "a," "i," and "r", followed by any number of characters, followed by the string "p," "l," "a," "n," and "e." In string-oriented search, the expression (`air^plane`) will match "airplane" but not "air plane" because no space character was specified in the search string. In general, the string-oriented mode is not as useful as the word-oriented mode. One of the few cases when this mode is useful is when you want to find all but some given forms. For example if you are looking for all the forms of the verb "kick" except the "ing" form, you can use the expression "kick*^! ^!ing" and the +g switch.

4. **+k**: Make analyses case-sensitive.

5. **+m**: By default **CLAN** leaves the output files in your current working directory. The +m switch tells **CLAN** to store output files in the directory where the corresponding input files were found.

6. **+o**: The +t switch is used to control the addition or deletion of particular tiers or lines from the input and the output to **COMBO**. In some cases, you may want to include a tier in the output that is not being included in the input. This typically happens when you want to match a string in only one dependent tier, such as the %mor tier, but you want all tiers to be included in the output. In order to do this you would use a command of the following shape:

```
combo  +t%mor  +s"*ALL"  +o%  sample2.cha
```

7. **+p**: Redefine the punctuation set.

8. **+r**: This switch has several different levels which allow you to specify how to treat omissions of parts of words, text replacement, prosodic delimiters, and retracings. For details see chapter 22.

9. **+s**: This option is used to specify a regular expression to search for in a given data line(s). This option should be immediately followed by the regular expression itself. The rules for forming a regular expression are discussed in detail earlier in this section.

10. **+t/-t**: Particular dependent tiers can be included or excluded by using the +t option immediately followed by the tier code. By default, **COMBO** excludes the header and dependent code tiers from the search and output. However, when the dependent code tiers are included by using the +t option, they are combined with their speaker tiers into clusters. For example, if the search expression is `the^*^kitten`, the match would be found even if "the" is on the speaker tier and "kitten" is on one of the speaker's associated dependent tiers. This feature is useful if one wants to select for analyses only speaker tiers that contain specific word(s) on the main tier and some specific code(s) on the dependent code tier. For example, if one wants to produce a frequency count of the words "want" and "to"

when either one of them is coded as an imitation on the %spa line, or "neat" when it is a continuation on the %spa line, the following two commands could be used.

```
combo   +s(want^to^*^%spa:^*^$INI*)+(neat^*^%spa:^*^$CON*)
+t%spa  +f  +d  sample.cha

freq  +swant  +sto  +sneat  sample.cmb
```

In this example the +s option specifies that the words "want," "to," and "$INI" may occur in any order on the selected tiers. The +t%spa option must be added in order to allow the program to look at the %spa tier when searching for a match. The +d option is used to specify that the information produced by the program, such as file name, line number and exact position of words on the tier, should be excluded from the output. This way the output is in a legal **CHAT** format and can be used as an input to another **CLAN** program, **FREQ** in this case. The same effect could also be obtained by using the piping feature which is discussed in the section on **FREQ**.

11. **+u:** Treat all specified files as one large file.

12. **+w/-w**: Define a window or lines around matching words.

13. **+x**: **COMBO** searches are sequential. If you specify the expression dog^cat, the program will match only the word "dog" directly followed by the word "cat". If you want to find clusters that contain both of these words, in any order, you need to use the +x option. This option allows the program to find the expressions in both the original order and in reverse order. Thus, to find a combination of "want" and "to" anywhere and in any order, you use this command:

```
combo  +swant^to  +x  sample.cha
```

14. **+y**: Work on nonCHAT files. The +y value works on lines and the +y1 value works on utterances as delimited by periods, question marks, and exclamation marks.

15. **+z**: Work on a specified range of words or utterances. See the description of +z in chapter 22 for ways of specifying ranges.

21.8. COOCCUR – Cooccurence Analysis

The **COOCCUR** program tabulates cooccurences of words. This is helpful for analyzing syntactic clusters. By default, the cluster length is two words, but you can reset this value just by inserting any integer up to 20 immediately after the +n option. The second word of the initial cluster will become the first word of the following cluster, and so on.

```
cooccur  +t*MOT  +n3  sample.cha  +f
```

The +t*MOT switch tells the program to select only the *MOT main speaker tiers. The header and dependent code tiers are excluded by default. The +n3 option tell the program to combine three words into a word cluster. The program will then go through all of *MOT main speaker tiers in the sample.cha file, three words at a time. When **COOCCUR** reaches the end of an utterance, it marks the end of a cluster, so that no clusters are broken across speakers or across utterances.

Coocurrences of codes on the %mor line can be searched using commands such as this example:

```
cooccur  +t%mor  -t*  +s*def  sample2.cha
```

The options for **COOCCUR** are:

1. **+d**: Strip the numbers from the output data that indicate how often a particular cluster occurred.

2. **+f/-f**: Send output to the screen or to a file. The default value of this switch is -f which sends output to the screen. If you want to send the output to a file, you must use the +f switch. The letters placed after the +f will be used as the file extension name. When you work on a collection of files, this switch sends each of the resultant analyses to a separate file. If you want a single merged analysis for a collection of files, use the redirecting symbols (> or >>) instead.

3. **+k**: Treat words in a case-sensitive fashion.

4. **+m:** By default **CLAN** leaves the output files in your current working directory. The +m switch tells **CLAN** to store output files in the directory where the corresponding input files were found.

5. **+n:** Set cluster length to a particular number. For example, +n3 will set cluster length to 3.

6. **+p:** Redefine the punctuation set.

7. **+r:** This switch has several different levels which allow you to specify how to treat omissions of parts of words, text replacement, prosodic delimiters, and retracings. For details see chapter 22.

8. **+s:** Select either a word or a file of words with @filename to search for.

9. **+t/-t:** Particular dependent tiers can be included or excluded by using the +t or -t options immediately followed by the tier code.

10. **+u**: By default, when the user has specified a series of files on the command line, the analyses are performed on each individual file. The program ends up reporting results for each data file separately. If the +u option is used, the program combines the input data found in all the specified files into one set and outputs results for that set as a whole.

11. **+y**: Work on non**CHAT** files. The +y value works on lines and the +y1 value works on utterances as delimited by periods, question marks, and exclamation marks.

12. **+z**: Work on a specified range of words or utterances. See the description of +z in chapter 22 for ways of specifying ranges.

21.9. DATES – Computing Ages and Dates

The **DATES** program takes two time values and computes the third. It can take the child's age and the current date and compute the child's date of birth. It can take the date of birth and the current date to compute the child's age. Or it can take the child's age and the date of birth to compute the current date. For example, if you type

```
dates +a 2;3.1 +b 12-jan-1962
```

you should get the following output:

```
@Age of Child:    2;3.1
@Birth of Child:    12-JAN-1962
@Date:    13-APR-1964
```

The options for **DATES** are:

1. **+a:** Following this switch, after a space, you can provide the child's age in **CHAT** format.

2. **+b:** Following this switch, after a space, you can provide the child's birthdate in day-month-year format.

3. **+d:** Following this switch, after a space, you can provide the current date or the date of the file you are analyzing in day-month-year format.

21.10.   DIST – Distances Between Codes

This program produces a listing of the average distances between words or codes in a file. **DIST** computes how many utterances exist between occurrences of a specified key word or code.

The exact calculation of average distance between occurrences for each word is:

$$\frac{\text{turn number of last occurrence - turn number of first occurrence}}{\text{total number of occurrences}}$$

The options for **DIST** are:

1. **+b**: This option allows you to specify a special character after the +b. This character is something like the colon which you have chosen to use to divide some complex code into its component parts. For example, you might designate a word as a noun on the dependent tier then further designate that word as a pronoun by placing a code on the dependent tier such as $NOU:pro. The program would analyze each element of the complex code individually and as a class. For the example cited earlier, the program would show the distance between those items marked with a $NOU (a larger class of words) and show the distance between those items marked with $NOU:pro as a subset of the larger set. The +b option for the example would look like this with a colon following the +b.

    ```
    dist  +b:  sample.cha
    ```

2. **+d**: Output data in a form suitable for statistical analysis.

3. **+f/-f**: Send output to the screen or to a file. The default -f value of this switch sends output to the screen. If you want to send the output to a file, you must use the +f switch. The letters placed after the +f will be used as the file extension name.

4. **+g**: Including this switch in the command line causes the program to count only one occurrence of each word for each utterance. So multiple occurrences of a word or code will count as one occurrence.

5. **+k**: Make analyses case-sensitive.

6. **+m**: By default **CLAN** leaves the output files in your current working directory. The +m switch tells **CLAN** to store output files in the directory where the corresponding input files were found.

7. **+o**: This option allows you to *only* consider words that contain the character specified by the **b** option, rather than all codes in addition to those containing your special character.

8. **+p**: Redefine the punctuation set.

9. **+r**: This switch has several different levels which allow you to specify how to treat omissions of parts of words, text replacement, prosodic delimiters, and retracings. For details see chapter 22.

10. **+s/-s**: This option is used to specify a word to search for in a given data line(s). This option should be immediately followed by the word itself. To refer to a set of words in a file use the form +s@filename.

11. **+t/-t**: Particular dependent tiers can be included or excluded by using the +t option immediately followed by the tier code.

12. **+u**: Treat all specified files as one big file.

13. **+y**: Work on nonCHAT files. The +y value works on lines and the +y1 value works on utterances as delimited by periods, question marks, and exclamation marks.

14. **+z**: Work on a specified range of words or utterances. See the description of +z in chapter 22 for ways of specifying ranges.

The following example demonstrates a use of the **DIST** program.

```
dist +t%spa -t* +b: sample.cha
```

This command line tells the program to look at the *%spa* tiers in the file "sample.cha" for codes containing the symbol ":". It then does a frequency count of each of these codes, as a group, and counts the number of turns between occurrences. The -t* option causes the program to ignore data from the main speaker tiers.

21.11.   DSS – Developmental Sentence Score

This program is designed to provide an automatic computation of the Developmental Sentence Score (DSS) of Lee (1974). This score is based upon the assignment of scores for a variety of syntactic, morphological, and lexical structures across eight grammatical domains. The current version of DSS is preliminary and incomplete. A fully automatic computation of the DSS will only be possible when we complete work on the PARS program. Until this additional work is finished, automatic computation of DSS must be carefully supplemented by manual correction of the automatically computed profile.

21.11.1.   CHAT File Format Requirements

For DSS to run correctly on a file the following CHAT conventions must be followed:

1. All utterances must have delimiters, and imperatives must end with an "!"
2. Incomplete or interrupted utterances must end either with the +... or the +/. codes.
3. Only the pronoun "I" and the first letter of proper nouns should be uppercase.
4. Utterances which contain a noun and a verb in a subject predicate relationship but which contain unusual word order must contain a [dss] code after the utterance delimiter.
5. DSS automatically excludes any child utterances which are imitations of the immediately preceding adult utterance. If, however, the analyst feels that there are additional child's utterances which are imitations which should be excluded from the analysis the [+ imit] postcode must be included for these utterances.

21.11.2.   Selection of a   50-sentence corpus

DSS scores are based upon analysis of a corpus of 50 sentences . The DSS program is designed to extract a set of 50 sentences from a language sample using Lee's six inclusion criteria.

1. **The corpus should contain fifty complete sentences**. A sentence is considered complete if it has a noun and a verb in the subject-predicate relationship. Imperatives such as "Look!" also are included. Imperative sentences MUST have an "!" terminator on the main speaker tier in the CHAT file. Immature sentences containing word order reversals such as "Car a garage come out, Hit a finger hammer Daddy" also should be included. However, these sentences MUST contain the [dss] code after the utterance delimiter on the main tier to be included in the analysis.

2. **The speech sample must be a block of consecutive sentences**. To be representative, the sentences comprising the corpora must occur consecutively in a block, ignoring incomplete utterances. The analyst may use his or her discretion as to which block of sentences are the most representative. The DSS program automatically includes the first fifty consecutive sentences in the transcript. To start the analysis at any other point in the transcript the user must insert an @dss header tier at the beginning of the file, and a @dss: start line at the point in the file where the user wants the DSS analysis to start instead.

3. **All sentences in the language sample must be different**. Only unique child sentences will be included in the corpora. Thus, **DSS** automatically analyzes each sentence and excludes any repeated sentences .

4. **Unintelligible sentences should be excluded from the corpus**. The **DSS** program automatically excludes any sentences containing unintelligible segments. Thus, any sentence containing xxx, xx, yyy, and yy codes on the main tier will be excluded from the analysis.

5. **Echoed sentences should be excluded from the corpus**. Since the DSS analysis focuses only on the child's "self-formulated" sentences, any sentence which is a repetition of the adult's preceding sentence is automatically excluded. Additionally, sentences containing a [+ imit] post-code also may be excluded by using the **-s** option.

6. **Incomplete sentences should be excluded**. Any sentence which has the "+..." or the "+/." sentence delimiters, indicating that they were either incomplete or interrupted sentences will not be included in the analysis.

7. (Not yet implemented) **DSS analysis should be used if and only if at least 50% of the utterances are complete sentences as defined by Lee**. If fewer than 50% of the sentences are complete sentences, then the Developmental Sentence Type analysis (DST) is appropriate instead. A warning message will be included on the **DSS** printout if this criteria has not been met.

21.11.3.   Automatic Calculation of DSS

In order to compute DSS, the user must must first complete a morphological analysis of the file using the **MOR** program with the **+c** option. **MOR** provides automatic morphological analysis of the words in an sentence and generates a corresponding dependent %mor tier. The new file containing the %mor tiers will have the extension "**.mor**". This will be the file that will be used with **DSS** .

Once the **MOR** analysis is complete, the user must run **DSS** to compute the Developmental Sentence Analysis. The **DSS** program has two modes: automatic and interactive. The automatic mode generates a DSS table *without* a final Developmental Sentence Score. The use of the **+e** option invokes the automatic mode. A basic automatic **DSS** command has this shape:

        dss +b*CHI +e   sample.mor

21.11.4.   Interactive Calculation

In the interactive mode, **DSS** analyzes each sentence in the corpora and then allows the user to add additional sentences points or attempt marks where appropriate. An additional sentence point is assigned to each sentence if it "meets all the adult standard rules" (Lee, p. 137). Sentence points also should be withheld for errors outside the 8 categories analyzed by **DSS**, such as errors in the use of articles, prepositions, plural and possessive markers, and word-order changes. In addition, sentence points should be withheld for semantic errors including neologisms such as "sitting-thing" for "chair" or "letterman" for "mailman" (Lee, p. 137).

Grammatical category points should be assigned only to those structures which meet all of Lee's requirements. If a grammatical structure is attempted but produced incorrectly then "attempt" marks should be inserted in the place of a numerical score. When using the interactive mode, the **DSS** program displays each sentence and asks the user to determine if it should or should not receive the additional sentence point and allows the user the opportunity to add attempt marks or edit the scoring.

```
           Sentence        |IP  |PP  |PV  |SV  |NG  |CNJ|IR  |WHQ|
  what  this  say.         | 1 |    |    |    |    |    |    | 2 |
```

To edit type: category +/- point value (e.g. np+4)
    or: p = sentence pt/continue; n = no sentence pt/continue
=>

The user has three options:
  1. to assign a point by typing "p" and continuing;
  2. to assign no sentence point by typing "n" and continuing; or
  3. to assign attempt marks or modify the point values for each of the categories by typing "e" and then typing "p" or "n".

The command to modify a category includes the categories, a plus or minus for addition or removal and a level number. Adding attempt marks or modifying a point values is done as follows:

To add the "-" attempt marker to primary verbs: **pv+0**

To remove the "-" attempt marker from primary verbs: **pv-0**

For example, in the sentence "what this say" the user might want to add attempt markers to both the primary verb (PV) and the interrogative reversal (IR) categories indicating the nature of the grammatical errors. To add an attempt mark for the Primary Verb category, the user would type: **pv+0** and get the following changes:

```
           Sentence        |IP  |PP  |PV  |SV  |NG  |CNJ|IR  |WHQ|
  what  this  say.         | 1 |    | - |    |    |    |    | 2 |
```

To edit type: category +/- point value (e.g. np+4)
    or: p = sentence pt/continue; n = no sentence pt/continue

To add an attempt mark for the Interrogative Reversal category the user would type:
    ir+0
and get the following changes:

```
           Sentence        |IP  |PP  |PV  |SV  |NG  |CNJ|IR  |WHQ|
  what  this  say.         | 1 |    | - |    |    |    | - | 2 |
```

To edit type: category +/- point value (e.g. np+4)
    or: p = sentence pt/continue; n = no sentence pt/continue

The **DSS** program allows the user to make multiple changes simultaneously. It is important therefore, that there should be no spaces between the "ir" the "+" and the "0". This interactive component also enables users to add or subtract point values from grammatical categories in the same way as adding or removing attempt marks.

Warning: The automatic form of **DSS** is unable to correctly assign points for three items. If these forms are present, they would have to be scored using interactive **DSS** after use of automatic **DSS**.

1. The pronominal use of "one" as in "One should not worry about one's life". These constructions should receive seven points as personal pronouns.

2. The distinction between non-complementing infinitive structures (e.g. I stopped to play) which receives 3 points as secondary verb and later infinitival complement structures (e.g. I had to go), which receive 5 points as secondary verbs. When these construction occur in the analysis the **DSS** program presents both the 3 and the 5 point value and the user needs to differentiate these.

3. Wh-questions with embedded clauses which do not contain a conjunction (e.g. Why did the man we saw yesterday call you?) in contrast to those where the embedded clause is marked with a conjunction (e.g What did the man *that* we saw yesterday say to you?)

21.11.5. DSS Output

Once all 50 sentences have been assigned sentence points, the **DSS** program automatically generates a table. For both the automatic and interactive modes each sentence is displayed on the left hand column of the table with the corresponding point values. For the interactive mode, the attempt markers for each grammatical category, sentence point assignments, and the DSS score also are displayed. The Developmental Sentence Score is calculated by dividing the sum of the total values for each sentence by the number of sentences in the analysis.

The output of the table has specifically been designed for users to determine "at a glance" areas of strength and weakness for the individual child for these eight grammatical categories. The low points values for both the indefinite and personal pronoun (IP, PP) categories in the table below indicate that this child used earlier developing forms exclusively. In addition, the attempt markers for the primary verb (PV) and interrogative reversal (IR) categories suggest possible difficulties in question formulation.

```
        Sentence      |IP |PP |PV |SV |NG |CNJ|IR |WHQ|S|TOT|
I like this.          |1  | 1 |1  |   |   |   |   |   |1|  4|
I like that.          |1  | 1 |1 .|   |   |   |   |   |1|  4|
I want hot dog.       |   |   |1 |1  |   |   |   |   |0|  2|
I like it .           | 1 | 1 |1  |   |   |   |   |   |1|  4|
what this say.        | 1 |   |- |   |   |   | - | 2 |0|  3|
```

Developmental Sentence Score: 4.2

21.11.6. DSS Summary

The **DSS** program has been designed to adhere as strictly as possible to the criteria for both sentence selection and scoring outline by Lee (1974). The goal of the **DSS** program is the calculation of DSS scores based upon Lee's (1974) criteria.   The DSS categories are outlined below.

Indefinite Pronouns (IP)
Score	Structure
1	it, this, that
3	no, some, more, all, lot(s), one(s), two (etc.) other(s), another
	something, somebody, someone
4	nothing, nobody, none, no one
7	any, anything, anybody, anyone,
	every, everything, everybody, everyone
	both, few, many, each, several, most, least, last, second, third (etc.)

Personal Pronouns (PP)
1	1st and 2nd person: I, me, my, mine, your(s)
2	3rd person: he, him, his, she, her(s)
3	plurals: we, us, our(s) they, them, their
	these, those
5	reflexives: myself, yourself, himself, herself, itself, themselves, ourselves
6	Wh-pronouns: who, which, whose, whom, what, that, how much
	Wh-word + infinitive: I know *what* to do, I know *who(m)* to take.
7	(his) own, one, oneself, whichever, whoever, whatever

Main Verb (MV)
1	uninflected verb
	copula, is or 's
	is + verb + ing
2	-s and -ed
	irregular past
	copula *am, are, was, were*
	auxiliary *am, are, was, were*
4	can, will may + verb
	obligatory do + verb
	emphatic do + verb
6	could, would, should, might + verb
	obligatory does, did + verb
	emphatic does, did +verb
7	passive including with *get*, and *be*
	must,shall + verb
	have + verb + en
	have got
8	have been + verb + ing, had been + verb + ing
	modal + have + verb + en
	modal + be + verb + ing
	other auxiliary combinations (e.g., should have been sleeping)

Secondary Verbs (SV)
2	five early developing infinitives
	I wanna see, I'm gonna see, I gotta see, Lemme see, Let's play
3	noncomplementing infinitives: I stopped *to play*
4	participle, present or past: I see a boy *running*
5	early infinitives with differing subjects in basic sentences:
	I want you *to come*
	later infinitival complements: I had *to go*

obligatory deletions: Make it [*to*] go
infinitive with wh-word: I know what *to get*
7 passive infinitive with *get :* I have *to get dressed*
   with *be*: I want *to be pulled.*
8 gerund: *Swinging* is fun.

Negative (NG)
1 it, this, that + copula or auxiliary is, 's + not: It's not mine.
   This is not a dog.
4 can't don't
5 isn't won't
7 uncontracted negatives
   pronoun-auxiliary or pronoun-copula contraction
   auxiliary-negative or copula negative contraction

Conjunction (CNJ)
3 and
5 but
   so, and so, so that
   or, if
8 where, when , how, while, whether, (or not), till, until, unless, since,
      before, after, for, as, as + adjective + as, as if, like, that, than
   obligatory deletions: I run faster that you [run].
   elliptical deletions (score 0)
   wh-words + infinitive
         I know *how* to do it.

Interrogative Reversal (IR)
1 reversal of copula: *is*n't *it* red?
4 reversal of auxiliary be: *Is* he coming?
6 obligatory -do, -does, -did *Do* they run?
   reversal of modal: *Can* you play?
   tag questions: It's fun *isn't* it?
8 reversal of auxiliary have: *Has he* seen you?
   reversal with two or three auxiliaries: *Has he been* eating?

Wh-question (WHQ)
2 who, what, what + noun
   where, how many, how much, what....do, what....for
5 when,. how, how + adjective
7 why, what it, how come, how about + gerund
8 whose, which, which + noun

The option for **DSS** are:

1. **+b**: Designates which speaker to be analyzed.

2. **+c**: Allows the user to determine the number of sentences to be included in analysis. The default for this option is 50 sentences .   These sentences must contain both a subject and a verb, be intelligible, and be unique and non-imitative. A strict criteria is used in the development of the corpora. Any sentences containing xxx yyy and www codes will be excluded from the corpora.

3. **+e**: Automatically generates a DSS table.

4. **+f/-f**: Send output to the screen or to a file. The default value of this switch is +f which sends output to a file. If you want to send the output to the screen, you must use the -f switch.

5. **+m:** By default **CLAN** leaves the output files in your current working directory. The +m switch tells **CLAN** to store output files in the directory where the corresponding input files were found.

6. **+u**: This switch merges all of the specified files together. This can be important if you do not have 50 sentences in a given file and need to combine several files in order to come up with a total of 50 sentences .

7. **+s/-s**: This switch has specific usage with **DSS**. To include sentences marked with the [dss] code the following option should be included on the command line: +s"[dss]". To exclude sentences with the [+ imit] postcode, the user should include the following option on the command line: -s"<+ imit>". These are the only two uses for the +s/-s option.

21.12.   FLO – Simplifying the Main Line

The **FLO** program constructs the flowing original rendition of the main speaker tier. This tier is an exact replica of the main speaker tier minus all special **CHAT** coding information. This tier is identified by the %flo code; and immediately follows the main tier from which it was created. The output of the **FLO** program is a **CHAT** formatted data file, which will consist of all the tiers found in the input data file(s). The **FLO** program completely removes all of the **CHAT** coding symbols to create a more "flowing" main line. The only symbols it leaves are the # and the +... symbols.

The following example demonstrates a possible use of the **FLO** program:

```
flo  +f  +t@  +d  sample.cha
```

This command creates a new file "sample.flo" with %flo lines replacing the old main lines.

The options for **FLO** are:

1.   **+d**:   This option tells the program to replace the main tier with the material that otherwise would have been placed onto the %flo tier in the output. If you do not use this switch, the %flo line will be added as a new dependent tier.

2.   **+f/-f**: Send output to the screen or to a file. The default value of this switch is -f which sends output to the screen. If you want to send the output to a file, you must use the +f switch. The letters placed after the +f will be used as the file extension name.

3.   **+m**: By default **CLAN** leaves the output files in your current working directory. The +m switch tells **CLAN** to store output files in the directory where the corresponding input files were found.

4.   **+t/-t**: Particular dependent tiers can be included or excluded by using the +t option immediately followed by the tier code. By default, headers and coding tiers are excluded.

Another way of simplifying the transcript is to delete particular types of lines. This can be done by using **KWAL** or **COMBO** for "limiting." For an explanation of how to do this, see the descriptions of those two programs.

21.13.   FREQ – Making Frequency Counts

One of the most powerful programs in **CLAN** is the **FREQ** program for frequency analysis. It is also one of the easiest programs to use and to a good program to start with when learning to use **CLAN**. The **FREQ** program constructs a frequency word count for user-specified files. A frequency word count is the calculation of the number of times a word, as delimited by a punctuation set, occurs in a file or set of files. The **FREQ** program produces a list of all the words used in the file, along with their frequency counts, and calculates a type-token ratio. The type-token ratio is found by calculating the total number of unique words used by a selected speaker (or speakers) and dividing that number by the total number of words used by the same speaker(s). It is generally used as a rough measure of lexical diversity. Of course, the type-token ratio can only be used to compare samples of equivalent size, because, as sample size increases, the increase in the number of types starts to level off.

21.13.1.   What FREQ Ignores

The **CHAT** manual specifies two special symbols that are used when transcribing difficult material. The xxx symbol is used to indicate unintelligible speech and the www symbol is used to indicate speech that is untranscribable for technical reasons. The **FREQ** program ignores these symbols by default. Also excluded are all the words beginning with one of the following characters: 0, &, +, -, #. If you wish to include them in your analyses, list them, along with other words you are searching for, in a file and use the +s/-s option to specify them on the command line. The **FREQ** program also ignores header and code tiers by default. Use the +t option if you want to include headers or coding tiers.

21.13.2.   Studying Lexical Groups

The easiest way of using **FREQ** is to simply ask it to give a complete frequency count for all the words in a transcript. However, **FREQ** can also be used to study the development and use of particular lexical groups. If you are interested, for example, in how children use personal pronouns between the ages of 2 and 3 years, a frequency count of these forms would be helpful. Other lexical groups that might be interesting to track could be the set of all conjunctions, all prepositions, all morality words, names of foods, and so on. In order to get a listing of the frequencies of such words, you need to put all the words you want to track into a text file and then use the +s switch with the name of the file preceded by the @ sign, as in this example:

```
freq  +s@articles  +f  sample.cha
```

This command would conduct a frequency analysis on all the articles that you have put in the file called "articles."

21.13.3.   Using Wild Cards with FREQ

Some of the most powerful uses of **FREQ** involve the use of wild cards. Wild cards are particularly useful when you want to analyze the frequencies for various codes that you have entered into coding lines. Here is an example of the use of wild cards with codes. One line of Hungarian data in "sample2.cha" has been coded on the %mor line for syntactic role and part of speech, as described in the **CHAT** manual. It includes these codes: N:A|duck-ACC, N:I|plane-ACC, N:I|grape-ALL, and N:A|baby-ALL, where the suffixes mark accusative and allative cases and N:A and N:I indicate animate and inanimate nouns.

If you want to obtain a frequency count of all the Animate Nouns (N:A) that occur in this file, use this command line:

```
freq  +t%mor  +s"N:A|*"  sample2.cha
```

The output of this command will be:

```
1  n:a|baby-all
1  n:a|ball-acc
1  n:a|duck-acc
```

Note that material after the +s switch is enclosed in double quotation marks to guarantee that wild cards will be correctly interpreted. For Macintosh and MS-DOS, the double quotes are the best ways of guaranteeing that a string is correctly interpreted. On UNIX, double quotes can also be used. However, in UNIX, single quotes are necessary when the search string contains a $ sign.

The next examples give additional search strings with asterisks and the output they will yield when run on the sample file. Note that what may appear to be a single underline in the second example is actually *two* underline characters.

String	Output
*-acc	1 n:a|ball-acc
	1 N:A|duck-acc
	1 N:I|plane-acc
*-a__	1 N:A|baby-all
	1 n:a|ball-acc
	1 N:A|duck-acc
	1 N:I|plane-acc
	1 N:I|grape-all
N:*|*-all	1 N:A|baby-all
	1 N:I|grape-all

These examples have shown the use of the asterisk as a wild card. When the asterisk is used, **FREQ** gives a full output of each of the specific code types that match.

If you don't want to see the specific instances of the matches, you can use the percentage wild card, as in the following examples:

String	Output
N:A|%	3 N:A|
%-ACC	3 -ACC
%-A__	3 -ACC
	2 -ALL
N:%|%-ACC	3 N:|-ACC
N:%|%	5 N:|

It is also possible to combine the use of the two types of wild cards, as in these examples:

String	Output
N:%|*-ACC	1 N:|ball-acc
	1 N:|duck-acc
	1 N:|plane-acc
N:*|%	3 N:A|
	2 N:I|

Researchers have also made extensive use of **FREQ** to tabulate speech act and interactional codes. Often such codes are constructed using a taxonomic hierarchy. For example, a code like $NIA:RP:NV has a three-level hierarchy. In the INCA-A system discussed in chapter 13, the first level codes the interchange type; the second level codes the speech act or illocutionary force type; and the third level codes the nature of the communicative channel. As in the case of the morphological example cited earlier, one could use wild cards in the +s string to analyze at different levels. The following examples show what the different wild cards will produce when analyzing the %spa tier. The basic command here is:

```
freq  +s"$*"  +t%spa  sample.cha
```

String	Output
$*	frequencies of all the three-level codes in the %spa tier
$*:%	frequencies of the interchange types
$%:*:%	frequencies of the speech act codes
$RES:*:%	frequencies of speech acts within the RES category
$*:sel:%	frequencies of the interchange types that have SEL speech acts

If some of the codes only have two levels, rather than the complete set of three levels, you need to use an additional % sign in the +s switch. Thus the switch

```
+s"$%:*:%%"
```

will find all speech act codes, including both those with the third level coded and those with only two levels coded.

21.13.4.   Directing the Output of FREQ

When **FREQ** is run on a single file, output can be directed to an output file by using the +f option:

```
freq +f sample.cha
```

This results in the output being sent to a file called "sample.frq". If you wish, you may specify a file extension other than .frq for the output file. For example, to have the output sent to a file with the extension .mot, you would specify:

```
freq +fmot sample.cha
```

Suppose, however, that you are using **FREQ** to produce output on a group of files rather than on a single file. The following command will produce a separate output file for each .cha file in the current directory:

```
freq +f *.cha
```

To specify that the frequency analysis for each of these files be computed separately but stored in a single file, you must use the redirect symbol (>) and specify the name of the output file. For example:

```
freq *.cha > freq.all
```

This command will maintain the separate frequency analyses for each file separately and store them all in a single file called freq.all. If there is already material in the "freq.all" file, you may want to append the new material to the end of the old material. In this case, you should use the form:

```
freq *.cha >> freq.all
```

Sometimes, however, researchers want to treat a whole group of files as a single database. To derive a single frequency count for all the .cha files, you need to use the +u option:

```
freq +u *.cha
```

Again, you may use the redirect feature to specify the name of the output file, as in the following.

```
freq +u *.cha > freq.all
```

21.13.5.   Limiting in FREQ

One of the most fundamental aspects of analysis through **CLAN** is the process of **limiting**. Limiting allows you to focus your analysis on the part of your data files that is relevant by excluding all other sections. Limiting is based on use of the +s, +t, and +z switches. Limiting is available in most of the **CLAN** programs, but cannot be done within special purpose programs such as **CHSTRING** or **CHECK**.

1. **Limiting by including or excluding dependent tiers**. Limiting can be used to select out particular dependent tiers. By using the +t and -t options, you can choose to include certain dependent tiers and ignore others. For example, if you select a particular main speaker tier, you will be able to choose the dependent tiers of only that particular speaker. Each type of tier has to be specifically selected by the user, otherwise the programs follow their default conditions for selecting tiers.

2. **Limiting by including or excluding main tiers**. When the -t* option is combined with a switch like +t*MOT, limiting first narrows the search to the utterances by MOT and then further excludes the main lines spoken by MOT. The -t* switch functions in a different way from -t*CHI which will simply exclude all of the utterances of CHI and the associated dependent tiers.

3. **Limiting by including or excluding sequential regions of lines or words**. The next level of limiting is performed when the +z option is used. At this level only the specified data region is chosen out of all the selected tiers.

4. **Limiting by string inclusion and exclusion**. The +s/-s options limit the data which is passed on to subsequent programs.

Here is an example of the combined use of the above four limiting techniques. There are two speakers, *NIC and *MOT, in "sample.cha". Suppose you want to create a frequency count of all variations of the $ini codes found on the %spa dependent tiers of *NIC only in the first 20 utterances. This analysis is accomplished by using this command:

```
freq  +t*NIC  +t%spa  +s"$INI*"  -t*  +z20u  sample.cha
```

The +t*NIC switch tells the program to select the main and dependent tiers associated only with the speaker *NIC. The +t%spa tells the program to further narrow the selection. It limits the analysis to the %spa dependent tiers and the *NIC main speaker tiers. The -t* option signals the program to eliminate data found on the main speaker tier for NIC from the analysis. The +s option tells the program to eliminate all the words which do not match the $INI* string from the analysis. Quotes are needed for this particular +s switch in order to guarantee correct interpretation of the asterisk. In general, it is safest to always use pairs of double quotes with the +s switch. The +z20u option tells the program to look at only the first twenty utterances. Now the **FREQ** program can perform the desired analysis. This command line will send the output to the screen only. You must use the +f option if you want it sent to a file. By default, the header tiers are excluded from the analysis.

21.13.6.   Studying Unique Words and Shared Words

With a few simple manipulations, **FREQ** can be used to study the extent to which words are shared between the parents and the child. For example, we may be interested in understanding the nature of words that are used by the child and not used by the mother as a way of understanding the ways in which the child's social and conceptual world is structured by forces outside of the immediate family. In order to isolate shared and unique words, you can go through three simple steps.

1. Run **FREQ** on the child's and the mother's utterances using these two commands:

```
freq  +d1  +t*mot  +f  *.cha
freq  +d1  +t*chi  +f  *.cha
```

The first command will produce a set of *.frq and the second will produce a set of *.fr0 files.

2. Next you should run **FREQ** on the output files:

```
freq  +y  +o  +u  01.f*
freq  +y  +o  +u  02.f*
. . .
```

The output of these commands is a list of frequencies with 1 and 2. All words with frequencies of 2 are shared and all words with frequencies of 1 are unique to either the mother or the child.

3. In order to determine whether a unique word is unique to the child or the mother, you can create a file of all the unique words and run this against the frequency list from the mother. All words with frequencies of 2 are unique to the mother. The words with frequencies of 1 are unique to the child.

The options for **FREQ** are:

1. **+c**: Find capitalized words only.

2. **+d**: Perform a particular level of data analysis. By default the output consists of all selected words found in the input data file(s) and their corresponding frequencies. The +d option can be used to change the output format. Try these commands:

```
freq  sample.cha  +d0
freq  sample.cha  +d1
freq  sample.cha  +d2  +t@ID=1.25*
```

Each of these three commands produces a different output.
+d0: When the +d0 option is used, the output consists of all selected words found in the input data file(s), their corresponding frequencies, and line numbers where each word is located in the file.
+d1: This option outputs each of the words found in the input data file(s) one word per line with no further information about frequency. Later this output could be used as an word list file for **KWAL** or **COMBO** programs to locate the context in which those words or codes are used.
+d2: With this option, the output is sent to a file in a very specific form that is useful for input to **STATFREQ**. This option also creates a "stat.out" file to keep track of multiple ".frq" output files. You do not need to use the +f option with +d2, since this is assumed. Note that you must include a +t specification in order to tell the +d2 option which speaker to track for the **STATFREQ** analysis. You can provide this specification either in the @ID form or in the +t*CHI form. For further discussion of the @ID codes, see the section on **STATFREQ**.
+d3: This output is essentially the same as that for +d2, but with only the statistics on types, tokens, and the type/token ratio. This option also creates a "stat.out" file to keep track of multiple ".frq" output files. Word frequencies are not placed into the output. You do not need to use the +f option with +d3, since this is assumed.
+d4: This switch allows you to output just the type/token information.

3. **+f/-f**: Send output to the screen or to a file. The default value of this switch is -f which sends output to the screen. If you want to send the output to a file, you must use the +f switch. The letters placed after the +f will be used as the file extension name. When you work on a collection of files, this switch sends each of the resultant analyses to a separate file. If you want a single merged analysis for a collection of files, use the redirecting symbol (>) instead (see Redirecting section above).

4. **+k**: Make analyses case-sensitive.

5. **+m:** By default **CLAN** leaves the output files in your current working directory. The +m switch tells **CLAN** to store output files in the directory where the corresponding input files were found.

6. **+o**: Normally, the output from **FREQ** is sorted alphabetically. This option can be used to sort the output in descending frequency. The +o1 level will sort to create a reverse concordance.

7. **+p**: Redefine the punctuation set.

8. **+r**: This switch has several different levels which allow you to specify how to treat omissions of parts of words, text replacement, prosodic delimiters, and retracings. For details see chapter 22.

9. **+s/-s**: This option, directly followed by a word, allows the user to determine the frequency of that particular word in a file. The use of metacharacters allows the program to locate other forms of the word being searched. (See the section on metacharacters for more information.) To track the frequencies of a group of words in a text file, use the form +s@filename.

10. **+t/-t**: Particular dependent tiers can be included or excluded by using the +t or -t options immediately followed by the tier code.

11. **+u**: By default, when the user has specified a series of files on the command line, the analyses are performed on each individual file. The program ends up reporting results for each data file separately. If the +u option is used, the program combines the input data found in all the specified files into one set and outputs results for that set as a whole.

12. **+y**: Work on nonCHAT files. The +y value works on lines and the +y1 value works on utterances as delimited by periods, question marks, and exclamation marks.

13. **+z**: Work on a specified range of words or utterances. See the description of +z in chapter 22 for ways of specifying ranges.

21.14.   FREQMERG - Merging FREQ Output

If you have collected a large number of **FREQ** output files and you want to merge these counts together, you can use **FREQMERG** to combine the outputs of several runs of the **FREQ** program. For example, you could run this command:

```
freq  sample*.cha  +f
```

This would create sample.frq and sample2.frq. Then you could merge these two counts using this command:

```
freqmerg  *.frq
```

The options for **FREQMERG** are:

1. **+f/-f**: Send output to the screen or to a file. The default value of this switch is -f which sends output to the screen. If you want to send the output to a file, you must use the +f switch. The letters placed after the +f will be used as the file extension name.

2. **+k**: Make analyses case-sensitive.

3. **+m:** By default **CLAN** leaves the output files in your current working directory. The +m switch tells **CLAN** to store output files in the directory where the corresponding input files were found.

4. **+o**: Search for a specific word on the main speaker tier. To search for a file of words use the form +o@filename.

5. **+p**: Redefine the punctuation set.

6. **+/-s**: This option is used to select file segments identified by words found on the @bg: tier. See the example given above for +g. To search for a group of words found in a file, use the form +s@filename.

21.15. GEM – Tagging Interesting Passages

The **GEM** program is designed to allow you to mark particular parts of a transcript for further analysis. Separate header lines are used to mark the beginning and end of each interesting passage you want included in your **GEM** output. These header tiers may contain "tags" that will affect whether a given section is selected or excluded in the output. If no particular tag information is being coded, you should use the header form @bg with no colon. If you are using tags, you must use the colon, followed by a tab. If you do not follow these rules, **CHECK** will complain.

By default, **GEM** looks for the beginning marker **@bg** without tags and the ending marker **@eg**, as in this example command:

```
gem  sample.cha
```

If you want to be more selective in your retrieval of "gems," you need to add code words or tags onto both the @bg: and @eg: lines. For example, you might wish to mark all cases of verbal interchange during the activity of reading. To do this, you must place the word "reading" on the @bg: line just before each reading episode, as well as on the @eg: line just after each reading episode. Then you can use the +sreading switch to retrieve only this type of gem, as in this example:

```
gem  +sreading  sample2.cha
```

Ambiguities can arise when one gem without a tag is nested within another or when two gems without tags overlap. In these cases, the program assumes that the gem being terminated by the @eg line is the one started at the last @bg line. If you have any sort of overlap or embedding of gems, make sure that you use unique tags.

GEM can also be used to retrieve responses to particular questions or particular stimuli used in an elicited production task. The @Bg entry for this header should show the number and/or description of stimulus. Here is an example of a completed header line:

```
@Bg:    Picture  53,  truck
```

One can then search for all of the responses to picture 53 by using the +s"53" switch in **GEM**.

The slash symbol / can be used on the @Bg line to indicate that a stimulus was described out of its order in a test composed of ordered stimuli. Also the & symbol can be used to indicate a second attempt to describe a stimulus, as in 1a& for the second description of stimulus 1a, as in this example:

```
@Bg:    1b  /
*CHI:   a  &b  ball.
@Bg:    1a  /
*CHI:   a  dog.
@Bg:    1a  &
*CHI:   and  a  big  ball.
```

Similar codes can be constructed as needed to describe the construction and ordering of stimuli for particular research projects.

When the user is sure that there is no overlapping or nesting of gems and that the end of one gem is marked by the beginning of the next, there is a simpler way of using **GEM**, which we can call "lazy **GEM**". Each gem is then marked by @G: with one or more tags and the +n switch is used. Here is an example:

```
@G:       reading
*CHI:     nice  kitty.
@G:       offstage
*CHI:     who  that?
@G:       reading
*CHI:     a  big  ball.
@G:       dinner
```

In this case, one can retrieve all the episodes of "reading" with this command:

```
gem  +n  +sreading
```

GEM also serves as a tool for limiting analyses. The type of limiting that is done by **GEM** is very different from that done by **KWAL** or **COMBO**. In a sense, **GEM** works like the +t switches in these other programs to select out particular segments of the file for analysis. When you do this, you will want to use the +d switch, so that the output is in **CHAT** format. You can then save this as a file or pipe it on to another program, as in this command.

```
gem  +sreading  +d  sample2.cha  |  freq
```

Note also that you can use any type of code on the @bg line. For example, you might wish to mark well-formed multi-utterance turns, teaching episodes, failures in communications, or contingent query sequences.

The options for **GEM** are:

1. **+d:** The +d0 level of this switch produces simple output that is in legal **CHAT** format. The +d1 level of this switch adds information to the legal **CHAT** output regarding file names, line numbers, and @ID codes.

2. **+f/-f:** Send output to the screen or to a file. The default value of this switch is -f which sends output to the screen. If you want to send the output to a file, you must use the +f switch. The letters placed after the +f will be used as the file extension name.

3. **+g:** If this switch is used, all of the tag words specified with +s switches must appear on the @bg: header line in order to make a match. Without the +g switch, having just one of the +s words present is enough for a match.

    ```
    gem  +sreading  +sbook  +g  sample2.cha
    ```

    This will retrieve all of the activities involving reading of books.

4. **+k:** Make analyses case-sensitive.

5. **+m:** By default **CLAN** leaves the output files in your current working directory. The +m switch tells **CLAN** to store output files in the directory where the corresponding input files were found.

6. **+n**: Use @g: lines as the basis for the search. If these are used, no overlapping or nesting of gems is possible and each @g must have tags. In this case, no @eg is needed, but **CHECK** and **GEM** will simply assume that the gem starts at the @g and ends with the next @g.

7. **+p**: Redefine the punctuation set.

8. **+r**: This switch has several different levels which allow you to specify how to treat omissions of parts of words, text replacement, prosodic delimiters, and retracings. For details see chapter 22.

9. **+s**: This option is used to select file segments identified by words found on the @bg: tier. Do not use the -s switch. See the example given above for +g. To search for a group of words found in a file, use the form +s@filename.

10. **+t/-t**: Particular dependent tiers can be included or excluded by using the +t or -t option immediately followed by the tier code. **GEM** output includes only main speaker lines unless you include +t% in the command. You can also specify a certain kind of dependent tier, such as +t%mor.

11. **+u:** Treat all the specified files as one combined file.

12. **+z**: Work on a specified range of words or utterances. See the description of +z in chapter 22 for ways of specifying ranges.

21.16.   GEMFREQ – Frequency Counts by Activity Types

This program combines the basic features of the **FREQ** and **GEM** programs. "Gems" are portions of the transcript that are marked off with @bg and @eg markers. For example, one could mark off a section of bookreading activity with "@bg bookreading" and "@eg bookreading". Once these markers are entered, you can then run **GEMFREQ** to retrieve a basic **FREQ**-type output for each of the various gem types you have marked. For example, you can run this command:

```
gemfreq  +sarriving  sample2.cha
```

and you would get the following output:

```
gemfreq  sample2.cha  +sarriving
Tue May  24  15:40:19  1994
gemfreq  (14-APR-94)  is  conducting  analyses  on:
   ALL  speaker  tiers
   and  ONLY  header  tiers  matching:  @BG:;  @EG:;
*****************************************
From  file  <sample2.cha>
    2    arriving:
       1 are
       1 fine
       1 how
       1 you
```

The options for **GEMFREQ** are:

1. **+d:** The d0 level of this switch produces simple output that is in legal **CHAT** format. The d1 level of this switch adds information to the legal **CHAT** output regarding file names, line numbers, and @ID codes.

2. **+f/-f**: Send output to the screen or to a file. The default value of this switch is -f which sends output to the screen. If you want to send the output to a file, you must use the +f switch. The letters placed after the +f will be used as the file extension name.

3. **+g:** If this switch is used, all of the tag words specified with +s switches must appear on the @bg: header line in order to make a match. Without the +g switch, having just one of the +s words present is enough for a match.

   ```
   gem  +sreading  +sbook  +g  sample2.cha
   ```

   This will retrieve all of the activities involving reading of books.

4. **+k**: Make analyses case-sensitive.

5. **+m:** By default **CLAN** leaves the output files in your current working directory. The +m switch tells **CLAN** to store output files in the directory where the corresponding input files were found.

6. **+n:** Use @g: lines as the basis for the search. If these are used, no overlapping or nesting of gems is possible and each @g must have tags. In this case, no @eg

is needed, and both **CHECK** and **GEMFREQ** will simply assume that the gem starts at the @g and ends with the next @g.

7.   **+o**:   Search for a specific word on the main speaker tier. To search for a file of words use the form +o@filename.

8.   **+p**:   Redefine the punctuation set.

9.   **+r**:   This switch has several different levels which allow you to specify how to treat omissions of parts of words, text replacement, prosodic delimiters, and retracings. For details see chapter 22.

10.   **+/-s**:   This option is used to select file segments identified by words found on the @bg: tier. See the example given above for +g. To search for a group of words found in a file, use the form +s@filename.

11.   **+t/-t**:   Particular dependent tiers can be included or excluded by using the +t or -t option immediately followed by the tier code. **GEMFREQ** output includes only main speaker lines unless you include +t% in the command. You can also specify a certain kind of dependent tier, such as +t%mor.

12.   **+u**:   Treat all the specified files as one combined file.

13.   **+z**:   Work on a specified range of words or utterances. See the description of +z in chapter 22 for ways of specifying ranges.

21.17. GEMLIST – Profiling "Gems" within Files

The **GEMLIST** program provides a convenient way of viewing the distribution of gems across a collection of files. For example, if you run **GEMLIST** on the sample.cha and sample2.cha, you will get this output:

```
From  file  <sample.cha>
   12  @BG
            3  main  speaker  tiers.
   21  @EG
            1  main  speaker  tiers.
   24  @BG
            3  main  speaker  tiers.
   32  @EG
From  file  <sample2.cha>
   18  @BG:         just  arriving
            2  main  speaker  tiers.
   21  @EG:         just  arriving
   22  @BG:         reading  magazines
            2  main  speaker  tiers.
   25  @EG:         reading  magazines
   26  @BG:         reading  a  comic  book
            2  main  speaker  tiers.
   29  @EG:         reading  a  comic  book
```

The options for **GEMLIST** are:

1. **+d**: Only summarize the data between the @bg and the @eg.

2. **+f/-f**: Send output to the screen or to a file. The default value of this switch is -f which sends output to the screen. If you want to send the output to a file, you must use the +f switch. The letters placed after the +f will be used as the file extension name.

3. **+m:** By default **CLAN** leaves the output files in your current working directory. The +m switch tells **CLAN** to store output files in the directory where the corresponding input files were found.

4. **+t/-t**: Particular dependent tiers can be included or excluded by using the +t or -t option immediately followed by the tier code. **GEMLIST** output includes only main speaker lines unless you include +t% in the command. You can also specify a certain kind of dependent tier, such as +t%mor.

21.18.   KEYMAP – Contingency Analysis

The **KEYMAP** program is useful for performing simple types of interactional and contingency analyses. **KEYMAP** requires users to pick specific initiating or beginning codes or *keys* to be tracked on a specific coding tier. If a match of the beginning code or key is found, **KEYMAP** looks at all the codes on the specified coding tier in the next utterance. This is the *map*. The output reports the numbers of times a given code maps onto a given key for different speakers. Here is an example of a set of codes that will be tracked by **KEYMAP**:

```
*MOT:     here you go.
%spa:     $INI
*MOT:     what do you say?
%spa:     $INI
*CHI:     thanks.
%spa:     $RES
*MOT:     you are very welcome.
%spa:     $CON
```

If you run the **KEYMAP** program on this data with the $INI as the +b key symbol, the program will report that $INI is followed once by $INI and once by $RES.

The key ($INI in the previous example) and the dependent tier code must be defined for the program. On the coding tier, **KEYMAP** will only look for symbols beginning with the $ sign. All other strings will be ignored. Keys are defined by using the +b option immediately followed by the symbol you wish to search for. To see how **KEYMAP** works, try this example:

```
keymap  +b$INI*  +t%spa  sample.cha
```

For UNIX, this command would have to be changed to quote metacharacters as follows:

```
keymap  +b\$INI\*  +t%spa  sample.cha
```

KEYMAP produces a table of all the speakers who used one or more of the key symbols, and how many times each symbol was used by each speaker. Each of those speakers is followed by the list of all the speakers who responded to the given initiating speaker, including continuations by the initial speaker, and the list of all the response codes and their frequency count.

The options for **KEYMAP** are:

1. **+b**: This is the beginning specification symbol.

2. **+f/-f**: Send output to the screen or to a file. The default value of this switch is -f, which sends output to the screen. If you want to send the output to a file, you must use the +f switch. The letters placed after the +f will be used as the file extension name.

3. **+k**: Make analyses case-sensitive. Normally, all search keys are converted to lower case characters. This means that $INI and $ini are seen as the same code. The +k option allows the program to judge upper and lower case as different

characters. Thus, using this option allows the $INI and $ini codes to be seen as unique.

4. **+m:** By default **CLAN** leaves the output files in your current working directory. The +m switch tells **CLAN** to store output files in the directory where the corresponding input files were found.

5. **+p:** Redefine the punctuation set.

6. **+r:** This switch has several different levels which allow you to specify how to treat omissions of parts of words, text replacement, prosodic delimiters, and retracings. For details see chapter 22.

7. **+s/-s:** This option is used to specify the code or codes beginning with the $ sign to treat as possible continuations. For example, in the sample.cha file, you might only want to track $CON:* codes as continuations. In this case, the command would be as follows.

```
keymap  +b$*  +s"$CON:*"  +t%spa  sample.cha
```

8. **+t/-t:** Particular dependent tiers can be included or excluded by using the +t or -t option immediately followed by the tier code, as in this example.

```
keymap  +b$*  +t%spa  sample.cha
```

If you want to look only at initiating codes by a particular speaker, you can use the +t switch in a way that is unique to **KEYMAP**. This way of using +t tracks the specified speaker as the initiator, but continuations by any subsequent speaker.

```
keymap  +t*MOT  +t%spa  +b$*  sample.cha
```

The output of this example will consist of the map from all the initiations found on the mother's %spa tier line to all continuations on following %spa lines from any following speaker.

9. **+u:** Treat all the specified files as one combined file.

10. **+z:** Work on a specified range of words or utterances. See the description of +z in chapter 22 for ways of specifying ranges.

21.19.   KWAL – Key Word and Line

The **KWAL** program outputs utterances that match to certain user-specified search words. The program also allows the user to view the context in which any given keyword is used. In order to specify the search words, use the +s option, which allows you to search for either a single word or a whole group of words stored in a file. It is possible to specify as many +s options on the command line as you like.

Like **COMBO**, the **KWAL** program works not on lines, but on "clusters." A cluster is a combination of the main tier and the selected dependent tiers relating to that line. Each cluster is searched independently for the given keyword. The program lists all keywords which are found in a given cluster tier. A simple example of the use of **KWAL** is:

```
kwal  +schalk  sample.cha
```

The output of this command tells you the file name and the absolute line number of the cluster containing the key word. It then prints out the matching cluster.

21.19.1.   Limiting in KWAL

Sometimes you may want to create new files in which some of the information in your original files is systematically deleted. For example, you may wish to drop out certain coding tiers that interfere with the readability of your transcript. In order to drop out a tier of %mor codes, you can use this command:

```
kwal  +o@  -t%mor  +d  +f  sample.cha
```

The +o@ switch will preserve the header tiers. Note that **KWAL** distinguishes between the +t switch which is used for limiting and the +o switch which is specifically used for formatting the shape of the output. In this process, the main lines and their dependent tiers are preserved by default. The -t%mor switch excludes the %mor tiers. The +d switch specifies that the output should be in **CHAT** format and the +f switch sends the output to a file. In this case, there is no need to use the +s switch. Try out this command with the sample file to make sure you understand how it works.

The options for **KWAL** are:

1. **+a**: Sort the output alphabetically. Choosing this option can slow down processing significantly. On MS-DOS machines which have less than 1MB of free memory, using this option can cause **CLAN** to crash.

2. **+d**: Normally, **KWAL** outputs the location of the tier where the match occurs. When the +d switch is turned on you can output each matched sentence without line number information in a simple legal **CHAT** format. The +d1 switch outputs legal **CHAT** format along with file names and line numbers. Try these commands:

    ```
    kwal  +s"chalk"  sample.cha
    kwal  +s"chalk"  +d  sample.cha
    kwal  +s"chalk"  +d1  sample.cha
    ```

    Using KWAL with +d for limiting: The +d and +d1 switches can be extremely important tools for performing analyses on particular subsets of a text. For example, in one project, a central research question focused on variations in MLU as a function of the nature of the addressee. In order to analyze this, each utterance was given a %add line along with a code that indicated the identity of the addressee. Using "sample.cha" as an example, the following **KWAL** line was used.

```
kwal +t%add +t*NIC +s"mot" +d sample.cha | mlu
```

This produces an MLU analysis on only those child utterances that are directed to the mother as addressee.

3. **+f/-f**: Send output to the screen or to a file. The default value of this switch is -f, which sends output to the screen. If you want to send the output to a file, you must use the +f switch. The letters placed after the +f will be used as the file extension name.

4. **+k**: Make analyses case-sensitive.

5. **+m:** By default **CLAN** leaves the output files in your current working directory. The +m switch tells **CLAN** to store output files in the directory where the corresponding input files were found.

6. **+o**: The +t switch is used to control the addition or deletion of particular tiers or lines from the input and the output to **KWAL**. In some cases, you may want to include a tier in the output that is not being included in the input. This typically happens when you want to match a string in only one dependent tier, such as the %mor tier, but you want all tiers to be included in the output. In order to do this you would use a command of the following shape:

```
kwal +t%mor +s"*ACC" +o% sample2.cha
```

7. **+p**: Redefine the punctuation set.

8. **+r**: This switch has several different levels which allow you to specify how to treat omissions of parts of words, text replacement, prosodic delimiters, and retracings. For details see chapter 22.

9. **+s/-s**: This option is used to specify a word to search for in a given data line(s). This option should be immediately followed by the word itself. In order to search for a group of words stored in a file, using the form +s@filename.

10. **+t/-t**: The user can specify which main speaker and its dependent tiers, if any, are to be included in the cluster. This is done by using the +t options. Only the main speaker tiers are included in the cluster by default. The main lines can be excluded using the -t* switch. However, this exclusion only affects the search process, not the form of the output. It will guarantee that no matches are found on the main line, but the main line will be included in the output. If you want to exclude the main lines from your output, you can use a simple **FLO** command such as

```
flo +t*NIC -t* +t%spa sample.cha
```

If you need to do more elaborate limiting, you can combine **FLO** and **KWAL**:

```
kwal +t*NIC +t%spa +s"$SEL*" -t* sample.cha +d |
    flo -t* +t%
```

To search for a keyword on the *MOT main speaker tiers and the %spa dependent tiers of that speaker only, include +t*MOT +t%spa on the command line, as in this command.

```
kwal  +s"$INI:*"  +t%spa  +t*MOT  sample.cha
```

11. **+u**: Treat the specified files as one combined file.

12. **+w/-w:** It is possible to instruct the program to enlarge the context in which the keyword was found. The +w/-w options let you specify how many clusters after/before the target cluster are to be included in the output. The +w/-w options must be immediately followed by a number. This number specifies how many clusters should be included before/after the target cluster. Windowing is particularly useful in the **KWAL** program. The following command looks for all cases of "chalk" in the sample.cha file.

```
kwal  +schalk  +w3  -w3  sample.cha
```

When the keyword is found, the cluster containing the keyword and the three clusters above (-w3) and below (+w3) it will be shown in the output.

13. **+y**: Work on non**CHAT** files. The +y value works on lines and the +y1 value works on utterances as delimited by periods, question marks, and exclamation marks.

14. **+z**: Work on a specified range of words or utterances. See the description of +z in chapter 22 for ways of specifying ranges.

21.20.   LINES – Adding Line Numbers

When working with a printed transcript, it is often helpful to be able to refer to parts of a transcript by using line numbers.   The **LINES** program allows you to add line numbers and then remove them. You must remember to remove the line numbers before doing any analysis of your files with **CLAN**.

The options for **LINES** are:

1.   **+f/-f**: Send output to the screen or to a file. The default value of this switch is -f which sends output to the screen. If you want to send the output to a file, you must use the +f switch. The letters placed after the +f will be used as the file extension name. When you work on a collection of files, this switch sends each of the resultant analyses to a separate file. If you want a single merged analysis for a collection of files, use the redirecting symbols (> and >>) instead.

2.   **+m**: By default **CLAN** leaves the output files in your current working directory. The +m switch tells **CLAN** to store output files in the directory where the corresponding input files were found.

3.   **+n**: Remove all the line/tier numbers that were inserted by an earlier run of **LINES**.

4.   **+t/-t**: Particular dependent tiers can be included or excluded by using the +t or -t options immediately followed by the tier code.

5.   **+u**: By default, when the user has specified a series of files on the command line, the analyses are performed on each individual file. The program ends up reporting results for each data file separately. If the +u option is used, the program combines the input data found in all the specified files into one set and outputs results for that set as a whole.

6.   **+z**: Work on a specified range of words or utterances . See the description of +z in chapter 22 for ways of specifying ranges.

21.21.   MAXWD – Tracking String Length

This program locates, measures, and prints either the longest word or the longest utterance in a file. **MAXWD** reads through a set of files looking for the longest word or utterance. When searching for the longest word, the **MAXWD** output consists of: the word, its length in characters, the line number on which it was found, and the name of the file where it was found. When searching for the longest utterance with the +g option, the output consists of: the utterance itself, the total length of the utterance, the line number on which the utterance begins, and the file name where it was found. By default, **MAXWD** only analyzes data found on the main speaker tiers. The +t option allows for the data found on the header and dependent tiers to be analyzed as well. Try out the following command which should report the longest word in "sample.cha."

```
maxwd  sample.cha
```

The options for **MAXWD** are:

1. **+b/-b:** You can use this switch to either include or exclude particular morpheme delimiters. By default the morpheme delimiters &, #, and - are understood to delimit separate morphemes. You can force **MAXWD** to ignore all three of these by using the -b#-& switch. You can use the +b switch to add additional delimiters to the list.

2. **+c:** This option is used to produce a given number of longest items. The following command will print the seven longest words in "sample.cha".

    ```
    maxwd  +c7  sample.cha
    ```

3. **+d:** The +d level of this switch produces output with one line for the length level and the next line for the word. The +d1 level produces output with only the longest words, one per line, in order in legal **CHAT** format.

4. **+f/-f:** Send output to the screen or to a file. The default value of this switch is -f which sends output to the screen. If you want to send the output to a file, you must use the +f switch. The letters placed after the +f will be used as the file extension name. Each file is searched for its longest word or utterance. The program thus reports the longest word or utterance for each data file.

5. **+g:** This switch forces **MAXWD** to compute not word lengths, but utterance lengths. It singles out the sentence which has the largest number of words or morphemes and prints that in the output. The way of computing the length of the utterance is determined by the number following the +g option. If the number is 1 then the length is in number of morphemes per utterance. If the number is 2 then the length is in number of words per utterance. And if the number is 3 then the length is in the number of characters per utterance.

    For example, if you want to compute the MLU and MLT of five longest utterances in words of the *MOT, you would use the following command:

    ```
    maxwd +g2 +c5 +d1 +t*mot sample.cha  |  mlu
    ```

    The +g2 option specifies that the utterance length will be counted in terms of numbers of words. The +c5 option specifies that ONLY the five longest utterances should be sent to the output. The +d1 option specifies that individual words, one per line, should be sent to the output. The | symbol sends the output to analysis by **MLU**.

6. **+k**: Make analyses case-sensitive.

7. **+m:** By default **CLAN** leaves the output files in your current working directory. The +m switch tells **CLAN** to store output files in the directory where the corresponding input files were found.

8. **+o**: If you have elected to use the +c switch, you can use the +o switch to further fine-tune its output so that only one instance of each length type is included in the output. Here is a sample command:

```
maxwd  +c8  +o  sample.cha
```

9. **+p**: Redefine the punctuation set.

10. **+r**: This switch has several different levels which allow you to specify how to treat omissions of parts of words, text replacement, prosodic delimiters, and retracings. For details see chapter 22.

11. **+s/-s**: This option is used to specify a word or a file of words to be included. This option should be immediately followed by the word itself. In order to search for a group of words stored in a file, use the form +s@filename.

12. **+t/-t**: Particular dependent tiers can be included or excluded by using the +t option immediately followed by the tier code. Usually you want **MAXWD** figures for individual speakers, not for a transcript as a whole. This means that you must use the +t switch. In our sample file there are two speakers, *MOT and *NIC. If you want **MAXWD** data for NIC, use the +t*NIC option.

13. **+u**: By default, when the user has specified a series of files on the command line, the analyses are performed on each individual file. The program ends up reporting results for each data file separately. If the +u option is used, the program combines the input data found in all the specified files into one set and outputs results for that set as a whole.

14. **+x:** This option allows you to start the search for the longest item at a certain item length, i.e. all the utterances or words longer than a specified number should not be included in a search. The length number should immediately follow the +x option. Try this command:

```
maxwd  sample.cha  +x6
```

15. **+y**: Work on non**CHAT** files. The +y value works on lines and the +y1 value works on utterances as delimited by periods, question marks, and exclamation marks.

16. **+z**: Work on a specified range of words or utterances. See the description of +z in chapter 22 for ways of specifying ranges.

21.22.   MLT – Mean Length of Turn

The **MLT** program computes the the mean number of utterances in a turn, the mean number of words per utterance, and the mean number of words per turn.   These computations are provided for each speaker separately.   Note that none of these ratios involve morphemes. If you want to analyze morphemes per utterances, you should use the **MLU** program.

The exact nature of the MLT calculation depends both on what the program includes and what it excludes.   The default principles that it uses are as follows:

1.   **MLT** excludes material in angle brackets followed by either [/] or [//].   This can be changed by using the **+r6** switch or by adding any of these switches:

     ```
     +s"</>"    +s"<//>"
     ```

2.   In order to exclude utterances with a specific postcode, such as [+ bch], you can use the -s switch:

     ```
     -s"[+  bch]"
     ```

3.   The following strings are also excluded:

     ```
     www  0*  &*  +*  -*  #*  $*.
     ```

     Here the asterisk indicates any material following the first symbol until a delimiter.

4.   The program considers the following symbols to be word delimiters:

     ```
     .  ?  !  ,  ;  [  ]  <  >
     ```

     The space is also a word delimiter.

5.   The program considers the following three symbols to be utterance delimiters:

     ```
     .  !  ?
     ```

     as well as the various complex symbols such as +..., which end with one of these three marks.

6.   The special symbols xxx and yyy are **not** excluded from the data. Thus if the utterance consists of those symbols only it will still be counted.

7.   Utterances with no speech on the main line can be counted as turns if you add the [+ trn] code, as in this example:

     ```
     CHI:     0.  [+ trn]
     %spa:    gestures  to  mother
     ```

     In order to count this "utterance" as a turn, you can use this switch:

     ```
     +s+"[+  trn]"
     ```

     The second plus after the "s" is used to mark the inclusion of something that is usually excluded.

The following example demonstrates a common use of the **MLT** program:

```
mlt   sample.cha
```

The options for **MLT** are:

1. **+cS**: Look for unit marker S. If you want to count phrases or narrative units instead of sentences, you can add markers such as [c] to make this segmentation of your transcript into additional units.

2. **+d**: You can use this switch, together with the ID specification described for **STATFREQ** to produce numbers for a statistical analysis, one per line. The command for the sample file is:

```
mlt   +d   +t@ID=1.25.8.2   sample.cha
```

The output of this command should be:

```
1.25.8.2  6  6  8  1.333  1.000  1.333
```

This gives these six numbers in this order:
 - the participant id
 - the number of turns
 - the number of words
 - words/turn
 - utterances/turn
 - words/utterance

In order to run this type of analysis you must have an @ID header for each participant you wish to track. Alternatively, you can use the +t switch in the form +t*CHI. In this case, all of the *CHI lines will be examined in the corpus. However, if you have different names for children across different files, you need to use the @ID fields.

+d1: This level of the d switch outputs data in another systematic format, with data for each speaker on a single line. However, this form is less adapted to input to a statistical program than the output for the basic +d switch. Also this switch works with the +u switch, whereas the basic +d switch does not. Here is an example of this output:

```
*NIC:      6      6      8    1.333    1.000    1.333
*MOT:      8      7     43    6.143    1.143    5.375
```

3. **+f/-f**: Send output to the screen or to a file. The default value of this switch is -f which sends output to the screen. If you want to send the output to a file, you must use the +f switch. The letters placed after the +f will be used as the file extension name.

4. **+g**: You can use the +g option to excludeutterances composed entirely of particular words. For example, you might wish to exclude utterances composed only of "hi", "bye", or both of these words together. To do this, you should place the words to be excluded in a file, each word on a separate line. The option should be immediately followed by the filename. That is to say, there should not be a

space between the +g option and the name of this file. If the filename is omitted, the program displays an error message: "No file name for the +g option specified!"

5.   **+k**: Make analyses case-sensitive.

6.   **+m:** By default **CLAN** leaves the output files in your current working directory. The +m switch tells **CLAN** to store output files in the directory where the corresponding input files were found.

7.   **+p**: Redefine the punctuation set.

8.   **+r**: This switch has several different levels which allow you to specify how to treat omissions of parts of words, text replacement, prosodic delimiters, and retracings. For details see chapter 22. For **MLT**, the +r6 switch includes rather than excludes retracings and repetitions.

9.   **+s/-s**: This option is used to specify a word to be used from an input file. This option should be immediately followed by the word itself. In order to search for a group of words stored in a file, use the form +s@filename. The -s value of this switch excludes certain words from the MLT count. This is a reasonable thing to do. The +s switch bases the count only on the included words. It is difficult to imagine why anyone would want to do such an analysis.

10. **+t/-t**: **MLT** provides separately counts for each speaker. If you only want data for one speaker, you can repress the additional information by using the +t switch. In our sample file there are two speakers, *MOT and *NIC. If you want the MLT for NIC only use the +t*NIC option.

11. **+u**: By default, when the user has specified a series of files on the command line, the analyses are performed on each individual file. The program ends up reporting results for each data file separately. If the +u option is used, the program combines the input data found in all the specified files into one set and outputs results for that set as a whole.

12. **+y**: Work on non**CHAT** files.   The +y value works on lines and the +y1 value works on utterances as delimited by periods, question marks, and exclamation marks.

13. **+z**: Work on a specified range of words or utterances. See the description of +z in chapter 22 for ways of specifying ranges.

21.23.   MLU – Mean Length of Utterance

The **MLU** program computes the the mean length of utterance, which is the ratio of morphemes to utterances.   This measure is widely considered (Brown, 1973) to be a measure of the level of language development.   The way in which symbols are processed by **MLU** is as follows.

1.   **MLU** excludes from all counts material in angle brackets followed by either [/] or [//].   This can be changed by using the +r6 switch or by adding any of these switches:

    ```
    +s"</>"   +s"<//>"
    ```

2.   In order to exclude utterances with a specific postcode, such as [+ bch], you can use the -s switch:

    ```
    -s"[+   bch]"
    ```

3.   The following strings are also excluded:

    ```
    xxx  yyy  www  uh  um  0*  &*  +*  -*  #*  $*
    ```

    where the asterisk indicates any material following the exclusion symbol.   By default the symbols **xx** and **yy** are not excluded.   If there is other material on the line, the utterance will be included in utterance count, but the particular excluded strings will not be included in the word or morpheme count.   If the utterance consists of only excludable material, the whole utterance will be ignored.

    In addition, suffixes, prefixes, or parts of compounds beginning with a zero are automatically excluded and there is no way to modify this exclusion.

4.   The program considers the following symbols to be word delimiters:

    ```
    .  ?  !  ,  ;  [  ]  <  >
    ```

    The space character is also a word delimiter.

5.   The program considers the following four symbols to be morpheme delimiters:

    ```
    &  -  #  ^
    ```

6.   The program considers the following three symbols to be utterance delimiters:

    ```
    .  !  ?
    ```

    as well as the various complex symbols such as +... which end with one of these three marks.

By default, **MLU** computes MLU counts for each speaker in the file separately on the basis of the main tier.   The following example demonstrates a common use of the **MLU** program:

```
mlu  sample.cha
```

Researchers often wish to conduct MLU analyses on particular subsets of their data. As discussed in greater detail in the section on **KWAL**, this can be done using commands such as:

```
kwal +t*NIC +t%add +s"mot" sample.cha +d | mlu
```

This command looks at only those utterances spoken by the child to the mother as addressee. **KWAL** outputs these utterances through a "pipe" to the **MLU** program. The pipe symbol "l" is used to indicate this transfer of data from one program to the next. If you want to send the output of the **MLU** analysis to a file, you can do this with the redirect symbol, as in this version of the command:

```
kwal +t*NIC +t%add +s"mot" sample.cha +d | mlu > file.mlu
```

The options for **MLU** are:

1. **+b/-b:** You can use this switch to either include or exclude particular morpheme delimiters. By default the morpheme delimiters &, #, and - are understood to delimit separate morphemes. You can force **MLU** to ignore all three of these by using the -b#-& switch. You can use the +b switch to add additional delimiters to the list.

2. **+c/-c**: For the program to calculate morphemes, words must be morphemically coded, according to **CHAT** format specifications. (See "Codes for Morphemicization" in the **CHAT** manual for further detail). Alnternatively MLU computation can be done off the %mor line. The -c option allows the program to ignore morphemicization symbols as delimiters, and instead view them as words. For example, by default, a word like un#read-able is seen as being composed of three morphemes: un read and able. By using the -c# option, the word un#read-able is now seen as being composed of two morphemes: un#read and able. By using the -c#- option, the word un#read-able is seen as one entity. Thus by specifying all the morphemicization symbols immediately following the -c option, the program will report the number of words, not morphemes, the number of utterances, and their ratio. The +c option allows you to add any symbol to the list of morphemicization symbols. Try these examples:

```
mlu +c+ sample.cha
mlu -c- sample.cha
```

3. **+d**: You can use this switch, together with the ID specification described for **STATFREQ** to produce numbers for a statistical analysis, one per line. The command for the sample file is:

```
mlu +d +t@ID=1.25.8.2 sample.cha
```

The output of this command should be:

```
1.25.8.2 5 7 1.400 0.548
```

This gives these five numbers in this order:
- the participant id
- the number of utterances
- the number of morphemes

- morphemes/utterance
- the standard deviation

In order to run this type of analysis you must have an @ID header for each participant you wish to track. Alternatively, you can use the +t switch in the form +t*CHI. In this case, all of the *CHI lines will be examined in the corpus. However, if you have different names for children across different files, you need to use the @ID fields.

+d1: This level of the d switch outputs data in another systematic format, with data for each speaker on a single line. However, this form is less adapted to input to a statistical program than the output for the basic +d switch. Also this switch works with the +u switch, whereas the basic +d switch does not. Here is an example of this output:

```
*NIC:      5      7     1.400     0.490
*MOT:      8     47     5.875     2.891
```

4. **+f/-f**: Send output to the screen or to a file. The default value of this switch is -f, which sends output to the screen. If you want to send the output to a file, you must use the +f switch. The letters placed after the +f will be used as the file extension name.

5. **+g**: You can use the +g option to exclude from the MLT analysis utterances composed entirely of particular words. For example, you might wish to exclude utterances composed only of "hi" or "bye." To do this, you should place the words to be excluded in a file, each word on a separate line. The option should be immediately followed by the filename. That is to say, there should not be a space between the +g option and the name of this file. If the filename is omitted, the program displays an error message: "No file name for the +g option specified!"

6. **+k**: Make analyses case-sensitive.

7. **+m:** By default **CLAN** leaves the output files in your current working directory. The +m switch tells **CLAN** to store output files in the directory where the corresponding input files were found.

8. **+p**: Redefine the punctuation set.

9. **+r**: This switch has several different levels which allow you to specify how to treat omissions of parts of words, text replacement, prosodic delimiters, and retracings. For details see chapter 22. For **MLU**, the +r6 switch includes rather than excludes retracings and repetitions.

10. **+s/-s**: This option is used to specify a word to be used from an input file. This option should be immediately followed by the word itself. In order to search for a group of words stored in a file, use the form +s@filename. The -s switch excludes certain words from the analysis. This is a reasonable thing to do. The +s switch bases the analysis only on certain words. It is more difficult to see why anyone would want to conduct such an analysis. However, the +s switch also has another use. One can use the +s switch to remove certain strings from automatic exclusion by **MLU**. The program automatically excludes xxx, 0, uh, and words beginning with & from the MLU count. This can be changed by using this command:

```
mlu  +s+uh  +s+xxx  +s0*  +s&*  file.cha
```

11. **+t/-t:** If you are only interested in calculating the MLU for one subject, you can use the +t switch. For example, if you use +t*NIC, you will only get an MLU for the speaker named NIC, not for the other speakers. If you want the MLU calculations to be performed on the %mor tier rather than on the main speaker tier, use the +t%mor switch. In that case, you will want to be careful to define how **MLU** treats punctuation on the %mor line.

12. **+u:** By default, when the user has specified a series of files on the command line, the analyses are performed on each individual file. The program ends up reporting results for each data file separately. If the +u option is used, the program combines the input data found in all the specified files into one set and outputs results for that set as a whole.

13. **+y:** Work on nonCHAT files. The +y value works on lines and the +y1 value works on utterances as delimited by periods, question marks, and exclamation marks.

14. **+z:** Work on a specified range of words or utterances. See the description of +z in chapter 22 for ways of specifying ranges.

Including and Excluding Utterances in MLU and MLT:

It is well known that certain sentence forms will artificially inflate or deflate MLU calculations, yet there is no clear consensus concerning which sentence forms should be included or excluded in an MLU calculation. The **CLAN MLU** program can accommodate differing approaches to MLU calculations if post codes indicating the utterance type are to be included on the main tier. Then the exclude (-s) switch must be used in conjunction with a file of words to be excluded. The exclude file should be a list of the post codes which you are interested in excluding from the analysis. For example, the "sample.cha" file is post coded for the presence of responses to yes/no questions [+ Q], imitations [+ I] and vocatives [+ V].

For the first MLU pass through the transcript you can calculate Nicolette's MLU on the entire transcript by typing

```
mlu    +t*NIC  sample.cha
```

For the second pass through the transcript you can calculate the child's MLU according to the criteria of Scarborough (1990). These criteria require excluding the following: routines [+ R], book reading [+ "], fillers [+ F], imitations [+ I], self repetitions [+ SR], isolated onomatopoeic sounds [+ O], vocalizations [+ V], and partially unintelligible utterances [+ PI]. To accomplish this, an exclude file must be made which contains all of these post codes. Of course, for the little sample file, there are only a few examples of a couple of these coding types. Nonetheless, by way of illustration, you can test this out an analysis using the Scarborough criteria by creating a file called "scmlu" with the relevant codes in angle brackets. Although postcodes are contained in square brackets in **CHAT** files, they are contained in angle brackets in files used by **CLAN**. The "scmlu" file would look something like this:

```
<+   R>
<+   ">
<+   V>
<+   I>
```

Once you have created this file, you then use the following command:

```
mlu  +t*nic  -s@scmlu  sample.cha
```

For the third pass through the transcript you can calculate the child's MLU using a still more restrictive set of criteria, also specified in angle brackets in postcodes and in a separate file. This set also excludes one word answers to yes/no questions [$Q] in the file of words to be excluded. You can calculate Nicolette's MLU using these criteria by typing:

```
mlu  +t*nic  -s@resmlu  sample.cha
```

In general, exclusion of these various limited types of utterances tends to increase the child's MLU.

21.24.   MODREP – Matching Words Across Tiers

The **MODREP** program matches words on one tier with corresponding words on another
tier. It works only on tiers where each word on tier A matches one and only one word on
tier B. When such a one-to-one correspondence exists, **MODREP** will output the
frequency of all matches. Consider the following sample file distributed with **CLAN** as
"modrep.cha":

```
@Begin
@Participants:   CHI  Child  Child
*CHI: I  want  more.
%pho: aI wan mo
%mod: aI want mor
*CHI: want  more  bananas.
%pho: wa  mo  nAnA
%mod: want  mor  bAn&nAz
*CHI: want  more  bananas.
%pho: wa  mo  nAnA
%mod: want  mor  bAn&nAz
*MOT: you excluded [//]  excluded [/]  xxx  yyy  www
      &d  do?
%pho: yu  du
%mod: yu  du
@End
```

You can run the following command on this file to create a model-and-replica analysis for
the child's speech:

```
modrep +b*chi +c%pho +k modrep.cha
```

The output of **MODREP** in this case should be as follows:

```
From  file  <modrep.cha>
   1 aI
        1 aI
   2 bAn&nAz
        2 nAnA
   3 mor
        3 mo
   3 want
        1 wan
        2 wa
```

This output tells us that "want" was replicated in two different ways, and that "more" was
replicated in only one way twice. Only the child's speech is included in this analysis and
the %mod line is ignored. Note that you must include the +k switch in this command in
order to guarantee that the analysis of the %pho line is case-sensitive. By default, all
CLAN programs are case-insensitive. However, on the %pho line, UNIBET uses
capitalization to distinguish between pairs of different phonemes.

21.24.1.   Exclusions and Inclusions

By default, **MODREP** ignores certain strings on the model tier and the main tier. These
include xxx, yyy, www, material preceded by an ampersand, and material preceding the
retracing markers [/] and [//]. To illustrate these exclusions, try this command:

```
modrep   +b*  +c%pho +k modrep.cha
```

The output of this command will look like this:

```
From file <modrep.cha>
  1 I
       1 aI
  2 bananas
       2 nAnA
  1 do
       1 du
  3 more
       3 mo
  3 want
       1 wan
       2 wa
  1 you
       1 yu
```

If you want to include some of the excluded strings, you can add the +q option. For example, you could type:

```
modrep   +b*  +c%pho +k modrep.cha +qwww
```

However, adding the "www" would destroy the one-to-one match between the model line and the replica line. When this happens, **CLAN** will complain and then die. Give this a try to see how it works. It is also possible to exclude additional strings using the +q switch. For example, you could exclude all words beginning with "z" using this command:

```
modrep   +b*  +c%pho +k modrep.cha -qz*
```

However, since there are no words beginning with "z" in the file, this will not change the match between the model and the replica.

21.24.2.   Using a %mod Line

A more precise way of using **MODREP** is to construct a %mod line to match the %pho line. In the "modrep.cha" file, a %mod line has been included. When this is done the following type of command can be used:

```
modrep +b%mod  +c%pho  +k  modrep.cha
```

This command will compare the %mod and %pho lines for both the mother and the child in the sample file. Note that it is also possible to trace pronunciations of individual target words by using the +o switch as in this command for tracing words beginning with /m/:

```
modrep +b%mod  +c%pho  +k  +sm*  modrep.cha
```

The +s switch can be combined with the +o switch in this way:

```
modrep +b%mod  +c%pho  +k  +sm*  +omo*  modrep.cha
```

21.24.3.   MODREP and COMBO -- Cross-tier COMBO

MODREP can also be used to match codes on the %mor tier to words on the main line. For example, if you want to find all the words on the main line that match words on the %mor line with an accusative suffix in the mother's speech in "sample2.cha", you can use this command:

```
modrep  +b%mor  +c*mot  +o"*ACC"  sample2.cha
```

The output of this command is:

```
From  file  <sample2.cha>
   1  n:a|ball-acc
         1  labda't
   1  n:a|duck-acc
         1  kacsa't
   1  n:i|plane-acc
          1  repu"lo"ge'pet
```

If you want to conduct an even more careful selection of codes on the %mor line, you can make combined use of **MODREP** and **COMBO**. For example, if you want to find all the words matching accusatives that follow verbs, you first select these utterances by running **COMBO** with the +d switch and the correct +s switch and then pipe the output to the **MODREP** command we used earlier.   This combined use of the two programs can be called "cross-tier **COMBO**."

```
combo  +s"v:*^*^n:*-acc"  +t%mor  sample2.cha  +d  |
modrep  +b%mor  +c*mot  +o"*acc"
```

The output of this program is the same as in the previous example. Of course, in a large input file, the addition of the **COMBO** filter can make the search much more restrictive and powerful.

The options for **MODREP** are as follows:

1. **+b**:   This switch is used to set the model tier name. There is no default setting. The model tier can also be set to the main line, using +b* or +b*chi.

2. **+c**:   You can use this switch to change the name of the replica tier. There is no default setting.

3. **+f/-f**: Send output to the screen or to a file. The default value of this switch is -f which sends output to the screen. If you want to send the output to a file, you must use the +f switch. The letters placed after the +f will be used as the file extension name.

4. **+k**:   Make analyses case-sensitive.

5. **+m:** By default **CLAN** leaves the output files in your current working directory. The +m switch tells **CLAN** to store output files in the directory where the corresponding input files were found.

6. **+o**: This switch limits the shape of the output from **MODREP** to some particular string or file of strings. For example, you can cut down the output to only those strings ending in "-ing" or with accusative suffixes, etc. If you want to track a series of strings or words, you can put them in a file and use the @filename form for the switch.

7. **+p**: Redefine the punctuation set.

8. **+r**: This switch has several different levels which allow you to specify how to treat omissions of parts of words, text replacement, prosodic delimiters, and retracings. For details see chapter 22. For this program the +r6 switch includes rather than excludes repeated and retraced material.

9. **+q/-q**: The +q switch allows you to include particular symbols such as xxx or &* that are excluded by default . The -q switch allows you to make further exclusions of particular strings. If you want to include or exclude a series of strings or words, you can put them in a file and use the @filename form for the switch.

10. **+t/-t**: Particular dependent tiers can be included or excluded by using the +t option immediately followed by the tier code.

11. **+u**: By default, when the user has specified a series of files on the command line, the analyses are performed on each individual file. The program ends up reporting results for each data file separately. If the +u option is used, the program combines the input data found in all the specified files into one set and outputs results for that set as a whole.

12. **+y**: Work on nonCHAT files. The +y value works on lines and the +y1 value works on utterances as delimited by periods, question marks, and exclamation marks.

13. **+z**: Work on a specified range of words or utterances. See the description of +z in chapter 22 for ways of specifying ranges.

21.25.   MOR – Morphological Analysis

The **MOR** program is used to generate a %mor tier for all main tiers in a **CHAT** file. Successful use of **MOR** requires a full understanding of the program, the process of lexicon building, and tools for improving the morphological analysis. This is not a program for the beginning or casual user. Rather, **MOR** is for the serious user who is willing to commit a large amount of effort to working with the program and the lexicon in order to achieve a major improvement in analytic capabilities. It is easy for a novice user of **MOR** to produce incorrect analyses that will lead to erroneous conclusions. For the **CLAN** programs in general and the **MOR** program in particular, the CHILDES center is willing to help users with correct use of the programs, but assumes no responsibility for erroneous analyses produced by users who have not fully learned how to use these tools.

The computational design of **MOR** was guided by Roland Hausser's MORPH system (Hausser, 1990). The system has been designed to maximize portability across languages, extendibility of the lexicon and grammar, and compatibility with the **CLAN** programs. The basic engine of the parser is language independent. Language-specific information is stored in separate data files.   The rules of the language are in data files that can be modified by the user. The lexical entries are also kept in ASCII files and there are several techniques for improving the match of the lexicon to a particular corpus. In order to avoid having too large a lexical file, only stems are stored in the lexicon and inflected forms appropriate for each stem are compiled at run time.

MOR automatically generates a %mor tier of the type described in Chapter 14. Words are labeled by their syntactic category or "scat", followed by the separator '|', followed by the word itself, broken down into its constituent morphemes.

```
*CHI:   the  people  are  making  cakes  .
%mor:   det|the  n|people  v:aux|be&PRES  v|make-ING
        n|cake-PL  .
```

The **MOR** program looks at each word on the main tier, without regard to context, and provides all possible grammatical categories and morphological analyses, as in the following example with the words "to" and "back". The "^" character denotes the multiple possibilities for each word on the main tier.

```
*CHI:   I  want  to  go  back.
%mor:   pro|I  v|want  inf|to^prep|to
        v|go  adv|back^n|back^v|back  .
```

In order to select the correct form for each ambiguous case, the user should edit the file in **CED** using Disambiguator mode.

For **MOR** to run successfully, there must be several files present in either the library directory or the current working directory.   The default names on the files are: eng.ar, eng.cr, eng.lex, and eng.clo. If you want to use alternative filenames, you will need to use the +g and +l switches.

1. **The allomorph rules file**. This file lists the ways in which morphemes vary in shape. The rules which describe these variations are called "arules". The extension on this file should be ".ar". The default name for this file is "eng.ar" which is the set of allomorphy rules for English.

2. **The concatenation rules file**. This file lists the ways in which morphemes can combine. The rules which describe allowable concatenations are called "crules". The extension on this file should be ".cr". The default name for this file is "eng.cr" which is the set of concatenation rules for English.

3. **The closed class file**. Since the affixes and clitics in a language are a small closed set that are needed for virtually all analyses, they are listed in a file with the extension ".clo". The default name for this file is "eng.clo" which is the set of closed class morphemes and affixes for English.

4. **The disk lexicon file**. This file lists the word forms in the language. The extension on this file should be ".lex". The default name of the file is "eng.lex" which is the lexicon for English. This file is what we call the "disk lexicon." The basic "eng.lex" file we distribute has about 24,000 words. When **CLAN** is distributed on diskettes, we include a smaller file called "engtoy.lex", since the full "eng.lex" file will not fit on a single diskette along with **CLAN**. Only machines with very large memories, such as UNIX or Macintosh machines, will be able to run this bigger lexicon. The average MS-DOS machine will not be able to handle such a large lexicon, because these machines typically have a limit of 640K of available memory.

5. **The disambiguation rules file**. **MOR** analyzes each word by itself. If the +b switch is used, the program will try to use the words in the utterance which are on the immediate left and right of the word being analyzed to choose among possible analyses. These rules are called "drules", and they are listed in the file with the extension ".dr". The default name for this file is "eng.dr" which is the set of disambiguation rules for English.

MOR uses the eng.ar, eng.lex, and eng.clo files to produce a "run-time lexicon" that is significantly more complete than eng.lex alone. **MOR** uses the run-time lexicon together with the concatenation rules file to analyze input words.

The first action of the parser program is to load the eng.ar file. Next the program reads in "eng.lex" and uses the rules in "eng.ar" to build the run-time lexicon. If your "eng.lex" file is fairly big, it will not be possible to run **MOR** on MS-DOS. However, if your "eng.lex" file is too small, much of the power of **MOR** will be lost. The best solution is to try to use a UNIX or Macintosh computer for this task. Once the run-time lexicon is loaded, the parser then reads in the eng.cr file, additionally, if the +b option is specified, the "eng.dr" file is also read in. Once the concatenation rules have been loaded the program is ready to analyze input words. As a user, you do not need to concern yourself about the run-time lexicon. Your main concern is about the entries in the lexicon files. The rules in the *.ar and *.cr files are only of concern if you wish to have a set of analyses and labelings which differs from the one given in Chapter 14, or if you are trying to write a new set of grammars for some language.

The options for **MOR** are:

1. **+b**: Use the disambiguation rules.

2. **+c**: With this option, clitics such as 'd, n't , 'll will be treated as separate words. This option *must* be used when creating the %mor tier for **DSS** analysis.

3. **+eN**: Set the level of diagnostic detail to N. This diagnostic feedback is mostly useful to users who are building new arule and crule files for a new language. The eight possible levels, in increasing order of terseness, are:
    1 - display application of all the rules.
    2 - display application of a rules.
    3 - display application of c rules.
    4 - display application of d rules.
    5 - display memory usage.
    6 - display d rules.
    7 - display c rules.
    8 - display a rules.

4. **+f/-f**: Send output to the screen or to a file. The default value of this switch for **MOR** is +f which sends output to a file with the extension name ".mor". If you want to send the output to the screen, you must use the -f switch.

5. **+g**: This switch enables the user to specify an alternative set of grammar files for different languages. The default for this option is "eng" for English. The English files are: eng.ar, eng.cr, and eng.dr. (Note: the ".dr" file is only used it the +b option is given). To specify an alternative set of grammar rules the +g option must be followed by the stem of the filename. Thus, the switch "+gdan" for Danish would tell mor to look at three files: dan.ar, dan.cr, and dan.dr. These files must be stored in the "lib" directory or the current working directory.

6. **+k:** This option controls the way in which **MOR** handles unknown words which begin with uppercase letters. By default, **MOR** labels these as proper nouns (n:prop). Use of this option will disable this feature.

7. **+l:** This option enables the user to determine which lexicons to use with the **MOR** analysis. The default for this option is "eng", and the files are "eng.lex" and "eng.clo". All lexicon files must be stored in the "lib" directory. In order to specify an alternative lexicon, such as "dan.lex", use the "+ldan" option.

8. **+m:** By default, **CLAN** leaves the output files in your current working directory. The +m switch tells **CLAN** to store output files in the directory where the corresponding input files were found.

9. **+xi**: Run **MOR** in interactive test mode. You type in one word at a time to the test prompt and **MOR** provides the analysis on line. To quit you type :q (colon plus q). To get help you type :h (colon plus h).

10. **+xl**: Run **MOR** in "build lexicon" mode. This mode takes a series of .cha files as input and outputs a small lexical file with the extension ".ulx" with entries for all words not recognized by **MOR**. This helps in the building of lexicons.

21.25.1.   MOR   Lexicons

Before running **MOR** on a set of **CHAT** files it is important to make sure that **MOR** will be able to recognize all the words in these files. This means that either the word itself or the stem of the word must be listed in the lexicon. It is extremely unlikely that every word in any large corpus of child language data would be listed in even the largest **MOR** lexicon. Therefore, users of **MOR** need to understand how to supplement the basic lexicons with additional entries. Before we look at the process of adding new words to the lexicon, we first need to examine the way in which entries in the disk lexicon are structured.

The disk lexicon contains truly irregular forms of a word, as well as citation forms. For example, the verb "go" is stored in the disk lexicon, along with the past tense "went", since this latter form is suppletive, and is not subject to regular rules. The disk lexicon contains any number of lexical entries, stored at most one entry per line. The lexicon may be annotated with comments, which will not be processed. A comment begins with the percent sign and ends with a new line.

A lexical entry consists of these parts:
1. The surface form of the word.
2. Category information about the word, expressed as a set of feature-value pairs. Each feature-value pair is enclosed in square brackets and the full set of feature-value pairs is enclosed in curly braces. All entries must contain a feature value pair which identifies the syntactic category to which the word belongs, consisting of the feature "scat" with an appropriate value. Words which belong to several categories will be followed by several sets of feature structures, each separated by a backslash.
3. If the word has multiple readings, each additional reading is entered by inserting a backslash and then putting the next reading on the next line.
4. Following the category information is optional information about the stem. If the surface form of the word is not the citation form of the word, then the citation form, surrounded by quotes, should follow the category information. If the word contains fused morphemes, these should be given as well, using the "**&**" symbol as the morpheme separator. The following are examples of lexical entries:

```
can     {[scat  v:aux]}   \
        {[scat  n}

a       {[scat  det]}

an      {[scat  det]}     "a"

go      {[scat  v]  [ir  +]}

went    {[scat  v]  [tense  past]}    "go&PAST"
```

When adding new entries to the lexicon it is usually sufficient to enter the citation form of the word, along with the syntactic category information.

21.25.2.   File Preparation

Before starting on the process of lexicon building, you need to verify that your files are in good **CHAT** format. You do this by running the **CHECK** program. At this point, it is important that you use the +g3 switch in **CHECK**, since this will detect many word-internal spelling errors. Cleaning up the various errors noted by **CHECK** will move you closer to being able to run **MOR** successfully.

After you have **CHECK**-ed your files, you will want to scan over the words in your corpus by eye. This can be done by running this **FREQ** command:

```
freq +r2 -s*@* +d1 +k +f +u *.cha
```

Here is a reminder of the meaning of all the switches:

+r2	show words with their parentheses such as loo(k) and look to make searching easier
-s*@*	ignore word with special form markers
+d1	makes a list of words, without the frequency numbers
+k	case sensitive to reveal inappropriate capitalization
+f	send to file
+u	all files go to one output

The output will go into a .frq file with a name derived from the first file in your file set. Capitalized words will appear at the beginning of this file. You should check over the capitalized words to make sure they are proper nouns. Also, you may run into words with apostrophes in them, such as o' which may mean "over" or "of". You can solve this ambiguity inside the file by filling in the missing information in parenthesis, as in o(ver) and o(f).

After you have cleaned up the spellings and typos, you will then need to find the words with @ signs and make decisions about whether or not they are appropriately marked. Typical problems with blurred @ sign assignations occur when unclear distinctions have been made between babbling/word play, neologisms, child forms, word play and familial forms. Forms ending in @n and @f need to be entered in the lexicon. Forms in @c or @wp do not. A true @c word is one that the child made up and used consistently. False @c words may need to be changed to @b, @w, or @o. Whenever possible, mispronounciations or shortening should be noted without special form markers, as in hossie@c => ho(r)sie faum@c => faum [: farm].

21.25.3.   Lexicon Building

Once the file is thoroughly **CHECK**-ed and its words have been scanned, you are ready to make a first run of **MOR**. The command is simply:

```
mor  +xl  *.mor
```

When **MOR** is run with the +xl flag, the output is a single file with the extension ".ulx" which contains templates for the lexical entries for all unknown words in a collection of files.   The following is an example of a set of entries from a .ulx file:

```
ta       {[scat  ?]}
tag      {[scat  ?]}
tags     {[scat  ?]}
talkative   {[scat  ?]}
tambourine  {[scat  ?]}
tag      {[scat  ?]}
```

Duplicates are removed automatically when **MOR** creates the .ulx file.

You must then go through this file and determine whether to discard, complete, or modify these entry templates. It is impossible to decide what category "ta" belongs to without examining where it occurs in the corpus.   In this example, a scan of the Sarah files in the Brown corpus, (from which these examples were taken), reveals that "ta" is a variant of the infinitive marker "to":

```
*MEL:  yeah  #  (be)cause  if  it's  gon  (t)a  be  a  p@l  it's
```

```
        got ta go that way.
```

Therefore, the entry for "ta" is amended to:

```
    ta {[scat inf]} "to"
```

The corpus includes both the form "tag" and "tags", but since the former can be derived from the latter, it is sufficient to have just the entry for "tag" in the lexicon. The forms "talkative" and "tambourine" are low-frequency items which are not included in the standard lexicon file "eng.lex". Inasmuch as these are real words, the ? should be replaced by the codes "adj" and "n", respectively. For the example fragment given above, the resulting .ulx file should look like this:

```
    ta        {[scat inf]} "to"
    tag       {[scat n]}
    talkative {[scat adj]}
    tambourine {[scat n]}
```

Once all words have been coded, you need to append these new words to a lexicon file. It is best to avoid entering forms directly into the standard eng.lex file. Instead, you can create your own supplementary lexicon file or group of lexicon files and call them up when you run **MOR** by using the +l switch as in this command:

```
    mor +leng2.lex sample.cha
```

This command will use both the standard eng.lex file and the supplementary eng2.lex file to analyze the input **CHAT** files.

21.25.4. Creating Rule Files

Users working with languages for which grammar files have already been built do not need to concern themselves with the remaining sections on **MOR**. However, users who need to develop grammars for new languages or who find they have to modify grammars for existing ones will need to understand how to create the two rule files themselves. In order to do this, they need to understand the basic principles underlying the arules in "eng.ar" and the crules in "eng.cr". This section provides this explanation.

Both arules and crules are written using a simple declarative notation. The following formatting conventions are used throughout:

1. Statements are 1 per line. Statements can be broken across lines by placing the continuation character '\' at the end of the line.

2. Comments begin with a '%' character, and are terminated by the newline. Comments may be placed after a statement on the same line, or they may be placed on a separate line.

3. Names are composed of alphanumeric symbols, plus these characters:
   ^ & + - _ : \ @ . /

Both rule files contain a series of rules. Rules contain one or more clauses, each of which is composed of a series of **condition** statements, followed by a series of **action** statements. In order for a clause in rule to apply the input(s) must satisfy all condition statements. The output is derived from the input via the sequential application of all the action statements.

Both condition and action statements take the form of equations. The left hand side of the equation is a keyword, which identifies the part of the input or output being processed. The right hand side of the rule describes either the surface patterns to be matched or generated, or the category information which must be checked or manipulated.

The analyzer manipulates two different kinds of information: information about the surface shape of a word, and information about its category. All statements which match or manipulate category information must make explicit reference to a feature or features. Similarly, it is possible for a rule to contain a literal specification of the shape of a stem or affix. In addition, it is possible to use a **pattern matching language** in order to give a more general description of the shape of a string.

Pattern-Matching Symbols: The specification of orthographic patterns relies on a set of symbols derived from the regular expression (regexp) system in UNIX. The rules of this system are:

1. The metacharacters are: * [ ] | . !
   All other characters are interpreted literally.

2. A pattern which contains no metacharacters will only match itself, for example the pattern "abc" will match only the string "abc".

3. The metacharacter '.' or period matches any character.

4. The metacharacter '*' allows any number of matches (including 0) on the preceding character. For example, the pattern '.*' will match a string consisting of any number of characters.

5. The bracket symbols '[' and ']' are used to indicate choice from among a set of characters. The pattern "[ab]" will match either 'a' or 'b'.

6. A pattern may consist of a disjunctive choice between two patterns, by use of the '|' symbol. For example the pattern will match all strings which end in "x", "s", "sh", or "ch".

7. It is possible to check that some input does not match a pattern by prefacing the entire pattern with the negation operator "!".

Variable notation: A variable is used to name a regular expression, and to record patterns that match it. A variable must first be declared in a special variable declaration statement. Variable declaration statements have the format: "VARNAME = regular-expression", where VARNAME is at most 8 characters long. If the variable name is more than 1 character, this name should be enclosed in parenthesis when the variable is invoked.

Once declared, the variable can be invoked in a rule by using the operator '$'. If the variable name is longer than a single character, the variable name should be enclosed in parentheses when invoked. For example, the statement X = .* declares and initializes a variable named "X". The name X is entered in a special variable table, along with the regular expression it stands for. Note that variables may not contain other variables.

The variable table also keeps track of the most recent string that matched a named pattern. For example, if the variable X is declared as above, then the pattern "$Xle" will match all strings which end in "le". In particular, the string "able" will match this pattern; "ab" will match the pattern named by "X", and "le" will match the literal string "le". Since the string "ab" is matched against the named pattern X, it will be stored in the variable table as the most recent instantiation of X, until another string matches X.

Category information operators: The following operators are used to manipulate category information: ADD [feature value], DEL [feature]. These are used in the category action statements. For example, the crule statement "RESULTCAT = ADD [num pl]" adds the feature value pair [num pl] to the result of the concatenation of two morphemes.

21.25.5. Arules

The function of the arules is to expand the entries in the disk lexicon into a larger number of entries in the on-line lexicon. Words which undergo regular phonological or orthographic changes when combined with an affix have only one disk lexicon entry. The arules are used to create on-line lexicon entries for all inflectional variants. These variants are called **allos**. For example, the final consonant of the verb "stop" is doubled before a vowel-initial suffix, such as "-ing". The disk lexicon contains an entry for "stop", while the on-line lexicon contains two entries: one for the form "stop" and one for the form "stopp".

An arule consists of a header statement, which contains the rulename, followed by one or more condition-action **clauses**. Each clause has a series of zero or more **conditions** on the input, and one or more sets of **actions**. Here is an example of a typical condition-action clause from the larger n-allo rule in the eng.ar file:

```
LEX-ENTRY:
LEXSURF  =  $Yy
LEXCAT   =  [scat  n]
ALLO:
ALLOSURF  =  $Yie
ALLOCAT   =  LEXCAT,  ADD  [allo  nYb]
ALLO:
ALLOSURF  =  LEXSURF
ALLOCAT   =  LEXCAT,  ADD  [allo  nYa]
```

This is one single condition-action clause, labeled by the header statement "LEX-ENTRY:". Conditions begin with one of these two keywords:
1. LEXSURF matches the surface form of the word in the lexical enry to an abstract pattern. In this case, the variable declaration is
    Y = .*[^aeiou]
    Given this, the statement: "LEXSURF = $Yy" will match all lexical entry surfaces which have a final "y" preceded by a non-vowel.
2. LEXCAT checks the category information given in the matched lexical item against a given series of feature value pairs, each enclosed in square brackets, and separated by commas. In this case, the rule is meant to apply only to nouns, so the category information must be [scat n]. It is possible to check that a feature value pair is not present by prefacing the feature value pair with the negation operator "!".

Variable declarations should be made at the beginning of the rule, before any of the condition-action clauses. Variables apply to all following condition-action clauses inside a rule, but should be redefined for each rule.

After the condition statements, come one or more action statements, labelled by "ALLO:" In most cases, one of the action statements is used to create an allomorph and the other is used to enter the original lexical entry into the run-time lexicon. Action clauses begin with one of these three keywords:

1. ALLOSURF is used to produce an output surface. In the first action clause, a lexical entry surface form like "pony" is converted to "ponie" to serve as the stem of the plural. In the second action clause, the original form "pony" is kept because the form "ALLOSURF = LEXSURF" causes the surface form of the lexical entry to be copied over to the surface form of the allo.

2. ALLOCAT determines the category of the output allos. The statement "ALLOCAT = LEXCAT" causes all category information from the lexical entry to be copied over to the allo entry. In addition these two actions add the morphological classes nYa and nYb in order to keep track of the nature of these allomorphs during the application of the crules.

3. ALLOSTEM is used to produce an output stem. This action is not necessary in this example, since this rule is fully regular and produces a non-inflected stem. However, the arule that converts "postman" into "postmen" uses this ALLOSTEM action:

ALLOSTEM = $Xman&PL

The result of this action is the the form postman&PL is placed into the %mor line without the involvement of any of the concatenation rules.

Every set of action statements leads to the generation of an entry for the on-line lexicon. Thus, if an arule clause contains several sets of action statements, each labeled by the header "ALLO:" then that arule, when applied to one entry from the disk lexicon, will result in several entries in the on-line lexicon. To create the on-line lexicon, the arules are applied to the entries in the disk lexicon. Each entry is matched against the arules in the order in which they occur in the arules file. As soon as the input matches all conditions in the condition section of a clause, then the actions are applied to that input to generate one or more allos, which are loaded into the on-line lexicon. No further rules are applied to that input, and the next entry from the disk lexicon is read in to be processed. The complete set of arules should end with a default rule to copy over all remaining lexical entries that have not yet been matched by some rule. This default rule is:

```
% default rule-   copy input to output
RULENAME:   default
LEX-ENTRY:
ALLO:
```

21.25.6.   Crules

The purpose of the crules is to combine stems and affixes. In these rules, sets of conditions and actions are grouped together into **if then** clauses. This allows a rule to apply to a disjunctive set of inputs. As soon as all the conditions in a clause are met, the actions are carried out. If these are carried out successfully the rule is considered to have "fired", and no further clauses in that rule will be tried.

There are two inputs to a crule: the part of the word identified thus far, called the "START"; and the next morpheme identified, called the "NEXT". The best way to think of this is in terms of a bouncing ball that moves through the word, moving items from the not-yet-processed chunk on the right over to the already processed chunk on the left. The output of a crule is called the "RESULT". The following is the list of the keywords used in the crules:

> *condition keywords*
> STARTSURF   check surface of start input against some pattern
> STARTCAT   check start category information
> NEXTSURF   check surface of next input against some pattern
> NEXTCAT   check next category information
> MATCHCAT   check that the the start and next have the same value for some feature
> *action keywords*
> RESULTCAT   output category information

Here is an example of a piece of a rule that uses most of these keywords:

```
S = .*[sc]h|.*[zxs]    % strings that end in affricates
O = .*[^aeiou]o    % things that end in o

% clause 1 - special case for "es" suffix
 if
 STARTSURF  =  $S
 NEXTSURF   =  es|-es
 NEXTCAT  =   [scat vsfx]
 MATCHCAT  [allo]
 then
 RESULTCAT  =  STARTCAT,  NEXTCAT  [tense],  DEL  [allo]
 RULEPACKAGE  =  {}
```

This rule is used to analyze verbs that end in -es. There are four conditions that must be matched in this rule:
1. The STARTSURF is a stem that is specified in the declaration to end in an affricate. The STARTCAT is not defined.
2. The NEXTSURF is the -es suffix that is attached to that stem.
3. The NEXTCAT is the category of the suffix, which is "vsfx" or verbal suffix.
4. The MATCHCAT [allo] statement checks that both the start and next inputs have the same value for the feature "allo".

The shape of the result surface is simply the concatenation of the start and next surfaces. Hence, it is not necessary to specify this via the crules. The category information of the result is specified via the RESULTCAT statement. The statement "RESULTCAT = STARTCAT" causes all category information from the start input to be copied over to the result. The statement "NEXTCAT [tense]" copies the tense value from the NEXT to the RESULT and the statement "DEL [allo]" deletes the value for the category [allo].

In addition to the condition-action statements, crules include two other statements: the CTYPE statement, and the RULEPACKAGES statement. The CTYPE statement identifies the kind of concatenation expected and the way in which this concatenation is to be marked. This statement follows the RULENAME header. There are two special CTYPE makers: START and END. "CTYPE: START" is used for those rules which execute as soon as one morpheme has been found. "CTYPE: END" is used for those rules which execute when the end of the input has been reached. Otherwise, the CYTPE marker is used to indicate which concatenation symbol is used when concatenating the morphemes together into a parse for a word. According to **CLAN** conventions, '#' is used between a prefix and a stem, '-' is used between a stem and suffix, and '~' is used between a clitic and a stem.

Rules with CTYPE START are entered into the list of startrules. Startrules are the set of rules applied as soon as a morpheme has been recognized. In this case, the beginning of the word is considered as the start input, and the next input is the morpheme first recognized. As the start input has no surface and no category information associated with it, conditions and actions are stated only on the next input.

Rules with CTYPE END are entered into the list of endrules. These rules are invoked when the end of a word is reached, and they are used to rule out spurious parses. In an endrule, the start input is the entire word which has just been parsed, and there is no next input. Thus conditions and actions are only stated on the start input.

The RULEPACKAGES statement identifies which rules may be applied to the result of a rule, when that result is the input to another rule. The RULEPACKAGES statement follows the action statements in a clause. There is a RULEPACKAGES statement associated with each clause. The rules named in a RULEPACKAGES statement are not tried until after another morpheme has been found. For example, in parsing the input "walking", the parser first finds the morpheme "walk", and at that point applies the startrules. Of these startrules, the rule for verbs will be fired. This rule includes a RULEPACKAGES statement which specifies that the rule which handles verb conjugation may later be fired. When the parser has further identified the morpheme "ing", the verb conjugation rule will apply, where "walk" is the start input, and "ing" is the next input.

21.26.   PAGE – Viewing Files One Page at a Time

The standard MS-DOS **TYPE** command does not allow you to page slowly through a document. So we have provided a utility for this function. You simply type:

```
page   filename
```

where "filename" stands for the name of the file you want to page through. To advance a page, press the space key. To exit back to DOS, type **q** for "quit." **PAGE** functions similarly on the Macintosh.

21.27.   PHONFREQ – Phonological Frequency Analysis

The **PHONFREQ** program tabulates all of the segments on the %pho line. For example, if you use **PHONFREQ** with no further options on the little file discussed under the **MODREP** program, the output would be as follows:

```
2    A       initial  =   0,  final  =   1,  other  =   1
1    I       initial  =   0,  final  =   1,  other  =   0
3    a       initial  =   1,  final  =   1,  other  =   1
2    m       initial  =   2,  final  =   0,  other  =   0
3    n       initial  =   1,  final  =   1,  other  =   1
2    o       initial  =   0,  final  =   2,  other  =   0
2    w       initial  =   2,  final  =   0,  other  =   0
```

This output tells you that there were two occurrences of the segment /A/, once in final position and once in other or medial position.

Alphabet File. If you create a file called "alphabet" and place it in your working directory, you can further specify that certain digraphs should be treated as single segments. This is important if you need to look at diphthongs or other digraphs in UNIBET. In the strings in the alphabet file, the asterisk character can be used to indicate any single character. For example, the string *: would indicate any sound followed by a colon. If you have three instances of a:, three of e:, and three of o:, the output will list each of these three separately, rather than summing them together as nine instances of something followed by a colon. Since the asterisk is not used in either UNIBET or PHONASCII, it should never be necessary to specify a search for a literal asterisk in your alphabet file. A sample alphabet file for English is distributed with **CLAN**. **PHONFREQ** will warn you that it does not find an alphabet file. You can ignore this warning if you are convinced that you do not need a special alphabet file.

If you want to construct a complete substitution matrix for phonological analysis, you need to add a %mod line in your transcript to indicate the target phonology. Then you can run **PHONFREQ** twice, first on the %pho line and then on the %mod line. To run on the %mod line, you need to add the +t%mod switch.

If you want to specify a set of digraphs that should be treated as single phonemes or segments, you can put them in a file with the name "alphabet." Each combination should be entered by itself on a single line. **PHONFREQ** will look for the alphabet file in either the working directory or the library directory. If it finds no alphabet file, each letter will be treated as a single segment. Within the alphabet file, you can also specify trigraphs that should override particular digraphs. In that case, the longer string that should override the shorter string should occur earlier in the alphabet file.

The options for **PHONFREQ** are:

1. **+b:** By default, **PHONFREQ** analyzes the %pho tier. If you want to analyze another tier, you can use the +b switch to specify the desired tier. Remember that you might still need to use the +t switch along with the +b switch as in this command:

```
phonfreq  +b*  +t*CHI  modrep.cha
```

2. **+d:** If you use this switch, the actual words that were matched will be written to the output. Each occurrence is written out.

3. **+f/-f**: Send output to the screen or to a file. The default value of this switch is -f which sends output to the screen. If you want to send the output to a file, you must use the +f switch. The letters placed after the +f will be used as the file extension name.

4. **+k**: In **PHONFREQ** the default analysis is case-sensitive. The +k switch here makes the analyses case insensitive. In most other programs, this switch has the opposite default setting.

5. **+m:** By default **CLAN** leaves the output files in your current working directory. The +m switch tells **CLAN** to store output files in the directory where the corresponding input files were found.

6. **+p**: Redefine the punctuation set.

7. **+r**: This switch has several different levels which allow you to specify how to treat omissions of parts of words, text replacement, prosodic delimiters, and retracings. For details see chapter 22.

8. **+s/-s**: This option is used to specify a word to be used from an input file. This option should be immediately followed by the word itself. In order to search for a group of words stored in a file, use the form +s@filename.

9. **+t/-t**: You should use the +b switch to change the identity of the tier analyzed by **PHONFREQ**. The +t switch is used instead to change the identity of the speaker being analyzed. For example, if you want to analyze the main lines for speaker CHI, you would use this command:

    ```
    phonfreq  +b*  +t*CHI  modrep.cha
    ```

10. **+u**: By default, when the user has specified a series of files on the command line, the analyses are performed on each individual file. The program ends up reporting results for each data file separately. If the +u option is used, the program combines the input data found in all the specified files into one set and outputs results for that set as a whole.

11. **+z**: Work on a specified range of words or utterances. See the description of +z in chapter 22 for ways of specifying ranges.

21.28.   POSFREQ – Positional Frequency Analysis

The **POSFREQ** program is essentially a minor variant of the basic **FREQ** program. What is different about **POSFREQ** is the fact that it allows the user to track the frequencies of words in specific positions in the utterance, including "first", "last", "second", and "other". This can be useful in studies of early child syntax. For example, using **POSFREQ** on the main line, one can track the use initial pronouns or auxiliaries. For open class items like verbs, one can use **POSFREQ** to analyze codes on the %mor line. This would allow one to study, for example, the appearance of verbs in second position, initial position, final position, and other positions.

To illustrate the running of **POSFREQ**, let us look at the results of this simple command:

```
posfreq  sample.cha
```

Here are the first six lines of the output from this command:

```
1   a              initial =  0, final =  0, other =  1
1   any            initial =  0, final =  0, other =  1
1   are            initial =  0, final =  1, other =  0
3   chalk          initial =  0, final =  3, other =  0
1   chalk+chalk    initial =  0, final =  1, other =  0
1   delicious      initial =  0, final =  0, other =  1
```

We see here that the word "chalk" appears three times in final position, whereas the word "delicious" appears only once and that is not in either initial or final position. In order to study occurrences in second position, we must use the +d switch as in:

```
posfreq  +d  sample.cha
```

The options available for **POSFREQ** include:

1. **+d**: Count words in either first, second, or other positions. The default is to count by first, last, and other positions.

2. **+f/-f**: Send output to the screen or to a file. The default value of this switch is -f which sends output to the screen. If you want to send the output to a file, you must use the +f switch. The letters placed after the +f will be used as the file extension name. When you work on a collection of files, this switch sends each of the resultant analyses to a separate file. If you want a single merged analysis for a collection of files, use the redirecting symbol (>) instead (see Redirecting section above).

3. **+g:** Displays only selected words in the output. The string following the +g can be either a word or a filename in the @filename notation.

4. **+k**: Make analyses case-sensitive.

5. **+m:** By default **CLAN** leaves the output files in your current working directory. The +m switch tells **CLAN** to store output files in the directory where the corresponding input files were found.

6. **+p**: Redefine the punctuation set.

7. **+r**: This switch has several different levels which allow you to specify how to treat omissions of parts of words, text replacement, prosodic delimiters, and retracings. For details see chapter 22.

8. **-s**: The effect of this option for **POSFREQ** is different from its effects in the other **CLAN** programs. Only the -s value of this switch applied. The effect of using -s is to exclude certain words as a part of the syntactic context. If you want to match a particular word with **POSFREQ**, you should use the +g switch rather than the +s switch.

9. **+t/-t**: Particular dependent tiers can be included or excluded by using the +t or -t options immediately followed by the tier code.

10. **+u**: By default, when the user has specified a series of files on the command line, the analyses are performed on each individual file. The program ends up reporting results for each data file separately. If the +u option is used, the program combines the input data found in all the specified files into one set and outputs results for that set as a whole.

11. **+y**: Work on non-**CHAT** files. The +y value works on lines and the +y1 value works on utterances as delimited by periods, question marks, and exclamation marks.

12. **+z**: Work on a specified range of words or utterances. See the description of +z in chapter 22 for ways of specifying ranges.

21.29.   RECALL – Command Entry and Batch File Construction

As you become more adept at composing **CLAN** commands, you will find that you often want to simply modify some previous command. Instead of having to type out a long complicated command from scratch, you can use the **RECALL** program to bring up an old command and then change it. On the Macintosh, the **RECALL** facility is built into **CLAN**. With MS-DOS, it is a memory-resident module that you install along with your general **CLAN** installation. The module was written by George Theall and is circulated as FreeWare. In order to test out this program, just type "recall -i". Then, issue a few commands to load up **RECALL**'s command memory. Now you can bring up old commands by pressing the "up" arrow ↑ on the numerical keypad. Repeated pressing of this key takes you up back through repeated old commands. To move the other way through the list of old commands, press the "down" key ↓ on the keypad. Once you have a command that you want to edit, use the arrow keys on the main part of the keyboard to move through the line to the point you want to change. Then just type over the material you want to change. When you are finished, hit the carriage return. You don't have to be at the end of the line to hit the carriage return.

If you want **RECALL** to work automatically, you should place a line in your "autoexec.bat" file which says "recall -i". After this is done and you have restarted the system, **RECALL** will always be automatically installed.   **RECALL** can be invoked with any one of four options.

-i = install in memory
-l = list command lines in recall buffer
-r = remove from memory
-? = display this help message

Only one option can be specified at a time. The complete set of keypad functions provided by **RECALL** is as follows:

Key	Action
←	Move cursor 1 character to left
→	Move cursor 1 character to right
\<PGUP\>	Move cursor 1 "word" to left
\<CTRL\>←	"
\<PGDN\>	Move cursor 1 "word" to right
\<CTRL\>→	"
\<HOME\>	Move cursor to start of line
\<END\>	Move cursor to end of line
↑	Display previous command in recall buffer
↓	Display next command in recall buffer
\<BS\>	Delete 1 character to left of cursor
\<DEL\>	Delete 1 character at cursor
\<CTRL\>\<PGUP\>	Delete to start of previous "word"
\<CTRL\>\<PGDN\>	Delete to start of next "word"
\<CTRL\>\<HOME\>	Delete to start of line
\<CTRL\>\<END\>	Delete to end of line
\<ESC\>	Delete entire line
\<INS\>	Toggle insert/overwrite mode

After you have worked for a while you may want to list command lines entered earlier. In this case, you can invoke **RECALL** with the -l option, and the current buffer contents will be displayed. You can redirect this output to a file, printer, or even another program using the DOS redirection characters >, >>, and l.

RECALL is a public domain memory-resident command line editor and history utility written and provided by George A. Theall of TifaWARE. Following Theall's request, the complete documentation and source code for the program is contained in the "recall.doc" zip file. The address of TifaWARE is 506 South 41st St., #3M Philadelphia, PA 19104, phone: (215) 662-0558, email: gtheall@penndrls.upenn.edu. Please do not contact George Theall or TifaWARE regarding problems with **RECALL**.

On the Macintosh, the functions parallel to those of **RECALL** can be accessed using the left and right arrows to move to the left and right and by using the ↑ and ↓ keys to scroll through previous commands. On the Macintosh, these functions are always automatically installed. UNIX users can achieve the similar results using the "history" facility.

Batch Files. An even more stable way of repeating a series of commands is to enter them into a "batch" file. A batch file is nothing more than a series of lines, each of which has a standard MS-DOS, Macintosh, or UNIX command. You use your text editor to create this file. If you wish to include variables in the script or batch file, you do this by using the percentage symbol on DOS and the Macintosh and the asterisk under UNIX. For example, the following batch file uses two variables, %1 and %2. The first variable (%1) is used to vary the speaker being tracked and the second variable (%2) is used to vary the file name. You provide values for these variables when you run the batch file.

```
freq  +t*%1  %2
mlt   +t*%1  %2
```

If you name this file now.bat and type the command:

```
now  FAT  kid10.cha
```

you will run **FREQ** and **MLT** on the father's speech in the kid10.cha file. Your %1 variable here is "FAT" and your %2 variable is "kid10.cha." You can then change speaker name and file name to any new values and continue to enter similar short commands, such as "now MOT kid*.cha" and so on.

Each of the operating systems has a unique way of identifying batch files and variables in batch files.
1. **MS-DOS**. You need to give the file a ".bat" extension, as in "mystuff.bat." Variables are indicated by the $ symbol. If you want the literal symbol % on MS-DOS, you must precede it with another % sign, as in +t%%spa.
2. **UNIX**. You need to make the file or "script" "executable" using the chmod +x command. Variables are indicated by the % symbol. If you want the literal dollar sign symbol $ under UNIX, you must precede it with a backslash.
3. **Macintosh**. You can use any name for the file. However, when you invoke a batch file, such as the "now" file discussed above, add the #symbol before it, so you would type:
   ```
   #now  FAT  kid10.cha
   ```
   Variables are indicated by the $ symbol. If you want the literal dollar sign symbol $ on the Macintosh, you must precede it with a backslash.

21.30.   RELY – Measuring Code Reliability

When you are entering a series of codes into files using the coder's editor facility of **CED**, you will often want to compute the reliability of your coding system by having two or more people code a single file or group of files. To do this, you can give each coder the original file, get them to enter a %cod line and then use the **RELY** program to spot matches and mismatches. For example, you could copy the "sample.cha" file to the "samplea.cha" file and change one code in the "samplea.cha" file. In this example, change the word "in" to "gone" in the code on line 15. They enter the command

```
rely  sample.cha  samplea.cha  +t%spa
```

The output in the sample.rly file will look like the basic "sample.cha" file, but with this additional information for line 15:

```
%spa:  $RDE:sel:non $RFI:xxx:gone:?"samplea.cha" $RFI:xxx:in:?"sample.cha"
```

If you want the program to ignore any differences in the main line, header line, or other dependent tiers that may have been introduced by the second coder, you can add the +c switch. If you do this, the program will ignore differences and always copy information from the first file. If the command is:

```
rely  +c  sample.cha  samplea.cha  +t%spa
```

then the program will use "sample.cha" as the master file for everything except the information on the %spa tier.

The options for **RELY** are:

1. **+c**: Do not check data on non-chosen tier.

2. **+f/-f**: Send output to the screen or to a file. The default value of this switch is -f which sends output to the screen. If you want to send the output to a file, you must use the +f switch. The letters placed after the +f will be used as the file extension name. When you work on a collection of files, this switch sends each of the resultant analyses to a separate file. If you want a single merged analysis for a collection of files, use the redirecting symbol (>) instead (see Redirecting section above).

3. **+k**: Make analyses case-sensitive.

4. **+m:** By default **CLAN** leaves the output files in your current working directory. The +m switch tells **CLAN** to store output files in the directory where the corresponding input files were found.

5. **+p**: Redefine the punctuation set.

6. **+t/-t**: Particular dependent tiers can be included or excluded by using the +t or -t options immediately followed by the tier code.

21.31.   SALTIN – Converting SALT Files

This program takes SALT formatted files and converts them to the **CHAT** format. SALT is a transcript format developed by Jon Miller and Robin Chapman at the University of Wisconsin. By default, **SALTIN** sends its output to a file. Here is the most common use of this program:

```
saltin  file.txt
```

There are still some bugs in this program, so please use it carefully. Errors may have to be fixed by hand. Please report any bugs or irregularities that you find in this program.

It may be useful to note a few details of the ways in which **SALTIN** operates on SALT files:

1. When **SALTIN** encounters material in parentheses, it translates this material as a unspecified retracing type, using the [/?] code.
2. Multiple comments are placed on separate lines on a single comment tier.
3. Times in minutes and seconds are converted to times in hours:minutes:seconds.
4. A %def tier is created for coding definitions.

The options for **SALTIN** are:

1. **+f/-f**: Send output to the screen or to a file. The default value of this switch is -f which sends output to the screen. If you want to send the output to a file, you must use the +f switch. The letters placed after the +f will be used as the file extension name.

2. **+h**: Some researchers have used angle brackets in SALT to enter comments. When the original contains text found between the < and the > characters this option instructs **SALTIN** to place it between [% and]. Otherwise, material in angle brackets would be coded as a text overlap.

3. **+k**:   Treat upper and lower case as different.

4. **+l**: Put all codes on a separate %cod line. If you do not select this option, codes will be placed on the main line in the [$text] format.

5. **+m**: By default **CLAN** leaves the output files in your current working directory. The +m switch tells **CLAN** to store output files in the directory where the corresponding input files were found.

21.32.   SLIDE – Viewing Files on a Time Line

Researchers often find that the top-to-bottom serial organization of a transcript imposes subtle limitations on the analytic process.   The offending element here seems to be the carriage return or "newline" notion. Words flow along nicely in a left-to-right fashion across the page or across the computer screen and then, suddenly, we force a reassessment and a break by jumping to the next line.   Given the notion of a "page", there is no simple way around this problem.   One can try to align overlaps a bit and one can try to place interlinear morphemic markings under their corresponding words, but this is a difficult and imperfect solution to the "newline" problem.   However, the dynamic nature of the display on a computer screen a totally different solution to this problem.   The best way to see how this works is to try **SLIDE** on the sample file, by typing:

```
slide  sample.cha
```

At first, you will see only the following display:

```
*MOT:    hey Nicky wanna [: want to] see what other neat toy-s there are ?
*NIC:                                                                      yeah.
```

However, it is now possible to "scroll" through this file not by moving downward, but by moving to the right. In effect, the whole interaction is now on a single linear display and the computer screen is now a window into that linear display. By moving the computer display left or right you can move linearly through that time line.

There are a variety of commands available for moving this display about. You can move by characters, by words, by screenfuls, or to the beginning and end of the whole file.

Control-e	move forward a screenful
Control-a	move backward a screenful
Control-f	move forward a single character
Control-b	move backward a single character
Escape-a	move to beginning of the file
Escape-e	move to end of the file
→	move forward a word
←	move backward a word
Control-u	repeat next argument N times, as in Control-u 33 Control-e to move forward 33 screenfuls
Control-q	quit **SLIDE**

Use the right arrow key to move to the end of the line and then you will see the material sliding over to the left, just as you would be advancing through a conversation. You will see that overlaps and turns are intuitively correct. If you want to attach morphemes to words, you simply type:

```
slide  +t%mor  sample.cha
```

SLIDE will also work well with other tiers such as the %pho line that have one-to-one correspondence with the main line or with the %err tier which uses the [*] marker to establish linear correspondences. It can produce poor results when displayed with tiers that have no clear correspondence with the main line, particularly when these include a lot of material, such as a heavily coded %spa tier.

The options for **SLIDE** are:

1. **+f/-f**: Send output to the screen or to a file. The default value of this switch is -f which sends output to the screen. If you want to send the output to a file, you must use the +f switch. The letters placed after the +f will be used as the file extension name. When you work on a collection of files, this switch sends each of the resultant analyses to a separate file. If you want a single merged analysis for a collection of files, use the redirecting symbol (>) instead (see Redirecting section above).

2. **+m:** By default **CLAN** leaves the output files in your current working directory. The +m switch tells **CLAN** to store output files in the directory where the corresponding input files were found.

3. **+p**: Redefine the punctuation set.

4. **+r**: This switch has several different levels which allow you to specify how to treat omissions of parts of words, text replacement, prosodic delimiters, and retracings. For details see chapter 22.

5. **+t/-t**: Particular dependent tiers can be included or excluded by using the +t or -t options immediately followed by the tier code.

6. **+u:** By default, when the user has specified a series of files on the command line, the analyses are performed on each individual file. The program ends up reporting results for each data file separately. If the +u option is used, the program combines the input data found in all the specified files into one set and outputs results for that set as a whole.

7. **+z**: Work on a specified range of words or utterances. See the description of +z in chapter 22 for ways of specifying ranges.

21.33.   STATFREQ – Outputting to Statistical Analyses

The **STATFREQ** program provides a way of producing a summary of word or code frequencies across a set of files. However, within each of the files, you can only look at one speaker at a time. This summary can be sent on as the input to statistical analysis by programs such as SAS or BMDP. Here is the output from a **STATFREQ** run on "sample.cha":

```
      a cat chalk+chalk fine here just minute mommy neat no not
that the uhhuh what's white yeah
1.25.8.2  0  0  1  0  0  0  0  1  1  0  0  1  0  0  1  0  2
1.26.8.2  1  1  0  1  1  1  1  0  0  1  1  0  1  1  0  1  0
```

In order to get this type of output, you need to go through three steps. The actual running of **STATFREQ** is the last of these three steps.

1.   First, you must assign appropriate @ID header line(s) to the files to be analyzed. Place a single @ID header lines into each file in a series of **CHAT** files. There can be only one @ID header per speaker. These lines take the following shape:

```
@ID:  1.25.8.2=NIC
```

There is a tab after the colon and there are no spaces around the equals sign. The material before the equals sign is the speaker ID and the material after the equals sign is the participant's three-letter code as given in the @Participants line.

2.   Next, run **FREQ** over the files using either +t and metacharacters, or +t* followed immediately by the appropriate speaker code. You must also use the +d2 option in the **FREQ** command line. This will produce a temporary file called stat.out. Here is an example of a **FREQ** command which outputs data for **STATFREQ** analysis:

```
freq  +d2  +t@ID=1.*.8.2    sample*.cha
```

The +t switch here has the special meaning of selecting out only those participants whose identification number matches the ID string. In this case, the use of the asterisk allows the programs to look at both 1.25.8.2 and 1.26.8.2 in these two sample files. If you had included @ID lines of the shape 1.*.8.2 for two speakers within a single file, **STATFREQ** would simply collapse the data for both of them into one line for the output. In most cases, this is not what you want, so be sure to keep your numbering system clear and consistent.

You may wish to organize your ID codes so that the header includes useful information about age, gender, etc. (see Chapter 3). In this way, you can generate a table of frequencies for all speakers of a particular age or gender by using the +t and metacharacters. For example, if you had assigned each target child an @ID header of the form @ID: 1.25.2, where the digit "1" represented "target child", the next two digits represented the file number, and the last represented age (1 = 14 months, 2 = 20 months), you could produce a table of frequencies for all target children by specifying +t@id=1.*.*. Similarly, specifying +t@id=1.*.20 would generate frequencies for all 20-month-old target children. When using this approach, the frequency data for a single speaker are identified in the **STATFREQ** output file by means of that speaker's unique speaker ID number.

If you do not want to go to the work of adding @ID fields to your files, and if you are always using the same three-letter code for a speaker across a set of files, you can use an alternative form of the +t switch. This alternative takes the form +t*CHI which instructs **STATFREQ** to merge across all speakers with the three-letter code "CHI." In this case, all of the *CHI lines will be examined in the corpus. However, if you have different names for children across different files, you need to use the @ID fields.

This special use of the +t switch can be combined with its standard uses. For example, if you wanted to do a **STATFREQ** analysis on only the %mor line for *CHI, you could use this command.

```
freq  +d2  +t*MOT  -t*  +t%mor  sample*.cha
```

3. **FREQ** will tell you to run **STATFREQ** by typing

```
statfreq stat.out
```

You should enter that command. If you want the output to go to a file, use the +f option:

```
statfreq +f stat.out
```

If the "@ID:" header is not found in a given file, the message "NO ID GIVEN" will be produced by the program.

You may wish to do some additional processing on the final output of **STATFREQ**. The best way to do this is to merge rows and columns within either a database management system or the data structure programs of statistical packages such as Minitab and SAS.

The options for **STATFREQ** are:

1. **+d:** This option removes the files headers so that the data can be sent directly into a program for statistical analysis. It also replaces missing values with a period, which is usually a symbol representing missing data for statistical analysis.

2. **+f/-f:** Send output to the screen or to a file. The default value of this switch is -f, which sends output to the screen. If you want to send the output to a file, you must use the +f switch. The letters placed after the +f will be used as the file extension name.

3. **+m:** By default **CLAN** leaves the output files in your current working directory. The +m switch tells **CLAN** to store output files in the directory where the corresponding input files were found.

21.34.   TEXTIN – Converting Unstructured Text to CHAT

The **TEXTIN** program is quite simple.   It takes a set of sentences in paragraph form and converts them to a **CHAT** file. Blank lines are considered to be possible paragraph breaks and are noted with @Blank headers.

As an example of the operation of **TEXTIN**, one could look at the results of running the program on the sentences in this section:

```
@Begin
@Participants:    T  Text
*T:    the textin program is quite simple.
*T:    it takes a set of sentences in paragraph form and
       converts them to a chat file.
*T:    blank lines are considered to be possible paragraph
       breaks and are noted with @blank headers.
@Blank
*T:    as an example of the operation of textin, one could
       look at the results of running the program on the
       sentences in this section:
@End
```

The options for **TEXTIN** are:

1. **+f/-f**: Send output to the screen or to a file. The default value of this switch is -f, which sends output to the screen. If you want to send the output to a file, you must use the +f switch. The letters placed after the +f will be used as the file extension name.

2. **+m:** By default **CLAN** leaves the output files in your current working directory. The +m switch tells **CLAN** to store output files in the directory where the corresponding input files were found.

21.35.   WDLEN – Graphs of Word Length

The **WDLEN** program tabulates word lengths and prints a histogram. The program reads through data files, tabulating the frequencies of various word and utterance lengths. The output consists of word lengths (in characters) and utterance lengths (in words), the frequencies of these lengths, and a histogram of these frequencies. The "Wdlen" in the output represents the "word length". The "Utt len" in the output represents the "utterance length." The basic use of the **WDLEN** program is as follows:

```
wdlen   sample.cha
```

The options for **WDLEN** are:

1. **+f/-f**: Send output to the screen or to a file. The default value of this switch is -f, which sends output to the screen. If you want to send the output to a file, you must use the +f switch. The letters placed after the +f will be used as the file extension name.

2. **+h**: When the frequency of either words or utterances exceeds 70, the dashes in the bar graph no longer have a one-to-one correspondence with the frequency count. The +h option allows you to extend the length of the longest line on the histogram.

3. **+k**: Make analyses case-sensitive.

4. **+m**: By default **CLAN** leaves the output files in your current working directory. The +m switch tells **CLAN** to store output files in the directory where the corresponding input files were found.

5. **+p**: Redefine the punctuation set.

6. **+r**: This switch has several different levels which allow you to specify how to treat omissions of parts of words, text replacement, prosodic delimiters, and retracings. For details see chapter 22.

7. **+s/-s**: This option is used to specify a single words or a set of words to be tracked. This option should be immediately followed by the word itself. In order to search for a group of words stored in a file, use the form +s@filename.

8. **+t/-t**: Particular dependent tiers can be included or excluded by using the +t option immediately followed by the tier code.

9. **+u**: If the +u option is used, the program combines the input data found in all the specified files into one set and outputs results for that set as a whole.

10. **+y**: Work on nonCHAT files. The +y value works on lines and the +y1 value works on utterances as delimited by periods, question marks, and exclamation marks.

11. **+z**: Work on a specified range of words or utterances. See the description of +z in chapter 22 for ways of specifying ranges.

22. CLAN **Options**

Let us now take a closer look at the various options or "switches" available for the CLAN programs. To see a list of options for **KWAL** just type "kwal." Each option begins with a plus or a minus. When you actually enter the command, you must include the hyphen and you must precede the plus with a space. Multiple options can be selected in any command. Options may occur in any order. Options on the command line must be separated by a space. For example, the command:

```
kwal +f +t*MOT sample.cha
```

would run a **K**ey **W**ord **A**nd Line analysis on the file "sample.cha". The selection of the +f option sends the output from this analysis into a new file called "sample.kwa". The +t*MOT option confines the analysis to only the lines spoken by the mother. The +f and +t switches can be placed in either order.

22.1. An Alphabetical Listing of Options

In this section we list each of the possible options and describe its role in the various programs.

+a   This switch is not yet used. It is being reserved for future functions.

+b   See the particular program for the use of this switch.

+c   See the particular program for the use of this switch.

+d   **Output Data Only**. Many programs insert some identifying information into the output. This can cause problems if you intend to use the output from one program as the input to a second program. The second program will try to analyze the identifying information inserted in the file as well as the data. The +d option allows the data to be displayed without the identifying information. There are different levels of information that could be excluded. Each level is represented by a single-digit number immediately following the +d option. Please see individual programs for more detailed information on each of the output levels.

+e   See the particular program for the use of this switch.

+f/-f   **Send Output to File or Screen**. By default, nearly all of the programs send the results of the analyses directly to the screen. You can, however, request that your results be inserted into a file. This is accomplished by inserting the +f option into the command line. The advantage of sending the program's results to a file is that you can go over the analysis more carefully, because you have a file to which you can later refer.

The -f switch is used for sending output to the screen. The advantage of sending the analysis to the screen (also called standard output) is that the results are immediate and your directory is less cluttered with nonessential files. This is ideal for quick temporary analysis. You only need to use the -f switch when you want the output to go to the screen for **CHSTRING, FLO,** and **SALTIN**. For all of the other programs, the output goes to the screen by default.

The string specified with the +f option is used to replace the default file name extension assigned to the output file name by each program. For example, the command:

```
freq  +f  file.ext
```

would create an output file "file.frq". If you want to control the shape of the extension name on the file, you can place up to three letters after the +f switch, as in this command:

```
freq  +fmot  file.ext
```

which would create an output file "file.mot." If the string argument is longer than *three characters* it will be truncated. For example, the command:

```
freq  +fmother  file.ext
```

would also create an output file "file.mot."

On the Macintosh, you can use the third option under the File Menu to set the directory for your output files. On MS-DOS you can achieve the same effect by using the +f switch with an argument, as in:

+fc:	This will send the output files to your working directory on c:
+f".res"	This sets the extension for your output files.
+f"c:.res"	This sends the output files to c: and gives them the extension .res.

Note: When you are running a command on several files and use the +f switch, the output will go into several files – one for each of the input files. If what you want is a combined analysis that treats all the input files as one large file, then use the +u switch. If you want all of the output to go input a single file for which you provide the name, then use the redirect option >. The redirect option can be used with or without +u, but not with +f.

+g See the particular program for the use of this switch.

+h See the particular program for the use of this switch.

+i See the particular program for the use of this switch.

+j This switch is not currently being used.

+k **Case-Sensitivity**. A case-sensitive program is one that makes a distinction between upper and lower case letters. The **CLAN** programs are not case-sensitive by default. The exception to this is **CHSTRING**. Use of the +k option overrides the default state and allows the other programs to become case-sensitive as well. For instance, suppose you are searching for the auxiliary verb "may" in a text. If you searched for the word "may" in a case-sensitive program, you would obtain all the occurrences of the word "may" in lower case only. You would not obtain any occurrences of "MAY" or "May." Searches performed for the word "may" using the +k option produce the words "may", "MAY", and "May" as a result.

+l   See the particular program for the use of this switch.

+m   **Controlling Output File Placement**. By default, CLAN leaves output
            files in your current working directory. The +m switch tells CLAN to store
            output files in the directory where the corresponding input files were found.
            This switch is particularly powerful if you are using a Macintosh, since all of
            the programs work recursively on the Macintosh. For example, you could run
            FREQ on the entire CHILDES database with a single command, such as:

                    freq +f +m *.cha

            If you use the +m switch, you will litter ".frq" files throughout your copy of the
            database.

+n   See the particular program for the use of this switch.

+o   See the particular program for the use of this switch.

+pF   **Defining a punctuation set**. Because most of the programs in the CLAN
            system are word-oriented, the beginning and ending boundaries of words must
            be defined. This is done by defining a punctuation set. The default punctuation
            set for CLAN includes the space and these characters:

                        , . ; ? ! [ ] < >

            This punctuation set applies to the main lines and all coding lines with the
            exception of the %pho and %mod lines which use the UNIBET and
            PHONASCII systems. Because those systems make use of punctuation
            markers for special characters, only the space can be used as a delimiter on the
            %pho and %mod lines.

            All of the word-oriented programs have the +p option. This option allows the
            user to redefine the default punctuation set. This is useful because the CHAT
            coding conventions use special characters that at times are used as delimiters
            and other times as parts of words. For example, sometimes the "-" character is
            used as a morpheme boundary marker and, therefore, should not be considered
            part of the word. This is also quite useful when you are working on a language
            that uses diacritics. To change the punctuation set, you must create a small file
            which lists all the punctuation marks present in the file. You do this by simply
            typing out all the punctuation marks one a single line with no spaces between
            them. This line will change the punctuation set of the main speaker tiers and the
            code tiers. The name of your new punctuation file should immediately follow
            the +p in the command line. Here is an example situation. Suppose you wish
            to change both the main speaker tier and the code tier punctuation sets from the
            default to the set in the file "newpunct.txt." The contents of the "newpunct.txt"
            file are as follows:

                    $ * & ^ !

            This line indicates the desired punctuation set for the main line and coding tier.
            You can now issue commands such as the following:

```
freq  +pnewpunct.txt  sample.cha
```

Note: If you use the +p switch with no file name, the programs look for a file called "punct.txt" in the current working directory. If you do not use the +p switch at all, the programs look for a punctuation file called "punct.def." If the "punct.def" file is not found, the program will then use the default built-in punctuation set. It is advisable to create a "punct.def" file when the punctuation characters of the language being analyzed are different from the default punctuation characters. The "punct.def" file should contain the new punctuation set and should be located in the current working directory. Because the "punct.def" file is referred to automatically, this feature allows you to change the punctuation set once for use with all the **CLAN** programs. If you do not want **CLAN** to ever change the default punctuation set, make sure you do not have a punct.def file in your current working directory and make sure you do not use the +p switch.

+q See the particular program for the use of this switch.

+r1 **Removing Parentheses.** Omitted parts of words can be marked by parentheses, as in "(be)cause" with the first syllable omitted. The +r1 option removes the parentheses and leaves the rest of the word as is.

+r2 **Leaving Parentheses.** This option leaves the word with parentheses.

+r3 **Removing Material in Parentheses.** This option removes all of the omitted part.

Here is an example of the first three +r options and their resulting outputs, if the input word is "get(s)":

Option	Output
"no option"	gets
"+r1"	gets
"+r2"	get(s)
"+r3"	get

+r4 **Removing Prosodic Symbols in Words.** Remove the #, /, and : symbols from words. The use of these symbols is discussed in chapter 7.

+r5 **Text Replacement.** By default, material in the form [: text] replaces the material preceding it in the string search programs. If you do not want this replacement to be done, use this switch.

+r6 **Retraced Material.** By default, material in retracings is included in searches and counts. However, this material can be excluded by using the +r6 switch. In the **MLU** and **MODREP** programs, retracings are excluded by default. For these programs, the +r6 switch can be used to include material in retracings.

+s/-s **Search for a word or a file.** The +s option allows you to specify the keyword you desire to find. You do this by putting the word in quotes directly after the +s switch, as in +sdog to search for the word "dog." You can also use the +s switch to specify a file containing words to be searched. You do this by putting the file name after the +s preceded by the @ sign, as in +s@adverbs, which will search for the words in a file called "adverbs." If you want to look for the literal character @, you need to precede it with a backslash as in +s"\@".

By default, the programs will only search for this string on the main line. Also, by default, this switch treats material in square brackets as if it were a single "opaque" form. In effect, unless you include the square brackets in your search string, the search will ignore any material that is enclosed in square brackets. The **COMBO** program is the only one that allows you to specify regular expressions with this option. The only programs that allow you to include delimiters in the search string are **COMBO**, **FREQ**, and **KWAL**.

It is possible to specify as many **+s** options on the command line as you like. Use of the **+s** option will override the default list. For example, the command

```
freq  +s"word"  data.txt
```

will search through the file "data.txt" looking for "word."

The +s/-s switch can be used with four types of material: (1) words, (2) codes or postcodes in square brackets, (3) text in angle brackets associated with particular codes within square brackets, (4) material associated with particular postcodes, and (5) particular postcodes themselves. The effect of the switch for the four different types is as follows.

	+ s	- s	+ s +
Word example:	only this word: **+s"dog"**	all words except: **-s"dog"**	all the words plus xxx **+s+xxx**
[code] example:	only this code: **+s"[//]"**	(default)	all text plus this code: **+s+"[//]"**
<code> example:	only text of this type: **+s"<//>"**	all text but this type: **-s"<//>"**	all text plus this type: **+s+"<//>"**
[+ code] example:	only this postcode: **+s"[+ imi]"**	(default)	all text plus this code: **+s+"[+ imi]"**
<+ code> example:	only utterances with this postcode: **+s"<+ imi>"**	all utterances except with this postcode: **-s"<+ imi>"**	all text plus this type: **+s+"<+ imi>"**

Multiple +s strings are matched as exclusive or's. If a string matches one +s string, it cannot match the other. The most specific matches are processed first. For example, if your command is:

```
freq  +s$gf%  +s$gf:a
```

and your text has these codes:

```
$gf  $gf:a  $gf:b  $gf:c
```

your output will be:

```
$gf%        3
$gf         1
```

Since $gf:a matches specifically to the +s$gf:a, it is excluded from matching +s$gf%.

Removal from Exclusion. One can also use the +s switch to remove certain strings from automatic exclusion. For example, the **MLU** program automatically excludes xxx, 0, uh, and words beginning with & from the MLU count. This can be changed by using this command:

```
mlu  +s+uh  +s+xxx  +s+0*  +s+&*  file.cha
```

+t/-t   **Select/Exclude Tier Code**. In **CHAT** formatted files, there exist three tier code types: main speaker tier(s) (denoted by *), speaker-dependent tier(s) (denoted by %), and header tier(s) (denoted by @). The speaker-dependent tiers are always attached to the main speakers. If, for example, you request to analyze the speaker *MOT and all the %cod dependent tiers, the programs will analyze all of the *MOT main tiers and only the %cod dependent tiers associated with that speaker.

The +t option allows you to specify which main speaker tiers, their dependent tiers, and header tiers should be included in the analysis. All other tiers, found in the given file, will be ignored by the program. For example, the command:

```
freq  +t*NIC  +t%spa  +t%mor  +t"@Group of Mot"  sample.cha
```

tells **FREQ** to look only at the *CHI main speaker tiers, their %spa and %mor dependent tiers, and @Situation header tiers. When tiers are included, the analysis will be done on only those specified tiers.

The -t option allows you to specify which main speaker tiers, their dependent tiers, and header tiers should be excluded from the analysis. All other tiers, found in the given file should be included in the analysis, unless specified otherwise by default. The command:

```
freq  -t*NIC  -t%spa  -t%mor  -t@"Group of Mot"  sample.cha
```

tells **FREQ** to exclude all the *CHI main speaker tiers together with all their dependent tiers, the %spa and %mor dependent tiers on all other speakers, and all @Situation header tiers from the analysis. All remaining tiers will be included in the analysis.

When the transcriber has decided to use complex combinations of codes for speaker ID's such as *CHI-MOT for "child addressing mother", it is possible to use the +t switch with the # symbol as a wild card, as in these commands:

```
freq  +t*NIC-MOT  sample.cha
freq  +t*#-MOT    sample.cha
freq  +t*NIC-#    sample.cha
```

When tiers are included, the analysis will be done on only those specified tiers. When tiers are excluded, however, the analysis is done on tiers **other** than those specified. Failure to exclude **all** unnecessary tiers will cause the programs to produce distorted results. Therefore, it is safer to include tiers in analyses than to exclude them, because it is often difficult to be aware of all the tiers present in any given data file.

If only a tier type symbol (*, %, @) is specified following the +t/-t options, the programs will include all tiers of that particular symbol type from the analysis. Using the option +t@ is important when using **KWAL** for limiting (see the description of the **KWAL** program), because it makes sure that the header information is not lost.

The programs search sequentially, starting from the left of the tier code descriptor, for exactly what the user has specified. This means that a match can occur wherever what has been specified has been found. If you specify *M on the command line after the option, the program will successfully match all speaker tiers that start with *M, such as *MAR, *MIK, *MOT, and so forth. For full clarity, it is best to specify the full tier name after the +t/-t options, including the ":" character. For example, to ensure that only the *MOT speaker tiers are included in the analysis, use the +t*MOT: notation.

As an alternative to specifying speaker names through letter codes, you can use the form:
```
+t@id=idcode
```
In this form, the "idcode" is any character string that matches the type of string that has been declared at the top of each file using the @ID header tier. Standards for constructing these idcodes have not yet been formalized. However, the eventual system that will be devised will code for information such as language, age, sex, etc.

All of the programs include the main speaker tiers by default and exclude all of the dependent tiers, unless a +t% switch is used.

+u   **Merge Specified Data Files Together**. By default, when the user has specified a series of files on the command line, the analysis is performed on each individual file. The program then provides separate output for each data file. If the command line uses the +u option, the program combines the data found in all the specified files into one set and outputs the result for that set as a whole. If too many files are selected, **CLAN** may eventually be unable to complete this merger.

+v   **Version Number**. This switch provides information on the date of the version of **CLAN** being used.

+w/-w   **Window Size**. This option can be used with two **CLAN** programs: **KWAL** and COMBO. These programs are used to display tiers that contain keyword(s) or regular expressions as chosen by the user. By default, **KWAL** and **COMBO** combine the user-chosen main and dependent tiers into "clusters." Each cluster includes the main tier and its dependent tiers. (See the +u option for further information on clusters.)

The -w option followed by a positive integer causes the program to display that number of clusters before each cluster of interest. The +w option followed by a positive integer causes the program to display that number of clusters *after* each cluster of interest. For example, if you wanted the **KWAL** program to produce a context larger than a single cluster, you could include the -w3 and +w2 options in the command line. The program would then output three clusters above and two clusters below each cluster of interest.

+x   See the particular program for the use of this switch.

+y   **Work on nonCHAT Files**. Most of the programs are designed to work best on **CHAT** formatted data files. However, the +y option allows the user to use these programs on nonCHAT formatted files. The program considers each line of a nonCHAT formatted file to be one tier. There are two values of the +y switch. The +y value works on lines and the +y1 value works on utterances as delimited by periods, question marks, and exclamation marks. Some programs do not allow the use of the +y option at all.

+z   **Setting a Range**. The programs perform analyses on the entire data file by default. The +z option allows the user to select any range of words, utterances or speaker turns to be analyzed. The range specifications should immediately follow the option. For example:

+z10w	analyze the first ten words only.
+z10u	analyze the first ten utterances only.
+z10t	analyze the first ten speaker turns only.
+z10w-20w	analyze 11 words starting with the 10th word.
+z10u-20u	analyze 11 utterances starting with the 10th utterance.
+z10t-20t	analyze 11 speaker turns starting with the 10th turn.
+z10w-	analyze from the tenth word to the end of file.
+z10u-	analyze from the tenth utterance to the end of file.
+z10t-	analyze from the tenth speaker turn to the end of file.

If the user has specified more items than exist in the file, the program will analyze only the existing items. If the turn or utterance happens to be empty, because it consists of special symbols and/or words that have been selected to be excluded, then this utterance or turn is not counted.

22.2. Metacharacters for Searching

Metacharacters are special characters used to describe other characters or groups of characters. Certain metacharacters may be used to modify search strings used by the +s/-s switch. However, in order to use metacharacters in the **CHSTRING** program a special switch must be set. The **CLAN** metacharacters are:

*	Any number of characters matched
%	Any number of characters matched and removed
%%	As above plus remove previous character
_	Any single character matched
\	Quote character

Suppose you would like to be able to find all occurrences of the word "cat" in a file. This includes the plural form "cats," the possessives "cat-'s," "cat-s'" and the contractions "cat-

'is" and "cat-'has." Using a metacharacter (in this case, the asterisk) would help you to find all of these without having to go through and individually specify each one. By inserting the string cat* into the include file or specifying it with +s option, all these forms would be found. Metacharacters can be placed anywhere in the word.

The (*) character is a "wild card" character; it will find any character or group of continuous characters which correspond to its placement in the word. For example, if b*s were specified, the program would match words like "beads," "bats," "bat-'s," "balls," "beds," "bed-s," "breaks," and so forth.

The (%) character allows the program to match characters in the same way that the (*) symbol does. Unlike the (*) symbol, however, all the characters matched by the (%) will be ignored in terms of the way of which the output is generated. In other words, the output will treat "beat" and "bat" as two occurrences of the same string, if the search string is b%t. Unless the (%) symbol is used with programs that produce a list of words matched by given keywords, the effect of the (%) symbol will be the same as the effect of the (*) symbol.

When the percentage symbol is immediately followed by a second percentage symbol, the effect of the metacharacter changes slightly. The result of such a search would be that not only the string matching (%) symbol will be removed but also any one character preceding the matched string will also be removed. Without adding the additional % character, a punctuation symbol preceding the wild card string will not be matched and ignored. Adding the second % sign can be particularly useful when searching for roots of words only. For example, to produce a word frequency count of the stem "cat," specify this command:

```
freq  +s"cat-%%"  file.cha.
```

The first % sign matches the suffixes and the second one matches the dash mark. Thus, the search string specified by the +s option will match words like: "cat," "cat-s," "cat-'s," and "cat-s" and **FREQ** will count all of these words as one word "cat." If the data file "file.cha" had consisted of only those four words, the output of the **FREQ** program would have been: 4 cat. The limitation of this search is that it will *not* match words like "cats" or "cat's," because the second percentage symbol is used to match the punctuation mark. The second percentage symbol is also useful for matching hierarchical codes such as $NIA:RP:IN.

The underline character (_) is similar to the (*) character except that it is used to specify any *single* character in a word. For example, the string b_d will match words like "bad," "bed," "bud," "bid," and so forth. For detailed examples of the use of the percentage, underline, and asterisk symbols, see the section on the **FREQ** program.

The quote character (\) is used to indicate the quotation of one of the characters being used as metacharacters. Suppose that you wanted to search for the actual symbol (*) in a text. Because the (*) symbol is used to represent any character, it must be quoted by inserting the (\) symbol before the (*) symbol in the search string to represent the actual (*) character, as in "string*string." To search for the actual character (\), it must be quoted also, i.e. "string\\string" will match "string" followed by "\" and then followed by a second "string."

23. Word Lists

Some of the most important uses of **COMBO**, **FREQ**, and **KWAL** are those that focus on the acquisition and use of particular lexical systems. In order to facilitate this analysis, this chapter provides a set of lists for some of the most important lexical groups in English. These lists are intended as starting points for more seriously constructed lists. Some of the lists were constructed from a search of the million-word spoken language corpus of Francis and Kucera (1982). However, there are surely forms that exist in the language that did not turn up in that corpus. Other lists are based on the symbols for nonstandard forms that were given in the **CHAT** manual. There will often be important theoretical reasons for reworking these lists. Please use these lists only as suggestive starting points, not as definitive characterizations.

Adjectives (Interrogative): what, whatever, which, whichever, whose, whosever.

Adverbs (Interrogative): how, however, howsabout, when, whenever, where, whereby, wherever, wherefore, wherein, whereof, whereon, wherever, wherewith, why.

Adverbs (Nominal): afar, here, then, downtown, east, Monday, Tuesday, Wednesday, Thursday, Friday, Saturday, Sunday, home, north, south, east, west, northeast, southeast, northwest, southwest, left, right, today, tomorrow, tonight, yesterday.

Adverbs (Phrasal): about, across, after, down, in , off, on, out, over, through, up.

Auxiliaries (Copula): ain't, am, are, aren't, be, been, being, is, isn't, was, wasn't, were, weren't.

Auxiliaries (Do): did, didn't, do, does, doesn't, doing, don't, done.

Auxiliaries (Have): had, hadn't, hafta, has, hasn't, have, haven't, having.

Auxiliaries (Modal): can, can't, could, couldn't, dare, may, might, must, need, needn't, ought, shall, should, shouldn't, will, won't, would, wouldn't.

Cardinal Numbers: zero, one, two, three, four, five, six, seven, eight, nine, ten, eleven, twelve, thirteen, fourteen, fifteen, sixteen, seventeen, eighteen, nineteen, twenty, twenty+one, twenty+two, thirty, forty, fifty, sixty, seventy, eighty, ninety, hundred, two+hundred+twenty+six, thousand, million, billion, trillion, quadrillion, quintillian, sextillion, septillion, octillion.

Conjunctions: after, again, against, albeit, although, and, as, (be)cause, before, but, during, either, else, except, for, if, lest, like, likewise, minus, neither, nevertheless, nor, notwithstanding, once, only, or, otherwise, plus, provided, providing, save, seeing, since, so, still, supposing, than, that, then, though, unless, (un)til, when, whence, whenever, where, whereas, whereupon, wherever, whether, while, whilst, without, yet.

Contractions: -'is, -'nt, -'re, -'s, -'d, -'t, -'ve.

Determiners: a, an, another, any, both, each, either, every, few, fewer, fewest, half, many, more, most, nary, neither, no, one, only, several, some, such, that, the, them, these, this, those.

Fused Forms: See the CHAT manual for forms like wanna and gimme.

Interactive and Communicative Markers: abracadabra, adieu, ah, aha, ahah, ahem, ahhah, ahoy, alas, all-right, alright, amen, anyway, atta-boy, augh, auh, aw, awoh, ay, aye, bah, bang, blimey, bong, boo, boohoo, boom, boom-boom-boom, bounce, bow-wow, boy, bravo, bullshit, bye-bye, careful, certainly, cheerio, cheers, chrissake, christ, come-on, crap, creepers, crunch, da-da-da-dum, daddy, dammit, damn, darling, darn, dear, doggone, drat, eek, egad, eh, farewell, fiddle-sticks, fiddlesticks, for-pete's-sake, gad, gawdamighty, gee, gee-up, glory, glory-be, go-ahead, god, goddammit, goddamn, golly, good, good-bye, good-morning, good-night, goodby, goodbye, goodmorning, goodnight, goody, gosh, guck, gucky, h'm, ha, hah, haha, hallelujah, hallo, haw, haw-haw, heehee, heh, hell, hello, help, hey, hi, hmm, hmpf, ho, honey, hoo, hooray, how, howdy, hubba, huh, huh-uh, hullo, hum, humbug, humph, hunhunh, hunmmm, hup, hurrah, hurray, hush, hush-hush, ick, icky, indeed, it-appears-so, it's-okay, jee, jeepers, jesus, kaboom, la, look, man, ma'am, mew, mhm, miaow, mmhm, mommy, morning, mum, mush, mushy, nah, never, no, nope, not-at-all, now, nuhuh, occasionally, of-course, oh, oh-good-right, oh-nuts, oh-oh, oh-yeah, oho, ok, okay, oops, ouch, out, ow, pah, perhaps, phew, phooey, please, poof, pooh, presto, probably, pshaw, pss, pugh, rah, roger, say, scrunch, see, see-here, sh, shalom, shh, shit, shoo, shucks, shush, sir, smoosh, so, sonuvabitch, ssh, sure, sure-sure, sweetie, ta, ta-ta, tehee, thank-you, that's wrong, that's-not-right, that's-ok, that's-right, there, thud, to-some-extent, toot, toot-toot, truly, tsk, tush, tut, tut-tut, tweet, ugh, um, umph, up-a-daisy, welcome, well, what, whee, whew, whirr, whoa, whoo, whoopee, whoosh, wo, woa, woof, wow, yah, yay, yea, yeah, yeah-sure, yeahhuh, yeek, yeh, yep, yes, yesiree, yick, yicky, yikes, yippee, yo, yoho, yoicks, you-see, yow, yuck, yucky, yum, yummy, yumyum, yup, zounds, zowie.

Particles: about, across, after, down, in , off, on, out, over, through, up.

Prefixes: a-, an-, anti-, arch-, auto-, be-, bi-, bio-, co-, contra-, counter-, de-, demi-, di-, dis-, double-, em-, en-, ex-, extra-, fore-, hemi-, hyper-, hypo-, il-, im-, in-, inter-, ir-, long-, lower-, mal-, mid-, middle-, mini-, mis-, mono-, multi-, neo-, non-, out-, over-, paleo-, pan-, poly-, post-, pre-, pro-, proto-, psuedo-, re-, semi-, short-, sub-, super-, tele-, tran-, tri-, ultra-, un-, under-, uni-, upper-, ur-, vice-.

Prepositions: aboard, about, above, abroad, according, across, afore, after, again, against, aloft, along, alongside, alongst, amid, amidst, among, amongst, and, anti, around, as, aside, astride, at, atop, before, behind, below, beneath, beside, besides, between, betwixt, beyond, but, by, concerning, considering, consisting, cross, depending, despite, down, downward, during, except, excepting, excluding, following, for, from, gainst, in, including, infra, inside, inter, into, involving, less, like, mid, midst, midway, minus, more, near, nearer, nearest, neath, next, notwithstanding, o'er, of, off, on, only, onto, opposite, or, out, outside, over, past, pending, per, plus, post, pursuant, rather, regarding, respecting, round, save, since, spite, than, through, throughout, thru, till, times, to, together, toward, towards, under, underneath, unless, unlike, until, unto, up, upon, upward, upwards, versus, via, vis-a-vis, with, within, without.

Pronouns (Interrogative): that, what, whatsoever, who, whoever, whom, whosoever

Pronouns (Nominal): anybody, anyone, anything, everybody, everyone, everything, naught, no-one, nobody, none, nothing, one, somebody, someone, something.

Pronouns (Object): her, him, it, you, us, them, me

Pronouns (Possessive): his, her, its, my, our, your, their.

Pronouns (Predicate Possessives): hers, his, mine, ours, theirs, yours.

Pronouns (Reflexive): herself, himself, itself, myself, oneself, ownself, yourself.

Pronouns (Subject): he, she, it, I, we, you, they, y'all, younz.

Qualifiers (General): These include hundreds of adverbs ending in -ly along with the following: all, almost, already, altogether, always, amply, any, aptly, as, awful, best, better, brand, close, cracking, damn, darned, dead, downright, even, ever, extra, far, farther, fast, flat, full, goddamn, great, half, half-way, halfway, head-and-shoulders, how, ill, indeed, just, kinda, least, less, little, long, lot, lots, many, midway, mighty, more, most, much, near, never, next, no, only, plain, plumb, pretty, quite, rather, raving, real, right, ruddy, second, so, soaking, softly, some, somewhat, sound, stark, still, straight, such, that, this, thus, too, two-thirds, very, way, well, wide, yet.

Qualifiers (Interrogative): how, however.

Qualifiers (Post): enough, indeed, still.

Quantifiers: all, any, both, each, either, enough, every, few, fewer, fewest, half, lots, many, more, most, much, neither, only, other, plenty, several, some, such.

Suffixes (inflectional): -s, -es, -ed, -ing.

Suffixes (derivational): -(i)an, -able, -age, -al, -ally, -ant , -ate, -atic, -ation, -ative, -dom, -ed, -ee, -eer, -en, -eous, -er, -ery, -es, -ese, -esque, -ess, -ette, -ful, -fy, -hood, -ial, -ible, -ic, -ical, -ify, -ine, -ing, -ious, -ise, -ish, -ism, -ist, -ity, -ive, -ize, -less, -let, -like, -ling, -ly, -ment, -ness, -ocracy, -or, -ous, -ren, -ry, -s, -ship, -ster, -uble, -ward(s), -ways, -wise, -y.

Irregular Plural Nouns:

1. Final -y -> -ies

2. Final -f, -fe -> -ves (Find list)

3. Final -ex -> -ices

4. Final -us -> -i

5. Final -um -> -a

6. Special forms: brother - brethren, child - children, die - dice, man - men, foot - feet, goose - geese, louse - lice, mouse - mice, tooth- teeth, woman - women.

Irregular Past Tenses and Participles:

Present	Past	Participle
abide	abode/abided	abode/abided
arise	arose	arisen
awake	awoke/awaked	awoken/awaked
bear	bore	borne
beat	beat	beaten/beat
become	became	become
befall	befell	befallen
beget	begot	begotten
begin	began	begun
behold	beheld	beheld
bend	bent	bent
bereave	bereft/bereaved	bereft/bereaved
beseech	besought/beseeched	besought/beseeched
beset	beset	beset
bestride	bestrode	bestridden/bestrode
bet	bet/betted	bet/betted
betake	betook	betaken
bid	bad/bade/bid	bade/bid/bidden
bind	bound	bound
bite	bit	bitten/bit
bleed	bled	bled
blow	blew	blown
break	broke	broken
breed	bred	bred
bring	brought	brought
broadcast	broadcast/broadcasted	broadcast/broadcasted
build	built	built
burn	burnt/burned	burnt/burned
burst	burst	burst
bust	bust/busted	bust/busted
buy	brought	bought
cast	cast	cast
catch	caught	caught
chide	chid/chided	chidden/chid/chided
choose	chose	chosen
cleave	cleft/clove/cleaved	cleft/cloven/cleaved
cling	clung	clung
come	came	come
cost	cost	cost
creep	crept	crept
cut	cut	cut
deal	dealt	dealt
deepfreeze	deepfroze/deepfreezed	deepfrozen/deepfreezed
dig	dug	dug
dive	dived/dove	dived
do/does	did	done

draw	drew	drawn
dream	dreamt/dreamed	dreamt/dreamed
drink	drank	drunk
drive	drove	driven
dwell	dwelt/dwelled	dwelt/dwelled
eat	ate	eaten
fall	fell	fallen
feed	fed	fed
feel	felt	felt
fight	fought	fought
find	found	found
fit	fit/fitted	fit/fitted
flee	fled	fled
fling	flung	flung
fly	flew	flown
forbear	forbore	forborne
forbid	forbade/forbad	forbidden/forbid
forecast	forecast/forecasted	forecast/forecasted
foresee	foresaw	foreseen
foretell	foretold	foretold
forget	forgot	forgotten/forgot
forgive	forgave	forgiven
forgo	forwent	forgone
forsake	forsook	forsaken
forswear	forswore	forsworn
freeze	froze	frozen
gainsay	gainsaid	gainsaid
get	got	got/gotten
give	gave	given
go	went	gone
grind	ground	ground
grow	grew	grown
hamstring	hamstrung	hamstrung
hang	hung/hanged	hung/hanged
have/has	had	had
hear	heard	heard
heave	heaved/hove	heaved/hove
hew	hewed	hewn/hewed
hide	hid	hidden/hid
hit	hit	hit
hold	held	held
hurt	hurt	hurt
inset	inset	inset
keep	kept	kept
kneel	knelt/kneeled	knelt/kneeled
knit	knit/knitted	knit/knitted
know	knew	known
lay	laid	laid
lead	led	led

lean	leant/leaned	leant/leaned
leap	leapt/leaped	leapt/leaped
learn	learnt/learned	learnt/learned
leave	left	left
lend	lent	lent
let	let	let
lie	lay	lain
light	lit/lighted	lit/lighted
lose	lost	lost
make	made	made
mean	meant	meant
meet	met	met
miscast	miscast	miscast
misdeal	misdealt	misdealt
misgive	misgave	misgiven
mishear	misheard	misheard
mislay	mislaid	mislaid
mislead	misled	misled
misspell	misspelt/misspelled	misspelt/misspelled
misspend	misspent	misspent
mistake	mistook	mistaken
misunderstand	misunderstood	misunderstood
mow	mowed	mown/mowed
offset	offset	offset
outbid	outbid	outbid/outbidden
outdo	outdid	outdone
outfight	outfought	outfought
outgrow	outgrew	outgrown
outrun	outran	outrun
outshine	outshone	outshone
overbear	overbore	overborne
overcast	overcast	overcast
overcome	overcame	overcome
overdo	overdid	overdone
overeat	overate	overeaten
overfeed	overfed	overfed
overhang	overhung	overhung
override	overrode	overridden
overrun	overran	overrun
oversee	oversaw	overseen
overshoot	overshot	overshot
oversleep	overslept	overslept
overtake	overtook	overtaken
overthrow	overthrew	overthrown
partake	partook	partaken
pay	paid	paid
plead	pleaded/pled	pleaded/pled
preset	preset	preset
prove	proved	proved/proven

put	put	put
quit	quit/quitted	quit/quitted
read	read	read
rebind	rebound	rebound
rebuild	rebuilt	rebuilt
recast	recast	recast
redo	redid	redone
remake	remade	remade
rend	rent	rent
repay	repaid	repaid
reread	reread	reread
rerun	reran	rerun
reset	reset	reset
restring	restrung	restrung
retell	retold	retold
rethink	rethought	rethought
rewind	rewound	rewound
rewrite	rewrote	rewritten
rid	rid/ridded	rid/ridded
ride	rode	ridden
ring	rang/rung	rung
rise	rose	risen
run	ran	run
saw	sawed	sawn/sawed
say	said	said
see	saw	seen
seek	sought	sought
sell	sold	sold
send	sent	sent
set	set	set
sew	sewed	sewn/sewed
shake	shook	shaken
shave	shaved	shaved/shaven
shear	sheared	shorn/sheared
shed	shed	shed
shew	shewed	shewn
shine	shone/shined	shone/shined
shit	shit/shat	shit
shoe	shod/shoed	shod/shoed
shoot	shot	shot
show	showed	shown/showed
shred	shredded/shred	shredded/shred
shrink	shrank	shrunk
shrive	shrived/shrove	shrived/shriven
shut	shut	shut
sing	sang	sung
sink	sank	sunk
sit	sat	sat
slay	slew	slain

sleep	slept	slept
slide	slid	slid
sling	slung	slung
slink	slunk	slunk
slit	slit	slit
smell	smelt/smelled	smelt/smelled
smite	smote	smitten
sow	sowed	sowed/sown
speak	spoke	spoken
speed	sped/speeded	sped/speeded
spell	spelt/spelled	spelt/spelled
spend	spent	spent
spill	spilt/spilled	spilt/spilled
spin	spun/span	spun
spit	spat/spit	spat/spit
split	split	split
spoil	spoit/spoiled	spoit/spoiled
spread	spread	spread
spring	sprang/sprung	sprung
stand	stood	stood
steal	stole	stolen
stick	stuck	stuck
sting	stung	stung
stink	stank/stunk	stunk
strew	strewed	strewn/strewed
stride	strode	stridden/strid/strode
strike	struck	struck
string	strung	strung
strive	strove/strived	striven/strived
swear	swore	sworn
sweat	sweat/sweated	sweat/sweated
sweep	swept	swept
swell	swelled	swollen/swelled
swim	swam/swum	swum
swing	swang/swung	swung
take	took	taken
teach	taught	taught
tear	tore	torn
telecast	telecast/telecasted	telecast/telecasted
tell	told	told
think	thought	thought
thrive	thrived/throve	thrived/thriven
throw	threw	thrown
thrust	thrust	thrust
transfer	transferred	transferred
tread	trod	trodden/trod
unbend	unbent	unbent
unbind	unbound	unbound
underbid	underbid	underbid/underbidden

undergo	underwent	undergone
understand	understood	understood
undertake	undertook	undertaken
underwrite	underwrote	underwritten
undo	undid	undone
unfreeze	unfroze	unfrozen
unmake	unmade	unmade
unwind	unwound	unwound
uphold	upheld	upheld
upset	upset	upset
wake	work/waked	woken/waked
waylay	waylaid	waylaid
wear	wore	worn
weave	wove	woven
wed	wedded/wed	wedded/wed
weep	wept	wept
wet	wet/wetted	wet/wetted
win	won	won
wind	wound	wound
withdraw	withdrew	withdrawn
withhold	withheld	withheld
withstand	withstood	withstood
wring	wrung	wrung
write	wrote	written

24. Testing, Bugs, and Modifications

24.1. Testing CLAN

It is important to make sure that **CLAN** is conducting analyses correctly. In some cases you may think that **CLAN** is doing something different from what it is actually designed to do. In order to prevent misinterpretations, you should set up a small test file that contains the various features you want **CLAN** to analyze. For example, if you are running a **FREQ** analysis, you can set a file with several instances of the words or codes for which you are searching. Be sure to include items that should be "misses" along with those that should be "hits." For example, if you don't want **CLAN** to count items on a particular tier, make sure you put some unique word on that tier. If the output of **FREQ** includes that word, you know that something is wrong. In general, you should be testing not for correct performance, but for possible incorrect performance.

In order to make sure that you are using the +t and +z switches correctly, make up a small file and then run **KWAL** over it without specifying any +s switch. This should output exactly the parts of the file that you intend to include or exclude.

24.2. Bug Reports

Occasionally, you may find **CLAN** provides incorrect results. When this occurs, the first thing to do is to reread the relevant sections of the manual to be sure that you have entered all of your commands correctly. If a rereading of the manual does not solve the problem, then you can send email to childes@andrew.cmu.edu to try to get further assistance. In some cases, there may be true "bugs" or program errors that are making correct analyses impossible.

The files "sample.cha" and "sample2.cha" are used throughout the manual. They are included on your **CLAN** diskettes so that you can run the **CLAN** programs as specified in the examples. If you run into problems with the running of a program, be sure to also test it out on the "sample.cha" file to make sure that the problem is with the program itself, rather than the input file. Also, running the program on the "sample.cha" file will help us in understanding the nature of the problem. Should the program not operate properly (according to the manual), please send email to childes@andrew.cmu.edu with the following information:

1. A copy of the file that the program was being run on.

2. The complete command line used when the malfunction occurred.

3. All the results obtained by use of that command.

4. The version number of your **CLAN** program.

24.3. Program Modification Requests

The **CLAN** programs have been designed in response to information we have received from users about the kinds of programs they need for furthering their research. Your input is important, because we are continually designing new programs and improving existing programs. If you find that these programs are not capable of producing the specific type of analysis that you are trying to achieve, contact us and we will do our best to help. Sometimes we can explain ways of using the current **CLAN** system to achieve your goals. In other cases, it may be necessary to modify programs or even to write entirely new programs. You can address inquiries by email to childes@andrew.cmu.edu.

We will need the following information as part of your request:
1. Examples of input file(s).
2. Examples of output(s) desired.
3. An explanation of why the modification is important or useful.

25. Database Introduction

The third major tool in the CHILDES workbench is the database itself. Not all researchers using the CHILDES tools need to make use of the database. If you are principally concerned with collecting and analyzing new empirical data, you will spend most of your time using **CHAT** and **CLAN**, and you will not need to focus your attention on the database. However, if you have research questions that can be addressed by looking at already transcribed data, you will want to learn how to use the database. In this case, the availability of a huge store of child language data can be of vital importance to furthering your research.

The role of the database can be understood best by considering the dilemma facing a researcher who wishes to test a detailed theoretical prediction that requires large naturalistic samples. For example, the researcher may wish to examine the interaction between language type and pronoun omission in order to evaluate the claims of parameter-setting models. Gathering new data that are ideal for the testing of a hypothesis may require months or even years of work. However, conducting an analysis on a small and unrepresentative sample may lead to incorrect conclusions. Because child language data are so time-consuming to collect and to process, many researchers may actually avoid using empirical data to test their theoretical predictions. Or they may try to find one or two sentences that illustrate their ideas, without considering the extent to which their predictions are important for the whole of the child's language. In some cases, conclusions about individual differences in child language have been based on analysis of as few as two children, and rarely on groups larger than 25. Because statistical tests based on three or four subjects have very little power, researchers often avoid the use of statistics altogether in corpora-based studies. This problem arises in particularly clear form when linguistic or psycholinguistic theory make predictions regarding the occurrence and distribution of rare events such as dative passives or certain types of NP-movement. Because of the rarity of such events, large amounts of data must be examined to find out exactly how often they occur in the input and in the child's speech. In these and other cases, researchers who are trying to focus on theoretical analyses are faced with the dilemma of having to commit their time to basic empirical work, rather than being able to focus on the development of acquisitional theory.

There is now a realistic solution to this dilemma. Using the CHILDES database, a researcher can access data from a number of research projects. The database includes a wide variety of language samples from a wide range of ages and situations. Although more than half of the data comes from English speakers, there is also a significant component of non-English data. The total size of the database is now approximately 150 million characters (150 megabytes). The corpora are divided into six major directories: English data, non-English data, story-telling or narrative data, data on language impairments, data from second language acquisition, and data that are not in **CHAT**.

25.1. Documentation and Quality Control

With the exception of a few corpora of historical interest, all of the files in the CHILDES database are in **CHAT** format and have been run through the **CHECK** program to guarantee adherence to the coding and transcription conventions of **CHAT**. Many of the files have full documentation of the conversational context, but for other files crucial details are missing. An attempt has been made to secure as much documentation as possible from the contributors. For editorial consistency, some of these descriptions have been rewritten into a common format, eliminating use of the first person and clarifying certain points. However, none of the factual elements of these documentation files have been changed.

None of the corpora collected before 1987 were transcribed initially in **CHAT**. Instead, we used computer programs and hand-checking to reformat these earlier corpora into the new standard. Since 1987, most of the corpora added to the database havebeen transcribed directly in **CHAT**. These new corpora have certain obvious advantages over the older corpora. First, the corpora that have been transcribed directly into **CHAT** make full use of the various contrasts available in that system. Second, because the new data did not go through a process of optical scanning and reformatting, they do not contain any reformatting errors . Some new corpora also have sonic **CHAT** files with digitized audio records available.

In continuing the construction of the CHILDES database, the overall goal is to achieve a continually higher standard of transcription accuracy and contextual documentation. In a sense the current shape of the database is both a statement about the impressive size of our current child language database and also about the many ways in which that database must be expanded and improved.

25.2.   Retrieving Materials through FTP

Access to the database is free and open. You can copy the CHILDES files, the CHILDES/BIB database, and the **CLAN** programs to your local machine using the FTP protocol over the InterNet. There is no charge for this. The procedure varies depending on the type of machine you are using and the type of files you wish to retrieve. However, in all cases, you first need to follow the basic rules for FTP connections:

1.   Connect to poppy.psy.cmu.edu (128.2.248.42) in Pittsburgh or atila-ftp.uia.ac.be in Antwerp using anonymous FTP. If you get an answer from poppy or atila-ftp, then you know that you have InterNet access. If you do not get an answer, you may not have access or access may be temporarily broken.
2.   When you receive the request for a username, enter "anonymous." Type in your name as a password.
3.   If you want to retrieve data files, type "cd childes" to move to the /childes directory. If you want to retrieve the CLAN programs, type "cd clan" to move to the /clan directory.
4.   Type "ls" to view the directory structure and use "cd" again as needed. It is easy to confuse directories with files. When in doubt type "cd filename." If that works, it was a directory. If not, it was a file.
5.   Type "binary" to set the transfer type. This transfer type will work for all types of files.
6.   Use the "get" command to pull files onto your machine.
7.   When you are finished, type "bye" to close the connection.

25.2.1.   Use of the TAR Program

Once the files are on your local machine, you must untar them. Before you can do this, you need to get a copy of the **TAR** program from poppy or atila-ftp. The Macintosh **TAR** program is in the /macintosh directory. You must "debinhex" it (see below) and then double-click to unstuff it. The MS-DOS **TAR** program is in the /msdos directory. UNIX has the **TAR** program built in. The tar command is something like:

```
tar -xvf eng.tar
```

Untarring the files will recreate the original directory structure. The names of the tar files correspond to divisions of the database as discussed in the manual. Some of the larger normal English corpora have been placed into their own tar files.

25.2.2.   Macintosh Retrieval of CLAN

In order to get the most recent version of CLAN along with certain Macintosh utilities, you should connect to poppy.psy.cmu.edu and use cd clan/macintosh to move into the directory with Macintosh programs and utilities. These files are all in BinHexed format, as indicated by the .hqx extension. The basic CLAN program, the lib files, and the **CED** editor are in clan.sea.hqx. The file manual.hqx has this current manual in MS-Word format. The tar program is in tar.sea.hqx. Once the files are on your machine, use any BinHex utility to decode them. Some FTP programs will run the debinhexing routine during the transfer, if you request this.

25.2.3.   MS-DOS Retrieval of CLAN

In order to get the most recent version of CLAN, connect to poppy.psy.cmu.edu in the way noted just above. Retrieve the tar.exe and clan.tar files using "get tar.exe" and "get clan.tar". Place these two files in \childes\clan and type "tar xvf clan.tar". This will extract all the CLAN programs.

25.3.   Obtaining Materials on CD-ROM

Another way to access the database and programs is by using a CHILDES CD-ROM. This single disk has the entire CHILDES database, the CHILDES/BIB database, the CDI database, and the CLAN programs. There is no charge for the CD-ROM disk itself, but you will have to have a CD-ROM drive in order to be able to use it. The drive unit connects directly into the SCSI port on the Mac. For the IBM-PC, you will need an adaptor card to provide a SCSI port. Often these are sold along with the CD-ROM drive.

25.3.1.   Direct Use of the CD-ROM on the Macintosh

One way of using the materials on the CD-ROM is to copy them over to your hard drive. On the Macintosh you can do this by just dragging whole folders. If you want to analyze files without moving them off the CD-ROM, you can use the "File" menu on the top menu bar in **CLAN** to set your "Working Directory" to some folder on the CD-ROM and your "Output Directory" to some folder on your hard drive. You cannot set the output of your analyses to go to the CD-ROM, because it is not possible to write to a CD-ROM. Once you have copied files and set up your "Working Directory", you should be able to use **CLAN** in the normal fashion.

25.3.2.   Direct Use of the CD-ROM on the IBM-PC

On the IBM/PC you may also decide to make use of the CD-ROM by copying over files to your hard drive. However, if you want to analyze files without copying them over, you must first make sure that you have set the path in your autoexec.bat file to find the **CLAN** programs. Next you should use the "cd" command to set your working directory to some particular directory on the CD-ROM. Then use "cd" to go to back to your working directory on the hard drive. Once you have done this, you can execute a command like:

```
freq +f e:*.cha
```

In this example, we are using e: as the drive designator for the CD-ROM. You can also use the redirect facility as in this command:

```
freq e:*.cha > newfile
```

This will throw all the files into a single file called "newfile" at the top of your hard drive.

To control the setting of your output directory, you can use the +f switch with an argument, as in

+fc:	This will send the output files to your working directory on c:
+f".res"	This sets the extension for your output files.
+f"c:.res"	This sends the output files to c: and gives them the extension .res.

25.4. World Wide Web Access

We have recently installed a World Wide Web (WWW) server on poppy.psy.cmu.edu that facilitates HyperText access to the database, this manual, and other materials. The URL for this server is http::/poppy.psy.cmu.edu/childes.html

25.5. Acknowledgments and Contributors

When researchers publish studies that make use of CHILDES data, we ask that they always provide acknowledgment first to the CHILDES system by citing MacWhinney and Snow (1990). In addition, they should acknowledge the work of the individual contributors of the corpora used in the analysis by citing the articles specified by those contributors. Each contributor has provided a set of one or more articles that should be cited in order to provide this acknowledgment. In a few cases, contributors have also requested that they be informed of the particular uses being made of their data, so that they can guard against inaccurate interpretations. In general, users should contact the original contributors whenever possible. The names and addresses of the primary contributors of the various CHILDES corpora are given in the following list:

Aksu-Koç, Ayhan
Department of Psychology
Bogazici University
80815 Bebek
Istanbul, Turkey
koc@boun.edu.tr

Albalá, José María
Departamento de Lengua Española
Univ. Nacional de Educ. a Distancia
Senda del Rey s/n
Madrid, Spain 28040

Bates, Elizabeth
Department of Psychology
University of California
La Jolla, CA 92093 USA
bates@amos.ucsd.edu

Berman, Ruth
Department of Linguistics
Tel-Aviv University
Ramat Aviv, Tel-Aviv 69978, Israel
rberman@ccsg.tau.ac.il

Bernstein-Ratner, Nan
Hearing and Speech Sciences
LeFrak Hall
University of Maryland
College Park, MD 20742 USA
nratner@bss1.umd.edu

Bliss, Lynn S.
Speech Communication
Wayne State University
585 Manoogian Hall
Detroit, MI 48202 USA
lbliss@cms.cc.wayne.edu

Bloom, Lois
Teachers College
Columbia University
525 West 120th St.
New York, NY 10027 USA
lmb32@columbia.edu

Bohannon, John Neil
Department of Psychology
Butler University
Indianapolis IN 46208 USA
bohannon@butler.edu

Brown, Roger
Department of Psychology
1510 William James Hall
Harvard University
Cambridge, MA 02139 USA

Burns-Hoffman, Rebecca
School of Education
University of Miami
5202 University Drive, Merrick 312
Coral Gables, Fl 33124
rburns@umiami.ir.miami.edu

Cappelli, Giuseppe
ILC (CNR)
Via della Faggiola, 32
Pisa 56100 Italy
beppe@icnucevm.cnuce.cnr.it

Carterette, Edward
Department of Psychology
University of California
Los Angeles, CA 90024 USA

Champaud, Christian
Laboratoire de Psych. CNRS
28, Rue Serpente
Paris 75006 France
champau@frmop22.cnusc.fr

Chapman, Robin
Department of Comm. Disorders
University of Wisconsin
1975 Willow Drive
Madison, WI 53706 USA
chapman@waisman.wisc.edu

Cipriani, Paola
IRCCS "Stella Maris"
INPE-Universitá di Pisa
Viale del Tirreno, 331
Calambrone (Pisa), Italy

Clahsen, Harald
Department of Linguistics
University of Essex
Colchester C04 3SQ England
harald@essex.ac.uk

Clark, Eve
Department of Linguistics
Stanford University
Building 100
Stanford, CA 94305 USA
eclark@psych.stanford.edu

Conti-Ramsden, Gina
Centre for Educational Guidance
Department of Education
University of Manchester
Manchester, England M13 9PL
gina.conti-ramsden@man.ac.uk

Cruttenden, Alan
Department of Linguistics
University of Manchester
Manchester M13 9PL England
a.cruttenden@manchester.ac.uk

De Houwer, Annick
Communicatiewetenschap
PSW - UIA
Universiteitsplein 1
Antwerp 2610 Belgium
vhouwer@uia.ua.ac.be

Demetras, Marty
Arizona University Affiliated Program
Assistive Tech. Program of Tucson
2600 N. Wyatt
Tucson, AZ 85712
demetras@nauvax.ucc.nau.edu

Deuchar, Margaret
Department of Linguistics
University of Cambridge
Sidgwick Avenue
Cambridge CB3 9DA England
md118@phx.cam.ac.uk

Deutsch, Werner
Institut für Psychologie
der TU Braunschweig
Spielmannstr. 19
3300 Braunschweig Germany

Elbers, Loekie
Department of Psychology
University of Utrecht
Heidelberglaan 1
3584 CS Utrecht Netherlands
elbers@fsw.ruu.nl

Evans, Mary Ann
Department of Psychology
University of Guelph
Guelph ON N1G 2W1 Canada
evans@psyadm.css.uoguelph.ca

Feldman, Heidi
Child Development Unit
Children's Hospital
3705 Fifth Ave.
Pittsburgh, PA 15213 USA
feldmah@chplink.chp.edu

Feldweg, Helmut
Max-Planck Institut für Psycholinguistik
Wundtlaan 1
6525 XD Nijmegen, The Netherlands
feldweg@sfs.nphil.uni-tuebingen.de

Fletcher, Paul
Department of Linguistic Science
University of Reading
PO Box 218
Reading RG6 2AA England
llsfletp@reading.ac.uk

Fosnot, Susan Meyers
4404 San Blas Ave.
Woodland Hills, CA 91364 USA
ibpysmf@mvs.oac.ucla.edu

Garvey, Catherine
Route 1, Box 255
Brooksville ME 04617 USA

Gathercole, Virginia C.
English Department
Florida International University
Miami, FL 33199 USA
gatherco@servax.fiu.edu

Gillis, Steven
University of Antwerp
Germaanse - Linguistiek
Universiteitsplein 1
B-2610 Wilrijk Belgium
gillis@uia.ac.be

Gleason, Jean Berko
Department of Psychology
Boston University
64 Cummington St.
Boston MA 02215 USA
gleason@bu-pub.bu.edu

Gopnik, Myrna
Department of Linguistics
McGill University
1001 Sherbrooke W.
Montreal, PQ H3A 1G5 Canada

Guthrie, Larry F.
Far West Laboratory
1855 Folsom St.
San Francisco, CA 94103 USA

Hall, William S.
Department of Psychology
University of Maryland
College Park, MD 20742 USA
whall@ucmd.edu

Hargrove, Patricia
Dept. of Communication Disorders
Mankato State University
Mankato, MN 56001 USA

Hayashi, Mariko
Institute of Psychology
University of Århus
Asylvej 4
Risskov, Denmark
psykhaya@aau.dk

Hayes, Donald
346 Uris Hall
Sociology Department
Cornell University
Ithaca, NY 14853 USA

Hemphill, Lowry
Harvard Graduate School of Education
703 Larsen Hall
Cambridge, MA 02125 USA
hemphilo@hugse1.harvard.edu

Hicks, Deborah
Department of Educ. Development
College of Education
University of Delaware
Newark, DE 19716 USA
hicks@brahms.udel.edu

Higginson, Roy P.
3089 Thorn Street
San Diego, CA 92104
rhigginson@ucsd.edu

Holland, Audrey
Department of Speech and Hearing
University of Arizona
Tucson, AZ USA
alh@ccit.arizona.edu

Hooshyar, Nahid
7818 La Verdura
Dallas, TX 75248 USA

Howe, Christine
Department of Psychology
Strathclyde University
155 George Street
Glasgow GIIRDUK Scotland

Korman, Myron
478 Pebble Ridge Court
Langhorne, PA 19047 USA

Kuczaj, Stan
Department of Psychology
Southern Methodist University
Dallas, TX 75275 USA

Leonard, Lawrence
Audiology and Speech Sciences
Purdue University
Heavilon Hall
West Lafayette, IN 47907 USA
xdxl@vm.cc.purdue.edu

Leveillé, Madeleine
Laboratoire de Psych. Experimentale
28 rue Serpente
Paris 75006 France
upec010@frors31.bitnet

Linaza, Jose L.
Psicologia de los procesos
Universidad Autonoma de Madrid
Cantoblanco
Madrid 34, Spain
jlinaza@ccuam3.sdi.uam.es

MacWhinney, Brian
Department of Psychology
Carnegie Mellon University
Pittsburgh PA 15213 USA
brian@andrew.cmu.edu

Marrero, Victoria
Departamento de Lengua Española
Univ. Nacional de Educ. a Distancia
Senda del Rey s/n
Madrid, Spain 28040
Victoria.Marrero@human.uned.es

Miller, Jon
Department of Comm. Disorders
Univ. of Wisconsin
1975 Willow Drive
Madison WI 53706
miller@don.waisman.wisc.edu

Montes, Rosa Graciela
Universidad Autonoma de Puebla
Apdo. Postal 1356
Puebla, Mexico 72001
rmontes@udlapvms.pue.udlap.mx

Narasimhan, R.
Tata Institute of Fundamental Research
Homi Bhabha Road
Bombay 400-005 India

Pan, Barbara
Harvard Graduate School of Education
Larsen Hall, Appian Way
Cambridge, MA 02138
snowbp@hugse1.harvard.edu

Peters, Ann
Department of Linguistics
University of Hawaii
1890 East West Road
Honolulu, HI 96822
ann@uhunix.uhcc.hawaii.edu

Pizzuto, Elena
c/o Virginia Volterra
Istituto di Psicologia CNR
Viale Marx, 15
Rome, Italy
pizzuto@kant.irmkant.rm.cnr.it

Plunkett, Kim
Department of Psychology
University of Oxford
Oxford England
plunkett@psy.oxford.ac.uk

Post, Kathy
134 Ridgeview Circle
Glenshaw, PA 15116 USA

Protassova, Ekaterina
Pelimannintie 21-23 F 27
Helsinki 00420 Finland

Roberts, Celia
National Center for Language Training
Havelock Road
Southhall, Middx UB2 4NZ England

Romero-Contreras, Silvia
University of the Americas
Puebla 223 Col. Roma
Mexico, D.F. 06700

Rondal, Jean
Laboratoire de Psychologie
Boulevarde du Rectorat, 5
Sart-Tilman
B-4000 Liege Belgium
u017301@vm1.ulg.ac.be

Sachs, Jacqueline
Department of Communication Science
University of Connecticut U-85
Storrs, CT 06268 USA
sachs@uconnvm.uconn.edu

Schaerlaekens, A.
Centrum voor Taalverwervingonderzoek
Kapucignenvoor 33
Leuven, 3000 Belgium

Schulze, H.
Sektion Phoniatrie und Paedaudiologie
Hals-Nasen-Ohrenklinik
Universität Ulm
Frauensteige 14a
7900 Ulm, Germany

Scliar-Cabral, Leonor
UFSC/LLV
Rua São Miguel 1106
Bairro Saco Grande
Florianópolís, Brazil 88030
fsc1cab@ibm.ufsc.br

Serra, Miquel
Departament de Psicologia Basica
Universitat de Barcelona
Adolf Florensa s/n
Barcelona, 08028 Spain
mserra@farmacia.ub.es

Slobin, Dan
Department of Psychology
University of California
Berkeley CA 94720 USA
slobin@cogsci.berkeley.edu

Snow, Catherine
Harvard Graduate Schl. of Ed.
703 Larsen Hall
Appian Way
Cambridge MA 02138 USA
snowcat@hugse1.harvard.edu

Stephany, Ursula
Institut fur Sprachwissenschaft
Universität zu Köln
D-5000 Köln 41, Germany
stephany@rs1.rrz.uni-koeln.de

Strömqvist, Sven
Department of Linguistics
University of Göteborg
Renstromsparken
Göteborg S-41298 Sweden
sven@hum.gu.se

Sulzby, Elizabeth
Center for Human Growth
300 N. Ingalls
University of Michigan
Ann Arbor, MI 48109-0406

Suppes, Patrick
Department of Philosophy
Stanford University
Stanford, CA 94305 USA

Van Houten, Lori
Department of Linguistics
Stanford University
Stanford, CA 94305 USA

van Kempen, Jacqueline
OTS, Trans 10
3512 JK Utrecht
The Netherlands
jacqueline.vankampen@let.ruu.nl

Wagner, Klaus
Universitat Dortmund
Fachbereich 15 - Kindersprache
Postfach 500500
Dortmund 4600 Germany

Warren-Leubecker, Amye
Department of Psychology
University of Tennessee
615 McCallie Ave
Chattanooga, TN 37403

Weissenborn, Jürgen
Max-Planck Institut
Wundtlaan 1
6525 XD Nijmegen Netherlands
weissenb@mpi.nl

Weist, Richard
Department of Psychology
SUNY Fredonia
Fredonia, 14063 USA
weist@a12t.cc.fredonia.edu

Wells, Gordon
OISE
252 Bloor St. West
Toronto ON M5S 1V6 Canada
gord_wells@oise.on.ca

Wijnen, Frank
Department of Linguistics
University of Groningen
Oude Kijk in 't Jatstraat 26
Groningen 9712 EK Netherland
f.n.k.wijnen@ppsw.rug.nl

Wilson, Bob
Department of State/FSI
1400 Key Blvd.
Suite 901
Arlington, VA 22209
statefsi@guvax.bitnet

Wode, Henning
Englishes Seminar
Christian-Albrechts-Universität
Olshausenstraße 40
D-2300 Kiel 1 Germany

Wolf, Dennis
Harvard Graduate School of Education
Larsen Hall
Cambridge, MA 02138
wolfde@hugse1.harvard.edu

Zeitlyn, David
University of Oxford
Institute of Social and Cultural Anthro.
51 Banbury Road
Oxford OX2 6PE England
zeitlyn@vax.ox.ac.uk

26. English Data

The directory of transcripts from normal English-speaking children constitutes about half of the total CHILDES database. The subdirectories are named for the contributors of the data.

26.1. Bates

This directory contains transcripts from the Bates/Bretherton Colorado longitudinal sample of middle-class children studied in Boulder, Colorado, between 1978 and 1980. There are four subdirectories: free20, free28, snack28, and story28. These names indicate the ages of the children in months and the nature of the activity in which they were engaged. Children were studied at four age levels: 10, 13, 20 and 28 months. The initial sample included 32 children;, but only 27 participated at all four ages. At each age level, data were collected in two sessions. The first session was always held in the home, followed by a session in the laboratory no more than 7 days later. Detailed transcriptions are available only for the laboratory session. At 20 months, there are only transcripts of mother–infant free play (the first 10–15 minutes of the session, a "warmup" for the sequence of structured procedures that followed). At 28 months, there are transcripts for three segments of mother–infant interaction:

1. **Free play** with the same instructions and the same toys used in the 20 month segment,
2. **Reading** of the book "Miffy in the Snow", and
3. **A snack**.

The children were all originally participants in a study of causal understanding in infancy (Carlson-Luden, 1979) involving an initial group of 48 infants with an average age of 0;10.11 (with a range from 0;10.0 to 0;10.28). At the end of the Carlson-Luden study, parents were asked if they would be willing to participate in our longitudinal study of language and symbolic development, up through 28 months of age. The parents of 32 children agreed, resulting in a starting sample of 16 boys and 16 girls. These infants were next seen at 13 months of age. Five children subsequently moved away. At 20 months, three new children were therefore invited to participate in the project, to bring the sample up to 15 boys and 15 girls. This sample of 30 children all participated in the final sessions at 28 months. Although the total sample varied from one session to another, 27 children participated at all four age levels. All the analyses in Bates, Bretherton, and Snyder (1988) are based on this constant sample of 27, including 13 boys and 14 girls. Thirteen children were first-born, ten were second-born, and four were third-born or later. Their average birthweight was 7.2 pounds., with a range from 5.5 to 9.0 lbs. Average age in days at the initial 10 month session was 311, with a range from 300 to 324. At all subsequent sessions, children were within two weeks on either side of the target range. A note regarding the demographic make-up of this sample: Although we did not select subjects systematically on the basis of race or socioeconomic level, the demographic characteristics of Boulder, Colorado are such that these selection criteria resulted in a sample of middle to upper-middle class Caucasian children (with the exception of one Black child from a middle-class family). This is, then, a very homogeneous and privileged group of children, a fact which of course limits the generalizability of our findings to other groups. If you make use of this corpus, please cite Bates, Bretherton, and Snyder (1988).

26.2.   Bernstein-Ratner

This directory contains data that were collected by Nan Bernstein-Ratner from nine children aged 1;1 to 1;11.   There are three samples from each child at three time points, all transcribed from high-quality reel-to-reel audiotapes in UNIBET notation.

Subjects. The subjects were nine mother-child dyads who were followed for a period of four to five months each. Each dyad has three transcripts. The mothers were all college-educated women, who were native born Americans with white collar husbands. The children (all girls) ranged in age from 1;1 to 1;9 at first taping. The ages of each child are posted on the very first line of each transcript file. Three of the children began the study as prelinguistic infants (Kay, Amelia and Dale). Three began as "holophrastic" language users (Alice, Cindy and Marie). Three began and finished as multi-word utterance producers (Lena, Gail and Annie). These names do not correspond to those listed in either Bernstein (1982) or some subsequent articles, due to the request by CHILDES to provide pseudonyms. Children in each of the first two groups made significant linguistic progress into higher language stages during the course of the study.

Procedure. Children and their mothers played for approximately 45 minutes at each session with the same selection of toys (blocks, stuffed animals, puppets, books, and so forth). Most of the sessions were followed by a parental interview. These interviews are collected in a subdirectory entitled "interview." The purpose of the interview was to gather a sample of the mothers' speech for comparison against the mother-child condition. In order to obtain exemplars of mother-adult words to match to the mother-child condition, the questioning sometimes wandered. In addition, to save transcription time, the mothers' responses to the investigator's questions are provided, but the investigator's comments are omitted.

Recording. These transcripts were derived from reel-to-reel audiotaped interactions carried out in a sound-proof playroom at the Massachusetts Institute of Technology Research Laboratory of Electronics during 1979-80. The original inquiry regarded phonetic characteristics of maternal speech. The quality of the audio recordings of both mothers and children is extremely fine. Mothers wore lavalier microphones with Sony ECM-50's and the interactions were taped on a Revox A77. These tapes will be made available to any researcher who requests them, with the provisos that the researcher receive some sort of authorship credit for subsequent research derived from them, and that the costs of materials/labor to duplicate the tapes be borne by the requesting researcher.

The children's language skills were not a primary focus of any of the research carried out to date using these samples. As a result, although phonetic transcriptions of the children have been provided, they are very rough. Given the notorious difficulty of obtaining reliability in the transcription of prelinguistic and early child phonetic strings, it is recommended that any researcher interested in doing a phonological analysis of the children's data request the original audiotapes. The children are transcribed in UNIBET, with minimal fine detail. To create uniformity, and to read as little as possible into the children's output, most of the children are phonetically transcribed, even when their productions appear to correspond to adult forms. The majority of the children's productions are phonetic, rather than phonemic, given the ages of the children. Some of the older children's transcripts include regular English orthography.

Miscellaneous notes. Amelia was a nonidentical twin. Her mother's speech to the other twin girl was also recorded for six months, but has not been provided. It is available on request. A series of three tapes of a mother conversing with a girl thought to be language-delayed and eliminated from the first and subsequent studies is available without transcript. Finally, a girl having linguistic skills similar to Lena, but with a more talkative mother, was taped for a manuscript in preparation and can be provided without transcription. Copies of the dissertation (Bernstein, 1982) can be obtained upon request, as can more information about particular subjects or other issues.

Please feel free to contact Dr. Bernstein-Ratner if you have any comments or questions regarding these samples. If you use these data, please cite one or more of these articles: Bernstein (1982), Bernstein-Ratner (1984a; 1984b; 1985; 1986; 1987) and Bernstein-Ratner and Pye (1984).

26.3. Bloom – 1973

This subdirectory contains a set of files from Bloom contributed by Lois Bloom of Columbia University Teacher's College. Allison was the subject of the study of language development reported in the appendices to Bloom (1973). Two additional files for Allison that did not appear in that book were contributed directly by Bloom (Allison5 and Allison6). The original collection and transcription of these data were made possible by research support provided by The National Institutes of Health to Lois Bloom. One copy of any published report or unpublished dissertation that make use of these data is to be sent to Lois Bloom at Teachers College, Columbia University, 525 West 120 Street, New York, NY 10027.

Details on the methods and material for video tape recording were given by Bloom in her introduction to the Appendix to (Bloom, 1973) which is repeated in its entirety as "0methods.doc." Allison was born on July 12, 1968. Her ages in the six samples are as follows:

Sample	Age	Sample	Age
1	1;4.21	4	1;10
2	1;7.14	5	2;4.7
3	1;8.21	6	2;10

If you use these data, please cite Bloom (1973).

26.4. Bloom – 1970

This directory contains files from three children.. The children are Peter, Eric, and Gia. Peter was born on December 27, 1969; Eric was born on July 2, 1964; and Gia was born on February 5, 1965.

The Peter subdirectory contains 20 files, recorded between the ages of one year, nine months and three years and two months. It was recorded during the years 1971 and 1973. Peter was one of the four subjects studied in the context of the project reported upon in "Language Development: Form and Function in Emerging Grammars." The other three children – Eric, Kathryn, and Gia – were recorded in the late 1960's, whereas Peter was recorded after the 1970 book was published. Additional data on hand-written sheets are available for Eric and Gia, as well as for a fourth child Kathryn.

Peter was an upper-middle class White child with college-educated parents. He was a first-born child living in a university community in New York City.

File	Age	File	Age	File	Age	File	Age
01	1;9.7	06	2;0.7	11	2;3.21	16	2;7.14
02	1;9.21	07	2;0.7	12	2;4.14	17	2;8.14
03	1;10.15	08	2;1.21	13	2;5.0	18	2;9.14
04	1;11.7	09	2;2.14	14	2;5.21	19	2;10.21
05	1;11.21	10	2;3.0	15	2;6.14	20	3;1.21

Eric was one of the three children studied in the context of the preparation of Bloom (1970). The file called "bookeric" has the material reported in the book. The other files, beginning when Eric is 19 months old, have been entered from handwritten transcripts.

Gia was one of the three children studied in the context of the preparation of Bloom (1970). The file called "bookgia" has the material reported in the book. The other files have been entered from handwritten transcripts. If you use these data, please cite Bloom (1970).

26.5.   Bohannon

These transcripts show the interaction of different adults with two children, Nat and Baxter. There were 17 adults interacting with Nat and 10 interacting with Baxter. The adults include 15 undergraduates, 5 graduates and the subject's mother. The data were collected in 1976–1977.

Subjects. Twelve undergraduates and five graduate students participated in the experiment. Nat was 2;8 (MLU = 3.59 morphemes) when he interacted with the undergraduates. He was 3;0 (MLU = 3.73 morphemes) when he interacted with the graduate students. Nat is the son of a college professor and a college graduate and probably verbally precocious.

Corresponding information regarding the Baxter study has not yet been provided.

Procedure. Students were given minimal instructions concerning the experiment. They were simply told to converse with the child and to try to draw him into conversation. The undergraduate students were sent to Nat's home in six teams of two students and one team of three students. The students visiting Baxter's home went singly. During each interaction, the noninteracting team members took contextual notes while the other team member interacted. The mother was present during all interactions. They were also accompanied by an experimental assistant to run the tape recorder. All interactions were recorded on Realistic Super Tape by means of a Realistic CTR-29 cassette deck. During the interaction several play materials (i.e. blocks, stuffed animals, and books around the house) were made available for assisting conversations. The average interaction lasted about 15 minutes, with one group of undergraduate students going a full hour. These transcripts were checked against the tapes for accuracy by Nat's mother and the authors.

Response Codes. Six of the transcribed files are coded for adult response types, errors and MLU on a %cod tier. These files are "claire.cha", "dan.cha", "elliott.cha", "harvey.cha", "ruth.cha", and "stephani.cha". The coding for "harvey.cha" is not complete. Here are the codes and the format for these codes.

The first number on the line is the MLU count for the above speaker's utterance. It is coded in the form $MLU=4. The next letter is the utterance type ($UT) which is coded as one of these five values:

d	declarative
q	question
i	imperative
wf	well-formed
if	ill-formed

If the utterance is ill-formed (if), then one of these error codes will follow it:

pr	pragmatic
sm	semantic
sy	syntactic
ph	phonetic

Thus, there will be codes such as $UT=if:pr and $UT=if:sm

The final cluster of codes refers to the adult response type ($ART) which can be:

cc	child contingent
cd	child dependent
ad	adult dependent
nc	non contingent
corr	correction
app	approval
oth	other

Or the final codes may refer to repetition types ($RT) which can be:

sf	self follows
cf	child follows

Both the $ART and the $RT codes may be further described by these qualifiers:

exct	exact
elab	elaborate
rcst	recast
cont	continuation

Thus, there are codes such a $ART=cc:exct and $RT=sf:elab.

Publications that make use of this corpus should cite Bohannon and Marquis (1977) and Stine and Bohannon (1983).

26.6. Braine

The 12 small files in this directory contain the early utterances from Andrew, David, Johnathan, Kendall, Odi, Seppo, Sipili, and Tofi published in Braine (1976). Only the child's utterances are entered, because no parental input was reported. It is necessary to use a "00depadd" file for Sipili and Seppo to pass **CHECK**, because Samoan has initial apostrophes. Publications that make use of this corpus should cite Braine (1976).

26.7. Brown

This subdirectory contains the complete transcripts from the three subjects Adam, Eve, and Sarah who were studied by Roger Brown and his students between 1962 and 1966. Adam was studied from 2;3 to 4;10, Eve from 1;6 to 2;3, and Sarah from 2;3 to 5;1. Brown (1973) summarized this research and provided detailed documentation regarding data collection, transcription, and analysis.

The corpora were scanned optically from the original typed sheets and then reformatted by program and extensively checked by hand. In 1989 the complete data set was checked for syntactic correctness by the CLAN program called CHECK. The basic level of transcription generally corresponds to minCHAT. However, the child's speech in the Adam and Eve corpora have also been coded for these five speech acts:

$RES	Response
$IMIT	Imitation
$EIMIT	Elicited Imitation
$MLR	Metalinguistic reference
$IMP	Imperative

Adam was the child of a minister and an elementary school teacher. His family was middle class and well-educated. Though he was Black, he was not a speaker of American Black English, but of Standard American. There are 55 files in the Adam corpus and his age ranges from 2;3 to 4;10. Also included in the corpus is a file called "00lexicon.doc" which contains some nonstandard lexical items that were used or invented by Adam.

File	Age	File	Age	File	Age	File	Age
01	2;3.4	15	2;10.2	29	3;4.18	43	4;1.15
02	2;3.18	16	2;10.16	30	3;5.0	44	4;2.17
03	2;4.3	17	2;10.30	31	3;5.15	45	4;3.9
04	2;4.15	18	2;11.13	32	3;6.9	46	4;4.0
05	2;4.30	19	2;11.28	33	3;5.29	47	4;3.13
06	2;5.12	20	3;0.11	34	3;7.7	48	4;5.11
07	2;6.3	21	3;0.25	35	3;8.0	49	4;6.24
08	2;6.17	22	3;1.9	36	3;8.14	50	4;7.0
09	2;6.17	23	3;1.26	37	3;8.26	51	4;7.29
10	2;7.14	24	3;2.9	38	3;9.16	52	5;2.12
11	2;8.0	25	3;2.21	39	3;10.15	53	4;9.2
12	2;8.16	26	3;3.4	40	3;11.0	54	4;10.2
13	2;9.4	27	3;3.18	41	3;11.14	55	4;10.23
14	2;9.18	28	3;4.1	42	4;0.14		

Eve was a linguistically precocious child. Unfortunately for the study, her family moved away from the Cambridge area after only 20 sessions were completed. Her speech developed very rapidly over these 9 months. In spite of the small amount of data, her record is especially rich. She began the study when she was 1;6 and left the study when she was 2;3.

Included with the Eve data are two files, "00lexicon.doc" and "00proper.doc". The 00lexicon.doc outlines nonstandard lexical items and the 00proper.doc file shows the proper nouns used by Eve. Eve's approximate ages in each of the 20 files are as follows:

File	Age	File	Age	File	Age	File	Age
01	1;6	06	1;9	11	1;11	16	2;1
02	1;6	07	1;9	12	1;11	17	2;2
03	1;7	08	1;9	13	1;12	18	2;2
04	1;7	09	1;10	14	2;0	19	2;3
05	1;8	10	1;10	15	2;1	20	2;3

Sarah was the child of a working class family. There are 139 files in the Sarah corpus covering the ages 2;3 to 5;1. There is also a "00lexicon.doc" file outlining nonstandard lexical items used by Sarah. Sarah's approximate ages for each of the 139 files are as follows:

File	Age	File	Age	File	Age	File	Age
001	2;3.5	036	2;11.2	071	3;7.30	106	4;4.25

002	2;3.7	037	2;11.17	072	3;8.6	107	4;5.4
003	2;3.19	038	2;11.23	073	3;8.12	108	4;5.8
004	2;3.22	039	2;11.30	074	3;8.20	109	4;5.14
005	2;3.26	040	3;0.18	075	3;8.27	110	4;5.22
006	2;3.28	041	3;0.18	076	3;9.3	111	4;5.29
007	2;4.10	042	3;0.27	077	3;9.18	112	4;6.5
008	2;4.12	043	3;1.3	078	3;9.26	113	4;6.11
009	2;4.17	044	3;1.10	079	3;9.26	114	4;6.17
010	2;4.19	045	3;1.17	080	3;10.1	115	4;6.24
011	2;4.26	046	3;1.24	081	3;10.9	116	4;7.0
012	2;5.7	047	3;2.2	082	3;10.16	117	4;7.11
013	2;5.15	048	3;2.10	083	3;10.30	118	4;7.17
014	2;5.25	049	3;2.16	084	3;11.9	119	4;7.24
015	2;5.30	050	3;2.23	085	3;11.16	120	4;8.7
016	2;6.4	051	3;3.7	086	3;11.29	121	4;8.13
017	2;6.13	052	3;3.7	087	4;0.5	122	4;8.20
018	2;6.20	053	3;3.13	088	4;0.14	123	4;9.4
019	2;6.30	054	3;3.20	089	4;0.28	124	4;9.12
020	2;7.5	055	3;3.28	090	4;1.4	125	4;9.19
021	2;7.12	056	3;4.1	091	4;1.11	126	4;9.26
022	2;7.18	057	3;4.9	092	4;1.18	127	4;10.6
023	2;7.28	058	3;4.16	093	4;1.28	128	4;10.21
024	2;8.2	059	3;4.26	094	4;2.1	129	4;10.27
025	2;8.25	060	3;5.1	095	4;2.9	130	4;11.4
026	2;8.25	061	3;5.7	096	4;2.16	131	4;11.13
027	2;9.0	062	3;5.13	097	4;2.23	132	4;11.19
028	2;9.6	063	3;5.20	098	4;2.28	133	4;11.26
029	2;9.14	064	3;6.6	099	4;3.7	134	5;0.2
030	2;9.20	065	3;6.16	100	4;3.13	135	5;0.10
031	2;9.29	066	3;6.23	101	4;3.19	136	5;0.16
032	2;10.5	067	3;6.30	102	4;3.26	137	5;0.25
033	2;10.11	068	3;7.9	103	4;4.1	138	5;0.30
034	2;10.20	069	3;7.16	104	4;4.11	139	5;1.6
035	2;10.24	070	3;7.23	105	4;4.18		

Publications that make use of this corpus should cite Brown (1973).

26.8. Carterette and Jones

This subdirectory contains the full text of the speech corpus in Carterette and Jones (1974) donated to the CHILDES by Edward Carterette of the University of California at Los Angeles in 1985. The data were taken from a computer tape from which the book had been made. The characters on that tape were translated first into ASCII and then into UNIBET. For a description of UNIBET notation, see chapter 10. The book is composed of a standard orthographic transcription of conversations and the corresponding text in phonetic orthography on the facing page.

Subjects. The data was collected from first, third and fifth grade students as well as adults. The adult sample was similar to the child samples in community, national and regional origin, and socioeconomic status. It was obtained from junior college classes of a city college in California. There were 54 first graders, 48 third graders, 48 fifth graders, and 24 adults. First graders did more giggling, interrupting, and drowning each other out, so more subjects were needed to provide a comparable amount of material.

Children from two different schools were used to reduce possible biases of unsuspected sorts. Both schools had children drawn largely from the middle socioeconomic level. The investigation of the effect of socioeconomic status on language development is an important one, but not the subject under investigation here. Moreover, it also requires a norm. It was just this norm for studies of language development of all sorts that this database provides. The sample used all children in a grade who were present when called and were not excused by reason of foreign language background, marked non-California dialect, or speech impediments. Because regions of the country differ in the phonemes used in speech, it was judged more in keeping with the aims of the study to include only one type of regional speech, which happened to be Southern Californian.

Data Collection Situation. A simple social situation was used. Three children were seated around a small table with a young, friendly adult. The adult greeted the children by name, told them she wanted to find out what children in their grade were interested in, and asked them to talk to each other about anything they wanted to talk about. Some groups required somewhat more encouragement; if so, the adult asked a question or two: "What do you do after school?," or "How many in your family?" Thereafter she said nothing. After the initial warm-up period, which was discarded for the transcription, the speech appeared to be children's normal speech. It was rapid; there were interruptions; it covered every conceivable topic; it was full of slang and noise words; there was give-and-take. This, then, was the situation in which all the child speech samples were recorded.

For the adults, the situation was structured differently. The participants were from elementary psychology classes, so their knowledge of psychological jargon was flattered. They were told that the experiment was investigating small group processes and that the situation was to be completely nondirective. Then they were introduced by first names and told they were at a party. The experimenter excused himself (psychologically) to get the snacks. Again groups of three were always used. Most of the adults did not know each other, whereas in the children's group, they did. The three-person interaction proved as useful for adults as for children, and the language produced was judged to be normal, everyday conversation, as rapid, slangy, and diverse as any in an unrecorded situation.

As many individuals and as many groups as possible were included, in order to reduce the effect of idiosyncrasies of vocabulary, topic, sentence constructions, pronunciation, and various aspects peculiar to spoken language. However, it was also important to allow sufficient time for each group to warm up and then become thoroughly engrossed in conversation, for otherwise many aspects of oral language suffer.

Jones and Carterette (1963) have shown that at least 6,000 words are necessary for stable statistical results, so the goal for the size of each sample was set at 10,000 words per level. It was felt that more than this would require too much time for phonemic transcription, which is very slow. Well over 10,000 words per level were actually transcribed, but more material than that was collected and remains untranscribed.

Transcription. Each tape was first transcribed by a typist, listening with binaural earphones. The instructions were to include all consecutive material, but if some part was incomprehensible to omit the entire utterance. Similarly, if some person was interrupted and did not pick up the thread of his utterance, the whole utterance was to be omitted, but if he did resume, then the interruption was to be omitted. The second step was to have the letter transcriptions checked by a research assistant. Next the phoneticians took over. Two formal reliability checks were made.

Warning. The %pho lines are missing from the last 15% of the adult.cha file. These are in the book and will have to be reentered eventually by hand.

Publications that make use of this corpus should cite Carterette and Jones (1974).

26.9. Clark

This subdirectory contains files from a short-term longitudinal study conducted by Eve Clark during 1976–1977. The data are from the child Shem and extend for a year from the age of 2;2 to 3;2. The transcripts pay close attention to repetitions, hesitations, and retracings.

Shem was seen on a near weekly basis by an observer (Cindy) who became a friend of the family over the course of the year's recording. The recordings were made at Shem's home, except on a few occasions when the parents made the recording because either Cindy or they were away on vacation so Shem would have missed more than one session. The child's name, Shem T– M– is a pseudonym, as are his address, Cresson Court, his sister's name Ana, the names of his parents, and the observer's name, Cindy, so as to preserve their confidentiality. The names of nearby places and institutions remain unchanged.

Shem was from a middle- to upper-middle class professional family in the Palo Alto area. He was an only child until just after the recordings began when his first sister, Ana, was born. He attended a local daycare center (Little Kids' Place) in the mornings, and occasionally went there for a short time in the afternoon. Most of the recording sessions took place at his home. Shem's age and the date (month and day) is noted at the top of each transcript. His date of birth was February 5, 1974. For convenience, the ages for each session are summarized here:

shem01	2;2.16	shem21	2;8.15
shem02	2;2.23	shem22	2;8.20
shem03	2;3.2	shem23	2;8.29
shem04	2;3.16	shem24	2;9.1
shem05	2;3.21	shem25	2;9.10
shem06	2;3.28	shem26	2;9.19
shem07	2;4.4	shem27	2;9.27
shem08	2;4.20	shem28	2;10.2
shem09	2;4.25	shem29	2;10.14/20
shem10	2;5.2	shem30	2;10.25
shem11	2;5.9	shem31	2;11.1
shem12	2;5.16	shem32	2;11.10
shem13	2;5.23	shem33	2;11.28
shem14	2;5.30	shem34	3;0.5
shem15	2;6.6	shem35	3;0.13
shem16	2;6.27/28	shem36	3;0.20
shem17	2;7.10	shem37	3;1.5
shem18	2;7.18	shem38	3;1.13
shem19	2;7.26	shem39	3;1.27
shem20	2;8.3	shem40	3;2.2

A few sessions are split into two parts – typically because they were slightly longer than usual, because most sessions lasted an hour.

Phonology. Shem's pronunciation at the beginning of the recording period was often unclear, and he frequently made more than one attempt to get himself understood. In the transcripts, all repairs are noted, but Shem's pronunciation has been largely normalized for representation in English orthography, except where his meaning remained unclear, or his pronunciation was critical to the overall form of an interchange. Typical features were voicing of all intervocalic voiceless stops (whether or not at word boundaries), omission of voiced final stops, voicing of voiceless initial stops, substitutions among fricatives, great variation in vowel quality, extensive reliance on schwa or syllabic /n/ for function words (the syllabic /n/ was typically, but not always a locative preposition), simplification of clusters with loss of post-consonantal /l/ and /r/; initial /l/ often /y/; initial /s/ often /d ~ t/, and final /s/ often /t/; final voiced stops often /n/ (e.g., /birn/ for "bird", /wen/ for "red", /bun/ or /bung/ for "bug"); voiceless final stops often replaced by glottal stops (especially /t/, and often /k/); occasional homorganic voiceless stops as releases to final nasals (e.g., /lawnt/ for "lawn").

Intonation is indicated by punctuation, with a period marking a terminal fall, a question mark marking interrogative rise, an exclamation mark indicating emphatic tone, and a comma indicating continuing or listing contour (slight pause, with sustained level tone, or slight falling but nonterminal tone). The bulk of the transcription is in English orthography for ease of reading, but a few persistent forms are left with glosses more or less in the form Shem produced them. On a few tapes, background conversations (e.g., on the telephone) are omitted from the final transcription.

The data collection was supported by an NSF grant (BNS 75-17126) to E. V. Clark. Publications that make use of this corpus should cite one or more of these publications: (Clark, 1978b), (Clark, 1978a), (Clark, 1979), (Clark, 1982a), and (Clark, 1982b).

26.10. Cruttenden

Alan Cruttenden of the University of Manchester has contributed phonologically transcribed data from two dizygotic twins, Jane and Lucy, from age 1;5 to 3;7. The data were collected at monthly intervals for a total of 25 files for each child. The two children transcribed here were dizygotic twins. No data was collected from months 4 and 5 and data collected from Month 23 onwards is sparse.

Error coding has only partially been carried out on this data. Errors which are clearly phonological have been systematically indicated but not coded. Inflectional errors have been indicated but no judgements have been made as to whether they are morphologically or phonologically induced. Syntactic errors have generally been indicated from the stage when the appropriate correct syntax was being used in other utterances. Comments on stress have been included on a comments line where this information is available.

26.11. Demetras – Trevor

This corpus contains 27 files of data collected by M. J. Demetras and John Umbreit between 1985 and 1987 from their son Trevor. Nine sets of four 20-minute conversations between Trevor and his father were recorded over a period of 35 months for a total of 28 sessions. All but one session were transcribed and included as part of this corpus. The context was free play and the participants used a somewhat standard set of toys through the duration of the recordings. Trevor was fairly intelligible and verbal at this stage in development. He also experienced two episodes of disfluency during this period, which was partially captured in the data. Trevor was born on June 3, 1983.

File	Age	File	Age
01	2;0.27	15	2;11.13
02	2;0.28	16	2;11.14
03	2;0.29	17	3;0.7
04	2;1.5	18	3;0.8
05	2;6.4	19	3;0.9
06	2;6.5	20	3;1.17
07	2;6.6	21	3;3.4
08	2;6.12	22*	3;3.10
09	2;8.3	23	3;3.12
10	2;8.5	24	3;10.22
11	2;8.7	25	3;10.23
12	2;8.10	26	3;10.24
13	2;10.4	27	3;11.27
14	2;11.11		

Publications that make use of this corpus may cite Demetras (1989). Audio and video recordings are available for copying to researchers interested in the data. Before using these data, please check with M. J. Demetras. Research based on the use of these data should cite Demetras (1989b). File 22 is not yet available.

26.12. Demetras – Working Parents

This directory contains data from three families each of which had a two-year-old son. In each family, both parents worked during the day and the children were in day care. Four 20-minute conversations between the boys and each of their parents were recorded within a two-week period of time. The context was free play and the toys varied from session to session. Sessons 2, 3, and 4 were transcribed and included in this corpus. The other sessions are available for future transcription. For one of the families, three additional sets of data (12 sessions) were collected and included in Demetras' (1989) longitudinal analysis of grammatical development and parent-child interactions. Thirteen of the 16 sessions collected for this family were transcribed and included in this corpus.

Elliot/Mom and Elliott/Father
DOB: 17-MAY-1983
File	Age
1	NT
2	2;2.18
3	2;2.20
4	2;2.22

David/Mom and David/Father
DOB: 07-MAR-1984
1	NT
2	2;1.30
3	2;2.1
4	2;2.6

Oliver/Mom and Oliver/Father
DOB: 20-JAN-1983

1	NT	9	2;6.29
2	2;2.15	10	2;7.2
3	2;2.20	11	2;7.4
4	2;2.24	12	2;7.5
5	NT	13	NT
6	2;4.28	14	2;9.16
7	2;4.29	15	2;9.22
8	2;4.30	16	2;9.23

NT = not transcribed

Publications that make use of these data may cite Demetras (1989b) for the longitudinal and Demetras (1989a) for the crossectional analyses. Audio and video recordings are available for copying to researchers interested in the data. Before using these data, please check with M. J. Demetras.

26.13. Evans

These transcripts are from 16 dyads of first grade children at indoor play. They were recorded by Mary Evans in Guelph, Ontario, Canada. The transcripts were prepared from ten minutes of interaction in about the middle of each play session as specified on the transcripts. The children in the dyads do not represent a random sample of children. Rather, children with ID numbers under 43 were described by their teachers as verbally quiet in kindergarten, whereas other children were consistently verbal or became verbal across the kindergarten year.

26.14. Fletcher

This subdirectory contains the Reading corpus of transcripts from 72 British children ages 3, 5, and 7. The participants in the project were Paul Fletcher, Michael Garman, Michael Johnson, Christina Schelleter, and Louisette Stodel. The project was entitled "The standardization of an expressive language assessment procedure" and was supported by Medical Research Council grant no. 68306114N and NATO Collaborative Research grant no. RG84/0135. The aims of this project were as follows:

1. To establish a computer data base of the expressive language of British children between 3;0 and 7;0.
2. To identify grammatical and lexical features of this database that were developmentally significant – which reliably distinguished older from younger children.
3. To apply this information in the identification, assessment and remediation of language-impaired children. This goal, which arises out of earlier work on LARSP (Crystal, Fletcher & Garman, 1989), affects all aspects of the database – choice of interlocutor, data collection methods, transcription decisions – and anyone using these data needs to be aware of this.

Elicitation. All data was collected in an interview situation between a female adult and the child. This was a deliberate attempt to mimic the typical initial encounter between a speech therapist and a child who is being assessed. All interviews took place in a quiet area of the nursery or school the child was attending, and lasted for approximately 45 minutes. The elicitation protocol for these sessions included these techniques:

1. Stick-on game (SG) Conversation takes place around a game (supplied by UNISET), consisting of a picture of either a house interior or a farmyard, and an appropriate set of stickers to be located at various points on these pictures.
2. Free/guided conversation (FC). There are no props for this part of the interview. The experimenter asks questions about the child's school and home experiences, and about significant past and future events in the child's life (Christmas, holidays, birthdays, Bonfire Night, and so forth) The aim is to encourage the child to talk, in as spontaneous a way as is possible within the constraints of the situation).
3. Balloon Story. The balloon story is a brief picture story, devised by Annette Karmiloff-Smith, to examine children's pronominal reference in discourse (Karmiloff-Smith, 1986).

Transcription and Segmentation. Conventions for transcription were the product of much discussion in the project team; their formal implementation was the work of M. Johnson.

Publications based on the use of this corpus should cite Fletcher and Garman (1988) and Johnson (1986).

26.15. Garvey

This directory contains a set of between-child conversational data collected by Catherine Garvey and donated to the CHILDES in 1986. The original corpus consists of 48 files of transcripts of dialogues between two children with no experimenter or other children present. All of the children's names have been replaced with pseudonyms. The children range in age from 2;10 to 5;7. In the original corpus, pairs of children belong to 16 triads of three children. Particular files are always dialogues between two members of each triad. Calling the children in a given triad A, B, and C, there are always three possible pairings: AB, AC, and BC. Data for triads 1, 3, 4, 6, 10, and 11 are not in the CHILDES database. Thus, the database contains a total of only 30 files from 10 triads. There is a file for each of these three pairings for each of the 10 triads.

Triad#1	Ages	Files	Triad #9	Ages	Files
Sue	4;4	suedon, suetim	Kay	3;6	kayben, kaydeb
Don	3;9	suedon, dontim	Ben	3;7	kayben, bendeb
Tim	4;1	dontim, suetim	Deb	3;7	kaydeb, bendeb
Triad #2			Triad #10		
Amy	3;6	amywes, amyann	Ned	5;2	nedima, nedmae
Wes	4;1	amywes, wesann	Ima	5;4	nedima, imamae
Ann	4;0	wesann, amyann	Mae	5;5	nedmae, imamae
Triad #3			Triad #11		
Hal	4;5	halpat, halivy	Bev	5;7	bevflo, bevguy
Pat	4;10	halpat, pativy	Flo	5;1	bevflo, floguy
Ivy	4;9	halivy, pativy	Guy	5;2	bevguy, floguy
Triad #4			Triad #12		

Ari	5;1	arigay, ariken	Ida	5;1	idabud, idazoe
Gay	5;2	arigay, kengay	Bud	5;1	idabud, budzoe
Ken	5;2	ariken, kengay	Zoe	5;0	idazoe, budzoe

Triad #5   Triad #13

Pia	4;9	piaval, piaabe	Peg	3;1	pegron, pegjan
Val	4;7	piaval, valabe	Ron	3;3	pegron, ronjan
Abe	4;9	valabe, piaabe	Jan	3;1	pegjan, ronjan

Triad #6   Triad #14

Glo	5;0	glojoy, globob	Sam	2;11	samian, samava
Joy	4;9	glojoy, joybob	Ian	2;10	samian, ianava
Bob	4;11	globob, joybob	Ava	3;2	samave, ianava

Triad #7   Triad #15

Fay	5;3	fayjay, faymeg	Max	3;1	maxnan, maxjim
Jay	5;0	fayjay, jaymeg	Nan	2;10	maxnan, nanjim
Meg	5;0	faymeg, jaymeg	Jim	3;0	maxjim, nanjim

Triad #8   Triad #16

Gus	4;0	gusleo, guseve	Roy	3;2	roykim, royada
Leo	4;0	gusleo, leoeve	Kim	3;0	roykim, kimada
Eve	3;11	guseve, leoeve	Ada	3;3	royada, kimada

The narrative section indicates when an interruption took place; it was sometimes necessary for the observers to intervene, to bring in another bag of toys, to turn on the light switch and caution the children not to turn off the light, or to take one or both children to the bathroom. Speech during these interruptions was not recorded. Conventional orthography is used with a few exceptions such as "gonna," "gotta," and "wanna." Some clearly distorted pronunciations are indicated, such as "beebe bottel" for "baby bottle." When periods, commas, or question marks appear in the text, they indicate utterance final intonation, nonterminal intonation, and interrogatory illocutionary force, respectively. In many scripts however, these punctuation marks are missing, as there was an (unfulfilled) plan to add transcription for intonation. The transcripts are heavily coded for actions, gestures, proxemics, timing, and intonation. The timing marks are missing for triad #4. Time is indicated in minutes and seconds with a colon separating the minutes and the seconds.

The file "0stats.doc" gives a variety of statistics computed for these 48 files by Catherine Garvey. These include total time, total words, total utterances, rate of utterance, percentage utterances in an exchange, percentage time in focused interaction, and number of episodes that are longer than nine exchanges. For each child in the pair, this file reports number of words, number of utterances, and words per utterance. A frequent code that occurs on the %com line is $CFA which stands for "common focus of attention." The symbol $/= followed by a number is used to indicate that some event or focus of attention continues for a certain number of lines. If you use this data please cite Garvey (1979). A further reference to these data is made in Garvey and Hogan (1973).

26.16. Gathercole

This directory consists of 16 files of cross-sectional data of children aged 2;9 to 6;6 donated to the CHILDES by Virginia Gathercole in 1987. There are four children at each age. These four children were observed at school while eating lunch with an experimenter present on four separate occasions. These data are arranged into 17 files, named by date of collection. Dr. Gathercole would like those researchers requesting the data to contact her to discuss the use of the data. The following is a list of the target participants in these files by age:

Subj.	Sex	Age	Sample #	Subj.	Sex	Age	Sample #
BRI	M	5;11	04	LUK	M	4;11	02
		6;2.15	07			5;2	06
		6;4.15	12			5;3	09
		6;6	16			5;5	14
ERI	M	3;2	11	MAT	M	4;7	02
		3;3	16			4;10	06
ERK	M	4;6	02			4;11	09
ERN	F	2;10	01			5;1	14
		3;0	05	MEG	F	3;6	03
		3;3	11			3;9	08
		3;4	13			3;10	10
GIL	M	4;3	02			4;0	15
		4;6	06	MIC	M	2;10	01
		4;7	09			3;0.15	05
		4;9	14			3;3	11
JEF	M	2;9	01			3;4	13
		2;11	05	NIC	F	5;4	04
LIL	F	3;10	03			5;7	07
		4;2	08			5;9	12
		4;3	10			5;10	16
		4;5	15	SAA	F	5;8	04
SAR	F	3;6	03			6;1	07
		3;9	08			6;0.15	12
		3;10	10			6;2	16
		4;0	15				

In addition, the files contain speech by various other nontargeted children and adults. Precise ages for these additional speakers have not been provided.

Child	Sex	Samples	Adult	Sex	Samples
BRY	M	03,06,07,09,12,16	BOB	F	all except 02
SHA	?	02	PAT	F	05,10
RAC	F	01-04,06-08,12,16	LLE	F	01-04,06,09
ALY	F	15	GAY	F	04,08
KEN	M	13	VIR	F	all (investigator)
KEI	M	01,04,05,09,	TEA	?	08,10,12,13
NAT	M	07,16	MOT	M	04
ALI	M	06	CHI	?	01,03,04,06,07
CON	F	01,08	UNC	?	02,04,11,15
CHR	?	01,02,06			

If you use this data, please cite Gathercole (1980).

26.17. Gathercole / Burns

Cross-sectional data were collected from 12 Scotttish children aged 3:0 to 6;4 at the Nursery of the Department of Psychology at the University of Edinburgh. There are four children at each of three age levels: three-year-olds (mean age 3;2.15), four-year-olds (mean age: 4;2), five-year-olds (mean age: 5;0). Four Scottish adults interacted with the children: two of the children's teachers, one sevitor of the nursery, and one mother of one of the children. The first three had educations through secondary school; the last had attended college. Each group of four Scottish children was videotaped in eight half-hour sessions for a total of 24 sessions. Each adult participated in two sessions with each group. The structured sessions involved block tasks and art tasks. All utterances were transcribed from the videotapes, along with extensive information on the non-linguistic contexts of the utterances. The data were reformatted into CHAT by Rebecca Burns. Users of these data should cite Gathercole (1986).

26.18. Gleason

This directory contains files donated to the CHILDES in 1988 by Jean Berko Gleason. The data were collected in the context of project called "Studies in the Acquisition of Communicative Competence," which was funded for three years by NSF grant #BNS 75-21909 to Jean Berko Gleason at Boston University. The subjects are 24 children aged 2;1 to 5;2 who were recorded in interactions (a) with their mother, (b) with their father, and (c) at the dinner table. The 24 subjects were recruited through nursery schools and similar networks, and were from middle class families in the greater Boston area. There were 12 boys and 12 girls. All families were white, and English was spoken as a first language in all families. Each child was seen three times: once in the laboratory with the mother; once in the laboratory with the father; and once at dinner with both mother and father. The laboratory sessions were videotaped and audiotaped, and the dinners were only audiotaped. Laboratory sessions included: (a) play with a toy auto, (b) reading a picture book, and (c) playing store.

The parent was encouraged to divide each 30 minute lab session about evenly among these activities. In addition, each child was presented with a small gift during the lab session, and the gift giving interchange (which followed a script on the part of our staff member) was also recorded.

Subject and File Information:

S#	Visit#	Date	Type	Code Name	Date of Birth	Age
1	1	6/11/76	Father	Andy	5/23/72	4;0.18
	2	6/25/76	Mother			4;1.2
	3	6/23/76	Dinner			4;2.0
2	1	6/15/76	Mother	Bobby	4/27/72	4;1.19
	2	9/24/76	Father			4;4.28
	3	6/28/76	Home			4;2.1
3	1	6/23/76	Father	Charlie	7/6/73	2;11.17
	2	7/14/76	Mother			3;0.8
	3	7/7/76	Dinner			3;0.1
4	1	6/26/76	Father	David	5/7/72	4;1.19

	2	7/10/76	Mother			4;2.3
	3	7/8/76	Dinner			4;2.1
5	1	7/13/76	Mother	Edward	4/1/72	4;3.12
	2	8/7/76	Father			4;4.6
	3	8/4/76	Dinner			4;4.3
6	1	7/14/76	Mother	Frank	5/14/71	5;2.0
	2	7/24/76	Father			5;2.10
	3	7/21/76	Dinner			5;2.7
7	1	7/23/76	Mother	Guy	7/3/73	3;0.20
	2	8/7/76	Father			3;1.4
	3	7/8/76	Dinner			3;0.5
8	1	7/27/76	Mother	Helen	8/25/71	4;11.2
	2	8/4/76	Father			4;11.10
	3	1/8/76	Dinner			4;4.14
9	1	9/22/76	Mother	Isadora	3/15/73	3;6.7
	2	10/16/76	Father			3;7.1
	3	10/6/76	Dinner			3;6.21
10	1	9/28/76	Mother	John	8/10/72	4;1.18
	2	10/27/76	Father			4;2.17
	3	11/2/76	Dinner			4;2.23
11	1	9/29/76	Mother	Katie	7/27/73	3;2.2
	2	10/18/76	Father			3;2.21
	3	unknown	Dinner			
12	1	9/30/76	Mother	Laurel	10/24/73	2;11.6
	2	11/13/76	Father			3;0.20
	3	11/16/76	Dinner			3;0.23
13	1	10/6/76	Mother	Martin	4/11/74	2;5.26
	2	10/23/76	Father			2;6.12
	3	11/3/76	Dinner			2;6.23
14	1	10/7/76	Mother	Nanette	9/3/74	2;1.4
	2	10/23/76	Father			2;1.20
	3	11/9/76	Dinner			2;2.6
15	1	10/16/76	Father	Olivia	8/4/73	3;2.12
	2	11/20/76	Mother			3;3.16
	3	11/2/76	Dinner			3;2.29
16	1	10/27/76	Mother	Patricia	5/18/74	2;5.9
	2	11/18/76	Father			2;6.0
	3	11/17/76	Dinner			2;5.30
17	1	10/28/76	Mother	Richard	2/10/74	2;8.18
	2	11/30/76	Father			2;9.20
	3	12/2/76	Dinner	(file missing)		2;9.22

18	1	1/14/77	Father	Susan	11/11/73	3;2.3
	2	2/1/77	Mother			3;2.21
	3	unknown	Dinner			
19	1	2/24/77	Mother	Theresa	2/24/73	4;0.0
	2	5/14/77	Father			4;2.20
	3	unknown	Dinner			
20	1	4/19/77	Father	Ursula	9/19/73	3;7.0
	2	5/14/77	Mother			3;7.25
	3	?	Dinner	(file missing)		
21	1	4/11/77	Mother	Victor	12/20/74	2;3.22
	2	5/23/77	Father			2;5.3
	3	unknown	Dinner			
22	1	5/3/77	Father	Wanda	5/10/73	3;11.22
	2	5/21/77	Mother			4;0.11
	3	unknown	Dinner			
23	1	2/15/78	Mother	William	11/27/75	2;2.16
	2	3/18/78	Father			2;3.22
	3	3/17/78	Dinner			2;3.21
24	1	3/4/79	Mother	Xavia	??	
	2	17/7/79	Father			
	3	12/9/79	Dinner			

Publications that make use of this corpus should cite one or more of these publications: Bellinger and Gleason (1982), Gleason (1980), Gleason and Greif (1983), Gleason, Perlmann, and Greif (1984), Greif and Gleason (1980), Masur and Gleason (1980), and Menn and Gleason (1986).

26.19. Haggerty

This directory contains a single file with data taken from Haggerty (1929). This source is a published article which records what a two-and-one-half-year-old child said in one day. Haggerty was on the faculty of the Department of Educational Psychology of the University of Minnesota. The child, Helen, was born in 1905 and thus this file also has a certain historical interest. The data was recorded by hand by the researcher and two assistants over the approximately 9.5 waking hours in her day. The following passage is taken from Haggerty's introduction to the article:

> The writer in the following pages reports the exact conversation carried on in the length of one day by her daughter, Helen, who was two years, seven and a half months old at the time. Helen was born in Anderson, Indiana, April 24, 1903. This record was made December 12, 1905. The record begins at seven o'clock in the morning when Helen awakened, and is continuous throughout the entire day, excepting for the period of the afternoon nap which occurred between 12:45 P.M. and 3:45 P.M. The record closes at 7:30 P.M., when Helen went to sleep for the night. With the aid of two others who gave occasional assistance, the writer was

able to record every word uttered by Helen during the day. This record therefore represents in entirety the linguistic expression of a two-and-a-half-year-old child during the approximate nine and a half hours of her waking day. This day was a representative day in Helen's life and was not unlike other days in that period of her life. The persons most frequently referred to were her father and mother, her baby sister, Margaret, who was one year and four days old, her grandmother, who was present, Carrie, a high school girl who lived in the home, and Nancy, a young seamstress, who took great interest in the children, and who was frequently employed in the home.

Researchers using this data should cite Haggerty (1929).

26.20. Hall

This directory contains a large database of conversational interactions from 39 children aged 4;6 to 5;0. The files were computerized by Bill Hall of the University of Maryland and donated to the CHILDES in 1984. They were first placed into **CHAT** format in 1987, but this work was redone from the originals in 1991 to clear up additional problems. Although the conversion to **CHAT** was generally straightforward, it was not possible to code overlaps by pairs. Instead, the overlap marked was coded by using the [%^] sign for without any attempt to indicate pairings of overlaps.

The corpus was collected with the purpose of providing a solid basis for comparing vocabulary usage in different socioeconomic and ethnic groups. This section describes how the corpus was collected in a way to ensure that spontaneous speech would be recorded in a variety of natural situations. We also characterize these situations in as much detail as possible, to provide users of these data with an accurate picture of the conditions under which they were collected.

Subjects were 39 preschool children (4;6 to 5;0) divided approximately equally according to race and socioeconomic status (SES) as follows: middle-class Black, middle-class-White, working-class Black, and working-class White. The working-class children in our sample were attending federally-funded preschools: the middle-class children were in private preschools. The working-class Black children were in all-Black classes, with Black teachers, whereas the middle-class Black children were in interracial classes with both Black and White teachers. None of the Black target children were in the same classes as any of the White target children in our sample.

Language samples were collected over two consecutive days for each child. On each day, an average of about two and a half hours of conversation were recorded, distributed among different situations. Most importantly, the situations in which the data were gathered were both natural and varied. Conversations were taped in a variety of situations at home, at school, and en route between the two. The children and their families were aware that they were being taped, but this seems to have caused little if any disruptions of normal activities. There are occasional references (although relatively few) to the fact that the tape recorder is on; but the conversations are natural. Reading the transcripts, one can clearly sense that the families are not "putting on an act" for the tape recorder; they tend to ignore it almost completely. Even if the presence of the tape recorder does exert some effect, the fact remains that there is no other method, apart from deception, that would offer a less obtrusive way of obtaining natural data.

The taping equipment was also chosen to minimize any disruption of normal conversation or activities. The children wore vests with wireless microphones sewn in;

their movements were not restricted, and they seemed quickly to forget about having them on. The use of wireless microphones made possible the inclusion of speech by the target children that might not otherwise have been recorded–for example, monologues spoken while the child was out of the hearing of any visible listener. Field workers clipped microphones to their ties. Although other adults and nontarget children in the study did not wear microphones, the two microphones used were, in general, sensitive enough to pick up significant verbal interaction with the children in the study. Portable tape recorders enabled data collection in a number of different settings, for example, in homes, shops, moving cars, and on sidewalks. The mobility achieved in this way would not have been possible with video-tapes; although video-tapes would provide more complete data in some respects, their use would have been far more disruptive.

The effects of the experimenter's race were minimized by using a Black field worker with Black families and a White field worker with White families. In the collection of data, the field worker tried to be as unobtrusive as possible. He rarely initiated conversations, but if spoken to, attempted to respond naturally. One of the field worker's responsibilities was to provide a verbal description of the contest. For the purposes of this research, the context included: where the recording took place, where the subject was, who the interactants were and what they were doing–both their verbal and nonverbal behavior. Futhermore, the descriptions of context often included what happened prior and subsequent to, as well as simultaneous with, the verbal interaction.

In order to sample situational variations in language, each child was recorded in a series of ten temporal situations, which can be grouped into three basic categories: Home, School, and Transition. The Home data consists of tapes made in the following situations: prior to school in the morning, arriving home from school, before dinner, dinner, and before bed. Each of these took place in or near the child's home, and includes approximately 30 minutes of conversation (15 minutes on each of the days taping was done). Particular segments of activities are missing from particular files. In BOO, the dinner segment was taped outside on the street. In TOS there is no dinner segment and 09 Before Dinner was coded instead. In JAF and ANC there are no directed activity segments.

The target children were between 4;6 and 5;0 during the taping. In each of the four groups, there were more male than female target children. The makeup of the families differs somewhat from one group to another. The social class and ethnic status of the children is as follows:

White Middle	ZOR, GRC, MAA, JUB, TOH, GAT, TOS, JOB, RAL
Black Middle	JAF, ANC, KIF, REF,VOH, MIM, BOM, BRD, DED, TRH, CHJ
White Working	SUT, STL, BOO, BRH, KAO, DAL, SAT, MIG, KAG
Black Working	ROG, ANL, TRC, KMF, KIG, PAG, DEG, ROJ, MIS, LEG

The distribution of the target children by gender is: White Middle – 6 boys, 3 girls; Black Middle Class – 9 boys, 2 girls, White Working Class – 7 boys, 2 girls Black Working Class – 6 boys, 4 girls. The following table gives the number (and percent) of families in each group that have various categories of speakers present. A speaker is considered present if there are more than 100 words spoken at home by speaker or speakers in that category. For example, there was a brother of the target child present in 5 of the 11 Black middle-class families in our sample, that is, in 45% of these families, but only in 3 (that is 30%) of the White working-class families. In all the families in our sample, both the experimenter and the target child spoke more than 100 words at home.

Speaker	Black	White	Black	White

Categories	Middle Class (N = 11)	Middle Class (N = 9)	Working Class (N = 10)	Working Class (N = 9)
Other Children				
Brother	5 (45)	4 (44)	6 (60)	3 (33)
Sister	4 (36)	0 (0)	6 (60)	1 (11)
Male Child	3 (27)	1 (11)	4 (40)	5 (56)
Female Child	3 (27)	0 (0)	3 (30)	2 (22)
Mother	10 (91)	9 (100)	10 (100)	8 (89)
Father	8 (73)	6 (67)	3 (30)	4 (44)
Grandmother	0 (0)	1 (11)	4 (40)	1 (11)
Grandfather	0 (0)	1 (11)	0 (0)	0 (0)
Male Adult	1 (9)	1 (11)	4 (40)	3 (33)
Female Adult	4 (36)	2 (22)	3 (30)	5 (56)

These transcripts were not coded originally in **CHAT** format. They have been reformatted into a modified version of **CHAT**. Please use caution when using the CLAN programs, because it is possible that some of these divergences from **CHAT** can lead to inaccuracies in certain analyses. A special code <original text> [*] [new text] is used to indicate any of three types of structures in this corpus:
1. errors
2. preferred speech (i.e., standard English for nonstandard forms)
3. estimated intent.

When reformatting the data into **CHAT**, it was impossible to distinguish these three types of codings from one another. It is clear that many of these notations in the corpus refer to alternatives rather than errors. In addition, the phonological transcriptions have not yet been changed to UNIBET. Overlaps were marked in the original, but the direction of the overlap was not marked. We have used the **CHAT** symbol [<>] for these overlaps. It means unclear overlap and not "overlap both precedes and follows" in this particular corpus.

Publications that make use of this corpus should cite Hall, Nagy, and Linn (1984), Hall, Nagy, and Nottenburg (1981), or Hall and Tirre (1979).

26.21. Higginson

The Higginson corpus contains 21 files, recorded in 1983 and 1984. These data were used in Roy Higginson's doctoral dissertation, "Fixing-Assimilation in Language Acquisition" completed at Washington State University. The data files are named according to the date they were recorded. These are naturalistic observations of mother–child interaction. The three female children are aged between 0;11 and 2;11. All of the children's utterances are coded phonetically in addition to the normalized main tier.

The project was funded in part by the Department of Anthropology at WSU, in part by the Sigma Xi Scientific Research Society, and in part from private funds of the researcher. The goals of the project were to examine the earliest stages of language development and to investigate the processes that children use to establish their lexica. Data was collected by making audio and video recordings of children in natural, unstructured play sessions in their homes. Each recording session was approximately 45 minutes long. First draft transcriptions were made from the videorecordings by the researcher and these were then checked against the audio recordings to verify the transcripts.   Phonetic transcriptions of the children's utterances were then prepared from the audio recordings and inserted into the transcripts at the appropriate places.   The material was entered onto floppy diskettes using the standardizations suggested by the Child Language Data Exchange System.

April was born April 22, 1981. She was studied between ages 1;10 and 2;11. She was the only child of an undergraduate student. Her mother and father are divorced; she lives with her mother at a land grant university. Her mother is a native English speaker. There are 3.15 hours of natural observations in the subject's home.

May was born March 14, 1982. She was 0;11 at the beginning of the study. She was the only child of graduate students. Her mother was well on in her second pregnancy. Both parents were native English speakers. They were both graduate students working on masters' degrees. There are 1.75 hours of natural observations in the subject's home.

June was born August 16, 1982. She was 1;3 at the beginning of the study and 1;9 at the end. She was the only child of graduate students. Both her mother and father were native English speakers. There are 12 hours of natural observations in the subject's home, which is in university accommodations.

Filename	Age	Filename	Age	Filename	Age	Filename	Age
apr01	1;10	may01	0;11	jun05	1;5	jun10	1;7
apr02	2;1	may02	0;11	jun06	1;5	jun11	1;8
apr03	2;1	jun01	1;3	jun07	1;6	jun12	1;8
apr04	2;9	jun02	1;4	jun08	1;7	jun13	1;8
apr05	2;10	jun03	1;4	jun09	1;7	jun14	1;9
apr06	2;11	jun04	1;5				

Publications that make use of this corpus should cite Higginson (1985).

26.22. Howe

This directory contains transcripts from 16 of the 24 Scottish mother-child pairs observed by Christine Howe while playing with toys in their homes in Glasgow. Each pair was recorded twice and the recordings are 40 minutes in duration. The data was coded extensively for actions and situations. The children are aged 1;6 to 1;8 at the first recording and 1;11 to 2;1 at the second recording. There are two files per subject, thus the corpus contains 32 data files.

The procedure for subject selection was to place a notice in the local newspaper. The most straightforward method of obtaining a reasonable sample of mothers and children would have been random or quota sampling from a local authority list. Unfortunately, the local authority in question refused to cooperate and more indirect methods had to be used. As a start, an article was written for the local newspaper explaining the aims of the study in deliberately vague terms and asking mothers to volunteer children in the age range of 15-18 months. Notices making similar requests were posted in likely public places, including doctors' waiting rooms, baby clinics, university common rooms and centres for further education. A social worker persuaded one of her clients to take part. Finally, a month after recruitment had started, health visitors from two of the baby clinics made contact with offers of help. One suggested sitting in on an afternoon session and asking attending mothers to participate. This was done. The other offerred names and addresses of every mother with a child of the right age in her area. The first eight in the alphabetical list were contacted and six said they were interested in taking part. By this time, some of the first volunteers had marshaled their friends into participating, and at the end of the period available for sampling, 33 mothers had volunteered their children. Two mothers were considered unsuitable because they had delegated childcare to a grandmother and an employed nanny. The remaining mothers had volunteered children in the age range of 13- to 21 months. It seemed sensible to choose the mothers with the 24 children nearest in age to the mean of 17 months and use others for pilot work.

Most of the final group lived in a small university-cum-market town or nearby villages. Despite the fact that sampling was anything but random, the group was represented well by gender, birth order and social class of family. Twelve children were boys and 12 were girls. Seven were only children, seven were the youngest of two, four were the oldest of two, four were the youngest of three and two were twins without other siblings. The fathers of 13 children had professional or managerial occupations, whereas the fathers of the remaining 11 children had skilled or semi-skilled manual occupations. The first group was designated "middle class" and the second group "working class"' The following table shows the sex, birth order, social class and recruitment method of the children in this directory (all identified by pseudonyms).

Name	Sex	Birth Order	Social Class	Method
Barry	Male	3rd of 3	Working	Clinic
Eileen	Female	Only	Working	Clinic
Faye	Female	1st of 2	Middle	Other Mother
Graham	Male	1st of 2	Middle	Notice
Ian	Male	2nd of 2	Working	Article
Jason	Male	1st of 2	Middle	Notice
Kevin	Male	2nd of 2	Middle	Article
Lucy	Female	2nd of 2	Middle	Other Mother
Melanie	Female	1st of 2	Working	Clinic
Nicola	Female	3rd of 3	Working	Clinic
Oliver	Male	Only	Middle	Other Mother
Philip	Male	2nd of 2	Working	Article
Richard	Male	2nd of 2	Middle	Article
Sally	Female	Only	Middle	Article
Wayne	Male	Only	Working	Article
Yvonne	Female	Only	Working	Social Worker

Each session was video-recorded in the home. The first 20 minutes consisted of a play session with the children's own toys and the second 20 minutes consisted of a play session with a special set of toys presented in the following order:

1. jigsaw puzzle,
2. plastic postbox with holes in the top for geometric shapes,
3. plastic doll with clothes teaset cot and brush,
4. lorry,
5. jeep and horsebox,
6. model zoo animals with fences cages and keeper,
7. interchangeable heads arms and legs which could be assembled into postmen, firemen, and policemen,
8. cardboard building blocks with pictures on every face,
9. fluffy puppet, and

10. picture story.

Once recording sessions were completed, the tapes were immediately transcribed. The videotapes were played back in the order of recording on a video taperecorder connected to a television screen and an audio tape recorder. The transcriber sat 6 feet from the screen holding an electrically powered pad that moved paper across a frame at the rate of 6 inches per minute. The rolls of paper used with this device had lines at 1/4-inch intervals. Thus, it was possible to know within 2 1/2 seconds when any mark on the paper was made, and 2 1/2 seconds became the basic time interval for analysis.

The moving paper device, the audio taperecorder set to record and the video taperecorder set to playback were started in that order. Watching only the child, the transcriber noted changes of action and object using a short-hand code. The code essentially used hieroglyphics to represent actions, including gaze, and the first two letters of names to represent the objects of actions. Every time the child vocalized, a dash was drawn on the left of the paper to be filled in later. Every vocalization, was being re-recorded on audio tape. The second tape was replayed and the child's behavior transcribed in the same way. Then the audio tape recorder was switched off and the whole procedure repeated for the mother. The transcription of all other participants required a third run.

The next stage was transcribing the the vocalizations and inserting them in the behavioral record. English words were transcribed as English words and other sounds were transcribed with some attempt to represent them using English syllables. Speakers varied in their intelligibility and the tapes varied in the amount of background noise. The mean percent of intelligible utterances was 94% for the children and 98% for the mothers. Reliability of transcription and coding completed a year later, resulted in 91% agreement for transcription and 83% agreement for the non-vocal behavior and speech in every 2 1/2 second period where speech occurred. Mean Length of Utterances and Type Token Ratios for each recording session are presented below:

Name	1st Recording		2nd Recording	
	MLU	TTR	MLU	TTR
Barry	1.30	0.27	2.56	0.20
Eileen	1.47	0.18	1.57	0.38
Faye	1.27	0.17	1.65	0.23
Graham	1.09	0.26	1.32	0.51
Ian	1.53	0.38	2.04	0.41
Jason	1.00	0.17	1.17	0.40
Kevin	1.16	0.45	1.87	0.50
Lucy	1.09	0.17	1.15	0.23
Melanie	1.19	0.43	1.55	0.41
Nicola	1.21	0.21	1.67	0.55
Oliver	1.53	0.23	2.04	0.23
Philip	1.22	0.17	1.54	0.26
Richard	1.30	0.16	2.13	0.19
Sally	1.33	0.39	1.98	0.44
Wayne	1.33	0.18	1.39	0.26
Yvonne	1.72	0.36	1.69	0.37

Publications that make use of this corpus should cite Howe (1981).

26.23. Korman

This subdirectory contains the speech of British mothers to infants during the first year. These data are from the Myron Korman's doctoral dissertation. The project focused on maternal speech interactions with preverbal infants. The data were collected in Britain from middle-class mothers with their first children. The children ranged in age from six weeks at the outset to sixteen weeks at the end of the project. The file "0functions.doc" provides detailed examples and reliability information.

These data focus on the language of mothers of infant children. They are useful for understanding the input to the infant, but not for studying the child's vocalizations, because these vocalizations are quite primitive and there is no attempt to capture the vocalizations in phonetic detail. Rather the focus is on the functions and pause characteristics of the maternal input.

The data were reformatted into **CHAT** in 1992. There are five files from each of the six mothers. The ages of the child for these five files are 6, 7, 11, 15, and 16 months. The main tier has utterances that are either marked as ATT for "attentional" or TUR for "turn-constructional." The codes for the %spa tier are given in the 0funct.doc file. In addition the codes $t and $c indicate repeitions of content or temporal structure. The recordings at 7, 11, and 15 months have a %tim tier which contains two types of timing information. The first number gives the length of phrase in seconds; the second number gives the length of the pause after the utterance in seconds. When the mother is not talking and the tape recorder goes on and off, an @New Episode marker is inserted.

Subjects. Subjects were six primiparous mothers from the greater Nottingham community. They had been contacted through introductions and referrals made by health visitors serving health centers local to their area. Mothers were told that the experimenter was interested in the development of their infant's vocalization over time. Some characteristics of the study sample are as follows:

	La.	Gl.	Cr.	Hi.	St.	Gi.
Mother Age:	27	26	23	25	27	25
Occup	Teacher	Clerical	Student	Nurse	Teacher	Chemist
Feeding:	Breast	Breast	Bottle	Bottle	Bottle	Breast
Husband:	Police	Chemist	Gas Board	Plumber	Photog	Chemist
Infant Sex:	Female	Female	Female	Male	Male	Male

Every effort was made to acquire a homogeneous, but balanced, study sample. All mothers were in their 20's and all were middle class. All (save one who had been completing a first degree) had worked prior to marriage and pregnancy. Three were breast feeders and three used a bottle. The infants were three boys and three girls. The table above provides an account of various "vital statistics" of each family in the study.

Data Collection. Recordings were made of each infant's auditory experience in the home for the whole of 24 hour periods. These recordings were made without an experimenter present and included a continuous record of the whole of all mother–infant engagements throughout the day. Video recordings were made of mother–infant free play in the home. Videotapings were limited to three monthly sessions nearest to the end, the midpoint, and the beginning of the period under investigation (at 7, 11, and 15 weeks). Audio records were made at fortnightly intervals beginning at 6 and ending at 16 weeks. The recording apparatus consisted of a Revox 4000 reel to reel tape recorder, a voice key and a small "lavalier" microphone with an attachment for pinning it on to things, and 50 feet of thin wire.

Audio Sessions. Audio records were made beginning at each infant's 6th week at fortnightly intervals ending in the 16th week. The sample was split into two groups of three infants each, and the groups were recorded on alternate weeks. It was explained that the study concerned the development of the infant's vocalization over time. Mothers were shown the operation of the device and asked to keep the microphone pinned near to the infant at all times. The apparatus was usually dropped off in mid-morning and picked up the following day at approximately the same time. In each household, a hiding place was found and the equipment, except for the wire and microphone, was always out of view. All households were on two floors and in each instance the length of wire was checked to see if it allowed access to all floors and rooms before recording began.

Video Sessions. Videotaping took place in the subjects' homes in a room of their own choosing (usually a front or "best" room). Sessions were held at a time of day that each mother had indicated their infant would be most alert and active. Most sessions took place around midday. Mothers were asked to "play with the baby as you would normally do" and no other instructions were given or restrictions imposed. There was no attempt to "standardize" the location of taping sessions or the positioning of mother and infant. Mothers were never discouraged from stopping to chat with the experimenter and short breaks in the play activity were common. Each mother was simply asked to play with the baby in their normal manner wherever, whenever, and however it suited them to do so. This is not to say that the purpose of these sessions was not clear to each mother (i.e., to play with the baby), but to point up the fact that control of the activity in each session was left as much as possible in the hands of the mothers. The sessions themselves were intended to be as relaxed and nonrestrictive as possible so as not to constrict or inhibit the mothers' natural responsiveness under the circumstances. Three toys were offered to provide an interactive alternative (a monkey hand puppet, a rattle, and a pop-up toy), but mothers were not encouraged to use them. In each session mothers also had the option to use their infants' own toys, which were usually close at hand. The play sessions were, for the most part, friendly social visits during which the mother was asked to play or interact with her infant while a video record was made. A typical session might consist of the experimenter and mother first having coffee and a chat, the mother preparing the area and the baby for play, the recorded play sessions themselves, which stopped at the mothers' convenience or the infant's continuance, and then perhaps another cup of coffee and a further casual discussion of the activity just finished, the infant's responsivity and growth generally, or the cost of coffee at Sainsbury's.

Pause Analysis. A pause was defined as: "any maternal silence of longer than 300 msec. which ended at: (a) another maternal utterance, (b) an interruption from the experimenter, or (c) an intruding and other than vocal interactive sound produced by the mother, such as rattle shaking or tapping noises." As a consequence this procedure resulted in the scoring of certain maternal pauses whose duration, although long, was none-the-less populated with some form of interactive behavior from one or the other of the partners in any exchange. Those especially long pauses that are scored will be made up of: a maternal vocal silence in anticipation of, or in response to, some infant behavior or some maternal activity that was done in complete silence.

Timing Procedures. The following timing procedures were used in analysis of the eighteen video observations of the present study. Video taped interactions were copied onto audio tape cassettes and timings were then undertaken with a hand held stop watch and a tape recorder. Maternal vocal behavior was timed from the perceived end of a phrase to the end of the next sequential phrase. Pauses were then timed from the end of the same first phrase to the onset of the second phrase and the durations of each sequential phrase and pause determined. Each set of timings was undertaken for a minimum of three trials until the experimenter was familiar with the sequence and satisfied with his result. The procedure was designed to familiarize the experimenter with the rhythmic and temporal patterning of the phrase/pause sequence about to be timed, and to help reduce the amount of time that might have been lost through guessing at the onset of a sequential vocalization. Average adult serial reaction time to auditory stimuli at irregular intervals is 335 msec to intervals of 500msec. All transcription and timing was later checked against the video tapes themselves to assess contextual accuracy.

Reliability. Three raters (undergraduates) were asked to transcribe one hundred sequential vocalizations of the same mother selected at random from available audio observations. That transcription resulted in a 97% agreement with the content and segmentation of the original transcript produced by the experimenter.

Six thirty-second exchanges were selected at random and the mothers' speech segmented and timed by this research assistant (an average of 21 phrases and pauses per mother; 126 in all). The resulting segmentation and the durations of phrases and pauses were then compared with measures of the experimenter. A comparison of segmentation resulted in 88.8% agreement. Those instances in which segmentation did not coincide (i.e., instances where two phrases were separated or joined by differing measurement of the same pause criteria) were later discarded from the final comparison of temporal durations (discarded were 14 phrases and 7 pauses of the original transcription). That final temporal analysis resulted in a comparison of 112 phrases and 119 pauses overall. In the measurement of phrase durations, agreement was 95.5% to within 300 msec. and 84.8% agreement to within 200 msec.

Publications that make use of this corpus should cite Korman (1984).

26.24. Kuczaj

This corpus consists of 210 files containing the diary study (1973-75) of Stan Kuczaj's son, Abe. Approximately one hour of Abe's spontaneous speech in his home environment was recorded each week (two one-half hour sessions per week) from age 2;4 to 4;1, and one-half hour of spontaneous speech was recorded each week from 4;1 to 5;0.

File	Age	File	Age	File	Age	File	Age
001	2;4.24	053	2;11.2	105	3;5.29	157	4;1.0
002	2;5.0	054	2;11.6	106	3;6.3	158	4;1.5
003	2;5.7	055	2;11.10	107	3;6.4	159	4;1.9
004	2;5.10	056	2;11.13	108	3;6.10	160	4;1.15
005	2;5.14	057	2;11.18	109	3;6.13	161	4;1.20
006	2;5.16	058	2;11.21	110	3;6.16	162	4;1.24
007	2;5.20	059	2;11.25	111	3;6.19	163	4;1.29
008	2;5.22	060	2;11.30	112	3;6.22	164	4;2.2
009	2;5.23	061	3;0.7	113	3;6.26	165	4;2.9
010	2;5.26	062	3;0.16	114	3;6.29	166	4;2.13
011	2;5.29	063	3;0.25	115	3;7.4	167	4;2.19
012	2;6.4	064	3;0.29	116	3;7.5	168	4;2.24
013	2;6.6	065	3;1.1	117	3;7.15	169	4;3.1
014	2;6.10	066	3;1.5	118	3;7.21	170	4;3.7
015	2;6.14	067	3;1.8	119	3;7.22	171	4;3.11
016	2;6.14	068	3;1.11	120	3;7.28	172	4;3.15
017	2;6.14/16	069	3;1.15	121	3;8.1	173	4;3.21
018	2;6.18	070	3;1.18	122	3;8.5	174	4;4.1

019	2;7.0	071	3;1.22	123	3;8.8	175	4;4.4
020	2;7.4	072	3;1.26	124	3;8.11	176	4;4.21
021	2;7.7	073	3;1.28	125	3;8.16	177	4;5.3
022	2;7.11	074	3;2.1	126	3;8.17	178	4;5.14
023	2;7.14	075	3;2.5	127	3;8.21	179	4;5.20
024	2;7.15	076	3;2.7	128	3;8.23	180	4;5.28
025	2;7.18	077	3;2.9	129	3;8.28	181	4;6.1
026	2;7.26	078	3;2.18	130	3;9.0	182	4;6.5
027	2;8.1	079	3;2.21	131	3;9.5	183	4;6.12
028	2;8.6	080	3;2.26	132	3;9.6	184	4;6.14
029	2;8.8	081	3;2.29	133	3;9.12	185	4;6.19
030	2;8.14	082	3;3.1	134	3;9.14	186	4;6.27
031	2;8.18	083	3;3.4	135	3;9.19	187	4;7.3
032	2;8.22	084	3;3.8	136	3;9.23	188	4;7.5
033	2;8.25	085	3;3.11	137	3;9.25	189	4;7.11
034	2;8.29	086	3;3.15	138	3;9.27	190	4;8.0
035	2;9.1	087	3;3.18	139	3;10.3	191	4;8.2
036	2;9.5	088	3;3.25	140	3;10.7	192	4;8.7
037	2;9.8	089	3;3.28	141	3;10.9	193	4;8.14
038	2;9.11	090	3;4.1	142	3;10.14	194	4;8.20
039	2;9.16	091	3;4.4	143	3;10.15	195	4;8.27
040	2;9.19	092	3;4.8	144	3;10.18	196	4;9.0
041	2;9.23	093	3;4.12	145	3;10.25	197	4;9.12
042	2;9.27	094	3;4.15	146	3;11.0	198	4;9.19
043	2;9.30	095	3;4.19	147	3;11.2	199	4;9.24
044	2;10.3	096	3;4.19/26	148	3;11.6	200	4;10.1
045	2;10.6	097	3;4.26	149	3;11.11	201	4;10.9
046	2;10.7	098	3;4.30	150	3;11.12	202	4;10.15
047	2;10.12	099	3;5.3	151	3;11.16	203	4;10.22
048	2;10.15	100	3;5.6	152	3;11.25	204	4;10.29
049	2;10.20	1101	3;5.13	153	4;0.3	205	4;11.5
050	2;10.22	102	3;5.17	154	4;0.15	206	4;11.13
051	2;10.27	103	3;5.23	155	4;0.16	207	4;11.21
052	2;10.30	104	3;5.24	156	4;0.25	208	4;11.27
						209	5;0.4
						210	5;0.11

Further documentation of this study is available in Kuczaj (1976). Publications that make use of this corpus should cite that source.

26.25. MacWhinney

This directory contains transcripts from MacWhinney's diary study of the development of his two sons, Ross and Mark. Ross was born on December 25, 1977 and Mark was born on November 19, 1979. Ross was recorded between the ages of 2;6 and 8;0 and Mark was recorded between 0;7 and 5;6. Because the experimenter is also the boys' father, these data represent a fairly natural record of the family's interactions. These data are still in a preliminary state and many files are not yet transcribed. MacWhinney has only double-checked the transcription of the files after ross53 and some of the earlier files. Although they are available for public use, users should be very much aware of their preliminary state. There is much descriptive information that has not yet been included in these files.

The files with the label "boys" include 29 files from Ross between the ages of 5;6 and 8;0 and from Mark between the ages of 3;6 and 6;0. The files with the label "ross" include 38 files from Ross between 2;6 and 5;4, when Mark is between 0;7 and 3;5. There is also a file (Ross01) that chronicles Ross's very early development. There is also a directory of 29 unfinished files from Ross and Mark. that is called "unfinished." Data were collected from 5;0 to 9;0, but they are not yet transcribed.

Publications that make use of this corpus do not need to cite anything.

26.26. New England

Subjects. This directory contains longitudinal data on 52 children whose language development was studied by Catherine Snow, Barbara Pan, and colleagues as part of the project "Foundations for Language Assessment in Spontaneous Speech," funded by the National Institutes of Health. Subjects were chosen from a larger sample of 100 children on whom language and other data were available from the MacArthur Individual Differences Project. A description of subject solicitation and other information about the original sample can be found in Snow (1989) and Dale, Bates, Reznick, and Morisset (1989) The present sample of 52 children from English-speaking families was chosen to include half girls and half boys, and equal proportions of children from families of lower-middle and upper-middle socioeconomic status. Children with indications of medical or other developmental problems were excluded.

Procedure. Each child-parent (generally the mother) dyad was brought to the laboratory at three ages: at 14 months, at 20 months, and again between the ages of 27-32 months. Transcripts at 14 and 20 months reflect spontaneous language data collected during a five minute warmup and several subsequent activities, each of which is described briefly here.

1. **Warm-up**. For the warm-up period, the mother and child were left alone in a small room with some toys, and the mother was instructed to take a few minutes to let her child become accustomed to the setting.

2. **Toy play**. Next there was a 5 minute period during which the child was given a variety of small toys to play with (Small-scale Activity) while the mother was filling out a form at a nearby table. Because the mother was instructed not to initiate interaction with the child during this period, this portion of the videotaped protocol was not transcribed.

3. **Forbidden object**. In the next task, the mother was seated beside the child at the table and instructed to try and keep the child from touching an attractive, moving object (Forbidden Object). Users of these transcripts should be aware that this part of the transcribed data involved some triadic (examiner-parent-child) interaction, and thus for certain analyses may not be comparable to the dyadic (parent-child) interaction which makes up the rest of the transcript.

4. **Boxes**. Finally, the mother was asked to spend about 10 minutes playing with her child using the contents of four successive boxes. She was not instructed how long should be spent on each box, but was told to try to get to all four, and to have only one box open at a time. The boxes contained, in order, a ball, a cloth for peekaboo, paper and crayons, and a book. The entire transcribed parent-child interaction averaged 20-25 minutes in duration.

The protocol for parent-child interaction at the third data point (age 27-32 months) involved only four boxes (no warm-up or forbidden object), and two substitutions were made to make the activities more age-appropriate: hand puppets and a Fisher-Price toy house replaced the ball and peekaboo cloth. Parent and child were videotaped by means of a camera located either at ceiling level in one corner of the room and operated by remote control, or located on the other side of a one-way mirror.

Transcription and coding. The transcripts in this corpus were prepared from the videotaped parent-child interaction by transcribers trained in the **CHAT** conventions. Users should note several specific transcription guidelines which were followed. Utterance boundaries were based on intonation contour. No attempt was made to distinguish the number of unintelligible words in a string; therefore xxx and yyy (rather than xx and yy) are used throughout. Where the phonological form could be represented, yyy was followed by a %pho tier and UNIBET transcription. Other nonverbal vocalizations were represented as 0 [=! vocalizes]. The audio quality of videotapes did not permit phonetic transcription. In general, no attempt was made to represent possible word omissions, nor to distinguish child-invented forms, family-specific forms, and phonologically consistent forms; rather the generic @ was used for all three. Pauses were transcribed as either # or #long, rather than in terms of precise duration. Words on the main tier were morphemicized so that MLU could be automatically computed in morphemes, and so that inflected forms of nouns and verbs would be counted not as separate word types, but as tokens of the uninflected stem.

Because it was anticipated that looking behaviors, especially in the 14 month olds, would often be used to direct the adult's attention, and would therefore be important to consider in coding infants' nonverbal communicative acts, it was decided that all looking behaviors (as well as points, head nods, etc.) would be recorded on %gpx tiers. Time at the beginning of each activity and the passage of each subsequent full minute were recorded on %tim tiers.

Research based on this corpus should cite (Dale et al., 1989) and (Snow, 1989).

26.27. Peters / Wilson

These are transcripts of audio tapes made by Dr. Bob Wilson of himself and his son Seth, who was born October 18, 1980. Although Wilson has placed this material in the public domain, it has not been censored as to personally sensitive material. Please be careful of this when using these transcripts and do not quote any questionable material. Wilson has chosen not to have the names changed. For coding conventions for the %spa line see the files "00spa.fat" and "00spa.chi" for the father and the child. The file "00coding.doc" has special codes for the %gls lines for Seth and for phonological forms placed on the main line for Seth. The files were reformatted into **CHAT** in June 1992 by Brian MacWhinney. They were then rechecked in 1994 by Ann Peters. However, there are still some deviations from standard **CHAT** format. These are currently being corrected.

These transcripts were made under the supervision of Dr. Ann Peters of the University of Hawai'i, with financial assistance from NSF grand BNS84-18272. Reference to these materials in documents to be circulated (published or unpublished) should acknowledge the above sources. Seth has a severe visual impairment. For more information see Wilson and Peters (1988) and Peters (1987).

26.28. Post

This study examined children from families living in Suwannee County, Florida. This area was chosen because it fits the criterion of being a rural, Southern community that has a predominantly white, working-class population. It is also the family home of this investigator's parents and numerous aunts, uncles and cousins. Through work on the qualifying paper, contacts had already been established at the Suwannee County Health Department to obtain access to the immunization records. In addition, the investigator's shared regional accent and shared cultural experiences allowed easy access to and ready acceptance by the study families.

Subjects. The subjects were three girls and their families. Two of the girls were approximately 19 months of age at the time of selection and the third was 22 months. One subject was the second-born, one was the third-born and the third subject was the fourth-born child in the family. The next-oldest sibling in each family was approximately 18 months older than the third- and fourth-born subjects and the older sibling was two years older than the second-born subject. All of the subjects are the products of normal pregnancies, were healthy at the time of taping and have no apparent hearing, speech or mental deficiencies. They were located through immunization records obtained from the Suwannee County Health Department and the records of a Pediatrician in Live Oak. The mothers were contacted by telephone and a meeting arranged to ascertain if the family met the criteria for the study.

Recruitment. At the initial meeting the mothers were told that the investigator was interested in observing how children change or develop over time. Since the families were selected according to the age of the younger child, the younger child was called the target child. It was emphasized, however, that we were interested in how both children developed over time, not just the younger one. It was explained to the families that they were entering a long-term commitment to the study. It was agreed that the sum of $100.00 would be paid to the families as an incentive to complete the study. Fifty dollars was paid to each family at the end of the first taping session and the remaining $50.00 was paid at the end of the final taping session. In addition, at the end of the fifth taping session, the investigator took the families out to lunch. The mothers also signed a consent form which appears in Appendix B. The mothers were interviewed periodically and asked their views on childrearing, how their children spend the day, methods of discipline, goals for their children, and other related issues. They were asked more specific questions on how they thought their children learn language, how the parents affect their children's language learning, how important language learning is, how they thought their children will do in school, what they thought their children should be able to do by the time they enter kindergarten, and what they perceived as the long-term and short-term effects of their children's education. In addition, the mothers were asked how they felt about their children watching television and if it should be regulated or not. In the ethnographic tradition, detailed descriptions of the community and the children and their families are provided. The descriptions help the reader understand the environment in which these children are learning language. The purpose of these portraits is to add a richness and completeness to the data.

Data Collection. Within one week of the initial meeting a taping session was conducted in the subject's home. Taping was accomplished with a Sony Video 8 AF portable video cassette recorder. Prior to the taping the recording equipment was brought into the subjects' homes to allow the children to examine the equipment to lessen the disruptive influence on the normal interaction. Occasionally, during the taping sessions, one of the children would come over to examine the camera, but generally, the camera was ignored once the toys were introduced. Each taping session lasted approximately sixty minutes. A toy bag provided by the investigator was introduced at the beginning of the session and the family played with whatever interested them. The toys were appropriate for the ages of the children and included such items as books, blocks, action figures, puzzles, pull-toys and one Fisher-Price playset. New toys and books were added over the taping sessions to maintain interest. Occasionally the subjects would bring out a favorite toy or book of their own. Taping sessions were scheduled at times which the mothers deemed most convenient and most likely to have the children in a receptive mood. Taping took place approximately every four weeks. Because of illness or vacations, occasionally the sessions were scheduled a little farther apart. A total of ten sessions was recorded for each family. Thus the language development of these three children was followed over a period of about nine months during the latter part of their second year and the early part of their third year. This age was chosen because during this time the child's language is expanding greatly in complexity of syntax and size of vocabulary.

The investigator was present for all of the tapings and made contextual notes to aid in transcription. The presence of an outsider and recording equipment no doubt affects the interaction among the family members. For this reason one "practice" taping session was made with each family, the data from which was not included in later analyses. It was observed that with repeated exposure to the taping situation the disruptive effects of the data collection methods were minimal.

Data Coding. Transcripts of the tapes were made as soon as possible after the session by the investigator. The data was transcribed in **CHAT**. In determining how to divide up maternal utterances, it was decided to use breath groups. That is, what the mother said on one breath was considered to be one utterance. One of the mothers tended to have longer utterances than the other two. On occasion, this mother (Darla) might take a quick supplemental breath, but the pause would be less than one second and it was clear that she was continuing the same utterance. The feedback data were obtained using the modified coding scheme described in Demetras (1986). Publications using these data should cite (Post, 1992) or (Post, 1994).

26.29. Sachs

This corpus consists of Jacqueline Sachs' longitudinal study of her daughter, Naomi, (born June 8, 1968). The transcripts cover the time from age 1;1 to 5;1. There is also a "0lexicon.doc" file, which is a list of nonstandard forms present in the data. The data various MLU Ranges are as follows:

MLU	Adult Utterances	Age
1-2	1340	1;8.0 to 1;10.17
2-2.5	1730	1;8.18 to 1;9.11
2.5-3	2300	1;9.12 to 2;2.0
3-3.5	920	2;2.25 to 2;4.0
3.5-4	3030	2;4.6 to 3;3.27
4-4.5	900	3;4.0 to 3;5.12
4-5;5	1050	3;6.0 to 3;8.19
5 up	730	4;7.28 to 5;1.20

Naomi's ages for the various files are as follows:

File	Age	File	Age	File	Age	File	Age
01	1;2.29	24	1;11.9	47	2;1.17	70	2;8.23
02	1;6.16	25	1;11.11	48	2;1.25	71	2;9.9
03	1;8.6	26	1;11.12	49	2;1.26	72	2;9.11
04	1;8.0	27	1;11.17	50	2;2.0	73	2;11.8
05	1;8.29	28	1;11.16	51	2;2.25	74	2;11.10
06	1;9.7	29	1;11.18	52	2;3.0	75	2;11.11
07	1;9.10	30	1;11.20	53	2;3.17	76	2;11.12
08	1;9.26	31	1;11.21	54	2;3.19	77	2;11.13
09	1;10.3	32	1;11.23	55	2;3.21	78	2;11.17
10	1;10.10	33	1;11.29	56	2;3.29	79	2;11.18
11	1;10.10	34	1;11.30	57	2;4.4	80	2;11.24
12	1;10.11	35	2;0.2	58	2;4.5	81	3;2.10
13	1;10.14	36	2;0.3	59	2;4.13	82	3;3.26
14	1;10.17	37	2;0.5	60	2;4.30	83	3;3.27
15	1;10.18	38	2;0.18	61	2;5.3	84	3;4.0
16	1;10.19	39	2;0.19	62	2;5.8	85	3;4.18
17	1;10.20	40	2;0.26	63	2;5.9	86	3;5.3
18	1;10.23	41	2;0.27	64	2;5.21	87	3;5.4
19	1;10.25	42	2;0.28	65	2;6.4	88	3;5.6
20	1;10.28	43	2;1.0	66	2;6.5	89	3;5.7
21	1;11.2	44	2;1.1	67	2;7.13	90	3;8.19
22	1;11.3	45	2;1.7	68	2;7.16	91	4;7.28
23	1;11.6	46	2;1.9	69	2;8.14	92	4;7.29
						93	4;9.3

Publications that make use of this corpus should cite Sachs (1983).

26.30. Snow

This corpus contains 30 files of data collected by Catherine Snow between 1979 and 1980 in Brookline, MA. The subject was her son, Nathaniel. He was 2;3 at the start of the study and 3;9 at the end. Before using the data, please check with Catherine Snow.

Nathaniel was, at this stage of development, a particularly unintelligible child. He also used many empty or semi-empty forms mixed with meaningful speech, such as duh-duh, da-da, dede. Accordingly, many of his transcribed utterances include syllables which were broadly phonetically transcribed, either because they had no meaning, or because they could not be interpreted. His mispronunciations had in some cases standardized themselves into lexical or semi-lexicalized items, used either standardly in the family (see "0lexicon.doc") or transiently within certain conversations (see "0lexicon.doc"). Unintelligible and empty syllables have been indicated in the text line by a yyy and the phonetic transcription is indicated on the %pho: tier.

File	Age	File	Age	File	Age	File	Age
01	2;5.18	08	2;6.25	15	3;0.19	23	3;4.10
02	2;6.0	09	2;7.1	16	3;0.22	24	3;4.10
03	2;6.0	10		17	3;1.6	25	3;4.18
04	2;6.0	11		18	3;2.27	26	3;4.21
05	2;6.3	12		19	3;4.8	27	3;4.21

06	2;6.19	13		20	3;4.8	28	3;7.14
07	2;6.19	14	2;8.20	21	3;4.9	29	3;9.2
				22	3;4.9	30	3;9.4

Publications that make use of this corpus do not need to cite anything.

26.31. Suppes

These data were contributed by Patrick Suppes. The child under study, named Nina, was 1;11 when the study began and 3;3 when it ended. The 52 files (4 were not included), consisting of 102,230 tokens, were collected between 1972 and 1973.

File	Age	File	Age	File	Age	File	Age
01	1;11.16	15	2;2.28	31	2;5.28	44	3;0.16
02	1;11.24	16	2;3.5	32	2;9.13	45	3;0.24
03	1;11.29	17	2;3.14	33	2;9.21	46	3;1.4
04	2;0.3	18	2;3.18	34	2;9.26	47	3;1.5
05	2;0.10	19	2;3.28	35	2;10.6	48	3;1.6
06	2;0.17	20	2;4.6	36	2;10.13	49	3;1.7
07	2;0.24	21	2;4.12	37	2;10.21	50	3;2.4
09	2;1.6	22	2;4.18	38	2;10.28	51	3;2.12
10	2;1.15	23	2;4.26	39	2;11.6	52	3;2.16
11	2;1.22	27	2;5.24	40	2;11.12	53	3;2.24
12	2;1.29	28	2;5.25	41	2;11.16	54	3;3.1
13	2;2.6	29	2;5.26	42	3;0.3	55	3;3.8
14	2;2.12	30	2;5.27	43	3;0.10	56	3;3.21

Publications that make use of this corpus should cite Suppes (1973).

26.32. Van Houten

These data were obtained from Lori Van Houten's doctoral dissertation, which studied differences in mother-child interaction between adolescent and older mothers. The mothers were followed from the time of the birth of their children. Data were collected at 4 months, 8 months, 2 years, and 3 years. Only the 2 year and 3 year data is on the computer.

Twos. The two year data are in the subdirectory "twos". The children were studied at home in three different situational contexts–lunchtime, a teaching session in which the mother attempted to teach the child a task, and a free play situation.

First there is a three minute segment of interaction while the child eats lunch. Videotaped for a half hour, mothers were instructed to try to ignore the camera and do whatever they would normally do during lunch. If the child finished lunch before the half hour was up mothers were instructed to do whatever they would normally do after eating lunch. The three minutes of tape following the first minute of interaction were transcribed for this study.

The second session was a teaching session in which the mother was instructed to teach the child three tasks from the Bayley Scales of Infant Development which were considered too difficult for the child's age. Mothers did not know the task was too difficult for the child. The tasks were: placing a block in specific locations (on, in, under, and so forth) around a cup and a small chair, stringing beads and sorting black and white buttons. The mothers were given one task at a time. The task was explained and the mother was given three minutes to teach each one. Only the first two minutes of the bead stringing and one minute of the sorting buttons task are transcribed.

The third session consisted of a half hour of play with a box of experimenter provided toys. Among the toys were: cloth books, a tea set, a truck with different-shaped blocks which fit in holes in the side of the truck, a miniature playground set with small characters, giant Legos, Ernie and Cookie Monster puppets and a chalk board/magnetic board with chalk and magnetic pieces. Mother and child played in an area in which they usually interacted. Also, mothers were requested to play only with the experimenter provided toys. The three minutes of interaction following the first minute of tape is transcribed.

Threes. The files for these data are in the subdirectory "threes." The children in this part of the study were between 3;2 and 3;7. In this segment of the study, 27 children were recorded during a free play situation and 25 children were recorded during a teaching activity in which the child attempts to teach the mother a simple task.

Thirteen of the children were children of adolescent mothers. All of the children, with the exception of Goose, have data at the 2 year level as well. Wilson, Doll, Dean, and Valley have 2 year transcripts but no 3 year data. The subject Park has two free play tapes. The child was generally uncooperative using the toys provided by the experimenter. A second file, entitled "Bestpark" is probably more representative of the child's true linguistic abilities as the child plays with his own toys. The reader will have to decide whether to opt for a more controlled sample on the same topic as the other files or for a more representative linguistic sample.

The children were seen in their homes by two experimenters. The mother was taken to another room where she was given a standard IQ test by one the examiners. The child remained with the other examiner and the McCarthy Scales of Children's Abilities and the Rhode Island Test of Language Structure were administered. The children's scores for each of these tests (McCarthy verbal and cognitive scores, RITLS number of errors out of 100) are given in the headers for each file. With the RITLS in particular, it sometimes took more than one visit to complete the test.

Free play. Following the tests, the examiner and the child engaged in at least 5 minutes of free play with an experimenter provided toy. The toy was a miniature park set including a slide, merry-go-round, park bench, some small figures, and a mother figure with a baby in a stroller. These interactions were audiotaped only. The goal of the interaction was to elicit a reasonable language sample in a fairly controlled setting. The examiner tried to use the same line of conversation with each child. Some of the children, however, responded better to some forms of conversation than others. For example, some children preferred to act out a story with the characters and others preferred to merely talk about the characters. The free play sessions were transcribed and coded using the same procedures used with the 2 year data.

Teaching. The second transcript for each child, and the last activity to take place during the home visit, consists of audiotapes of the child trying to teach the mother a given activity. The mother joined the experimenter and child. The mother was instructed to "close her eyes and cover her ears" while the examiner taught the child a simple task. The examiner taught the child the task (manipulating the small characters from the park set and stringing beads) in such a way as to insure that the child could perform the task, and to offer a verbal model of how to teach the task. The child was then told to teach the mother the task. Throughout the teaching the investigator encouraged the child to teach the mother the task and then have the mother perform the task. The investigator again tried to use similar procedures and utterances with each child. We were interested in looking at whether the child chose to demonstrate the task, to teach it verbally or used a combination of the two techniques. The final goal was to compare the child's teaching technique with what the mothers had done at 2 years in a similar situation. These teaching segments were not timed and each transcript may be of a different length. A separate coding system was devised for this segment.

Coding System for Twos. This coding system is appropriate for use with children from approximately Stage 1 to about 4 years. It is based on the premise that there are elements of interaction beyond the sentence level which may affect the course and rate of language acquisition. There are three main components to the coding system: Structural Complexity (MLU and Number of Main Verbs), Discourse Role (Initiate, Respond, Continue Turn, and so forth) and Pragmatic Role (Request Information, Report, Clarification, Control/Restrict, and so forth). These are coded for both mother and child (although some of the pragmatic variables pertain only to the mother or child) in an attempt to characterize the reciprocal nature of the interaction. A brief summary of the codes used is as follows:

Grammatical Complexity:

MLU	MLU
Number of Main Verbs	NMV

Discourse Role

Initiate	Ini
Continue Turn	Con
Null	Nul
Respond	Res
(mother only)	
Respond Expressive	Rex
Respond Collaborative	Rco
Respond Report	Rre
Respond Learning	Rle
Respond Desire	Rde
Respond Ego-Enhancing	Reg
Respond Possession	Rpo
Respond Joining	Rjo
Respond Request for Info	Rri
Respond to Action	Rta

Pragmatic
  (Mother only)

Clarification	Cla
Explication	Exp
Confirm/Acknowledge	C/A
Accomodate	Acc
Collaborative	Col
Control/Restrict	C/R
Request for Action	Rfa
Request for Information	Rfi
Report	Rep
Teach	Tea

Routine Score	Rsc	
(Child only)		
Routine Score	Rsc	
Expressive		Epr
Desire	Des	
Possession Rights	Pos	
Ego-Enhancing	Ego	
Self-Referring	Sel	
Joining	Joi	
Request for Information	Rfi	
Collaborative	Col	
Learning Implementing	Lim	
Report	Rep	

As mentioned above the target of this coding system is to describe the interaction between mother and child. All behaviors of mother and child are transcribed, both verbal and nonverbal. Also child utterances when the child is "talking to himself" are transcribed. In the study described here, only the behaviors of mother and child are of interest. If there is any interaction between, for example, the father and one of the target participants this is noted but not transcribed or coded. Child and maternal utterances to the camera person or other people in the room are not transcribed. Also, the mother's phone conversations are not transcribed. The fact that the mother is on the phone or spoke to someone else in the room may be noted in the situation line if they bear on some further element of the interaction. Otherwise, they are not mentioned.

If the child says something like: "wa da ober dere?", this will be transcribed as "What that over there?" If the child's utterance is completely unintelligible and no accurate gloss can be determined from context, xxx is written in the utterance slot. On the coding line this is not coded for structural complexity but is coded for discourse and pragmatic role (if it can be determined from context). Therefore, it is important to include that the child has said something even if it is not intelligible.

The situation line is under the utterance line. On this line, any contextual elements are noted. For example, pointing, gesturing, entrances and exits, gaze, tone of voice (anger, whining), laughing, and so on are all included in the situation line. If two utterances are said simultaneously this is noted in the situation line of both utterances. Not every utterance has a situation line. Only when it makes the dialogue easier to follow or makes the coding more transparent is it included. Another purpose for the situation line is to describe child behaviors which the mother responds to although the child did not intend his behaviors to be communicative. This is the case, for example, if the child silently strings a bead and the mother says 'very good'. The mother's utterance is contingent on the child's previous behavior. The child's contribution is noted with a zero in the utterance line and the behavior is described in the situation line. There is no other coding for this type of child behavior.

Coding for Threes. The coding system used for the teaching situation at 3 years is different from that used with free play. It was designed specifically for use with these transcripts with several questions in mind. First, how well does the child adhere to the the teaching procedure in terms of the type of utterances used and the structure of the teaching situation? Secondly, what role do the adults play in this interaction? Finally, how do the utterances in teaching differ from those used in free play? Based on these questions, a coding system was developed that included rough measures of grammatical complexity, variables representing the various segments of the teaching situation, and variables coding the pragmatic role of both adults' and the child's utterances. The following is a list of the variable names and the three letter codes used for each. This is followed by a description of each variable:

Grammatical Complexity

Mean Length of Utterance	MLU
Number of Main Verbs	NMV

Teaching Segments

Teach Mother	Tmo
Teach Child	Tch
Closing	Clo

Pragmatics

(adult only)

Directive	Dir
Request for Information	Rfi
Evaluate Teaching	Evt
Evaluate Performance	Evp
Teach	Tea
Accommodate/Acknowledge	A/A
Control/Restrict	C/R
Explication of Child Teaching	Ext
Learning Implementing	Lim
Quizzing	Qui
Clarification	Cla
Correction	Cor
Report	Rep
Routine Score	Rsc

(child only)

Teach	Tea
Teach, Respond to Question	Trq
Control/Restrict	C/R
Request for Information	Rfi
Report	Rep
Evaluate	Eva
Routine Score	Rsc

The interaction is divided in terms of who is teaching whom and, in general, what the purpose of the interaction is. To this end, the following segments are used:

1. Teach Mother (Tmo): By far the largest portion of the interaction, this segment includes all utterances by the examiner and mother exhorting the child to teach the mother, all the child's utterances surrounding the teaching process, and all utterances evaluating the mother's performance of the task.

2. Teach Child (Tch): Some children forget what they are supposed to teach. The examiner interrupts the interaction to teach the child the task again.

3. Closing (Clo): Includes any closing statements, usually evaluations of the child's teaching techniques, following the teaching of the task.

These segment markers are the third item entered on the coding line following the two grammatical complexity measures. The final measure considers the pragmatic role of the individual utterance.

Headers. In addition to the standard CHAT headers such as Participants, Sex and Situation, there are some project-specific headers.

1. Mother's Age Group: The mother's status as an adolescent or older mother is provided.

2. Mother's SES: Socioeconomic status based on the Hollingshead four factor index is given for each mother. The information necessary for calculating SES was collected when the child was 8 months old.

3. Mother's Education: Maternal educational level. 1=completed junior high, 2=completed high school, 3=some post-secondary education. Again this is based on the mother's educational status at 8 months. Not too many of the adolescents had continued with school after the birth of their child and none of the older mothers were students. Therefore, these figures can be considered reasonably accurate.

4. McCarthy-Cognitive: (3 year data only) The child's IQ based on his performance on the McCarthy Scales of Infant Development.

5. McCarthy-Verbal: (3 year data only) The child's scaled score on the verbal portion of the McCarthy Scales of Infant Development.

6. RITLS: (3 year data only) The total number of errors out of 100 on the Rhode Island Test of Language Structure, a standardized test of comprehension of various simple and complex syntactic structures. Utilizing a picture identification task, the test requires children to choose from an array of three the one picture which most closely exemplifies the examiner's stimulus sentence.

Results. The repeated measures ANOVAs at both age levels demonstrate main effects for maternal age but no significant interactions between maternal age and situation. At two years, teenage mothers confirmed or acknowledged children's utterances significantly less and had fewer teaching utterances. These results, combined with other trends in the data, suggest that adolescent mothers did not differ significantly from children of older mothers in their general linguistic competencies. Thus, despite differences in the nature of their input, adolescent and older mothers provided at least the minimum amount of the right kind of input to insure that acquisition proceeded at a "normal" rate. A review of mother's instructional strategies revealed that teenage mothers were less likely to use the decontextualized, syntactically complex, language of the classroom. Lack of familiarity with this form of discourse may have contributed to the children's poor performance. Thus, adolescent mothers' communicative strategies with their language learning children could be associated with the children's lack of success in school and school-related tasks. Publications that make use of this corpus should cite VanHouten (1986).

26.33. Van Kleeck

These data were contributed by Ann Van Kleeck of the University of Texas at Austin. They are from 37 normal three-year-olds in a laboratory setting. The children are from the Austin area and are native English speakers. This sample was not controlled for race or socio-economic status. Each child participated in two one-half hour sessions.

We have received only a small amount of information concerning the files. Each individual file is headed with identifying information on the child, the file names represent the child's name (usually first, but last initial or name has been used where there is duplication of the first name), and the session number. Each child participated in two one-half hour sessions, creating the first file (Bree1) for the first session and the second file (Bree2) for the second session. We hope to eventually receive further details regarding the subjects and data collection procedures.

26.34. Warren-Leubecker

This subdirectory contains data from 20 children interacting either with their mothers or their fathers. The families are white and middle-class, but nonprofessionals. One group of children is aged 1;6 to 3;1 and the other group is aged 4;6 to 6;2. The data were contributed by Amye Warren-Leubecker. Ten of the children are in the "older" group, (Mean age of 64.7 months, SD = 8.25, range from 4;6 to 6;2) and ten are in a "younger" group (Mean age of 26.5 months, SD = 5.99, range from 1;6 to 3;1). Half of the children in each age group are boys and half are girls. Each child spoke to his or her mother and father in successive dyadic, separate sessions. The order in which they spoke to mother or father was randomized. The sessions took place in the child's home, normally in a living room or den area, with the child's own toys or books present to facilitate conversation. The experimenter was either not present in the room (set up the tape recorder and left it behind) or was in an isolated part of the room where the child could not easily see her. Parents were instructed to play/with or talk to their children as naturally as possible. They were instructed to bring out the child in conversation, and the only limitation was that neither child or parent was to actually read to the other.

The parents were told that the experimenter was interested in how language develops, and thus was tape recording children of various age for a project. Actually, the purpose of the project was to examine the fundamental voice frequencies used by mothers versus fathers when speaking to children, and the parents were subsequently informed that the experimenter was less interested in the child's speech than in their own. Because voice frequency was the primary measure to be used, the recording had to be high quality. A Revox reel-to-reel recorder and omni-directional microphone were used and all home background noise was eliminated (TVs or radios off, siblings physically removed and so forth). Each session with mother or father lasted at least 15 minutes, possibly up to half an hour. Thus, each child conversed for at least half an hour. The resulting recordings were transcribed verbatim by the experimenter using the common English alphabet (not the phonetic alphabet). Phonetic approximations were used for any uninterpretable speech segments, and for common "slang" phrases (e.g., "Gonna", "Wanna", "Doin", "Uh-huh"). Moreover, care was taken to approximate dialectical variation in pronunciation. All of the parents live in the suburbs of Atlanta, Georgia, but most were not born or raised in this area and thus do not have "Southern" accents. None of the parents or children had any obvious speech disfluencies, and none of the children were language delayed. The transcripts were compared for mother–father differences in prosodic, structural, and functional features of child-directed speech.

Publications that make use of this corpus should cite Warren-Leubecker and Bohannon (1984) or Warren-Leubecker (1982) where further analyses can be found.

26.35. Wells

This extensive corpus contains 299 files from 32 British children (16 girls and 16 boys) aged 1;6 to 5;0 recorded in a naturalistic setting. The data are taken from a project by Gordon Wells and colleagues entitled "The Bristol language development study: language development in pre-school children" (1973–1977). The original intent of the study was to provide a normative survey of British children growing up in an urban environment. The samples were recorded by taperecorders that turned on for 90 second intervals and then automatically turned off.

Approximately 1000 names were drawn at random from the record of births held by the City Medical Officer, and the families of all these children were approached initially by health visitors and subsequently by members of the research team. Details relevant to the classification of family background were obtained from all families, including a small minority who declined to take part in the study. At the same time, information was obtained which allowed us to exclude a number of categories of children: multiple births, children with known handicaps, those in full-time day care and those whose parents did not speak English as their native language. These categories were excluded, not out of any lack of interest in the problems that such children might be expected to encounter, but because their numbers in a sample of this size could not be expected to be large enough to permit meaningful comparisons to be made with the "normal" population.

Then, finally, names of those children whose families had agreed to take part were picked at random to fill the cells in the sample design, and a number of reserves were picked in a similar manner. During the following four years several families withdrew from the study, but when the schedule of recordings was finally completed, the sample still numbered 129 children.

Each child was observed a total of ten times at three-monthly intervals, each observation consisting of a recording in the child's home and the administration of a number of tests at the Research Unit in the university. In addition, the parents of each child were interviewed when he or she was aged 3;6, to obtain information about the long-term environment provided by the home and about the parents' beliefs and practices concerning their role in the upbringing of their children.

The recording of spontaneous occurring conversation was the main part of each observation. The decision was made at the outset to obtain recordings in conditions that reduced to the minimum the possibly distorting effect of the actual observation process. To this end, special equipment was constructed which could be delivered to the child's home on the day before the observation was to be made and left there to work quite automatically until after the observation was completed. In the morning, when the child was being dressed for the day, a lightweight harness containing a radio microphone was put under the child's top garment. This transmitted continuously all speech produced by the child and any speech by others that was loud enough for him to hear. It also, of course, picked up and transmitted a large range of other noises, such as doors shutting, footsteps, and even the bubbles of the goldfish in the aquarium. Because the microphone was linked to the tape recorder by radio, it caused no impediment to the child's freedom to move around, and reception remained good up to a range of 100 meters.

At the other end of the radio link in an out-of-the-way room or cupboard was a box containing the rest of the equipment: a radio receiver, a tape recorder and a rather complex timing mechanism which was programmed to record 24 examples of 90 seconds' duration at approximately 20-minute intervals between 9 a.m. and 6 p.m. The intervals between samples were irregular so that parents would not be tempted to plan activities in regular 20-minute cycles. In fact, they were completely unaware of the precise time at which recordings were to be made, and the programme was changed for each observation. The result was that, as far as is humanly possible within the limits set by ethical considerations, we recorded samples of these families' normal spontaneous conversation without their being aware that they were being observed.

There was, of course, a price to be paid. By choosing to give priority to naturalness, we had to forgo the making of on-the-spot notes about the context in which the conversations occurred. To a considerable extent we were able to compensate for this by playing the recording back to the parents in the evening and asking them to recall, in as much detail as possible, the location, participants and activity for each of the recorded 90-second samples. An experiment carried out to compare this procedure with the more traditional procedure of a researcher being present during the recording revealed little difference in terms of the amount of contextual information that could be recovered; in some cases the mother was able to make more sense of an episode when she listened to it in the evening than the observer had been able to do while it was actually occurring. Once the observation had been made, the recording was transcribed and checked and then each child utterance was analyzed using the framework described earlier.

Sample	Age	Sample	Age	Sample	Age
abigai02	1;5.28	geofre04	2;2.29	nancy08	3;0.6
abigai03	1;8.27	geofre05	2;2.29	nancy09	3;3.3
abigai04	2;0.1	geofre06	2;5.29	neil02	1;6.4
abigai05	2;3.0	geofre07	2;9.4	neil03	1;9.5
abigai06	2;6.2	geofre08	3;0.12	neil04	1;11.28
abigai07	2;9.3	geofre09	3;3.9	neil05	2;2.25
abigai08	3;0.2	geofre10	3;6.11	neil06	2;6.1
abigai09	3;3.0	geofre21	4;11.22	neil08	3;0.2
abigai10	3;6.6	gerald02	1;6.6	neil09	3;3.1
abigai21	4;8	gerald03	1;8.29	neil10	3;6.1
benjam02	1;5.21	gerald04	2;0.15	nevill02	1;5.25
benjam03	1;8.27	gerald05	2;3.5	nevill03	1;9.15
benjam04	1;11.30	gerald06	2;6.5	nevill04	2;0.7
benjam05	2;3.3	gerald07	2;9.1	nevill05	2;3.0
benjam06	2;5.28	gerald08	2;11.26	nevill06	2;5.21
benjam07	2;9.1	gerald10	3;5.0	nevill07	2;9.0
benjam08	2;11.29	gerald21	4;9.5	nevill08	3;0.1
benjam09	3;2.29	harrie02	1;6.2	nevill09	3;4.12
benjam10	3;6.3	harrie03	1;9.1	nevill10	3;5.27
benjam21	5;0.24	harrie04	2;0.1	olivia02	1;6.0
betty02	1;6.3	harrie05	2;3.2	olivia03	1;9.4
betty03	1;9.4	harrie06	2;6.1	olivia04	1;11.27
betty04	2;0.3	harrie07	2;9.0	olivia05	2;3.5
betty05	2;3.2	harrie08	3;0.0	olivia06	2;5.25
betty06	2;5.28	harrie09	3;3.0	olivia07	2;8.21
betty07	2;8.27	harrie10	3;6.1	olivia08	2;11.26
betty08	3;0.9	harrie21	4;10.3	olivia09	3;3.10
betty09	3;3.2	iris02	1;6.0	olivia10	3;5.22

betty21	4;11.2	iris03	1;8.5	penny02	1;6.9
darren02	1;6.2	iris04	2;0.2	penny03	2;9.5
darren03	1;9.0	iris05	2;2.30	penny04	1;11.27
darren04	2;0.6	iris06	2;3/2;9?	penny05	2;3.0
darren05	2;2.26	iris07	2;9.13	penny06	2;6.0
darren06	2;6.1	iris08	3;0.6	penny07	2;9.18
darren07	2;8.29	iris09	3;2.29	penny08	2;11.27
darren08	3;0.3	iris10	3;5.27	penny09	3;3.7
darren09	3;3.11	iris21	4;8.4	penny10	3;5.26
darren10	3;6.4	jack02	1;5.26	rosie02	1;5.29
darren21	4;10.6	jack03	1;9.4	rosie03	1;9.19
debbie02	1;6.9	jack04	2;0.2	rosie04	2;0.13
debbie03	1;8.30	jack05	2;2.25	rosie05	2;2.27
debbie04	1;11.29	jack06	2;5.13	rosie06	2;6.3
debbie05	2;3.20	jack07	2;9.24	rosie07	2;9.10
debbie06	2;6.6	jack08	2;11.26	rosie08	0;0.3
debbie07	2;9.5	jack09	3;3.8	rosie09	3;3.0
debbie08	3;11.28	jack10	3;5.23	rosie10	3;6.11
debbie09	3;3.4	jack21	4;9.1	samant02	1;6.6
debbie10	3;6.24	jason02	1;6.0	samant03	1;9.7
debbie21	1;11.25?	jason03	1;9.0	samant04	1;11.30
ellen02	1;5.26	jason04	2;0.8	samant05	2;2.29
ellen03	1;9.0	jason05	2;3.1	samant06	2;6.0
ellen04	1;11.29	jason06	2;6.1	samant07	2;9.3
ellen05	2;2.21	jason07	2;9.29	samant08	3;0.4
ellen06	2;5.21	jason08	3;0.2	samant09	3;2.27
ellen07	2;8.30	jason09	3;3.6	samant10	3;6.11
ellen08	2;11.28	jason10	3;5.30	sean02	1;6.11
ellen09	3;3.4	jason21	5;0.19	sean03	1;8.30
ellen10	3;6.1	jonath02	1;6.5	sean04	1;11.29
ellen21	4;9.22	jonath03	1;8.26	sean05	2;2.28
elspet02	1;5.30	jonath04	1;11.29	sean06	2;6.5
elspet03	1;8.23	jonath05	2;2.26	sean07	2;9.4
elspet04	2;0.2	jonath06	2;6.2	sean08	3;0.11
elspet05	2;2.29	jonath07	2;9.1	sean09	3;2.28
elspet06	2;6.6	jonath08	2;11.29	sean10	3;6.9
elspet07	2;8.28	jonath09	3;2.28	sheila02	1;11.25?
elspet08	3;0.4	jonath10	3;5.24	sheila03	1;9.2
elspet09	3;2.30	jonath21	4;7.14	sheila04	1;11.30
elspet10	3;6.5	laura02	1;6.1	sheila05	2;3.4
elspet21	5;0.3	laura03	1;9.7	sheila06	2;5.27
frances02	1;6.1	laura04	2;0.6	sheila07	2;9.0
frances03	1;8.30	laura05	2;4.16	sheila08	2;11.28
frances04	2;0.1	laura06	2;6.3	sheila09	3;3.4
frances05	2;3.2	laura07	2;9.13	sheila10	3;6.25
frances06	2;6.3	laura08	3;0.7	simon02	1;5.21
frances07	2;8.30	laura09	3;3.0	simon03	1;9.2
frances08	2;11.28	laura10	3;6.2	simon04	1;11.13
frances09	3;3.0	lee02	1;5.28	simon05	2;3.5
frances10	3;6.0	lee03	2;2.3	simon06	2;6.0
frances21	4;10.8	lee04	1;11.26	simon07	1;9.1
gary02	1;6.0	lee05	2;3.1	simon08	3;0.1
gary03	1;9.2	lee06	2;6.1	simon09	3;3.9
gary04	2;0.4	lee07	2;9.24	simon10	3;5.22

gary05	2;3.4	lee08	3;0.1	stella02	1;6.8
gary06	2;6.3	lee09	3;3.0	stella03	1;9.3
gary07	2;9.5	lee10	3;5.29	stella05	2;2.30
gary08	3;0.4	martin02	1;5.26	stella06	2;6.2
gary09	3;3.3	martin03	1;9.2	stella07	2;8.25
gary10	3;5.25	martin04	2;0.8	stella08	2;11.27
gary21	4;9.0	martin05	2;3.3	stella09	3;3.7
gavin02	1;6.21	martin06	2;5.26	stella10	3;5.30
gavin03	1;9.4	martin07	2;8.24	tony02	1;5.26
gavin04	1;11.30	martin08	3;0.4	tony03	1;8.26
gavin05	2;4.4	martin09	3;3.5	tony04	1;11.14
gavin07	2;10.5	martin10	3;5.28	tony05	2;3.10
gavin08	3;0.6	nancy02	1;6.2	tony06	2;5.26
gavin09	3;3.19	nancy03	1;9.4	tony07	2;9.2
gavin10	3;7.27	nancy04	2;0.1	tony08	2;11.23
gavin21	4;9.18	nancy05	2;3.12	tony09	3;3.21
geofre02	1;6.0	nancy06	2;5.27	tony10	3;6.8
geofre03	1;9.6	nancy07	2;8.25		

Publications that make use of this corpus should cite Wells (1981).

26.36. Wisconsin

This directory contains files from 48 children in the age range around 1;6 studied by Jon Miller and Robin Chapman. Documentation on this database is not yet available.

26.37. Additional English Data Elsewhere in the Database

In addition to the English data in this chapter, the database also has several sets of data from normal English-speaking children that were studied as controls for language-impaired children. These corpora are from Bliss, Conti-Ramsden, Feldman, Hooshyar, and Rondal. They are described in the chapter discussing data on language impairments. Also the Cornell corpus in the non-CHAT directory has some data from English first language acquisition.

27. Non-English Data

Currently, the CHILDES database is heavily weighted with data from English-speaking children. However, it is a basic commitment of the CHILDES system to increase the coverage of other languages. If we want to understand which aspects of language learning are universal and which are language and culture specific, non-English data are essential. Fortunately, we now have corpora from many other languages and there are ongoing projects in many countries that plan on adding new non-English data to the database.

Researchers will only be able to make skillful use of corpora from languages which they themselves know. In some cases, it is possible that a group of researchers working together can examine a set of languages for which each is an expert. With the exception of the data from Polish and Tamil, the various non-English data sets have no English glosses or morphemic codings. These glosses and codings do not allow researchers who do not know a language to make full use of the corpora. Rather, they allow researchers who already know the language to perform a variety of automatic syntactic and lexical analyses. Thus, the addition of glosses and morphemic codings is not a prerequisite for the addition of data to the non-English database.

27.1. Brazilian Portuguese

These data were collected, transcribed and examined during Leonor Scliar-Cabral's doctoral thesis work in 1974. The records were reviewed during the adaptation to CHILDES in 1993. They consist of one Brazilian Portuguese child's 5530 utterances in broad phonetic transcription (including intonational patterns) collected in three sessions:
1. Age 1;8.21, MLU 1.45 (5 hours of recording, 1320 utterances) ;
2. Age 1;10.20, MLU 2.22 (6 hours of recording, 2245 utterances)
3. Age 2;2.8, MLU 2.40 (6 hours of recording, 1966 utterances).

The corpus collected during the first session is the first to be sent to CHILDES archives. The other ones will follow, as soon as the adaptation is ready. The phonetic transcription was made by Scliar-Cabral, who has phonological training. Three speech therapy students checked the transcriptions.

The intonational patterns which were transcribed in the original version were not adapted to CHILDES, but this information will be added in the future. Notes were taken for describing the situational context and/or any relevant information. The child's mother and father were helpful in translating his lexical creations. No videotapes were made. The following measures were computed: MLU, utterance types, utterance tokens, type/token ratio, upper bound, number of imitations, percentage of imitations, lexicon size, number of nouns, verbs, adjectives, locatives, and pronouns, functors required, functors present, and percentage of functors present. Other classes computed were: copulas; modals; pivotal operators; discourse operators; tags; interjections; onomatopoeias; stereotypes. Pronouns were subclassified as possessive, demonstrative and interrogative. MLU was computed using the criteria suggested by Brown (1973) and Bowerman (1973). Utterances were only coded as imitations if they had an identical intonation to the previous utterance, as well as a complete lexical overlap. Omitting imitations and onomatopoeias, the **MLU** computed by **CLAN** matched that computed by hand.

The child was a Brazilian Portuguese native speaker, living in an upper-middle class suburb of São Paulo. He attended a part day upper-middle class nursery where Brazilian

Portuguese was spoken. His parents were of upper-class Jewish background: although the father was a fluent speaker of French, the parents only spoke Brazilian Portuguese with their child. The father is a professor of linguistics at the University of São Paulo; the mother is a psychologist. There were frequent and tight contacts with other relatives, like uncles, aunts, and grand-parents who also used Brazilian Portuguese. As is common among Brazilian uper-middle class families, there was a house-keeper and a nanny who used a lower-class sociolinguistic variety, sometimes from different regions of Brazil. Excluding these inputs, all the other adults used the Brazilian Portuguese variety of São Paulo city and its surroundings.

27.2. Danish

This directory contains longitudinal corpora from two Danish children – Anne and Jens – studied by Kim Plunkett of Århus University during 1982–1987. The data were contributed to CHILDES in 1989. The children's ages during the study were 8 months to 6 years for Anne and 11 months to 6 years for Jens. In addition to the **CHAT** transcripts, results from the Uzgiris-Hunt Assessment Scales are available for both children during the first year of the study, as are results of various comprehension tests. Copies of the original videotapes can be made available.

The data were collected in the context of a project entitled "Projekt Bärnesprøg," which is a longitudinal investigation of Danish children's linguistic, cognitive, and social development. The main purpose of the study is to establish a profile of young Danish children's language development in relationship to their developing cognitive and social skills using the techniques of developmental psycholinguistic analysis. Even with a sample of just four children, individual differences in development demand a more refined account than the generalist approaches prevalent during the 70's.

The study began when the two children – a boy and a girl – were 0;11.15 and 0;8.1. respectively. Data collection continued until both children were 6;0. The girl has a sister who is 2 1/2 years older. Both parents had completed a university education. The boy is a single child. The father is a skilled worker and the mother had just started on a university education. Both children have spent a good deal of time in nursery school. The children were visited in their homes fortnightly. Each visit consisted of an interview, testing procedures, and a free play session. The interview focused on the parents' observations of their child's language behavior since the previous visit; whether any new words had emerged; whether the child had begun using old words in new ways; whether the child's social and communicative skills had developed in any way; finally, any other noteworthy developments the parents may have observed. To this end, the parents were asked to keep a diary of the various aspects of their child's development on a week- to-week basis. The contents of the diary formed the basis of much of the discussion in the interview session. The testing procedures were taken from the Uzgiris-Hunt Infant Assessment Scales (Uzgiris & Hunt, 1975). The rationale for these scales is based on Piaget's (1952) theory of the sensorimotor period. The object permanence and means-ends sub-scales were administered on each visit. The remaining sub-scales were administered less frequently. In the final free play session, parent and child were encouraged to engage in a variety of social situations. An attempt was made to establish some regularity in the kind of situations observed across visits (feeding time, solving a problem together, story-telling). However, importance was attached to collecting naturalistic data and so coercion was avoided. The entirety of each visit, which lasted approximately 1 1/2 hours, was recorded on video-tape. Transmitting microphones were used to collect the vocal data from child and parent.

After the visit, a transcription was made of the videotape. A standard orthographic transcription was made of all the verbal behavior during the session together with a transcription of any nonverbal activity that might aid in the interpretation of the verbal behavior. The speech of all participants was analyzed into utterances after Snow's (1972) guidelines. On this view, utterances are not defined in terms of adult grammatical structures like the sentence, but according to the pauses and intonational patterns in the dialogue. Utterances were then analyzed into morphemes. for children this can be a problematic process. For example, "What is that" may be uttered by the child as a single undifferentiated formula. In such cases, utterances are coded as containing only a single morpheme. The criteria used for deciding the morphemic breakdown of an utterance are based on articulatory and fluency criteria (Peters, 1983). A distinction between idiosyncratic expressions, lexicalized morphemes and formulaic expressions is made explicit in the coding of the transcription such that a variety of different analyses can be performed on the same database. For example, it is an easy matter using the CLAN programs to observe the effect of including or excluding a child's idiosyncratic expressions in an MLU count. .

File	Date	Age	File	Date	Age
anne01.cha	04-NOV-82	0;8.12	jens01.cha	29-OCT-82	0;11.15
anne02.cha	19-NOV-82	0;8.27	jens02.cha	12-NOV-82	0;11.28
anne03.cha	03-DEC-82	0;9.11	jens03.cha	25-NOV-82	1;0.11
anne04.cha	08-JAN-83	0;10.16	jens04.cha	10-DEC-82	1;0.26
anne05.cha	22-JAN-83	0;11.2	jens05.cha	07-JAN-83	1;1.23
anne06.cha	??-FEB-83	1;0	jens06.cha	20-JAN-83	1;2.6
anne07.cha	21-FEB-83	1;0.1	jens07.cha	04-FEB-83	1;2.20
anne08.cha	07-MAR-83	1;0.15	jens08.cha	04-MAR-83	1;3.20
anne09.cha	21-MAR-83	1;1.1	jens09.cha	25-MAR-83	1;4.11
anne10.cha	11-APR-83	1;1.19	jens10.cha	08-APR-83	1;4.24
anne11.cha	25-APR-83	1;2.5	jens11.cha	20-APR-83	1;5.6
anne12.cha	16-MAY-83	1;2.24	jens12.cha	06-MAY-83	1;5.22
anne13.cha	06-JUN-83	1;3.14	jens13.cha	27-MAY-83	1;6.13
anne14.cha	20;JUN-83	1;4-0	jens14.cha	10-JUN-83	1;6.26
anne15.cha	06-JUL-83	1;4.14	jens15.cha	28-JUN-83	1;7.14
anne16.cha	21;JUL-83	1;5.1	jens16.cha	15-JUL-83	1;8.1
anne17.cha	16-AUG-83	1;5.24	jens17.cha	02-AUG-83	1;8.18
anne18.cha	29-AUG-83	1;6.9	jens18.cha	18-AUG-83	1;9.4
anne19.cha	10-SEP-83	1;6.18	jens19.cha	30-AUG-83	1;9.16
anne20.cha	24-SEP-83	1;7.4	jens20.cha	16-SEP-83	1;10.2
anne21.cha	08-OCT-83	1;7.16	jens21.cha	28-SEP-83	1;10.14
anne22.cha	29-OCT-83	1;8.9	jens22.cha	12-OCT-83	1;10.28
anne23.cha	12-NOV-83	1;8.20	jens23.cha	29-OCT-83	1;11.15
anne24.cha	29-NOV-83	1;9.9	jens24.cha	16-NOV-83	2;0.2
anne25.cha	17-DEC-83	1;9.25	jens25.cha	07-DEC-83	2;0.23
anne26.cha	07-JAN-84	1;10.15	jens26.cha	20-DEC-83	2;1.6
anne27.cha	08-FEB-84	1;11.16	jens27.cha	05-JAN-84	2;1.21
anne28.cha	16-DEC-84	2;9.24	jens28.cha	25-JAN-84	2;2.11
anne29.cha	01-MAR-84	2;0.9	jens29.cha	09-FEB-84	2;2,25
anne30.cha	15-MAR-84	2;0.23	jens30.cha	28-FEB-84	2;3.14
anne31.cha	29-MAR-84	2;1.9	jens31.cha	13-MAR-84	2;3.29
anne32.cha	05-APR-84	2;1.13	jens32.cha	29-MAR-84	2;4.15
anne33.cha	26-APR-84	2;2.6	jens33.cha	05-APR-84	2;4.21
anne34.cha	10-MAY-84	2;2.20	jens34.cha	17-APR-84	2;5.3
anne35.cha	29-MAY-84	2;3.9	jens35.cha	26-APR-84	2;5.12

anne36.cha	missing		jens36.cha	10-MAY-84	2;5.26
anne37.cha	missing		jens37.cha	24-MAY-84	2;6.10
anne38.cha	05-JUL-84	2;4.13	jens38.cha	07-JUN-84	2;6.21
anne39.cha	07-AUG-84	2;5.15	jens39.cha	25-JUN-84	2;7.11
			jens40.cha	missing	
			jens41.cha	19-JUL-84	2;7.5
			jens42.cha	14-AUG-84	2;8.0

Publications that make use of this corpus should cite Plunkett (1986) or Plunkett (1985).

27.3. Dutch

27.3.1. Gillis

This directory contains a longitudinal corpus from a boy learning Dutch. The corpus was donated to the CHILDES by Steven Gillis, Department of Germanic Linguistics, University of Antwerp, Belgium. The data are in **CHAT** format without English glosses.

The child, Maarten, was a Flemish boy learning Dutch. Bi-weekly video-recordings were taken at the child's home between the ages of 0;11.15 and 1;11.28. Recordings began when the child's vocalizations exhibited what Dore, Franklin, Miller, and Ramer (Dore, Franklin, Miller & Ramer, 1976) called phonetically consistent forms. They lasted until the child's MLU exceeded 1.5 for three consecutive sessions. The entire corpus consists of 29,324 intelligible child utterances. The child was recorded for an average of 3 hours a week for a total of 104 hours of recording (average: 1:18 hours per recording, with a range of 0:15:18 hours to 3:44:52 hours). The sessions included interactions between the child and an adult (usually his mother) as well as solitary play. All recordings were made in an unstructured regular home setting.

The video recordings were transcribed according to the **CHAT** conventions and include the child's vocalizations in Dutch UNIBET transcription (see chapter 10) on the %pho tier. There are no adult glosses of the child's utterances. The transcripts also include the adults' utterances in normal graphemic transcription on the main tier and the child's and the adults' nonverbal behavior (gestures, gaze direction, object manipulation, etc.), notes on the synchronization of the verbal and the nonverbal behaviors, and description of the context. All this information can be found on the %sit tier, which is at the present written in Dutch .

In the %sit line, dashes separate actions. The match of actions to the phonology is sometimes indicated. Three-letter codes indicate the actor and the addressee. For example, MXA means that M did X to A. MXA &1 MYB means that M did X to A and while this is going on M does Y to B. In order to get these files to pass **CHECK**, these three symbols must be added to the %sit line in the depfile:
&*   to mark the cooccurrence of actions
-       to separate sequential actions
'*   for certain Dutch words
The '* symbol must also be added to the main line.

Overview of the Observational Sessions:

The first table gives the individual sessions. The second is grouped by months.

File	Date	Age	Length	# interpretable utterances

1	12-02-81	0;11.18	1:38:42	30
2	17-02-81	0;11.23	O:39:48	8
3	19-02-81	0;11.25	0:40:04	17
4	25-02-81	1;00.00	1:17:28	29
5	11-03-81	1;00.14	0:48:47	68
6	16-03-81	1;00.19	0:57:52	210
7	18-03-81	1;00.21	0:11:09	10
8	23-03-81	1;00.26	0:57:37	256
9	30-03-81	1;01.05	1:26:32	97
10	01-04-81	1;01.07	0:16:35	93
11	07-04-81	1;01.13	0:52:43	75
12	23-04-81	1;01.29	0:29:28	15
13	28-04-81	1;02.03	0:47:25	40
14	30-04-81	1;02.05	0:16:47	25
15	07-05-81	1;02.12	0:34:30	15
16	11-05-81	1;02.16	1:12:22	69
17	15-05-81	1;02.20	0:20:07	63
18	20-05-81	1;02.25	1:08:45	196
19	26-05-81	1;03.01	1:02:02	306
20	29-05-81	1;03.04	1:21:16	285
21	03-06-81	1;03.09	0:13:15	37
22	05-06-81	1;03.11	0:13:26	89
23	09-06-81	1;03.15	0:36:00	40
24	16-06-81	1;03.22	0:59:31	159
25	21-06-81	1;03.27	0:15:18	68
26	22-06-81	1;03.28	0:55:09	205
27	25-06-81	1;04.00	0:42:21	164
28	01-07-81	1;04.06	0:59:41	271
29	08-07-81	1;04.13	1:04:31	245
30	12-07-81	1;04.17	1:01:06	334
31	16-07-81	1;04.21	0:21:50	73
32	21-07-81	1;04.26	2:09:51	539
33	29-07-81	1;05.04	1:27:14	600
34	05-08-81	1;05.11	1:36:04	561
35	12-08-81	1;05.18	1:04:18	260
36	17-08-81	1;05.23	0:46:43	147
37	26-08-81	1;06.01	0:40:55	400
38	02-09-81	1;06.08	0:38:02	199
39	05-09-81	1;06.11	0:20:54	158
40	07-09-81	1;06.13	0:39:18	332
41	10-09-81	1;06.16	1:24:40	344
42	12-09-81	1;06.18	1:10:42	435
43	17-09-81	1;06.23	0:34:09	271
44	24-09-81	1;06.30	1:20:27	201
45	29-09-81	1;07.04	0:58:20	198
46	01-10-81	1;07.06	0:55:47	281
47	07-10-81	1;07.12	0:51:43	331
48	10-10-81	1;07.15	0:55:28	249
49	15-10-81	1;07.20	0:43:57	221
50	19-10-81	1;07.24	0:29:13	323
51	21-10-81	1;07.26	1:54:51	363
52	26-10-81	1;08.01	0:41:14	200
53	29-10-81	1;08.04	1:01:20	292

54	04-11-81	1;08.10	1:08:03	173
55	06-11-81	1;08.12	1:33:06	538
56	10-11-81	1;08.16	1:43:10	385
57	12-11-81	1;08.18	1:49:34	828
58	18-11-81	1;08.24	1:50:15	670
59	20-11-81	1;08.26	1:37:43	827
60	23-11-81	1;08.29	1:10:02	308
61	26-11-81	1;09.01	1:06:31	376
62	30-11-81	1;09.05	1:29:17	516
63	03-12-81	1;09.08	1:18:24	357
64	07-12-81	1;09.12	1:41:24	540
65	10-12-81	1;09.15	1:44:10	483
66	16-12-81	1;09.21	2:30:48	515
67	18-12-81	1;09.23	1:48:49	302
68	22-12-81	1;09.27	1:58:40	430
69	26-12-81	1;10.01	3:44:52	1061
70	28-12-81	1;10.03	1:52:12	803
71	04-01-82	1;10.10	2:29:46	624
72	08-01-82	1;10.14	3:29:51	1369
73	13-01-82	1;10.19	3:29:23	1377
74	19-01-82	1;10.25	2:53:33	982
75	26-01-82	1;11.01	2:57:02	1037
76	29-01-82	1;11.04	3:05:18	1085
77	02-02-82	1;11.08	3:05:18	1176
78	09-02-82	1;11.15	1:53:51	661
79	21-02-82	1;11.27	3:05:18	n.t.

Month	Sessions	Ages	Length	Length per session
1	1 - 5	0;11.18 to 1;00.17	5:04:49	1:00:58
2	6 - 11	1;00.18 to 1;01.17	4:42:28	0:47:04
3	12 - 16	1;01.18 to 1;02.17	3:20:32	0:40:06
4	17 - 23	1;02.18 to 1;03.17	4:54:51	0:42:07
5	24 - 30	1;03.18 to 1;04.17	5:57:37	0:51:05
6	31 - 34	1;04.18 to 1;05.17	5:34:59	1:23:44
7	35 - 41	1;05.18 to 1;06.17	5:34:50	0:47:50
8	42 - 48	1;06.18 to 1;07.17	6:46:36	0:58:05
9	49 - 56	1;07.18 to 1;08.17	9:14:54	1:09:21
10	57 - 65	1;08.18 to 1;09.17	13:47:20	1:31:55
11	66 - 72	1;09.18 to 1;10.17	17:54:58	2:33:34
12	73 - 78	1;10.18 to 1;11.17	17:24:25	2:54:04
13	79	1;11.18 to 1;11.17	3:05:18	

The first 65 files are not yet in the CHILDES database. Publications that make use of the Antwerp corpus should cite Schaerlaekens and Gillis (1987).

27.3.2.   Schaerlaekens

These data were originally collected by A.M. Schaerlaekens in 1969 and 1970. The data were collected by recording the spontaneous dialogues of two triplets. For this purpose, the children were wearing small wireless transmitters which were sewn into their aprons. Further details of the procedure can be found in Schaerlaekens (1973).

Subjects. The original database consists of the spontaneous language of two triplets between the ages of 1;10.18 and 3;1.7 for the first triplet and 1;6.17 and 2;10.23 for the second triplet. Gijs, Joost en Katelijne are non-identical triplets, two boys and one girl. They were born in the following order: Joost, Katelijne, Gijs. At the age of eighteen months, they were administered the Gesell developmental scales, showing no perceptible differences as to psychomotor development. At the age of four years and two months they participated in a non-verbal intelligence test (Snijders-Oomen), which yielded an above average IQ.

The children were recorded at monthly intervals. Due to problems with the equipment, however, there are no data available for particular months. An overview of the observations is given in Table 1. Arnold, Diederik and Maria are also non-identical triplets, two boys and a girl. They were born in the following order: Diederik, Arnold, Maria. When they were eighteen months, the Gesell developmental scales were administered, showing no perceptible differences as to psychomotor development. At the age of four years and two months they participated in a non-verbal intelligence test (Snijders-Oomen), which yielded an above average IQ. The data for Arnold, Diederik and Maria are summarized in table 2.

Table 1: Data For Gijs (GIJS), Joost (JOOST) and Katelijne (KAT)

Session	Date	Age
1	1-3-1969	1;8.29
2	29-4-1969	1;9.24
3	29-5-1969	1;10.24
4	10-6-1969	1;11.5
5	2-7-1969	1;11.27
6	17-7-1969	2;0.12
7	23-9-1969	2;2.18
8	29-12-1969	2;5.24
9	28-1-1970	2;6.23
10	24-2-1970	2;7.19
11	24-3-1970	2;8.19
12	28-5-1970	2;10.23

Table 2: Data For Arnold (ARNOLD), Diederik (DIEDE) and Maria (MAR)

Session	Date	Age
1	11-7-1969	1;10.18
2	11-9-1969	2;0.19
3	25-9-1969	2;1.2
4	16-10-1969	2;1.23
5	25-11-1969	2;3.2
6	6-1-1970	2;4.14
7	10-2-1970	2;5.18
8	17-3-1970	2;6.22
9	23-4-1970	2;8.1
10	21-5-1970	2;8.28
11	11-6-1970	2;9.19
12	21-7-1970	2;10.28
13	30-9-1970	3;1.7

Transcription and coding. The speech of the children was graphemically transcribed. The original transcription can be found on the %tra tier in the files. The main tiers contain a conventionalized transcription. Unfortunately the language of the children's parents was not transcribed and the audiotapes could not be used anymore for transcription in 1992.

The data were reformatted into **CHAT** in 1993. On the %mor-tier, words are coded for their part-of-speech and for their morphosyntactic properties. The coding was done with a Dutch version of the **MOR** program. A preliminary syntactic coding was performed using the following categories and abbreviations:

S	Subject
D	Direct Object
I	Indirect Object
P	Prepositional Phrase
C	Complement
B	Adverbial Complement
Neg	Negation
X	Other

Verbs were further coded as:

V	Main (lexical) verb
Aux	Auxiliary
Cop	Copula

For each of these categories the markers "f" for "finite verbform" and "nf" for "non-finite verbform" were added. Agreement was coded on the %agr tier. The following categories (and numeric codes) were used:

1	correct agreement
2	incorrect agreement
3	no agreement: subjectless sentence
4	other (a.o. verbless sentences)

Publications that make use of these data can cite Gillis and Verhoeven (1992), Schaerlaekens (1972), Schaerlaekens (1973) or Schaerlaekens and Gillis (1987).

27.3.3.   Utrecht

The Utrecht corpus is based on weekly home tapings of two Dutch boys, named Thomas and Hein, between the ages of roughly 2;3 and 3;1. The corpus was compiled by Loekie Elbers and Frank Wijnen (University of Utrecht), with assistance from Joke van Marle, Trudy van der Horst, Herma Veenhof-Haan and Inge Boers. The recordings were made by the children's mothers. The data were used in two projects focusing on the relation between language acquisition and developmental disfluency. Both Hein and Thomas show an increase of disfluency around age 2;7-2;8. In Thomas, the disfluency is mild, in Hein it is severe. In both children, the frequency of disfluencies drops subsequently, until it reaches a level comparable to that in the initial samples.

The recordings were generally made in unstructured settings. Usually, the target child and an adult interlocutor (mostly the mother) were engaged in some everyday routine, such as having breakfast, playing, getting dressed, or looking through picture books. Both children are regularly presented with a particular picture book, entitled "The little giantess", in order to attain some standardization of the recording conditions in some sessions. The use of this book is indicated in the @Situation or @Activities header. A description of the pictures in the book as well as the complete text (and its translation in English) can be found in the file "0pict.doc". In most instances where the book is used, the transcriptions contain explicit references to the picture book pictures by means of

@Stim headers. In some of the recordings of Thomas, his mother uses a puppet (Kermit the Frog) to stimulate (or motivate) the conversation.

An overview of the available material and some indications of progress in processing the data is given below. Some 71 hours of recordings were collected. All usable samples of Thomas and Hein are transcribed. Generally, samples involving other children in addition to the target child were not transcribed.

The number and character of reliability checks on the transcriptions are indicated by the number after "lit" [= "literal transcription"] in the "Progress" column. A zero (0) indicates that the file contains an initial transcription that has not been checked. One (1) means that the initial transcription is checked, either by the person who made the initial transcription, or by somebody else. A two (2) indicates that the session was transcribed by two independent coders, and that the final version was constructed by means of a consensus procedure. In the "lit2" files, data on which the first and second transcriber could not reach an agreement are represented with "xxx". The presence of "hes" or "mor" in the "Progress" column indicates that a full %hes line was coded for hesitations or that a %mor line was coded for morphology.

The presence of other participants, as well as other salient or exceptional characteristics of the tapings are mentioned in the "Remarks" column.

Table of Contents -- Thomas

Tape	Dur	Date	Age	Progress	Remarks
T01	60	800716	2;3.22	lit2 mor hes	
		800717	2;3.23	lit2 mor hes	
		800719	2;3.25	lit2 mor hes	
T02	90	800722	2;3.28	lit2 mor hes	
		800724	2;4.0	lit2 mor hes	
		800727	2;4.3	lit2 mor hes	
T03	60	800730	2;4.6	lit2 mor hes	
		800801	2;4.8	lit2 mor hes	
T04	90	800801	contin	lit2 mor hes	
		800803	2;4.10	lit2 mor hes	
		800804	2;4.11	lit2 mor hes	
		800807	2;4.14	lit2 mor hes	
		800809	2;4.16	lit2 mor hes	
T05	60	800819	2;4.26	lit0	+Doortje
		800820	2;4.27	lit0	
		800823	2;4.30	lit0	
T06	60	800827	2;5.3	lit2 mor hes	
		800828	2;5.4	lit2 mor hes	
		800830	2;5.6	lit2 mor hes	
T07	60	800903	2;5.10	lit0	
		800904	2;5.11	lit0	
		800907	2;5.14	lit0	
		800908	2;5.15	lit0	
T08a	45	800909	2;5.16	not transcribed	+Hella
T09	60	800910	2;5.17	lit2 mor hes	
		800912	2;5.19	lit2 mor hes	
		800914	2;5.21	lit2 mor hes	

T10	60	800918	2;5.25	lit2 mor hes	
		800920	2;5.27	lit2 mor hes	
T08b	45	801019	2;6.25	lit0	
		801022	2;6.28	lit0	
T11	60	801025	2;7.1	lit2 mor hes	
		801026	2;7.2	lit2 mor hes	
T12	60	801101	2;7.7	lit2 mor hes	
		801102	2;7.8	lit2 mor hes	
T13	60	801102	contin	lit1 mor hes	
		801106	2;7.12	lit1 mor hes	
		801108	2;7.14	lit1 mor hes	
T14	60	801114	2;7.20	lit1 mor hes	
		801116	2;7.22	lit1 mor hes	
T15	60	801121	2;7.27	lit1 mor hes	
		801122	2;7.28	lit1 mor hes	
T16	60	801126	2;8.2	lit2 mor hes	
		801129	2;8.5	lit2 mor hes	
T17	60	801130	2;8.6	lit2 mor hes	
		801202	2;8.8	lit2 mor hes	+Doortje
		801204	2;8.10	lit2 mor hes	
		801205	2;8.11	not transcribed	+visitors
		801209	2;8.15	lit2 mor hes	
T18	60	801210	2;8.16	lit2 mor hes	
		801211	2;8.17	lit2 mor hes	
		801213	2;8.19	lit2 mor hes	
		801214	2;8.20	lit2 mor hes	
		801217	2;8.22	lit2 mor hes	
T19	30	801218	2;8.24	lit2 mor hes	
		801220	2;8.26	lit2 mor hes	
T20	60	801226	2;9.2	lit2 mor hes	
		801228	2;9.4	lit2 mor hes	
		801229	2;9.5	lit2 mor hes	
T21	60	810101	2;9.8	lit1 mor hes	
		810103	2;9.10	lit1 mor hes	
		810105	2;9.12	lit0	
		810108	2;9.15	lit0	
T21A	60	810117	2;9.24	not transcribed	+Kim
		810119	2;9.26	lit0	T-O-T
T22	60	810126	2;10.2	lit1 mor hes	
		810128	2;10.4	lit1 mor hes	
		810130	2;10.6	lit0	
		810201	2;10.8	lit0	
T23	60	810207	2;10.14	lit0	
		810208	2;10.15	lit0	
		810212	2;10.19	lit0	
T24	60	810216	2;10.23	lit2 mor hes	
		810219	2;10.26	lit2 mor hes	+Opa
T25	60	810222	2;10.29	lit2 mor hes	
		810223	2;10.30	lit2 mor hes	
		810225	2;11.1	lit2 mor hes	
		810226	2;11.2	lit2 mor hes	
		810304	2;11.8	lit2 mor hes	
T26	60	810314	2;11.18	lit2 mor hes	
		810315	2;11.19	lit2 mor hes	

Table of Contents -- Hein

Tape	Dur	Date	Age	Progress
H01	60	800725	2;4.11	lit1 mor hes
		800728	2;4.14	lit1 mor hes
		800730	2;4.16	lit1 mor hes
		800801	2;4.18	lit1 mor hes
		800804	2;4.21	lit1 mor hes
H02	60	800804	contin	lit1 mor hes
		800806	2;4.23	lit1 mor hes
		800808	2;4.25	lit1 mor hes
H03	60	800825	2;5.11	lit1
		800828	2;5.14	lit1 mor hes
		800831	2;5.17	lit1
H04	60	800902	2;5.19	lit1 mor hes
		800904	2;5.21	lit1
		800907	2;5.24	lit0
H05	60	800916	2;6.2	lit1 mor hes
		800919	2;6.5	lit0
		800921	2;6.7	lit0
H06	60	800922	2;6.8	lit1 mor hes
		800924	2;6.10	lit0
		800928	2;6.14	lit0
H07	60	800930	2;6.16	lit1 mor hes
		801003	2;6.19	lit0
		801007	2;6.23	lit0
H08	60	801011	2;6.27	lit1 mor hes
		801012	2;6.28	lit0
		801015	2;7.1	lit1 mor hes
H09	60	801019	2;7.5	lit1 mor hes
		801021	2;7.7	lit1 mor hes
		801026	2;7.12	not transcribed +Susan
H10	60	801028	2;7.14	lit1 mor hes
		801031	2;7.17	lit1 mor hes
		801103	2;7.20	lit1 mor hes
		801105	2;7.22	lit1 mor hes
H11	60	801110	2;7.27	lit1 mor hes
		801113	2;7.30	lit1 mor hes
		801116	2;8.2	lit1 mor hes
H12	60	801118	2;8.4	lit1 mor hes
		801121	2;8.7	lit0
		801124	2;8.10	lit0
H13	60	801128?	2;8.14	lit1 mor hes
		801130	2;8.16	lit1 mor hes
		801202	2;8.18	lit0
H14	60	801204	2;8.20	lit1 mor hes
		801207	2;8.23	lit0
		801209	2;8.25	lit0
		801212	2;8.28	lit0
H15	60	801215	2;9.1	lit1 mor hes
		801221	2;9.7	lit0

		801225	2;9.11	lit0
H16	60	801228	2;9.14	lit1 mor hes
		801230	2;9.16	lit0
		810108	2;9.25	lit0
H17	60	810111	2;9.28	lit1 mor hes
		810114	2;10.0	lit0
		810119	2;10.5	lit0
H18	60	810121?	2;10.7	lit1 mor hes
		810124?	2;10.10	lit0
		810126	2;10.12	lit0
H19	60	810202	2;10.19	lit1 mor hes
		810207	2;10.24	lit1 mor hes
		810209	2;10.26	lit1 mor hes
		810213	2;10.30	lit0
H20	60	810215	2;11.1	lit1 mor hes
		810216	2;11.2	lit0
		810217	2;11.3	lit0
		810221	2;11.7	lit0
		810222	2;11.8	lit0
H21	60	810226	2;11.12	lit1 mor hes
		810302	2;11.16	lit0
		810304	2;11.18	lit0
H22	60	810312	2;11.26	lit1 mor hes
H23	60	810321	3;0.7	lit1 mor hes
		810325	3;0.11	lit1 mor hes
		810403	3;0.20	lit1 mor hes
H24	60	810409	3;0.26	lit1 mor hes
		810413	3;0.30	lit1 mor hes
		810417	3;1.3	lit1 mor hes
		810423	3;1.9	lit1 mor hes
H25	60	810423	contin	lit1 mor hes
		810430	3;1.16	lit1 mor hes
		810508	3;1.24	lit1 mor hes

The files are labelled in accordance with the date of recording. For instance, t800716.cha represents the recording of Thomas made on July 16, 1980.

The main lines of both the children and adult speakers contain various codes for non-fluencies and hesitations. Usually, the standard CHAT diacritica are used. You may however also find some non-standard codes, e.g. [$I] (interrupted word) or [$B] (block). Additionally, these square-bracketed entries indicating aspects of prosody are provided:

[=! rising]   rising contour
[=! falling]   falling contour
[=! contin]   continuation contour

[=! f]   loud
[=! ff]   very loud
[=! p]   soft
[=! pp]   very soft (whispered)

The codes included on the %hes line and their meanings are as follows:

$REP: repetitions

$rep|wrd:	word repetition
$rep|wst:	word string repetition
$rep|isg:	initial segment(s) repetition
$rep|isy:	initial syllable repetition
$rep|cpx:	a composite of several of the above

$COR: self-corrections

$cor|dx_ry:	a self-correction involving a delay of x words and a retracing span of y words.

$WBR: word break
$BLK: block
$UPS: unfilled (silent) pause
$FPS: filled pause (uh)
$SSI: senseless sound insertion

For $UPS, $FPS, and $SSI, scoping numbers indicate the position of the word following the disfluency. For $WBR and $BLK, the scoping number indicates the position of the affected word. For $COR and $REP, the scoping number indicates the beginning of the repetition or retracing.

If needed for the disambiguation and interpretation of the text or the non-fluencies and errors, phonetic UNIBET-transcriptions are supplied on %pho tier. The UNIBET used in this corpus conforms by and large to the table for Dutch in the manual. A complete overview of the IPA-ASCII conversion table is provided in the file "0phon.doc". Please note that not all speech errors have yet been explicitly coded on %err tiers, particularly in the corpus of Thomas.

In the corrected transcriptions (lit1 and lit2), word classes of the words produced by the children are coded on %mor tiers in a one-to-one fashion. This is indicated by the entry "mor" in the "Progress" column. The morphological codes have the general format:

        <i>$AAA=BBB|CCC_DDD_etc

<i> : scoping
AAA   syntactic class, such as DET.
      Also "zero derivations" may be marked by this part of the code,
          e.g. "N=V" = nominalized verb.
BBB   lexical class, such as N, V or PREP.
CCC   subclassifications for tense, person, etc.

The code COMM stands for Dutch "common" gender. The article "een" (a) is usually transcribed as "'n", in order to distinguish it from "een" (one). The transcription of "het" may be "'t", depending on the pronunciation.

Publications that make use of these data can cite (Elbers, 1985; Elbers & Wijnen, 1992; Wijnen, 1988; Wijnen, 1990a; Wijnen, 1992). The compilers would very much appreciate getting copies/offprints of research reports that make use of these data.

27.3.4.   Van Kampen

The Van Kampen corpus is based on tapings of two Dutch girls. Laura was studied from the age of 1;9.18 to 5;10.9 and Sarah from 1;6.16 to 6;0. The recordings were made roughly once or twice every month by the mother of the children (Jacqueline van Kampen). The Laura corpus exists of 80 45-minutes recordings. The corpus will be completely transcribed and checked by 1996. The collection of the data is funded by the Netherlands Organization of Scientific Research (NWO), project 300-171-027 "The acquisition of WH-questions". Assistance was provided by Christel de Heus, Evelien Krikhaar, Jacky Vernimmen and Simone Boezewinkel.

The recordings were made using a Prefer OCC/1121 microphone and a Nakamichi 350 recorder. The transcribers used a Sanyo TRC 9010 with foot pedal. The recordings were made in unstructured, regular home settings between the target child and the mother. There has been no explicit use of %mor or %syn tiers. Only in the cases that the child used non-adult words or incomprehensible utterances, the %pho tier was used. Utterances containing the tag-question marker "he" at the end have not been given a question mark. This is done to distinguish them from real questions with inversion.

An overview of the available data is given below. The initial transcription is done by one of the assistants. The final version is always checked by Van Kampen.

Tape	Date	Age
L01	100288	1;9.4
L02	240288	1;9.18
L03	090388	1;10.3
L04	160388	1;10.10
L05	010488	1;10.25
L06	140488	1;11.8
L07	270488	1;11.21
L08	110588	2;0.5
L09	250588	2;0.19
L10	080688	2;1.2
L11	160688	2;1.10
L12	030788	2;1.27

Publications based on the use of these data can cite (Van Kampen, 1994).

27.3.5.   Wijnen

The Wijnen Corpus was compiled by Frank Wijnen and Herma Veenhof-Haan. The corpus is based on home tapings of one Dutch boy, Niek, between the ages of 2;7 and 3;10. The recordings were made by Niek's father (Frank Wijnen). The data were mainly used in a project focusing on the relation between language acquisition and developmental disfluency.

Niek was a slow starter in language, both with respect to grammar and to phonology. The first sample in the corpus, at age 2;7, yields an MLU (in words) of 1.72. Some details of Niek's grammatical development are given in Wijnen (1993). Further information is available on request. Niek's phonological development was also slow. Particularly, he persisted in various substitution processes, most notably "fronting", i.e., the substitution of alveolar consonants for back obstruents and clusters. This behavior gradually disappeared during the period of observation. At approximately age 4;6, he had developed into a fluent and competent speaker, intelligible for adults other than his parents.

The recordings were generally made in unstructured settings. Usually, the target child and an adult interlocutor (mostly the father) were engaged in some normal everyday routine: playing (often with Lego), looking through picture books, etc.

An overview of the available material and some indications of progress in processing the data is given below. Some 31 hours of recordings were collected. A subset of these, amounting to 23 hours, were transcribed. The presence of participants other than one of the parents, as well as other salient or exceptional characteristics of the tapings are mentioned in the "Remarks" column. Additional aspects of the coding and transcription techniques can be found in the description of the "Utrecht" corpora.

Tape	Date	Age
N01	840213	3;0.21
	840219	3;0.27
	840220	3;0.28
	840225	3;1.2
	840227	3;1.4
N02	840228	3;1.5
	840306	3;1.12
	840310	3;1.16
N03	840312	3;1.18
	840319	3;1.25
	840405	3;2.13
N07	840524	3;4.1
	840601	3;4.9
N08	840604	3;4.12
	840610	3;4.18
N09	840616	3;4.24
	840618	3;4.26
N10	840619	3;4.27
	840623	3;5.0
N15	840723	3;6.0
	840725	3;6.2
	840727	3;6.4
	840730	3;6.7
N16	840731	3;6.8
N17	840812	3;6.20
	840813	3;6.21
N18	840820	3;6.28
	840826	3;7.3
N21	840924	3;8.1
	840925	3;8.2
	841001	3;8.8
N22	841022	3;8.30
	841029	3;9.6
N23	841105	3;9.6
	841112	3;9.13
	841117	3;9.25
N24	841119	3;9.27
	841126	3;10.3
N25	841210	3;10.17

The data files are labeled in accordance with the subject's age at the date of recording. For instance, "nie31017.cha" represents the recording made at age 3;10.17.

Publications based on the use of these data can cite (Wijnen, 1988; Wijnen, 1990b; Wijnen, 1992).

27.4.   French

27.4.1.   Champaud

This subdirectory contains data that were videotaped, transcribed, and coded in **CHAT** by Christian Champaud, Chargé de Recherches at the C.N.R.S. (UA 316). The subject of the study is Grégoire. The work was done in collaboration with Grégoire's family with particular assistance from his mother Dominique. Thanks are due to Catherine Marlot, Danièle Boussin and Françoise Roland for transcription, rechecking, and typing. This work is still in progress and new data are still being added to the corpus.

Grégoire is the third child of Dominique (mother, born on 3-AUG-46) and Michel (father, born on 5-APR-48, whose usual name is Kôfy). Grégoire was born on 28-APR-86. His elder brother, Adrien, was born on 21-APR-80. The other brother, Victor, was born on 16-JUN-83. Grégoire's parents live in Paris, France, and the only spoken language in the family is French. Both parents have college degrees. Dominique was a professor of French, who left her job in order to take care of her family. She has experience in developmental psycholinguistics (investigations conducted with Laurence Lentin) and in linguistics. Michel is a professor of German at the University of Paris III. The socioeconomic status of Grégoire's family can be characterized as upper-middle.

Space insertion. In French, when a word begins with a vowel, this leads in some cases to the disappearance of the final vowel of the preceding word: l'ami and not le ami. The vowel -e is elided, and in the spelling, the two words are linked together by an apostrophe. This is the case for a determiner preceding a noun, or for a clitic pronoun preceding a verb, etc. It is important to add a space after the apostrophe in these cases. It allows to make searches for some determiners or articles, for pronouns, and for the words that follow, as whole words. It allows also to include them in frequency counts, or to take them into account for computing the MLU in words. This decision implies that, in French **CHAT** transcriptions, the following strings must be obligatorily followed by a space: c' , d' , j' , l' , m' , n' , qu' , s' , t' , and y' . Presently, this has only been done with some transcriptions.

In hyphenated words like abat-jour, the hyphen (-) must be replaced by a plus (+): abat+jour, in order to avoid confusions with suffixes. In French, the hyphen symbol is sometimes used between words, like in est-ce que; in these cases, the hyphen symbol must be omitted and replaced by a space: est ce que, for similar reasons, and also to insure that all words are included in frequency counts.

Phonology. In order not to create an unreadable transcript and in order to avoid overinterpretation often inherent in error analysis, a decision was made to rely on the %pho tier for the definitive form of words. It is then possible to revise interpretations on the main line without returning to the videotape.

There are plans to add an %eng tier, but this goal is only partially fulfilled for the first files. A native speaker of English with good knowledge of French and of the domain will be needed to do this correctly. In order to allow for convenient computer searches, certain diacritical signs are preceded and followed by a space; / ^ ! [_] # ## . | are examples of such signs; ":" (sign of lengthening or geminate), contrary to the preceding signs, must immediately follow the phoneme to which it applies. Also, whenever possible, strings on the %pho tier must be segmented in sequences corresponding to meaningful productions of the child, particularly to "words" or word-like utterances (child's words, not adult ones that appear on the main line); so, /papwOp/ will be considered as a single word for the child, even if it is written in the adult form "pas propre" on the main line. For the moment, searches on the %pho tier are just considered as controls in order to improve our coding. Persons interested in the actual form of the word must search it in the *%pho* tier. For instance, the word "plus" is indeed pronounced /pY/ by Grégoire, as by all young French children, but appears on the form "plus" on the main line.

The coding of the %pho tier is not intended to appropriately document the phonological development of Grégoire. In any case, any serious research of this kind may be considered only on double-checked data. It is necessary because, as a native Occitan speaker (and hence a Southerner), the researcher does not hear certain distinctions made in speech, particularly for vowels, even though he was once trained in phonetics. For instance, he does not segment the continuum between /e/ and /E/, or /o/ and /O/, in the same manner a Northerner does. The problem is less acute or less bothersome for consonants. At the moment only some files have been double-checked by a Northerner. So, even though these questions of phonemics are not central in our study, some general remarks on the realizations of French consonants, such as gliding and deletion of /l/ and /r/ whether they are initial, intervocalic, final, simple or clustered, are available only on draft notes.

file name	date	age
Available:		
greg01.cha	16-FEB-1988	1;9.18
greg02.cha	1-MAR-1988	1;10.3
greg03.cha	22-MAR-1988	1;10.24
greg04.cha	19-APR-1988	1;11.21
greg05.cha	3-MAY-1988	2;0.5
greg06.cha	22-JUN-1988	2;1.24
greg07.cha	28-JUL-1988	2;3.0
greg08.cha	29-SEP-1988	2;5.1
greg09.cha	11-OCT-1988	2;5.13
greg10.cha	25-OCT-1988	2;5.27

An additional directory called GREGX contains observations and notes of the parents or investigator for which no audio recording is available and no double-checking can be done. These files begin when Gregoire is 1;9 and run for about 28 months.

27.4.2.   Leveillé

This directory contains files from a longitudinal study of a single French child. The study was conducted by Madeleine Leveillé of the CNRS in Paris and Patrick Suppes of Stanford University. The data was donated to CHILDES by Patrick Suppes in 1985. The data are in **CHAT** format without English glosses. The subject of the study – Phillipe – was the only child of academic parents in their thirties. He was in close association only with native French speakers. His parents were willing to submit to the rather demanding rule that all they said, as well as what their child said, would be recorded for one hour a week over an indefinite period of time.

Philippe was born on March 3, 1969. In the first visit, Philippe was 25 months and 19 days old. He was a sociable little boy who was not shy, even with strangers. During the period of data collection, he often went to the Faculty of Sciences with this father who taught there. He also visited his mother in a laboratory of psychology where she worked, and he occasionally participated in experiments in the laboratory. Usually he attended nursery school; when he did not stay there the whole day, a lady in her forties stayed with him at his house. Both his mother and father talked a lot with him and provided him with a verbally and intellectually stimulating environment.

During the first period, April 22 through June 24, 1971, the observer (M. Leveillé) visited Philippe in his house one hour a week. A group of 10 sessions was completed by June 24, 1971, before summer vacation began. After an interruption of nearly three months (83 days) when Philippe went to the country, the sessions continued at the same frequency through December 18, 1971. There was a lapse of 14 days between September 30, 1971 and October 14, 1971 due to a strike on the Metro, which paralyzed Paris. At that time 21 hours had been recorded. Then the visits became less frequent – one every fortnight. Between December 18 and January 6, 1972, and between March 23 and May 6 a total of 63 days elapsed because Philippe was on vacation. Session 33 was the last one, because Philippe was leaving Paris for his summer vacation. The complete schedule of recording sessions is as follows.

File	Date	Age	File	Date	Age
phil01	4-22-71	2;1.19	phil17	11-4-71	2;8.1
phil02	4-29-71	2;1.26	phil18	11-11-71	2;8.8
phil03	5-6-71	2;2.3	phil19	11-18-71	2;8.15
phil04	5-13-71	2;2.10	phil20	11-25-71	2;8.22
phil05	5-20-71	2;2.17	phil21	12-2-71	2;8.29
phil06	5-29-71	2;2.26	phil22	12-18-71	2;9.15
phil07	6-3-71	2;3.0	phil23	1-6-72	2;10.3
phil08	6-10-71	2;3.7	phil24	1-20-72	2;10.17
phil09	6-17-71	2;3.14	phil25	2-3-72	2;11.0
phil10	6-24-71	2;3.21	phil26	2-10-72	2;11.7
phil11	9-16-71	2;6.13	phil27	2-24-72	2;11.21
phil12	9-23-71	2;6.20	phil28	3-9-72	3;0.6
phil13	9-30-71	2;6.27	phil29	3-23-72	3;0.20
phil14	10-14-71	2;7.11	phil30	5-6-72	3;2.3
phil15	10-21-71	2;7.18	phil31	5-18-72	3;2.15
phil16	10-28-71	2;7.25	phil32	6-1-72	3;2.29
			phil33	6-15-72	3;3.12

For practical reasons, recording sessions always took place in the morning, generally not long after Philippe had awakened. Each session, with a few exceptions, lasted one hour. Although the recording periods were relaxed and informal, Philippe was asked not to leave the room in which the tape recorder was installed for any significant time. Usually the tape recorder was set up in the living room, which was at the center of the apartment. Only the microphone was moved to the kitchen during breakfast. If Philippe wanted to play in his bedroom, the tape recorder was taken there and Philippe was asked not to go into the other rooms too often or too long.

Publications that make use of this corpus should cite Suppes, Smith, and Leveillé (1973).

27.4.3. Rondal

A third French corpus was contributed by Jean Rondal of the University of Liège. This directory contains a set of 120 files of interactions between Jean Rondal's son Stephane and his Mother René Rondal. Stephane was 2;3 at the time of the recording session in 01a.cha and 4;9 at the time of the last recording session found in 48.cha. Stephane was born on 28-JUN-1972 and was the only child during the time of these recordings. Stephane has agreed to the use of his name in the files. Between the ages of 1;2 and 4;3, the child was living in the United States in St. Paul, Minnesota with his parents. The language spoken in the family was French with only a few sentences from English from time to time. Between 4;4 and 4;9, the child was back in French-speaking Belgium with his family. From approximately 3;2 to 4;3, Stephane attended nursery school in St. Paul. His French MLU dropped in the first half of this period of time from 4.50 to 3.25, as he was struggling to learn to speak more English. Non uninterestingly, the Mother's MLU stagnated and even dropped about .50 MLU during the same period of time.

The transcription and segmentation of utterances was done in accord with the principles discussed in Rondal, Bachelet, and Peree (1985). The files were converted into **CHAT** in 1992. The bulk of the sentences are produced either by the child (CHI) or the mother (MOT). Occasional sentences from the father or other adults are marked as Other (OTH). The mother's sentences are transcribed in standard French orthography. The child's sentences are transcribed in a non-standard form in order to capture more closely the actual phonetics of the child's productions. The departures from standard French orthography are as follows:
1. A colon (:) following a vowel indicates lengthening.
2. The tilde (~) following the vowel "e" indicates an oral unrounded vowel with relatively high tongue position, as in the French word for "tea."
3. e= is a lowered front oral unrounded vowel as in "paix."
4. i= is a lowered front nasal unrounded vowel as in "pain."
5. u= is a lowered front nasal rounded vowel as in brun."
6. o= is a lowered back nasal rounded vowel as in "bon."
7. a= is a low back nasal rounded vowel as in "blanc."
8. oe is a lowered front rounded oral vowel as in "peur."
9. eu is an high front oral rounded vowel as in "peu."
10. o" is a lowered back oral rounded vowel as in "peau."
11. o is a lowered back oral rounded vowel as in "part."
12. w indicates a rounded voiced velar semi-vowel or glide, as in "Wallon."

No attempt has been made or will be made to convert this system to UNIBET. Elisions are indicated by the apostrophe. Word stressing and pauses are marked. There are no comments or situational notes. Articles that make use of this corpus should cite Rondal (1985).

27.5. German

27.5.1. Clahsen

This corpus was contributed by Harald Clahsen. Please inform Dr. Clahsen when using these data. Details about data collection techniques and sociobiographical status of the informants are given in the attached excerpt from Clahsen (1982). The data were transferred to **CHAT** by Helmut Feldweg at the Max-Planck-Institute in 1990.

Please note that the data in this subdirectory is only a subset of the total amount of data collected for the three informants. The remaining data have not yet been entered into the computer.

Filenames and corresponding ages of informants:

Daniel:
>   dan17.cha: 2-9-28
>   dan18.cha: 2-10-14
>   dan19.cha: 2-11-14
>   dan21.cha: 3-0-21
>   dan22.cha: 3-1-21
>   dan23.cha: 3-2-14
>   dan24.cha: 3-3-21
>   dan25.cha: 3-4-21
>   dan26.cha: 3-5-21
>   dan27.cha: 3-6-28

Julia:
>   jul21.cha: 1-11-21
>   jul22.cha: 2-0-21
>   jul23.cha: 2-1-14
>   jul24.cha: 2-2-21
>   jul25.cha: 2-3-21
>   jul26.cha: 2-4-21
>   jul27.cha: 2-5-28

Mathias:
>   mat17.cha: 2-9-7
>   mat18.cha: 2-10-14
>   mat19.cha: 2-11-14
>   mat21.cha: 3-0-21
>   mat22.cha: 3-1-21
>   mat23.cha: 3-2-14
>   mat24.cha: 3-3-21
>   mat25.cha: 3-4-21
>   mat26.cha: 3-5-21
>   mat27.cha: 3-6-28

The three children in this study came from a family that lived in the neighborhood of the investigator. Daniel and Mathias were twins and Julia was their younger sister. The family was upper middle-class. The father was born in 1942. The mother was born in 1944. He was a well-paid lawyer and she was a doctor.

The twins had perinatal anoxia that led to a mild paresis that was successfully treated with gymnastics exercises. In their second year, the twins also had diarrhea for several weeks. Julia was always healthy. A Kramer IQ test yielded scores of 128 for Matthias, 123 for Daniel, and 121 for Julia. Matthias was demanding and sometimes aggressive. Daniel was more introverted. Julia was more normal in her temperament.

Following Brown (1973), video recordings of 45 to 60 minutes length were made at regular intervals of two or three week periods. Recordings were made in the home with the mother present. A small portable video camera with an attached microphone was used to minimize interference with the natural situation. Recordings were transcribed and double-checked within a week.

27.5.2.   Wagner

This directory contains a set of thirteen mini-corpora collected by Klaus R. Wagner of the University of Dortmund and his students and coworkers.   As indicated in the following table, the ages of the subjects ranged from 1;5 to 14;10.

No.	Subject	Age	Researcher	Length of Sequence in Minutes
1	Katrin	1;5	Schwarze	202
2	Nicole	1;8	Kadatz	241
3	Andreas	2;1	Wahner	213
4	Carsten	3;6	Hoffmann-Kirsch	189
5	Gabi	5;4	Brinkmann	152
6	Frederick	8;7	Häussermann	193
7	Roman	9;2	Otto	311
8	Kai	9;6	Corzillius/Landskröner/Koort	869 (one day)
9	Teresa	9;7	Wagner	804 (one day)
10	Regina	10;7	Giljohann	1430 (6 mornings at school)
11	Markus	11;4	Brünner	188
12	Christiane	12;2	Pagels/Gasse	430
13	Axel	14;10	Vette	254

The subjects wore a transmitting microphone and were therefore free to move about as they wished. This is of immense importance for studies aiming at eliciting and describing the spontaneous speech of children. Within a radius of 300 meter around the recording apparatus, the child can move freely, play, skip, climb trees, drive a go-cart, and so forth. The transcription system is that used in the pilot study (Wagner, 1974, pp. 147-179) with certain improvements after Ehlich & Rehbein (1976). The transcripts include all the subjects' utterances verbatim, including paralanguage; all interlocutor utterances in full as far as they concern the subject, otherwise abbreviated; and detailed information on the communicative setting (place, action, particular circumstances).

The following list gives two further types of information about the corpora: the communication situations in which subjects found themselves during recording and parental social status.

(1) *Schwarze corpus: Katrin   (1;5)*. The situations include: breakfast, playing (tap, milk lorry, dolls), helping to sort crockery, playing with bricks and dolls, nappy change, looking at guinea pigs, lunch, and monologues in bed. Social status: mother (researcher) is qualified in child care; father is a parson; upper middle-class.

(2) *Kadatz corpus: Nicole (1;8)*. The situations include: waking up, playing and jumping about in parents' bed, on her potty and getting dressed, breakfast and playing in her high-chair, at the kitchen window, painting, clearing the table, painting and playing with a toy clock, playing with a big doll, playing a board game, on her potty, playing a board game, eating, getting undressed, and monologues in bed. Social status: mother is a saleswoman; father (researcher) is a trainee teacher; upper working-class.

(3) *Wahner corpus: Andreas (2;1)*. The situations include: eating a sandwich, playing (metal foil, animals, helicopter, toothbrushes, spinning top), playing with granddad and Caesar the rabbit (doll), playing with granddad and a Santa Claus doll, reciting a poem, looking at a picture book with brother and aunt (researcher), playing with a Lego tank, a candle, matches, drinking juice, and playing football with a beachball. Social status: mother stopped working after the birth of her first child (subject's elder brother); father

is a supervisor of apprentices in an electrical workshop and is studying electrical engineering to become an electrical technician; upper working-class or lower middle-class.

(4) *Hoffmann-Kirsch corpus: Carsten (5;4)*. The situations include: playing (role-playing, driving a car, 'writing' = drawing), cutting up a birthday card, eating chocolate and looking at pictures with grandma, going into the cellar, playing at being a dog, going to the milkman, buying yogurt, eating yogurt, looking at and talking about pictures, having lunch, cuddling and talking to grandma, playing with cars (role-playing), cuddling and talking to his mother (researcher), crying (after being bumped), and being comforted by grandma. Social status: mother (researcher) is a trainee teacher; father is a car salesman; middle-class.

(5) *Brinkmann corpus: Gabi (5;4)*. The situations include: talking about her brother's birthday, breakfast, playing dominoes, eating Nutella (chocolate spread), playing dominoes again, and drawing. Social status: mother is a housewife; father is a lawyer; upper middle-class.

(6) *Häussermann corpus: Frederik (8;7)*. The situations include: waiting for the end of break; lessons: understanding things, mathematics, German, understanding things, German composition; break; lesson: braille; end of school, being driven home, arriving at home, collecting Andreas (playmate), and playing with a racing car set. Social status: mother (researcher) is a trainee teacher, entrance qualifications gained through further education, upper working-class or lower middle-class.

(7) *Otto corpus: Roman (9;2)*. The situations include: playing monopoly with Georg (younger brother), getting ready to go out, at the sports ground, relaxed conversation, playing with little cars, drive to the camp site, at the camp site, going home, going on with the game of monopoly with Georg, watching television (sports programme), and playing with racing car set. Social status: mother is a gymnastics teacher; father (researcher) has 12 years in the armed forces as a sergeant and is now a trainee teacher; middle-class.

(8) *Corzillus/Landskruöner/Koort corpus: Kai (9;6)*. The situations include: getting up, putting on the microphone transmitter, breakfast, going to school in the car, lessons (drawing, understanding things, mathematics (test), language, reading, singing) with breaks, going home, lunch, playing monopoly, driving a go-cart, playing in a Citroën 2CV, soldering, drawing, making a tassel, collecting food, watching television, and memory game. Social status: mother: landlady; father (researcher): draughtsman, invalid, died when subject was 3 years old, upper working-class.

(9) *Wagner corpus: Teresa (9;7)*. The situations include: waking up, getting dressed, sewing on the microphone transmitter, breakfast, packing her bag, drive to school, before lessons, lessons (arithmetic, language), 10 o'clock break, prizegiving, drive home, clearing things away, reading the mail, Teresa's file, picking gooseberries, playing with girl-friends (catching the cat, dressing up, clowns, ballet kidnappers), lunch, picking and cleaning gooseberries, homework, having coffee, clearing away toys, playing with Anke (coffee table, climbing a tree, playing on the grass, hopping on the patio, gold investigators, eating, ducat gold thieves), watching television, skipping, having dinner, watching television news, and going to bed. (For a more detailed discussion of speech situations see Wagner (1974: 203-38).) Social status: mother was a teacher for eight years, then housewife; father (researcher) was a secondary school teacher in various school types, later university lecturer; middle-class.

(10) *Brunner corpus: Markus (11;4).* The situations include: making a veteran car (toy car made by cutting out and pasting cardboard), and using a microscope. Social status: mother (researcher) is a trainee teacher; father is a certified engineer, architect, professor; upper middle-class.

(11) *Pagels/Gasse corpus: Christiane (12;2).* The situations include: saying hello, making a crib, lunch, continuing work on the crib, skating, playing a word game, doing crochet, having coffee, singing Advent songs, reading aloud, conversation, watching television, drawing, having dinner, and doing schoolwork. Social status: mother spent 10 years working in business, then housewife; father was a skilled art metal worker, retrained as a teacher of art and vocational preparation at a school for mentally handicapped children; upper working-class or lower middle-class.

(12) *Vette corpus: Axel (14;10).* The situations include: talking about cassette recorders, solving arithmetical problems, playing table tennis, having coffee, playing cards, recording music, and playing table tennis. Social status: mother is a housewife; father is a moulder in an iron-foundry; working-class.

If you use these data, please cite Wagner (1985) and inform Dr. Wagner of the nature of the results.

27.5.3. Weissenborn

The third German corpus is a set of protocols taken from older children by Jürgen Weissenborn of the Max-Planck-Institut in the context of experimental elicitations of route descriptions. This corpus contains verbal protocols taken from a route-description task administered to German children and adults. The experiment carried out consisted of a route description task with pairs of German children of the same age - 7, 8, 9, 10, 11, 14 years – and adults. Within each age group, six to ten pairs of subjects were tested.

The participants could not see each other. Each had an identical model of a small town in front of him and the direction giver had to specify for the other participant the route of a toy car through the town. The task material consisted of two identical three-dimensional wooden models of towns (0.60m by 0.70m). The houses, with red or blue roofs and two different sizes, were organized symmetrically (mirror-image) around a central axis. Four different paths (A, B, C and D) of equal difficulty (same number of subpaths and turning points) were defined and each was then successively described by one child to another under three different conditions:

1. with supplementary landmarks (trees, animals, cars) destroying the symmetry of the display and with gestures (the children were allowed to use their hands freely during the description);
2. without landmarks and with gestures; and
3. without landmarks and without gestures (the children were sitting on their hands).

These conditions were combined with paths A to C as follows: 1A-2B-3C; 2B-1C-3A; and so forth. Path D was always described by the child to the experimenter under condition 2. The descriptions were videotaped.

The symmetrical design of the model was chosen because the referential determinacy of any path description that refers to it is only guaranteed if these descriptions are embedded in a verbal reference frame that has jointly been defined by the participants. For example a description like "You pass under the bridge" would not suffice given that there are two bridges. The same holds for every other building. In order to resolve this indeterminacy the use of relational expressions like "left" and "right", "in front of" and "behind" is required. But, as we have seen above, the reference of these terms is itself indeterminate between the deictic and the intrinsic perspective when applied to oriented objects. Thus, when applied to the toy car that the child drives along the path, "left" and "right" coincide with the describer's perspective as long as the car moves away from him; when the car moves towards him this is no longer the case so that, at least for this instance, the describer has to specify explicitly which perspective he has chosen if he wants to avoid misunderstandings.

This is only possible if these alternative perspectives are discriminated and if the ensuing necessity to coordinate the speaker's and listener's perspective is recognized. Notice that the two perspectives or reference frames are not equivalent in terms of cognitive complexity. The deictic perspective is based on the projection of the body schema of the speaker onto the experimental display whereas in the intrinsic perspective it is first mentally transposed onto the oriented object (i.e., the toy car) and then projected onto the display thus necessitating the constant coordination between the original deictic and the transposed intrinsic use. Thus the structure of the experimental display asking for the use of these spatial terms has necessary conversational implications in that it requires the negotiation of the rules of use of these terms in order to establish a shared frame of reference and action.

What has been said so far about the consequences of the experimental design for the task solution applies in particular to condition 2. The task requirements are obviously quite different in condition 1 where the symmetrical design is destroyed by the introduction of additional landmarks. In this condition an unambiguous description of the path could be achieved by relying mainly on the information provided by these elements without necessarily using relational terms like "left" and "right". That is, these landmarks furnish a concrete and fixed frame of reference, external to the describer. Condition 3 was designed to study the influence of the absence of gestures on the child's descriptive abilities.

In order to evaluate the describer's ability to establish a coherent frame of reference a certain number of parameters have been defined that are considered to characterize each individual describer's performance, that is completeness of the path description defined in terms of adequate characterization of the turning points and the connections between them, prevailing perspective, perspective awareness, and so forth. A detailed presentation and quantitative analysis of these parameters can be found in Weissenborn and Stralka, in preparation. Publications that use this corpus should cite (Weissenborn, 1985) and (Weissenborn, 1986).

27.5.4.   Wode

The fourth German corpus is a set of transcripts of noncontinuous interactions collected by Henning Wode of the University of Kiel with a chief focus on his son Lars and daughter Inga. Both were acquiring German as their first language.

The material was gathered in a longitudinal day-by-day routine involving both notes taken spontaneously and tape recordings using a portable Uher tape recorder. Data were collected while the children were engaged in all kinds of activities, including meals, games, walks, and sports. The written notes contain phonetic details of the utterances and comments about the situational context. A rigid data collection procedure, involving fixed intervals or time limits for recording sessions, was not maintained.

The participants in these interactions are:

BAR   Barbara Wode, wife of Henning and mother of Heiko, Birgit, Lars, and Inga. She was born in 1945.
HEN   Henning Wode, husband of Barbara and father of the four children. Born in 1937.
HEI   Heiko Wode, the oldest child (son), born in May 1966.
BIR   Birgit Wode, second child (daughter), born in May 1967.
LAR   Lars Wode, third child (son), born in May 1969.
ING   Inga Wode, fourth child (daughter), born in May 1971.
BEL   Belinda, an American visitor with the family, born 1960.

Some of the special codings in the original version include "korrigiert" for corrected and "erneut" for a new start. These have not yet been changed to [//] in **CHAT**. Comments were originally marked with @@ and overlaps with @*@.

Publications based on this corpus include Wode (1974; 1977; 1978; 1979; 1980; 1981; 1987) and Wode and Allendorff (1981). Papers using these data should cite one or two of these articles.

27.6.   Greek

The Greek child data in this corpus were donated by Ursula Stephany. They were collected between 1971 and 1974 in natural speech situations in the homes and/or Kindergarten from four monolingual Greek children growing up in Athens, Greece.
The boy Spiros was observed at 1;9.
The girl Maria was observed at 2;3 and 2;9.
The girl Mairi was observed at 1;9, 2;3, and 2;9.
The girl Janna was observed at 1;11, 2;5, and 2;9.

File names (e.g. MAI21A1.CHA) are structured as follows:
Child's name: SPI, MAR, MAI, JAN
Child's age in months
Period of observation: A (1;9 or 1;11), B (2;3 or 2;5), C (2;9)
Running number of file at period A, B, or C.

The transcription is phonetic/phonemic. Capital letters have been used for the interdental fricatives (D voiced, T, unvoiced) and the voiced velar fricative (G). Grammatical coding is to be found on the %mor line; phonetic detail is indicated on the %phon line; adult correspondences are indicated on the main line or on the %err line.

Papers based on the use of these data can cite Stephany (1986; 1992; 1995).

27.7. Hebrew

There are three Hebrew corpora – all from the Tel Aviv group headed by Ruth Berman.

27.7.1. Ravid

This directory contains 37 files collected by Dorit Ravid from her daughter Sivan between the ages of 1;8 and 6;10. The recordings were made between May 1980 and April 1985 Sivan (SIV), was a first-born female, born June 14, 1978. Her brother Asaf (ASA) was born July 30, 1979.   The mother (MOT) is a linguist. The father (FAT) is Arik. The family lives in an apartment in a high rise building in a provincial town called Yahud in the center of Israel (Tel Aviv metropolitan area). Their mother is a (second generation) native Hebrew speaker, their father came to Israel as a small child, and the children were definitely monolingual Hebrew speakers throughout the period of the recordings.   The family background and lifestyle is typical of well-educated, literate Israeli middle-class salaried professionals.   The recordings were made by the mother when the children were playing at home in their bedroom or the living room - sometimes just the two of them, most of the time one or both of them with one or both of their parents, occasionally with (maternal) grandparents or with another child from the same neighborhood. Sivan, the older child, was linguistically highly precocious with an unusually developed metalinguistic feel for language, and in these recordings she did not often give her brother much floor space!

Asaf was 0;9.16 in file 111a. There is not much speech from him until file 206b when he is 1;4:8.

File	Age of Siv	Total utterances	Date
111a	1;11.2	600	16/05/80
111b	1;11.12	87	26/05/80
202a	2;2.18	223	02/09/80
202b	2;2.19	264	03/09/80
203a	2;3.5	112	19/09/80
203b	2;3.12	195	26/09/80
204a	2;4.3	848	17/10/80
205a	2;5.7	1075	21/11/80
205b	2;5.24	1036	08/12/80
207a	2;7.20	495	04/02/81
207b	2;7.29	501	13/02/81
300a	3;0.23	1100	07/07/81
301a	3;1.2	156	16/07/81
301b	3;1.27	147	11/08/81
303a	3;3.26	66	10/09/81
304a	3;4.5	41	19/10/81
304b	3;4.10	200	24/10/81
304c	3;4.14	308	28/10/81
304d	3;4.17	229	31/10/81
304e	3;4.18	377	01/11/81
306a	3;6.11	371	25/12/81
306b	3;6.21-29	209	05/01/82
307a	3;7.9	40	25/01/82
307b	3;7.18	197	02/02/82

307c	3;7.21	499	05/02/82
404a	4;4.22	188	06/11/82
404b	4;4.24	390	08/11/82
404c	4;4.24-29	547	08/11/82
407a	4;7.17	116	01/03/83
407b	4;7.21	511	05/03/83
410a	4;10.6	482	20/04/83
410b	4;10.9	442	23/04/83
505a	5;5.12	572	26/11/83
505b	5;5.25	192	09/12/83
506a	5;6.11	754	25/12/83
603a	6;3.22	542	06/10/84
611a	6;11.4	405	08/05/85

For Hebrew morphological coding one must add *-* to the depfile for the main line.

27.7.2. Na'ama

This corpus contains files from a Hebrew-speaking child between ages 1;7 and 2;6. Na'ama was the firstborn child of middle-class fairly educated native-speaking parents. She was recorded by Dafna Kaplan, a friend and neighbor of the family, as part of her M.A. studies in linguistics at Tel Aviv University in 1983. The recordings were all done in her home, with or without the mother present.

File	Age
1	1;7.8
2	1;7.27
3	1;8.25
4	1;9.2
5	1;10.0
6	1;11.0
7	2;0.10
8	2;0.24
9	2;1.12
10	2;2.12
11	2;3.2
12	2;3.23
13	2;4.14
14	2;5.4
15	2;5.8
16	2;6.0
17	2;6.4

27.7.3. BSF

The materials in this Hebrew data set were gathered during the first phase of a crosslinguistic project on the development of tense-aspect funded by a grant from the United States-Israel Binational Science Foundation (BSF) awarded to Ruth A. Berman, Tel Aviv University as principal investigator and Dan I. Slobin, University of California, Berkeley, for three years starting in September 1982. The first undertaking of this study was to collect together as much as possible in the form of naturalistic speech samples for Hebrew preschool children. This was done in some cases by recordings and transcriptions carried out by members of the project team (native speakers of Hebrew majoring in linguistics - including Inbal Gozes, Galia Hatab, Yona Neeman, and Ziva Wijler); in others by typing up transcriptions of students doing seminar and other research papers under the aegis of Dr. Esther Dromi of the School of Education and Dr. Anita Rom of the School of Communications Disorders - both at Tel Aviv University; and in yet others by materials collected in the course of work on graduate theses by students of Ruth Berman (e.g. Dafna Kaplan, Shoshana Rabinowitch, Batya Zur). Around 160 transcripts varying from under 50 to over 500 utterances in length were collected and typed up in this way. The ones which allowed for this were then optically scanned and reformatted at CMU for entry on CHILDES, whereas the rest were entered onto an IBM-clone PC computer at Tel Aviv University according to the current **CHAT** format. The data are without English glosses.

All this material was then reviewed and checked by Ruth Berman (when on sabbatical at Berkeley in 1985-1986), and 100 of the best, most reliable transcripts were selected for inclusion in CHILDES, providing a data-set of approximately 100 individual transcripts for each year–group from ages 1;2 years, 2;3, 3;4, and 5;6.

The children all come from middle-class homes and are monolingual Hebrew speakers whose parents are in most cases also native speakers of Hebrew. They come mainly from metropolitan Tel Aviv and its environs, and are from urban and rural backgrounds, where "rural" refers to children who are raised on the communal settlements (kibbutzim) or in the cooperative villages (moshavim) which constitute part of the middle to upper-middle class stratum of Israeli society.

1 -- AGES 1;6 to 1;11

File	Investigator	Role	child utterances	comment
alita18.cha	M.Hirsch	MYR	280+	problematic
gadi111.cha	E.Dromi student	INV	350	few combinations
keren11.cha	E.Dromi	MOT	60	early one-word
keren13.cha	E.Dromi	MOT	150	rich one-word
keren15.cha	E.Dromi	MOT	120	few comb
*liro111.cha	A.Rom student	FAT	125	basic syntax
mixal16.cha	E.Dromi student	INV	109	combinations
noa111.cha	A.Rom student	INV	132	some syntax
ran19.cha	E.Dromi student	INV	63	few combinations
uris11.cha	Y.Strassberg		48	mainly one-word
uris12.cha	Y.Strassberg		15	several strings
yifat11.cha	E.Dromi w/mother	ETT	300+	mainly input
yifat14.cha	E.Dromi student	INV	56	
yifat16.cha	E.Dromi student	INV	108	mainly one-word

2A -- AGES 2;0 to 2;6 (This directory is currently missing)

File	Investigator	Role	utterances
hay26.cha	N.Shoham	MOT	180
kobi21.cha	E.Dromi student	INV	203
nimro22.cha	E.Dromi student	INV	141
nimro23.cha	E.Dromi student	INV	101
ori20.cha	L.Dganit		61
ori21.cha	L.Dganit		71
ori22.cha	L.Dganit	MOT	186
ori23.cha	L.Dganit	MOT	60
ori245.cha	L.Dganit	MOT	72
roi23.cha	A.Rom student	INV	129

ronit20.cha	B.Zur		61	
sharo20.cha	A.Rom student	INV	80	
urik25.cha	D.Kaplan	MOT	112	
urik26.cha	D.Kaplan	MOT	86	
yahel23.cha	A.Rom student	INV	75	
zohar26.tem	Z.Wijler	ZIV	72	
tomer27.cha	M.Hirsch	MYR	265	
maya29.cha	A.Rom student	INV	242	
urik211.cha	D.Kaplan	MOT	220	
yael211.cha	Z. Wijler	MOT	90	

2 -- AGES 2;0 to 2;11

adi26.cha	D.Kaplan	DAF	198
asaf26.cha	A.Rom student	INV	105
chen211.cha	M. Hirsch	MYR	320
eran26.eng	A.Rom student	INV	135
hay22.cha	N.Shoham	MOT	203
hay24.cha	N.Shoham	MOT	225

3 -- AGES 3;0 to 3;11

amit30.cha	B.Zur	BAT	50
avi36.cha	B.Zur		31
aviad31.cha	Mirit/Rom	RES	153
boy36.cha	Sara/Rom	RES	102
chen31.cha	M.Hirsch	MYR	253
dani311.cha	A.Rom	ANI	46
debby35.cha	S.Rabin		
dotan31.cha	S.Rabinowich	SHO	103
guy311.cha	Z.Wijler	ZIV	239
inbar36.cha	D.Kaplan	DAF	78
keren36.cha	S.Rabinowitz	SHO	128
limor311.cha	M.Hirsch	MYR	159
limor40.cha	M.Hirsch	MYR	78
*mayan39.cha	Y.Neeman	YON	204
merav38.cha	G.Hatab	GAL	582
mixal33.cha	B.Zur		52
mor310.cha	M.Hirsch	MYR	265
*mor311.cha	M.Hirsch	MYR	100
moti311.cha	B.Zur	BAT	50
rafi211.eng	D.Kaplan	DAF	157
rafi30.cha	D.Kaplan	DAF	198
ravit38.cha	B.Zur		49
reut32.cha	M.Hirsch	MYR	208
shlom36.cha	D.Kaplan	DAF	323
smadr37.cha	Z.Wijler	ZIV	201
yael32.cha	S.Rabinowich	SHO	80
yotam30.cha	Smadar/Rom	RES	151

4 -- AGES 4;1 to 4;11

adi43.cha	S.Rabinowitz	SHO	67	long narratives
adit41.cha	A.Rom	INV	32	

arel42.cha	A.Rom	INV	11 +18	
avi47.eng	A.Rom	INV	32	
barux42.cha	A.Rom	INV	21	
dana41.cha	S.Rabinowitz	SHO	83	
dudi41.cha	A.Rom	INV	19	
elad43.cha	A.Rom	INV	26	long utterances
eran43.cha	I.Gozes	INB	275	
girl46.cha	B.Zur	INV	45	some narrative
ido46.cha	S.Rabinowitz	SHO	104	
keren44.cha	B.Zur	INV	43	
or411.cha	Z.Wijler	ZIV	330	long utterances
oren410.cha	B.Josman	BAR	15	
oshra41.cha	A.Rom	INV	43	
saa47.cha	A.Rom			
shar411.cha	A.Rom	INV	32	
shay410.cha	A.Rom	INV	37	
tali46.cha	B.Josman	BAR	190	
yaron42.cha	A.Rom	INV	28	
yifat42.cha	B.Zur	INV	40	narrative
yoni44.cha	S.Rabinowitz	SHO	123	
yonit45.cha	B.Josman	BAR	178	
yuval46.cha	Z.Wijler	ZIV	197	
ziv41.cha	B.Zur	INV	45	narrative

5--AGES 5;0 to 5;11

amnon53.cha	S.Rabinowitz	SHO	168	plus narratives
*ari56.cha	S.Rabinowitz	SHO	65	
aron511.cha	A.Rom	INV	23	picture description
asaf51.cha	S.Rabinowitz	SHO	88	
ben51.cha	S.Rabinowitz	SHO	79	
david55.cha	B.Josman		15	story retelling
elad56.cha	B.Josman	BAR	15	story retelling
gil52.cha	A.Rom		29	long utterances
gilad54.cha	B.Zur		42	stilted
girl52.cha	B.Zur		31	narratives
idit58.cha	A.Rom		19	picture description
*keren50.cha	G.Hatab	GAL	160	
*oren52.cha	B.Josman	BAR	15	long utterances
shar510.cha	A.Rom	INV	29	
tal54.cha	A.Rom		29	long utterances
yifat54.cha	B.Zur		32	narratives
*yonat56.cha	B.Josman	BAR	23	part narrative

* Files marked with asterisks have English glosses for the Hebrew.

Publications based on these data should cite Berman and Dromi (1984) and Berman (1985).

27.8. Hungarian

These data were collected by Brian MacWhinney in Hungary during the 1970–1971 academic year. They were donated to the CHILDES in 1985. The children studied were Zoli, Moni, Andi, Gyuri, and Eva – children in the nursery school of the National Institute for Nursery School Methodology (BOMI). The children all came from middle-class families with two working parents. The recordings were made by using a wireless microphone and a radio receiver. The microphone was sewn into a pocket in one of the standard nursery school aprons worn by the child. The particular apron used had the figure of a fox on it and the children often competed to be allowed to wear the "fox apron." Recording began in November when it was already too cold for the children to go outside and continued through March. There was a one month break during April. When recording resumed in May, the children were often outside playing in the garden.

Activities at the nursery school were very highly structured. Each child had a symbol that identified a particular closet, a particular chair, a particular towel, and so on. There were only a few children under the age of 1;3 in the school. Those children were kept in cribs in a special room. The children between 1;3 and 2;0 were in a second play group. Zoli, Andi, and Moni were in that group. The older play group had children from 2;0 to 3;0 and Eva and Gyuri were in that group.

Most of the interactions are with a dyad of children and the investigator. Some of the interactions, particularly those with Zoli, involve only the investigator and the target child. The nursery school teachers only rarely engaged the children during the recordings. The investigator is not a native speaker of Hungarian and, particularly during the first few months of the recording, the investigator's use of Hungarian was fairly weak. Listening back to the tapes, it is difficult to detect any influence that this had on the children who seemed more interested in the investigator's moustache and the toys that he was carrying than in the rather nonstandard nature of his language.

MacWhinney (1975) conducted a detailed analysis of the syntactic patterns for Zoli, Moni, and Andi with particular emphasis on the relative contributions of word-based positional patterns and general topic-comment patterns to word ordering. MacWhinney (1974) provides additional information on data collection and transcription.

Zoli was born July 5, 1969. Samples 1 and 2 are not complete. They were kept in a separate notebook which now appears to be missing.

Sample	Age	Hours	Utterances	MLU	Dates
Zoli 1	1;5.2-5	4	51	1.10	Dec 7-8
Zoli 2	1;6.29-30	6	228	1.58	Feb 3
Zoli 3	1;8.6-8	8	2675	1.60	March 11-16
Zoli 4	1;10.0-6	7	1911	1.87	May 5-11
Zoli 5	2;0.0-5	6	835	2.58	July 1-7
Zoli 6	2-2-0-3	7	1826	2.50	Aug 31-Sept 3
Moni 1	1;11.18-27	8	1478	1.53	
Moni 2	2;2.0	8	576	1.28	
Moni 3	2;4.16-17	5	797	1.15	
Moni 4	2;5.20-23	8	700	1.03	

Publications that make use of this corpus should cite MacWhinney (MacWhinney, 1974).

27.9.   Italian

There are two major Italian corpora. The first is from the CNR Psychology group in Rome. The second is from the Stella Maris Calambrone group working with the CNR Computational Linguistics group in Pisa.

27.9.1.   Calambrone

The first Italian database includes data on both normal and disordered language development. The normal data come from six subjects (2 boys and 4 girls) whose speech samples were collected at home. Each child was recorded bimonthly and every session lasted from 30 to 45 minutes. The data from children with language disorders were collected at the Stella Maris Institute and include longitudinal as well as cross-sectional data on clinical syndromes (developmental dysphasia, genetic and chromosomal disorders). The longitudinal subjects are three dysphasic children, observed from the age of three. Their linguistic production was limited to holophrases and few word associations. Their speech was videotaped during monthly 30-minute sessions.

 This database is the result of research conducted from 1985 to 1990 in the laboratory of "Fisiopatologia del linguaggio in etá evolutiva" in which many people have taken part: Piero Bottari, Anna Maria Chilosi, Lorena Cittadoni, Alessandro Ciuti, Anna Maccari, Natalia Pantano, Lucia Pfanner, Paola Poli, Stefania Sarno, Luca Surian, and Paola Cipriani as coordinator.   Pietro Pfanner is the Scientific Director of the Institute. Giuseppe Cappelli of the Institute for Computational Linguistics (directed by Antonio Zampolli) was responsible for the computational aspects of the project. Data collection was supported by the grant 6 500.4/ICS/62.1/1135 (13/08/85) assigned to the Stella Maris Scientific Institute by the Italian Ministry of Health.

All transcripts were derived from videotaped interactions recorded with a videocamera (Hitachi VM 200E or Nordmende V150). Each session was also audiotaped with a Sony TCM-6 recorder with Sony ECM-150T personal microphone. Transcripts were filed on floppy disks of IBM personal computer by one researcher, and the level of mutual evaluation agreement was checked by two independent transcribers.

Normal Subjects. The six normal subjects were: Rafaello, a first-born boy from a family of high SES: followed from 1;7.08 to 3;3.00 (39 videotapings); Rosa, a second-born girl from a middle-low SES, followed from 1;3.00 to 3;3.23 (43 videotapings); Martina, the only daughter from a family of middle SES, followed from 1;7.00 to 3;0.00 (20 videotapings); Guglielmo, a second-born boy from a family of middle-high SES, followed from 2;1.00 to 2;11.00 (13 videotapings); Viola, a second-born girl from a family of middle SES, followed from 1;10.00 to 3;0.14 (23 videotapings); and Diana, a first-born girl from a family of middle SES, followed from 1;6.07 to 3;0.19 (26 videotapings).

Subject	Ages	Files	Kbytes	Words	Child Words
Normal Subjects:					
Rafaello	1;7,22 - 2;11.23	19	429	42203	7810
Rosa	1;7.13 - 3;3.23	21	553	14634	14862
Martina	1;7.18 - 2;7.15	13	451	36444	7580
Guglielmo	2;2 - 3;0	9	238	22397	6469

Viola	2;0.14 - 2;10.04	9	259	24255	4329
Diana	1;8.05 - 2;6.16	9	188	16253	7974
TOTAL		80	2547	90766	49024

Longitudinal Language-Impaired Subjects:

Marco	6;2 - 9;4	13	296	30587	8027
Sara	4;11 - 6;5	12	257	32735	8216
Davide	5;8 - 6;11	4	73	9191	4490
TOTAL		29	626	72513	20733

Cross-sectional Language-Impaired Subjects:

Manolo	7	1	5	489	489
Angela	8;2	1	5	307	307
Jessica	10;3	1	6	469	469
Romina	8;3	1	7	497	497
Paola	10;7	1	5	234	234
Ketty	11;10	1	4	270	270
Francesca	7;9	1	11	1179	674
Emanuele	9;3	1	5	654	400
TOTAL		8	48	4179	3420

The language samples from children and interacting adults were transcribed in **CHAT** format with a minimum context contained in dependent tiers (%act; %gpx; %exp); the main lines of the children contain the real speech produced, with some coding for special forms of lexicon, punctuation and pauses. At a second stage some new lines were added in order to code errors, omissions and pre-syntactic devices. The focus of our first analysis was on lexical and morphological acquisition by normal and language-impaired children, looking in depth for transitional phenomena and stages of global language development.

Publications using this corpus should cite Cipriani et al. (1989).

27.9.2.   Roma

The second Italian database is from Rome. Elena Pizzuto of the CNR in Rome has contributed data in **CHAT** from a longitudinal study of a single child originally studied by Antinucci and Volterra.. The data are in **CHAT** format without English glosses. The Italian corpus contains six data files, a "00readme.doc" file and a "00words.doc" file. This corpus was collected in 1969 and 1970 as part of a language acquisition project at the Istituto di Psicologia in Rome. The male subject's name is Francesco. He was tape-recorded between 1;4 and 4;0. The data is morphemically coded. The data collected had as focus the child's spontaneous language production with adults and the relevant contextual information during interaction. The transcription was morphemic rather than phonological and no attention was given to other features, such as paravocal.

Francesco was a bright, healthy child from middle-class, university educated parents living in Rome. Francesco's mother worked part-time as a biochemist. During her absence, Francesco was cared for by a working-class maid. The maid spoke a lower-class Roman version of Italian and this might be considered as a possible influence on Francesco's speech. Francesco attended preschool during the morning in the period from 2;6 (2 years, 6 months) through his fourth birthday. Francesco was a first-born child. His sister was born slightly before his third birthday. The mother's pregnancy is an isue that clearly concerned him and is discussed several times in the records from about 2;6 to 3;0.

Francesco was studied from 1;4 to 4;0. He was visited in his home approximately every two weeks, and two-hour audiorecordings were made at each visit. The observer was well known to the family, and the children were accustomed to the recording equipment. Sessions were for the most part spontaneous and unplanned, although the adults present tended to initiate games or other activites that encouraged the children to talk. Because both were highly verbal children, such encouragement was rarely necessary.

Transcriptions of the recording sessions include all child speech, all adult speech relevant to the child's utterances (e.g. no record is kept of adult-adult conversations ignored by the child), and information concerning the nonverbal context. The latter includes descriptions of the child's play activities, actions by the adult which prompt comment by the child, and any contextual or background information clarifying the child's communicative intentions. In Francesco's case, observer Virginia Volterra was also a family friend present on many occasions outside the research periods. Hence her background notes and interpretations are a particularly rich and accurate source.

When coding the transcripts into **CHAT**, several simplifications were made. First, a variety of types of data were noted on a %cri line. The abbreviation "cri" here stands for "context-relevant information" including gesture, situation, proxemics, and so forth. Second, the symbol @ was used without any further extensions for nonstandard forms. In general, these transcripts contain insufficient information to be used to study phonological development, intonation, retracings, or speech acts.

Publications that make use of this corpus should cite Antinucci and Parisi (1973), Antinucci and Volterra (1978), Volterra (1972), Volterra (1976), or (1984).

27.10. Mambila

This data has been prepared as part of an ESRC funded project "Kinship and language: a computer-aided study of social deixis in conversation" (grant no R000233311) which has funded Andrew Wilson's employment. Dr. David Zeitlyn, the project director, is a British Academy Research Fellow at the Institute of Social and Cultural Anthropology, Oxford and a Research Fellow at Wolfson College, Oxford.

Introduction to Mambila. The Mambila lie on either side of the Nigeria/Cameroon border, the bulk of them living on the Mambila Plateau in Nigeria. A smaller number (c. 12,000) are to be found in Cameroon, especially at the foot of of Mambila Plateau escarpment, on the Tikar Plain. The fieldwork was restricted to these latter groups, and in particular to the village of Somie. Somie had a population of approximately one thousand (based on the official 1986 tax census) at the time of fieldwork. Self-sufficient in food, the villagers have grown coffee as a cash crop since the early 1960s. Cameroonian Mambila on the Tikar Plain have adopted the Tikar institution of the chiefship, yet their social structure otherwise closely resembles that described for the Nigerian village of Warwar by Rehfisch (1972) based on fieldwork in 1953. Nigerian Mambila did not have the same type of institutionalized chiefship as is found in Cameroon. In Nigeria, villages were organised on gerontocratic principles, and largely lacked political offices. The system of exchange marriage described by Rehfisch (1960) has now vanished, and with it the two sorts of named group which recruited through different combinations of descent, marriage type (exchange or bridewealth) and residence. Marriage is viripatrilocal, and is increasingly on the basis of courtship although bridewealth is still a major factor. However, bridewealth may be paid in instalments over a number of years. It is not cited as a reason for the failure of young men to marry. Most people in the village are members of either the Catholic or Protestant church. Zeitlyn (1993) gives some information about the kinship terminology. A short transcript from that paper plus digitized audio recording may be found at the following URLusing gopher rsl.ox.ac.uk within the anthropology corner or at the following URL for the World Wide Web: http://rsl.ox.ac.uk/isca/mambila/mambila.html.

Introduction to the data. The Mambila transcript that accompanies this file has been transcribed according to **CHAT** guidelines, with the exceptions and constraints noted below. First the utterances have been segmented according to the principles described in Stiles (1992). We note that this is controversial and for many other purposes we feel the turn or the phase may be safer albeit harder to define - a spoken phrase may be crudely understood to be a turn or an utterance begining and ending either with a turn transition or a pause.

Developmental psychologists familiar with **CHAT** should note that the data was not collected and coded with developmental issues in mind. It is hoped that it may still prove of some interest to them nonetheless. The transcription of Mambila follows Perrin's work on the phonology with some modification since I work in the village of Somie which has a slightly different phonology. Characters are used with their standard IPA values plus the following charactors which I have redefined to make my own Mambila font:

ASCII value	Phonetic value
198	velar nasal 'ng'
239	Upper-case velar nasal 'Ng'
191	Mid-low back rounded vowel 'aw'
207	mid-centra! vowel 'shuwa'
96	Low tone
94	High-low tone
171	High tone
164	Mid-low tone

The database includes a copy of the Mam-Times font which is a Macintosh composite postscript font created by David Zeitlyn that assumes you have Times-Roman installed in your system (if you want high quality printing). Even without Times-Roman installed, it should display adequately on screen. The Man-TImes font needs to be installed in your system.

The transcript records a conversation in the house of Michel Sondue on 15-DEC-1990. Therecording was made, in Zeitlyn's absence, by Sondue and comments made during the course of the conversation show that those present were not unaware of its presence. Neither Zeitlyn nor Sondue can ascertain any significant difference between this conversation and others which were not recorded. The transcription procedures deserve some mention. Soon after making the recording Zeitlyn went through it with Sondue. At this stage as well as making some contextual notes they made a second recording - Sondue repeated each utterance into a second tape recorder, speaking slowly and clearly. To do this he used both his undertsanding as a native speaker and the fact that he was an actor in the conversation to understand parts of the recording that were (and remain) extremely indistinct to my foreign ears. In the course of making this second recording he explained various idioms and vocabulary items that were new to Zeitlyn. Zeitlyn subsequently transcribed the second recording in the UK and then returned to the original recording. The transcript was then coded in the UK following a scheme developed in a pilot study by Blum-Kulka and Snow (1992) elaborated in Wilson and Zeitlyn (in press). In the course of the coding, the English translation was revised so that the use of pronouns and names was parallel to their use in the Mambila original - although there are obvious problems in this such as a gender neutral third person and some (rare) compound pronouns. The coding process turned up some further problems which were resolved during a further fieldtrip in May 1994. The result is a robust transcript. This is not to say that it is not theory-laden (Ochs, 1979) and inevitably it could be improved, in particular the absence of a visual channel combined with the free passage of children (and adults) in and out of the house makes it uncertain just who the non-participating audience is at any one time. In addition there are often the voices of children at play in the background. Most of the time these have proved too indistinct to be able to trancribe. Almost any recording one makes in Somie will have the voices of children playing somewhere in the background!

Header tiers and background information. The conversation is taken from a household in Somie village, West Cameroon. The tape-recorder has been left with the father of the household (MIS) to minimise any effects due to the presence of the investigator (DZ). The participants are predominantly family of MIS and his wife TBL, with the exception of two visitors, DAN and MBM. Most of the family members are co-resident with MIS and TBL, except for their eldest daughter ANG and her young child NKB. Throughout the conversation there is a general procession of participants in and out of the house. These tend to consist of the younger children who are playing outside. This causes two problems: a) it is often unclear who is speaking or what is being said when the voice comes from outside the range of the microphone range, b) without a visual record of what is happening, it has proved difficult to track the wherabouts of the participants, hence causing difficulties with the addresse tier. In particular cases of doubt or confusion, the file has been checked and re-checked with the participants themselves.

Main tiers. Many turns in this conversation have been segmented into several distinct utterances which are coded individually. The motivation for this segmentation comes from our own research interests and the need to have a conceptually viable unit of conversation over which to score frequencies over certain linguistic and illocutionary items. The criteria by which we performed this segmentation comes from the work of Stiles (1992) and his concept of speech act. Stiles has presented a taxonomy that he claims is an improvement on the traditional attempts in being based on principles of classification whereas "most other systems have been developed empirically-by examining samples of a particular domain of discourse"(p.31). This will not only ensure that the taxonomy is both mutually exclusive and exhaustive (every possible utterance is categorised uniquely) but is more likely to be applicable to all languages, a feature of great interest to anthropologists doing cross-cultural comparisons, so long as the principles themselves are universally applicable. This will depend on the theoretical under-pinnings of the taxonomy.

Stiles, a clinical psychologist, conceives every utterance (1) "to concern either the speaker's or the other's experience, with 'experience' understood broadly to include thoughts, feelings, perceptions, and intentional actions"(p.14), (2) to either make presumptions about the other's experience or not to presume anything of the other's experience (ibid.), and (3) to "represent the experience either from his or her own personal viewpoint or from a viewpoint that is shared or held in common with the other"(p.15). These three principles of classification he calls "source of experience", "presumption about experience" and "frame of reference" respectively and are dichotomous in having the value "speaker" or "other". Hence we have a possible eight categories (2 X 2 X 2), or Verbal Response Modes (V.R.M.s for short), which he labels Disclosure (D), Edification (E), Advisement (A), Confirmation (C), Acknowledgement (K), Interpretation (I), and Reflection (R), according the table below. He is careful to make clear that these names are only for convenience and the category classification should not be confused with their everyday connotations, although he uses the considerable overlap with natural categories as evidence that his principles are salient.

This is further discussed in our review of Stiles (Wilson and Zeitlyn 1994). Applying these criteria often requires that what seem to be normal sentences are split into two or more phrases that constitute separate utterances. On the main tiers we have paid liitle attention to tonal and prosodic information, but have incorporated information such as interruptions, pauses, overlaps and retraces. Retraces are further discussed below.

Dependent tiers.

%eng: Each main line has a free English translation. These tiers look like main tiers in that they preserve the main line informationin CHAT format (except for the ID code). This will permit certain analyses to be completed on the basis of the English translation alone. In particular the translation attempts to preserve the person referrring expressions (i.e. pronouns, names, kin term) used.

%spa: All utterances are coded for their speech act. The taxonomy we have adopted for this purpose is the VRM taxonomy of Stiles (1992), which is easily applied to natural conversations. See Wilson and Zeitlyn (1994) for a full review.

%add: Addressee. This conversation is a multi-party conversation, so most utterances have several candidates for addressee, since there are several people whom can reasonably be expected to hear the utterance. Coding this aspect is achieved by a series of hierarchial cues which, when applied, will cut down the set of potential addressees to the set of actual addresses. The cues are as folllows (see Wilson and Zeitlyn 1994 for a fuller discussion).

1. Physical constraints that determine the candidates who are within ear-shot.
2. The presence of vocatives which will uniquely identify the addressee.
3. The subsequent turn, if it follows appropriately (i.e. is an answer to a question) reveals addressee, even though it may have been 'negotiated' or unintended.
4. Informational content: the addressee is the set of persons for whom the utterance is maximally informative (e.g. telling a story to a visitor, since the rest know the story already) The addressees are coded by the id code. If there are more than one addressee, the codes are split by a colon; the names are always coded in the order as they are introduced on the header tier.

%top: This tier records any changes in the topic or content of the conversation. Notoriously had to pin down, we have adopted a rather intuitive approach to this aspect, coding on each utterance a change ($new) or reversal ($rev) of topic as it occurs.

%fta   Face threatening act. An attempt to capture the intuitions of face work and linguistic politeness (Brown and Levinson 1987) within this natural conversation has led to our coding ot any utterance that is reckoned to threaten the face of others (addressee or not, we have not included face threats, e.g. insults, to absent third parties). Each code is presented in the following order: the face threatener, usually the utterer, though not always, the threatened, the imposition of the face threat (on a crude ordinal scale of 1 (weak) to 3 (strong), and whether the face threatened was positive or negative (see Brown and Levinson (1987), Wilson and Zeitlyn (1994) for more details. Thus the code $mis:gun:2+ve tells us that in that utterance, MIS has threatened GUN's positive face to a value of 2.

%nte and %ftn: these tiers provide additional information that might be of help in understanding the significance or meaning of certain parts of the conversation. For example, reference to third parties are eloborated upon, along with some general ethnographic information, as well as any breaks in the tape recording.

%pre: this tier provides a code for all person referring expressions that occur in any one utterance. Three aspects of person referring expressions ('PREs') have been coded for, the category of expression, the actual linguistic form, and the status of the referent relative to the utterance. These three aspects are coded together and separated with colons.

We have distinguished the following five categories of expression: pronoun, kin terms, names, titles, and descriptive expressions. The distinction can be operationalised both on semantic grounds and on syntactic grounds (see Wilson and Zeitlyn 1994). For each category, the linguistic form is coded in a different way as follows:

1.   Pronouns ($pro:) The Mambila system of pronouns is roughly comparable to the English system, that is there are three persons (first, second and third) that can be either singular or plural. We have marked these by a number followed by 's' (singular) or 'p' (plural). In addition we noted if the pronoun is a possesvive (e.g. $pro:2spos). In addition there are other pronouns that do not have simple translations in English. For example, "Bubu" is a compound pronoun that refers to two persons, and "nyi" is an anaphoric pronoun used to refer to the speaker of reported speech. In these cases the Mambila form has been maintained in the coding tier.

2.   Names ($nam:) With names the actual linguistic realisation is maintained on the tier to allow immediate inspection without reference to the main tier from which it came. There are some cases in which the form of the name is often varied, possibly to act as a mitigator (e.g. "Celistine" and "Celi"). These changes have been coded in the following way. The 'unmarked' version is of the name is determined by examining which is the most common version. Thereafter any variation of that name ('marked' forms) are coded with a (+) or (-) depending on whether they appear to be marked in a positive, more intimate, direction, or a negative direction. For instance, DAN is sometimes addressed as "Dan-e" This has been coded as $nam:dan-e(+).

3.   Kin terms ($kin:) The linguistic form of kin terms are coded in the same way as names, that is by preserving the original form and adding any intimacy marker where necessary.

4.   Titles ($tit:) The linguistic form of titles is maintained on the coding ti= er.

5.   Descriptive expressions ($des): These expressions too are preserved on the coding tier. Often a descriptive phrase will be made up of two or more words. In these cases the words or linked on the coding tier with a _ (e.g.$des:bˋø_nùàr_taar_dœ). This preserves the expressions when conducting any FREQ searches. Some linguistic expressions are made up from combinations of these simple expressions. These can either consist of a series of simple expressions that refer to the some person which we term compound expressions (e.g. "Aunt Sally, or Sir Brian") or a series of simple expressions which achieve ultimate reference by referring to others, termed oblique expressions (e.g. "my brother's daughter"). These combinations are coded by coding the simple expressions connected with a & sign (e.g. $kin:tele:abs&$pro:1s:utt). In the case of compound expressions, where only one person, or set of persons, are referred to, the conversational status (explained below) is included only once.

The third aspect of this %pre tier is the conversational status of the referent, and requires coding the referent according to how he or she stands in relation to the utterance. This code rests on the following distinction.

1. Utterer (utt): the expression can refer to self (e.g. "me")

2. Addressee (adr): the expression can refer to the addressee (e.g. you or an explicit vocative).

3. Participant (cnv): the expression can refer to someone in the conversation who is not being addressed with that utterance.

4. Overhearer (aud): the expression can refer to someone within ear-shot, though not participating in the conversation.

5. Baby (bby): the utterance can refer to smeone or something who does not have the ability to comprehennd or reply. This category includes pets or small babies.

6. Absentee (abs): the expression can refer to someone who is absent (or dead).

7. Rhetorical (rhe): the expression can refer only in a rhetorical sense.

It is, of course, possible to refer to more than one individual with any simple expression (e.g. "they", "sisters" etc.). Thus it is possible for the referrents to have different conversational statuses. For instance, "we" will often refer to utterer and addressee or utterer and absentee. This outcome is coded by combining the status codes in the order given above, separated with a + sign. For instance $pro:1p:utt+cnv+abs.

One final piece of information required when coding the person referring expressions is to whether the expression was uttered as part of a retrace or not. If any p.r.e. is then retraced or coded, it is flagged with a - at the end of the code. This allows the analyst the choice of considering attempts to refer (an illocutionary concept) or with linguistic data exactly as uttered. For instance:

```
*TBL:   <Dan-o ke ka> [/] Dan-o, ke ka!
%eng:   <Dan-o Look> [/] Dan-o Look!
%pre:   $nam:dan-o:adr- $nam:dan-o:adr
```

27.11. Polish

Richard Weist has contributed these data in **CHAT** from three children learning Polish. There are six files for each child. The children were taperecorded at the following ages: Marta at 1;7, 1;8, 1;8, 1;9, 1;9, and 1;10. 2; Bartosz at 1;7, 1;7, 1;8, 1;8, 1;11, and 1;11; and Kubus at 2;1, 2;2, 2;2, 2;4, 2;4, and 2;6. All of the children were from middle class families raised in the urban environment of Poznan, Poland. In general, their parents were highly educated. The children were recorded in their homes (typically an apartment) by two experimenters. One of the experimenters carried a small bag containing the tape recorder and the other took context notes which were integrated during transcription. In addition to the three child language data sets, we have included a description of the coding. The basic unit of data was a text line, a gloss, and a translation. Context notes are included where available. Because of the use of morphemic glosses, the data are coded morphemically in a way that is very useful for comparative analysis.

This project was supported by NSF, NICHHD, and the Kosciuszko Foundation. Zbigniew Nadstoga and Emilia Konieczna-Tou entered the data. Publications that use these data should cite Weist, Wysocka, Witkowska-Stadnik, Buczowska, and Konieczna (1984) or Weist and Witkowska-Stadnik (1986).

27.12. Russian

Ekaterina Protassova of the Russian Academy of Education has contributed data from recordings of her daughter Varvara, born on October 1, 1982, in Moscow, the first and the only child in the family. Her father Alexander (Sasha) is a book illustrator and her mother Ekaterina (Katja) is a psycholinguist. The child was brought up at home. Some days of the week grandparents have taken care of hers, sometimes she spent several hours in a family with two children and a dog. Her grandparents lived at the time in the same flat, both were scientists. The girl's name is Varvara, which is a Russian equivalent for Barbara, a more common short variant is Varja, diminutives are Varen'ka, Varjusha, Varjunja, Varjushen'ka, maybe others, appelative is Var', Varjun', Varjush. At seven months, Varvara used her first word which was to call herself Ain'ka, so sometimes this name is used by parents.

All of the recordings were taken during 90 minute periods in the usual situations at home or in the summer house by a simple recorder and written down immediately afterwards in Russian. The lag between recordings is about 1.5 months between the first records and about 6 months between the last records. The roman transliteration and the English translation (for the three first seances, which are most difficult to understand) or comments date from the recent time. Childish sound modifications and shortenings of the conventional words are usually transmitted, at least until the forth session.

27.13. Spanish

27.13.1. Linaza

Jose Linaza of the University of Madrid has contributed data from a longitudinal case study of his son Juan between ages 2 and 4. Juan's younger brother Jaime also talks in the files collected at the later ages. The names of the files reflect Juan's ages in years and months. The data were reformatted into **CHAT** in 1992. Most of the files have the father as the major interlocutor. However, the mother and another researcher speak with the child on some of the tapes. Juan's speech is often transcribed in a way that captures phonological deletions. For example, "Orge" is used for "Jorge" and so on. Before doing analyses for lexical items, the researcher take a good look at these alternative spellings. The marking of clauses or utterances in the original was not always consistent, so counts such as MLU would not be appropriate.

27.13.2. Marrero

These 12 files are the first part of a corpus on Spanish child language in CHAT format. The aim of our work is the linguistic analysis (at the phonic, morphologic, syntactic, semantic and pragmatic levels) of the language of six normal children, from 1.8 to 8 years old. This longitudinal study started at the end of 1990. Transcription is orthographic, when it is possible. When the child form does not correspond to a standard word, but we can identify the unit, the transcription is as close as feasible to the orthographic representation.

We don't use the error mark ([*]) on the main line; instead, we employ the "%err" dependent tier, with the following structure:

<locus> non standard word = standard word

Files beginning by IDA belong to a child living in the Canary Islands, where a specific dialect of Spanish is spoken (similar, in some aspects, to the Caribbean Spanish). The trancription was made, however, maintaining the orthographic rules of standard Spanish, but indications about the pronunciation of some sounds are attached.

27.13.3.   Montes

The data being contributed consist of transcripts of thirteen 30-45 minute audio recordings of a Spanish speaking child interacting with her parents in the child's home. The earliest recording was made when the child was 1;7.20 years of age and the last one when she was 2;11.14.

Biographical data. Koki is the first child of a middle-class professional couple. Both parents are linguists. At the time the tapes were made the parents had research and teaching jobs in a linguistics program in Patzcuaro, Mexico. The mother was out of the house from 9 to 1 and then again from 4 to 8 every evening. The father worked mostly at home. At the time the tapes were made Koki was the only child; however, during some of the later tapes, the mother is pregnant with her second child, and reference is made to this baby in some of the tapes.

Language background. The child, Koki, who is the researcher's own child, was acquiring Spanish as a first language. The father is American, his native language is English and he was learning Spanish at the time that the tapes were being made. However, even when he was not fluent in the language, he usually addressed Koki in Spanish. The mother is Argentine, her native language is Spanish, but she had acquired English as a child living in various English speaking countries. The parents spoke in English to each other but both spoke mostly in Spanish to Koki. Koki was born in Poland, where her parents were teaching. When she was six months old the family left Poland and went on an extended trip to Argentina where they stayed until just before Koki's first birthday. During this time they lived with the mother's family in a Spanish-speaking household. The family lived briefly in the States, for a period of two months (Koki 1;1 - 1;3) and then moved to Patzcuaro, Michoacan, in Mexico, where the recordings were made. At the time the recordings were started they had been living in Patzcuaro for 4 and 1/2 months (Koki 1;7.20).

To summarize Koki's language background: she is acquiring Spanish as a first language. Everybody in the house speaks to her in Spanish, including her father who is learning Spanish. The Spanish spoken in her surroundings is Mexican Spanish; however, the mother speaks Argentine Spanish. Koki's Spanish seems to be mostly Mexican. At first, the earlier tapes, there are some phonological features from Argentine Sp. and also lexical items. In the later tapes there are Argentine lexical items, but her phonology is mostly Mexican. Her regular contacts with Mexican speakers include a Mexican woman who comes in daily to help around the house and two little girls, slightly older, who live down the street and with whom Koki plays often.

The parents did not keep a diary record of Koki's language development, but notes indicate that her first "words" were at around 10 months. A lexicon of her productive vocabulary drawn up on June 15, one month before the first recording, lists approximately 60 words.

Data collection. The data were gathered with no particular purpose other than to document the development of the child's "communicative competence". The tape recorder was turned on during "play sessions" or daily routines (lunch, bath, etcc.) and no attempt was made to elicit any forms or test her competence. The tape recorder was always in full view and was a big source of interest although it did not appear to inhibit the child. However, it did have some influence on the interaction since very often when the child would make moves to grab the microphone or the tape recorder the mother would attempt to distract her by calling attention to some other objects or would initiate some other activity. These play sessions are "naturalistic", but they are also special child-centered situations. The adults tend to follow the child's lead and the child, in general, is the one who proposes and initiates activities. When both parents are together they tend to each interact with the child rather than with each other. Talk between the parents was tacitly assumed to be some sort of interruption. Note that when the tape recorder was not on the same type of activity often occurred. Thus, the recorded events were felt to be natural or typical of that type of situation. However, unrecorded play sessions were more susceptible to outside interruptions than were recorded ones.

Transcription. The transcripts presented are in **CHAT** format. Pauses are indicated by # plus seconds and tenths of seconds in brackets. Following suggestions in the literature for conversations with young children, only pauses between utterances greater than 2secs. were marked. The transcripts were made from audio-recordings. During the recording sessions one of the parents (usually the mother) made notes about the context of utterances, concurrent actions, etc. However, these notes usually note major, salient actions and details are lost which often are crucial for giving a full interpretation of what went on.

Contents:

File	Date	Age	Duration
K01	21 Jul 1980	1;7.20	30 mins
K02	19 Sep 1980	1;9.18	30 mins
K03	26 Nov 1980	1;11.25	30 mins
K04	30 Jan 1981	2;1.29	30 mins
K05	28 Feb 1981	2;2.27	30 mins
K06	22 Mar 1981	2;3.21	10 mins
K07	19 Apr 1981	2;4.18	30 mins
K08	25 May 1981	2;5.24	45 mins
K09	11 Jun 1981	2;6.10	30 mins
K10	11 Jul 1981	2;7.10	30 mins
K11	10 Aug 1981	2;8.9	30 mins
K12	19 Sep 1981	2;9.18	30 mins
K13	15 Nov 1981	2;11.14	45 mins

K01 and K13 are the end-points of the tapes done with this child, however there are about twenty additional tapes of in-between stages in the process of transcription.

Publications that make use of this corpus should cite Montes (1987; 1992). The author would appreciate receiving a citation notice of any use made of this corpus, and, if possible, a copy of the paper or article.

27.13.4.   Romero-Contreras

This project has been funded by the researchers themselves and the University of the Americas.   This corpus is part of a data base that we are gathering of Spanish as a first language in naturalistic contexts, for the development of descriptive studies of the process of the construction of communicative competence in Spanish monolinguals.

Data Collection. Data were collected of the child in daily interaction with his family at his/her home. Samples were videotaped. Children in this project are selected according to the age range defined (6 months to 7 years). They, as well as their parents, have to be native Spanish speakers, residents of Mexico City for the last 5 years. Subjects have to be free of any condition that may suggest abnormal development or a family history that may indicate a language impairment.   Children should be free of strong cultural influences other than Mexican; therefore, those children attending bicultural schools are not eligible.

Transcription procedure. Transcription was done directly from the videotapes with the aid of field diaries for other contextual information. Several passes of the video were often necessary. Regular spelling was the rule, except for uninteligible or child specific utterances. No translation into English has been included. All min**CHAT** conventions have been followed and other **CHAT** codes, when necessary, have been used. Warning: Contextual information is still limited; copies of videos are available under request.

In the filename, the first and second digits stand for the lower limit of the age range of the child at the beginning of the study, expressed in years (first digit) and months (second digit). The third and fourth digits stand for sex. Twelve children are included in each age range, therefore numbers used are from 00 to 11, odd numbers are females, even numbers are males. The fifth digit stands for the child's school option, this is, the kind of school the child attends or is going to attend: 0 = public school, 9 = private school. The sixth digit stands for the part of the corpus in the file, this data is coded progressively: 1 = first part, 2 = second part, and so forth.

Three @Stim codes are used: Sinclair lógica, Sinclair fisica, and Sinclair simbólico. These codes refer to specific tasks used with the children in order to assess their cognitive development taken from Sinclair (1982)

Biographical Data for subject in file 200691.   Subject's age at the beginning of the study was 2 years. He was a male. He had one older and one younger sisters. He was enrolled in a private preschool.   His parents were middle upper class.   The father was a biochemichal engineer currently working in the Foreign Trade Division of a Foreign bank. The mother was a Speech and Language therapist. They were Catholics.

All the familiy, except for the father who grew in Monterrey, Nuevo Leon, until some years before getting married, has always lived in Mexico City.   The family lives in an urban home with all facilities: kitchen, three bathrooms, four bedrooms, garage, garden, etc.   The child, at the moment of the study, shared his room with his older sister (5 years) and had for himself and his siblings a game-room full of toys of all kinds. The child likes to watch movies, the same ones over and over. His favorite activities include ball games, playing musical toy instruments, story telling, book reading and other age appropriate games.

Users of this corpus are asked to cite (Romero, Santos & Pellicer, 1992). We ask potential users of our data to give notice in advance to the authors, outlining the purpose of the study and specific uses to the corpus.

Pseudonyms: no pseudonyms have been used, nor need to be used. Informants have given consent for the use of their data.

27.14. Swedish

The 74 computerized transcription files contained in this second release of the Swedish corpus relate to the project "Databasorienterade studier i svensk barnspraaksutveckling" (Database oriented studies of Swedish child language development), in which the language development in five monolingual Swedish children is analysed. The project is supported by the Swedish Research Council for the Humanities and Social Sciences (HSFR), grant F 783/91 and F 517/92. The project leader is Sven Strömqvist; research assistants are Ulla Richtoff, Åsa Nordqvist, and Lennart Andersson, all at the Department of Linguistics, University of Göteborg, Sweden. A comprehensive guide to the Swedish corpus is presented in Strömqvist et al. 1993.

The five children under study grow up in middle-class families on the west coast of Sweden. The families speak standard Swedish with a modest touch of the regional variant. The recorded material relates to a wide range of activity types: everyday activities in the home (such as meals, bedtime procedures, cooking, washing, etc); freeplay; story telling; as well as adult-child interaction; child-child interaction; and soliloquy.

Data collection for two of the children - a boy Markus from 1;3.19 to 6;0.09, and a girl Eva from 1;0.21 to 3;9.23 - is already completed. The data from Markus and Eva, who are siblings, constitute a sub-corpus of the Swedish corpus "Strömqvist's corpus". Data collection from the other three children - two boys Anton and Harry and a girl Thea - is in progress. Data collection started at 1;11.08 for Anton, at 1;5.26 for Harry and at 1;0.02 for Thea. The data from and Harry and Thea, who are siblings, and from Anton, who relates to a different family, constitute a second sub-corpus - "Richtoff's corpus".

Index. The name of each of the computerized transcription files reflects the name of the child and his age (in months and days) at the time of the recording. The present release of the corpus contains 74 transcription files: 28 from Markus (ma15_19.cha to ma33_29.cha), 20 from Anton (ant23_08.cha to ant34_04.cha) and 26 from Harry (har18_20.cha to har35_07.cha). Below, we list these three sets of files together with the corresponding MLU values for the child tiers.

Markus	MLU
ma15_19.cha	1.885
ma16_27.cha	1.287
ma18_10.cha	2.158
ma19_25.cha	1.395
ma20_05.cha	1.183
ma21_03.cha	1.151
ma21_07.cha	1.574
ma22_14.cha	1.815
ma22_25.cha	1.993
ma23_00.cha	2.751
ma23_12.cha	3.013
ma23_25.cha	3.556
ma24_09.cha	4.257
ma24_16.cha	4.132
ma24_25.cha	3.545
ma26_05.cha	3.878
ma26_10.cha	4.440
ma26_17.cha	4.148
ma27_09.cha	4.689
ma27_28.cha	4.549
ma28_09.cha	3.828
ma28_18.cha	4.125
ma30_20.cha	4.320
ma30_25.cha	3.700
ma31_24.cha	3.817
ma32_02.cha	4.584
ma32_08.cha	5.468
ma33_29.cha	6.224

Anton	MLU
ant23_08.cha	1.035
ant24_13.cha	1.176
ant24_26.cha	1.168
ant25_21.cha	1.371
ant26_10.cha	1.478
ant27_00.cha	1.492
ant27_21.cha	1.376
ant28_03.cha	1.415
ant28_15.cha	1.575
ant28_28.cha	1.573
ant29_08.cha	1.568
ant30_02.cha	1.952
ant30_15.cha	2.142
ant31_03.cha	2.151
ant31_19.cha	1.867
ant32_02.cha	2.269
ant32_11.cha	2.428
ant32_29.cha	2.539
ant33_18.cha	2.300
ant34_04.cha	2.546

Harry	MLU
har18_20.cha	1.223
har19_09.cha	1.121
har20_26.cha	1.143
har21_15.cha	1.201
har22_18.cha	1.231
har23_18.cha	1.213
har24_16.cha	1.301
har25_10.cha	1.409
har26_00.cha	1.455
har26_18.cha	1.482
har27_09.cha	1.824
har28_02.cha	2.088
har28_23.cha	2.596
har29_17.cha	2.439
har30_10.cha	2.066
har31_04.cha	2.543
har31_23.cha	3.248
har32_11.cha	3.603
har32_25.cha	3.927
har32_27.cha	3.027
har33_08.cha	3.435
har33_10.cha	3.845
har33_24.cha	3.449
har33_26.cha	4.324
har34_18.cha	3.638
har35_07.cha	3.969

Transcription conventions, lexicon files, and coding. All main tiers (both child and adult) have been morphologically segmented by means of the symbols # (prefix), + (lexical compound) and - (suffix). The utterance delimiters ! and ? indicate exclamation and question, respectively. A full stop is used as a default utterance delimiter and but has no specific linguistic meaning. It should be read as ambiguous with respect to functions like statement, request, etc. Utterances have been identified on intonational criteria. In the present release, only the 28 Markus files are checked for reliability. The reliability check indicates a breaking point at 18;10. In the transcripts before ma18_10.cha the two project transcribers agreed on utterance segmentation in 80-85% of the cases, whereas after 18_10 they agreed in 96-99% of the cases.

The transcripts are morphologically oriented and take Swedish orthography as a point of departure but allow for deviations from the orthographic norm in order to capture qualities of spoken Swedish. In particular, we have tried to avoid the fallacy of overrepresenting or underrepresenting the child's knowledge of morphology in terms of the adult norm. The three children so far transcribed vary considerably in acquisition structure and way of speaking and this is reflected in the transcripts. The word forms in the transcripts of Markus are, as a rule, sufficiently transparent to be succesfully interpreted by a speaker of Swedish. In contrast, several of the early transcripts of Harry are less transparent and the majority of the transcripts of Anton are rather opaque. As a guide to these opaque word forms we have constructed a set of lexicon files for Harry and Anton. Each of Harry's 26 and Anton's 20 transcript files is matched with a lexicon file containing a list of the opaque word forms in the transcript file, the transcriber's interpretation of the opaque word form in terms of the closest adult/target word form (the child's form is often ambiguous and several interpretations/target forms are rendered) and the token frequency of the opaque word form. There is a strong tendency for ambiguous forms to be among the most frequent forms, generally. The file "har32_25.cha" has a matching lexicon file "har32_25.lex", which, among many other entries and lines, contains the line "27 e aer/en/ett" which means: 27 tokens of the transcribed form "e" which is used by the child as sometimes "aer" (copula:PRES), sometimes "en" (indefinite article:common gender), and sometimes "ett" (indefinite article:neuter gender).

In the present version of the text files, three things are coded: time, word accents, and feedback. First, a %tim tier is used to indicate the temporal location of an utterance in minutes and seconds from the start of the recording (e.g. "32:12" means 32 minutes and 12 seconds). Second, a %wac: word accent tier is used to code word accents. So far, the marked word accent, "accent 2" (grave), is coded only when it occurs in utterance focus position. The code used for marking accent 2 in focus position is WAC2:FOC. Unclear cases are marked WAC2:FOC?. (The auditive identification of accent 2 contours is far from unproblematic. The presence of only a %wac tier indicates an instance of accent 2 on which the two transcribers agreed. For cases where there was a disagreement between the two transcribers, an additional %wan tier is used to indicate a conflicting judgment.) Third, a %nfb tier is used to code so-called narrow feedback morphemes. Only feedback giving morphemes (such as hm, naehae) have been coded so far. The code used for marking feedback givers is ``FBG''. Unclear cases are marked ``FBG?''. In addition to the three coding tiers mentioned, a fourth %aaf tier is used to indicate that one or several word forms on the main tier have been subjected to acoustic analysis and are stored in an acoustic analysis file. The acoustic analysis tier provides information necessary for the identification of the matching aaf file(s). See further below for more information on the acoustic archive containing these files. Whereas %tim: is a standard option from the CHILDES manual, %wac:, %nfb:, and %aaf: are not. The three latter codes have so far only been used for project internal purposes.

An acoustic archive. In addition to the computerized transcription files, we have created a computerized acoustic archive containing a sample of a little more than 500 disyllabic word forms from Markus 18;10 to 26;10. The archive is created in MacSpeech Lab environment. The sample contains both monomorphemic and dimorphemic word forms, the latter being either lexical compounds or stems plus an inflectional suffix. Further, the sample contains word forms which make up one-word utterances as well as word forms from the initial, medial or final position in multi-word utterances. Copies of the acoustic archive can be obtained from Sven Strömqvist who welcomes comments and questions relating to the Swedish corpus.

Publications that make use of these data should cite (Plunkett & Strömqvist, 1992) and (Strömqvist, Richtoff & Anderson, 1993).

27.15. Tamil

The files in this directory are from a longitudinal study of a single Tamil child conducted by Dr. R. Narasimhan of the Tata Institute of Fundamental Research in Bombay and by R. Vaidyanathan of the Audiology and Speech Therapy School of the Nair Hospital in Bombay. They were contributed to the CHILDES in computerized form in 1984 and reformatted into **CHAT** in 1986. The files are taken from language interaction between a child and her parents during unstructured caretaking situations.The interactions were audiotaped in her home over a period of 24 months, from the time the child was 9 months old to the time she was 33 months old. The recording relates to 25 sessions in all at approximately biweekly intervals. The typed transcripts of the corpus are about 450 pages. The language is Tamil – one of the Dravidian languages spoken in South India. Transcription has been done phonemically. Complete English glosses and contextual notes are provided.

Subject. Vanitha, the target child in these transcripts, was born on June 6, 1979. She is the first born child – and the only child during the period of the data collection – of a Tamil-speaking couple living in Bombay. Both the father and the mother of the child are graduates and are employed. The father is an engineering graduate and works as a civil engineer. The mother, a graduate of science, works as a research officer in a forensic laboratory. The child's father was born and brought up in Tamilnadu, while her mother was born and brought up in Nagpur. The family belongs to the middle socioeconomic group.

During the data collection period, when the parents were away working, Vanitha was looked after by a caretaker whose mother tongue was the same as that of the family. The caretaker was the mother of a 15-year-old girl and 12-year-old boy. When at home, during holidays, Kiran, the neighbor's child (girl) used to visit Vanitha and play with her. Although Kiran's mother tongue was Telugu she used to interact with Vanitha in Hindi.

Vanitha's mother was transferred to Nagpur when the child was 20 months old. The mother and child stayed in Nagpur for ten months. During this period they came to Bombay to visit the father every two months, at least. Vanitha joined a nursery class at Nagpur when she was 25 months old. The medium of instruction in the class was English. Sree, Vanitha's maternal uncle's daughter of the same age, also attended the class with her. Vanitha's maternal uncle and aunt work as doctors in two different hospitals in Bombay. And they used to visit Vanitha's family often. Her grandmother used to visit her family frequently also.

Recording Procedure. Data collection of the parent-child interaction was started when Vanitha was almost exactly nine months old. Home visits were made by R.V. for data collection at intervals of approximately two weeks (but with some gaps when the child was away from the city). R.V. was a stranger to the household till the start of this field study. The home visits lasted for about two hours during which time about 45 minutes of audio recording was made using a portable cassette recorder (Orion, model MC) with a built-in condenser microphone.

The parents were informed that they and the child were being audio-taped for a field-study of parent-child interaction in the early stages of language behavior acquisition. They were asked to interact with the child as they would normally do in the absence of the observer. The recordings were made inside the house while the parents were involved in unstructured caretaking (feeding, dressing, and so forth) and free play situations. During the recording sessions R.V. was essentially a silent observer of the parent-child interactions. The audio recordings were supplemented by manually written notes. The observer kept a running account of the child's and parents' actions, and of all interactions including the objects and events referred to in them. Comments were noted down on the situational contexts in which utterances were made and also the nonverbal behavior of the interacting partners.

Transcription. Phonemic transcriptions of the utterances from the tapes as well as the manual notes, including intonations (where relevant), were made by R.V. using his linguistic background: (R.V. is a trained linguist who works in the Audiology and Speech Pathology Division of one of the major hospitals in Bombay). Initial typescripts prepared by him of his transcriptions were keyed into a computer (DEC 1077 system at NCSDCT) using a text-processing and text-composition software, DIP, developed at NCSDCT. The printouts from the computer were then used as working copies by three research students to verify the completeness and correctness of the transcribed corpus against the original tape recordings.

The corpus consists of transcriptions of the language behavior interaction in the verbal dimension only. Intonation contours are not marked (except rarely, to identify questions), nor are the gestural accompaniments of speech. Clearly both these are important and relevant inputs to language behavior acquisition. They are not included in the corpus, because our primary interest is in the analysis of the corpus in the verbal dimension

The English translations of the utterances that accompany their phonemically transcribed Tamil originals should be used with great caution. These are primarily intended to give a rough idea of the on-going interaction. The English translations do not convey the structures and patterns of the originals faithfully. Hence, all inferences about the syntax and semantics of the parent-child interaction should be drawn only from the original Tamil versions. Nursery terms/idioms in Tamil have not been translated into "equivalent" ones in English because such correspondences for the most part are not valid. Many Tamil expressions are very culture-dependent and quite often untranslatable into English "oral speech". In some cases Tamil terms have been left untranslated and a directory of translations has been separately provided.

Segments of conversations between the parents, and of conversations in Hindi (between Vanitha and her parents, or between Vanitha and her friends) have been omitted in this corpus, except where they blend with and are necessary to establish and maintain context. Also, nonverbal vocalizations, singing and other rhythmic/ rhyming vocal behavior have not in general been transcribed except when they form an integral part of the context for the ongoing verbal interaction.

Several ancillary files provide additional information about this corpus. Special words are found in 0lexicon.doc. The phonemic inventory of Tamil is presented in 0phon.doc. And the file 0pragindex.doc is an index to each of the various scenes in the corpus in terms of the nature of the detailed pragmatic activity occurring in each.

Publications that make use of this corpus should cite Narasimhan (1981).

27.16. Turkish

This directory contains data collected by Ayhan Aksu and Dan Slobin in Turkey. The "frogs" directory has descriptions of a picture book describing the adventures of a boy and his frog. The "Berkeley" directory has files from the project conducted in the early 1970's comparing semantic development across cultures.

27.16.1.   Berkeley

These data were gathered in 1972-73 in Istanbul, under the direction of Dan I. Slobin, with support from The Grant Foundation. All of the children came from urban, professional families in which at least one parent had a college education. They were selected at four-month age intervals, from 2;0 to 4;4. Some of the children were visited a second time, four months later, resulting in a full age range of 2;0 to 4;8. The first visit occurred within one week on either side of the day of the month corresponding to the child's birthday. Children were visited in their homes or preschools over the period of a week, during which they were given a battery of cognitive and language tasks, as described in Slobin (1982). The overall study included Turkish, Serbo-Croatian, Italian, and English. The Turkish phase of the study was designed in collaboration with Ayhan Aksu-Koc'.

These transcripts represent all of the adult-child spontaneous and guided conversation during the course of those visits. (A number of standardized comprehension questions are interspersed in the conversations.) The interviewer was female (either Ayla Algar or Alev Alatli'); as indicated at the top of each sample, other adults and children took part in some sessions.   All words are in lower case; only proper names are capitalized. Uncertain transcriptions are enclosed in parentheses; standard equivalents of child or colloquial forms are given in square brackets. Child utterances are separated into morphemes by hyphens. Diacritics are marked by the apostrophe which indicates umlaut following o and u, dot following I, dotless following i, macron following g, and cedilla following c and s.

These data were entered onto computer and coded with support from the National Science Foundation (BNS-8812854), using facilities provided by the Institute of Cognitive Studies and the Institute of Human Development of the University of California at Berkeley. The transcripts were typed and morphemicized by Abdul Bolat and Mine Ternar; they were checked and grammatically coded by Aylin Ku'ntay. Public use of these data should credit Dan I. Slobin, The Grant Foundation, and NSF. Further information can be obtained from Dan I. Slobin.

27.16.2.   Frogs

This directory has descriptions of the "Frog Story" picture book by Turkish children and adults. The data was collected and contributed by Ayhan Aksu-Koc'.

28. Narrative Data

The data in this directory are narratives, currently mostly derived from retellings of stories in books and movies.

28.1. Gopnik

This directory contains data that were contributed by Myrna Gopnik of McGill University to the CHILDES in August of 1988. They include story book descriptions from normal children between the ages of 2 and 5.

The filenames use this syntax:

        Storytype = f (free) or p (prompted) or q (questionnaire) or g (game)
        StudentID = 3 digit number
        Booktype = 1 (free) 2-5 (one of four books)
        Session   = 1, 2, or 3 (which test session)

ID	Sex	Birthdate	Teacher	Verified
01	F	27-10-78	LS	Y
02	F	12-08-78	LS	Y
03	F	01-07-79	LS	Y
04	F	10-02-79	LS	Y
05	M	29-11-78	LS	Y
06	M	23-10-78	LS	Y
07	M	31-08-78	LS	Y
08	F	17-08-79	LS	Y
09	M	06-12-79	BL	Y
10	M	13-12-79	BL	N
11	M	14-11-80	LD	N
12	M	19-01-81	LD	N
13	M	26-05-81	BL	N
14	M	25-07-80	BL	Y
15	M	05-01-80	BL	Y
16	F	20-08-79	LS	Y
17	F	29-03-79	LS	N
18	F	19-02-80	BL	Y
46	F	21-01-81	LD	Y
47	M	02-04-80	HD	N
48	M	01-03-81	LD	N
49	F	17-02-82	LG	N
50	F	01-06-80	XY	N
51	F	09-10-79	BL	N
52	M	18-02-82	SG	N
53	F	20-04-82	SG	N
54	M	28-01-80	BL	N
55	F	01-01-80	XY	N
56	M	12-10-80	BL	N
57	F	19-03-82	LG	N
58	M	28-05-80	BL	N
59	F	06-03-81	LD	N

| 60 | M | 31-08-82 | LG | Y |
| 61 | F | 11-03-82 | XY | N |

Publications that make use of this corpus should cite Gopnik (1989).

28.2. Hicks

The narratives in this directory were collected by Deborah Hicks in the context of a study of primary school children's narrative genre skills, focusing on their ability to produce a range of kinds of narratives. They were donated to the CHILDES in 1988. In the study, children from three primary grade levels – first, second, and fifth – were shown a shortened version of the silent film, "The Red Balloon." After viewing the film, children were asked to tell the film's events in three different ways: as a factual news report, an ongoing event case, and a more embellished story. These three narrative genres are representative of what Heath (1983) terms "key" narratives, or narratives which are found crossculturally in children's language learning environments. The narrative data were coded by utterances for linguistic forms that might mark genre differences.

This directory contains four subdirectories: 1st, 2nd, 5th, and del. The first three are taken from first, second, and fifth graders in a Cambridge, Massachusetts. The fourth is taken from a lower-class group in Delaware. For comparison with the Delaware children, these 12 files in the 1st grade directory were used: 4, 5, 12, 16, 27, 29, 30, 35, 38, 39, 40, and 42.

The children with files in the subdirectories called 1st, 2nd, and 5th were first grade, second grade, and fifth grade students in a private elementary school in Cambridge, Massachusetts. The majority of students attending this school were members of middle class families in which one or both parents were working professionals, so that these children could be considered members of mainstream culture (Heath, 1983). The classrooms were somewhat progressive in nature, so that children were free to choose from a range of activities those that they would work on. Many of the activities which children performed regularly were language activities, such as recounting on tape a story of how the world was created, writing about "what we did in science class", and recounting personal experiences during sharing time episodes. The narrative genre tasks were thus presented to the children as one of the many options available, and in all but a few cases, children were willing and eager to leave the room for the tasks.

Before performing any of the narrative tasks, children were told that they would watch a film and would then tell what happened in the film in three different ways. In the case of the online narration task, children listened to the experimenter saying "This is [child's name] and Deborah, sportscasters, and we're gonna say everything we see happening in the film. I'm gonna start off and then [child's name] is gonna take over." The child then watched the 3-minute segment of the film and then the experimenter started the narration by saying "The little boy and the red balloon are going past a church steeple. And they're coming to a bakery shop. The little boy is looking inside the bakery shop. Now he's checking in his pocket to see if he has enough money to buy something to eat. Looks good. Now he's walking into the bakery shop." Then the experimenter turned to the child and asked, "Can you take over now and be the sportscaster?" The order of the report and event cast tasks was randomly selected within grade levels.

The storytelling task was performed separately from the report and event cast, in a session that took place approximately one hour after the completion of the first two tasks.

This particular research design was chosen on the grounds that performance of three consecutive tasks would be too demanding for many of the children in the study, particularly the five year old children. For the storytelling task, the leading given by the experimenter was "This is [child's name] and Deborah, and we're gonna be storytellers and tell the story of The Red Balloon. I'm gonna start off and then [child's name] is gonna take over." During this, the experimenter holds a "storybook" which has on the front cover a picture from the film but which has neither words nor pictures inside. The experimenter then says "The Red Balloon. Once upon a time there was a little boy who lived in Paris, France. One day, on his way to the bus stop, he found this big beautiful red balloon. He wanted the balloon to be his friend." Then the experimenter turns to the child and says, "Can you take over now and be the storyteller?" At this point, the experimenter passes the storybook to the child.

In an attempt to create some degree of homogeneity in the data, in addition to providing an interaction with the highest possible degree of ecological validity, children were provided with a great deal of contextual support for the tasks. As was noted in the introductory section to this chapter, children were reminded before each task of the particular narrative "voice" they were to assume: that of a news reporter, a sportscaster, or a storyteller. For the storytelling task, children were also given a storybook containing only a single picture on the outside cover, which they were encouraged to hold during the story narration.

The data obtained from the study were transcribed in **CHAT** and analyzed using the **CLAN** computer programs for child language analysis. The entire narration was divided into clauses with one clause on each line of the **CHAT** transcript. The segmentation of the narrative data was done on the basis of clause units of analysis, following Berman and Slobin (1986). Clause units were defined as any linguistic utterance containing a predicate, so that the following would all be considered separate units of analysis: "he climbed up the stairs", "when the boy was inside the bakery shop", and "the boys who stole the balloon". Segmentation of complement clauses was done following Chomsky (1969) so that the utterance "he saw the balloon floating by the door" was segmented into "he saw" and "the balloon floating by the door." Utterances containing verbs with three arguments such as "he told the balloon to stay by the door" were segmented as "he told the balloon" and "to stay by the door".

The narrative data were examined in terms of children's use of specific linguistic forms representing three basic subsystems: a) syntactic constructions, b) temporal expressions and/or event relationships, and c) indexical clauses, or clauses referring to setting, atmosphere, and character internal states (see the coding manual). The analysis of syntactic constructions was designed to assess possible genre differences in the syntactic complexity of event casting, reportative, and story narratives. The analysis of expressions of temporality and event relationships was designed to examine genre differences in how temporal and logical relationships between events were expressed in the discourse. Finally, the analysis of indexical clauses was an attempt to assess genre differences in how children went beyond the basic narration tasks to provide evaluative and/or descriptive information about events in the narrative.

The file "0codes.doc" contains further information on coding for temporality, events, indices, and intensifiers. Publications that make use of this corpus should cite Hicks (1990).

28.3. Wolf-Hemphill

This directory contains longitudinal data on 30 children whose discourse development from ages 6-8 was studied by Dennis Palmer Wolf and Lowry Hemphill. The work was funded by a larger project, "Foundations for Language Assessment in Spontaneous Speech," funded by the National Institutes of Health.

Subjects. Subjects were selected at age 1 from a larger sample of 100 children participating in the MacArthur Individual Differences Project. Information about subject recruitment and characteristics of the original sample can be found in Snow (1989) and Dale, Bates, Reznick, and Morisset (1989). The present sample of 30 children is 50% girls and 50% boys; all are white English-speakers. Fourteen of the children are from working class families; sixteen are from middle class families. All attained milestones for early language development (e.g., MLU) at appropriate ages.

Procedure. Children were videotaped in their home each year at 6, 7, and 8, participating in a range of narrative and other discourse tasks. This corpus includes data only for the wordless picturebook narration task. Procedures for eliciting the narratives were to have the child look through Mercer Mayer's wordless "frog story" picture book entitled "A Boy, a Dog, A Frog," to develop a sense of the entire story depicted. Then the experimenter asked, "Can you tell me the story, looking through the book?" If the child seemed to have trouble producing narration at any point, the experimenter asked, "What happened next?"

Transcription. Transcribers trained in **CHAT** conventions prepared the transcripts, using the vidoetaped frog story narrations. Utterance boundary decisions were based on intonation contours and pauses. Utterances are broken into grammatical clauses using [c] as a marker of clause boundaries. Each clause is coded for narrative function (e.g., event, reported speech, durative/descriptive), for verb forms, and for use of connectives. Research based on this corpus should cite Miranda, Hemphill, Camp, and Wolf (1992).

29. NonCHAT Data

The CHILDES database also includes the complete text of several books and articles. In each case, the system has been granted permission from the publishers and/or authors to include these books in the database. Working with the CHILDES, Roy Higginson of Iowa State University has also developed an extensive computerized bibliography of research in child language development which is included as a part of the database.

29.1. Cornell Corpus

Donald Hayes of the Cornell Sociology Department has donated a large collection of text files from a variety of printed and spoken sources. The corpus is designed not for the study of conversational interaction, but for the analysis of lexical usage. Accordingly, the files utilize an entirely minimal form of encoding. The written texts are often small samples from larger books. The texts are first stratified into ten segments of equal length. For each segment, a simple random sample is drawn to identify the page (and where on that page) the sample is to begin. A 100-word sample is then taken, in complete consecutive sentences, making each sample text 1000 or more words in length. The majority of a category's texts come from its most common forms (e.g., according to Neilson ratings on TV; or from the highest circulation magazines and newspapers).

The types of books in the corpus are as follows:

1. Texts designed for preschoolers (preschbk).
2. Children's books for ages 9-12 (childbk).
3. British advanced books for ages 10-14 (britbkad).
4. British easy books for ages 10-14 (britbkez).
5. Basal readers (basalrds).
6. Comic books (comics).
7. Magazines for adolescents (adolmags).
8. Top 20 magazines (top20mag).
9. Specialty magazines (specmags).
10. Newspapers (newpapr).

The types of media recordings include:

1. Preschool TV programs (preschtv).
2. Song lyrics from popular music (lyrics).
3. TV re-runs popular with children (childtv).
4. Prime-time adult TV shows (adulttv).
5. TV cartoon shows (cartoons).
6. News and Educational TV (hibrowtv).

The samples of informal speech are distributed in the English directory. Some samples are taken from the Kuczaj, MacWhinney, and Sachs corpora in the CHILDES database.

The samples of formal speech are mostly from trials. The first five are from the Patty Hearst trial in 1976.

1. Defense psychiatrist (patybail).
2. Prosecution psychiatrist (patypros).

3. Other witnesses (otherwit).
4. Expert witnesses (exprtwit).
5. The judge (judge).
6. U.S. Senate Hearings on abortion (abortion).
7. A civil trial in Ithaca, NY in 1940 (1940tril).

Papers that make use of these data should cite Hayes (1988).

29.2. Isaacs

This directory contains the complete text of Isaacs (1930) <u>Intellectual Growth In Young Children</u> and Isaacs (1933) <u>Social Development in Young Children</u>. Isaacs recorded interesting interactions with children often in nearly verbatim form. These data are rich guides to many aspects of cognitive development, reasoning skills, inferencing, and scientific reasoning in school aged children. The children's ages range from 2;11 to 7;5. There are selections from both boys and girls. These are upper-middle and upper-class British children in a school setting. These selections are entered into the computer as a series of dated episodes. Please cite Isaacs (1930) or Isaacs (1933) when using these data.

29.3. MacBates

These data were gathered using a picture description task developed and used by Brian MacWhinney and Elizabeth Bates in 1975 in English, Italian, and Hungarian with adults and children aged 3, 4, and 5 years. The complete description of this study is given in MacWhinney and Bates (1978). The subjects saw nine sets of pictorial stimuli which could be described in terms of simple sentences. For example, Series 2 consists of three pictures of the same boy, which can be described by these three sentences:

> (a) A boy is running.
> (b) A boy is skiing.
> (c) A boy is swimming.

Series	Structure	
1	S V	A bear (mouse, bunny) is crying.
2	S V	A boy is running (swimming, skiing).
3	S V O	A monkey (squirrel, bunny) is eating a banana.
4	S V O	A boy is kissing (hugging, kicking) a dog.
5	S V O	A girl is eating an apple (cookie, ice cream).
6	S V L	A dog is in (on, under) a car.
7	S V L	A cat is on a table (bed, chair).
8	S V O I	A lady is giving a present (truck, mouse) to a girl.
9	S V O I	A cat is giving a flower to a boy (bunny, dog).

In this listing, the following abbreviations are used for the major elements of a sentence: S=subject, V=verb, O=object, L=object of the locative preposition and I=indirect object.

The three pictures in each series will be called frames. For example, (a) is the first frame, (b) is the second frame, and (c) is the third frame. In this particular series, the subject increases in givenness across the frames whereas the verb increases in newness. In Series 6 and 7, the verb is taken to include both the copular and the locative preposition. (In Hungarian the locative is a postposition or suffix rather that a preposition.)

In the 1978 experiment, there were 120 subjects: 40 Americans, 40 Hungarians, and 40 Italians. Within each language community, there were ten 3-year-olds, ten 4-year-olds, ten 5-year-olds, and ten adults. The chief focus of attention was upon the development in the 3-6 year period. The adult subjects were included as controls to see if any further developmental changes might be present after age 6 in use of these devices. Each group of ten subjects included five females and five males. The children were enrolled in nursery schools in Denver, Budapest, and Rome. There is every reason to believe that the children at each age were generally equal in terms of overall linguistic ability, because they were all normal, middle-class members of the majority culture and all resided in large metropolitan areas within what is commonly known as Western culture. Unfortunately, no cross-culturally valid measure of general linguistic ability is yet available, and is therefore difficult to show conclusively that the groups were equal in overall ability.

Before a subject was tested, the pictures were placed into the order in which they were to be administered. The order of the nine series of pictures within each series was also randomized. Following each series, a picture of a common object such as a bottle or a sailboat was inserted. This was done to break up any set (*Einstellung*) effects. Subjects were examined individually. Each subject was first seated next to the the experimenter at a table. The subject was told that he would be asked to tell about what he saw in some pictures. Adults were told to describe the pictures in a simple direct fashion. The experimenter showed the pictures to each subject one at a time in the sequence determined by the randomization procedure. Two probes were used: "Tell me about this picture" and "What's happening in this picture?" Use of the two probes was also randomized. Each session was tape-recorded in its entirety. If you use these data, please cite MacWhinney and Bates (1978).

29.4. Sterns

This German corpus is a nonCHAT set of diary notes by Clara and Wilhelm Stern on the development of their three children. These data were entered from original hand-written notes into computer files by Werner Deutsch of the Max Planck Institut in Nijmegen. They were contributed to the CHILDES in 1988. There are no plans to reformat the files into **CHAT**. The files have the following composition:

Hilde Stern (born April 7,1900)

Number	From - To	Age	Pages
I	07.04.1900 - 06.10.1901	0;00,00 - 1;05,30	177
II	11.10.1901 - 21.01.1902	1;06,04 - 1;09,14	229
III	21.01.1902 - 30.05.1902	1;09,14 - 2;01,23	187
IV	30.05.1902 - 09.02.1903	2;01,23 - 2;10,02	220
V	02.02.1903 - 17.10.1903	2;09,25 - 3;06,10	183
VI	13.10.1903 - 08.02.1904	3;06,12 - 3;10,01	187
VII	08.02.1904 - 21.08.1904	3;10,01 - 4;04,14	188
VIII	23.08.1904 - 05.05.1905	4;04,17 - 5;00,29	188
IX	11.05.1905 - 27.06.1906	5;01,04 - 6;02,20	216
X	14.07.1906 - 29.01.1908	6;03,07 - 7;09,22	186
XI	24.02.1908 - 25.06.1909	7;10,17 - 9;02,18	187
XII	11.08.1909 - 21.05.1912	9;04,04 - 12;01,14	205
XIII	09.07.1912 - 04.05.1913	12;03,02 - 13;00,27	105
Appendix "Wie ich Hilde sehe"			16

Günther Stern (-Anders) (born July 12, 1902)

Number	From - To	Age	Pages
I	13.07.1902 - 31.05.1904	0;00,01 - 1;10,19	205

II	04.06.1904 - 27.04.1905	1;10,23 - 2;09,15	189
III	04.05.1905 - 11.02.1907	2;10,22 - 4;06,30	190
IV	21.02.1907 - 30.06.1908	4;07,09 - 5;11,11	205
V	23.06.1908 - 16.04.1909	5;11,11 - 6;09,04	192
VI	15.05.1909 - 30.10.1909	6;10,03 - 7;03,18	197
VII	31.01.1911 - 27.07.1912	8;06,19 - 10;00,15	189
VIII	14.08.1912 - 23.02.1918	10;01,02 - 17;07,11	239

Eva (Michaelis-)Stern (born December 29, 1904)

Number	From - To	Age	Pages
I	15.01.1905 - 30.06.1908	0;00,18 - 3;06,01	282
II	03.07.1908 - 27.06.1912	3;06,04 - 7;05,28	215
III	08.12.1912 - 26.11.1915	7;11,09 - 9;10,28	258

Publications that make use of this corpus should cite Stern and Stern (1907).

29.5. Sulzby

These data were collected by Elizabeth Sulzby of Northwestern University in the project "Children's Emergent Abilities to Read Favorite Stories," (CEARFS) funded by the Spencer Foundation in 1981–1982. They contain discussions with children about their favorite books and narratives from the children about these books. They were collected in a nursery school setting. Some children were interviewed only once and some were interviewed a second time about 3 months later. This data is to be used only with the permission of the contributor. The ages of the children, the dates of the interviews, and their ages are as follows:

Sample	Age	Sample	Age	Sample	Age
Adam1	4;1.4	Eliza	3;5.19	Megan	3;7.16
Adam2	4;3.13	Erin	4;4.2	Michael	4;7.26
Amarie1	3;7.16	Gaby1	4;2.2	Milton	4;6.14
Amarie2	3;8.24	Gaby2	4;4.11	Patrick	2;7.19
Amy1	3;2.0	Jason	3;2.23	Ramin	4;7.22
Amy2	3;4.9	Jenni1	3;5.19	Rani	4;2.1
Andrew1	5;1.1	Jenni2	3;7.28	Raphael	4;7.10
Andrew2	5;3.8	Jessica.	2;4.17	Robert	3;11.0
Brian	4;7.26	Jillian	4;4.27	Robin	4;6.14
Bridget	3;4.20	Joanna1	4;3.28	Ryan	3;1.29
Chris1	2;7.19	Joanna2	4;6.5	Sapna	4;2.1
Chris2	2;9.29	Jose	4;7.22	Scott	4;3.10
Cindy	4;3.16	Joy	3;2.0	Scotty	4;5.18
Colin1	4;2.7	Kathy	4;3.28	Sean	3;10.4
Colin2	4;4.14	Kenny	4;4.9	Shawna1	4;3.16
Cory	3;10.4	Kevin	4;2.7	Shawna2	4;5.23
Danny.	4;4.9	Kimberly	3;6.24	Susan	3;9.27
Denise.	3;9.27	Laura	3;6.24	Terra	3;4.11
Dennis.	3;11.0	Leecie	3;1.29	Timmy	4;3.10
Devin1	3;4.20	Maria	4;2.2	Tina	3;7.16
Devin2	3;6.27	Mark	4;1.4	Wyatt1	3;2.23
		Matt	5;1.1	Wyatt2	3-4-30

30. Language Impairments

The directory on language impairments currently includes data both from children suffering from some form of language impairment and from adults suffering from aphasia. The data on aphasia will eventually be expanded. This expanded data set will then be linked with the CHILDES database and the expanded second language acquisition database into a larger database called TEXS (Text Exchange System).

30.1. Bliss

The Bliss directory consists of transcripts from 8 normal children and 7 language impaired children collected by Lynn Bliss at Wayne State University and formatted in **CHAT**. These data are not intended as comprehensive documentations of particular types of language disorders, but simply as illustrations of language disordered children from different ages and their normal comparisons. Dr. Bliss would like researchers to provide her with the results of any analyses that use these data.

Normal	Age	Impaired	Age
Aimee	5;4.0	Denise	5;7.0
Gary	11;8.0	Fred	5;9.0
Justin	4;6.0	Jim	8;0.0
Marjorie	2;3.0	Joel	3;0.0
Melissa	3;4.0	John	6;4.0
Meredith	2;5.0	Sarah	11;8.0
Trevor	4;3.0	Terra	4;11.0
Willie	6;1.0		

Publications that make use of this corpus should cite Bliss (1988).

30.2. CAP

This subdirectory contains transcripts gathered from 60 English, German, and Hungarian aphasics along with normal controls in the Comparative Aphasia Project directed by Elizabeth Bates. The transcripts are in **CHAT** format and large segments have full morphemic coding and error coding. Additional normal comparison groups for these data can be found in the \childes\noneng\macbates directory, which contains the data from MacWhinney and Bates (1978) on English, Italian, and Hungarian children and adults.

Procedure. All of the data were collected using a common procedure which is the "given-new" picture description task of MacWhinney and Bates (1978). This procedure was varied only slightly to allow the aphasic subjects to see three pictures in a series at once. Subjects saw nine sets of pictorial stimuli which could be described in terms of simple sentences. For example, Series 2 consists of three pictures of the same boy, which can be described by these sentences:
> (a) A boy is running.
> (b) A boy is skiing.
> (c) A boy is swimming.

Series	Structure	Sentences
1	S V	A bear (mouse, bunny) is crying.
2	S V	A boy is running (swimming, skiing).
3	S V O	A monkey (squirrel, bunny) is eating a banana.
4	S V O	A boy is kissing (hugging, kicking) a dog.
5	S V O	A girl is eating an apple (cookie, ice cream).
6	S V L	A dog is in (on, under) a car.
7	S V L	A cat is on a table (bed, chair).
8	S V O I	A lady is giving a present (truck, mouse) to a girl.
9	S V O I	A cat is giving a flower to a boy (bunny, dog).

In this listing, these abbreviations are used for the major elements of a sentence: S=subject, V=verb, O=object, L=object of the locative preposition and I=indirect object. The three pictures in each series will be called frames. For example, (a) is the first frame, (b) is the second frame, and (c) is the third frame. In this particular series, the subject increases in givenness across the frames whereas the verb increases in newness.   In Series 6 and 7, the verb is taken to include both the copular and the locative preposition. (In Hungarian the locative is a postposition or suffix rather that a preposition.)

The order of the nine series of pictures was randomized. Following each series, a picture of a common object such as a bottle or a sailboat was inserted. This was done to break up any set (Einstellung) effects. Subjects were examined individually. Each subject was seated next to the experimenter at a table. The subject was told that he would be asked to tell about what he saw in some pictures. The experimenter showed the pictures to each subject in groups of three, varying the placement of particular pictures left, middle, and right across subjects. Two probes were used: "Tell me about this picture" and "What's happening in this picture?" Use of the two probes was also randomized. Each session was tape-recorded in its entirety.

Subjects. All of the subjects were right-handed. All of the aphasic subjects had left lateral lesions. The transcripts in the CHILDES database are from either Broca's aphasics, Wernicke aphasics, or anomics. The characterization of these syndromes is as follows:

1.   Broca's aphasics are nonfluent patients, displaying an abnormal reduction in utterance length and sentence complexity, with marked errors of omission and/or substitution in grammatical morphology – all in the presence of comprehension abilities that appear to be normal in free conversation.

2.   Wernicke's aphasics are patients suffering from marked comprehension deficits, despite fluent or hyper-fluent speech with an apparently normal melodic line; these patients are expected to display serious word finding difficulties, usually with semantic and/or phonological paraphasias and occasional paragrammatisms.

3. Anomics are fluent patients, with apparently normal comprehension abilities in free conversation, suffering primarily from word-finding problems (in the absence of severe paraphasias or paragrammatism).

Patients were referred for testing by neurologists and speech pathologists at the respective research sites, with one of the above diagnoses. In support of each classification, we were provided with neurological records (including CT scans in many cases), together with the results of standard aphasia batteries that used at the respective research sites (e.g. the Boston Diagnostic Aphasia Examination in the United States and the Aachen Aphasia Battery in Europe. To eliminate the possibility that a patient had changed status since the diagnosis provided at referral, patients were all screened in a biographical interview administered and recorded prior to testing. In addition, we excluded all patients with one or more of the following conditions:

1. history of multiple strokes,
2. significant hearing and/or visual disabilities,
3. severe gross motor disabilities,
4. severe motor-speech involvement such that less than 50% of the subject's speech attempts are intelligible, or
5. evidence that subject is neurologically or physically unstable and/or less than 3 months post onset.

Patient groups were defined within each language according to their fit to a prototype used by neurologists and speech pathologists in that community. For example, a prototypic Broca's aphasic would show reduced fluency and phrase length, and a tendency toward omission of functors– relative to normals in that language. Hence patients are matched across languages only in the sense that they represent different degrees of deviation from a prototype developed out of observed variation within each language group. This permits comparison of the "best" and the "worst" patients across languages, as well as those who fit the mean.

English

Subject–ID	Sex	Onset	Test Lag	Etiology	Ed.	Occupation
B1-71	M	58	2 years	CVA	12	telephone engineer
B2-73	M	31	1 year	CVA	16	engineer
B3-76	M	61	5 years	CVA	-	telephone repair
B4-66	M	43	8 years	CVA	18	accountant
B5-74	M	33	34	Trauma	15	electronics
B6-72	M	44	1 year	CVA	-	-
W1-82	M	47	2 months	CVA	16	insurance
W2-83	M	81	1 year	CVA	-	build. maintenance
W3-84	M	56	1 month	CVA	11	-
W4-81	M	53	1 year	CVA	16	parish priest
W5-85	M	61	3 weeks	CVA	18	army colonel

German

Subject	Sex	Onset	Test Lag	Etiology	Ed.	Occupation
B08	F	57	2 months	CVA	13+	speech therapist
B41	F	55	1 year	CVA		
B42	F	42	4 years	CVA	13+	technician
B43	F	25	6 years	Trauma	9	sales clerk
B44	F	40	7 years	CVA	9	housewife
B45	F	59	2 years	CVA	9+	office clerk
B46	F	36	7 years	CVA	11	dressmaker
B47	F	52	20 months	CVA	9	kitchen help
B48	M	47	8 years	CVA	16	engineer
B161	M	62	9 years	CVA	9+	business
W31	F	43	8 years	Trauma	9+	office clerk
W32	M	52	11 years	CVA	9+	electrician
W33	M	70	20 months	CVA	9+	foundry worker

W34	F	36	8 years	Trauma	9+	sales clerk
W35	M	59	4 years	CVA	9+	accountant
W36	M	47	3 years	CVA	13+	merchant
W37	F	65	4 years	CVA	9	housewife
W38	M	64	5 years	CVA	9+	service manager
W39	M	71	3 years	CVA	9	
W40	F	49	7 weeks	CVA		housewife

Hungarian

Subject	Etiology	Locus	WAB-AQ	WAB Fluency	WAB Comp.
B1	trauma	centro-parietal	73	4	9.0
B2	CVA	MCA	50.2	4	6.4
B5	thrombosis	MCA	33.6	3	6.7
B7	thrombosis	MCA	70.8	4	8.2
B9	trauma	fronto-temporal	59.8	2	8.1
B10	CVA	MCA	45.4	5	6.9
B11	trauma	fronto-temporal	43.4	5	7.4
B12	thrombosis	fronto-temporal	65.4	6	8.6
B13	CVA	fronto-temporal	67.0	4	9.2
B14	aneurism	fronto-temporal	66.6	4	6.4
W2	abscess	centro-parietal	33	6	6.6
W4	meningeoma	occipital	58	7	5.6
W5	tumor	ant-temporal	56	8	5.6
W9	thrombosis	MCA	51.2	8	5.5
W11	ischemia	MCA	49.4	6	6.7

Subject	Onset Age	Testing Lag	Sex	Occupation	Grades
B1	37		Female		6
B2	36	4 years	Male	worker	8
B5	44	7 months	Male	ironworker	university
B7	55	7.5 months	Female	engineer	8
B9	18	25 months	Male	accountant	8
B10	53	8 months	Male	student	8
B11	26	2 years	Male	ironworker	8
B12	55	4 years	Male	fireman	university
B13	34	7.5 years	Female	engineer	8
B14	41	4 months	Male	telex	8
W2	51	5 months	Female	mechanic	12
W4	55	4 months	Female	teacher	12
W5	37	2 months	Male	clerk	university
W9	76	2 months	Male	engineer	12
W11	63	3 months	Female	accountant	6
		3 months		xeroxer	

A1	F	R	39	39	vascular	8th grade
A2	F	R	18	18	vascular	high school
A3	F	R	48	48	vascular	high school
A4	M	R	57	57	vascular	8th grade
A5	M	R	18	18	trauma	8th grade
A6	M	R	31	33	tumor	high school

A7	M	R	64	64	vascular	8th grade
A8	F	R	29	29	angioma	high school
A10	F	R	57	57	tumor	5th grade
A11	M	R	59	59	vascular	8th grade

Published studies based on the normal and impaired subjects include Bates, Friederici, and Wulfeck (1987b), Bates, Friederici, and Wulfeck (Bates, Friederici & Wulfeck, 1987a), Bates, Friederici, Wulfeck, and Juarez (1988), Bates, Hamby, and Zurif (1983), Bates and Wulfeck (1989a), Bates and Wulfeck (1989b), MacWhinney and Bates (1978), and Wulfeck, Bates, Juarez, Opie, Friederici, MacWhinney, and Zurif (1989). Publications that make use of this corpus should cite one or more of these studies.

30.3. Conti-Ramsden

This corpus includes data from five British language-impaired children and their younger MLU-matched siblings in the age range from 4;0 to 9;0.

Subjects. Two groups of children and their mothers participated in this study. Five subjects were language-impaired children and five were their normally developing younger siblings. The families were drawn from a larger study of parent-child interaction conducted by Conti-Ramsden in England. The study had a two-stage screening procedure for the recruitment of subjects. First, families were contacted through a network of speech therapists and professional colleagues who were informed by letter of the criteria for participation. Second, each language-impaired subject referred was matched with his or her younger, normally developing sibling on the basis of MLU during a home visit. This part of the screening consisted of audiotaping a language sample for each of the two children while playing at home in order to obtain a rough idea of their MLU. It is not often that one finds an older language-impaired child at the same expressive language stage as his or her younger normally developing sibling. For the Conti-Ramsden project in England 36 families were contacted of which only 5 met the standards of language match required in this study. The five families participating in this study were white, intact (both father and mother living together at home), and monolingual.

All parents had secondary education (two fathers had further education but did not hold university degrees). The mothers were all housewives. Based on the father's occupation, the families belonged to social class II (ancillary workers with occupations between professional and skilled), III (Skilled manual workers), or IV (semi-skilled manual workers), as indicated in the following summary.

FED	MED	FSEG	SE Group	Subjects
Secondary	Secondary	skilled manual	III(M)	Rick and Rose
Further	Secondary	managerial	II	Clay and Charles
Further	Secondary	managerial	II	Abe and Ann
Secondary	Secondary	manual	IV	Kate and Kyle
Secondary	Secondary	skilled manual	III(M)	Sean and Susan

The language-impaired children ranged in age from 4;9 to 6;9 years. All five language-impaired children presented with severe expressive language delays as measured by MLU. The language-impaired children fell within Brown's (1973) Stage I and II of linguistic development, although according to their chronological age they should have been functioning post Stage V. In addition all language-impaired children appeared to have nonverbal abilities within normal limits as measured by the Leiter International Performance Scale (Leiter, 1969). These data, along with the child's sibling position in the family are as follows:

Subject	Group	Sex	Age	Position	M.A.	I.Q.
Rick	LI	M	6;9	3/4	6;6	101
Rose	SIB	F	3;2	4/4	3;3	108
Clay	LI	M	5;10	1/2	4;9	86
Charles	SIB	M	2;4	2/2	2;0	91
Abe	LI	M	5;3	2/3	5;9	115
Ann	SIB	F	1;11	3/3	1;10	101
Kate	LI	F	4;9	1/3	4;3	95
Kyle	SIB	M	2;4	3/3	2;3	101
Sid	LI	M	4;9	1/2	5;0	110
Susan	SIB	F	2;5	2/2	2;3	98

Interestingly, the children's comprehension status varied depending on which aspect of comprehension was being measured. The following table gives the results for three standardized tests. Results of the Preschool Language Scale (PLS-C) (Zimmerman, Steiner & Pond, 1979), a developmental test of auditory comprehension, revealed all language-impaired children to be functioning within normal limits (quotients ranging from 82 to 105). Results for the receptive vocabulary test, The British Picture Vocabulary Scale (BPVS) (Dunn, Dunn, Whetton & Pintillie, 1982), a test in which the child points to one picture out of four choices, revealed all language impaired children to have difficulties with receptive vocabulary (percentile scores ranging from 6% to 26%). Finally, findings of The Test of Reception of Grammar (TROG) (Bishop, 1982), a test of the comprehension of grammatical structures, revealed some language-impaired children to have difficulties in this area, although others appeared to be functioning normally (percentile scores ranging from no measurable comprehension of grammar to 50%). The results on these three tests were as follows:

Subject	Group	CA	PLS-C	BPVS	TROG
Rick	LI	6;9	6;6 (96)	4;6 (6%)	5;0 (10%)
Rose	SIB	3;2	2;9 (87)	2;8 (28%)	*
Clay	LI	5;10	5;4 (91)	4;7 (22%)	4;9 (20%)
Charles	SIB	2;4	2;4 (98)	*	*
Abe	LI	5;3	5;6 (105)	4;4 (26%)	5;0 (40%)
Ann	SIB	1;11	2;7 (131)	*	*
Kate	LI	4;9	3;10 (82)	3;0 (7%)	See note
Kyle	SIB	2;4	2;1 (91)	*	*
Sean	LI	4;9	4;10 (103)	2;10 (6%)	5;0 (50%)
Susan	SIB	2;5	2;3 (93)	*	*

* = Too young to be tested.
Note: Kate (LI) did not reach the lowest age equivalent of 4;0 for the TROG test.

In addition, younger siblings ranged in age from 1;11 to 3;2 years. All younger siblings appeared normally developing (IQ ranging from 91 to 108) with age-appropriate language in terms of MLU (MLU in Stages I and II) and general auditory comprehension (PLS-C quotients ranging from 87 to 131).

All children participating in the study had hearing within normal limits as determined by pure tone audiometry screening bilaterally (at 500, 1,000 and 2,000 Hz at 25 dB). Through the use of a questionnaire and parent interview, it was ascertained that no child had a history of chronic middle ear problems that necessitated regular otological treatment. In addition, all children presented uneventful case histories with respect to severe neurological and/or emotional problems.

Furthermore, as can be seen in the following summary, all language-impaired children were receiving speech therapy in the clinic or were enrolled in language-based classrooms for specific language-disordered children (language units). In these classrooms, the children received help from their language teacher and speech-language pathologist who worked together to develop a program for each individual child. In England, both speech-language pathologists and teachers are in continual contact with the children's parents via home visits and visits by the parents to the clinic or the language units in the school. Nonetheless, none of the parents participating in this study had attended a parent training program.

Subject	Started Therapy	Months in Therapy	Type of Provision
Rick	4;0	33	Clinic 4;0 - 5;3
			Language-Unit 5;3 - 6;9
Clay	2;6	44	Clinic 2;6 - 4;6
			Language Unit 4;6 - 5;8
Abe	3;0	27	Clinic 3;0 - 4;6
			L-Unit 4;6 - 5;3
Kate	4;6	3	Clinic 4;6 - 4;9
Sean	3;2	21	Clinic 3;2 - 4;2
			L-Unit 4;2 - 4;9

"Clinic" refers to weekly therapy in a clinic. Despite severe problems, Kate appears to have fallen through the health service net as she was not referred to therapy until she attended nursery school.

Procedures. After a warm up period of two to ten visits, each language-impaired child and younger sibling were videorecorded interacting individually with their mothers in a free play situation in the subjects' home. The videorecorder was not turned on until the participants were ready and playing comfortably. Each dyadic play interaction lasted approximately 15 minutes. The order of interactions was determined by each family given everyday restrictions such as older sibling's possible school attendance, children's willingness, and so forth. In addition, each family chose the toys they wanted to play with and were only instructed to "do what you normally do." The present project attempted to gather ecologically valid, everyday interactions, thus, it was desirable to minimize the amount of structure imposed on the families' everyday activities.

Transcription. The transcription process involved two phases. In the first phase, 10-minute samples of continuous play interaction were transcribed from the videotape recordings. Transcriptions included verbal and nonverbal events and the context in which these event occurred. These initial transcriptions were done by two native speakers of British English using paper and pencil and following an early version of **CHAT**. In the second phase, the paper and pencil transcriptions were computerized, verified, enriched with gestures, indications of nonverbal communicative activity, gaze, and some broad phonetic information required for the analyses, and formatted in accordance with **CHAT**.

When using these data, please cite Conti-Ramsden & Dykins (1989).

30.4. Feldman

This subdirectory contains a set of **CHAT** files collected by Heidi Feldman at Children's Hospital in Pittsburgh from four sets of twins in which one twin suffered early brain damage and the other did not. There are 22 data files in the twins directory from a pilot study conducted in 1985–1986. The subjects were 1;2 to 3;0. The children had incurred some brain injury at birth and are at risk for language impairment. The study was conducted in the subjects' homes with an experimenter present and experimental protocols were used. The data was coded for speech acts according to the system outlined in the file 0codes.doc. Publications that make use of this corpus should cite Keefe, Feldman, and Holland (1989) or Feldman, Keefe, and Holland (1989).

30.5. Flusberg

This directory contains files from children with autism and children with Down Syndrome. The data were contributed by Helen Tager-Flusberg and reformatted into **CHAT** by Pam Rollins. The full description of this project can be found in (Tager-Flusberg et al., 1990).

30.6. Fosnot

This directory contains a group of files from children in the age range of 0;6 to 3;0. Half of the subjects are at risk for stuttering and half are not. The data were contributed by Susan Meyers Fosnot. Articles based on the use of these data should cite (Fosnot & Spajik, 1994).

30.7. Hargrove

This subdirectory contains a set of interviews in **CHAT** format between a speech therapist and six language-impaired children in the age range of 3 to 6. The files were contributed by Patricia Hargrove. Publications that make use of this corpus should cite Hargrove, Holmberg, and Zeigler (1986).

30.8. Holland

The language transcripts were gathered under the direction of Drs. Audrey Holland and O.M. Reinmuth as part of research project funded by NINCDS entitled "Early Language Recovery Following Stroke". They were donated by Dr. Holland to the CHILDES in 1986 and reformatted from SALT to **CHAT** in 1988. Patients were seen for 15 minutes a day, 6 days/week throughout the course of their hospitalization, beginning at 24 to 72 hours post-stroke. The daily visits were conducted by two trained speech-language pathologists: one to converse with the patient and the other to observe, tape-record, and tally features of the interaction. For each patient there are three transcribed conversations, representing 5-minute segments from the first, middle, and last visits made during the patient's hospitalization. The filename includes a number that will indicate which visit it is. For example, there are these files for the patient coded as Wilde:

wilde1.cha, wilde9.cha, and wilde17.cha. In this case, the patient had 17 total visits: wilde1 is the first, wilde9 the ninth, and wilde17 the seventeenth and last.

Pseudonym	Onset Age	Side	Initial Type of Disorder
Athos	51	R	normal
Atkins	79	L	Wernicke
Barrie	19	B	uncertain + apraxia of speech
Basil	72	R	dysarthria + uncertain
Boris	38	B	unresponsive
Brown	59	L	global
Collin	75	L	global
Cyert	35	L	global/mixed
Davis	85	L	Wernicke
Getty	76	L	uncertain + dysarthria
Godot	77	R	R hem cog + L neglect + dysarthria
Gruman	45	L	Broca + apraxia of speech + dysarthria
Hector	74	L	anomia + confusion
Henley	75	L	thalamic neglect + confusion
Holmes	64	L	conduction
Horace	60	L	uncertain
Jones	69	L	apraxia of speech + uncertain
Kirk	48	L	global
Malone	35	L	transcortical motor
Miles	76	L	Wernicke
Milan	61	L	global
Milton	74	R	normal
Murray	71	R	thalamic neglect + R hem cog
Neil	68	L	conduction
Norman	33	L	apraxia of speech + uncertain
Oliver	45	B	R hem cog
Parker	81	L	Wernicke
Robert	77	R	L neglect + R hem cog + dysarthria
Rudolf	69	L	conduction
Rupert	74	L	dysarthria
Scott	80	L	dysarthria + R neglect
Seller	61	L	Broca + dysarthria
Spade	93	L	Wernicke
Stone	40	L	uncertain + dysarthria
Stuart	61	L	uncertain
Taylor	55	B	unresponsive
White	73	L	uncertain + dysarthria
Wilde	82	L	global
Wilson	64	R	R hem cog + L neglect + dysarthria
Young	65	L	dysarthria
Zenith	76	L	uncertain
Zipps	82	L	global

Publications that make use of this corpus should cite Holland, Miller, Reinmuth, Bartlett, Fromm, Pashek, Stein, and Swindell (1985).

30.9. Hooshyar

This directory contains files from Down Syndrome children and their mothers collected by Nahid Hooshyar in the context of a project entitled "Language Interactions between Mothers and Their Nonhandicapped Children, Mothers and Their Down Syndrome Children, and Mothers and Their Language-Impaired Children." The data from the nonhandicapped and language-impaired children are not in CHILDES. The data were collected during 1984-86 and contributed to the CHILDES system in 1988. They were originally formatted in SALT (Miller & Chapman, 1983), but were reformatted to **CHAT** by the SALTIN program. The project was supported by Grant No. 8402115 and CFDA 84.023D from the Department of Education.

The major goal of this study was to isolate and identify patterns occurring in language interactions between mothers and their nonhandicapped (NH), Down Syndrome (DS), or language-impaired (LI) children. The study explored the nature of such language interactions and attempted to determine whether there were consistently recurring patterns within a group, and if so, whether these patterns were the same across groups. More specifically, this study was designed to investigate the following questions:

1. What kinds of language teaching strategies do mothers of nonhandicapped, Down Syndrome, and language- impaired children utilize in language interactions with their children in "real life" situations?

2. What kinds of language learning strategies do nonhandicapped, Down Syndrome, and language- impaired children bring into language learning situations?

3. Can contextual variables be identified that serve to evoke and/or control these strategies?

Subjects. Three groups of mother-child dyads participated in this study: nonhandicapped children and their mothers, children with Down Syndrome and their mothers, and children with language impairment and their mothers. Names of potential subjects were obtained from a number of cooperating school systems and day-care centers in the Dallas/Fort Worth Metroplex, the Down Syndrome Guild, and the Callier Center for Communication Disorders of the University of Texas at Dallas. Mothers were mailed an introductory letter explaining the nature of the study and a parental consent form. The introductory letter was followed by telephone contact during which mothers were given more detailed information about the tasks and time involved in this study. Mothers were asked to volunteer if their children could produce at least 10 words but were not yet regularly producing multiword utterances. The final criterion for inclusion of a child in the study was the child's level of linguistic development as measured by the mean length of utterance (MLU) as defined by Brown [, 1973 #539]. Only children with MLU between 1 and 3 were included in this study.

Initial Interview. In order to insure that children of the three groups were equal in their expressive and and receptive language, the Vineland Adaptive Behavior Scale (VABS) (Sparrow, Balla & Cichetti, 1984) was administered. Three to five days after the telephone contact, a member of the research team called each of the mothers to arrange an appointment for a home visit. During this visit, the same research assistant interviewed the mother using a family background and demographic characteristics questionnaire and the VABS. The purpose of this interview was to encourage communication, to allow the interviewer to study the attitudes of the mothers toward the child and to form other subjective observations useful in subsequent contacts with the mothers. The visit lasted between 3 to 4 hours. Although the purpose of the study was stated in the letter sent to the mothers, it was reiterated during the initial visit in the following format: "We are researchers at the University of Texas at Dallas and we would like to learn about the language development among three groups of children: nonhandicapped, Down Syndrome, and language-impaired. We feel we will get a typical language sample if we observe children interacting with their mothers in their familiar environment. We would like to carry on your daily activities as you ordinarily do."

Videotaping. Videotaping sessions were conducted in the participants' home and were scheduled at the mothers' convenience. Participants were videotaped while engaged in each of the three activities (play time, story time, and meal time) for approximately 20 minutes. All sessions were completed during one home visit that lasted two to three hours. In most of the sessions only the child and the mother were present. However, in about 25% of the cases there was another child or adult present also. Two to three weeks after the videotaping session, each mother was mailed a questionnaire to assess the effects of the videotaping and the presence of the observer on the mother and child behavior.

Instruments. Mothers' rating of their child's social and adaptive behavior was assessed by the VABS survey form. This scale contains 297 items which measure adaptive behavior in four domains: (1) communication, (2) daily living skills, (3) socialization, and (4) motor skills. In interview form, it is designed to be used with parents of individuals aged zero to 18 years 11 months or of low-functioning adults. The scale was standardized on the performance of a representative national sample of handicapped and nonhandicapped individuals. Reported internal consistencies range from 0.89 to 0.98, and test-retest reliabilities range from 0.76 to 0.93.

For the purpose of this study, a detailed demographic characteristic and family background questionnaire was developed. The questionnaire consisted of 65 items grouped into eight categories: identifying information, demographic information, marital status, source of financial support,occupation, number of children, child-care, health of the child, reading, TV viewing, physical environment, and experience outside of the home. Questions included such areas as birth order, educational attainment, employment, and marital history of the parents. A second questionnaire was developed consisting of an open-ended question asking mothers to describe their feelings and thoughts about the videotaping session and the observer.

Subjects. The final sample consisted of 40 NH (21 female, 19 male), 31 DS (14 female, 17 male),and 21 LI (7 female, 14 male) children and their mothers. Only the data from the Down Syndrome group is in the CHILDES database. Of the children with Down Syndrome, the Karyotype of 30 were diagnosed as Trisomy 21 and one as Translocation. The LI children were of normal intelligence with language or speech production problems including articulation problems attributed primarily to middle ear infection, cleft palate (surgically corrected), and nonspecified causes.

All subjects were Caucasian, English speaking, middle-class, as defined by Hollingshead Index of Social Status. Table 3 presents the birth order of the children. All mothers were currently married, living with a spouse, and primary caregivers of their children. The mean age for the mothers of the NH children was 30.0 years (SD = 0.80; Range = 20 to 45 years) and the mean age for the mothers of the two other groups was 36.0 years (SD= 1.34 and Range = 20 to 46 years for mothers of DS children; SD = 0.94 and Range 20 to 45 years for mothers of LI children). The educational level ranged from high school to postgraduate education for mothers of NH children and from partial college preparation to B.A. or B.S. degree for the other two groups. The mean parity, as defined by Ryder and Westhoff (1971), was 1.81 for families with NH children, 3.09 for families with DS

children or B.S. degree for the other two groups. The mean parity was 1.81 for families with NH children, 3.09 for families with DS, and 2.05 for families with LI children. The mean age for NH children was 26.75 months (SD = 4.24; Range = 16 to 35 months), for DS children was 64.48 months (SD = 17.87; Range = 38 to 138 months), and for LI children was 44.84 months (SD = 9.23; Range = 32 to 69 months). The mean MLU for NH children was 1.85 (SD = 0.61; Range = 1.07 to 2.98), for DS children was 1.64 (SD = 0.63; Range = 1.01 to 2.95), and for LI children was 1.98 (SD = 0.66; Range = 1.04 to 3.00).

The mean Adaptive Behavior Composite (ABC) score on the VABS for NH children was 37.60 (SD= 46.53; Range= 17 to 32), for DS it was 44.35 (SD= 17.33; Range= 18 to 75), and for LI it was 41.33 (SD= 10.05 ; Range= 21 to 64). The mean Expressive Communication on the VABS for NH children was 29.05 (SD= 8.73; Range= 13 to 53), for DS it was 38.00 (SD= 21.36; Range= 12 to 89), and for LI it was 36.00 (SD= 12.12; Range= 17 to 62). The mean Receptive communication on the VABS for NH children was 39.82 (SD= 9.54; Range= 18 to 47), for DS it was 53.41 (SD= 27.88; Range= 14 to 94), and for LI it was 46.52 (SD= 17.66; Range= 30 to 94). The NH children were functioning significantly above their chronological age (CA) in expressive and receptive communication (t= 2.48 and t= 9.2 with P= 0.02 and 0.001 respectively). Children with DS were significantly delayed in their adaptive behavior, expressive and receptive communication functioning (t= 8.06, 8.01, 4.53 with P < 0.001 for the three scores). For LI children, the mean ABC and expressive communication scores were significantly delayed (t= 2.22 and t= 3.67 with P= 0.04 and 0.002, respectively).

Files. Each subject was videotaped during three different settings: play time, story time, and meal time. Only the playtime and storytime transcripts are in the CHILDES database. The names of the files with playtime dialogs all begin with the letter "p" and the names of the files with storytime dialogs all begin with the letter "s." The subject numbers, pseudonyms, ages in months, ages in years, dates of recordings (for the story files), and dates of birth are as follows:

Code	Name	Months	Age	Date of Recording	Date of Birth
041	Shally	81	6;8.24	10-MAR-1985	16-JUN-1978
042	John	79(77)	6;7.0	4-APR-1985	
043	Alicia	86	7;6.0	30-MAR-1985	
044	Ruth	37(38)	3;1.0	18-APR-1985	
045	David	107	8;11.0	17-MAY-1985	
046	Beverly	55(46)	4;7.0		
047	Jerald	58	4;10.0	3-JUN-1985	
048	Robert	41	3;5.0	14-JUN-1985	
049	Cheryl	38	3;2.0		
050	Steve	56	4;8.0	29-MAY-1985	
051	Mary	95	7;10.0	4-JUN-1985	
052	Michael	42	3;6.0	17-JUN-1985	16-DEC-1981
053	Barton	95	7;10.25	14-JUN-1985	20-JUL-1977
054	Marilyn	40	3;5.9	19-JUL-1985	10-FEB-1982
055	Mark	40	3;4.18	8-AUG-1985	21-MAR-1982
056	Edward	65	5;5.0	20-AUG-1985	20-MAR-1980
057	Craig	45	3;9.0	22-AUG-1985	
058	Kim	102	9;4.0		
059	Taffie	47	3;10.3	2-OCT-1985	30-DEC-1981
060	Rick	52	4;5.9	3-JAN-1986	25-AUG-1981
061	Donald	47	3;11.16	7-FEB-1986	19-FEB-1982

062	Jack	38	3;2.0	18-FEB-1986	
063	James	138	11;6.0	14-APR-1986	
064	Barbara	99	8;3.0	8-AUG-1986	
065	Adam	108	9;5.0	7-AUG-1986	
066	Eileen	120	9;11.0	13-AUG-1986	
067	George	96	8;10.7	29-AUG-1986	22-OCT-1977
068	Sandra	108	9;7.10	23-OCT-1986	13-
MAR-1977					
069	Jody	108			
070	Ronald	96	7;11.13	20-AUG-1986	7-SEP-1978
071	Lynelle	84	7;0.5	23-AUG-1986	18-AUG-1979

All of the names given above are pseudonyms. The data from Subject 069 (Jody) were not yet provided to CHILDES.

Transcribing. Five research assistants participated in transcribing the video- recording. In order to have a uniform transcription, transcribers were trained to use SALT (Miller & Chapman, 1983) for preparing and marking the transcripts. Sample transcripts were jointly reviewed in conferences to clarify and answer questions about instructions. An utterance-by-utterance reliability of the transcription was estimated by having the transcribers independently transcribe 10 representative videotapes. Only after interrater agreement approached unity were the remaining videotapes transcribed. All transcriptions were made in ordinary English orthography with phonetic notation used in cases where an English word could not be identified. Normal English punctuation was used to denote intonation patterns, to make the meaning of a sentence clear , or to indicate the pauses and stops which the speaker made in speaking. The mood of each utterance was identified primarily on the basis of intonation and secondarily, on the basis of structural features. For example, declarative sentences that ended in rising intonation were coded as interrogative mood. Seven assistants entered the transcribed records into the computer using WordStar. Finally, observers checked the transcripts of their own videotaping sessions to verify the accuracy and add necessary contextual information. The final product was a complete record of verbal and behavioral events and the context in which these occurred. In 1988, the SALT files were converted to **CHAT** format, using the **SALTIN** program.

Speech Act Codes. Every utterance was coded for its overall speech act function and specific value. The functions and their specific values were as follows:

1. Queries: leading, coaching, information request.
2. Declaratives: labeling, announcing, informing, explaining, idle chat.
3. Imperatives: request attention, request action, proposal for joint action.
4. Feedbacks: informative feedback, evaluative feedback, corrective feedback, verbal disapproval, granting permission.
5. Performatives: demonstrating, pointing, guiding, affect, joshing.
6. Imitations: exact, reduced, expanded, modified.
7. Self-repetition: exact, reduced, expanded, modified.
8. Syntactic well-formedness: sentence fragment, complete sentence, minor abbreviations.
9. Sentence types: yes-no question, wh-question, imperative, declarative.
10. Speech style: disfluent, run-on, unintelligible, stock expression.

These data can only be used with the expressed permission of Dr. Hooshyar who requests that she be included as co-author on any publications utilizing her data. Publications that make use of this corpus should also cite Hooshyar (1985) and Hooshyar (1987).

30.10. Leonard

The eleven children whose transcripts are provided here were diagnosed as specifically language-impaired (SLI). All scored above 85 on the Arthur Adaptation of the Leiter International Performance Scale and more than 1 standard deviation below their age on the composite (Picture Vocabulary, Oral Vocabulary, Grammatical Understanding, Sentence Imitation, Grammatical Completion) of the Test of Language Development-Primary. All children passed a hearing screening, a test of oral-motor function, showed no evidence of frank neurological impairment, and displayed no signs of emotional disorder. Samples were obtained as the child played with an adult female research assistant. Common toys and picture books were the chief source of conversation. Only the utterances of the child appear in the transcripts. Transcripts were coded for Brown's fourteen morphological categories. Word order was not preserved.

Ages are in years; months. IQ scores are from Leiter International Performance Scale, Arthur Adaptations. TOLD-P and TELD scores are composite z-scores:

Childe	Age	Sex	IQ		
SLI-A	5;0	M	110	TOLD-P	-2.20
SLI-B	4;3	F	120	TOLD-P	-1.40
SLI-C	5;0	M	92	TOLD-P	-1.86
SLI-D	4;4	M	100	TOLD-P	-1.87
SLI-E	4;6	F	105	TOLD-P	-1.87
SLI-F	4;6	M	98	TOLD-P	-1.86
SLI-G	5;3	F	86	TOLD-P	-1.60
SLI-H	3;8	M	134	TELD	-1.00
SLI-I	5;7	M	99	TOLD-P	-2.53
SLI-J	4;11	F	127	TOLD-P	-1.40
SLI-K	3;9	M	125	TELD	-1.47

30.11. Rondal

This directory contains files from 21 Down syndrome children (12 girls and 9 boys), along with a set of files from 21 children in the normal control group. The data were collected from children in Minnesota by Jean Rondal. A fairly full report on the project is given in Rondal (1978). The samples are matched for mean length of utterance. The original study was designed to examine differences in maternal speech directed to normal and Down syndrome children.

Subjects. The subjects of this study were 21 Down syndrome children and their natural mothers and 21 normal children and their natural mothers. As a condition for participating in the study it was required that none of the mothers in the two groups had been or were currently engaged in any early education curriculum for parents with special emphasis on promoting early language abilities in children. All of the normal children and their mothers and 14 of the identified Down syndrome children lived in the Minneapolis-St. Paul area. The seven remaining Down syndrome children and their mothers lived in other towns in Minnesota. Karyotypes were obtained for all the Down syndrome children and all were reported to be Trisomy 21's. There were 12 girls and 9 boys among the Down syndrome children, and 8 girls and 13 boys among the normal children. No effort was made to balance the two groups of children for gender, as it was thought not to be an important variable.

In order to participate in the study, the children could not have any debilitating heart condition, obvious sensory impairment, or more generally any medical condition (other than Down syndrome for the Down syndrome children) that might seriously limit their development, and their speech had to be reasonably intelligible. The normal and Down syndrome children were matched on linguistic development as measured by MLU. The children's MLU was computed using the criterion given in Brown [, 1973 #539], a count based on morphemes. The only exception to Brown's criterion was that MLU was based on the total sample (i.e., one-hour speech recording) rather than the first 100 utterances. On the basis of the children's MLU, the mother-child pairs were divided into three language-level categories for each population of normal and Down syndrome children. Specified MLU ranges for the three language levels were 1.00-1.50, 1.75-2.25, 2.50-3.00. The following table lists child and mother MLU for the Down and normal children along with the child's chronological age in months at the three language levels.

Child	sex	CA	Down Mother MLU	Child MLU		sex	CA	Normal Mother MLU
Language Level 1:								
1 Stella	f	47	3.69	1.41	Tansy	f	23	4.39	1.15
2 Jon	m	49	4.46	1.52	Shelly	f	20	5.07	1.54
3 Mel	m	36	3.36	1.04	Lana	f	22	4.38	1.43
4 Baxter	m	38	3.90	1.04	Josh	m	22	4.16	1.05
5 Selma	f	37	4.99	1.11	Carla	f	26	3.55	1.52
6 Kevin	m	52	3.98	1.12	Ken	m	22	3.56	1.06
7 Abby	f	54	3.30	1.55	Billy	m	25	4.53	1.10
mean			3.95	1.25				4.23	1.26
s.d.			-----	.228				-----	.222
Language Level 2:								
8 Bob	m	56	3.94	1.72	Carl	m	24	4.89	1.76
9 Cheryl	f	57	3.52	1.79	Elbert	m	27	4.32	1.74
10 Silvia	f	94	3.48	2.03	Dirk	m	28	4.40	1.94
11 Dan	m	56	4.90	1.96	Caleb	m	27	4.60	1.75
12 Janet	f	55	4.48	1.75	Vance	m	28	4.24	2.14
13 Corrie	f	84	4.10	2.09	Marvin	m	25	5.21	2.24
14 Paul	m	62	6.27	2.22	Murray	m	27	4.81	2.07
mean			4.38	1.94				4.64	1.95
s.d.			-----	.187				-----	.206
Language Level 3:								
15 Mat	m	146	6.32	2.93	Lina	f	32	6.44	2.78
16 Ava	f	121	5.39	3.06	Jane	f	31	4.39	2.48
17 Kimmy	f	134	4.99	2.92	Andy	m	30	3.45	2.98
18 Rhoda	f	100	4.88	2.70	Martin	m	29	5.20
3.01								
19 Missy	f	135	5.08	2.85	Jed	m	29	4.60	3.03
20 Cassy	f	128	5.33	3.04	Kelly	f	29	5.65	2.87
21 Donald	m	74	5.53	2.59	Joel	m	28	4.14	2.97
mean			5.36	2.87				4.84	2.88
s.d.			-----	.136				-----	.192

There are two **CHAT** files from each child with the exception of Martin and Stella. The files for these two children were lost in 1976 and cannot be recovered. All of the names given are pseudonyms. The mothers of normal children and the mothers of Down syndrome children were matched on the following criteria: ethnic group (Caucasian), familial monolingualism, familial structure (both husband and wife living at home), mother free of any major sensory handicap, maternal intelligence not obviously outside of the normal range (no intelligence test given), and socioeconomic status (the families selected for the study were predominantly drawn from the middle class). Perhaps more important than socioeconomic status (usually based on occupational and educational level of the head of the household) for research of this type, is the mother's educational level. The mothers selected for this study were matched on the Educational Scale supplied by Hollingshead in his two factor Index of Social Position. The overall means of the mothers of Down syndrome children on the Hollingshead's Educational Scale was 2.67 (SD 1.02) versus 2.71 (SD .90) for the mothers of normal children. This difference was found to be not significant. No effort was made to match mothers of normal and retarded children for age, nor to match normal and retarded children for birth order, number of siblings, and age differences between the children in the family as it is known that in the cases of Trisomy 21, the mean age of the mother at the birth of the child is significantly older than in control populations. This, in turn affects birth order and family composition for Down syndrome children as they are more likely to be later-born children than are normal children. The average age of the mothers of Down syndrome children in this study was 514.86 months (SD 100.84 months) versus 338.29 months (SD 49.42 months for the mothers of normal children. The average birth order was 3.76 (SD 2.30) for the Down syndrome children and 1.76 (SD .89) for the normal children. From language level 1 to language level 3 respectively, approximately 12 to 40% of the siblings of the Down syndrome children were no longer living in the family home at the time of the study.

Subjects are identified by first names and with a three-digit code. In this code the first number is for the group level with "1" indicating Down syndrome and "2" indicating normal; the second number is for the language level, and the third number is for the subject number within the particular cell.

Data Collection. The verbal interaction between mother and child was tape recorded at home in a free-play situation. The investigator was present in the home during the tape recording and made every effort to keep his presence as discreet as possible. The mothers were told that the study was primarily about child language development in a plausible attempt to keep them as unconcerned as possible about their own speech. Moreover, the mothers were asked not to engage the investigator in conversation during actual recording.

It is possible that mother-child interaction in the presence of an observer are somewhat different from what they are "behind closed doors." Even if mothers modified their behavior toward the children in the observer's presence, it is improbable that they would be able to invent, at once, new and different mother-child interaction patterns (Moerk, 1972). Besides, there is no reason to expect the observer's presence to affect differentially the verbal behavior of mothers of normal and Down syndrome children.

In order to preserve as much spontaneity and naturalness in the mother-child interactions as possible, no specific instruction other that "do what you usually do when you play and talk with the child and use whatever kind of toys or material you want to use, only avoid recitations" was given to the mothers as to what they should do with the children during the free-play situation. It turned out the the free-play situations and the material used by the mothers were surprisingly similar from home to home, particularly for those normal and Down syndrome children at language levels 1 and 2. The use of Play-doh games, shape-matching or shape-folding games, play-action games such as the farm game, the airport, the village, the school, Sesame Street and McDonald's games by Fisher-Price, PlaySkool and others, looking at picture and storybooks, alternated in one way or the other during all recording sessions. The contents of the free-play situations were somewhat more heterogeneous for the two groups of children at the third language level, with several mothers of normal and Down syndrome children spending part or all of the two recording sessions in conversation with the child using toys and pictures as a support for conversation. There were two recording sessions each lasting half an hour for each mother and child pair. The two recording sessions took place on two different days at approximately a one-week interval. They were preceded, on another day, by a 20-minute "get acquainted session" during which the investigator familiarized himself with the mother and the child, obtained first-hand information on the child's language level, and gave the child an opportunity to extinguish most of his or her orientation reactions to the tape recorder by have in it displayed and functioning in the room, which additionally supplied information on the effects of the acoustics of the room on the tape recording. Publications that make use of this corpus should cite Rondal (1978).

30.12. Ulm

These data were contributed by H. S. Johannsen, H. Schulze, D. Rommel, A. Haege, and J. Sieron from the phoniatric outpatients' clinic of the University of Ulm, Germany. The data are a set of protocols taken from preschool and primary school children in the context of an experimental playing situation in which the children play half an hour with her mothers in the laboratory of the phoniatric clinic. The playing material is a farm building kit in all cases. All assessed children came to the phoniatric clinic because of more or less severe stuttering and take part in a longitudinal study of the relations between different variables and the development of stuttering in childhood using CLAN. The transcribed language is not standard German but a Swabian dialect spoken in the region round Ulm. In order to protect the data privacy all names were removed or shortened to one character, while dates are original.

Please inform the authors when using these data. More details about the data and their context can be requested in case of interest. Publications that make use of this corpus should cite (Johannsen, Schulze, Rommel & Häge, 1992).

31. Bilingual Acquisition

31.1. De Houwer

This directory contains a longitudinal corpus of a girl acquiring English and Dutch as her two first languages. The corpus was contributed by Annick De Houwer, University of Antwerp, Belgium. The data are in **CHAT** format, but no English glosses have been provided for the Dutch material in the corpus. All child utterances have been fully coded on the morphological and syntactic levels.

The subject of this study is an only child, named Kate, who was exposed to English and Dutch virtually from birth onwards. Kate lived with both her parents up to and including the period of investigation and was usually addressed in a different language by each parent. Kate's American mother spoke English to her, while her Flemish father used Dutch with her. Kate's parents used English with each other. Apart from short intervals when one of the parents was away on a trip, or when Kate and her mother were in the United States without Kate's father, exposure to two languages was a nearly daily occurrence for Kate. The family's home base has mostly been Antwerp, a fairly large city in Belgium (for more detailed biographical information see the file "0bio.doc").

In total, 19 one hour audio-recordings were made. The age period studied covers the 8 months from 2;7 to 3;4. Data collection was carried out in the child's home using a good quality portable cassette-recorder with a built-in multi-directional microphone. Most frequently, interactions were recorded while Kate was playing with the investigator in the kitchen while Kate's mother was cooking. The investigator used her native Dutch with Kate but conversations between the investigator and Kate's mother were in English. Many of the interactions recorded involve three-way conversations (for more detailed information on the recording sessions see the file "0rec.doc").

All child–adult interactions were transcribed in full, including hesitations, false starts, repetitions, self–made songs, and nonsense utterances. Extended conversations between the adults that did not include the child in any way were not transcribed, but all other adult utterances were included in the transcription. (For more detailed information on the transcription see the file "0hist.doc".)

After the initial transcription, all child utterances were entered on computer disks, coded along various dimensions, and analyzed using specially designed programmes. When the data were converted into **CHAT** format, the adult utterances were added.

Each child utterance in the corpus is always followed by %mph, %gl1 and %gl2 tiers Sometimes a %stx tier is also added. Code lines %gl1 and %gl2 contain codes that refer to characteristics of the relevant utterance as a whole (hence gl for "global"). Code lines %mph and %stx contain word-per-word codes on the morphological and syntactic levels respectively (for more detailed information on the codes used see file "0cod.doc").

Warnings.
1. For the adult Dutch utterances, note that verb forms and plural nouns with a stem + {-e(n)} may have been transcribed in two fashions: - as stem + en, e.g. "peren" or "eten". This notation does not necessarily mean that the final "n" was in fact pronounced: it could have been present or not - as stem + e(n), e.g. "pere(n)" or "ete(n)". This notation does indicate that the bracketed "n" was in fact not pronounced.

2. Note that English contracted negative verb forms (e.g. "doesn't"), which CLAN treats as single words, actually have been coded on the %mph line using two morphological codes, viz. a verb code and the code "neg". In other words, for utterances containing English contracted negative verb forms there will be no one-to-one correspondence between the number of words and the number of morphological codes.
3. These data are not suitable for analyses of speaker overlappings and/or interruptions, since these aspects were not transcribed consistently.
4. Users of these data should be familiar with both Dutch and English. No English glosses are provided for Dutch (parts of) utterances. Dutch abbreviations (no capitals used in text of course)

Dutch abbreviations were handled in the following way. For each, the exact status needs to be determined for child utterances:

1. 'T is short, colloquial version of HET in input.
2. NIE is short, colloquial version of NIET in input.
3. DA is short version of DAT in input.
4. ES is short, colloquial version of EENS in input.
5. WA'S is short, colloquial version of WAT IS in input.
6. WA is short version of WAT in input.
7. DA'S is short, colloquial version of DAT IS in input.
8. K is short version of IK in input.
9. G' is short version of GE/GIJ in input.
10. 'N is short version of EEN in input.
11. Z' is short version of ZE/ZIJ in input.

The following table lists the ages at which each recording session took place, as well as the distribution of language use by Kate per recording session. The language or each utterance was coded as either Dutch, English, mixed, or non-language specific (NLS).

Tape	Age	Dutch	English	Mixed	NLS	totals
1	2;7.12	68.8	23.4	7.8	0.0	77
2	2;7.17	42.7	38.2	18.8	0.3	335
3	2;8.8	45.9	27.0	21.6	5.4	37
4	2;9.0	94.7	0.5	3.2	1.6	374
5	2;10.5	60.8	36.6	0.9	1.7	232
6	2;10.13	95.8	0.4	3.6	0.2	527
7	2;10.28	69.3	26.1	4.1	0.4	241
8	2;11.14	72.5	20.8	6.7	0.0	284
9	3;0.6	52.3	38.6	9.1	0.0	88
10	3;0.11	52.3	36.2	11.5	0.0	130
11	3;0.17	16.2	68.4	15.4	0.0	117
12	3;1.6	45.2	48.8	6.0	0.0	84
13	3;1.12	52.7	45.1	2.2	0.0	91
14	3;1.13	5.2	85.8	6.7	2.2	134
15	3;1.18	10.7	77.2	5.4	6.7	224
16	3;1.26	53.5	36.0	3.5	7.0	258
17	3;2.7	55.9	38.8	3.3	2.0	245
18	3;3.9	88.3	1.1	5.5	5.1	274
19	3;3.16	89.3	2.6	7.9	0.3	392
Totals		65.2	26.5	6.5	1.7	4144

The Kate data are not useful for studying the onset of morphosyntactic development in bilingual children, since Kate was already well into this development when data collection started. At the end of the study Kate had started to use complex sentences. Researchers using these data should cite De Houwer (1990).

31.2. Deuchar

The subject of this corpus is Manuela, a girl born in Brighton, England on 24-JUN-1985. Manuela lived in Brighton and was an only child during the period under investigation. Her mother, Margaret Deuchar, is the investigator, and is a linguist. Her father is a civil engineer. Her mother was born and brought up in England, speaking English, and learned Spanish in early adulthood. Her English is standard with an RP accent slightly modified by southern English features (most of her childhood was spent in Hampshire). Her father was born in Cuba where he lived until age 7, after which he lived mostly in the Dominican Republic and Panama, most of that time being spent in the latter until early adulthood, when he moved to England. He was brought up by Cuban parents speaking Cuban Spanish; his Spanish is also influenced by that spoken in Panama, where he spent his middle and later childhood. He learned English as a second language, starting in secondary school. From the time of their marriage (four years before Manuela's birth) the parents spoke Spanish with one another. During the period of data collection Manuela was exposed to Spanish from both parents in the home, and English from caregivers in the creche and from her maternal grandmother, who spent one day per week with her, and speaks standard English with a fairly conservative RP accent. At age 1;3, Manuela heard, on the average, English, 48% of the time, and Spanish, 52% of the time (calculated on the basis of 12 waking hours per day, 7 days per week).

Data collection. Video and audio recordings were made weekly of spontaneous interactions between Manuela and her Spanish-speaking father on one hand, and Manuela and her English-speaking grandmother on the other. Manuela's mother was also present at some of the recordings in both languages. Audio recordings were made under studio conditions at age 1;11 and monthly from age 2;3 onwards in order to obtain elicited data of sufficient quality for the voicing study. Daily diary records were also kept by Manuela's mother when interacting with Manuela and were supplemented by observations in the creche attended by Manuela. Most of the recordings took place at home in rectangular room - half of which was the living room and half, the dining room. There was no partition separating the two areas.

Sampling Procedure. The corpus here represents only a small sample of the recordings made, of which there are in total 95 made with an English-speaking interlocutor, mostly the maternal grandmother, and 125 with a Spanish-speaking interlocutor, mostly the father. These recordings were made weekly over a two year period from age 1;3 to 3;3. Many of the recordings have not yet been transcribed; others, although transcribed, do not yet meet the **CHAT** conventions. Diary and creche records are also not yet available in the **CHAT** format.

Warnings for all files:
1. In %pho: lines the $ symbol is used inconsistently to indicate word boundaries.
2. There is a tendency for Manuela's utterances to be represented as "yyy" in the main tier.
3. The form "ae" should be changed to "&" and "ao" should be changed to "Q" in the %pho tier in all files.
4. The form "Manuela" is used invariably in the main tier of the child's speech, pronunciation of this being given in %pho tier as "m i n a". In adult speech,

where no %pho tier is included, the actual pronunciation of "Manuela" is indicated by the spelling.

5.   Adult sentences are in general very long, as many sentences have been linked by pause symbols (#) instead of being delimited by utterance terminators.

Pseudonyms were not used. All adults involved gave informed consent for the use of their data.

Goals of the Project. The major goal was to determine, by means of a case study of an infant acquiring English and Spanish simultaneously between the ages of 1;3 and 3;3, whether the child had an initial linguistic system which subsequently divided into two, or whether a division corresponding to the two sources of linguistic input could be ascertained from the beginning of linguistic production.

Transcription. Recorded data were transcribed, using phonetic transcription in PHONASCII for the child utterances. The transcriber was competent in English and Spanish and phonetic transcription, and was trained in the **CHAT** conventions. Transcriptions were typed directly into computer files while video tapes were viewed and audio tapes listened to: the transcriber operated computer, video recorder and audio recorder at the same time while doing transcription. The %pho tier was the only one recorded for each utterance by Manuela; other tiers, such as those coding nonverbal or situational information, were included when the transcriber judged that they gave useful additional information. Prosody was not transcribed. In the Spanish transcriptions, each utterance was given a tier with a translation into English. Random spot reliability checks were done: these, however, affected a fairly small portion of the data. The only file checked and corrected in exhaustive detail is 861002e.gra.   No project-specific codes were used.

English Transcripts:
1) 861002e.gra	2-OCT-1986	1;3.8
2) 861023e.gra	23-OCT-1986	1;3.29
3) 861127e.gra	27-NOV-1986	1;5.3
4) 870402e.gra	2-APR-1987	1;9.9
5) 870528e.gra	28-MAY-1987	1;11.4
6) 870728e.ray	28-JUL-1987	2;1.4
7) 870823e.jos	23-AUG-1987	2;1.30
8) 871126e.gra	26-NOV-1987	2;5.2
9) 880114e.gra	14-JAN-1988	2;6.21

Spanish Transcripts:
1) 860928s.fat	28-SEP-1986	1;3.4
2) 861025s.fat	25-OCT-1986	1;4.1
3) 870329s.fat	29-MAR-1987	1;9.5
4) 870531s.fat	31-MAY-1987	1;11.7
5) 870720s.kes	20-JULY-1987	2;0.26
6) 870829s.par	29-AUG-1987	2;2.5
7) 871129s.fat	29-NOV-1987	2;5.5
8) 871226s.fat	26-DEC-1987	2;6.2

* Note: The labels "s" or "e" in the file names refer to the language spoken by the adult in the recording session.

Researchers using this corpus should cite (Deuchar & Clark, 1992). Copies of articles that make use of the data should be sent to Margaret Deuchar. Newnham College, Cambridge,

CB3 9DF. This project was supported by grants from the Economic and Social Research Council (ref. no. C00232393) and the British Academy.

31.3. Guthrie

This subdirectory contains data from a detailed examination of the language use of a group of Chinese-American first-graders and their two teachers. The files were collected by Larry Guthrie of the Far Western Research Laboratory and donated to the CHILDES in 1985. They were reformatted into CHAT in 1986.

Goals. Although considerable information is available on language use in monolingual classrooms, and to a lesser extent, on that in Hispanic bilingual situations, very little is known about how Chinese children and their teachers construct interactions. The focus of the research was a bilingual class of students that alternated each half-day between a Chinese bilingual teacher and a teacher who did not speak Chinese. This provided the unique opportunity to examine the language of the same Limited English Speaking (LES) children with two different teachers. The first of these teachers not only spoke the students' first language, Cantonese, but was also of the same cultural background. A woman in her early 20's, she had immigrated to the United States at the age of nine. Both her Cantonese and English were native-like. The other teacher was an Anglo male who had taught in Spanish-English bilingual programs, but had little prior experience with Chinese students.

Three basic questions directed the research. The first of these sought an in-depth description of the classroom interaction between Chinese-American children and their teachers. How do teachers orchestrate lessons and how, in turn, do students respond? What variation, in both teacher and student language, is found across student English language proficiency groups? Second, we compared the interaction in the two classrooms. What differences occur between the ways in which the two teachers orchestrate lessons? What differences emerge in student language use? How do these differences compare across linguistic proficiency groups? Third, we asked what variations in teacher and student language might be found when this group of children moved on to second grade. Did these students experience difficulty in crossing the "border" between first and second grade, or in adjusting to the rule system of the new teacher?

Method. Sociolinguistic methods were used to seek answers to these questions and to uncover the ways in which Cantonese-speaking children and their teachers constructed their interactions and used language. The study was conducted in three phases. In the first phase, target students and speech events (lessons) were identified. In the second phase recordings of sample lessons were collected, transcribed, and analyzed. The third phase involved additional recording in reading lessons after target students had progressed to second grade. The procedures employed within each phase are described in more detail later. First, however, is a description of the setting in which the study was conducted.

Subjects. The setting for the study was an elementary school with a predominantly Chinese population. The school was located near a large Chinatown community on the West Coast. There were approximately 644 students enrolled in Chinatown Elementary at the time of this study. The school population is relatively stable, but there are periodic influxes of new immigrant and refugee populations. Almost half (44.6%) of the school population was Chinese; the remainder of the students were largely Spanish surname (19.9%), other Oriental (20.5%), and Black (11.6%). Because of the ethnic quota system operative within the district, the school is now officially "closed" to new Chinese students, except those who live within the most immediate neighborhood. Most of the Chinese students at Chinese Elementary are classified as either Limited-English-Speaking (LES – 28%) or Non-English-speaking (NES – 61%). These students, in turn, are placed in either a bilingual or regular class.

Within the Chinese community, the school has a good reputation. Most Chinese parents seem to feel more secure if their children are attending a school that is predominantly Chinese and has Chinese teachers. There have been reports of parents who submitted a falsified address, or used that of a relative, in order that their child might be allowed to attend the school.

The subjects in Phase 1 were eleven first-grade Chinese-American students, selected on the basis of English language proficiency. Prior to data collection, each teacher was asked to rank all students in the class on a four-point scale of oral English language proficiency. The bilingual teacher also provided similar information on students' Chinese proficiency. These judgements were then verified through observations of potential target students. In this way, five students ranked at the low end of the scale (1-2), four ranked at the middle of the scale (3), and two fluent English speakers were selected.

Lessons. As mentioned earlier, the two participating teachers in the study taught in a half-day alternation bilingual program. Each teacher met with the students in the target class for half of each school day, and alternated between mornings and afternoons. One teacher was bilingual and biliterate in Chinese and English, and although the other spoke no Chinese, he did speak Spanish and had taught a self-contained Spanish bilingual class the year before. Both teachers had several years of experience.

Two types of lessons were selected for analysis in this report, Reading with the bilingual teacher and oral language in the Anglo teacher's class. Although the lesson content and focus differed somewhat across the teachers' lessons, they were in many respects comparable. For two weeks prior to taping, classroom observers took descriptive fieldnotes and coded for activity structures. These two lessons were found to be compatible in that they were both teacher-directed, student membership was approximately the same, and both teachers organized lessons around a basic question/answer format. Descriptions of the typical organization of each teacher's lesson follow.

Reading. The bilingual teacher divided students into four instructional groups for reading: Flintstones, Roadrunners, Bugs Bunnies, and Snoopies. Each group met with the teacher for 15 to 20 minutes during each reading period, rotating according to the schedule set up by the teacher. Reading lessons are conducted in much the same way with each group. The teacher usually began by writing a list of vocabulary words on the board near the reading table. She then would introduce each word and ask students to read and say the words as a group. Individual students were then called on to read all the vocabulary words aloud. The next activity included story posters. Each poster contained a picture on the top and a story below. When she used the poster, the teacher would ask the students to look at the picture first, then ask them to describe the picture. Together, they would then read the story on the poster. When she used the book, she adopted the same approach as with the poster, beginning with a description of the picture, followed by reading. The final step in the typical reading lesson would be to ask the children to read the text silently, after which she asked them comprehension questions. To answer these, students were allowed to read an appropriate phrase or sentence from the text. Throughout the reading lesson, if students stumbled over a word, the teacher read it out and asked the student to repeat it.

Oral Language. The Anglo teacher divided his class for oral language into two instructional groups on the basis of oral English proficiency, Low and a combination of Middle and High. However, during the oral language period, only that group being taught by the teacher remained in the classroom; the other group met with another instructor in a different room. The overall procedures employed with each group were much the same. The Low group consisted of six students who sat in their assigned seats. For oral language, the teacher would join the group by pulling up an additional chair. Very often the lesson began with picture flash cards, which students were required to identify and describe. The Middle/High group was composed of nine students. They all sat at a table in the center of the room, where only the Middle group students normally sat. The teacher brought his own chair when he joined the group. Once again, the teacher usually began with picture flashcards, which the students were to identify. Chinese lessons taught by the bilingual teacher as well as seatwork in the other teacher's class were recorded as well.

Phase Two. In Phase Two, teachers and target students were recorded in different lessons: oral language and seatwork in the Anglo teacher's class and reading and Chinese in the bilingual teacher's class. There were transcribed, coded, and analyzed. The following is an overall description of the activities within this phase of the study. Audiotape recordings were made through the use of a Marantz recorder, with two lavaliere microphones placed in the middle of each group's table. All data collection for Phase Two was conducted over a two-month period in the Spring of 1982.

Two data collectors were present during each taping session, both fluent speakers of Cantonese, Mandarin, and English. One data collector took fieldnotes on the activities of the focal group, recording information on the physical arrangement of the group, important nonverbal behaviors, the text and/or materials used, and other contextual information. The other data collector, meanwhile, monitored the audiotape through earphones. Because of incidental noise in the class and the voices of students in other groups, the earphones enabled the data collector to hear the speech of the teacher and target students much better. This data collector wrote down names and utterance fragments of speakers throughout the interaction to aid in subsequent transcription.

The audiotape recording of each lesson was transcribed by the data collector who monitored that taping session. The handwritten transcript was then entered into an IBM Personal Computer used for the analysis. Those utterances in Chinese were transcribed in Chinese, and an English translation was provided in brackets. Descriptions of nonverbal behavior were included in parentheses.

Recordings took place between February, 1982 through October, 1982 Lessons 1-28 were recorded while students were in first grade. Lessons 30-38 were recorded while students were in second grade.

Code	Child's name	Sex	Age
*WYM	Wyman	M	7;8
*PHU	Phung Ngoc	F	6;11
*AHT	Ah Tay	F	?
*AHN	Ah Ngat	F	6;10
*AHP	Ah Phang	F	6;6
*MEO	Mei Oanh	F	8;0
*STE	Steven	F	7;5
*HOW	Howie	M	7;10
*HIE	Hieu Nghi	F	6;7

*ANT	Anton	M	?
*CAO	Carolina	F	6;5
*JAC	Jackie	F	6;4
*CHR	Christopher	M	7;1
*CLI	Clifton	M	?

The following are other children in the class:

*AMY	Amy	F
*MEN	Mei-Ngoc	F
*LIS	Lisa	F
*JUS	Justin	M
*JOS	Joseph	M
*KEA	Kearny	M
*YVO	Yvonne	F
*ANH	Anh Tu	F
*WAI	Wai Yee	F
*CAL	Carletta	F
*HEN	Henrietta	F
*SUB	Subnum	F
*STU	Unidentified Student 1	
*STU	Unidentified Student 2	
*SEV	Several	

The following are adults interacting with the students:

*MAR	Mary	(bilingual teacher, Teacher A)
*LAR	Larry	(Teacher B)
*ELA	Elaine	(Mary's aide)
*ELL	Ellen	(Larry's aide)
*TRA	Tracy	(Mary's student teacher)
*JUN	June	
*BEA	Beatrice	
*FOO	Miss Foo	

Files. There are three subdirectories. The "Larry" subdirectory contains the files from the monolingual Anglo teacher's class of first graders. The "Mary" subdirectory contains the files from the first grade class of the bilingual teacher. The "Maisie" subdirectory contains the files from the second grade teacher's class in the follow-up study. The teacher was observed on three different days with three reading groups on each day. For the "Maisie" subdirectory, the following additional codes are used:

Speaker Number	Speaker Code	Name of Speaker	Identity
09	MAI	Maisie Dea	Teacher
10	QUO	Quoc-Hung	Student
17	SAM	Sam-Day	Student
18	ELI	Elizabeth	Student
19	XYZ	*	Student
20	KIM	Kim-Lien	Student
27	RIT	Rita	Student
28	CHI	Chin	Student
29	EDW	Edwin	Student
30	TIN	Tina	Student
33	ANG	Angela	Student

37	PUI	Pui-Chin	Student
39	NGH	Nghi-Ma	Student
54	VEL	Velma	Student
91	STU	Unknown	Student
92	STU	Unknown	Student
93	STU	Unknown	Student
99	SEV	Several	Students

*There is no positive identification of speaker XYZ's name, however the speaker may be "Sui-Wai"

Please contact Dr. Guthrie before conducting analyses using the conversation act coding system. This coding system is delineated in the file 0codes.doc and in 0orig.doc. Articles published from this data include Guthrie (1983), Guthrie (1984), and Guthrie and Guthrie (1988).

31.4. Hayashi

This corpus includes longitudinal data from a child growing up in a Japanese-Danish bilingual family in the age range of 12-29 months. The data were collected by Mariko Hayashi, University of Aarhus, Denmark, in the context of her Ph.D. study investigating language development in bilingual children. Pseudonyms have been used to preserve informant anonymity. The child is called "Anders". Anders is a first born boy, and had no siblings during the period studied. The father had an university education, the mother college education, thus the family belongs to the educated middle class.

Anders' mother is Japanese and father Danish. The family resided in Denmark, where the community language is Danish. The parents have spoken their respective native tongue to the child from the beginning. Occationally code-switching by the parents, especailly by the father, does occur to a certain extent. The parents speak mainly English, and occasionally Japanese and Danish to each other. Anders and his mother spent summer vacation in Japan at the child's age of 21-23 months. In this period Anders was exposed exclusively to Japanese.

Anders was taken care of by his mother in the day time. He had a couple of Danish speaking playmates he was occasionally together with. In the evenings and the weekends the father took care of the child as well. The father's parents, who speak Danish, lived in the neighborhood, and visited the family regularly. People who visited the mother spoke either Japanese or English to her, as the mother did not understand much Danish. The father and the mother, as mentioned above, speak mainly English to each other. Otherwise, the child was not exposed to English.

The language Anders was exposed most to was Japanese, as it was the mother who took care of him in the day time. He also spent a three-month summer vacation in Japan, where he was exposed exclusively to Japanese. In his productive vocabulary Japanese began to be dominant at 20 months. The dominance of the Japanese language became especially clear while and after his visit to Japan. Although Anders did not show any clear sign for comprehending English, he did pick up a few English expressions such as "see you" and "two".

Monthly video-recordings of the child of about an hour's duration were made in the age range of 11-38 months. All recordings were made in the child's own home by Hayashi. With a few exceptions, both parents were present at each session. Each visit included until a certain time testing on the Uzgiris-Hunt Infant Assessment Scales (1978) as well. For a certain period, the parents were asked to keep a record of the child's production of lexicalized items, which was used as a supplement to the video-recordings. The mother made audio-recordings during their stay in Japan as well.

30 minutes of each session was transcribed based on standard orthography by Hayashi, who is a native speaker of Japanese as well as a fluent speaker of Danish. All transcripts were checked by a native speaker of Danish. Three or four different situations, typically dining situation, free play and book reading, were selected for transcription. Furthermore, care was taken so that the mother and the father were more or less equally included in the portion of recording to be transcribed. The Plunkett method (1990) is applied for identifying utterances and units of speech. That is, utterances are identified after prosodic criteria such as intonation and pauses, whilst utterances themselves are divided into units based on clarity of articulation and fluency. Limited attention is paid to overlapping, retracings, and hesitations. A deviated phonological form is described in the phonetic tier. However, it does not provide a precise phonetic analysis. Speech errors are not coded. All transcripts are formatted after the ChiLDES method (MacWhinney 1991).

The corpus contains the following 17 files.

File name	Date of recording	Age of the target child
and03.cha	02-NOV-1986	1;0.15
and04.cha	07-DEC-1986	1;1.20
and05.cha	18-JAN-1987	1;3.1
and06.cha	15-FEB-1987	1;3.28
and07.cha	08-MAR-1987	1;4.21
and08.cha	12-APR-1987	1;5.25
and09.cha	04-MAY-1987	1;6.17
and10.cha	31-MAY-1987	1;7.14
and11.cha	29-JUN-1987	1;8.12
and12.cha	03-AUG-1987	1;9.16
and13.cha	05-SEP-1987	1;10.18
and14.cha	31-OCT-1987	2;0.14
and15.cha	28-NOV-1987	2;1.11
and16.cha	07-JAN-1988	2;2.20
and17.cha	14-FEB-1988	2;3.27
and18.cha	17-MAR-1988	2,5.0
and19.cha	15-APR-1988	2;5.28

Warnings:

1. Overlapping is not accurately transcribed in these data.
2. Retracings and hesitations are not accurately transcribed in these data.
3. These data contain limited information regarding the context.
4. Repetitions of identical units/utterances are transcribed twice at most.
5. Productive units within an utterance are identified on the basis of articulation and fluency criteria.
6. The phonetic tier is used to describe more accurately the child's pronunciation of a given sound. However, it does not provide a precise phonetic analysis.
7. Regular inflections of nouns and verbs are preceded by a dash in the main text line. Irregularly inflected nouns and verbs are not divided into morphemes.
8. Two (or more) different words, which are spelled identically, are distinguished by @ followed by English explanation. Note that only the one word of the two in

each pair, which is assumed to be used less often, is marked. @d stands for Danish word, @j for Japanese word, and   @fp for @final particle.

9.   There are three alphabet letters in Danish, which cannot be typed onto the computer. Based on the conventional method, these letters are replaced by ae, oe, and aa respectively.

Publications that make use of this corpus can cite (Hayashi, 1993; Klausen, Subritzky & Hayashi, 1992).

31.5.   Serra

This study examined ten children in Barcelona learning Spanish, Catalan, or both from the ages of 1;0 to 3;0. The title of the project is "Language Acquisition in Spanish and Catalan Children" directed by Miquel Serra of the University of Barcelona and Rosa Solé of the Autonomous University of Barcelona with support from grant CAICYT PR84-0455, DGICYT PB0317 and DGICYT PB91-0851. The children were studied during the period from 1986 to 1989. Assistants on the project include Elisabet Serrat, Vicens Torrens, and Cristina Vila. The children include one monolingual Spanish child (Eduard), five monolingual Catalan children (Alvar, Gisela, Guillem, Laura, and Pep), and four bilingual children (Antoni, Caterina, Josep, and Marti). The situation of the sessions are natural: children speak with their mothers or caretakers in spontaneous speech. All of the sessions were videotaped.

31.6.   Snow / Velasco

Subjects in this study were Puerto Rican bilinguals who were enrolled in the bilingual program at the public schools in New Haven, Connecticut. Subjects were selected on the basis of teacher ratings. Teachers were asked to rate each of the children on their reading and writing skills, and on their speaking and listening skills on a five point scale in both languages. Eighty children were selected for participation in this study; half were third and half were fifth graders. Half in each grade were identified as relatively poor readers (in Spanish) and the other half as good readers. All the children were either born in Puerto Rico or on the mainland of Puerto Rican parents, and all spoke Spanish predominantly or exclusively at home. The files are organized into four directories, each corresponding to a group of children:

    3PR 3rd grade poor readers
    3GR 3rd grade good readers
    5PR 5th grade poor readers
    5GR 5th grade good readers

Within each directory files are identified for the language used (S or E) in the first position of the filename, the task (dpt = decontextualized picture description, def = definitions) and then the subject number. Thus, to compare the English and Spanish files for one child one must select (for example) EDPT277.cha and SDPT277.cha.

The children were attending public school bilingual classrooms in a school system which had adopted a "pairing model" for bilingual education. Within this model, each child spends half the day with a Spanish-speaking teacher receiving instruction in Spanish, and the other half with an English-speaking teacher receiving instruction in English. The Spanish half of the day is devoted primarily to reading and content area instruction, whereas the English half of the day includes repetition in English of some of the content already presented in Spanish, English reading, and some ESL instruction. In the third grade the bilingual classrooms which the subjects attended contained about 30-35 children. By fifth grade, classes were much smaller, because most of the normally progressing children had been mainstreamed. Fifth grade classes consisted of two groups: more recent arrivals from Puerto Rico and children with persistent difficulties in acquiring English. The selection criteria guaranteed that:

1. All students had been in this bilingual program for at least two years.
2. All students qualified for the free lunch program (indicator of poverty status, based on per capita family income). Parents were in general engaged in unskilled labor or unemployed.
3. California Test of Basic Skills (Spanish) reading scores fell between the 60th to 89th percentile (for the good readers) or the 11th to 40th percentile (poor readers). Means (standard deviations) were: third grade poor readers 33 (7); third grade good readers 70 (9); fifth grade poor readers 30 (9); and fifth grade good readers 75 (10).
4. All participants had adequate (i.e., third grade equivalent) English decoding skills, as assessed by the Word Recognition Achievement Test.

Testing procedure: Oral language performance in both Spanish and English was assessed using two different tasks. Testing was done in separate sessions for each language. Half of the subjects in each grade were tested first in Spanish, half were tested first in English. Testing in both languages was carried out by Patricia Velasco, a fluent bilingual. The subjects were also administered a reading comprehension test (Velasco & Snow, 1990)
.

Definitions. The definitions task was designed to test the child's ability to give formal definitions (Davidson, Kline & Snow, 1986). The procedure is identical to that prescribed in the WISC-R instructions, and the first ten nouns in the WISC-R were used. Specific instructions were: "What does ____ mean?" The Spanish version of this is, "Qué quiere decir _____?"

Picture description. To assess children's ability to respond to the needs of a distant listener, a picture description task was used. Children were shown a picture that included 3-4 children of the same gender engaged in play or household activities. Instructions were: "Please describe this picture so that another child that will be coming after you can draw a picture exactly like this one but without looking at it, just by listening to you. The Spanish version of this was, "Por favor describe lo que está pasando en este dibujo, para que el niño que venga después de ti pueda hacer un dibujo igual a este, pero sin verlo, solo escuchandote a ti."

The picture description files contain a coding line that reflects coding for various features presumed to be of importance in distinguishing more complete, more explicit, and more narrative descriptions from the rest. For complete coding instructions, see Velasco (1989), Velasco & Snow (1990) or Davidson, Kline & Snow (1986). Briefly, the categories coded with their abbreviations were:

VE	verb, present tense
VN	nonpresent tense verb
NP	noun phrase
LX	lexical noun phrase
AJ	adjective
UC	unusual conjunction (i.e., not 'and' or 'and then')
SL	specific locative
CM	clarificatory marker (post nominal clarification)
RL	relative clause
RE	revision, self correction

CO   communicatively effective revision
OP   opening--an explicitly narrative opening
TP   saying explicitly 'this picture'
CL   closing--some conventional closing (the end; that's all)
NC   naming characters--assigning proper names to characters
XP   extrapictorial element--mention of something not in picture
IS   internal state--reference to internal state of character
CF   conversational features--intrusions of child as speaker
DI   dialogue--instances in which character is quoted directly
LS   language switch--word from other language
CW   creation of words--use of words not either Spanish or English

The data were recorded onto audiotape and then transcribed into a minCHAT format. Papers that use these data should cite Velasco (Velasco, 1989) and Velasco and Snow (1990).

32. CHILDES/BIB

Roy Higginson has compiled a rich computerized bibliography of research in child language development. The entry of the bibliography was supported by the MacArthur Foundation and NIH grants to CHILDES at Carnegie Mellon University. The research staff at Iowa State University who assisted Dr. Higginson in the data entry were: Kyunghee Hong, Kate Kasten, Kyoko Mizuno, Mack Staton, and Alexis Walker. The Society for Research in Child Development gave permission to include materials from the *Child Development Abstracts* in the database, the Linguistic Society of America gave permission to use materials previously published in *Language*. Adele Abrahamsen gave permission to include references from Abrahamsen (1977) and Dan I. Slobin gave permission to use materials from Slobin (1972). The CHILDES system wants to thank the SRCD, the LSA, Indiana University Press, University Park Press, Adele Abrahamsen, and Dan I. Slobin for their generous cooperation. Without these permissions, construction of this bibliographic database would have been impossible.

The CHILDES/BIB system provides fast electronic access to references for research articles in child language research. The system includes full bibliographic information and abstracts for over 16,000 articles. The electronic version of the CHILDES/BIB system was redesigned in June of 1993 to utilize the EndNote Plus database system developed by Niles and Associates. A demo version of EndNote is provided with the database. The full version of EndNote can be purchased for approximately $150 either through mail order or from:

> Niles and Associates
> 2000 Hearst Ave., Suite 200
> Berkeley, CA 94709, U.S.A.
> phone (510) 649-8176 fax (510) 649-8179

Niles and Associates have allowed us to distribute a limited version of EndNote for use with the CHILDES/BIB database. The EndNote application works in a fairly intuitive fashion. If you have questions regarding its use, please consult the "ReadMe" file distributed with the EndNote program. The file "0cats.doc" provides a listing of the keywords used in the database. The CHILDES/BIB system is distributed through FTP and CD-ROM, as discussed in Chapter 27.

Publications that make use of this bibliographic tool should cite Higginson and MacWhinney (1990).

33. Research Based on CHILDES

The availability of the CHILDES database and programs has facilitated the publication of hundreds of new empirical studies of language learning. These new publications are not mindless recitations of numerical distributions and frequency counts. Instead, they are high quality analyses that link the classic issues in language learning to this new, stronger empirical foundation.

Publications based on use of the CHILDES system divide into a number of general categories. The six categories include: grammatical development, input studies, computational modeling and connectionism, lexical learning, narrative structure, language and literacy, language impairments, and phonological development. Let us review the work produced in each of these six categories.

33.1. Grammatical Development

One of the most active topics of investigation has been the development of the marking of grammatical categories. The theoretical perspectives adopted here range from functional analyses to formal syntax inside the G-B framework. Much of this work is crosslinguistic. Languages studied have included German, English, French, Inuktitut, Swedish, Spanish, Polish, and Hebrew. Some of this work examines the development of specific syntactic categories, while other work looks at overall issues in learnability, phrase structure development, functional categories, or parameter-setting. Additional work on the acquisition of grammatical categories can also be found in the section that lists published articles on language impairments.

Allen, S. (1994). *Acquisition of some mechanisms of transitivity alternation in arctic Quebec Inuktitut.* Unpublished doctoral dissertation, McGill University.

Allen, S., & Crago, M. B. (1993). The acquisition of passives and unaccusatives in Inuktitut. *McGill Working Papers in Linguistics*, 9, 1-29.

Andersson, A. (1992). Second language learners' acquisition of grammatical gender in Swedish. *Gothenburg Monographs in Linguistics*, 10.

Andersson, A. B., & Strömqvist, S. (1990). Adult L2 acquisition of gender - a crosslinguistic and cross-learner type perspective. *Gothenburg Papers in Theoretical Linguistics*, 61.

Andersson, E., & Richtoff, U. (1991). Relativkonstrukionernas ontogenes - en fallstudie. *Gothenburg Papers in Theoretical Linguistics*, 17.

Behrens, H. (1993). *Temporal reference in German child language.* Unpublished doctoral dissertation, University of Amsterdam.

Bentivoglio, P. (1992). Linguistic correlations between subjects of one-argument verbs and subjects of more-than-one argument verbs in spoken Spanish. In P. Hirschbuhler, & K. Koerner (Eds.), *Romance Languages and Modern Linguistic Theory*. Amsterdam: John Benjamins.

Berman, R. A. (1990). On acquiring an (S)VO language: Subjectless sentences in children's Hebrew. *Linguistics*, 28, 1135-1166.

Berman, R. A. (1993). Marking of verb transitivity by Hebrew-speaking children. *Journal of Child Language*, 20, 641-669.

Berman, R. A. (1994). Developmental perspectives on transitivity: A confluence of ideas. In Y. Levy (Ed.) *Other childre, other languages: Issues in the theory of language acquisition* . Hillsdale, NJ: Erlbaum.

Bloom, P. (1989b). Why do children omit subjects? *Papers and Reports on Child Language Development, 28,* 57-64.

Bloom, P. (1990a). *Semantic structure and language development.* Unpublished doctoral dissertation, MIT.

Bloom, P. (1990b). Subjectless sentences in child language. *Linguistic Inquiry, 21,* 491-504.

Bloom, P. (1990c). Syntactic distinctions in child language. *Journal of Child Language, 17,* 343-355.

Bloom, P. (1993a). Grammatical continuity in language development: The case of subjectless sentences. *Linguistic Inquiry, 24,* 721-734.

Bloom, P. (1993b). Theories of subjectless sentences in language development. In *Proceedings of the 1992 Western Conference on Linguistics..*

Bloom, P. (1994). Semantic competence as an explanation for some transitions in language development. In Y. Levy (Ed.) *Other children, other languages: Issues in the theory of language acquisition* . Hillsdale NJ: Erlbaum.

Bloom, P. (in press-a). Subjectless sentences in child languages. *Linguistic Inquiry.*

Bloom, P. (in press-b). Syntactic distinctions in child language. *Journal of Child Language.*

Bloom, P., Barss, A., Nicol, J., & Conway, L. (1994). Children's knowledge of binding and coreference: Evidence from spontaneous speech. *Language, 70,* 53-71.

Brent, M. (1994). Surface cues and robust inference as a basis for the early acquisition of subcategorization frames. *Lingua, 92,* 433-470.

De Houwer, A. (1990). *The acquisition of two languages: A case study.* New York: Cambridge University Press.

de Villiers, J. (1991). Why questions? In B. Plunkett, & T. Maxfield (Eds.), *The acquisition of wh.* Amherst MA: University of Massachusetts.

de Villiers, J. (1992). On the acquisition of functional categories: A general commentary. In J. Meisel (Ed.) *The acquisition of verb placement: Functional categories and V2 phenomena in language development..* Dordrecht: Kluwer.

de Villiers, J., Roeper, T., & Vainikka, A. (in press). The acquisition of long distance rules. In L. Frazier, & J. de Villiers (Eds.), *Language processing and acquisition..* Amsterdam: Kluwer.

Deprez, V., & Pierce, A. (1993). Negation and functional projections in early grammar. *Linguistic Inquiry, 24,* 25-67.

Drozd, K. (1994). *A unification categorial grammar of child English negation.* Unpublished doctoral dissertation, University of Arizona.

Eisenberg, S. (1989). *The development of infinitives by 3-, 4-, and 5-year-old children.* Unpublished doctoral dissertation, CUNY Graduate Center.

Gordon, P., & Chafetz, J. (1990). Verb-based vs. class-based accounts of actionality effects in children's comprehension of passives. *Cognition, 36,* 227-254.

Gropen, J., Pinker, S., Hollander, M., & Goldberg, R. (1991). Syntax and semantics in the acquisition of locative verbs. *Journal of Child Language, 18,* 115-151.

Gropen, J., Pinker, S., Hollander, M., & Goldberg, R. (in press). The semantics of direct objects in the acquisition of verb argument structure. *Cognition* .

Gropen, J., Pinker, S., Hollander, M., Goldberg, R., & Wilson, R. (1989). The learnability and acquisition of the dative alternation in English. *Language, 65,* 203-257.

Hyams, N., & Wexler, K. (1993). On the grammatical basis of null subjects in child language. *Linguistic Inquiry, 24,* 421-459.

Ihns, M., & Leonard, L. (1988). Syntactic categories in early child language: Some additional data. *Journal of Child Language, 15,* 673-678.

Ingham, R. (1992). *Syntactic input and verb transitivity in L1 acquisition.* Working Papers. Unpublished manuscript, Department of Linguistic Science, University of Reading.

Kim, J., Marcus, G., Pinker, S., Hollander, M., & Coppola, M. (1994). Sensitivity of children's inflection to grammatical structure. *Journal of Child Language*, *21*, 173-209.

Kim, J., Pinker, S., Prince, A., & Prasada, S. (1990). Why no mere mortal has ever flown out to center field. *Cognitive Science*, *15*, 173-218.

MacWhinney, B. (1993b). How to set parameters: Arguments from language change. *Applied Psycholinguistics*, *14*, 418-421.

Marcus, G. (in press). Children's overregularization of English plurals: A quantitative analysis. *Journal of Child Language* .

Marcus, G., Ullman, M., Pinker, S., Hollander, M., Rosen, T., & Xu, F. (1992). Overregularization in language acquisition. *Monographs of the Society for Research in Child Development*, *57* .

Maxfield, T. (1991). Children answer echo questions how? In B. Plunkett, & T. Maxfield (Eds.)., *The acquisition of wh*. Amherst MA: University of Massachusetts.

O'Grady, W., Peters, A., & Masterson, D. (1989). The transition from optional to required subjects. *Journal of Child Language*, *16*, 513-529.

Ono, S. (1994). A corpus of a Japanese girl: Arisa (1;6.2): Part 1. *The Bulletin of Aichi Shukutoku Junior College*, *33*, 81-108.

Pinker, S. (1989). *Learnability and cognition: the acquisition of argument structure*. Cambridge: MIT Press.

Pinker, S. (1994a). Grammar puss. *The New Republic*, *210*, 19-26.

Pinker, S. (1994b). *The language instinct.*. New York: William Morrow.

Pinker, S., Lebeaux, D., & Frost, L. A. (1987). Productivity and constraints in the acquisition of the passive. *Cognition*, *26*, 195-267.

Pizzuto, E., & Caselli, M. (1993). The acquisition of Italian morphology: A reply to Hyams. *Journal of Child Language*, *20*, 707-712.

Pan, B. (1994). Basic measures of child language. In J. Sokolov, & C. Snow (Eds.), *Handbook of research in language acquisition using CHILDES* . Hillsdale NJ: Erlbaum.

Plunkett, K., & Strömqvist, S. (1992). The acquisition of Scandinavian languages. In D. I. Slobin (Ed.), *The crosslinguistic study of language acquisition: Volume 3*. Hillsdale, NJ: Lawrence Erlbaum Associates.

Poeppel, D., & Wexler, K. (1993). The full competence hypothesis of clause structure in early German. *Language*, *69*, 1-33.

Roeper, T., & de Villiers, J. (in press). Ordered decisions in the acquisition of wh-movement. In H. Goodluck, J. Weissenborn, & T. Roeper (Eds.), *Proceedings of the Berlin Conference*. Hillsdale, NJ: Erlbaum.

Sano, T. (1989). *A mechanism of language acquisition: A preliminary study of the acquisition of grammatical relations*. Unpublished doctoral dissertation, Tokyo Gakugei University.

Sera, M. (1992). To be or to be: Use and acquisition of the Spanish copulas. *Journal of Memory and Language*, *31*, 408-427.

Shirai, Y. (1994a). On the overgeneralization of progressive marking on stative verbs: Bioprogram or input? *First Language*, *14*, 67-82.

Shirai, Y. (1994b). *Tense/aspect marking by L2 learners of Japanese*. Boston University Conference on Language Development, Boston .

Slobin, D. I. (Ed.) (1992). *The crosslinguistic study of language acquisition, Vol. 3*. Hillsdale, NJ: Lawrence Erlbaum.

Slobin, D. I. (1993). Coding child language data for crosslinguistic analysis. In J. A. Edwards, & M. D. Lampert (Eds.), *Talking data: Transcription and coding of spoken discourse*. Hillsdale, NJ: Erlbaum.

Slobin, D. I. (1994a). Crosslinguistic aspects of child language acquisition. *Sophia Work Papers in Linguistics*, *35* .

Slobin, D. I. (1994b). Passives and alternatives in children's narratives in English, Spanish, German, and Turkish. In B. Fox, & P. Hopper (Eds.)., *Voice: Form and function*. Amsterdam: Benjamins.

Slobin, D. I. (1994c). Talking perfectly: Discourse origins of the present perfect. In W. Pagliuca, & G. Davis (Eds.), *Perspectives on grammaticalization*. Amsterdam: Benjam

Slobin, D. I. (in press-a). Converbs in Turkish child language: The grammaticalization of event coherence. In M. Haspelmath, & E. Koenig (Eds.), *Converbs in crosslinguistic perspective*. Berlin: Mouton de Gruyter.

Stephany, U. (1992). Grammaticalization in first language acquisition. *Zeitschrift für Phonetik, Sprachwißenschaft, und Kommunikationsforschung, 45*, 289-303.

Stephany, U. (1995). The acquisition of Greek. In D. I. Slobin (Ed.), *The crosslinguistic study of language acquisition. Vol. 4*. Hillsdale, NJ: Lawrence Erlbaum.

Stromswold, K. (1988). Linguistic representations of children's wh-questions. *Papers and Reports on Child Language Development, 27*, 107-114.

Stromswold, K. (1989). How conservative are children?: Evidence from auxiliary errors. *Papers and Reports on Child Language Development, 22*, 25-35.

Stromswold, K. (1991). *Learnability and the acquisition of auxiliaries*. ESCOL '91, Ohio State.

Stromswold, K. (1993). *Learnability and the acquisition of auxiliaries*. Unpublished doctoral dissertation, MIT.

Stromswold, K. (1994). Using spontaneous production data to assess syntactic development. In D. McDaniel, C. McKee, & H. Cairns (Eds.), *Methods for assessing children's syntax*. Cambridge: MIT Press.

Stromswold, K. (in press). The acquisition of subject and object wh-questions. *Language Acquisition*.

Stromswold, K. (1995b). The cognitive and neural bases of language acquisition. In M. Gazzaniga (Ed.) *The cognitive neurosciences*. Cambridge: MIT Press.

Stromswold, K., Pinker, S., & Kaplan, R. (1985). Cues for understanding the passive voice. *Papers and Reports on Child Language, 24*.

Thomas, M. (1994). Young children's hypotheses about English reflexives. In J. Sokolov, & C. Snow (Eds.), *Handbook of research in language development using CHILDES*. Hillsdale, NJ: Lawrence Erlbaum Associates.

Weist, R. (1990). Neutralization and the concept of subject in child Polish. *Linguistics, 28*, 1331-1349.

Weist, R. (in press). Split intransitivity in child language. In M. Bowerman (Ed.) *MPI Conference on verb argument structure*.

Xu, F., & Pinker, S. (in press). Weird past tense forms. *Journal of Child Language*.

33.2. Input Studies

Within the larger topic of grammatical development, there has recently been particular interest in better understanding the degree to which language development is driven by either parental input or an internal BioProgram. Are children provided with negative evidence, is this evidence consistent enough to support learning, and do children make any use of the negative evidence they receive? Can learning be faciliated by recasts and expansions? The analysis of CHILDES transcripts has played an important role in the examination of these issues.

Anderson, R., & Shirai, Y. (1994). Discourse motivations for some cognitive acquisition principles. *Studies in Second Language Acquisition, 16*, 133-156.

Bever, T., Newport, E., Aslin, R., Mintz, T., Juliano, C., & LaMendola, N. (in preparation). Computational studies of motherese.

Bohannon, N., MacWhinney, B., & Snow, C. (1990). No negative evidence revisited: Beyond learnability or who has to prove what to whom. *Developmental Psychology*, 26, 221-226.

Bohannon, N., & Stanowicz, L. (1988). The issue of negative evidence: Adult responses to children's language errors. *Developmental Psychology*, *24*, 684-689.

Chafetz, J., Feldman, H., & Wareham, N. (1992). There car: Ungrammatical parentese. *Journal of Child Language*, *19*, 473-480.

Crain, S. (1991). Language acquisition in the absence of experience. *Behavioral and Brain Sciences*, *14*, 597-611.

Kuntay, A., & Slobin, D. I. (in press). Listening to a Turkish mother: Some puzzles for acquisition. In D. I. Slobin, J. Guo, & A. Kyratzis (Eds.), *Social interaction, social context, and language: Essays in honor of Susan Ervin-Tripp.* Hillsdale NJ: Erlbaum.

Marcus, G. (1993). Negative evidence in language acquisition. *Cognition*, *46*, 53-85.

Mintz, T., Newport, E., & Bever, T. (1994). *Distributional regularities of grammatical categories in speech to infants.*

Morgan, J. (1989). Learnability considerations and the nature of trigger experiences in language acquisition. *Behavioral and Brain Sciences*, *12*, 352-353.

Morgan, J., & Travis, L. (1989). Limits on negative information in language input. *Journal of Child Language*, *16*, 531-552.

Morgan, J. L., Meier, R. P., & Newport, E. L. (1989). Facilitating the acquisition of syntax with cross-sentential cues to phrase structure. *Journal of Memory and Language*, *28*, 360-374.

Oshima-Takane, Y. (1989). Effects of older siblings on early language development. In *Proceedings of the 31st Annual Convention of Japanese Association of Educational Psychology.* Tokyo: Japanese Association ofEducational Psychology.

Oshima-Takane, Y. (1992). Parental interaction style and language development. In *Proceedings of the 56th Annual Convention of Japanese Psychological Association.* Tokyo: Japanese Psychological Association.

Oshima-Takane, Y., & Derevensky, J. (1990). *Do later-born children delay in language development?* Unpublished manuscript, Paper presented at the International Conference on Infant Studies, Montreal.

Oshima-Takane, Y., Goodz, E., & Derevensky, J. L. (In press). Birth order effects on early language development: Do second children learn from overheard speech? *Child Development*,

Post, K. (1994). Negative evidence. In J. Sokolov, & C. Snow (Eds.), *Handbook of research in language development using CHILDES*. Hillsdale, NJ: Lawrence Erlbaum Associates.

Richards, B., & Robinson, P. (1993). Environmental correlates of child copula verb growth. *Journal of Child Language*, *20*, 343-362.

Sokolov, J. (1990). *Conversational interaction and competition in child language.* Unpublished doctoral dissertation, Carnegie Mellon University.

Sokolov, J. (1992). Linguistic imitation in children with Down Syndrome. *American Journal on Mental Retardation*, *97*, 209-221.

Sokolov, J. (1993). A local contingency analysis of the fine-tuning hypothesis. *Developmental Psychology*, *29*, 1008-1023.

Sokolov, J., & MacWhinney, B. (1990). The CHIP framework: Automatic coding and analysis of parent-child conversational interaction. *Behavioral Research Methods, Instruments, and Computers*, *22*, 151-161.

Sokolov, J., & Moreton, J. (1994). Individual differences in linguistic imitativeness. In J. Sokolov, & C. Snow (Eds.), *Handbook of research in language development using CHILDES*. Hillsdale, NJ: Lawrence Erlbaum Associates.

Van Houten, L. (1988). *Role of maternal input in the acquisition process: The communicative strategies of adolescent and older mothers with their language learning children*. Phd. Thesis, Harvard University.

33.3. Computational Modeling and Connectionism

Recent interest in connectionist networks, cue-based learning, and statistical models has provided another venue for use of the CHILDES database. Both proponents and opponents of connectionist theory have used these data to support their respective positions.

Anderson, J., & Schooler, L. (1991). Reflections of the environment in memory. *Psychological Science*, *2*, 396-408.

Indefrey, P., & Goebel, R. (1993). The learning of weak noun declension in German: Children vs. artificial network models. In *Proceedings of the Fifteenth Annual Conference of the Cognitive Science Society*. Boulder, CO: Lawrence Erlbaum.

Karmiloff-Smith, A. (1992). Nature, nurture and PDP: Preposterous Developmental Postulates? *Connection Science*, *4*, 253-269.

Kazman, R. (1994). Simulating the child's acquisition of the lexicon and syntax: Experiences with Babel. *Machine Learning*, *16*, 87-120.

MacDonald, J. (1993). The acquisition of categories marked by multiple probabilistic cues. In G. Bower (Ed.) *Psychology of Learning and Motivation- Advances in Research and Theory*. New York: Academic.

Pinker, S., & Prince, A. (1988). On language and connectionism: Analysis of a Parallel Distributed Processing Model of language acquisition. *Cognition*, *29*, 73-193.

Plunkett, K. (1986). Learning strategies in two Danish children's language development. *Scandinavian Journal of Psychology*, *27*, 64-73.

Plunkett, K. (1993). Lexical segmentation and vocabulary growth in early language acquisition. *Journal of Child Language*, *20*, 43-60.

Plunkett, K., & Sinha, C. (1992). Connectionism and developmental theory. *British Journal of Developmental Psychology*, *10*, 209-254.

Redington, M., Chater, N., & Finch, S. (1993). Distributional information and the acquisition of linguistic categories: A statistical approach. In *Proceedings of the Fifteenth Annual Conference of the Cognitive Science Society*. Hillsdale, NJ: Lawrence Erlbaum.

33.4. Lexical Learning

Another major area of investigation in child language studies has been the acquisition of the meanings or concepts underlying words in areas as diverse as color words, contrast terms, place names, connectives, aspect, mental verbs, and politeness terms. In addition to studies of specific lexical fields, several articles and books have examined overall patterns of lexical development across ages.

Au, K. T., & Laframboise, D. E. (1990). Acquiring color names via linguistic contrast: The influence of contrasting terms. *Child Development*, *61*, 1806-1823.

Au, T. K., & Song, Y. K. (1994). Input vs. constraints: Early word acquisition in Korean and English. *Journal of Memory and Language*, *33*, 567-582.

Bartsch, K., & Wellman, H. (1994). *Children talk about the mind*. New York: Oxford University Press.

Bassano, D., & Champaud, C. (1989). The argumentative connective "même" in French: An experimental study in 8-year-old to 10-year-old children. *Journal of Child Language*, *16*, 643-664.

Bates, E., & Carnevale, G. (1993). New directions in research on language development. *Developmental Review*, *13*, 436-470.

Bates, E., Marchman, V., Thal, D., Lenson, L., Dale, P., Reznick, S., Reilly, J., & Hartung, J. (1994). Developmental and stylistic variation in the composition of early vocabulary. *Journal of Child Language*, *21*, 85-123.

Becker, J. (1994). "Sneak-shoes," "sworders," and "nose-beards": A case study of lexical innovation. *First Language*, *14*, 195-211.

Bodin, L., & Snow, C. (1993). What kind of a birdie is this? Learning to use superordinates. In J. Sokolov, & C. Snow (Eds.), *Handbook of research in language development using CHILDES*. Hillsdale, NJ: Lawrence Erlbaum Associates.

Boloh, Y. (1989). Time reference in conditional sentences. *Cahiers de Psychologie Cognitive*, *9*, 265-276.

Boloh, Y., & Champaud, C. (1993). The past conditional verb form in French children: the role of semantics in late grammatical development. *Journal of Child Language*, *20*, 169-189.

Byrnes, J. P., & Duff, M. A. (1989). Young children's comprehension of modal expressions. *Cognitive Development*, *4*, 369-387.

Champaud, C., & Bassano, D. (1994). French concessive connectives and argumentation: An experimental study in eight- to ten-year-old children. *Journal of Child Language*, *21*, 415-438.

Clark, E. (in press). Early verbs, event-types, and inflections. In J. Gilbert, & C. Johnson (Eds.), *Trieste IASCL Meeting*. Hillsdale, NJ: Erlbaum.

Clark, E., & Carpenter, K. (1989a). The notion of source in language acquisition. *Language*, *65*, 1-30.

Clark, E., & Carpenter, K. (1989b). On children's uses of "from," "by," and "with" in oblique noun phrases. *Journal of Child Language*, *16*, 349-364.

Clark, E. V. (1994). *Thematic roles in language acquisition: The case of Source*. In preparation.

de Acedo, B. (1994). Early morphological development: The acquisition of articles in Spanish. In J. Sokolov, & C. Snow (Eds.), *Handbook of research in language development using CHILDES*. Hillsdale, NJ: Lawrence Erlbaum Associates.

Dickinson, D. K., Cote, L., & Smith, M. W. (in press). Learning vocabulary in preschool: Social and discourse contexts affecting vocabulary growth. In C. Daiute (Ed.) *The development of literacy through social interaction*. San Francisco: Jossey-Bass.

Ely, R., & Gleason, J. B. (in press). The coin of the realm: Parents' and children's conversations about money. *Journal of Child Language* .

Ely, R., Gleason, J. B., & McCabe, A. (in press). "Why didn't you talk to your Mommy, Honey?". *Research on Language and Social Interaction* .

Ely, R., Gleason, J. B., Narasimhan, B., & McCabe, A. (in press). Family talk about talk: Mothers lead the way. *Discourse Processes* .

Ely, R., & McCabe, A. (1993). Remembered voices. *Journal of Child Language*, *20*, 671-696.

Ely, R., & McCabe, A. (1994). The language play of Kindergarten children. *First Language*, *14*, 19-35.

Estes, D., Wellman, H., & Woolley, J. (1989). Children's understanding of mental phenomena. *Advances in Child Development and Behavior*, *22*, 41-87.

Farrar, J., Friend, M., & Forbes, J. (1993). Event knowledge and early language acquisition. *Journal of Child Language*, *20*, 591-606.

Gleason, J. B., Ely, R., Perlmann, R., & Narasimhan, B. (1994). Patterns of prohibitions in parent-child discourse. In D. I. Slobin, J. Gerhardt, A. Kyratzis, & J. Guo (Eds.), *Social interaction, social context, and language: Essays in honor of Susan Ervin-Tripp*. Hillsdale, NJ: Erlbaum.

Gleason, J. B., Perlmann, R. Y., Ely, R., & Evans, D. W. (1994). The babytalk register: Parent's use of diminutives. In J. Sokolov, & C. Snow (Eds.), *Handbook of research in language using CHILDES*. Hillsdale NJ: Erlbaum.

Goldfield, B., & Snow, C. (1992). "What's your cousin Arthur's mommy's name?": Features of family talk about kin and kin terms. *First Language*, *12*, 187-205.

Harris, P. L., Banerjee, M., & Sinclair, A. (in press). Early understanding of emotion: Evidence from natural language. *Cognition and Emotion*,

Hu, Q. (1994). A study of some common features of mother's vocabulary. In J. Sokolov, & C. Snow (Eds.), *Handbook of research in language development using CHILDES*. Hillsdale, NJ: Lawrence Erlbaum Associates.

Jackson-Maldonado, D., & Thal, D. (in press). Lenguaje y cognicion en los primeros años de vida: Resultados preliminares. *Psicologia y Sociedad* .

Johnson, C., & Harris, P. (1994). Magic: Special but not excluded. *British Journal of Developmental Psychology*, *12*, 35-51.

Li, P. (1990). *Aspect and Aktionsart in child Mandarin*. Dordrecht: Foris.

Logan, J. (1992). *A computational analysis of young children's lexicons*. Unpublished doctoral dissertation, Indiana University.

Nelfelt, K. (1991). The development of definite singular in a Swedish boy. *Gothenburg Papers in Theoretical Linguistics*, *17* .

Scholnick, E., Hall, W. S., Wallner, K. E., & Livesey, K. (1993). The languages of affect: Developmental and functional considerations. *Merrill-Palmer Quarterly*, *39*, 311-325.

Scholnick, E., & Wing, C. S. (1992). Speaking deductively: Using conversation to trace the origins of conditional thought in children. *Merrill-Palmer Quarterly*, *38*, 1-20.

Sinha, C., Thorsen, L. A., Hayashi, M., & Plunkett, K. (in press). Comparative spatial semantics and language acquisition: evidence from Danish, English and Japanese. *Journal of Semantics* .

Slobin, D. I. (in press-c). Typology and rhetoric: Verbs of motion in English and Spanish. In M. Shibatani, & S. Thompson (Eds.), *Essays in semantics*. Oxford: Oxford University Press.

Slobin, D. I., & Hoiting, N. (in press). Reference to movement in spoken and signed languages: Typological considerations. *Proceedings of the Twentieth Annusal Meeting of the Berkeley Linguistic Society* .

Snow, C. (1987). Language and the beginnings of moral understanding. In J. Kagan, & J. Dunn (Eds.), *Moral development..* Cambridge: Harvard University Press.

Snow, C., Perlmann, R., Gleason, J., & Hooshyar, N. (1990). Developmental perspectives on politeness: Sources of children's knowledge. *Journal of Pragmatics*, *14*, 289-305.

Soja, N. (1987). *Ontological constraints on 2-year-olds' induction of word meanings*. Unpublished doctoral dissertation, MIT.

Soja, N. N. (1994). Evidence for a distinct kind of noun. *Cognition*, *51*, 267-284.

Soja, N. N., Carey, S., & Spelke, E. S. (1990). Ontological categories guide young children's inductions of word meaning: object terms and substance terms. *Cognition*, *38*, 179-211.

Tomasello, M. (1992). *First verbs: A case study of early grammatical development*. Cambridge: Cambridge University Press.

Wellman, H. (1991). From desires to beliefs: Acquisition of a theory of mind. In A. Whiten (Ed.) *Natural theories of mind: The evolution, development, and simulation of everyday mindreading*. Oxford: Basil Blackwell.

Wellman, H. M. (in press). Young children's conception of mind and emotion: Evidence from English speakers. In J. A. Russell (Ed.) *Everyday conception of emotion*. Dordrecht: Kluwer.

Wellman, H., & Banerjee, M. (1991). Mind and emotion: Children's understanding of the emotional consequences of beliefs and desires. *British Journal of Developmental Psychology*, *9*, 191-214.

Wellman, H., & Bartsch, K. (1994). Before belief: Children's early psychological theory. In C. Lewis, & P. Mitchell (Eds.), *Origins of an understanding of mind*. Hove: Earlbaum.

Wellman, H., & Bartsch, K. (1994). *Children talk about the mind*. Oxford: Oxford University Press.

Wellman, H., Harris, P., Banerjee, M., & Sinclair, A. (1994). Early understanding of emotion: Evidence from natural language. *Cognition and Emotion*, in press.

Wellman, H., & Hickling, A. (in press). The Mind's "I": Children's conception of the mind as an active agent. *Child Development* .

Windsor, J. (1993). The functions of novel word compounds. *Journal of Child Language*, *20*, 119-138.

Wolf, D., Moreton, J., & Camp, L. (1994). Children's acquisition of different kinds of narrative discourse: Genres and lines of talk. In J. Sokolov, & C. Snow (Eds.), *Handbook of research in language development using CHILDES*. Hillsdale, NJ: Lawrence Erlbaum Associates.

Woolley, J., & Wellman, H. (1990). Young children's understanding of realities, nonrealities, and appearances. *Child Development*, *61*, 946-961.

Woolley, J., & Wellman, H. (1994). Children's use of "real" and "really": the appearance/reality distinction in everyday communication. *Developmental Psychology*, in press.

33.5. Narrative Structure

Within the CHILDES system, a variety of tools have been developed to facilitate the study of the development of narrative structure. These include the **CHAINS**, **KEYMAP**, **DIST**, **GEM**, **GEMFREQ**, **GEMLIST**, and **KWAL** programs. These tools have been used in a large number of articles and theses.

Arlington, J., Brenninkmeyer, S., Arn, D., & O'Connell, D. (1992). A usual extreme case: Pause reports of informal spontaneous dialog. *Bulletin of the Psychonomic Society* .

Beals, D. E. (1993). Explanatory talk in low-income families' mealtime conversations. *Applied Psycholinguistics*, *14*, 489-513.

Beals, D. E., & De Temple, J. M. (1993a). Home contributions to early language and literacy development. In D. J. Leu, & C. K. Kinzer (Eds.), *Forty-second Yearbook of the National Reading Conference*. Chicago: National Reading Conference.

Beals, D. E., & De Temple, J. M. (1993). *The where and when of whys and what: Explanatory talk across settings*. SRCD Meeting, New Orleans.

Beals, D. E., De Temple, J. M., & Snow, C. E. (1991). *Reading, reporting and repast: Three R's for co-constructing language and literacy skills*. Submitted for publication.

Beals, D. E., & Snow, C. E. (1994). "Thunder is when the angels are upstairs bowling": Narratives and explanations at the dinner table. *Journal of Narrative and Life History*, *4*, 331-352.

Beals, D. E., & Tabors, P. O. (1994). *Talk at home: Extended discourse and rare vocabulary use at mealtimes.*. Paper presented at the Annual Meetings of the American Education Research Association, New Orleans.

Beals, D. E., & Tabors, P. O. (in press). Arboretum, bureaucratic, and carbohydrates: Preschoolers' exposure to rare vocabulary at home. *First Language* .

Berman, R. A., & Slobin, D. I. (1994). *Relating events in narrative: A crosslinguistic developmental study*. Hillsdale, NJ: Erlbaum.

Hickmann, M. (1991). The development of discourse cohesion: Some functional and cross-linguistic issues. *Pragmatics and Beyond*, 157-185.

Hickmann, M., & Liang, J. (1990). Clause-structure variation in Chinese narrative discourse: a developmental analysis. *Linguistics*, *28*, 1167-1200.

Hicks, D. (1990a). Kinds of texts: Narrative genre skills among children from two communities. In A. McCabe (Ed.) *Developing narrative structure*. Hillsdale, NJ: Lawrence Erlbaum.

Hicks, D. (1990b). Narrative skills and genre knowledge: Ways of telling in the primary school grades. *Applied Psycholinguistics*, *11*, 83-104.

Hicks, D. (in press). Genre skills and narrative development in the elementary school years. *Linguistics and Education*..

Hendriks, H. (1993). *Motion and location in children's narrative discourse*. Unpublished doctoral dissertation, University of Leiden.

Min, R.-F. (1994). *The acquisition of referring expressions by young Chinese children*. Unpublished doctoral dissertation, University of Nijmegen.

Minami, M. (1994). *Narrative styles of Japanese mothers and their children*. Unpublished doctoral dissertation, Harvard University.

Miranda, E., Camp, L., Hemphill, L., & Wolf, D. (1992). *Developmental changes in children's us of tense in narrative*. Paper presented at the Boston University Conference on Language Development, Boston.

Ninio, A., Snow, C., Pan, B., & Rollins, P. (1994). Classifying communicative acts in children's interactions. *Journal of Communicative Disorders*, *27*, 157-188.

Slobin, D. I. (1991). Learning to think for speaking: Narrative, language, cognition, and rhetorical style. *Pragmatics*, *1*, 7-26.

Slobin, D. I. (in press-b). From "thought and language" to "thinking for speaking". In J. J. Gumperz, & S. Levinson (Eds.), *Rethinking linguistic relativity*. Cambridge: Cambridge University Press.

Snow, C., & Dickinson, D. (1990). Social sources of narrative skills at home and at school. *First Language*, *10*, 87-103.

33.6.   Language and Literacy

The same computational tools that are used to study narrative development and lexical development have also been brought to bear on the study of the development of literacy.

Davidson, R. (1993). *Oral preparation for literacy: Mothers' and fathers' conversations with precocious readers*. Unpublished doctoral dissertation, Harvard University.

De Temple, J. M., & Beals, D. E. (1991). Family talk: Sources of support for the development of decontextualized language skills. *Journal of Research in Childhood Education*, *6*, 11-19.

De Temple, J. M., & Snow, C. (in press). Styles of parent-child book-reading as related to mothers' views of literacy and children's literacy outcomes. In J. Shimron (Ed.) *Literacy and education: Essays in honor of Dina Feitelson*. New York: Hampton Press.

Dickinson, D. K., & Beals, D. E. (1984). Not by print alone: Oral language supports for early literacy. In D. Lancy (Ed.) *Children's emergent literacy: From research to practice*. Westport, CT: Praeger.

Dickinson, D. K., Hirschler, J. A., & Smith, M. W. (1992). Book reading with preschoolers: Co-construction of text at home and at school. *Early Chilhood Research Quarterly*, *7*, 323-346.

Dickinson, D. K., & Moreton, J. (1993). Preschool classrooms as settings for the acquisition of emergent literacy and literacy-related language skills. *Merrill-Palmer Quarterly*,

Dickinson, D. K., & Smith, M. W. (1991). Preschool talk: Patterns of teacher-child interaction in early childhood classrooms. *Journal of Research in Childhood Education, 6*, 20-29.

Dickinson, D. K., & Tabors, P. O. (1991). Early literacy: Linkages between home, school and literacy achievement at age five. *Journal of Research in Childhood Education, 6*, 30-46.

Dickinson, D. K., & Smith, M. W. (1993). Long-term effects of preschool teachers'book readings on low-income children's vocabulary and story comprehension. *Reading Research Quarterly, 29*, 104-122.

Hebert, L. R., & Hadley, P. A. (submitted). *Variation in reading styles of Head Start teachers.*.

Koopmans, M. (1988). *Reasoning in two languages: An assessment of the effects of language proficiency on the syllogistic performance of Puerto Rican bilinguals.* Unpublished doctoral dissertation, Harvard Graduate School of Education.

Snow, C. E. (1991). The theoretical basis for relationships between language and literacy in development. *Journal of Research in Childhood Education, 6*, 5-10.

Snow, C. E., De Temple, J., Tabors, P. O., & Kurland, B. (1994). *Literacy across two generations.* APA Conference, Los Angeles.

Snow, C. E., & Kurland, B. (in press). Sticking to the point: Talk about magnets as a preparation for literacy. In D. Hicks (Ed.) *Child discourse and social learning: An interdisciplinary perspective.* New York: Cambridge University Press.

Snow, C. E., Perlmann, R., & Nathan, D. (1994). Why routines are different: Toward a multiple-factors model of the relation between input and language acquisition. In K. Nelson, & A. v. Kleeck (Eds.), *Children's Language.* Hillsdale, NJ: Erlbaum.

Snow, C. E., & Tabors, P. O. (1993). Home: Where children get ready for school. *Harvard Graduate School of Education Alumni Bulletin, 37*, 7-9.

Snow, C. E., Tabors, P. O., Nicholson, P., & Kurland, B. (1994). SHELL: A method for assessing oral language and early skills in kindergarten and first grade children. *Journal or Research in Childhood Education*.

Strömqvist, S. (1988). Svenska i ett ontogenetiskt perspektiv. In P. Linell, V. Adelsvärd, & L. Gustavsson (Eds.), *Svenskans beskrivning*. Linköping: Department of Communication Studies.

Strömqvist, S. (1992). Nordens språk som förstaspråk. In M. Axelsson, & Å. Viberg (Eds.), *Nordens språk som andraspråk*. Stockholm: University of Stockholm.

Strömqvist, S. (1993). Barns språk. In *Aktuell Forskning*. Gothenburg: University of Gothenburg.

Strömqvist, S. (1994a). Language acquisition, processing and change - perspectives on speech, sign, and writing. In I. Ahlgren, & K. Hyltenstam (Eds.), *Bilingualism in deaf education*. Hamburg: Signum.

Strömqvist, S. (in press). Language acquisition, speech, sign, and writing. *Scandinavian Working Papers in Bilingualism*.

Strömqvist, S. (1994c). Language development - a Scandinavian perspective. In A. Allwood (Ed.) *Proceedings from the XIVth Scandinavian Conference of Linguistics*. Göteborg.

Strömqvist, S., & Hellstrand, Å. (1994). Tala och skriva i lingvistiskt och didaktiskt perspektiv - en projecktbeskrivning. *Didaktisk Tidskrift, 1-2*.

Strömqvist, S., Ragnarsdóttir, H., Toivainen, K., Toivainen, H., Simonsen, G., Peters, A., Engstrand, O., Jondóttir, H., Lanza, E., Leiwo, M., Nordqvist, Å., Plunkett, K., & Richtoff, U. (in press). The inter-Nordic study of language acquisition. *Nordic Journal of Linguistics*.

Tabors, P. O., & Beals, D. E. (1993). *Learning new words from books: Context or conversation.* Harvard mss.

Velasco, P. (1989). *The relationship between decontextualized oral language skills and reading comprehension in bilingual children.* Unpublished doctoral dissertation, Harvard Graduate School of Education.

33.7.   Language Impairments

The application of CHILDES tools to the study of language impairments has been particularly active in the last four years. These analyses use basic **CLAN** tools for lexical counts, MLU analyses, and syntactic analyses to compare the language development of children with language impairments to that of normally-developing children.

Conti-Ramsden, G., & Dykins, J. (1991). Mother-child interactions with language-impaired children and their siblings. *British Journal of Disorders of Communication*, *26*, 337-354.

Conti-Ramsden, G., Hutcheson, G. D., & Grove, J. (in press). Contingency and breakdown: Specific Language Impaired children's conversations with their mothers and fathers. *Journal of Speech and Hearing Research* .

Craig, H., & Evans, J. (1993). Pragmatics and SLI: Within-group variations in discourse behaviors. *Journal of Speech and Hearing Research*, *36*, 777-789.

Feldman, H., Evans, J., Brown, R., & Wareham, N. (1992). Early language abilities of children with periventricular leukomalacia with and without developmental delays. *American Journal on Mental Retardation*, *97*, 222-234.

Feldman, H., & Holland, A. (1991). *Language development with and without left hemispheric damage.* Unpublished manuscript, SRCD Yearly Meeting: St. Louis.

Feldman, H., Holland, A., Kemp, S., & Janosky, J. (1992). Language development after unilateral brain injury. *Brain and Language*, *42*, 89-102.

Feldman, H., Keefe, K., & Holland, A. (1989). Language abilities after left hemisphere brain injury: A case study of twins. *Topics in Special Education*, *9*, 32-47.

Feldman, H., Scher, M., & Kemp, S. (1990). Neurodevelopmental outcome of children with evidence of periventricular leukomalacia on late MRI. *Pediatric Neurology*, *6*, 287-360.

Feldman, H. M. (1994). Language development after early unilateral brain injury: A replication study. In H. Tager-Flusberg (Ed.) *Constraints on language acquisition.* Hillsdale NJ: Erlbaum.

Feldman, H. M., Janosky, J. E., Scher, M. S., & Wareham, N. L. (1994). Language abilities following prematurity, periventricular brain injury, and cerbral palsy. *Journal of Communicative Disorders* , *27*, 71-90.

Fletcher, P. (1992). *The grammatical characterisation of specific language impairment: Theoretical and methodological issues.* Unpublished manuscript, Department of Linguistic Science, University of Reading.

Friel-Patti, S. (1992). Research in child language disorders: What do we know and where are we going? *Folia Phoniatrica*, *44*, 126-142.

Hadley, P. (1993). *A longitudinal investigation of the auxiliary system in children with Specific Language Impairment.* Unpublished doctoral dissertation, University of Kansas.

Hadley, P. A., & Rice, M. L. (submitted). Categorical distinctions between early markers of finiteness: Evidence from children with Specific Language Impairment.

Hemmer, V., & Bernstein-Ratner, N. (1994). Communicative development in twins with discordant histories of recurrent otitis media. *Journal of Communication Disorders*, 27, 91-106.

Hemphill, L. (in press). Conversational abilities in mentally retarded and normally developing children. *Applied Psycholinguistics* .

Hemphill, L., Feldman, H. M., Camp, L., Griffin, T. M., Miranda, A. B., & Wolf, D. P. (1994). Development changes in narrative and non-narrative discourse in children with and without brain injury. *Journal of Communicative Disorders*, 27, 107-134

Hemphill, L., Picardi, N., & Tager-Flusberg, H. (1991). Narrative as an index of communicative competence in mildly mentally retarded children. *Applied Psycholinguistics*, 12, 263-279.

Keefe, K., Feldman, H., & Holland, A. (1989). Lexical learning and language abilities in preschoolers with perinatal brain damage. *Journal of Speech and Hearing Disorders*, 54, 395-402.

LeNormand, M., Leonard, L., & McGregor, K. (1993). A cross-linguistic study of article use by children with specific language impairment. *European Journal of Disorders of Communication*, 28, 153-163.

Levy, Y. (in press-a). Language acquisition in children with focal brain lesions: Implications for normal development. In H. Tager-Flusberg (Ed.) *Language in atypical populations*. Hillsdale, NJ: Erlbaum.

Levy, Y. (in press-b). Morphological development in a child with a congenital LH infarct. *Cognitive Neuropsychology* .

Levy, Y., Amir, N., & Shalev, R. (1994). Morphology in a child with a congenital left-hemisphere brain lesion: Implications for normal acquisition. In H. Tager-Flusberg (Ed.) *Constraints on language acquisition*. Hillsdale, NJ: Erlbaum.

MacWhinney, B., & Osman-Sági, J. (1991). Inflectional marking in Hungarian aphasics. *Brain and Language*, 41, 165-183.

MacWhinney, B. (1994). Using CHILDES to study language disorders. *Journal of Communication Disorders*, 27, 67-70.

Muma, J., Morales, A., Day, K., Tackett, A., Smith, S., Daniel, B., Logue, B., & Morriss, D. (1989). *Toward a posteriori assessment: Rationale, theory, and evidence*. Unpublished manuscript, Texas Tech University.

Murray, L., & Holland, A. (in press). The language recovery of acutely aphasic patients receiving different therapy regimens. *Aphasiology* .

Nicholas, J. G. (in press). Sensory aid use and the development of communicative function. In A. E. Geers, & J. Moog (Eds.), *Effectiveness of cochlear implants and tactile aids for deaf children: A report of the CID study*. Washington D.C.: Alexander Graham Bell Association.

Rescorla, L., & Schwartz, E. (1990). Outcome of toddlers with Specific Expressive Language Delay. *Applied Psycholinguistics*, 11, 393-407.

Rollins, P. (1994). Language profiles of children with specific language impairment. In J. Sokolov, & C. Snow (Eds.), *Handbook of research in language development using CHILDES*. Hillsdale, NJ: Lawrence Erlbaum Associates.

Rollins, P., Pan, B., Conti-Ramsden, G., & Snow, C. (1990). Communicative skills in specific language impaired children: A comparison with their language-matched siblings. *Journal of Communication Disorders*, 27, 189-206.

Schley, S. (1994). *Language proficiency and the bilingual education of deaf children.* Unpublished doctoral dissertation, Harvard University.

Stemmer, B., Giroux, F., & Joanette, Y. (1994). Production and evaluation of requets by right-hemisphere brain-damaged individuals. *Brain and Language*, 47, 1-31.

Tager-Flusberg, H. (1994). Dissociations in form and function in the acquisition of language by autistic children. In H. Tager-Flusberg (Ed.) *Constraints on language development*. Hillsdale NJ: Erlbaum.

Tager-Flusberg, H., & Calkins, S. (in press). Does imitation facilitate the acquisition of grammar? Evidence from a study of autistic, Down syndrome and normal children. *Journal of Child Language* .

Tait, M., & Shillcock, R. (1993). Syntactic theory and the characterization of dysphasic speech. *Clinical Linguistics and Phonetics*, *7*, 237-239.

Thal, D., Bates, E., Zappia, M., & Oroz, M. (in press). Ties between lexical and grammatical development: Evidence from early talkers. *Journal of Child Language* .

Thal, D., Oroz, M., & McCaw, V. (in press). Phonological and lexical development in normal and late talking toddlers. *Applied Psycholinguistics* .

Tingley, E., Berko Gleason, J., & Hooshyar, N. (1994). Beyond good: Mothers' use of internal state words with Down syndrome and normally developing children at dinner time. *Journal of Communication Disorders* , *27*, 135-156.

Watkins, R., & Rice, M. (1991). Verb particle and preposition acquisition in language-impaired preschoolers. *Journal of Speech and Hearing Research*, *34*, 1130-1141.

33.8. Phonological Development

Perhaps the most underdeveloped aspect of the CHILDES system has been its application to the study of phonological development.   There are two reasons for the lesser impact of CHILDES in this area.   The most important is the fact that there are only two publicly available computerized corpora that record phonological detail.   Moreover, one of these two corpora only became available in 1994.   The second reason is that the computational tools available inside the CHILDES system for the study of phonology are not as well developed as those for the study of lexicon, grammar, and discourse.

Bernstein-Ratner, N. (1993b). Interactive influences on phonological behavior: A case study. *Journal of Child Language*, *20*, 191-197.

Bernstein-Ratner, N. (1993c). Phonological analysis of child speech. In J. Sokolov, & C. Snow (Eds.), *Handbook of research in language development using CHILDES*. Hillsdale, NJ: Lawrence Erlbaum Associates.

Engstrand, O., Williams, K., & Strömqvist, S. (1991). Acquisition of the Swedish tonal word accent contrast. In *Actes du XIIème Congres International des Sciences Phonétiques*. Aix-Marseille: Université de Provence.

Peters, A. M., & Strömqvist, S. (1994). The role of prosody in the acquisition of grammatical morphemes. In J. Morgan, & K. Demuth (Eds.), *From signal to syntax*. Hillsdale NJ: Erlbaum.

Wijnen, F. (1988). Spontaneous word fragmentations in children: Evidence for the syllable as a unit in speech production. *Journal of Phonetics*, *16*, 187-202.

Wijnen, F. (1990). The development of sentence planning. *Journal of Child Language*, *17*, 550-562.

Wijnen, F. (1992). Incidental word and sound errors in young speakers. *Journal of Memory and Language*, *31*, 734-755.

Wijnen, F., & Elbers, L. (1993). Effort, production skill, and language learning. In C. Ferguson, L. Menn, & C. Stoel-Gammon (Eds.), *Phonological development*. Timonium, MD: York.

33.9. Articles about CHILDES

The last set of articles examines the CHILDES system itself. Most of these articles are devoted to promoting access to the database, programs, and bibliographic tools.   Others examine issues of coding reliability, phonological notations, and data distribution.   In addition there are several publications that translate the CHILDES materials into other languages or interpret the CHILDES tools for speakers of other languages.

Allen, G. (1988). The PHONASCII system. *Journal of the International Phonetic Association*, *18*, 9-25.

Bernstein-Ratner, N. (1993a). *The CHILDES Project: Tools for analyzing talk.* Language in Society, 22, 307-313.

Biber, D., Conrad, S., & Reppen, R. (1994). *Corpus-based approaches to issues in applied linguistics.* Applied Linguistics, 15, 169-189.

Deutsch, W. (1994). *The observing eye: A century of baby diaries.* Human Development, 37, 30-35.

Edwards, J. (1992). *Computer methods in child language research: four principles for the use of archived data.* Journal of Child Language, 19, 435-458.

Edwards, J. (1993). *Perfecting research techniques in an imperfect world.* Journal of Child Language, 20, 209-216.

Higginson, R. (1988). *The ISU/CHILDES database – a bibliographic addition to CHILDES.* Journal of Child Language, 15, 175-177.

Higginson, R. (1990). An update on the CHILDES/BIB (formerly ISU/CHILDES) database. *Journal of Child Language*, *17*, 473-480.

Higginson, R., & MacWhinney, B. (1990). *CHILDES/BIB: An annotated bibliography of child language and language disorders.* Hillsdale, NJ: Erlbaum.

Higginson, R., & MacWhinney, B. (1994). *CHILDES/BIB 1994 Supplement.* Hillsdale, NJ: Lawrence Erlbaum.

MacWhinney, B., & Snow, C. (1990). *The Child Language Data Exchange System.* ICAME Journal, 14, 3-25.

MacWhinney, B., & Snow, C. (1990). *The Child Language Data Exchange System: An update.* Journal of Child Language, 17, 457-472.

MacWhinney, B. (1991). *The CHILDES database.* Dublin, OH: Discovery Systems.

MacWhinney, B. (1991). *The CHILDES project: Tools for analyzing talk.* Hillsdale, NJ: Erlbaum.

MacWhinney, B., & Snow, C. (1992). *Tools for analyzing child language corpora.* In A. Mackie, T. McAuley, & C. Simmons (Eds.), For Henry Kucera: Studies in Slavic philology and computational linguistics. Ann Arbor: Michigan Slavic Publications.

MacWhinney, B., & Snow, C. (1992b). *The wheat and the chaff: Or four confusions regarding CHILDES.* Journal of Child Language, 19, 459-472.

MacWhinney, B. (1993). *The CHILDES Database: Second Edition.* Dublin, OH: Discovery Systems.

MacWhinney, B. (1994). *The CHILDES system.* In W. Ritchie, & T. Bhatia (Eds.), Handbook of language acquisition. New York: Academic Press.

MacWhinney, B. (1994). *Computational tools for analyzing language.* In P. Fletcher, & B. MacWhinney (Eds.), Handbook of child language research. London: Blackwells.

MacWhinney, B. (1994). *New horizons for CHILDES research.* In J. Sokolov, & C. Snow (Eds.), Handbook for research in language development using CHILDES. Hillsdale, NJ: Lawrence Erlbaum Associates.

MacWhinney, B. (1994). Tools for studying language disorders through spontaneous interactions. *Journal of Communication Disorders* .

Miyata, S. (1994). MinJ-CHAT 0.9 Hebon: CHILDES yoo nihongo deeta nyuuryoku foomatto [MinJ-CHAT 0.9 Hepburn style: A format for the input of Japanese language data into CHILDES]. *The Bulletin of Aichi Shukutoku Junior College*, *33*, 153-166.

Noldus, L. P., van de Loo, E. H., & Timmers, P. H. (1989). Computers in behavioural research. *Nature*, *341*, 767-768.

Plunkett, K. (1990). Computational tools for analysing talk. *Nordic Journal of Linguistics*, 1-13.

Oshima-Takane, Y., & MacWhinney, B. (1994). *Japanese CHAT Manual.* Unpublished manuscript, McGill University.

Pizzuto, E., & D'Amico, S. (1990). Il programma CHILDES: Strumenti per lo studio del linguaggio naturale e simulato. *Giornale Italiano di psicologia*, *17*, 537-551.

Pizzuto, E., & MacWhinney, B. (1994) *Italian CHILDES Manual.* CNR: Rome.

Serra, M., & MacWhinney, B. (1993) *Spanish CHILDES Manual.* University of Barcelona: Barcelona.

Sokolov, J., & MacWhinney, B. (1990). *The CHIP framework: Automatic coding and analysis of parent-child conversational interaction.* Behavioral Research Methods, Instruments, and Computers, 22, 151-161.

Sokolov, J., & Snow, C. (Eds.). (1994). *Handbook of research in language development using CHILDES.* Hillsdale, NJ: Erlbaum.

34. Future Directions

Although we have completed a great deal of work in the past seven years, there is still an enormous amount to be done. Our plans for the future focus on seven areas: database development, user-friendliness, exploratory reality, phonological analysis, discourse analysis, lexical analysis, and morphosyntactic analysis.

34.1. Database Development

We need to continue the expansion of the database in terms of both increased coverage and quality of data. In terms of coverage, we want to have data from more languages, more children, more subgroups, and more ages. In terms of quality, we want our data to begin to include full audio and even video records, precisely linked to increasingly high quality transcripts. As our work in database development proceeds, we want to think in terms of a more general database of all the many varieties of spoken human language. Thinking in terms of the database of the next century, we want to plan the formation of a database for the Human Speechome.

It will be difficult to match our desires for improvements in the database to the realities of increasingly tight fiscal restrictions. To maximize the use of our scant resources, we need to rely more and more on the use of computational technologies to achieve increases in precision and economies in storage and analysis. In addition, individual researchers can help by treating the contribution of new corpora to the database as a basic scientific responsibility. This is particularly true for research projects which have been supported by public funds. If each researcher accepts this responsibility, we will see a continuing natural growth in the quality and coverage of the database.

Currently, complete copies of **CHAT**, **CLAN**, and the database can be obtained over the InterNet from a machine in Pittsburgh (poppy.psy.cmu.edu) and a machine in Antwerp (atila-ftp.uia.be). More interactive access to the database and manual is provided by using a program like NetScape or Mosaic to connect to this WWW (World Wide Web) address: http://poppy.psy.cmu.edu/www/childes.html.

Administrative and technical electronic mail for the CHILDES system can be sent to childes@andrew.cmu.edu. Mail of more general interest can be posted to info-childes@andrew.cmu.edu – a mailing list which reaches about 350 child language researchers. Researchers interested in having their name added to the info-childes list should send mail to info-childes-request@andrew.cmu.edu.

We have attempted to supplement electronic communications and printed materials with face-to-face tutorials sessions and workshops. In 1988, we ran three small workshops at Carnegie Mellon designed to familiarize researchers with the use of **CHAT** and **CLAN**. In June 1989 and October 1991, we ran larger workshops at Harvard University. Two-day workshops were conducted at the International Child Language Association Meetings in 1990 in Budapest and in 1993 in Trieste. In 1994, a four-day workshop was conducted in the framework of the Lisbon meeting for the study of Romance Child Language Research. There have also been CHILDES workshops in Puebla, Ann Arbor, Purdue, Honolulu, Montreal, Brazil, Venezuela, Barcelona, Antwerp, Pisa, Göteborg, and Århus. We have also delivered brief presentations of key aspects of the system at child language conferences in Stanford, Austin, and Boston.

To further deepen the use of **CHAT** and **CLAN** in both teaching and research Sokolov and Snow (1994) have compiled a group of studies the illustrate the applications of the CHILDES tools to specific research projects. A combined use of the Sokolov and Snow tutorials with the CHILDES CD-ROM can form an important part of the curriculum in courses that deal with language acquisition or general principles of language analysis.

34.2. User-Friendliness

The **CLAN** programs are well-debugged and accurately documented. However, they are not yet very user-friendly. There is a command line interface that requires the user to remember a fairly arbitrary set of switches, rules, and values. The opaque nature of this interface makes it difficult for new users to learn **CLAN** quickly.

To improve the user-friendliness of the programs we have constructed a Macintosh user interface that relies on dialog boxes and pop-up menus. The current version of CLAN on the Macintosh now allows users to construct **CLAN** commands using dialogs. It will be more difficult to develop a parallel set of tools for MS-DOS.

Linked to the construction of a user-friendly menu interface is the restructuring of the 16 individual programs into a single program. This restructuring has already been completed on the Macintosh. However, for MS-DOS and UNIX, each of the 16 programs is compiled separately, although each relies on a core set of C utilities. As we move toward the construction of a consistent user interface, we will also combine the set of programs into a single program. Doing this also means that we will need to have **CLAN** issue basic DOS commands such as **dir**, **del**, **cd**, and **copy** into **CLAN**, so that the user will not have to continually shift between **CLAN** and DOS.

34.3. Exploratory Reality

Currently, the programs and the database rely primarily on typed transcripts as the sole guide to the nature of the original interaction. Because it would be so tedious to load up an original videotape or audiotape to explore details of the interaction, we usually base our analyses entirely on this secondary representation of the original reality. However, the emergence of digitized audio and video formats on microcomputers now opens up possibilities for a more intimate relation between the transcript and a fuller record of the original interaction. We can call this new relation "Exploratory Reality".

On the lowest level, Exploratory Reality is nothing more than the digitization of audio and video signals. But the computerization of the video and audio signals allows us the kind of direct access to interactional details that has never before been possible. Attempts to analyze interactions in great detail (Dore, 1977; Ervin-Tripp, 1979; Pittenger, Hockett & Danehy, 1960) have yielded interesting results, but the data underlying these analyses have not been made publicly available and there is seldom any way of verifying the conclusions reached by these researchers. In the area of phonology, the lack of public tools for digitizing and analyzing audio records has meant that it is virtually impossible to build a database grounded on the primary data used in the field.

It is now possible to use **CED** to link a transcript directly to both audio and video records. The realities of current storage technology makes this most reasonable for linkage to the audio records. For a detailed discussion of this way of constructing Exploratory Reality, see the section on "sonic **CHAT**" in the description of **CED**. The **CED** program also provides support for direct access to videotape segments through the use of time code markings and S-video control. In practical terms, this requires use of a video playback unit priced at over $4500. Until video compression technology advances to the point at which large segments of video can be stored on optical disks, we will need to continue to focus on attention primarily on tools for audio analysis. However, the rapid progress of compression technologies should make the extension of these tools to video processing practical within a few years.

Work on sonic **CHAT** is still not complete. Much of the work involved in building up the sonic capacities of **CED** is fairly technical in nature. In particular, some of our basic programming tasks include:

1. **Scrolling linkage**. Currently, scrolling of the wave form window in sonic CHAT is not linked to scrolling of the text window. We need to tighten this relation so that the user always knows where the insertion point is in both windows.
2. **Windowing**. Currently, CED lacks a very basic tool that will be needed in many further developments. This is the ability to open multiple windows. Because we are working on three parallel platforms, we plan to build this facility from the bottom, rather than simply using system-dependent toolbox routines.
3. **Porting** to Windows and UNIX. Most aspects of **CED** have been ported to MS-DOS and UNIX, but we have not yet ported the sonic features to these other systems and we need to build up a Windows version of **CED** from the bottom up.
4. **Coding tools**. A variety of tools for phonological and prosodic coding have been developed at MIT, Kiel, and Bielefeld. Currently, these tools require use of the UNIX-based WAVES system. We want to link these tools to sonic CHAT and extend their applicability to Macintosh and Windows.
5. **Help facilities**. We hope to make a variety of Tutorial and Help facilities available from **CED**. For example, as a part of the process of entering IPA codes, we will make accessible to the user a complete digitized reference set of standard IPA sounds. By matching IPA characters to standard digitized sound values we can play back a crude approximation of the target value of the transcription being entered. Second, as a part of standard discourse transcription, we will provide the user with a complete list of **CHAT** codes and examples of their use in digitized samples.

34.4. Phonological Analysis

A fully coded sonic **CHAT** file provides rich material for a wide variety of new analytic systems. One new set of programs currently being developed focuses on automatic **pause analysis**. Using the temporal values entered on the %snd line through sonic **CHAT**, we will develop programs that compute for each speaker indices such as: time spent in overlaps, time spent in utterance-internal pausing, time spent in between-utterance pausing, and total speaking time. These measures can be used to study conversational behavior and socialization. Parallel measures will be developed for the temporal study of code-switching phenomena.

In addition to the programs for pause analysis, we will extend the current programs for **phonological analysis**. Currently, there are four **CLAN** programs that facilitate phonological analysis. These programs compute phonological frequencies, positional inventories, and model-and-replica analyses. We will broaden our coverage by including programs for computing homonymy, correctness, phonetic product per utterance (Bauer, 1988; Nelson & Bauer, 1991) and phonological process analyses.

## Chapter 34

34.5. Discourse Analysis

Many researchers want to track the ways in which discourse influences ways of expressing topic, anaphora, tense, mood, narrative voice, ellipsis, embedding, and word order (Halliday & Hasan, 1976; MacWhinney, 1985). They want to track shifts in narrative voice, transitions between discourse blocks, and foreground-background relations in discourse. They are also interested in the ways in which particular speech acts from one participant give rise to responsive or nonresponsive speech acts in the other participant.

CLAN cannot code these relations automatically. Decisions about shifts in narrative voice or categorizations of utterances according to a speech-act taxonomy (Ninio & Wheeler, 1986) cannot be done by a computer program. However, the Coder's Editor component of **CED** provides a consistent and fast way of entering codes throughout a transcript. Programs like **FREQ, COMBO, DIST, KEYMAP, RELY**, and **CHAINS** can be invaluable aids in discourse analysis. Once a set of legal **CHAT** codes have been entered in a transcript, **CLAN** programs will track the frequencies of these codes, their distribution in terms of response pairs, runs of particular types of codes, resumptions of runs, and other series analyses. In addition, **CLAN** programs will be devised that will help the coder enter legal codes according to a particular coding scheme.

There are a variety of ways in which the examination of discourse and narrativestructures within **CLAN** could be improved. Perhaps the most promising line of development is to link **CHAT** files and the **CLAN** programs with a program of the type developed in the field of Exploratory Sequential Data Analysis (ESDA) in the area of Human-Computer Interaction (HCI). A particularly interesting program in this area is the MacShapa program developed by Penelope Sanderson. This program permits a variety of displays of profiles of different types of acts and has many tools for making reports of the distributions of these acts across a transcript.

34.6. Lexical Analysis

Analyses of lexical development in both normally-developing and language impaired children have been hampered by difficulties in obtaining large, consistently transcribed corpora for various clinical groups. Even with the advent of the CHILDES corpora and programs, studies of lexical development have been slowed by the fact that full analyses of many files have overloaded the memories of smaller computers and been slow even on larger computers. To correct this problem and to advance the analyses of lexical development, we need to construct a computerized retrieval key to the complete CHILDES database. This key will allow immediate retrieval of particular words or classes of words through pre-stored pointers to occurrences in individual files. This new program will be called **LEX**.

The completion of a key to the lexical structure of the database would facilitate compilation of new word frequency dictionaries. The only available frequency count based on actual spoken usage from English-speaking children is Rinsland (1945). That count was based on a small set of data and is now badly out of date. Using the **LEX** database, we can construct a frequency count that includes both the input to children and the forms the children use at different age levels. The lexicon will include more than simply a listing of words and their frequency. It will also include:
1.   for the more common words, those words with which they cooccur as arguments,
2.   common pronunciation variations from phonologically transcribed corpora,

3.   statistics on morphophonological and phonological errors for each word,
4.   information relevant to estimating the frequency of different polysemes of a word, and
5.   for the less common words, pointers to the locations of those words in the full CHILDES corpus.

This lexicon will be published in both a computational form that allows it to be used both as an independent research tool and in a more limited hard copy version.

The **LEX** facility can also be used as a basis to compute a Lexical Rarity Index (LRI). Currently, the major index of lexical diversity is the type-token ratio (TTR) of Templin (1957). A more interesting measure would focus on the relative dispersion in a transcript of words that are generally rare in some comparison data set. The more that a child uses "rare" words, the higher the Lexical Rarity Index. If most of the words are common and frequent, the LRI will be low. In order to compute various forms of this index, the **LRI** program would rely on values provided by **LEX**.

34.7.   Morphosyntactic Analysis

The final set of goals relates to analyses conducting primarily from the %mor and %syn tiers. Here, we need to continue development of the **MOR** program. For corpora that have a complete %mor tier, we can begin to automate a variety of programmatic analyses that earlier had been computed by hand. Computation of the DSS is already possible through use of the **DSS** program. Other indices that we will program include LARSP (Crystal et al., 1989), IPSyn (Scarborough, 1990), and productivity analyses of the type proposed by Braine (1976), MacWhinney (1975), and Ingram (1989).

34.8.   A Final Word

We encourage researchers to join us in working toward these new goals, to make full use of the current CHILDES tools, and to propose new directions and possible improvements to the system. It is important for all researchers to understand that further development of the CHILDES tools depends entirely on funding support from government agencies and private foundations. Currently, support for the system comes from the National Institute of Child Health and Human Development at the National Institutes of Health. The best way to argue for such support is to show that the CHILDES tools are being used productively. This means that we need to get frequent and complete feedback at the Pittsburgh Center from users regarding articles that have been published using CHILDES data or projects that are underway using the **CHAT** and **CLAN** tools. Please address correspondence to Child Language Data Exchange System, Department of Psychology, Carnegie Mellon University, Pittsburgh PA 15213 USA or send electronic mail to childes@andrew.cmu.edu.

References

Abrahamsen, A. (1977). *Child language: An interdisciplinary guide to theory and research* . Baltimore, MD: University Park Press.

Allen, G. (1988). The PHONASCII system. *Journal of the International Phonetic Association*, *18*, 9-25.

Antinucci, F., & Parisi, D. (1973). Early language acquisition: A model and some data. In C. Ferguson & D. Slobin (Eds.), *Studies in child language development.* New York: Holt.

Antinucci, F., & Volterra, V. (1978). Lo sviluppo della negazione nel linguaggio infantile: uno studio pragmatico. In L. Camaioni (Ed.), *Sviluppo del linguaggio e interazione sociale.* Bologna: Il Mulino.

Bates, E., Bretherton, I., & Snyder, L. (1988). *From first words to grammar: Individual differences and dissociable mechanisms* . Cambridge, MA: Cambridge University Press.

Bates, E., Friederici, A., & Wulfeck, B. (1987a). Grammatical morphology in aphasia: Evidence from three languages. *Cortex*, *23*, 545-574.

Bates, E., Friederici, A., & Wulfeck, B. (1987b). Sentence comprehension in aphasia: A cross-linguistic study. *Brain and Language*, *32*(1), 19-67.

Bates, E., Friederici, A., Wulfeck, B., & Juarez, L. (1988). On the preservation of word order in aphasia: Cross-linguistic evidence. *Brain and Language*, *33*, 323-364.

Bates, E., Hamby, S., & Zurif, E. (1983). The effects of focal brain damage on pragmatic expression. *Canadian Journal of Psychology*, *37*, 59-84.

Bates, E., & MacWhinney, B. (1982). Functionalist approaches to grammar. In E. Wanner & L. Gleitman (Eds.), *Language acquisition: The state of the art.* New York: Cambridge University Press.

Bates, E., & Wulfeck, B. (1989a). Comparative aphasiology: A crosslinguistic approach to language breakdown. *Aphasiology*, *3*, 11-142.

Bates, E., & Wulfeck, B. (1989b). Crosslinguistic studies of aphasia. In B. MacWhinney & E. Bates (Eds.), *The crosslinguistic study of sentence processing.* New York: Cambridge University Press.

Bauer, H. (1988). The ethologic model of phonetic development: I. Phonetic contrast estimators. *Clinical Linguistics and Phonetics*, *2*, 347-380.

Bellinger, D., & Gleason, J. (1982). Sex differences in parental directives to young children. *Journal of Sex Roles*, *8*, 1123-1139.

Berman, R. (1985). The acquisition of Hebrew. In D. I. Slobin (Ed.), *The crosslinguistic study of language acquisition.* Hillsdale, NJ: Lawrence Erlbaum Associates.

Berman, R., & Dromi, E. (1984). On marking time without aspect in child language. *Papers and Reports on Child Language Development*, *23*, 23-32.

Berman, R., & Slobin, D. (1986). *Coding manual: Temporality in discourse*. Berkeley, CA: University of California.

Bernstein, N. (1982). *Acoustic study of mothers' speech to language-learning children: An analysis of vowel articulatory characteristics.* Unpublished doctoral dissertation, Boston University.

Bernstein-Ratner, N. (1984a). Patterns of vowel modification in mother–child speech. *Journal of Child Language*, *11*, 557-578.

Bernstein-Ratner, N. (1984b). Phonological rule usage in mother-child speech. *Journal of Phonetics*, *12*, 245-254.

Bernstein-Ratner, N. (1985). Dissociations between vowel durations and formant frequency characteristics. *Journal of Speech and Hearing Research*, *28*, 255-264.

Bernstein-Ratner, N. (1986). Durational cues which mark clause boundaries in mother child speech. *Journal of Phonetics*, *14*, 303-309.